Saint Pius V

Roberto de Mattei

Saint Pius V

The Legendary Pope Who Excommunicated Queen Elizabeth I, Standardized the Mass, and Defeated the Ottoman Empire

Translated by Giuseppe Pellegrino

SOPHIA INSTITUTE PRESS
Manchester, New Hampshire

Cover design by LUCAS Art & Design, Jenison, MI.

On the cover: *Alliance of Filippo II of Spain, Doge Venier, and Pope Pius V against the Turks*, 1571, by Alessandro Maganza © Bridgeman Archives (DGA644123).

Sophia Institute Press
Box 5284, Manchester, NH 03108
1-800-888-9344

www.SophiaInstitute.com

Sophia Institute Press® is a registered trademark of Sophia Institute.

paperback ISBN 978-1-64413-461-0

ebook ISBN 978-1-64413-462-7

Library of Congress Control Number: 2021934488

First Printing

O you, historian, the ink of your pen
Honestly describes our horrendous history
And tells our children about our terrible misfortune
So that, when they read what you wrote, they join in
our suffering
And turn away from their fathers' sins
So as not to share the same misery.

—Pierre de Ronsard, *Discours des misères de ce temps* (1562)

Contents

Acknowledgments

I would like to express my deep gratitude to those who made this book possible: Fr. Ezra O'Sullivan; John Murdock, with whom I have discussed parts of this work and who has supported it; Manuela Faella, for her careful editorial collaboration; and my English translator, Giuseppe Pellegrino.

Foreword

The Christian victory of Lepanto on October 7, 1571, whose 450th anniversary is commemorated in 2021, is closely tied to the name of St. Pius V. Not only was he the architect of the Holy League against the Turks, but it was also to his prayers, and in particular to the Holy Rosary, that his contemporaries attributed that triumph, which still today is a symbol of the militant spirit that should never leave the Christian. It is not by chance that the Church on earth is called the Church Militant, inseparably united in the communion of saints with the Church Triumphant that rejoices eternally in Paradise. The words of Pope Pius XII are memorable: "We belong to the Church militant; and she is militant because on earth the powers of darkness are ever restless to encompass her destruction."[1]

The life of every Christian is a battle, from the last of the faithful to the Supreme Pastor, and St. Pius V offers us a luminous example of this militancy. His pontificate between 1566 and 1572 took place in the heart of the sixteenth century, an era in which the Catholic Church faced two terrible enemies. The first was an external enemy, the Ottoman Turks, who after the conquest of Constantinople in 1453, enlarged their domains, both on land and at sea, and whose ultimate objective was the city of Rome itself.

[1] Pio XII, *Discorso per l'inaugurazione della nuova sede del Pontificio Collegio Americano del Nord* del 14 ottobre 1953, in *Discorsi e Radiomessaggi di Sua Santità Pio XII*, vol. 15, p. 400.

The second, the internal enemy, was the Protestant Revolution, which, exploding on the ground prepared by humanism and the Renaissance, tore apart Christendom and sought to overthrow the Roman papacy. Pius V not only barred the path against these two enemies, preserving the Church and Christendom from great catastrophes, but with a supernatural spirit he also initiated an authentic reform of the customs of the Church, applying the decrees of the Council of Trent with rigor and restoring Catholic liturgy.

The most insidious enemy he had to fight, however, was the false Catholic reform, which deluded itself that it could find a "third way" between Catholic orthodoxy and heresy by pushing Catholics toward an attitude of psychological disarmament. Faced with this crypto-heresy, St. Pius V used all his zeal and experience as an inquisitor. The Benedictine Cardinal Domenico Serafini, archbishop of Spoleto and Assessor of the Holy Office, when asked to commemorate Pius V during the celebrations for the second centenary of his canonization in 1912, affirmed the following:

> If I consider him as a religious in his cell, centered on piety and study, Pius V appears to me as the perfect disciple of the great patriarch Dominic. If I consider him as inquisitor, he seems to me to emulate the many members of the illustrious Order of Preachers who gave their sweat, blood and lives in the defense of the faith. If I consider him as a shepherd of souls, he is the model of pastors. Finally, if I gaze on him raised up on the Chair of Peter, his brief pontificate is so packed full of grandiose works that few can equal it, especially in the 16th century; none surpass it.[2]

With the competence as a historian that is proper to him, but also with the spirit of faith that is necessary for the Catholic historian in studying the life of the Church, Professor Roberto de Mattei shows us in this book

[2] Domenico Serafini, *Discorso in onore di S. Pio V. Recitato nella cappella del S. Uffizio il 22 maggio 1912*, Tipografia Poliglotta Vaticana, Roma 1912, p. 5.

the true face of St. Pius V, the defender of the Faith against heresy, the architect of the victory of Lepanto, the reformer of the Church, and the restorer of its liturgical life.

This book, which appears in a dramatic epoch for the Church and for all of society, can be of precious help in understanding the crisis of the present time in the light of the past, and in working accordingly. In order to act, we need models to imitate, and the models *par excellence* are the saints. Who better than a holy pope like Pius V can show us the right way, even to those who have, or will have in the future, supreme responsibilities in the Church?

I hope that Roberto de Mattei's book will have the widespread distribution it deserves, and that it will do good for many souls, encouraging them to remain faithful to the Church and to fight for the Kingdom of Jesus and Mary in time and in eternity.

—Bishop Athanasius Schneider
Auxiliary Bishop of Astana

Preface

Until now there have been approximately thirty biographies written about St. Pius V, in various languages and of unequal value.[3] The first to be printed[4] was the *Vita del Gloriosissimo Papa Pio V* by Girolamo Catena,[5] the secretary of Cardinal Michele Bonelli, Pope Ghislieri's nephew. The work was published in 1586, fourteen years after the pontiff's death, and it was reprinted the following year, with the personal support of Pope Sixtus V. This work served as the basis for all subsequent biographies, because of its rich documentation and the important collection of the letters of Pius V that it contains. This work was followed by the *Vida y Echos de Pio* (1595) by the Spanish priest Antonio de Fuenmayor—the

[3] Cf. Ludwig von Pastor, *I biografi di Pio V*, in *Storia dei Papi*, vol. VIII, pp. 627–632; Miguel Gotor, *Le vite di San Pio V dal 1572 al 1712 tra censura, agiografia e storia*, in *Pio V nella società e nella politica del suo tempo*, edited by Maurilio Guasco and Angelo Torre, Il Mulino, Bologna, 2005, pp. 207–250.

[4] The oldest is actually the short biography composed immediately after the pope's death by Tommaso Porcacchi (1532–1576), which remained unedited until it was published by Fr. François Van Ortroy in *Analecta Bollandiana*, vol. 33, pp. 207–217.

[5] Girolamo Catena, *Vita del gloriosissimo papa Pio quinto dedicata al santissimo signor nostro Sisto quinto. Con una raccolta di lettere di Pio V a diversi Principi e le risposte*, by Alessandro Gardano and Francesco Coattino, Rome, 1587.

first work in a foreign language[6]—and the *De Vita et Rebus Gestis Pii V*[7] (1605) by the Barnabite Giovanni Antonio Gabuzio, which was originally planned to be a Latin translation of the work by Girolamo Catena, but which was then enriched with new documentation. These works formed the foundation for the work of the Dominican Arcangelo Caraccia di Rivalta d'Acqui, the procurator of Pius V's cause of beatification, in his *Vita del Beatissimo Pontefice Papa Pio V* (1615).[8]

Following the beatification of Pius V, which was decreed by Clement X on May 1, 1672, the centenary of his death, there appeared in Paris the *Vie du très Saint Pape Pie V*[9] by the Dominican Jean-Baptiste Feuillet. In the year of Pius's canonization, which was done by Clement XI on May 22, 1712, two other important works were published: the *Vita di S. Pio V*[10] by Paolo Alessandro Maffei, which was nearly five hundred pages long in eight volumes, published first in Venice (Tommasini) and then in Rome (Gonzaga); and, also in 1712, the short *Vita S. Pii V Summi Pontificis*,[11] written in Latin by the Dominican Tommaso Maria Minorelli. (A translation with the Latin text on the facing page was published in

6 Antonio de Fuenmayor, *Vida y hechos de Pio Quinto dividida en seis libros, con algunos notables sucesos de la christiandad del tiempo de su pontificado*, Luis Sanchez, Madrid, 1595; then Pedro Escuer, 1633; Aldus, Madrid, 1953. Cf. Miles Pattenden, *Antonio de Fuenmayor's Life of Pius V: A pope in early modern Spanish historiography*, "Renaissance Studies," 32 (2) 2018, published online.

7 Giovanni Antonio Gabuzio, *De vita et rebus gestis Pii V*. Pont. Max. libri sex., 1605. Rome, Ex typographia Aloisij Zannetti, Rome, 1605. The work was included by the Bollandists in the *Acta sanctorum* (edited by D. Papebrochius and G. Henschenius, XII, Maii I, Antverpiae 1680, pp. 616–714).

8 F. Arcangelo Caraccia da Rivalta, *Vita del beatissimo pontefice papa Pio V. Dell'ordine de' Predicatori. ... descritta dal* M. R. P. *maestro del medesimo ordine*, Giacomo Ardizzoni, Pavia, 1615.

9 Jean-Baptiste Feuillet, *La vie du B. pape Pie V de l'Ordre des FF. Prêcheurs*, André Cramoisy, Paris, 1674.

10 Paolo Alessandro Maffei, *Vita di S. Pio V*, Giacomo Tommasini, Venice, 1712.

11 Tommaso Maria Minorelli, *Vita di San Pio V*, (1712), edited by Fabio Gasti, Ibis, Pavia, 2012.

2012, on the occasion of the third centenary of the canonization of Ghislieri, edited by Fabio Gasti.)

The volumes dedicated to St. Pius V by two French historians, the viscount Alfred de Falloux in 1884[12] and the Abbé (later cardinal) Georges Grente in 1905,[13] are in my opinion still valid and interesting, and do not merit the severe judgment reserved for them by Baron Ludwig von Pastor, who is too dependent on the German historical-critical school; however the eighth volume of his *History of the Popes*,[14] gives us, to date, the best overview of the pontificate of St. Pius V.

In the nineteenth century two anti-Catholic but well-documented works should be recalled: a biography by Joseph Mendham,[15] a deacon of the Church of England, and the collection of St. Pius V's letters by Louis de Potter.[16]

In the twentieth century there were several biographies dedicated to Pope Ghislieri and written in a popular but well-informed style: *The Sword of Saint Michael* (1943) by Lillian Browne Olf (1943);[17] *San Pio V. Il pontefice di Lepanto, del rosario e della liturgia tridentina* (1997) by Fr. Innocenzo Venchi;[18] and *San Pio V "Il Papa della S. Messa e di Lepanto"* by Don Ugolino Giugni (2004);[19] as well as the brief profile *St. Pius V*

[12] Alfred de Falloux, *Histoire de Saint Pie V, pape de l'ordre des frères prêcheurs*, Sagnier et Bray, Paris, 1844.

[13] Card. Georges Grente, *Pius V*, Victor Lecoffre, Paris, 1905. The work was republished with the title *Le Pape des grands combats. Saint Pie*, by Arthème Fayard, Paris, 1956.

[14] Ludwig von Pastor, *Storia dei Papi dalla fine del Medioevo*, Desclée, Rome, 1926–1963.

[15] Joseph Mendham, *The Life and Pontificate of Saint Pius V. Subjoined is a reimpression of a historic deduction of the episcopal oath of allegiance of the Pope*, in *The Church of Rome*, James Duncan, London, 1832.

[16] De Potter, *Lettres de Saint Pie V*.

[17] Lillian Browne Olf, *The Sword of Saint Michael. The Life of Saint Pius V*, The Bruce Publishing Company, Milwaukee, 1943.

[18] Innocenzo Venchi, O.P. *San Pio V. Il pontefice di Lepanto, del rosario e della liturgia tridentina*, Edizioni Studio Domenicano, Rome, 1997.

[19] Don Ugolino Giugni, *San Pio V "Il Papa della S. Messa e di Lepanto,"* Centro Librario Sodalitium, Verrua Savoia, 2004.

by the English writer Robin Anderson (1973),[20] the more challenging volume *Saint Pie V* by the French historian Nicole Lemaître (1994),[21] and the recent hagiography *Saint Pie V, le pape intempestif* by Philippe Verdin (2018).[22]

Among more recent academic studies there should be noted the collective volumes *San Pio V e la problematica del suo tempo*;[23] *Pio V nella società e nella politica del suo tempo*, edited by Maurilio Guasco and Angelo Torre (2005);[24] the acts of the symposium held in Bosco Marengo in 2004, *Il tempo di Pio V. Pio V nel tempo*, edited by Fulvio Cervini and Carla Enrica Spantigati (2006);[25] and those of the 2012 symposium held on the occasion of the third centenary of the canonization, *San Pio V nella storia*, edited by Carlo Bernasconi.

The sometimes-repetitive entries by Simona Feci in the *Enciclopedia dei Papi*,[26] in the *Dizionario Biografico degli Italiani*,[27] and in the *Dizionario storico dell'Inquisizione*[28] are also useful for the bibliographies they include.

As for primary sources, the seven volumes of the *Magnum Bullarium*,[29] edited by G. Mainardi and C. Coquelines (1733–1762), are fundamental,

[20] Robin Anderson, *St. Pius V: His Life, Times, Virtues and Miracles*, TAN Books, 1973–1978, republished 2009.

[21] Nicole Lemaître, *Saint Pie V*, Fayard, Paris, 1994.

[22] Philippe Verdin, *Saint Pie V, le pape intempestif*, Le Cerf, 2018.

[23] *San Pio V e la problematica del suo tempo*, Cassa di Risparmio di Alessandria, Alessandria, 1972.

[24] *Pio V nella società e nella politica del suo tempo*, edited by Maurilio Guasco and Angelo Torre, Il Mulino, Bologna, 2005.

[25] *Il tempo di Pio V. Pio V nel tempo*, edited by Fulvio Cervini and Carla Enrica Spantigati, Edizioni dell'Orso, Alessandria, 2006.

[26] Simona Feci, *Pio V*, in *Enciclopedia dei Papi*, Istituto della Enciclopedia Italiana, Rome, 2000, vol. 3; pp. 160–180.

[27] Simona Feci, *Pius V* in DBI, vol. 83 (2015), pp. 814–825.

[28] Simona Feci, *Pio V*, in *Dizionario Storico dell'Inquisizione*, edited by A. Prosperi, V. Lavenia, J. Tedeschi, Edizioni della Normale, Pisa, 2010, vol. 3, pp. 1213–1215.

[29] *Magnum Bullarium*, edited by G. Mainardi and C. Coquelines, 32 vol., 1733–1762, then *Bullarium diplomatum et privilegiorum sanctorum romanorum pontificum*, S. and H. Dalmezzo, Turin, 1860, vol. 7.

as they gather a considerable number of bulls by Pius V; and the volume of the *Epistolae ad principes*,[30] dedicated to St. Pius V and edited by Tomislav Mrkonjić, contains all of the necessary information for archival research.

As for my own work, I have followed the method already utilized in my preceding volumes on Pius IX[31] and Leo XIII.[32] First of all, I have sought to insert the figure of Pius V into his historical context, exploring sources and bibliography that concern him, even if only in an indirect manner. Every pope, just like every great figure of history, can be understood only in relation to his time, and the more this aspect of historical context is clear, the easier it is to grasp the meta-historical dimension of their work. In the second place, I have enriched the notes not only with bibliographical details but also biographical and informative information, in order to make it easier for non-specialists to understand the events narrated.

I believe that, like my preceding works, the greatest contribution that this work can make is to the interpretation of the figure of St. Pius V in relationship to his time, but also in relation to ours—that is, in his significance as the model of a saintly pontiff: an interpretation which certainly diverges from that of most twentieth-century historians and which is, if anything, closer to that of the first biographers. But I have often tried to affirm the contributions of contemporary historians, even by those on the opposing side, when they are serious and documented.

I use the term "the opposing side," because there is no such thing as "neutrality" for a historian. What exists is the historic truth that transcends the personality of historians and ought to be sought after scrupulously and with objectivity, without ever manipulating the facts or the sources.

30 *Epistolae ad principes*: *Epistolae ad principes*, vol. 2, *S. Pius V-Gregorius XIII (1566-1585)*, edited by Tomislav Mrkonjić, Vatican Secret Archive, Vatican City, 1994.

31 Roberto de Mattei, *Pio IX e la Rivoluzione italiana*, Piemme, Casale Monferrato, 2000, republished by Cantagalli, Siena, 2012, and now Fiducia, Rome, 2020.

32 Roberto de Mattei, *Il ralliement di Leone XIII. Il fallimento di un progetto pastorale*, Le Lettere, Florence, 2014.

The Catholic historian is not afraid of the truth. In this sense I reject the definition of my book as an "apologetic work," if this term means a distortion of historical reality for partisan interests. I do accept the term if it instead refers to my position as a militant Catholic, different from that of a large number of contemporary Catholic and secular historians. The historian demonstrates his objectivity and impartiality not by renouncing any expression of his own ideas, but rather when he refuses to deform or manipulate the facts in order to justify a preconceived thesis.

As a Catholic and as a historian, I submit these pages to the judgment of the Church, and I am ready to retract any concept, phrase, or word that either she condemns or is biased in her favor. My work desires in fact to be an act of service to the Truth, but also an act of service to the Catholic Church, which is the infallible guardian of Truth, because she has been founded and is held in life by He who is the only Way, Truth, and Life (John 14:6).

Saint Pius V

1

The Church in the First Half of the Sixteenth Century

1. The Church in the Age of Humanism and the Renaissance

During the fourteenth and fifteenth centuries, Italy was the center of a profound transformation of mentality and customs, which progressively extended to include all of Christianity. This cultural revolution took the name Humanism, because it had its origin in the cult of classical literature, *humanae litterae*, and placed man at the center of the universe, substituting earthly happiness, based on love of self, in lieu of supernatural happiness, oriented to the love of God. The artistic expression of this movement was called the Renaissance, but the two terms Humanism and Renaissance are often used interchangeably as synonyms.[33]

[33] There is an abundance of discussion on the concepts of Humanism and the Renaissance, but little that is significantly new has been contributed since the synthesis of WALLACE K. FERGUSON, *The Renaissance in Historical Thought*, Houghton Mifflin, Cambridge, Massachusetts, 1948. On the relationship between the popes and Humanism, a fundamental source is the first volume of *Storia dei Papi dalla fine del Medioevo* by LUDWIG VON PASTOR (16 vol., Desclée, Rome, 1926–1963). For a general overview, see JAKOB BURCKHARDT, *Die Kultur der Renaissance in Italien* (1860), Italian translation, *La civiltà del Rinascimento in Italia*, Avanzini e Torraca, Rome, 1967; ABY WARBURG, *The Renewal of Pagan Antiquity*, Getty Research Institute for the History of Art and the Humanities, Los Angeles, 1999; EUGENIO GARIN, *L'umanesimo italiano*, 3rd ed., Laterza, Rome-Bari, 2000.

In the Middle Ages, the spirit of sacrifice knew its highest expression in the Crusades, a spiritual movement of souls in which all of Christianity embraced the Cross of Christ and fought and died in its name. Humanism did not deny Christian truths in principle but proposed a hedonistic ideal that in reality denied the redemptive value of the Sacrifice of the Cross. It was the beginning of a process that would lead step-by-step in a consistent and consequent way to the dissolution of Christendom.[34]

The new spirit was denounced by men of God like Blessed Giovanni Dominici,[35] who, in his *Lucula Noctis* (*Firefly*), contrasted divine Wisdom with the worldly knowledge of the humanists, but it nonetheless penetrated in the fifteenth century into the midst of the Catholic Church. In the brief pontificate of Innocent VII (1404–1406) the historian Ludwig von Pastor already saw the new humanistic and worldly direction of the Roman Curia asserting itself.[36] The cult of Beauty, freed from the True and the Good, led to the refusal of asceticism and the primacy of sensual delight, exalted as the only motive for human action by authors like Lorenzo Valla.[37]

In response, St. Catherine of Siena had traced out a plan of governance for the popes that would always be relevant: that of reforming

[34] See MSGR. JEAN-JOSEPH GAUME, *La Révolution. Recherches historiques sur l'origine et la propagation du mal en Europe depuis la Renaissance jusqu'à nos jours*, Gaume frères, Paris, 1856, 12 vol., and, for a synthetic but magistral analysis of this process, PLINIO CORRÊA DE OLIVEIRA, *Rivoluzione e Contro-Rivoluzione*, Italian translation, Sugarco, Milan, 2009.

[35] Blessed Giovanni Dominici (1357–1419), Dominican of the Priory of Santa Maria Novella in Florence, archbishop of Ragusa in Dalmatia (1407) and cardinal (1408), dedicated his energies to fighting the spirit of nascent Humanism and to extinguishing the schism that tore apart the Western Church. See *Johannis Dominici Lucula noctis*, edited by Edmund Hunt, University of Notre Dame Press, Notre Dame, Indiana, 1940.

[36] PASTOR, *Storia dei Papi*, vol. 1, p. 173.

[37] The humanist Lorenzo Valla (1405–1447), apostolic secretary under Pope Callistus III (1455–1458), is the author of, among other works, *De voluptate* (1431), in which he combats both Stoic and Christian morality, celebrating pleasure all the way up to *divina voluptas*.

the papal Curia and renouncing every ambition to power and human greatness in order to follow Jesus Christ on the Way of the Cross. But above all beginning with the election of Pope Sixtus IV (1471–1484), the humanist faction dominated the papacy and "the worldly element prevailed in the College of Cardinals, in the papal curia, in the higher clergy and consequently in all of Christian life."[38]

The eleven-year pontificate of Alexander VI,[39] against which Girolamo Savonarola[40] raised his voice, seemed to signal the apex of this process of becoming more and more worldly. Alexander VI, Rodrigo Borgia, never thought of anything else in his life, writes Cardinal Hergenröther, besides "satisfying his passions, enriching and enhancing his family," and "in his time as pope he continued for a long time in this kind of life," "whence his pontificate served to throw the Holy See, which he profaned, into discredit before the whole world."[41]

However, the worst was yet to come, and the scourges of war, famine, and epidemics seemed to announce a period of new crisis in the Church

38 Agostino Saba, *Storia della Chiesa*, UTET, Turin, 1938–1940, vol. 3, p. 219.

39 Alexander VI (Rodrigo Borgia: 1431–1503) was one of the most controversial popes because of his scandalous life, but without putting into question the orthodoxy of his doctrine. For more on his life see the extensive article of Giovanni Battista Picotti, Matteo Sanfilippo, in EP, vol. 3, pp. 13–22; Barbara Briganti, Claudio Crescentini, Massimo Miglio, Claudio Strinati, Marie Viallon, *Les Borgia et leur temps: de Léonard de Vinci à Michel-Ange*, Gallimard, Paris, 2014.

40 There is still great controversy within the Catholic world about Girolamo Savonarola (1452–1498), of the Order of Preachers. See Roberto Ridolfi, *Vita di Girolamo Savonarola*, 4th enhanced edition, Sansoni, Florence, 1974; on the contrast with Alexander VI: Ricardo García Villoslada, S.J. – Bernardino Llorca, S.J., *Historia de la Iglesia Católica*, III, *Edad Nueva (1306-1648). La Iglesia en la época del Renacimiento y de la reforma Católica*, BAC, Madrid, 1967, pp. 444–469; for a comprehensive bibliography: Lauro Martines, *Savonarola. Moralità e politica a Firenze nel Quattrocento*, Mondadori, Milan, 2008.

41 Joseph Hergenröther, *Storia universale della Chiesa*, Libreria Editrice Fiorentina, Florence, 1907–1911, vol. 5, p. 314.

after the terrible period of the Great Western Schism. Ludwig von Pastor observes:

> The three horsemen of the Apocalypse, war, famine, and death, which Dürer had designated at the end of the 15th century as a prophecy of what must come, made their terrible journey throughout Italy. The fury of war raced through the country like a mighty hurricane, destroying houses and fields and kidnapping men. In the end the garden of Europe was transformed into a battlefield sown with corpses, which soon became focal point of plague. The frightening cases, the unheard of sufferings, threw the popular soul into a powerful excitement, which was continually increased by prophesying hermits.[42]

The plague was joined by the disease of syphilis. The debauchery of customs and established mores led to a rapid spread of the illness, which was also called the "French evil" because it was brought into Italy by the army of Charles VIII, King of France: "Just as in the other countries of Europe, so also in Italy the new illness was considered as a just punishment for the sins of men and for their great shamelessness."[43]

At the beginning of the sixteenth century, the city of Rome, the seat of the Catholic Church, offered the spectacle of a great development of the arts but also that of a profound moral decadence. "In no other place did artistic creation have such a great development, in a sort of frenzy for novelty, for spectacular decorations; in no other place were so many basilicas restored and constructed, so many beautiful temples," writes the historian Jacques Heers. He continues: "It was an exceptional flowering that owed everything absolutely to the ecclesiastical courts, the court of the sovereign pontiff, the courts of the cardinals and their families, of their clients and allies, of their bankers, money lenders, and suppliers."[44]

[42] Pastor, *Storia dei Papi*, vol. 4, pt. 2, p. 582.

[43] Pastor, *Storia dei Papi*, vol. 3, p. 8.

[44] Jacques Heers, *La vita quotidiana nella Roma pontificia ai tempi dei Borgia e dei Medici*, BUR, Milan, 2017, p. 263.

The climate of the papal household was the same as all the other principal courts of Italy such as Naples, Venice, Florence, or Urbino, with an alternation of banquets, hunting, and pagan-flavored parties. The popes lived like princes, patrons of the arts, diplomats, leaders, and they seemed to be concerned with the temporal interests of their states more than with the supernatural good of souls.[45]

Alexander VI died on August 19, 1503. After the brief but edifying pontificate of Pius III, Francesco Piccolomini, Cardinal Giulio della Rovere, the nephew of Sixtus IV, ascended to the papal throne with the name of Julius II.[46] The Venetian ambassador, Girolamo Lippomano, depicted him as "of terrible heart and soul," and he was named "The Terrible" by his contemporaries and his historic successors.[47] In addition to being an able politician and warrior, Julius II was also a great patron of the arts. Under his pontificate Michelangelo began painting the frescoes of the Sistine Chapel, Raphael began decorating the Vatican parlors, and the Constantinian basilica of St. Peter was demolished to make room for the new basilica, which was being designed by Bramante.[48] The ancient basilica was a world sanctuary, full of treasures and votive memorial offerings, guilty of having been built in a "barbarian" age. The very tomb of St. Peter itself would have been profaned if Julius II had not personally acted to protect it.[49] These acts of artistic "vandalism" express the

[45] See Emmanuel Rodocanachi, *La première renaissance: Rome au temps de Jules II et de Léon X*, Librairie Hachette & Cie, Rome, 1912. For a general overview, beyond the work of Pastor, see volume 15 of *Storia della Chiesa* by Fliche-Martin, *La Chiesa e il Rinascimento*; Denys Hay, *The Church in Italy in the Fifteenth Century*, Cambridge University Press, New York, 1971; Marco Pellegrini, *Il papato nel Rinascimento*, Il Mulino, Bologna, 2010.

[46] On Julius II (Giuliano della Rovere: 1443–1513), see the study of Alessandro Pastore, in DBI, vol. 57 (2001), pp. 17–26; Ivan Cloulas, *Jules II*, Librairie Arthème Fayard, Paris, 1990; Christine Shaw, *Julius II: The Warrior Pope*, Blackwell, Oxford, 1996.

[47] Villoslada, *La Iglesia en la época del Renacimiento y de la reforma Católica*, p. 488.

[48] Pastor, *Storia dei Papi*, vol. 1, p. 519; vol. 3, pp. 891–892.

[49] Pastor, *Storia dei Papi*, vol. 3, pp. 898–899.

mentality of an age in which artistic splendor became an end in itself, thereby inflicting grave loss on public and religious pieties and overall civic moral sense.

2. The Pontificate of Leo X

Upon the death of Julius II on February 21, 1513, he was succeeded by the thirty-eight-year-old Giovanni de' Medici, the son of Lorenzo the Magnificent, who took the name Leo X.[50] Although he was a cardinal, he was only a deacon, and so the new pope received priestly ordination and episcopal consecration before being crowned as pope, with a ceremony that "offered the most splendid spectacle that Rome had witnessed since the imperial age."[51] The procession was opened by two hundred lancers on horseback, followed by musicians who wore the papal livery: white, red, and green. The great red gonfalon, or banner, of Rome, with the letters S.P.Q.R. (*Senatus Populusque Romanus*, the Senate and People of Rome) inscribed in gold was carried by Giovanni Giorgio Cesarini, followed by the procurator of the Teutonic Order with the white banner on which stood a black cross, and by the prior of the Order of Rhodes, with the red silk flag and the white cross. Then came the gonfalons of the general captain and the gonfalonier of the Church and a group of the nobility of Rome and Florence on horseback, all in gala dress. The pontifical ecclesiastical court offered a no-less-colorful portrait, with the tabernacle of the Most Blessed Sacrament mounted on a white horse. Two hundred fifty abbots, bishops, and archbishops preceded the cardinals, ordered according to their various ranks. The Swiss guard with their picturesque uniforms finally announced the pope,

[50] Leo X (Giovanni de'Medici: 1475–1521), created cardinal when he was only thirteen years old, continued the policies of Julius II. On his character, see M. Pellegrini, in DBI, vol. 64 (2005), pp. 513–523; Guglielmo Roscoe, *Vita e pontificato di Leone X*, Sonzogno, Milan, 1805, 12 vol.; Rodocanachi, *La première renaissance*; Bonner Mitchell, *Rome in the High Renaissance: The Age of Leo X*, University of Oklahoma Press, Norman, 1973.

[51] Pastor, *Storia dei Papi*, vol. 4, pt. 1, p. 24.

the last in the procession because he was the first in order of importance. Under a canopy carried by Roman citizens, with the tiara studded with gems on his head, Leo X rode upon a white Turkish steed. The streets of the procession route were decorated with rich tapestries embroidered in gold, the windows crowded with spectators, the people massed along the streets. Among the triumphal arches erected by the rich bankers, the most sumptuous was that of Agostino Chigi. Written upon it in gold letters was, "Once upon a time Venus ruled; then followed Mars the god of war; now august Minerva, the time for you begins."[52] After the pontificates of Alexander VI, who evoked Venus by his dissolute private life, and Julius II, the general, symbolized by Mars, Minerva heralded the reign of a humanist pope, whose ambition was to make of Rome what his father, "the Magnificent," had made of Florence: the most active intellectual center of Italy and the world.[53] The protector gods were those of paganism.

The Medici pope, who had been formed in the climate of the neoplatonic *Accademia*,[54] gathered around him the most celebrated artists and writers and sent hand-picked scholars throughout Europe in search of the most precious Latin manuscripts. Like his predecessors, Leo X lived totally immersed in a worldly life. He loved music and dramatic productions, often licentious ones, but his favorite entertainment was hunting. Leo X dedicated the month of October each year to this pastime, wandering through the Roman countryside with his well-trained falcons, who captured quail, partridges, and pheasants. An entourage of society notables numbering in the hundreds joined him, with Venetian

52 Ibid., p. 27.

53 VILLOSLADA, *La Iglesia en la época del Renacimiento y de la reforma Católica*, p. 514.

54 The neoplatonic *Accademia* was a cultural institution founded in Florence in 1462 by the philosopher and astrologer Marsilio Ficino (1433–1499) on behalf of Cosimo I de' Medici. See ERWIN PANOFSKY, *Il movimento neoplatonico a Firenze e nell'Italia settentrionale*, in *Studi di iconologia* (1939), Einaudi, Turin, 1999, pp. 184–235; OSKAR KRISTELLER, *Il pensiero filosofico di Marsilio Ficino*, Le Lettere, Florence, 2005.

ambassadors carefully cataloging the hunts in detail, including the happy participation of numerous cardinals, prelates, and writers.[55]

Leo X seemed insensitive to the ongoing calls for a reform of customs and clerical discipline that by now had echoed for more than a century within the Church. Shortly before his death in 1512, Julius II had convened the Fifth Lateran Council[56] in order to discuss the reform of the life of the Church. The superior general of the Augustinians, Egidio of Viterbo, had said to the assembly that he saw "ignorance, ambition, shamelessness, and libertinism triumph in the Holy Place, where shameful vices ought to be carefully banished,"[57] while a disciple of Savonarola, Gianfrancesco Pico della Mirandola,[58] had presented to the Council Fathers a prayer in which, after having described the grave corruption of customs, he called upon the pope to remedy the serious abuses existing in the Church, declaring that if Leo X allowed the crimes of ecclesiastics to continue to go unpunished, there was need to fear that God himself "would strike and scatter the sick members with fire and sword."[59]

The Fifth Lateran Council concluded on March 16, 1517. On October 31 of the same year, Martin Luther affixed his Ninety-Five Theses on

[55] Pastor, *Storia dei Papi*, vol. 4, pt. 1, pp. 385–389.

[56] On Lateran V, see Karl Joseph Von Hefele, *Histoire des Conciles d'après les documents originaux*, Letouzey et Ané, Paris, 1907, vol. 8, pt. 1, pp. 239–548; Pastor, *Storia dei Papi*, vol. 3, pp. 820–825, 837–839; vol. 4, pt. 1, pp. 529–547; Richard Schoeck, *The Fifth Lateran Council: Its Partial Success and Its Larger Failures*, in *Reform and Authority in the Medieval and Reformation Church*, edited by G. F. Lytle, Catholic University of America Press, Washington, D.C., 1981, pp. 99–126.

[57] *Storia religiosa di mons. Claude Fleury*, Vincenzo Pazzini Carli, Siena, 1782, p. 238.

[58] Giovanni Francesco II Pico della Mirandola (1469–1503) is the author of a dialog in three books—*Strix, sive de ludificatione daemonum* (Bologna, 1523); translated by the Dominican Leandro degli Alberti with the title *La Strega, overo de le Illusioni del Demonio* (Geronimo de Beneditti, Bologna, 1524)—considered to be one of the first treatises on demonology.

[59] Pastor, *Storia dei Papi*, vol. 4, pt. 1, p. 543.

the door of the church of the castle of Wittenberg. When he received news of the Lutheran revolt, Pope Leo simply shrugged his shoulders, not understanding the implications. Ludwig von Pastor concluded the volume of his history of the popes dedicated to Leo X by saying that since he was "of a light and joyful disposition, he continued to dedicate himself without thinking to very worldly pleasures, even after the great storm was already set off that would strip the Roman See of a third of Europe. In everything a true son of the age of the Renaissance, Leo X, surrounded by his artists, poets, musicians, comedians, buffoons and similar courtiers, abandoned himself with frightening ease to the vortex of the life of the world, caring not whether his pleasures were agreeable or not to a spiritual lord."[60]

The corruption was certainly worse under Alexander VI, a pope who was not responsible for any doctrinal errors but whose pontificate "was a disgrace for the Church, to whose prestige he dealt the most profound wounds."[61] For Pastor, however, the worldliness of Leo X was "more dangerous for the Church" because it was "much more difficult to combat." "His pontificate, exaggeratedly raised to the heavens by humanists and poets, glorified by the brilliant art of Raphael, was fatal to the Roman See."[62]

3. The Revolution of Luther

A bleak presentiment of the future always precedes major catastrophes. Among all of the catastrophes of the sixteenth century, the most terrible was the Protestant Revolution, initiated by Martin Luther in 1517.[63] The occasion for the tragedy was the so-called question of indulgences.

[60] Ibid., p. 575.

[61] Ibid., p. 576.

[62] Ibid., p. 577.

[63] On the person and work of Martin Luther (1483–1546), we recommend the studies of the Dominican Fr. Denifle and the Jesuit Fr. Grisar, who drew their work from the original sources: Friedrich Heinrich Denifle, O.P. (1844–1905), *Luther und Luthertum in der Ersten Entwickelung*, 3 vol., Franz Kirchheim, Mainz, 1905–1906; Hartmann Grisar, S.J. (1845–1932),

In 1514, Leo X, in order to raise funds needed for the construction of the new St. Peter's Basilica, instituted a large new indulgence for all of Europe. An indulgence, according to Catholic doctrine, is the total or partial remission of the temporal punishments incurred for a sin that has been committed. The indulgence is granted thanks to the treasury of infinite merits of Jesus Christ and the merits of the Blessed Virgin and the saints, which the Church administers. In order to obtain an indulgence, it is necessary to be in the state of grace, to make a good confession and receive Holy Communion, and also to carry out some good works such as prayers, pilgrimages, or almsgiving. These good works are simply conditions for the fruit of the indulgence; they are not the *cause* of the indulgence. But the preaching of this new indulgence of Leo X throughout Germany encouraged a true and proper market-trading mentality on the part of those who collected the alms and sent them to Rome. Seizing on this abuse, in his theses against indulgences that he affixed to the door of the church of Wittenberg castle, Martin Luther, an Augustinian monk without a true vocation, not only condemned the venality of ecclesiastics but also denied the existence of the treasury of merits of the Church, declaring instead that the infinite merits of the Blood of Christ were enough for the salvation of souls.

Luther's gesture stirred up an enormous outcry, in part because he was encouraged by the humanist movement and by the political maneuverings of German princes, who wished to further consolidate their power by emancipating themselves from both the yoke of the Church of Rome and the Holy Roman Empire. The Protestant historian Roland H. Bainton affirms that Luther became an international personality thanks to the support of the humanists: "His call to return to the simplicity of the New

---

Luther, 3 vol., Herder, Freiburg im Breisgau, 1921–1930. Among more recent works are: RICARDO GARCIA VILLOSLADA, *Martin Lutero*, IPL, Milan, 1985; and ROBERT VON FIEDEBURG, *Luther's Legacy: The Thirty Years War and the Modern Notion of "State" in the Empire, 1530s to 1790s*, Cambridge University Press, New York, 2016.

Testament, his annoyance with scholastic subtleties, his denunciation of indulgences, of the veneration of relics, of the cult of the saints, all accorded perfectly with the humanist program."[64] And Bernd Möller writes, "The humanists were the first to accept Luther and ensure that he had a lasting following. They were the ones who first made his cause a far-reaching movement. Without them, he would have failed as many failed before him who sought to rise up against the old church. We can say this with certainty: without Humanism, there would have been no Reformation."[65]

At the end of 1518, Luther formed his new doctrine of salvation by means of faith without works, and in 1520 he formed his other principle according to which Sacred Scripture is the only source of truth, without the mediation of the Church. The fundamental concept for Luther is that human nature is radically corrupted by Original Sin, the center and source of every evil in man; sin is invincible; not even Baptism can cancel it out. Thus man is not justified by the observance of the law through his good works but rather by faith alone, without works. God has given man a law that he cannot observe, so that through awareness of the nothingness of his works, faith may be born within man. The phrase "*pecca fortiter, crede fortius*," (*sin greatly, but believe still more greatly*) is a very good summary of Luther's thought.

The doctrines of Luther were finally condemned on June 15, 1520, by Leo X's bull *Exsurge Domine*.[66] But Luther, even before he knew of this document, had written to a friend: "The die has been cast. I despise forever both the furor and the favor of Rome." On August 1, 1520, he

[64] ROLAND H. BAINTON, *La riforma protestante*, Italian translation. Einaudi, Turin, 1964, p. 64. On the relationship between Luther and Humanism, see among others: LEWIS W. SPITZ, *The Protestant Reformation 1517–1559*, Harper and Row, New York, 1985; HELMAR JUNGHANS, *Der Einfluss des Humanismus auf Luthers Entwicklung bis 1518*, in "Luther-Jahrbuch," 37 (1970), pp. 37–101.

[65] BERND MÖLLER, *Imperial Cities and the Reformation*, Fortress Press, Philadelphia, 1972, p. 36.

[66] DENZ-H, nn. 1451–1492.

published a manifesto, *To the Christian Nobility of the German Nation*, in which he proclaimed the equality of all Christians because of the universal priesthood, and recourse to the Bible alone as the source of truth. In October of the same year he published a new work, *On the Babylonian Captivity of the Church*, in which he reduced the number of the sacraments to two—Baptism and the Lord's Supper—while declaring that their efficacy depended only on a faith that justifies.

4. The Spread of Protestantism in Europe

On January 3, 1521, Leo X decreed the excommunication of Luther with the bull *Decet Romanum Pontificem*. Emperor Charles V summoned Luther to the diet which opened at Worms on January 28, 1521, and with the Edict of Worms the following May 26, he banned the heretic from the empire. At that time, Charles V[67] reigned over a vast territory of which it was said that the sun never set on it, because it stretched from the extreme eastern borders of Europe across the oceans to the new colonial possessions in America. His dream of recovering the universal empire of Charlemagne was shattered, among other reasons, because of his indulgence toward Luther, who obtained a safe-conduct from him and thus was able to leave the Diet of Worms undisturbed. On his way back, Prince Frederick the Wise of Saxony protected Luther by having him kidnapped by a group of knights and brought to his castle, the Wartburg, where the heresiarch remained for ten months, employed in the composition of various writings and in the translation of the Bible into German. During this period, an extreme left wing began to emerge among his followers, which sought to push the nascent movement toward radical positions: priests got married, monks left their abbeys, the

[67] Charles V (1500–1558) became Prince of the Low Countries as Duke of Bourgogne in 1506, King of Spain in 1516, and Emperor of the Germanic Holy Roman Empire from 1519 until his abdication in 1555. See the biographies of Karl Brandi, *Carlo V*, Italian translation, Einaudi, Turin, 2008; and Alfred Kohler, *Carlo V*, Italian translation, Salerno, Rome, 2005.

Mass was changed, and altars, images of the saints, and crucifixes were demolished.[68] The preaching of Luther also ignited the flame of religious and social revolt, but the so-called "Peasants' Revolt" between 1524 and 1525 was severely repressed by the German princes, with the approbation of Luther.

In 1526 the Diet of Speyer was convoked, in which Charles V granted to princes and to the other free cities of the empire the right to embrace Protestantism. Taking advantage of this faculty, various German states converted to the new religion, including East Prussia, which was a fiefdom of an ancient chivalric order, the Teutonic Order, which had distinguished itself in battle in the Crusades and in the conversion of the Baltic nations. The apostasy of the Grand Master Albrecht von Hohenzollern laid the foundation for what would later become the Prussian state.

The term "Protestant" entered history on April 19, 1529, when a new Diet of Speyer confirmed the Edict of Worms against Luther. It was then that the states that had already been conquered by the new ideas presented a solemn *protest*, signed by five princes and fourteen cities of the empire. On December 25, 1530, the Lutheran states united together at Schmalkalden, in Thuringia, forming a league that made Lutheranism a political and military power. After fierce military clashes, on September 25, 1555, the Peace of Augsburg was concluded between Catholics and Protestants by the Emperor Ferdinand, brother of Charles V. The Peace of Augsburg established the right of princes to choose their religious confession, obligating their subjects to adopt the same religion as their sovereigns (*cuius regio, eius religio*: "whoever rules the region chooses the religion"). The religious division of the empire was thus officially sanctioned, and Lutheranism conquered about two-thirds of Germany.

[68] On the "Radical Reform," see George Hunston Williams, *The Radical Reformation*, Westminster Press, Philadelphia, 1962; Ugo Gastaldi, *Storia dell'anabattismo*, 2 vol. Claudiana, Turin, 1972–1981; Roberto de Mattei, *A sinistra di Lutero*, Solfanelli, Chieti, 2017.

The work of Luther was developed in Switzerland by the apostate pastor Ulrico Zwingli,[69] and above all by John Calvin,[70] who published his *Institutio Religionis Christianae* in 1536, in which he brought the Lutheran doctrine on predestination to its extreme consequences. Luther began from the total corruption of human nature and so concluded that salvation comes by faith alone. Calvin completely denied human freedom and conceived of faith as a gift given by God only to his elect. If everything depends on God, without the cooperation of man, it is God who decides infallibly whom to save and whom to condemn. Human freedom is thus annulled. Like Luther, Calvin reduced the number of sacraments to only two, Baptism and the Eucharist, but he went beyond Luther, reducing the Eucharist to a merely symbolic commemoration. Calvin further succeeded in instituting a religious dictatorship in Geneva, by which he imposed on all its citizens a tenor of life that was inspired by the strictest rigorism. Those who did not observe the prescribed norms were inexorably persecuted and killed. Swiss Calvinism spread into France, the Low Countries, Germany, and Scotland. It was then brought to America by English emigrants.

[69] Ulrich Zwingli (1484–1531) died in 1531 in the Second War of Kappel, in which the Protestant cantons were defeated by the Catholic ones. His body, recovered after the battle, was quartered by the executioner, and his ashes were thrown to the wind. The only work of Zwingli in which his doctrine is systematically laid out is his *Commentary on True and False Religion*. He adopted the core of Lutheranism as his own but accentuated its spiritualist and anti-sacramental character.

[70] John Calvin (1509–1564), who was directed by his father toward an ecclesiastical career, had to renounce it because of a crime he committed for which he received a sentence of death, but which was later commuted to being given a brand of infamy on his shoulder. Between 1533 and 1536 he composed the *Institutio Christianae Religionis* (1536), the "*summa*" of "reformed" Protestantism, the first edition of which was published at Basel in six chapters. Little by little it grew until the final edition (1650), which contained four volumes and eighty chapters. According to the Protestant historian Bainton, "Calvin's conception of man was just as dismal—and perhaps even more catastrophic—than that of Luther and the anabaptists" (*La riforma protestante*, p. 109).

If in Germany Protestantism began with a heresy and ended with a schism, in England the opposite happened: the rupture with the Church began with schism and ended with heresy. Henry VIII, who ascended to the throne in 1509, was a young and brilliant prince. When Luther began to attack the doctrine of the Church, Henry VIII refuted him with a work in which he defended the sacraments, and so in 1521 Pope Leo X conferred on him the title of *Defensor Ecclesiae*. But a few years later, the sad question of his marriage exploded, when the king divorced Catherine of Aragon and married Anne Boleyn in 1533, even though the pope forbade it. Pope Clement VII refused to recognize the marriage, and the following year Henry VIII made Parliament vote in favor of the Act of Supremacy, with which the Kingdom of England separated itself from the Roman Catholic religion and formed a national church, later called the Anglican Church, whose supreme head was the king.

For Bossuet, in his *Histoire des variations des Eglises protestantes* (1688),[71] there are four great groups of "Protestants": Lutherans, Zwinglians, Calvinists, and Anglicans. However, these religious confessions were bypassed on the left by a swarm of sects, modeled by the Anabaptists, so named because they denied the validity of Baptism administered to infants and readministered it only to adults. Within this group there later developed a rationalist current called Socinianism after its founders Lelio and Fausto Socino of Siena, who in the name of the principle of free examination dissolved all dogmas, beginning with the Trinity. Based on this same principle, the Anabaptists and the Socinians concluded that each member of the faithful was free not only to place every belief under examination but also to practice the morals of his liking. The unique element common to all the Protestant variations is the rejection of the Roman Church, the Mystical Body of Jesus Christ. As the Spanish philosopher Jaime Balmes

[71] JACQUES-BÉNIGNE BOSSUET, *Histoire des variations des Eglises protestantes*, printed by the widow of Sebastien Marbre-Cramoisy, Paris, 1688. For a pointed criticism of the development of Protestant doctrines, see the important work of Fr. GIOVANNI PERRONE, S.J., *Il protestantesimo e la regola della fede*, 2 vol., *La Civiltà Cattolica*, Rome, 1853.

observes, these variations demonstrate that the constitutive principle of the Protestant heresy is purely destructive and dissolving.[72]

Protestantism, deprived of an objective rule of faith, moved toward a religious self-fragmentation, and the spiritual unity of Europe was now compromised.

5. Catholic Reform and Counter-Reform

What history has labeled the Protestant Reformation was in reality a religious revolution and thus a pseudo-reform. The Catholic Church opposed this revolution with a vast effort encompassing religion, politics, culture, and the arts.[73] Protestant and liberal historiography called this Catholic reaction the "Counter-Reformation" in order to imply that it was a movement without a soul, purely repressive. But the term "Counter-Reformation," like the term "medieval," has today lost all negative meaning and may be tranquilly used to indicate the authentic Catholic Reform of the sixteenth century, which was caused not by the Protestant Revolution but rather by the supernatural principle that constitutes the soul of the Church and never abandons her.[74] The reform movement within the

[72] Jaime Balmes, *El protestantismo comparado con el catolicismo*, in *Obras completas*, La Editorial Católica, Madrid, 1948, vol. 4, p. 17. See also Giovani Turco, *Protestantesimo e modernità Soggettivismo religioso e soggettivismo politico nell'analisi di Balmes, de Maistre e Taparelli*, in "Espíritu," 142 (2011), pp. 311–377.

[73] For a panoramic vision, see Daniel Rops, *L' Eglise de la Renaissance et de la Réforme*, Fayard, Paris, 1955; Léon Cristiani, *La Chiesa al tempo del Concilio di Trento*, in Fliche-Martin, vol. 17, pp. 1–579.

[74] "*Reformatio catholica non determinata est a reformatione protestantica (...) Causa prima est principium vitae supernaturalis, vis spiritualis intera, quae semper agit in Ecclesia, quia semper in ea vivit et agiit eius Fundatoris*" (Fredegando Callaey, *Praelectiones historiae ecclesiasticae mediae et modernae*, Pontificium Urbanum de Propaganda Fide, Rome, 1950, p. 340). The concept of "early modern Catholicism" proposed by John W. Malley does not grasp the essence of the vast phenomenon (*Trent and All That: Renaming Catholicism in the Early Modern Era*, Harvard University Press, Cambridge, Massachusetts, 2000). The distinction between the Reform and Counter-Reform proposed by Hubert Jedin in his essay *Katholische*

Catholic Church began in fact well before Luther, and the emergence of Protestantism only served to increase it and better define it.

In the fifteenth century, religious orders like the Dominicans, Franciscans, and Benedictines sought to reform themselves, thanks to the emergence and vast influence of numerous great preachers, theologians, and spiritual masters. Among the Franciscans, there were St. Bernardine of Siena, St. John of Capistrano, and St. James of Marca; among the Dominicans, Blessed Giovanni Dominici and St. Antonino of Florence, without forgetting Cardinal Thomas de Vio (also known as Gaetanus or Cajetan), appointed as general of the order in 1508, who promoted the full observance of the rule in all the houses of the order. Among the Benedictines, three reformed congregations stand out: San Benito of Valladolid in Spain, Bursfeld, near Hannover, in Germany, and Santa Giustina in Italy. Among the "White Benedictines" or Cistercians, two reformed branches emerged, one in Castile and the other at Chiaravalle in Lombardy. In 1520 Blessed Paolo Giustiniani founded a new congregation of Camaldolese who took the name of the hermitage of Montecorona that was its center. Among the spiritual authors of this period we should also recall the Dominican Battista of Crema[75] and his disciple Serafino of Fermo of the Canons Regular of the Lateran Basilica, while in 1528 the Capuchin order was formed, based on the ancient Franciscan rule, through the work of Ludovico Tenaglia and then of Matteo of Bassi, the

Reformation oder Gegenreformation?, Josef Stocker, Lucerne, 1946, also seems to be artificial.

75 Battista da Crema (baptized Giovanni Battista Carioni: ca. 1460–1534), was a widely read but also very controversial religious Dominican of the pre-Tridentine period. In 1554 his works were placed by Paul IV on the Index of Forbidden Books with the accusation of semi-pelagianism, but they were taken off at the beginning of the twentieth century, after the canonization (1897) of St. Anthony Maria Zaccaria, who was his disciple. See I. Colosio, *Jean-Baptiste Carioni*, in DSp, vol. 1, cols. 153–156; Luigi Bogliolo, *Battista da Crema. Nuovi studi sopra la sua vita, i suoi scritti, la sua dottrina*, SEI, Turin, 1952; and Mauro Regazzoni, *L'epoca della Riforma e della Controriforma*, in *Storia della spiritualità italiana*, a cura di Pietro Zovatto, Città Nuova, Rome, 2002, pp. 276–281.

vicar general of the Franciscan Order of Friars Minor. However, in the fourteenth century, the rich array of new religious institutes that would characterize the next century was lacking. In this sense, as Fr. Innocenzo Colosio observes, the fifteenth century was one of the most sterile centuries in the history of the Church.[76]

Among the exceptions was the Calabrian St. Francis of Paola,[77] the founder of the Minims, who died in 1507 at the age of ninety-one in the convent of Plessis-lez-Tours in France. In response to a century immersed in disorder and hedonism, Francis imposed the practice of severe Lenten abstinence on the new order, which was to be practiced in every time and place throughout one's entire life. The life of St. Francis of Paola was an uninterrupted series of prodigies, such as when he crossed the Straits of Messina on his mantle placed over the waves. King Louis XI made him come to his court so that he could be assisted by an authentic saint, and Francis remained in France for twenty-four years as a living reproof against the pagan spirit of Humanism.[78] St. Robert Bellarmine writes that on the eve of the Protestant heresy, the Lord wanted in a certain way to contrast the severe mortifications of St. Francis of Paola with the rebellious sensualism of Luther, showing what could have been the path of an authentic Christian reform.[79]

[76] I. Colosio, *I Mistici italiani dalla fine del Trecento ai primi del Seicento*, in GAF, vol. 9 (1964), p. 2161.

[77] On St. Francis di Paola (1416–1507), canonized on May 1, 1519, only twelve years after his death, see the biographies dedicated to him by the Minimist Frs. Giuseppe Maria Perrimezzi (*La vita di S. Francesco da Paola, fondatore dell'ordine de'Minimi*, Tipografia Francesco de Angelis, Naples, 1842) and Giuseppe Roberti (*S. Francesco di Paola*, Curia Generalizia dei Minimi, Rome, 1963).

[78] L. Cristiani, *L'insurrection protestante. L'Eglise de 1450 à 1623*, Librairie Fayard, Paris, 1961, p. 40.

[79] "*Lutherus docuit nihil valere ieiunium et ciborum delectum esse superstitiosum; Franciscus Ordinem instituit, in quo qui vivere volunt frequenter ieiunare, et perpetuo a carnibus et lacticiniis se abstinere debent*" (S. Roberto Bellarmino, *Conciones habitae*, Coloniae Agrippinae, Lovanii, 1615, *Concio VI*, p. 544).

The dawn of the new century opened with the birth of groups of ardent piety, the Confraternities or Companies of Divine Love.[80] Under the influence of the preaching of the Franciscan Bernardino of Feltre,[81] a group formed in Vicenza in 1500 called "The Secret Company of St. Jerome," or the Oratory of Divine Love, composed of laity dedicated to works of piety and charity, above all toward those sick with the plague and syphilis.[82] In Liguria, under the influence of the same St. Bernardino, who had preached in Genoa, and of a great mystic, St. Catherine Adorno de' Fieschi,[83] a Company of Divine Love developed, which was initiated by the notary Ettore Vernazza. The purposes of the sodality were expressed in its Chapters: "*Our Fraternity is instituted for no other reason than to root and plant divine love in our hearts, that is, charity.*"

80 Villoslada, *La Iglesia en la época del Renacimiento*, vol. 3, pp. 587–599. *I Capitoli della Confraternita del Divino Amore* were published by Fr. Pietro Tacchi Venturi in *Storia della Compagnia di Gesù in Italia: La vita religiosa in Italia durante la prima età della Compagnia di Gesù*, Civiltà Cattolica, Rome, 1930, pp. 223–238. See also Daniela Solfaroli Camillocci, *I devoti della carità. Le confraternite del Divino Amore nell'Italia del primo Cinquecento*, La Città del Sole, Naples, 2002.

81 Blessed Bernardino of Feltre (1439–1494) was a disciple of St. James of La Marca (1393–1476), who in his turn continued the spirit and preaching of St. Bernardine of Siena (1380–1444) and of St. John of Capistrano (1386–1456). See Lodovico da Besse, *Il beato Bernardino da Feltre e la sua opera*, 2 vol., Tip. Pontificia S. Bernardino, Siena, 1905.

82 On St. Cajetan of Thiene (1480–1547), canonized by Clement X in 1671, see the perspective of Gaetano Greco, in DBI, vol. 51 (1998), pp. 203–207; René de Maulde La Clavière, *San Gaetano di Thiene e la Riforma cattolica italiana*, Italian translation edited by Giulio Salvadori, Desclée, Rome, 1911; Pio Paschini, *San Gaetano di Thiene, Gian Pietro Carafa e le origini dei chierici regolari teatini*, Storia e Letteratura, Rome, 1926; and Gabriel Lompart, *Gaetano da Thiene. Estudios sobra un reformador religioso*, in "Regnum Dei," 24 (1968), pp. 1–325.

83 St. Catherine Fieschi Adorno (1447–1510), known as Catherine of Genoa, is considered one of the greatest figures of Christian mysticism. On her life, see Umile Bonzi da Genova, *Catherine de Gênes*, in DSp, vol. 2 (1953), cols. 290–325; Bonzi da Genova, *Santa Caterina Fieschi Adorno*, 2 vol., Marietti, Turin, 1960–1962.

Wherever the Companies of Divine Love developed, they promoted personal sanctification, divine worship, and the works of mercy. The fruit of the Company of Divine Love of Genoa was the foundation of the Hospital of the Incurables or the Chronically Ill, whose statutes were approved by the Senate of the Republic of Genoa on November 27, 1500. Two other hospitals were soon added in Rome and Naples. As Fr. Garcia Villoslada observes, "there was no Company of Divine Love without a hospital in which its members could practice charity."[84]

The Company of Divine Love in Rome had its most fervent, humble, and charitable member in the priest Cajetan of Thiene,[85] from Vicenza in the Venetian Republic, who carried out his role as protonotary apostolic in the Curia and who became the great initiator of the Catholic reform of the sixteenth century. One of Cajetan's collaborators was the Neapolitan priest Gian Pietro Carafa, who was of a very different temperament but just as pious and zealous. Cajetan was proclaimed a saint by Clement X in 1671. Carafa became pope in 1555, taking the name Paul IV. Together these two reformers founded the Congregation of Clerics Regular in 1524, later more commonly known as the Theatines because Carafa, the first superior of the new religious order, was bishop of Chieti (*Episcopus Theatinus*). Theatine spirituality was centered on abandonment to Divine Providence and an ardent eucharistic zeal.

6. The Church Preserves the Gift of Holiness

The Theatines inaugurated a new form of religious life, that of clerics regular, who practiced the evangelical counsels, professed public vows, and lived a common life following a rule, but without a cloister. The same

[84] Villoslada, *La Iglesia en la época del Renacimiento*, p. 595.

[85] Cristiani, *La Chiesa al tempo del Concilio di Trento*, pp. 24–26. Alongside St. Cajetan of Thiene at Rome there was also the distinguished theologian, later bishop, Giuliano Dati (1445–1524), who placed his own church of Santa Dorotea in Trastevere at the disposition of the Company, until it obtained the hospital of San Giacomo in Augusta.

model of life was embraced by St. Anthony Mary Zaccaria,[86] who in 1530 founded the Clerics Regular of St. Paul, or the Barnabites, named after the first church they possessed, St. Barnabas. The Barnabites restored liturgical life, attracting people to the churches with the beauty of worship and the majesty of various ceremonies such as public adoration of the Most Blessed Sacrament. From the altar, where he often celebrated Mass in ecstasy, their founder passed to the confessional, the pulpit, hospitals, and prisons. Following Zaccaria's spirit, the Countess of Guastalla, Ludovica Torelli, after being widowed for the second time at twenty-five years old, founded the Institute of the Angeliche in Milan, while St. Angela Merici formed the "Company of the Discharged of St. Ursula" in Brescia, known as the Ursulines, with the purpose of the moral and religious education of women and offering spiritual and material assistance to sick and wayward women.

In 1532 St. Jerome Emiliani,[87] a soldier who was wounded in combat and converted after a long imprisonment, founded the Order of the Somaschi Fathers, named after the village near Bergamo that became the center of the order. Jerome, who remained in the lay state, died on February 8, 1537, the victim of his heroic dedication to plague victims. His institute was approved by Paul II three years later, in 1540.

In the same year, 1540, the pope approved the Society of Jesus, founded by St. Ignatius of Loyola.[88] The Society was a sort of militia gathered

[86] On St. Anthony Mary Zaccaria (1502–1539), see FRANCESCO TRANQUILLINO MOLTEDO, *Vita di S. Antonio Maria Zaccaria fondatore de' Barnabiti e delle Angeliche*, Tipografia M. Ricci, Florence, 1897; PAOLO PRODI, *Antonio Maria Zaccaria*, in DBI, vol. 3 (1961), pp. 586–590.

[87] Jerome Emiliani (1486–1537), founder of the order of Clerics Regular of Somasca, was canonized by Clement XIII in 1767. The best biography is GIUSEPPE LANDINI, *S. Girolamo Miani. Dalle testimonianze processuali, dai biografi, dai documenti editi e inediti fino ad oggi*, Ordine dei Chierici Regolari Comaschi, Rome, 1947.

[88] On St. Ignatius of Loyola (1491–1556), canonized by Gregory XV in 1622, there is an immense literature. See IGNACIO IPARRAGUIRRE – MANUEL RUIZ JURADO, *Orientaciones bibliograficas sobre S. Ignacio de Loyola*, 3 vol., Institutum Historicum S. I., Rome, 1965–1989.

around the standard of the Cross, that had as its goal the propagation of the Faith and works of charity. In addition to the three vows of poverty, chastity, and obedience, the Jesuits also had to make a fourth vow to obey the Roman Pontiff in all the tasks he gave them to accomplish. Thanks to its militant spirit and ironclad organization, the Jesuits spread rapidly throughout Europe. They soon took over important positions in the courts and universities of Europe and in the spiritual direction of princes and sovereigns. The model of their educative system was the Roman College, founded in 1551.[89]

At the center of the spirituality of the Society of Jesus were the *Spiritual Exercises* of St. Ignatius,[90] an inspired book that according to St. Francis de Sales produced more saints than the number of individual letters of the alphabet it contains. Among these were Sts. Peter Faber and Peter Canisius who, in opposition to Lutheranism, renewed the Christian spirit in Germany, while St. Francis Xavier undertook a prodigious missionary activity in India and Japan between 1540 and 1552. When St. Ignatius died at Rome on July 31, 1556, the Society of Jesus included more than one thousand professed religious, divided into four national regions and twelve provinces, with one hundred houses and colleges.

In 1540, St. John of God[91] had founded a congregation in Spain called the *Fatebenefratelli* because, when he was begging for the sick, St. John was often heard to say in the streets: "*Fate bene fratelli*—Do good brothers, for you and for the love of God." Along with him in Spain, St. Thomas of Villanova and St. John of Avila formed, along with St. Ignatius, a triad

[89] CRISTIANI, *La Chiesa al tempo del Concilio di Trento*, pp. 31–35. See also JACQUES CRÉTINEAU-JOLY, *Histoire religieuse, politique et littéraire de la Compagnie de Jésus, composée sur les documents inédits et authentiques*, Mellier, Paris, 1844–1846; and TACCHI VENTURI, *Storia della Compagnia di Gesù in Italia*.

[90] See JOSEPH DE GUIBERT, S.J., *La spiritualità della Compagnia di Gesù*, Italian translation, Città Nuova, Rome, 1992, pp. 77–100.

[91] St. John of God (1495–1550), founder of the Hospitaller Order, also called the *Fatebenefratelli*, was canonized by Alexander VIII in 1690. See JOSÉ LUIS MARTÍNEZ GIL, *San Juan de Dios fundador de la Fraternidad Hospitalaria*, Biblioteca Autores Cristianos, Madrid, 2002.

of prominent representatives of the Catholic reform, with initiatives, styles, and consequences opposed to Lutheranism.[92]

In the same years, the figure of Philip Neri[93] dominated Rome, a very different saint from Ignatius of Loyola but closely tied to him. St. Ignatius, who loved him in a special way, compared him to a bell that calls the people to church even though it remains in the bell tower.[94] Little by little he gathered a group of people around him called the Oratory, which met in the Church of San Girolamo della Carità and then in the "*Chiesa Nuova*" of Santa Maria in Vallicella. Philip gained souls through catechesis, spiritual conferences, and religious practices such as the "Seven Churches" pilgrimage and the "Forty Hours" devotion that he introduced to Rome. During the Jubilee Year 1550, the Pilgrims' Confraternity of the Trinity, founded by St. Philip, offered asylum and assistance to over fifty thousand pilgrims who were poor or whose health was in a precarious condition.[95]

[92] M. Ruiz Jurado, *Storia della spiritualità: secoli XV–XVI*, Pontificia Università Gregoriana, Rome, 2000, pp. 26–37; Camilo Abad, *Ascetas y místicos españoles del siglo de oro anteriores y contemporáneos al V.P. Luis de la Puente*, in "Miscelánea Comillas," 10 (1948), pp. 27–127. St. Thomas of Villanova (1486–1555), archbishop of Valencia, was a great restorer of discipline and ecclesiastical formation, prior to the decrees of the Council of Trent. St. John of Avila (1499–1569), the apostle of Andalusia, was a counselor of bishops in planning and carrying out the reform of the Church desired by the Council of Trent.

[93] On St. Philip Neri (1515–1595), canonized by Gregory XV in 1622, beyond the work of Fr. Antonio Gallonio, *Vita beati p. Philippi Neri Florentini Congregatione Oratorio fondatoris in annos digesta*, published *apud* Aloysium Zannettum, Rome, 1600 (critical edition in the care of the Presidency of the Council of Ministers, Rome, 1995), see also Louîs Ponnelle e Louis Bordet, *Saint Philippe Néri et la société romaine de son temps*, Bloud et Gay, Paris, 1928; Antonio Cistellini, *San Filippo Neri, l'Oratorio e la Congregazione oratoriana, storia e spiritualità*, 3 vol., Morcelliana, Brescia, 1989.

[94] René François Rohrbacher, *Storia universale della Chiesa cattolica*, Italian translation, Giacinto Marietti, Turin, 1969, vol. 13, p. 37.

[95] Luigi Fiorani, *Il carisma dell'ospitalità*, in *La storia dei Giubilei*, Giunti, Rome, 1998, vol. 2, pp. 308–325.

This veritable legion of saints flowered before, during, and after the Council of Trent, which was the great Catholic response to the Lutheran Revolution. While Protestantism's conquests finally ceased, "God," writes Dom Guéranger, "was pleased to show that the Roman Church had not lost anything because it had preserved the gift of holiness."[96]

7. Adrian VI and the Sack of Rome

The first pope who understood the need for a reform of the Church was the successor of Leo X, Adrian Florent of Utrecht,[97] who reigned for only twenty months as Adrian VI (1522–1523). "However," Pastor observes, "to him remains the imperishable merit of having been the first one to place his finger on the wound with heroic courage and indicate the way forward for the future."[98] The two guiding ideas of this pope, laid out in his enthronement speech, were the continuation of the Crusades against the Turks and the reform of the Curia, prepared by a commission of cardinals instituted in February 1523. Adrian VI undertook a "gigantic war against the swarm of abuses that deformed the Roman Curia as well as almost the entire Church,"[99] and he openly denounced the men of the Church for their responsibility for the abuse, as emerges clearly from an instruction that the nuncio Francesco Chieregati read in Adrian's name to the Diet of Nuremburg on January 3, 1523. In this unprecedented document, the pope said:

> We know well that also for years now many detestable things have been happening in this Holy See: abuses in ecclesiastical matters,

[96] Dom Prosper Guéranger, *Le sens chrétien de l'histoire*, in *Jésus-Christ roi de l'histoire*, Association Saint-Jérôme, Saint-Macaire, 2005, p. 48.

[97] Adrian Florent (1459–1523) of Utrecht, professor of theology at Louvain, tutor and later counselor of Charles V, created cardinal by Leo X in 1517, was elected pope on January 9, 1522. On his life, see Pastor, *Storia del Papi*, vol. 4, pt. 2, pp. 3–148; Mario Rosa, *Adriano VI*, in EP, vol. 3 (2000), pp. 64–70; Robert E. McNally, *Pope Adrian VI (1522–23) and Church Reform*, in "Archivum Historiae Pontificiae," vol. 7 (1969), pp. 253–285.

[98] Pastor, *Storia del Papi*, vol. 4, pt. 1, p. 6.

[99] Ibid., vol. 4, pt. 2, p. 141.

injuries to the precepts; indeed, everything had changed for the worse. It is therefore no wonder that the disease has spread from the head to the members, from the Pope to the prelates. All of us, prelates and clergy, have deviated from the path of the righteous, and for a long time there was no one who did good. Therefore we ought to all give honor to God and humble ourselves before Him: each one should meditate so that he may repent and reform himself before he is judged by God on the day of his wrath. Therefore in our name you shall promise that we want to see with all diligence that the Roman Court be improved before all else, from which perhaps all these other evils have originated; then, just as the disease began here, so also the recovery will begin here, to which we consider ourselves all the more obliged because everyone wants such reform.[100]

Adrian VI died on September 14, 1523. At that time Philip de Villiers de l'Isle Adam,[101] the Grand Master of the Order of Hospitallers (later the Order of Malta), had come to the Vatican seeking refuge. The order had tried in vain to defend the island of Rhodes from the Turks. He was the living testimony of a threat that continued to loom over Christianity.

On November 19, 1523, Cardinal Giulio de' Medici, the cousin of Pope Leo X, succeeded Adrian VI as pope with the name of Clement VII (1523–1534).[102] With him, Burckhardt writes, "the horizon of Rome was

[100] Ibid., pp. 87–88.

[101] Philippe de Villiers de l'Isle-Adam (1464–1534) became Grand Master of the Order of Hospitallers of St. John in 1521, and immediately he had to deal with the defense of Rhodes against the assault of Sultan Suleiman. After a heroic resistance that lasted six months, he accepted a capitulation and left the island. Emperor Charles V granted him Tripoli and Malta in 1530. The name of the Order of Malta dates to that year.

[102] Clement VII (Giulio de' Medici: 1478–1534), natural son (later legitimized) of Giuliano, who was assassinated in the Pazzi conspiracy a month before Giulio's birth, was made a cardinal in 1513, and he carried out the role of vice-chancellor during the pontificate of his cousin Leo X. See Roger Mols, *Clement VII*, in DHGE, vol. 5 (1958), cols. 1241–1244; Adriano Prosperi, *Clemente VII*, in DBI, vol. 26 (1982), pp. 222–259.

covered with heavy vapors resembling the leaden veil of the *scirocco* that at times makes the last months of summer so dangerous."[103]

It was during Clement VII's pontificate that the terrible Sack of Rome[104] took place on May 6, 1527, at the hands of the *Landsknechts* of Emperor Charles V. It is difficult to describe how many and great were the sacrileges and devastations carried out during this event, which surpassed the Sack of Rome by Alaric in 410 in its brutality. The sack raged with particular brutality against priests and religious: nuns were raped, priests and monks were killed and sold as slaves, palaces and churches were destroyed. The unlimited license to steal and kill lasted eight days and the occupation of the city lasted nine months. "Hell is nothing compared to the garment that Rome now wears," reads a Venetian account written on May 10, 1527, quoted by Pastor.[105]

According to the German historian, "the Sack signaled the end of the Renaissance, the end of the Rome of Julius II and Leo X."[106] Catholics universally interpreted the event as a merited chastisement for their sins. "The recognition that God had punished with fire and sword the failure of the Eternal City that had called for heaven's revenge led many to come

[103] J. BURCKHARDT, *La civiltà del Rinascimento*, p. 145. The *scirocco* is a hot, dusty, rainy wind and fog that blows from North Africa across the Mediterranean to southern Europe.

[104] The Sack of Rome was the consequence of the decision by Pope Clement VII in May 1526 to support an anti-Habsburgian alliance called the League of Cognac. In addition to the king of France, the league included the Duchy of Milan, the Republics of Venice and Genoa, and Medicean Florence. The conflict quickly turned in favor of Charles V, whose troops entered Rome on May 6, 1527. The protagonists of the sack of the city were above all the German *Landsknechts*, the majority of whom were Lutheran. See UGO BONCOMPAGNI LUDOVISI, *Il Sacco di Roma*, Fratelli Strini, Albano Laziale, 1928; PASTOR, *Storia dei Papi*, vol. 4, pt. 2, pp. 253–281; ERIC RUSSELL CHAMBERLIN, *The Sack of Rome*, Dorset, New York, 1979; ANDRÉ CHASTEL, *Il Sacco di Roma*, Italian translation, Einaudi, Turin, 1983.

[105] PASTOR, *Storia dei Papi*, vol. 4, pt. 2, p. 261.

[106] Ibid., p. 582.

to their senses";[107] Catholic sentiment understood that it was a divine punishment.[108] And yet the hour of punishment was also, as always, the hour of mercy. After the terrible sack, the life of Rome changed profoundly. The climate of moral and religious relativism was dispelled, and the general misery gave the Sacred City an austere and penitential air, favoring the work of Catholic reform undertaken by the saints. "Crowned amid great hopes, Clement VII died ten years later amid sufferings that tormented both his physical person as well as the Mystical Body of the Church: his disappointing pontificate ended up becoming dramatic and was the darkest moment in the history of the papacy of that era."[109]

Pope Clement VII thought that a work of art in the Vatican should evoke the drama that befell the Church in those years, so he commissioned Michelangelo to paint the *Last Judgment* in the Sistine Chapel. The work was executed between 1535 and 1541, during the pontificate of his successor, Paul III,[110] Alessandro Farnese, who ascended to the throne on October 13, 1534.

8. Paul III and the Opening of the Council of Trent

Paul III has been called the last pope of the Renaissance and the first of the Counter-Reform.[111] The fulcrum of his pontificate was the Council of Trent, which gave an official and definitive form to the movement of authentic reform and reaction against the false Protestant reform that

[107] Ibid., p. 583.

[108] Chastel, *Il Sacco di Roma*, pp. 187–196.

[109] François Fossier, *Clemente VII*, in DSP, p. 330 (pp. 330–333).

[110] Paul III (Alessandro Farnese, 1468–1549), was made a cardinal in 1493 by Alexander VI. His sister Giulia Farnese was the "favorite" mistress of Alexander VI. He was consecrated bishop the following July 2 by Leo X and was the pope's representative at the Fifth Lateran Council. See Gigliola Fragnito, *Paolo III*, in DBI, vol. 81 (2014), pp. 98–107; Guido Rebecchini, *After the Medici. The New Rome of Pope Paul III Farnese*, in *I Tatti Studies*, 11 (2007), pp. 147–200.

[111] Giacomo Martina, *Storia della Chiesa*, "Ut Unum Sint," Rome, 1980, p. 250. Guido Rebecchini, *After the Medici.*

appeared in the Church during the first half of the sixteenth century.[112] At the beginning the popes were less favorable to this initiative than Charles V. They recalled the unhappy experience of the Councils of Constance (1414–1418) and Basel (1431), whereas the emperor saw in a general assembly of Christianity the possibility of finding a compromise, if possible, between Catholics and Lutherans in order to calm the religious warfare that was tearing the empire apart. When the possibility of an agreement collapsed at the Imperial Diet of Augsburg (1530), Paul III convoked a general council at Mantua, but the war between Charles V and King Francis I of France prevented it from taking place. Finally, with a bull issued on May 12, 1542, Pope Paul III convoked the nineteenth ecumenical council of the Catholic Church at Trent. On July 21 of the same year, at the suggestion of Cardinal Carafa, Paul III instituted the Roman Inquisition, which was the central authority for the battle against Protestantism in Italy. In the consistory of July 15, 1541, the pontiff placed Cardinal Carafa in charge of the reorganization of the Inquisition. With the bull *Licet Ab Initio*[113] of July 21, 1542, Paul III appointed a central commission composed of six inquisitorial cardinals, competent in matters of faith and given jurisdiction over the entire Christian world.

The Council of Trent opened on December 13, 1545,[114] "to the praise and glory of the Holy and Undivided Trinity, Father, Son, and Holy Spirit, for the increase and exaltation of the faith and Christian religion, for

[112] VILLOSLADA, *La Iglesia en la época del Renacimiento*, vol. 3, p. 771.

[113] *Bullarium diplomatum et privilegiorum sanctorum romanorum pontificum (=Bullarium Romanum)*, S. e H. Dalmezzo, Turin, 1860, pp. 344–346.

[114] On the Council of Trent, a fundamental work remains that of Fr. FRANCESCO SFORZA PALLAVICINO, *Storia del concilio di Trento*, 6 vol., Angelo Bernabò, Rome, 1656–1657. By contrast, great caution should be used in consulting the imposing work of Fr. HUBERT JEDIN, *Geschichte des Konzils von Trient*, 4 vol., Herder, Freiburg im Breisgau, 1949–1975 (*A History of the Council of Trent*, 2 vol., Herder Book Company, London, 1957 and 1961); and, more recently, the works of ALAIN TALLON, *Le concile de Trente*, Editions du Cerf, Paris, 2000; and JOHN W. O'MALLEY, *Trent: What Happened at the Council*, The Belknap Press of Harvard University Press, Cambridge, Massachusetts, 2013.

the extirpation of heresy, for the peace and union of the Church, for the reform of the clergy and the people, for the repression and extinction of the enemies of the Christian name."[115]

It was discussed among the Council Fathers whether the doctrinal or pastoral aspect should prevail, whether the focus should be on theological definition and the condemnation of doctrinal errors or on the reform of discipline and ecclesiastical customs. It was decided that the two aspects were inseparable, but that in a moment of doctrinal confusion such as the one the Church was living through it was necessary to define the truth and condemn errors. The Nicene-Constantinopolitan Creed was considered as the unique and unshakeable "firmament" of Christian unity.[116]

In the fourth session (April 8, 1546), the "Decree Concerning the Canonical Scriptures" was promulgated, in which the Council restated the necessity of the two sources of Revelation: Scripture and Tradition. The normative truth of the gospel "is contained in the written books and in the unwritten traditions, which, received from the Apostles themselves from the mouth of Christ himself, or by the same Apostles under the inspiration of the Holy Spirit, transmitted as if from hand to hand, have finally come down to us."[117] Regarding Sacred Scripture, the Council established that all the books that compose it were written under the inspiration of the Holy Spirit and do not contain errors. The text that was approved was the Vulgate of St. Jerome, which would be published in 1582. Of equal importance was the decree of June 17, 1546, on Original Sin, which distinguished between the Original Sin that injures all men and concupiscence that remains in man after Baptism, as a trial but not as a sin.[118]

[115] *Conciliorum Oecumenicorum Decreta*, edited by the Istituto per le Scienze Religiose, bilingual edition, EDB, Bologna, 2002, p. 660.

[116] Concilium Tridentinum, *Diariorum, actorum, epistularum, tractatuum nova collectio*, Societas Görresiana, Herder, Freiburg im Breisgau, vol. 4, 1904, pp. 579–580.

[117] Denz-H, n. 1501.

[118] Ibid., nn. 1510–1516.

The sixth session of January 13, 1547, solemnly published the Decree on Justification.[119] The Council condemned the Lutheran doctrine of justification by faith alone, restating that one is saved by means of both faith and works, and striking with an anathema those who say that "for the man who is justified and established in grace, the commandments of God are impossible to observe.[120] "God does not command the impossible; but when he commands he admonishes to do what you can, to ask for the grace to do what you cannot, and he helps you so that you can."[121]

In the seventh session, finally, the errors of Luther regarding the sacraments were condemned, anathematizing anyone who denies that "the sacraments of the new law were not all instituted by Christ our Lord, or that they are more or less than seven."[122]

Paul III died at the age of eighty-two on November 10, 1549. Luther had died on February 18, 1546, after having launched outrageous attacks condemning the pope of Rome. In March 1545 his final work was published, entitled *Against the Papacy of Rome Founded by the Devil*, in which he unleashed all of his hatred against Rome, affirming that "the Pope was defecated in the Church by all the devils of hell," and calling him "head of the damned multitude of the worst rascals on earth, the lieutenant of the devil, the enemy of God, the adversary of Christ, the destroyer of all the Christian churches, the master of all lies, blasphemies, and idolatries."[123]

9. The Conclave of 1549 and Gian Pietro Carafa

The conclave that opened on November 30, 1549, after the death of Paul III, was certainly one of the most dramatic in the history of the Church.[124]

[119] Ibid., nn. 1520–1583.
[120] Ibid., n. 1568.
[121] Ibid., n. 536.
[122] Ibid., nn. 1600–1630.
[123] See GARCIA VILLOSLADA, *Lutero*, vol. 2, *In lotta contro Roma*, pp. 742–743.
[124] On the conclave that elected Julius III, see THOMAS F. MAYER, *The War of the Two Saints: The Conclave of Julius III and Reginald Pole*, in *Cardinal Pole in European Context: A Via Media in the Reformation*, edited by the

The English cardinal Reginald Pole[125] was considered by everyone as the favorite thanks to his noble birth and the support of the Habsburgs. The papal garments were already prepared for him and he had already shown someone the speech he had prepared giving thanks for his election.

On December 5, 1549, Pole was only one vote short of obtaining the papal tiara, when Cardinal Gian Pietro Carafa stood up in front of the entire astonished assembly and publicly accused him of heresy, reproving him, among other things, for having welcomed the heretic Marcantonio Flaminio as a guest in his home, of advocating the marriage of priests, and of supporting the crypto-Lutheran doctrine of double justification. Carafa was known for his doctrinal integrity and for his life of piety. The votes for Pole collapsed and, after many long controversies, on February 7, 1550, Cardinal Giovanni del Monte was elected, taking the name of Julius III.[126]

---

same, Ashgate, Aldershot, 2000; and MASSIMO FIRPO, *La presa di potere dell'Inquisizione romana 1550–1553*, Laterza, Bari, 2014, pp. 3–51. According to Firpo, Mayer does not understand the doctrinal nature of the conflict during the conclave, reducing it instead to a simple "battle between France and imperial factions" (pp. 38–39).

125 Cardinal Reginald Pole (1500–1558) was related to the English royalty. Made a cardinal in 1536, he promoted conciliation with the reformers and, in 1545, he was one of the papal legates to the Council of Trent. Julius III named him papal legate to England, and with the rise to the throne of Mary Tudor he was consecrated archbishop of Canterbury (1556) and became the principal counselor of Queen Mary in matters of religious policy. Accused of heresy, he was referred to a tribunal of the Inquisition, but he died before the end of the trial. See DAVIDE ROMANO, in DBI, vol. 84 (2015), pp. 526–533; PAOLO SIMONCELLI, *Il caso Reginald Pole. Eresia e santità nelle polemiche religiose del cinquecento*, Edizioni di Storia e Letteratura, Rome, 1977; T. F. MAYER, *Cardinal Pole, Prince & Prophet*, Cambridge University Press, Cambridge-New York, 2000.

126 Julius III (Giovanni Maria Ciocchi del Monte, 1487–1555) was created cardinal in 1536 by Paul III, with whom he was a close collaborator. With the bull of February 22, 1545, he was appointed papal legate to the Council of Trent, which he would preside over until 1548, including during its phase in Bologna. See PASTOR, *Storia dei Papi*, vol. 6, pp. 3–299.

The accusation of heresy that for the first time was made in a conclave against a cardinal reflected the divisions of Catholics with regard to Protestantism. There was an intransigent wing that refused to make any compromise with heresy, and there was a moderate wing that was willing to compromise. If Cardinal Carafa was the champion of the first line of thought, the second tendency had its most notable exponents in Cardinals Reginald Pole and Giovanni Morone. They cultivated an irenicist Christianity and proposed reconciling Lutheranism with the institutional structure of Roman Church. Pole had created a heterodox circle in Viterbo; when Morone was bishop of Modena from 1543 to 1546 he had chosen preachers who were all successively tried for heresy. The Holy Office investigated them.

Julius III ordered the Council to be reopened at Trent on May 1, 1551, but he did not succeed in bringing it to completion. In the thirteenth session, on October 11 of that year, the Council issued its solemn definitions on the Real Presence of Our Lord, on the Most Holy Eucharist, on transubstantiation, and on the true worship of the Most Blessed Sacrament.[127] It condemned Protestants of every persuasion by declaring anathema "whoever denies that in the Most Blessed Sacrament of the Eucharist there are contained truly, really, and substantially the Body and Blood of Our Lord Jesus Christ, together with his Soul and Divinity, and thus Christ whole and entire."[128] The fourteenth session defined the matter of the sacrament of Penance[129] and Extreme Unction, considered by the Fathers as "the perfection not only of penance but of the entire Christian life, which ought to be a perpetual penance."[130]

Julius III died on March 23, 1555, and was succeeded by Cardinal Marcello Cervini, who chose to preserve his baptismal name, calling himself Marcellus II.[131] His pontificate was one of the shortest in history,

[127] Denz-H, nn. 1635–1681.

[128] Ibid., n. 1651.

[129] Ibid., nn. 1657–1719.

[130] Ibid., n. 1694.

[131] Marcellus II (Marcello Cervini, 1501–1555), created cardinal on December 19, 1539, presided over the Council of Trent in its first sessions. See

lasting only twenty-two days between April and May 1555. It was to him that Pier Luigi da Palestrina dedicated his famous *Missa Papae Marcelli* (Pope Marcellus Mass).

On May 23, 1555, Cardinal Gian Pietro Carafa was elected pope, taking the name of Paul IV,[132] surpassing Cardinal Morone by the thinnest of margins. He was seventy-nine years old and was still quite strong both physically and mentally. As bishop of Chieti he had sought to improve his diocese by means of his own example and the transformation of life of his own collaborators, in conformity with the motto he had chosen:

PASTOR, *Storia dei Papi*, vol. 6, pp. 303–340; WILLIAM V. HUDON, *Marcello Cervini and Ecclesiastical Government in Tridentine Italy*, Northern Illinois University Press, DeKalb, 1992; *Papa Marcello II Cervini e la Chiesa della prima metà del '500*, edited by C. Prezzolini and V. Novembri, Le Balze, Montepulciano, 2003; and CHIARA QUARANTA, *Marcello II Cervini (1501–1555). Riforma della Chiesa, Concilio, Inquisizione*, Il Mulino, Bologna, 2010.

[132] Born into an illustrious Neapolitan family, Gian Pietro Carafa was appointed bishop of Chieti in 1505 and was nuncio to England and Spain between 1513 and 1518. In 1518 he was made archbishop of Brindisi. Chosen by Adrian VI as a collaborator in his planned universal reform of the Church, after Adrian's death he decided to resign his episcopates and founded the Theatine Order with St. Cajetan of Thiene. Created cardinal by Paul III in 1536, he was from the very beginning a member and driving force of the Roman Inquisition established by the same pope. An important work on his life is the biography by the Theatine Fr. ANTONIO CARACCIOLO (1565–1642), *De vita Pauli IV Pont. Max. Collectanea Historica*, Johann Kinckius, Colonia, 1612; the text of this work was then reutilized by CARLO BROMATO for his *Storia di Paolo IV*, 2 vol., Anton Maria Landi, Ravenna, 1748–1753. See also BERNARDO LAUGENI, *Una vita per la Chiesa: Gian Pietro Carafa – Paolo IV, il Pontefice della riforma cattolica*, Curia dei Chierici Regolari teatini, Morlupo, 1995; ALBERTO AUBERT, *Paolo IV, Politica inquisizione e storiografia*, Le Lettere, Rome, 1999; DANIELE SANTARELLI, *La riforma della Chiesa di Paolo IV nello specchio delle lettere dell'ambasciatore veneziano Bernardo Navagero*, in "Annali dell'Istituto Italiano per gli Studi Storici," 20 (2003/2004), pp. 81–104; ANDREA VANNI, *"Fare diligente inquisitione": Gian Pietro Carafa e le origini dei chierici regolari teatini*, Viella, Rome, 2010.

"It is time that the judgment begins with my own house."[133] The primary objective of his life had always been the battle against heresies and the true reform of the Church. After having founded the order of the Theatines with Cajetan of Thiene, he had dedicated himself to the organization and development of the order, settling in Venice in 1527. His stay in the Republic of Venice, where he helped his friend Matteo Giberti,[134] the bishop of Verona, in the reform of his diocese, was the occasion of a deep reflection on the situation of the Church at that time, expressed in his essay *De Lutheranorum haeresi reprimenda* (On the Heresies of the Lutherans to be Repressed), which he sent to Clement VII in 1532. He condemned the spread of heresies and the corruption of the clergy and suggested what should be done to remedy these ills. The program he described was laid out in the course of his pontificate, which was austere and without compromise. Once he was elected pope, Gian Pietro Carafa fought with vigor against simony, imposed on bishops the obligation of residing in their own dioceses, re-established monastic discipline, gave strong support to the Tribunal of the Inquisition, and instituted the Index of Forbidden Books.

On the political level, Pope Carafa opposed Charles V, reproving him for being too tolerant with the German Protestants and for having favored the heresy of the *alumbrados* in Spain, but he valued the new sovereign Philip II of Spain for the support he gave to the Inquisition. When he discovered, at the end of his pontificate, the embezzlement of his nephew Charles, whom he had made a cardinal, Paul IV dismissed him from all his offices and, together with his two brothers, exiled him from Rome. On June 1, 1557, he informed the cardinals that he had ordered the imprisonment of Cardinal Giovanni Morone in Castel Sant'Angelo

[133] Pastor, *Storia dei Papi*, vol. 4, pt. 2, pp. 557–558.

[134] Gian Matteo Giberti (1495–1543), who became bishop of Verona in 1524, undertook a profound reform of the life of his diocese after the Sack of Rome in 1527. See L. Cristiani, *La Chiesa al tempo del Concilio di Trento*, pp. 40–67; Adriano Prosperi, *Tra evangelismo e controriforma: Gian Matteo Giberti (1495–1543)*, Edizioni di Storia e Letteratura, Rome, 2011.

on suspicion of heresy.[135] The pope made the same accusation against Cardinal Pole, who was in England, and he was dismissed from the office of papal legate. Morone was freed only in August 1559 when, on the eve of his sentencing, Pope Carafa died, thus permitting Morone to recover his liberty. He was acquitted by Pius IV the following March.

On February 15, 1559, Paul IV issued the bull *Cum ex apostolatus officio*, which decreed that any cardinal who had given rise to suspicions of heresy was ineligible for the papal throne. The bull declares that "if it ever happens at any time that ... prior to his promotion as cardinal or his elevation as Roman Pontiff, he has deviated from the Catholic faith or had fallen into any heresy (or has been part of a schism or incited one), his promotion or elevation is null, invalid, and without any value, even if it happened with the agreement and unanimous consent of all the cardinals."[136]

The figure of Paul IV has been vilified by Protestant and Modernist historiography, but he was first and foremost a reformer pope, like Adrian VI and St. Pius V. He has been accused of a lack of balance and prudence,

[135] Cardinal Giovanni Gerolamo Morone (1509–1580) was made bishop of Modena by Clement VII (1529), cardinal by Paul III (1542), and bishop of Novara by Julius III (1552). After having been incarcerated for heresy (1557–1559), he was acquitted of these accusations by Pius IV, and in 1563 he was sent as papal legate to direct the last sessions of the Council of Trent. He died in Rome on December 1, 1580, as dean of the sacred college, and was buried in the Basilica of Santa Maria sopra Minerva (his tomb today cannot be found). See M. Firpo, *Morone Giovanni*, in DBI, vol. 77 (2012), pp. 66–74; Firpo, *Inquisizione romana e Controriforma. Studi sul cardinal Giovanni Morone (1509–1580) e il suo processo d'eresia*, Morcelliana, Brescia, 2005 (1992); Firpo, *Giovanni Morone. L'eretico che salvò la Chiesa*, Einaudi, Turin, 2019; and the critical edition *Processo Morone*. On the book dedicated by Firpo to the "Morone case," see don Francesco Ricossa, *L'eresia ai vertici della Chiesa*, in "Sodalitium," 93 (1994), pp. 33–46.

[136] See *Bullarium Romanum*, vol. 6, pp. 551–556. See Elena Bonora, *Giudicare i vescovi. La definizione dei poteri nella Chiesa postridentina*, Laterza, Bari, 2007, pp. 238–286; F. Ricossa, *La Bolla "Cum ex apostolatus officio" di Paolo IV. Noterelle storiche*, in "Sodalitium," nn. 70–71 (2020), pp. 22–30.

but the situation of the Church in his time was disastrous, and only a man like him who combined an indomitable energy with an unblemished life could have faced it. As Pastor observes, "he always represented the Church's rigid point of view without regard."[137] In the battle against corruption and heresy his pontificate opened the way for St. Pius V.

10. Pius IV and the Conclusion of the Council of Trent

When Paul IV died on August 18, 1559, groups of troublemakers stormed the Inquisition building, plundered the papers, and freed the prisoners. On December 25 of the same year, after seventy-one ballots and the longest conclave of the century (September 25–December 25, 1559), the Milanese Cardinal Gianangelo de' Medici was elected pope, taking the name of Pius IV.[138] His pontificate openly contrasted with the preceding one, and began with a sensational trial against the nephews of Paul IV, the cardinals Carlo and Alfonso Carafa, and the Duke of Paliano, Giovanni Carafa, who were arrested in June 1559 with the accusation of violence, homicide, abuse of power, and injured majesty. In a consistory held on March 3, 1560, the pope presented the case to the college of cardinals and secured their consent to a guilty sentence. Carlo and Giovanni were condemned to death, the first by strangulation, the second by beheading, and their goods were confiscated.[139] Unable to obtain their

[137] PASTOR, *Storia dei Papi*, vol. 6, p. 587.

[138] Pius IV, Gianangelo de' Medici (1499–1565), archbishop of Ragusa in 1545, was created cardinal by Paul III in 1549. See PASTOR, *Storia dei Papi*, vol. 7, and the fundamental work of JOSEF ŠUSTA, *Die römische Kurie und das Koncil von Trient unter Pius IV*, 4 vols., Hölder, Vienna, 1901–1914. There was no link between the Medici family of Florence and the Medici family of Milan to which Pius IV belonged.

[139] On the trial of the Carafas, see PASTOR, *Storia dei Papi*, vol. 7, pp. 123–130; RENÉ ANCEL, *La disgrace et le procès des Carafa d'après des documents inèdits, 1559–1567*, in "Revue Bénédictine," 22 (1905), pp. 525–535; 24 (1907), pp. 224–253, 479–509; 25 (1908), pp. 194–224; 26 (1909), pp. 52–80, 189–220, 301–324. See also R. DE MAIO, *Alfonso Carafa cardinale di Napoli*, Libreria Editrice Vaticana, Vatican City, 1961; DE MAIO, *Riforme e miti nella Chiesa del Cinquecento*, Guida, Naples, 1973, pp. 93–139; A.

assent to capital punishment for Alfonso Carafa, Pius IV was forced to release him after he paid a fine of 100,000 scudi. The real goal of the trial was to discredit the image of Paul IV and simultaneously to rehabilitate Cardinal Morone, whom Pope Carafa had accused of heresy.[140] Morone was absolved of all guilt with a sentence that was issued in the consistory of March 13, 1560, and immediately announced to all the princes of Christendom.

If the hatred displayed against the Carafas, and implicitly against Paul IV, was a stain on the pontificate of Pius IV, his greatest merit was the reopening of the Council of Trent on January 18, 1562. Over the course of nine sessions, the assembly promulgated fundamental decrees, including five on the practice of Communion, the Canon, and the ceremonies of the Sacrifice of the Mass, the sacrament of Holy Orders,[141] and Matrimony.[142]

In the twenty-fifth and final session of December 3–4, 1563, the decrees on Purgatory, indulgences, and the cult of the saints and their relics and image were added. In addition, the institution of seminaries was created, and the obligation of residence for bishops in their dioceses was established. On March 2, 1563, Cardinal Gonzaga, the presiding cardinal of the Council, died, and Pius IV nominated Cardinal Morone as his successor. The final decrees of the Council were signed by 225 Council Fathers, including cardinals, patriarchs, archbishops, bishops, abbots, and generals of religious orders. Finally, on December 4, 1563, Cardinal Morone declared the Council closed. As the *acclamationes* composed by the cardinal of Lorena filled the cathedral of Trent to announce the conclusion of the Council's work, many of the Fathers could not hold back their tears. "The greatness of the moment," writes

---

AUBERT, *Paolo IV*, pp. 45–108; MILES PATTENDEN, *Pius IV and the Fall of the Carafa: Nepotism and Papal Authority in Counter-Reformation Rome*, Oxford University Press, Oxford, 2013.

140 AUBERT, *Paolo IV*, pp. 41–42.

141 DENZ-H, nn. 1763–1771.

142 Ibid., nn. 1797–1816.

Pastor, "took hold of everyone, making them sense that the hand of God had turned a page in the history of the Church."[143]

Many celebrated theologians participated in the Council of Trent, such as the Jesuits Diego Laynez and Alfonso Salmeron and the Dominicans Melchor Cano and Domenico Soto. Among the saints who promoted it and increased its impact were Peter Canisius, Ignatius of Loyola, and Charles Borromeo.

With the bull *Benedictus Deus* issued on January 26, 1564,[144] Pius IV announced his full approbation of the canons and Tridentine decrees.[145] A few months later, on November 13, the pope issued the bull *Iniunctum Nobis*,[146] with which he promulgated the *Professio Fidei Tridentinae*, which was to be the foundation of the reform. On March 24, 1564, Pius IV issued the first *Index Librorum Prohibitorum*[147] (the Index of Forbidden Books, listing those books suspected of heresy). These measures, which contrasted with the accommodating nature of Pius IV, were taken above all thanks to the influence of the secretary of state and nephew of the pope, Charles Borromeo. When Pius IV died on the evening of December 9, 1559, St. Charles Borromeo, who had just arrived from Milan, was at his bedside to assist him. He administered Extreme Unction to the pope and received his last wishes relative to his successor.

[143] Pastor, *Storia dei Papi*, vol. 7, p. 263.

[144] Denz-H, nn. 1847–1850.

[145] Albert Michel, *Les décrets du Concile de Trente*, Letouzey et Ané, Paris 1938; *The Canons and Decrees of the Council of Trent*, edited by Henry-Joseph Schröder, TAN Books, Rockford, Illinois, 1978.

[146] Denz-H, nn. 1862–1870.

[147] Ibid., nn.1851–1861.

2

Vicar of Christ and Sovereign Pontiff

1. The Conclave of 1565

On December 20, 1565, the conclave opened in the Apostolic Palace of the Popes to elect the successor of Pius IV, who died on December 9 of that year after a pontificate of six years. No one in Rome could remember such a tranquil atmosphere preceding a papal election, perhaps because it was the days right before Christmas, the day on which the Savior first saw the light of this world and brought peace to it. In an effort to reinforce this tranquility, severe prescriptions had been issued: no one could enter into Rome from outside, every dispute had to be suppressed, and anyone who drew his sword would lose his hand.[148]

The conclave[149] was solemnly opened on the morning of December 20 with the Mass of the Holy Spirit celebrated by Cardinal Francesco

[148] PASTOR, *Storia dei Papi*, vol. 7, pp. 1–2.

[149] The term conclave derives from the Latin *cum clave* (closed with the key) and designates the gathering of the college of cardinals that has the task of naming the pontiff. In the course of history there have been different legislative directives given by the popes on the conclave. See ALBERTO MELLONI, *Il conclave*, Il Mulino, Bologna, 2001; FREDERIC J. BAUMGARTNER, *Behind Locked Doors: A History of the Papal Elections*. Palgrave Macmillan, New York, 2003; MARIA ANTONIETTA VISCEGLIA, *Morte e elezione del papa. Norme, riti e conflitti. L'Età moderna*, Viella, Rome, 2013; MILES PATTENDEN, *Electing the Pope in Early Modern Italy, 1450–1700*, Oxford University Press, Oxford, 2017; AGOSTINO PARAVICINI BAGLIANI, M. A. VISCEGLIA,

Pisani, dean of the sacred college. Toward noon the cardinals reached the Pauline Chapel, where the oath took place for all those inside the conclave, which was placed under the surveillance of Prince Flaminio Savelli, marshal of the Holy Roman Church. Then the bull *In Eligendis*[150] of October 9, 1562, was read, with which Pius IV had intended to prescribe more severe rules for the election of the Supreme Pontiff. The constitution of Pius IV provided for the possibility of four electoral systems: the *scrutiny*, in which voting by ballot occurred until the canonical majority was achieved; the *accession*, which permitted each cardinal at the end of a scrutiny to transfer his vote and "accede" to a candidate who needed his vote in order to be elected; the *compromise*, which delegated the choice to a restricted number of cardinals as "great electors"; and the *inspiration*, or *adoration*, as an act of extraordinary acclamation. The ban on anyone entering the conclave was reiterated, as well as the severity of the enclosure and the prohibition on communicating in any way with the outside world. The entrances were strictly monitored, to guarantee isolation from the outside world.

There were at that moment seventy-one cardinals of the Church. Many of them were far from Rome, and so only forty-eight entered into the conclave. In the following days others arrived, and the number rose to fifty-three. Only one, Cardinal Pisani, dated back to the era of Leo X.[151] The others had received the red hat from the seven popes who had succeeded from 1522 to 1565. However, it was difficult to surmise which of them would be elected.

Il Conclave. Continuità e mutamenti dal Medioevo ad oggi, Viella, Rome, 2018.

150 *Bullarium Romanum*, vol. 7, pp. 230–236.

151 Francesco Pisani (1494–1570), of an aristocratic Venetian family, was created cardinal by Leo X in 1517. After playing a decisive role in the conclaves that elected Paul IV and Pius IV, he participated in the conclave of 1565 with his nephew Alvise (1522–1570), created cardinal by Pius IV on March 12 of the same year. See LINDA BOREAN, *I cardinali Francesco e Alvise Pisani: ascesa al potere, magnificenza e vanagloria*, in CATERINA FURLAN, PATRIZIA TOSINI (ed.), *I cardinali della Serenissima. Arte e committenza tra Venezia e Roma (1523–1605)*, Silvana, Cinisello Balsamo, 2015, pp. 105–127.

The eyes of all the European courts were fixed on Rome, but in the conclave of 1565 the political pressure proved to be less strong than it had been for the elections of the preceding popes. Maximilian II, the son of Emperor Ferdinand of Austria, had held the supreme temporal authority of Christianity for only one year and held an ambiguous position between Catholics and Protestants. Catherine de' Medici, regent for her fifteen-year-old son, Charles IX, governed with difficulty a France that had been divided by the wars of religion. The queen of England, Elizabeth Tudor, was struggling with the queen of Scotland, Mary Stuart, who contested her legitimacy. The king of Spain, Philip II, who had inherited the American and Italian dominions of his father, Charles V, in 1556, was the only one who, because of the integrity of his faith and the power of his kingdom, could have used his power to influence the conclave, but out of respect toward the sacred college he renounced using it.[152]

The king of Spain, however, carefully followed the events and asked his ambassador, Luis de Requesens,[153] to compose an opinion on the upcoming papal election. In Requesens's opinion, the favorite seemed to be Cardinal Giovanni Morone, who at the age of fifty-seven was at the height of his strength and had extensive diplomatic experience. But, Requesens wrote to Philip II, "*es tenido por hombre muy hondo e doblado y que jamas muestra lo que tiene en el echo.* (He is considered to be a man who is very deep and bent over, who never shows what he has in his action)."[154] Among the names that were in discussion, Requesens also mentioned that of Cardinal Michele Ghislieri, called "the Alexandrian cardinal" after the Piedmontese city of Alessandria closest to

[152] Pastor, *Storia dei Papi*, vol. 8, p. 9.

[153] Luis de Requesens y Zúñiga (1528–1576) was the representative of the king of Spain to Rome. In 1571 he participated in the Battle of Lepanto with Don Juan of Austria. He was appointed governor of the state of Milan (1572–1573) by Philip II and then governor of the Low Countries (1573–1576). See Adro Xavier, *Luis de Requesens en la Europa del siglo XVI*, Vassallo de Mumbert, Madrid, 1984.

[154] Quoted in Firpo, *Inquisizione romana e controriforma*, Il Mulino, Bologna, 1992, pp. 473–474.

the region where he was born. But Requesens believed it was impossible that Ghislieri could be chosen, because he was considered too rigid in his views. Furthermore, some did not consider him to be up for such a demanding task because of his limited experience in managing political and economic affairs.[155]

Just as in every papal election, everything would depend on the "party leaders," the cardinals who, thanks to their personalities and their ecclesiastical relations and policies, controlled the highest number of votes. In 1565, these were Cardinals Alessandro Farnese, Ippolito d'Este, and Charles Borromeo.

The ancient house of Farnese had experienced a rapid ascent thanks to Pope Paul III, who had appointed Pier Luigi of the Farnese family as the gonfalonier of the Holy Roman Church,[156] the Duke of Castro and, in 1545, the Duke of Parma and Piacenza. Alessandro Farnese[157] was the son of Pier Luigi, who was assassinated in 1547. Alessandro was created cardinal by Paul III at the age of only fourteen. Like all the members of his family, the cardinal was a lover of the arts and a generous patron. He lived in his splendid palace, surrounded by a princely court. He used to say that he had made three unattainable things: the Palazzo Farnese, the

[155] Tommaso Maria Minorelli, *Vita di San Pio V*, (1712), edited by Fabio Gasti, Ibis, Pavia, 2012, p. 65.

[156] The office of gonfalonier of the Church (in Latin *Vexillifer Ecclesiæ*) was one of the highest offices of the Papal States. Innocent XI (1676–1689) replaced the position of the gonfalonier with the *Vessillifero*, or Standard Bearer of the Holy Roman Church, making this office honorary and hereditary. He conferred it on Marquis Giovanni Battista Naro, in whose family (which became by succession Patrizi Naro Montoro) remained until the motu proprio *Pontificalis Domus* of Paul VI in 1968, by which the Pontifical Noble Guard was abolished.

[157] Alessandro Farnese, called "the Youth" (1520–1589), whom history would recall as "*il Gran cardinale*," was, from 1535 until his death, vice chancellor of the Holy Roman Church, the highest office after the pope. His tomb is in the Church of the Gesù, which he had built for himself. See Clare Robertson, *Il Gran Cardinale Alessandro Farnese: Patron of the Arts*, Yale University Press, New Haven, 1992. On the Farnese family: Edoardo del Vecchio, *I Farnese*, Istituto di studi romani editore, Rome, 1972.

Church of the Gesù, and his natural daughter, Clelia,[158] whom Michel de Montaigne called "*sans comparaison la plus aimable femme qui fut pour lors à Rome* (without comparison the kindest woman then living in Rome)."[159]

The dynasty of the Este family was just as noble and influential. The cardinal of Ferrara, Ippolito d'Este,[160] was the son of Duke Alfonso I and Lucrezia Borgia. If the paternal grandfather of Cardinal Farnese was Paul III, the maternal grandfather of Ippolito d'Este was Alexander VI. And if Cardinal Farnese would pass into history for the Farnese Palace and the Farnese Gardens that he created on the ruins of the Palatine Hill, Cardinal Ippolito would be remembered for the magnificent Villa d'Este built at Tivoli, where he was governor for life. Created cardinal by Paul III, Cardinal Ippolito set himself the goal of ascending to the papal throne in order to secure greater glory for a family that had not yet given popes to the Church. He had participated without success in the conclaves that had elected Julius III, Marcellus II, Paul IV, and Pius IV, and he hoped finally to succeed in his undertaking. Paul IV had compared him to Simon Magus for his simoniacal maneuvering.[161]

[158] So wrote Giacinto Gigli (1594–1671) in his diary on September 13, 1613, recalling the death of Clelia Farnese, whom the cardinal had sired by the French duchess Claude de Beaune. See PATRIZIA ROSINI, *Clelia Farnese la figlia del Gran cardinale*, Sette Città, Viterbo, 2010.

[159] MICHEL DE MONTAIGNE, *Journal de voyage en Italie par la Suisse et l'Allemagne en 1580 et 1581*, Les Belles lettres, Paris, 1946, p. 486.

[160] Cardinal Ippolito d'Este (1509–1572), appointed archbishop of Milan in 1519 when he was only ten years old, renounced the pastoral governance of the archdiocese in 1550, but he reassumed apostolic administration in 1555 and renounced it again on December 16, 1556. In 1552 he was appointed governor of Siena. See LUCY BYATT, *Este, Ippolito d'*, in DBI, vol. 43 (1993), pp. 367–374; VINCENZO PACIFICI, *Ippolito II d'Este, Cardinal di Ferrara*, Società di Storia e d'Arte in Villa d'Este, Tivoli, 1984 (1923). On the Este family, one of the most ancient and long-lived Eurpoean dynasties, see LUCIANO CHIAPPINI, *Gli estensi. Storia di mille anni*, Corbo Editore, Ferrara, 2001.

[161] PASTOR, *Storia dei Papi*, vol. 6, p. 453. Simon Magus, a contemporary of the apostles, practiced the magic arts in Samaria and wanted to purchase the powers of St. Peter and the apostles, but he crashed to the ground as

Another cardinal was more a balance needle than a party leader: Cardinal Francesco Gonzaga,[162] the son of Ferrante I Gonzaga, the sovereign of the countship of Guastalla and the nephew of Cardinal Ercole Gonzaga. He was related to Cardinal Borromeo by marriage, because his eldest brother, Cesare, was married to Borromeo's sister Camilla. He had fought for the establishment of peace between the Gonzaga and Farnese families, divided by an ancient rivalry, and reconciliation took place in 1560 before Pius IV, who made Gonzaga a cardinal on February 26, 1561.

2. The Role of St. Charles Borromeo

The key figure, however, was Carlo Borromeo,[163] a twenty-eight-year-old cardinal, of noble birth but also valued by many for his ability and piety. Carlo was the son of count Gilberto Borromeo and Margherita de' Medici, the sister of Pius IV. He was born on October 2, 1538, at Arona, the family castle, on the left shore of Lago Maggiore. In the consistory of January 31, 1560, when he was only twenty-two, his uncle made him

he was trying to rise into the air with the help of the devil (Acts 8:9–10). This story is the origin of the term "simony," understood as the buying and selling of sacred things. The historian Eusebius of Caesarea and the first Fathers of the Church say that the roots of *gnosis* and of heresy go back to Simon Magus. See JULIEN RIES, *Gnostici e manicheismo. Gli gnostici. Storia e dottrina*, Italian translation, Jaca Book, Milan, 2010; JULIEN RIES., *Gnosticisme*, in DHGE, 21 (1986), cols. 264–281; STEPHEN HAAR, *Simon Magus: The First Gnostic?*, Walter de Gruyter, Berlin, 2003.

[162] Francesco Gonzaga (1538–1566), the son of Ferrante I and Isabella di Capua, was created cardinal by Pius IV in 1561 and bishop of Mantova on May 15, 1565, with a dispensation for not having yet reached the canonical age for the appointment. On the Gonzaga family, see RENATA SALVARANI, *I Gonzaga e i papi. Roma e le corti padane fra Umanesimo e Rinascimento (1418–1620)*, Libreria Editrice Vaticana, Rome, 2014.

[163] On Carlo Borromeo (1538–1584), archbishop of Milan beginning in 1564 and canonized in 1610 by Pope Paul V, only twenty-six years after his death, see MICHEL DE CERTEAU, *Borromeo*, in DBI, vol. 20 (1970), pp. 260–269; PASTOR, *Storia dei Papi*, vol. 7, pp. 82–94; 322–328. For a bibliography, see R. MOLS, DHGE, XII, (1953), cols. 530–534; and H. JEDIN, *Carlo Borromeo*, Istituto della Enciclopedia Italiana, Rome, 1971, pp. 63–71.

a cardinal and soon after his secretary of state. His conduct was always irreprehensible, but his deep conversion took place only after the sudden death of his eldest brother, Federico. Everyone in Rome thought that Carlo would continue the family, but after making the spiritual exercises of St. Ignatius, he turned his back on a future of wealth and pleasure, receiving priestly ordination on July 17, 1563. On May 12, 1564, Pope Pius IV appointed him archbishop of Milan, where he arrived in September 1565 with an entourage of one hundred people and escorted by a company of knights—as was befitting for bishops, "*in militia Christi imperatores* (commanders of Christ's army)."[164] When the pope became ill in December, Borromeo immediately returned to Rome, and in December he was able to administer Extreme Unction to his uncle.

On his deathbed, Pius IV said to Borromeo that he desired to be succeeded by a cardinal he had created. Borromeo did not have strength to impose his own candidate, but he controlled about twenty votes in the conclave, enough to impede the election of a candidate who was displeasing to him. Yet he never threw his votes to either Cardinal Este or Cardinal Farnese, both of whom he considered too worldly. He favored Cardinal Morone, who had been tried for heresy by Pope Carafa, but who had been exonerated in 1559 by Pius IV, who held him in high regard. Morone was not worldly, he was an able diplomat, and he had the merit of having brought the Council of Trent to a close, which Borromeo had participated in during the sessions of 1562–1563. Borromeo thought that while he might not make a holy pope, he would certainly be a serious pope.

Borromeo was convinced that he had the election in hand, but he had not reckoned with Cardinal Michele Ghislieri, who had no personal ambition of his own but only one candidate to whom he was opposed: Giovanni Morone. Ghislieri said that in conscience he could not elect Morone as pope, since Morone had been suspected of heresy by Paul IV;[165] he had proof of it. With these words, Cardinal Alessandrino, who

[164] *Acta Ecclesiae Mediolanensis*, edited by Achille Ratti, vol. 3, Pontificia Sancti Iosephi, Mediolani, 1897, p. 857.

[165] Bromato, *Storia di Paolo IV*, vol. 2, p. 407.

had received the doctrinal inheritance of Paul IV, brought to light the existence of a division within the sacred college between two parties that had opposed each other in the preceding years and that corresponded to two different ways of facing the Protestant heresy.

The party faithful to the memory of Paul IV, Pope Carafa, maintained that no compromise with the Protestants was possible. Its manifesto was the letter *De Lutheranorum haeresi reprimenda*, written by Cardinal Carafa to Clement VII on October 4, 1532, which affirmed that in the "spiritual war" that was taking place "we must not be sleeping!" and that "the truth is this: heretics must be treated as heretics."[166]

The party that followed Pius IV, the pope who had just passed away, instead advocated a more political line, which in modern terms could be called the "outstretched hand." On March 25, 1538, Giovanni Morone, who was then bishop of Modena, wrote a letter to Jacopo Sadoleto in which he said that it would be "much better to proceed with these modern heretics with meekness than to want to irritate them with insults, and if this had been done at first perhaps less effort would be presently needed to unite the Church."[167] On May 14, 1539, Morone suggested to the pope that "the means enacted to reduce the Lutherans" should not be sought in arms but in the meeting of the Council, in the concession of the marriage of priests and communion under both species [*sub utraque*], and especially in refraining from writing "contumeliously" against the heretics.[168]

Ghislieri, on the other hand, said that he did not understand how Morone could be supported in good conscience, knowing that he had been prosecuted for heresy. He was convinced that, if certain points of accusation had been more attentively examined, the Milanese cardinal

[166] *Concili Tridentini Tractatum*, edited by Vincentius Schweitzer, vol. 12, Herder, Freiburg im Breisgau, 1930, p. 68 (pp. 67–77).

[167] Walter Friedensburg, *Giovanni Morone und der Brief Sadolets an Melanchthon vom 17. Juni 1537*, in "Archiv für Reformationsgeschichte," I (1903), p. 380 (pp. 372–380).

[168] Franz Dittrich, *Nuntiaturberichte aus Deutschland*, Perthes, Gotha-Berlin, 1892–1981, vol. 4, pp. 405–407.

would not have been acquitted so easily; after all, even the mere suspicion of heresy was enough to exclude him from the papal dignity. When it was said to him that Paul IV had tried Morone because he had ill will toward him, Ghislieri replied that Pius IV had acquitted him without sufficient knowledge because he had too much good will toward him.[169] Ghislieri knew what he was talking about, since he had been a member of the commission that oversaw the trial against Morone. In his capacity as Grand Inquisitor it was he who had collected depositions and documents and directed the interrogations of Cardinal Morone.

After the death of Paul IV, the new pope, Pius IV, had published in consistory a sentence of absolution that annulled the preceding trial. Ghislieri, at the insistence of Pius IV, had signed the sentence, but in 1565 he brought with him into the conclave the procedural papers against the Milanese cardinal, which remained in his possession.

Ghislieri's intervention in the conclave disrupted Borromeo's plans and instead reinvigorated Cardinals Ippolito d'Este and Alessandro Farnese who were opposed to him, flanked by Cardinals Francesco and Alvise Pisani. Borromeo decided to make an effort, however, and over the course of the night of December 22, he worked strenuously for the candidacy of Morone. But at the first scrutiny on the morning of December 23, Morone obtained only twenty-six votes, a number still far distant from the required two-thirds majority.

Seeing the election of Morone fade away, Cardinal Farnese thought his moment had come, and he met with Borromeo to obtain his support, but without any success. Farnese then thought of forcing the situation. If he had obtained twenty-eight to thirty votes for himself, which was still insufficient for election, his adherents would have been able to have recourse to election through *adoration*, which consisted in placing him on the papal throne and having him sit there until the other cardinals recognized him as pope. He counted on the support of Cardinal Gonzaga who, however, died unexpectedly on the evening of January 6. His body,

[169] Pastor, *Storia dei Papi*, vol. 8, pp. 18–19, quoting from the firsthand testimony of the time.

placed on a stretcher and taken out of the conclave at one o'clock in the morning, was then buried in his titular church, San Lorenzo in Lucina.

3. The Election of Pius V

The circle of possibilities was so restricted that Borromeo was obligated to break the silence with an alternative candidate, and on the morning of January 5, 1566, he proposed the name of Guglielmo Sirleto,[170] an educated and pious cardinal, who was one of the most faithful collaborators of Pope Marcellus II during the Council of Trent. Ghislieri, who esteemed Sirleto, promised his vote. At this point Borromeo, with fifteen cardinals, went to Cardinal Farnese and begged him to elevate Sirleto by *adoration*, which Farnese had in vain asked Borromeo for himself. But Farnese, in retaliation, was immovable in demanding that the election be done by scrutiny, and Sirleto himself, who was sick in bed, asked to be spared the burden of the papacy. It was January 7, 1566, and, after eighteen days of conclave, there had been no success in reaching any agreement. His failure with Sirleto led Borromeo to a decisive step with Farnese. On the afternoon of January 7, he met Farnese once again to try to convince him to renounce the papacy, since he would never have enough votes. Instead of keeping the whole world waiting, Borromeo said to Farnese, he should behave as a Christian and make an agreement with him for the election of a good pope. Cardinal Farnese, irritated, responded that the splendor of the house of Borromeo was due to Pius IV, who had become a cardinal thanks to the support of Paul III. But, because the nephew of Pius IV refused to return the favor and was denying the papacy to the nephew of Paul III, now Farnese proposed to him a list of four names from which to choose the new pontiff: Cardinals Ricci,[171]

[170] Guglielmo Sirleto (1514–1585) enjoyed the trust of Paul IV, and after his death he retired at the formation house of the Theatines at San Silvestro in Quirinale, where he became an instructor of Greek and Hebrew, counting Charles Borromeo among his students. At the proposal of Borromeo, Pius VI appointed Sirleto a cardinal on March 12, 1565.

[171] Giovanni Ricci (1497–1574) was created cardinal by Julius III in 1551. Ricci was opposed by St. Charles Borromeo, who considered him

Dolera,[172] Scotti,[173] and Ghislieri. Borromeo, after having attentively meditated, judged Cardinal Ghislieri the most worthy of receiving the supreme authority and employed himself in every way in order to garner as many votes for him as possible.[174]

In the early afternoon of January 7, the cardinals came to the cell of Cardinal Ghislieri and almost by force and against his will led him to the Pauline Chapel. The Dominican tried in vain to withdraw himself. The cardinals genuflected before him and implored him to accept election, which took place by acclamation. Cardinal Pisani rose first, saying, "I, Cardinal Francesco Pisani, Dean of the Sacred College, elect as pope my most reverend lord Michele, called the Alessandrian Cardinal." After Pisani, Morone rose, giving his vote in a similar way, and then all the others. When they reached the number of fifty-one they stopped, because the only one left was Cardinal Ghislieri, who could not vote for himself. After the proclamation there was a long silence, until Ghislieri was heard to murmur, "*Sono content* (I am content)."[175]

---

unworthy because of a son he had by a Portuguese woman and then legitimized.

[172] Clemente Dolera (1501–1568), a Franciscan theologian, was created cardinal in 1557 and was inquisitor general under Paul IV.

[173] Giovanni Bernardino Scotti (1478–1568), from Rieti, participated in the Roman chapter of the Oratory of Divine Love and was one of the founders of the Theatines. Paul IV, who esteemed him greatly, made him archbishop of Trani and cardinal, and in 1559 wanted him to be a member of the Sacred Council, the organ that was to concern itself with the governance of the Papal States. Between 1557 and 1558 Scotti participated in the posthumous trial of Girolamo Savonarola, and in 1558 he served as judge in the first trial against Cardinal Morone. See ANDREA VANNI, *Da chierico teatino a cardinale inquisitore. Breve profilo di Bernardino Scotti* in "Rivista di Storia della Chiesa in Italia," 65 (2011) 1, pp. 101–119.

[174] Borromeo was flanked in the conclave by Cardinal Marco Sittico Altemps (1533–1595), the son of Wolfgang Dietrich and Chiara Medici, the sister of Pius IV. Although he was at first opposed to the election of a friar, Altemps later decisively supported the candidacy of the Dominican Ghislieri.

[175] PASTOR, *Storia dei Papi*, vol. 8, p. 29.

Michele Ghislieri, the 225th successor of Peter, was elected with the name of Pius V on January 7, 1566. He was seventy-two. It would have been natural for the Alessandrian cardinal to take the name of his protector, Paul IV, but out of regard for Cardinal Borromeo, the nephew of Pius IV, he took the name of the deceased pope, even thought he had not been favored by him. "With this magnanimous decision," Pastor observes, "the new pope manifested a self-abnegation similar to that of Carlo Borromeo."[176]

In a letter of January 27, 1566, to King Philip II, Borromeo wrote: "With determined will I gave myself to doing everything I could to see his exaltation."[177] And in a subsequent letter to the king of Portugal, St. Charles wrote: "I decided to take nothing into account so much as religion and faith. And since I had great esteem for the singular piety, integrity, diligence, and all the holy sentiments of the Alessandrian cardinal, I estimated that the Christian republic could be very well and divinely governed by him, if he was raised to the pontificate. And so I worked with all my soul and strength so that he would be made Pope."[178]

The certainty with which Borromeo, a man who was always truthful, referred to himself in the role of "Great Elector" of Pius V spurs us to reflection. Knowing the diplomatic ability of the Milanese saint, it is licit to think that, from the beginning his candidate *in pectore* was Ghislieri, but that he did not want to show his cards in order not to burn them, and also out of respect for the last wishes of his uncle, who had probably indicated to him the name of Morone.

Be that as it may, it was neither the first nor the last unexpected election in history. Cardinal Pedro Pacheco wrote to Philip II on January 7, 1566, that the election was evidently the work of the Holy Spirit, because many of the cardinals who entered into the conclave preferring to have

[176] Ibid.

[177] S. CARLO BORROMEO, *Lettera al re di Spagna Filippo II*, quoted in PASTOR, *Storia dei Papi*, vol. 8, p. 30.

[178] S. CARLO BORROMEO, *Lettera del 26 febbraio 1566 al Re di Portogallo*, in GIOVANNI PIETRO GIUSSANO, *Vita di S. Carlo Borromeo*, Tip. Gaetano Motta, Milano, 1821, vol. 1, pp. 77–79.

their feet cut off than vote for Ghislieri were among the first to concur in his election.[179] The general of the Jesuits, Francis Borgia, wrote to the provincial superiors of the Society that the new pope was appointed with great admiration by those who had elected him, and they confessed that "*a Domino factum est istud et est mirabile in oculis nostris*. (This is the LORD's doing; it is marvelous in our eyes.)" (Ps. 118:23)[180]

The election of Pius V was surrounded by many signs and prodigies. St. Philip Neri, when everyone said that Ghislieri could not possibly be elected pope, announced that he would be elected on a Monday at the time of Vespers, as in fact happened.[181] The day before his election, Cardinal Francesco Gonzaga, as he lay dying, suddenly woke up from his slumber and reproved his servants for not having told him of the election of Cardinal Ghislieri as pope.[182] Furthermore, during those days a frightening comet appeared in the sky above London: it looked like a hand of fire holding a sword over the island: "an express symbol of the blazing zeal of the Blessed Pope Pius V, who lashed the tyrannical Elizabeth with excommunication and other ecclesiastical censures."[183]

On his first night as pope, January 7, 1566, the new pope slept for eleven hours straight, which was unusual for him, both because of the austerity of his life and because of the evils that afflicted him. But, as Fr.

[179] PASTOR, *Storia dei Papi*, vol. 8, p. 29.

[180] SAN FRANCESCO BORGIA, *Lettera ai prepositi provinciali della Compagnia*, in *Monumenta Historica Societatis Jesu*, vol. 38, *Sanctus Franciscus Borgia*, vol. 4, Gabrielis Lopez del Horno, Matriti, 1910, p. 163.

[181] *Ristretto della vita, virtù e miracoli del Beato Pio V*, Niccolò Angelo Tinassi, Rome, 1672, pp. 46–47.

[182] MINORELLI, *Vita di San Pio V*, pp. 67–69.

[183] *Ristretto della vita, virtù e miracoli del Beato Pio V*, pp. 48–49. The phenomenon was also reported by ALFONSO DE ULLOA, who, in his *Historie di Europa* (Bolognino Zaltieri, Venice, 1770, p. 168), writes that on January 12, 1566, two comets were seen in London that followed the sun "and after there a hand was seen coming out above the clouds, holding a sword extended toward the sun, and this prodigy continued for three days." See also FELICE GIRARDI, *Diario delle cose più illustri seguite nel mondo. Diviso in quattro libri*, Presso Roberto Mello, Naples, 1653, p. 48.

Venchi observes, Pius V went to bed at peace with God and men; he had not sought the honor of the papacy, but God and men had wanted it.[184]

There exists among Catholics a tendency to believe that, in a conclave, the election is the exclusive or quasi-exclusive work of the Holy Spirit. In reality, the assistance of the Holy Spirit does not take away the freedom of the papal electors. The cardinals are only *assisted*, in a non-imposing way, which does not take away their freedom. No theologian, but also no Catholic, can maintain that the cardinals who elected the immoral popes of the Renaissance were illuminated by the Holy Spirit. The Holy Spirit did not fail to assist them, but it can happen that the cardinals gathered in the conclave reject the influence of the Holy Spirit. This does not mean that the Holy Spirit is defeated by men or by the devil. God, and God alone, is capable of drawing good out of evil and thus Providence guides every affair of history. In the case of the conclave, as Cardinal Journet[185] explains in his treatise on the conclave, the assistance of the Holy Spirit means that even if the election was the result of an evil choice, it is certain that the Holy Spirit, who assists the Church by guiding even what is evil toward the good, permits this to happen for greater and mysterious purposes. In the case of the conclave of 1565, the decisive role was played by a saint, Carlo Borromeo. And thanks to his correspondence to grace, another saint was elected, Michele (Michael) Ghislieri.

4. The Family and Childhood of Michael Ghislieri

Michael Ghislieri was born on January 17, 1504, in Bosco, a fortified village not far from Alessandria, which at the time was part of the Duchy of Milan and the Diocese of Tortona. The pope in those years was Julius II, and the emperor was Maximilian I of Austria. The Ghislieri family, originally from Bologna, was of noble origin but lived in a poor condition

[184] INNOCENZO VENCHI, O.P., *San Pio V. Il pontefice di Lepanto, del rosario e della liturgia tridentina*, Edizioni Studio Domenicano, Rome, 1997, pp. 20–21.

[185] CHARLES JOURNET, *L'Eglise du Verbe incarné*, Desclée de Brouwer, Paris, 1941, vol. 2, p. 625.

as a result of the internal battles that had torn apart the city, between the Guelphs, who were tied to the Church, and the Ghibellines, who were tied to the empire.[186] In 1445, as a result of the triumph of the Ghibelline faction, the Ghislieri family, faithful to the papacy, were expelled from Bologna and despoiled of their possessions. One branch of the family transferred to Rome, taking the name of Consiglieri, while the branch of the firstborn son transferred to the Piedmont, to Bosco. Paolo Ghislieri and Domenica Augeri named their son Antonio, because he was born on the feast of St. Antony the hermit. Only subsequently, after he entered into religion, did he take the name Michael.

The childhood home of the saint is still visible: it is a modest habitation composed of four rooms, with a stairway in the middle and a portico connected to a barn. The young Antonio was taking care of his father's flock when through the secret designs of Providence two Dominicans came to Bosco.[187] They interacted with him and were so struck by the

[186] The Ghislieri family, in addition to St. Pius V, includes two Blesseds: Filippa, a companion of St. Clare of Assisi; and Bonaparte, a disciple of Blessed Raniero da Perugia. Ludovico Iacobilli, *Vite del Ss. S.P. Pio V, del B. Bonaparte, etc.*, Vincenzo Galeffi, Todi, 1661, pp. 1–14. Returning to Bologna, the Ghislieris had senatorial dignity and later the title of count and marquis. The family coat of arms was three red bands in a silver field. Innocenzo Ghislieri, who died in Rome in 1765 without a direct descendant, was the last representative of the Roman branch of the family (Elisabetta Mori, *I Ghislieri a Roma da Pio V all'Ottocento: vicende familiari e patrimoniali ricostruite attraverso il riordinamento del loro archivio*, in "Bollettino dei Musei Comunali di Roma," 2, 1988, pp. 35–46; Mori, *L'Archivio del ramo romano della famiglia Ghislieri*, "Archivio della Società Romana di Storia Patria," 18 [1995], pp. 118–171). Luigi Bruzzone in his *Storia del Comune di Bosco*, Tip. Franchini, 1861–1863, vol. 2, p. 308, presents the family tree of the branch of the Ghislieri family in Bosco.

[187] The Order of Friars Preachers (O.P.) is a religious institute recognized by Pope Honorius III with the bull *Religiosam Vitam* (1216). The friars who belong to it are called Dominicans, after their founder, St. Dominic Guzmán (1170–1221). See Massimo Carlo Giannini, *I domenicani*, il Mulino, Bologna, 2016; Giannini, *Intellettuali militanti: i frati predicatori tra censura e Inquisizione nel Cinquecento*, in *Libri e biblioteche: le letture*

lively spirit of the youth, which was accompanied by a great modesty, that they asked him if he wanted to continue on the way with them, offering to receive him into the Dominican order and assist him in his studies. With the approval of his parents, Antonio followed them to their convent of Santa Maria della Pietà in Voghera, in Lombardy,[188] an edifice immersed in the silence of the country amidst vineyards, meadows, and woods, where after two years he received the black and white Dominican habit.

From Voghera the youth went to the convent of San Pietro Martire in Vigevano, where he began the novitiate and professed his solemn vows on May 18, 1521. When the prior asked the youth what religious name he wished to take, he replied: Michael of Bosco. The prior, perhaps thinking that the name of such an unknown locality did not give any prestige to the new name, replied: "What do you mean "of Bosco"? Because you are from the environs of Alessandria, from now on you will be called Brother Michael of Alessandria."[189]

Brother Michael of Alessandria, known as the Alessandrian, received priestly ordination in 1528 in the Church of Santa Maria di Castello in Genoa, in the ancient heart of the city. After deepening his study of theology at the University of Bologna, because of his intellectual talents Brother Michael was sent to be a teacher. He was a lecturer of philosophy and theology in different *studia* of the order, including San Tommaso in Pavia, the city where he would establish the college that today bears the name of the Ghislieri family. His lectures were rich not only in knowledge

---

dei frati mendicanti tra Rinascimento ed Età moderna, Fondazione Centro Italiano di Studi sull'Alto Medioevo, Spoleto, 2019, pp. 327–354; Gianni Festa, Marco Rainini (a cura di), *L'ordine dei predicatori. I domenicani: storia, figure e istituzioni* (1216–2016), Laterza, Rome-Bari, 2016. See also Giuseppe Villa, Paolo Benedicenti, *I domenicani della 'Lombardia Superiore' dalle origini al 1891*, Editore Valerio Ferrua, Turin, 2002.

188 Paolo Alessandro Maffei, *Vita di S. Pio V*, Giacomo Tummassini, Venice, 1712, p. 6.

189 Girolamo Catena, *Vita del gloriosissimo papa Pio V*, Filippo de' Rossi, Rome, 1647, p. 13.

but also in spirituality, so much that it was said of him that he knew how to "unite the thorns of scholasticism with those of Calvary."[190]

As a newly ordained friar, the Alessandrian was sent to the Dominican friaries of Pavia, Vigevano, Soncino, and Alba, where he quickly showed himself to be an exemplary religious and was subsequently elected as prior many times. His main character traits of boldness in faith and courage were evident from the start, which allowed him to face every difficult event of his life with deep equanimity. For example, the friars of the friary of Alba, where he was vicar, found themselves one day exposed to the fury of three hundred roaming French soldiers who wanted to sack the monastery.[191] Fra Michele threw himself before the soldiers and threatened them with the judgment of God with words so strong and fiery that it was only his presence that succeeded in preventing sacrilegious violence that day.[192]

There was already such veneration for him that he was called the new St. Bernardine, because he resembled the saint not only in his appearance but above all in his ascetical spirit.[193] The proof of the reputation he enjoyed is that on the occasion of provincial chapter of the order, which was held at Parma in 1543, he was chosen to present thirty-six theological theses to his brothers, the majority of which concerned the defense of the Roman primacy and the refutation of heresies. As Fr. Maffei observes, the words that St. Basil applied to St. Gregory of Nyssa may be adapted to Brother Michael: "*Inclytus bellator Ecclesie, ambidexter per utramque eruditionem in adversarios armatus*"; that is, he was a generous defender of the Church who, with both his hands armed to combat the monstrous errors of his time, "studied the controversies and wisely united

[190] Card. Giorgio Grente, *Il Pontefice delle grandi battaglie*, Italian translation, Paoline, Rome 1937, p. 11.

[191] The French troops, commanded by Francois de Bourbon (1519–1546), had invaded Piedmont during the Italian war of 1542–1546 between the French and the Spanish. See Michael Mallett - C. Shaw, *The Italian Wars, 1494–1559: War, State and Society in Early Modern Europe*, Pearson Education Limited, Harlow, 2012.

[192] Maffei, *Vita di S. Pio V*, p. 16.

[193] Minorelli, *Vita di San Pio V*, p. 47.

positive and scholastic theology, made excellent refutation of all those heretics with whom he happened to enter into a discussion or a dispute, and served as a model for his religious brothers on which in the future good and true theologians could be formed for the benefit of the Church and for the edification of the Christian world."[194]

5. *Summus ac perpetuus Inquisitor*

The fame of Fra Michele Ghislieri for doctrine and rigor, first of all toward himself, was such that on October 11, 1542, the Holy Office in Rome entrusted him with the role of commissioner and vicar of the Inquisition for the city of Pavia. It was the beginning of a career inside the Church that led him to assume, in 1550, the role of Inquisitor of the Diocese of Como. One of his brothers wrote that he "accepted with enthusiasm: he could commit himself more deeply, inflamed as he was with zeal to defend the Catholic religion and to eliminate lethal errors."[195]

In Italy heresy was spreading. The task of the Inquisition was to repress it. If any outbreak of heresy was reported to him, Brother Michael intervened to stamp it out. According to his biographer Catena, "the beginning of his greatness" dates back to these difficulties and the sufferings that he had to undergo in performing his office.[196] "Whoever wants to serve God in the Holy Office," Fra Ghislieri warned in 1556, "must not be afraid of threats but must have only God, the truth, and justice before his eyes."[197]

The territory under his jurisdiction extended to Valtellina and the Grisons, where over the course of 1550, Brother Michele went to ascertain the validity of the accusations of heresy brought by the Archpriest of Sondrio, Bartolomeo von Salis, against the bishop, Thomas Planta. The inquisitor demonstrated the unworthiness of the prelate. In Como, a bookseller clandestinely distributed forbidden books. Brother

[194] Ibid., p. 10.

[195] Ibid., *Vita di San Pio V*, p. 49.

[196] Catena, *Vita del gloriosissimo papa Pio V*, p. 7.

[197] Quoted in Simona Feci, *Pio V*, DSI, vol. 2, p. 1213.

Michael confiscated them. The bookseller was supported by the vicar of the diocese and the chapter of canons, who opposed the seizure of the books, but Ghislieri excommunicated both the vicar and the chapter. The canons appealed to the governor of Milan, Ferrante Gonzaga, who ordered Ghislieri to present himself before him. On the road to Milan the heretics had prepared an ambush, but Brother Michael reached the city by means of secret paths, leaving the assassins to wait in futility. He met the governor, resisted all pressure, and took the road to Rome in order to report to the Holy Office.

On December 24, 1550, Brother Michael Ghislieri, exhausted by his travels, entered the Eternal City for the first time. He went to the Dominican friary of Santa Sabina, but the prior, seeing his miserable appearance, took him for a vagabond who had come to the papal court to try his fortune, and received him coldly, asking at a certain point with mockery: "What are you looking for here, Father? Perhaps you have come here to see if the college of cardinals wants to make you pope?" "I have come to Rome," Ghislieri responded, "because the interests of the Church have called me here. I will leave as soon as my task is done. Until then, I ask you only to grant me brief hospitality and a little hay for my mule."[198]

Ghislieri's meeting with Cardinal Gian Pietro Carafa, the Prefect of the Holy Office, was decisive for his life. The Theatine cardinal was a man of vast knowledge and irreproachable behavior, and he sensed the extraordinary qualities of the Dominican friar. A fellowship was born between the two men that would never fail. The cardinal gave him full liberty to come and go from his house, where the two spent many hours a day discussing how best to fight heresy.[199] The Dominican was sent to Bergamo, where a lawyer of a noble family, Giorgio Medolago, favored Protestantism. Fra Michele imprisoned him and instituted the process.[200]

[198] ALFRED F. P. DE FALLOUX, *Histoire de Saint Pie V, Pape de l'ordre des Frères Precheurs*, Sagnier et Bray, Paris, 1844, vol. 1, p. 17.

[199] *Ristretto della vita, virtù e miracoli del Beato Pio V*, p. 30.

[200] PIER ANTONIO UCCELLI, *Dell'eresia in Bergamo nel* XVI *secolo e di frate Michele Ghislieri inquisitore in detta città indi col nome di Pio V pontefice massimo e santo*, in "La Scuola cattolica," 3 (1875), pp. 222–236, 249–262, 559–569;

The man was protected by the crypto-heretic bishop of the city, Vittore Soranzo.[201] When Ghislieri returned to Bergamo, the bishop hired ruffians to kill the Dominican, but once again he managed to escape the attack and secretly make his way back to Rome. The biographers of Pius V pass over this episode rapidly, or even ignore it, even though it was very serious for its time. Bishop Soranzo, of an illustrious family, was an acclaimed personality and enjoyed the support of the Republic of Venice. Fra Michele showed energy and uncommon courage in confronting him, with the help of laity of great doctrinal formation and exemplary habits, such as the patrician of Como, Bernardo Odescalchi, and Count Giovanni Girolamo Albani.[202] The latter saved Ghislieri's life, hiding him in the fortress of Urgnano when, after a violent uprising in Bergamo, the heretics tried again to assassinate Fra Michele.

Bishop Soranzo was arrested and transferred to Rome on March 24, 1551, following an investigation by Fra Ghislieri, who had confiscated two cases belonging to the bishop containing the works of Luther, Protestant texts, and anti-papal pamphlets. This was one of the actions that earned

---

GEREMIA PACCHIANI, *Manifestazioni protestantiche a Bergamo*, in "La Scuola cattolica," 63 (June 1935), pp. 323–347.

[201] Vittore Soranzo (1500–1558), bishop of Bergamo from 1547, was tried for heresy in 1551. Julius III imposed his absolution on the Holy Office, after receiving a secret oath from him, but Paul IV made him stand trial again and sentenced him *in absentia*, a few weeks before his death. See LUIGI CHIODI, *L'eresia protestante a Bergamo nella prima metà del Cinquecento e il vescovo Vittore Soranzo*, in "Rivista di Storia della Chiesa in Italia," 35 (1981), pp. 456–485; M. FIRPO, *I processi inquisitoriali di Vittore Soranzo (1550–1558). Edizione critica* (in collaboration with Sergio Pagano), 2 vol., Vatican Secret Archive, Vatican City, 2004; FIRPO, *Vittore Soranzo, vescovo ed eretico. Riforma della Chiesa e Inquisizione nell'Italia del Cinquecento*, Laterza, Rome-Bari, 2006.

[202] Giovanni Gerolamo Albani (1509–1591), of a noble family of Bergamo, was a renowned jurist to whom Fra Michele Ghislieri often had recourse. When he became pope, he called his former advisor and benefactor back to Rome, where he became an ecclesiastic and was awarded the dignity of protonotary apostolic and governor of the Marca di Ancona. On May 17, 1570, Pius V made him a cardinal. His candidacy for the papacy was put forward in the conclaves of 1585 and 1590.

Fra Michele the appointment to head the Inquisition.[203] The first commissioner general of the Inquisition, the Calabrian Dominican Teofilo Scullica, was dying. Cardinal Carafa rejected the names proposed by the master general of the Dominicans, Francesco Romeo, and proposed to Julius III the name of Ghislieri, who on June 3, 1551, was appointed commissioner general of the Holy Office. The duty of Fra Michele was not only to investigate and judge heretics but also to assist them when they were condemned. Every morning he went down into the prisons to visit the accused, sparing no effort to bring them back to Christ. His mercy often succeeded in conquering the hardest hearts, convincing them to abjure their mistakes.[204]

On March 23, 1555, Julius III died. The sacred college elected Cardinal Carafa as pope, but he, although an octogenarian, said that his hour had not yet come and used his authority to see Cardinal Cervini raised to the papal throne, who took the name Marcellus II. Twenty-two days later the Holy See was again vacant, and on May 14, 1555, Cardinal Carafa accepted the tiara, taking the name of Paul IV. Among the first acts of the new pope was the appointment of Fra Michele Ghislieri as bishop of Sutri and Nepi on September 4, 1556. The Dominican asked the pope to free him from this responsibility, but Paul IV replied: "I will put on your feet a chain so strong that the idea of returning to your convent will no longer pass through your head." Fra Michele replied that His Holiness had lifted him out of Purgatory to put him in Hell.[205] And since the office of commissioner general of the Inquisition was not compatible with that of bishop, Ghislieri was appointed prefect of the Palace of the Inquisition. On March 15, 1557, Paul IV made him cardinal of the church of Santa Maria sopra Minerva, which he later changed to another Dominican church, Santa Sabina on the Aventine Hill.

[203] Pierroberto Scaramella, *Pio V e la repressione dell'eresia nell'Italia meridionale*, in *Pio V nella società e nella politica del suo tempo*, a cura di Maurilio Guasco e Angelo Torre, Il Mulino, Bologna, 2005, p. 86.

[204] Ugolino Giugni, *San Pio V*, Centro Librario Sodalitium, Verrua Savoia, 2004, p. 15.

[205] Catena, *Vita del gloriosissimo papa Pio V*, p. 12.

Paul IV wanted to give him a still greater authority, never conferred on anyone else, and in the consistory[206] of December 14, 1558, he appointed him *summus ac perpetuus inquisitor*: Inquisitor General for Life, of all of Christendom, subjecting to his jurisdiction all the inquisitors and the bishops themselves. Among the first trials with which Ghislieri concerned himself was the prosecution of Girolamo Savonarola, which Paul IV wanted. The Alessandrian cardinal assumed a prudent position, which historians have called rather "innocent," limiting the accusations against the Dominican to the disciplinary realm.[207] Much more rigorous were the doctrinal accusations made against the prelates whom Ghislieri had arrested between the middle of 1557 and August 1559 and in some cases condemned: the bishop and cardinal Giovanni Morone, the bishops Giovanni Tommaso Sanfelice, Andrea Centanni, Vittore Soranzo, Giovanni Francesco Verdura, Pietro Antonio Di Capua, and Egidio Foscarari, and the protonotary apostolic Pietro Carnesecchi. The Alessandrian cardinal, however, explained his zeal only after he became pope.

6. The Alessandrian Cardinal and Pope Pius IV

In 1559, Paul IV died and was succeeded by Pius IV. The position of Cardinal Ghislieri became difficult, because the direction taken by Pius IV with regard to the Inquisition was in contradiction to his own views.[208] The new pope, while leaving Cardinal Ghislieri in his position, wanted to remove him from Rome, and on March 27, 1560, he appointed him

[206] The consistory is an assembly of cardinals convoked by and presided over by the pope in order to address matters of great importance. It may be secret, public, or semipublic.

[207] M. Firpo, P. Simoncelli, *I processi inquisitoriali contro Savonarola (1550) e Carnesecchi (1566–1567). Una proposta di interpretazione*, in "Rivista di Storia e Letteratura religiosa," 18 (1982), n. 2, pp. 220–221.

[208] Pastor, *Storia dei Papi*, vol. 8, p. 35. As Elena Bonora finds, the studies of the last thirty years on the religious aspect of sixteenth-century Italy have brought to light the contrast between the policies of Paul IV and those of Pius IV, precisely starting from the role attributed to the Inquisition (*Giudicare i vescovi*, pp. 154–155).

as bishop of Mondovì in Piedmont.[209] Ghislieri made his entrance on August 7, 1561, but immediately went to Turin and then returned to Rome before the end of the year. A second voyage in 1564 was made impossible by the loss of all his baggage at the hands of corsairs who plundered the ship that was carrying them.

One of the first initiatives of the new bishop was to turn to Duke Emanuele Filiberto of Savoy, to ask his help against the magistrates of Mondovì, who had shown themselves to be little inclined to follow the dispositions of the Holy Office. The Savoyan prince was in turn not very inclined to follow the strong line of the Dominican. In those years a group of French bishops were compromised with the Huguenot heretics. At the mandate of Pius IV, the Alessandrian cardinal directed eight bishops, including Jean de Monluc, François de Noailles, and Antonio Caracciolo to present themselves within six months at the Holy Office in order to clear themselves of the suspicion of heresy. The bishops were protected by Catherine de' Medici, but the pope took Ghislieri's position, declared them heretics, and deprived them of the episcopal dignity.[210]

The Alessandrian cardinal was among the few who dared to resist Pius IV. During a banquet in 1563, the pope expressed his desire to confer the red hat on the young princes Ferdinando de' Medici,[211] who was thirteen years old, and Federico Gonzaga,[212] who was twenty-one.

[209] *Una città e il suo vescovo. Mondovì al tempo del cardinale Michele Ghislieri*, edited by Giancarlo Comino, Giuseppe Griseri, in "Bollettino della Società per gli studi storici, archeologici e artistici della provincia di Cuneo," n. 133 (2005), pp. 7–113.

[210] Antoine Degert, *Procès de huit évêques français suspects de calvinisme*, in "Revue des Questions Historiques," 38 (1904), pp. 61–108.

[211] Ferdinando de' Medici (1549–1609), the son of the Grand Duke Cosimo, was created cardinal by Pius IV in 1562, but after the sudden death of his brother Francesco in 1587 he left the ecclesiastical life and became the third Grand Duke of Tuscany, a title he held until his death. In 1589 he married Christine of Lorena, with whom he had nine children.

[212] Federico Gonzaga (1540–1565), the last son of Federico II Gonzaga and the nephew of Cardinal Ercole, was created cardinal by Pius IV on January 6, 1563, and bishop of Mantua in 1565, shortly before his death.

Ghislieri, with respectful firmness, told the pope that the appointment of youths to the government of the Church was contrary to the recent decrees of the Council, and also that it was not an appropriate moment for a decision of such importance.[213] The pope was struck by Ghislieri's frankness, but he yielded to the requests of the Medicis. In 1587, Cardinal de' Medici's brother died, and he left the ecclesiastical life to become the third Grand Duke of Tuscany. The Alessandrian cardinal at least could have the satisfaction of seeing that his reasons for opposing his selection as cardinal were well-founded. And when the Florentine ambassador, during a visit of protocol, thanked him together with the sacred college for having adhered to the will of the pope, Cardinal Ghislieri responded boldly: "Lord Ambassador, do not thank me for the promotion, because I opposed it as much as I could, because I could not betray my conscience, which did not allow me to consent to the elevation of a thirteen-year-old boy to the cardinalate."[214]

One of the points of greatest conflict between Pius IV and Cardinal Ghislieri was the battle against heresy, which the pope wanted to be softer and the Alessandrian cardinal wanted more diligent and rigorous. It was for this reason that, during a full consistory, Ghislieri attacked the policy of Pius IV in France, opposing the assignment of the Avignon legation to Cardinal Charles de Bourbon, a relative of the heretics.[215]

His resistance to the will of Pius IV, however, made him fall into disgrace, and the pope wanted to downsize his role as Grand Inquisitor. With a brief issued on October 14 and a motu proprio issued on October 31, 1562, Pius IV redesigned the competence of the Holy Office, which, according to Elena Bonora, was reduced "to a discredited institution turned

[213] MAFFEI, *Vita di S. Pio V*, pp. 55–57.

[214] Ibid., p. 58.

[215] CATENA, *Vita del gloriosissimo papa Pio V*, p. 19; ELENA BONORA, *Inquisizione e Papato tra Pio IV e Pio V*, in *Pio V nella società e nella politica del suo tempo*, cit., pp. 62–63. Cardinal Charles de Bourbon-Vendôme (1503–1590), archbishop of Rouen, was the younger brother of Antoine de Bourbon and thus the uncle of Henri IV. At that time the Bourbons sided with the Huguenot heretics.

in on itself, although still securely in the hands of Cardinal Ghislieri."[216] The Venetian ambassador to Rome, Paolo Tiepolo, informed the Council of Trent that "the supreme authority of the Inquisition is no longer in the hands of the Illustrious Alessandrian, but His Holiness has deputized seven cardinals with equal authority who are looking after matters of the Inquisition, who are dividing the trials among themselves."[217] In 1564 Cardinal Ghislieri thought of retiring to his diocese of Mondovì. In addition to the "mal della pietra"[218] which he had suffered from for years, his overall health had worsened to the point that, in view of the death that he believed to be near, he had a tomb built for himself in Santa Maria sopra Minerva.

Then, on January 7, 1566, the unexpected election as pope changed the course of his life. The supreme office to which he was elevated seemed like a heavy cross to him, which he feared would crush him, but he accepted it with immense trust in divine help. He asked his family members how the news of his ascent to the pontificate had been received. When he was told that the people had been more saddened than happy, he responded: "We trust in God who will give us the grace to comport ourselves in such a manner that sadness the people will feel over our death will be greater than the displeasure they now feel over the dignity we have received."[219]

7. The Sovereign of Rome

The coronation of Pius V took place with the usual solemnity in St. Peter's Basilica on January 17, 1566, his birthday. The ceremony began with a solemn procession that accompanied the newly elected pope from the Apostolic Palace on the *sedia gestatoria* to the Altar of the Confession.

[216] BONORA, *Giudicare i vescovi*, p. 64.

[217] Quoted in BONORA, *Inquisizione e Papato tra Pio IV e Pio V*, p. 55.

[218] The "mal della pietra" or "stoneache," today known as kidney stones, is one of the oldest and most painful illnesses that afflicts human beings. St. Pius V cured it with donkey's milk, whose healing qualities have been known since antiquity (MAFFEI, *Vita di S. Pio V*, p. 164).

[219] CATENA, *Vita del gloriosissimo papa Pio V*, p. 16.

Along the length of the basilica, a pontifical master of ceremonies knelt three times before the pope, carrying a silver baton topped by a flaming ball of tow, reciting the words, "*Sancte Pater, sic transit gloria mundi* (Holy Father, thus passes worldly glory)," the first time in a low voice, then in a stronger voice, and finally in a loud voice. At the end of the solemn pontificals, while the choir sang the ancient hymn *Corona aurea super caput eius*, the cardinal proto-deacon imposed the *Triregno*, or papal tiara, pronouncing the following formula in Latin: "Receive the tiara adorned with three crowns, and know that you are the father of princes and kings, the rector of the world, the vicar on earth of Our Lord Jesus Christ, to whom is honor and glory for ever and ever."

Some practices that accompanied this ceremony were, however, modified. As the procession returned, the officials of the militia used to throw money to the crowds, to assure that the newly elected pope would have the sympathies of the people, but it happened that not a few people were crushed and killed in the crowd. Pius V wanted this practice to be abolished, and he ordered instead that the money be distributed wisely to poor families. The evening banquet in honor of the cardinals and ambassadors was also made less solemn, and the money thus saved was distributed to needy monasteries.

It is necessary to recall that the pope, in the sixteenth century, was not only the supreme spiritual authority of Christianity but also the temporal sovereign of a state that was not limited to the city of Rome but extended over forty thousand square kilometers, from Romagna to the Gulf of Gaeta.[220]

The Roman people flocked to St. Peter's to see what their new sovereign looked like, who up until then had led a secluded life, without the luxury and ostentation of the other princes of the Church. Most of the depictions of Pius V[221] that have come down to us show him in

[220] See Mario Caravale-Alberto Caracciolo, *Lo Stato pontificio da Martino V a Pio IX*, UTET, Turin, 1978.

[221] Antonino Silli, O.P., *San Pio V. Note agiografiche ed iconografiche*, Biblioteca B. Angelico, Rome, 1979, p. 21.

pontifical robes, with a red velvet mozzetta and, often, with a red camauro[222] on his head. The pope is recognizable by the characteristic lines of a sharp face, adorned with a flowing white beard, an aquiline nose, and deep blue eyes.[223] Ludwig von Pastor writes that the life of Michael Ghislieri, conducted in untiring work amidst penances and privations of every sort, had left clear traces in his physique: "Although he was only 62 years old, that slender man with a bald head and a long very white beard gave the impression of being an old man."[224] The general conviction was that he would not live very long, because of his health, affected by chronic bladder pain. He was a man of a sober and austere life, demanding of himself and of others. He dedicated a good deal of his day to prayer, above all when he had to make particular decisions. He was mainly concerned with perfect truthfulness, and anyone who told a lie lost his favor forever.[225] Further, Pastor adds, "he did not allow himself to be swayed by the first impression, but as soon as he had formed a strong opinion, it was almost impossible to make him reconsider it."[226] Neither worldly calculations nor the worst threats could detach him from what he felt was right.

[222] The camauro is a traditional headdress of the popes, made of red velvet and edged with ermine fur during the winter or red satin during the summer. The last popes to wear it were John XXIII and Benedict XVI, who wore it during two general audiences on December 21 and 28, 2005. See MORONI, *Dizionario di erudizione*, vol. 6, p. 308.

[223] Among these portraits, one of the best is that done by the painter Scipione Pulzone, which is in the Gallery of the Palazzo Colonna in the Piazza Santi Apostoli. Scipione Pulzone (1540–ca.1598), called Gaetano or of Gaeta, after his native place, was one of the most appreciated artists in Rome in the second half of the sixteenth century. The portraits of Pius V that are kept in the Collegio Ghislieri in Pavia and in the monastery of the Most Holy Rosary in Rome are attributed to him (SILLI, *San Pio V*, pp. 38–40). See FEDERICO ZERI, *Pittura e controriforma. L'"arte senza tempo" di Scipione da Gaeta*, Neri Pozza, Venice, 1957.

[224] PASTOR, *Storia dei Papi*, vol. 8, p. 36.

[225] CATENA, *Vita del gloriosissimo papa Pio V*, pp. 32–34; PASTOR, *Storia dei Papi*, vol. 8, p. 44.

[226] Ibid., p. 45.

The new pope appeared to be a man moved only by the desire to restore the ancient splendor of the Holy See by means of improving customs and battling against errors. Four days prior to taking possession of the Lateran, on January 12, 1566, a consistory was held in which Pius V announced reforms for the clergy and for the people of Rome. For the reform of the secular Roman clergy, a cardinalatial commission was instituted by Cardinals Borromeo, Savelli, Alciati, and Sirleto, which was to examine the knowledge, life, and customs of all priests. On this occasion, the pope exhorted the cardinals to rigorously keep watch over the members of their household, notifying them of the abolition of the right of asylum everywhere, since justice had to be able to place its hands on the guilty, even within the Apostolic Palace.[227] Under the pain of excommunication, a motu proprio imposed on all the cardinals a catalog of their income and benefices obtained from Pius IV, because Pius V said that he did not want to help rich cardinals. Since the accounts of many expenses of Pius IV were not found, the general treasurer of that pope, Matteo Minali, was put on trial and found guilty of embezzlement. In 1568, Minali, who confessed to the crime, was condemned to perpetual rowing service, the confiscation of his goods, and public flogging in Campo de' Fiori.[228]

On the day, when Pius V was making his way, with great solemnity, to take possession of the Lateran Basilica, as he passed in front of the professed house of the Society of Jesus, the pope saw Fr. Francis Borgia, surrounded by his entire community. He called him, stopped the procession, cordially embraced him, and spoke with him for some time.[229] On January 12, 1566, writing to his Jesuit brother Alfonso Salmeron, Borgia observed that with Pius V "the matters of the Reform and the Inquisition

[227] PASTOR, *Storia dei Papi*, vol. 8, p. 50.

[228] Matteo Minali, who died in prison in Ostia in July 1560, had been nominated Treasurer General of the Apostolic Camera by Pius IV on July 30, 1560. See MASSIMO CARLO GIANNINI, *Minali, Donato Matteo*, in DBI, vol. 74 (2010), pp. 555–557.

[229] PIERRE SUAU, *San Francesco Borgia (1510–1572)*, Desclée, Rome, 1909, p. 164.

will go very far."[230] St. Francis Borgia himself relates that in his first meeting with the cardinals, Pius V advised them that there were three things that they should never ask of him, because he would always deny them: "the first, if there were things against divine service; the second, if against the Council of Trent; the third, if against the order and good of the Church." The pope added that, "if someone, by deceiving him or informing him badly, would make him fall into error, against one of the things just said, he would cite him before the judgment seat of Christ Our Lord, and the wrath of God would fall upon him, because he would not have deceived a man, but the Vicar of Christ."[231]

In the allocution that he addressed to the cardinals on January 23, 1566, Pius V said that he did not intend to treat them as slaves but as brothers, observing however that the wicked lives of ecclesiastics had made no little contribution to the origin and spread of heresy. The pope exhorted them to change their lives, affirming that he would comply with the prescriptions of the Council of Trent. He ordered every bishop to leave Rome and to go and reside at the place of their own proper church, and he expressed his desire that the cardinal bishops would stay there for at least six months. His thought, he said, was directed solely toward maintaining peace between the Christian princes, annihilating heresies, and procuring help against the Turks.[232]

Pius V was convinced that the Roman Church, the mother of all the churches, was supposed to give to the world an example of holiness, order, and discipline. He therefore gathered the penitentiaries, canons, and all the priests of the Eternal City, exhorting them to fulfill their ministry in a holy way,[233] but he wanted to begin the reform of the Church with himself and his collaborators. He did not purchase new vestments but made use of those that Pius IV had used, and he never took off his Dominican

[230] Giovanni Romeo, *Pio V nelle fonti gesuite*, in *Pio V nella società e nella politica del suo tempo*, p. 114.

[231] San Francesco Borgia, *Lettera ai prepositi provinciali della Compagnia*, p. 164.

[232] Pastor, *Storia dei Papi*, vol. 8, p. 47.

[233] Maffei, *Vita di S. Pio V*, p. 82.

habit. Thus he was the first of the series of "white-robed" popes.[234] He often slept with his habit on, in order to make it easier to rise for prayer during the night. He began his day at dawn with the Holy Mass, and every Sunday and Thursday he granted public audiences, in which the poor had precedence.[235] In those days Pius V sat still and listened to the people who presented themselves to him, even for ten hours at a time. "The audience, which began early in the morning by candlelight, despite the displeasure of the officials, would last until three hours after midday, without the Holy Father taking any refreshment other than a little soup or some fruit."[236]

As early as 1566, the Spanish ambassador judges that the Church had not had a better head for three hundred years. Repeatedly in the reports this observation is made: "this Pope is a saint."[237]

8. The First Acts of the Pontificate

One of the problems that the new pope faced was choosing his closest collaborators. He wanted them to be few and faithful. Pius V was accustomed to giving his trust only to people who sought nothing for themselves. The figure of the "cardinal nephew," equivalent to a secretary of state, had at that time become an institution of the Church. Cardinal Borromeo had filled this role, but he was a man of the highest integrity, and no one had ever thought of criticizing Pius IV for this choice. At the beginning, Pius V wanted to diminish this position, and he limited himself to appointing as his "personal secretary" his former secretary Girolamo Rusticucci,[238] who was unconditionally devoted to him. He

[234] Innocenzo Venchi, O.P., *San Pio V*, Rome, 1997.

[235] Catena, *Vita del gloriosissimo papa Pio V*, p. 10.

[236] Grente, *Il Pontefice delle grandi battaglie*, p. 51.

[237] Pastor, *Storia dei Papi*, vol. 8, p. 43.

[238] Girolamo Rusticucci (1537–1603) was created cardinal by Pius V on May 17, 1570. In 1577 he was appointed vicar of the City of Rome by Gregory XIII, and during the pontificate of Sixtus V he lived together with Cardinal Michele Bonelli in the Vatican palaces, actively collaborating with the pontiff. See Giampiero Brunelli, *Rusticucci Girolamo*, in DBI, vol. 89 (2017), pp. 360–362.

conferred the office of Secretary of State on Cardinal Reumano,[239] who like him belonged to the school of Pope Carafa. When it was suggested to him in the first days of his reign that he should promote his relatives, Pius V responded, "God has called me to serve the Church, not the Church to serve me."[240]

The pope had two great-nephews who at the time were living in Rome as students at the German College, the sons of Domenica Bonelli, who was the daughter of the pope's sister, Gardina Bonelli. Pius V told them that they should continue their studies and that he would take care of them if they remained modest and humble, without expecting much from him. The pope had another great-nephew who had his same baptismal name, Antonio, who had entered into the Dominican order and had also taken the religious name of Michele. At the consistory of March 6, 1566, Pius V yielded to the requests of the College of Cardinals, made Fra Michele a cardinal, and appointed him Superintendent General of the Ecclesiastical State.[241] In this capacity, he had to deal with the temporal affairs of the Papal States and diplomatic relations with foreign powers. This new prince of the Church was given the name "the Alessandrian," just like his great-uncle.

When Cardinal Reumano died on April 28 of the same year, the pope entrusted the office of Secretary of State to his great-nephew Michele Bonelli, who together with Rusticucci became his closest collaborator, reserving for himself the true direction of the affairs of governance. Pius V watched closely over the behavior of his nephew and expressly

[239] Jean Suaux (1503–1566), born in Rheims, France, was also called Giovanni Reumano, through an Italianization of his birthplace. He was created cardinal by Paul IV in 1555, and was included among the cardinal members of the Holy Office, but he was not reconfirmed in his post by Pius IV because of his too-rigid position in line with Pope Carafa and Cardinal Ghislieri.

[240] Pastor, *Storia dei Papi*, vol. 8, p. 53.

[241] Michele Bonelli (1541–1598), created cardinal on March 6, 1566, was a member of the Congregation of the Index and the Congregation of the Council, and from 1580 until his death was cardinal protector of the Dominican Order. Cf. A. Prosperi, in DBI, vol. 10 (1969), pp. 766–774.

forbade him to use silk clothes, precious furniture, and silver vessels.[242] On November 2, 1566, St. Francis Borgia related in a letter to the Polish Cardinal Hosio that the pope had gone to the apartment of his nephew Michele Bonelli, and seeing a silk curtain on his bed, had exclaimed: "*Quid tibi, pauperi monacho, cum huiusmodi ornatu?* (What have you, a poor monk, to do with this sort of adornment?)." The cardinal replied that the curtain had been placed there by his butler without his permission, but Pius V wanted it to be removed immediately.[243]

The pope's other relatives were treated with equal rigor, including Paolo Ghislieri, his brother's son, whom Pius V freed from a Turkish prison and appointed as commander of the guard and governor of the Borgo in May 1567. When he heard that his nephew was leading a dissolute life, the pope issued a sentence declaring that Paolo Ghislieri had lost all of his offices and had to leave the Vatican within two days, the Borgo within three days, and the Papal States within ten days. All attempts by the young man to obtain the revocation of this exile failed.[244] This moral rigor and firmness toward his relatives soon ensured the respect and veneration of the Roman people for the new pope.

In the consistory of January 23, 1566, the pope spoke not only of the need for a reform of the clergy but also of his intention to proceed against blasphemy and concubinage. In order to accomplish this, on April 1, 1566, he published an edict that established the most rigid penalties against the disturbance of divine worship, the profanation of Sundays, simony, blasphemy, sodomy, and concubinage,[245] and in July of 1566 he issued an ordinance for the limitation of luxury in clothing and extravagant banquets, followed by other decrees in 1566 and 1567. The pope further wanted to remove the plague of beggars from the city of Rome, and all vagabonds and gypsies were expelled from the Papal States.[246]

[242] Maffei, *Vita di S. Pio V*, p. 74; Pastor, *Storia dei Papi*, vol. 8, p. 53.
[243] Grente, *Il Pontefice delle grandi battaglie*, p. 54.
[244] Pastor, *Storia dei Papi*, vol. 8, p. 59.
[245] *Bullarium Romanum*, vol. 7, pp. 434–438.
[246] Pastor, *Storia dei Papi*, vol. 8, p. 61.

With the bull *Supra Gregem Dominicum*[247] of March 8, 1566, the pope confirmed the decree *Cum Infirmitas*[248] of Pope Innocent III, in which he imposed on doctors the obligation of exhorting the sick to receive the sacraments. The bull established that after the first visit of the doctor, the sick person had to go to Confession within three days, or else the doctor could not return. The relatives, family members, and servants of the sick person were admonished to notify the parish priest of the illness of their relative or servant, and that they themselves should exhort the sick person to go to Confession in good time. Doctors who did not observe these prescriptions were deprived of the title of doctor, expelled from the medical colleges and universities, along with monetary fines that were to be established by the episcopal ordinary of the place. No college or university could confer a doctorate in medicine if it had not first publicly sworn before a notary and other witnesses that it would observe the papal decree.

Another plague afflicted the Papal States: prostitution. The pope decided to expel prostitutes from Rome in order to eliminate the great dishonor that they brought against the holiness of the city. When a protest was raised by the *Conservatores Urbis*, the magistrates who, together with the Senate, administered the city, the pope publicly declared that he himself and the entire papal court would sooner leave Rome than tolerate such shamefulness in the city that was supposed to give exclusively holy example to the whole world.[249] At the end of June 1566, the prostitutes were driven out of the Borgo around St. Peter's, and a subsequent edict of July 22 established that the most well-known "courtesans" must leave Rome within six days, unless they had married or entered into the convent of penitents.[250] Pius V proposed to also fight against the numerous

[247] *Bullarium Romanum*, vol. 7, pp. 430–431. The bull followed by several years a decree of Paul III that St. Ignatius of Loyola had advocated for, by which the decretals of Innocent III for the city of Rome were restored to their full force.

[248] LATERAN COUNCIL IV, chap. 22, *Gli infermi provvedano prima all'anima poi al corpo*.

[249] MINORELLI, *Vita di San Pio V*, p. 79.

[250] PASTOR, *Storia dei Papi*, vol. 8, pp. 62–63.

cases of adultery, establishing severe penalties for those who committed it. One of the richest and most reputable bankers of Rome, Signore de Vecchi of Siena, who was guilty of adultery, was flogged in the public square in December 1568 as an example to warn the nobles against committing this crime.[251]

9. Pius V and the Jews

At this point, it is necessary to speak of certain restrictive provisions of Pius V toward the Jews. With the bull *Romanus Pontifex*[252] of April 19, 1566, the pope, renewing Paul IV's bull *Cum Nimis Absurdum*[253] of July 14, 1555, confirmed the establishment of the ghetto, a section of the city, closed in by walls, which was reserved for the Jews, and prescribed for them a "*certum modum vivendi* (specific way of living)" within the city of Rome. With his subsequent bull *Cum Nos Nuper*[254] of January 17, 1567, Pius V ordered that the Jews of the Papal States must sell all of their real estate, which had been acquired by the concession of Pius IV, under penalty of confiscation. With the bull *Hebraeorum Gens*[255] of February 26, 1569, Pius V finally ordered the Jews to leave the Papal States within two months, with the exception of those who lived in the ghettos of Ancona and Rome.

[251] Ibid., p. 65.

[252] *Bullarium Romanum*, vol. 7, pp. 438–440.

[253] *Bullarium Romanum*, vol. 6, p. 498. With the establishment of the ghetto, Jews in Rome had to live in one or two connected streets, separated from the dwellings of Christians. This imposition was accompanied by various other clauses, including a ban on having Christian slaves, a ban on having any business other than selling rags and used clothing, and the obligation for all Jewish men and women to wear a yellow hat or scarf. See also E. Rodocanachi, *Le Saint-Siège et les juifs. Le Ghetto à Rome*, Firmin-Didot, Paris, 1891.

[254] *Bullarium Romanum*, vol. 7, p. 514.

[255] Ibid., pp. 740–741. The last regulation concerning the Jews in Rome was enacted by Pius VI, with his Edict on the Jews of April 5, 1775. See the text in Abraham Berliner, *Storia degli ebrei a Roma*, Rusconi, Milan, 1992, pp. 264–275.

With regard to these limitations, what escapes many historians is the distinction between the two distinct roles of the pope as head of the Universal Church and as sovereign of the Papal States. As head of the Church, the pope exercises a canonical jurisdiction over every baptized Christian in the world, but not over Jews, who belong to a different religion. It is therefore imprecise to link the Jews to the tribunal of the Inquisition, which concerned itself with them only indirectly, since they were not baptized. As the most attentive historians emphasize, "the Roman Inquisition was founded to oppose the spread of the Reformation, and it was directed against Christian heresies, not against the Jews, since these latter were considered as infidels who were *extra gremium Ecclesiae*."[256]

As sovereign of the Papal States, Pius V made a series of decisions of a political nature that must be contextualized within this historical period. The policy of segregation or expulsion of the Jews was analogous to that of other nations, such as the Kingdom of Spain and the Republic of Venice, where beginning in 1516, the Major Council created the first ghetto in Italy. In an era in which religious freedom did not exist in any European city, it would have been strange if it had existed in Rome, Christendom's holy city.[257]

Economic historians such as Giacomo Todeschini have further noted "the entirely political decision to establish the ghettos," which was complementary in Italy to the birth of the Monti di Pietà (pawnshops established to assist the poor) and the effort by governments to regulate credit.[258] With the development of the modern economy, the Monti di Pietà were Christian lending institutes that were intended to oppose

[256] Pietro Ioly Zorattini, *Ebrei*, in DSI, vol. 2, pp. 523–524.

[257] Kenneth R. Stow, in *Theater of Acculturation. The Roman Ghetto in the Sixteenth Century*, University of Washington Press, Seattle-London 2001, emphasizes the aspect of Rome as "a holy city following the heavenly archetype" (pp. 39–40).

[258] Giacomo Todeschini, *La banca e il ghetto. Una storia italiana (secoli XI-V-XVI)*, Laterza, Bari, 2016, p. 207 and *passim*. The assets confiscated from the Jews who had transgressed the restrictive measures of Pius V were supposed to be used to increase the Roman pawnshop (Monte di Pietà, founded in 1539) and the *Casa dei Catecumeni* (ibid., p. 210). See *Monti*

then-existing usury practices by Jews. The expulsion of the Jews from the Papal States was a political decision, certainly influenced by what happened in Spain, where the Jews had been expelled for reasons of social order, such as the excessive charging of interest on loans, which were viewed to especially damage the most humble classes of the population. In Italy these measures had been extended by Charles V and Philip II to the territories subject to Spain (Sicily, Sardinia, the Vice-Kingdom of Naples, and the State of Milan), while the Jews lived freely in other states within Italy.

All this has nothing to do with modern anti-Semitism, which originated in the Protestant sphere and developed after the French Revolution as ideological hatred against the figure of "the Jew." For the Church, the Jews are the Chosen People, called to reenter the Church prior to the end of the world. Pius V did not depart from this traditional perspective, and in his politics there is none of the ambivalence that Kenneth Stow seems to see in one of his essays.[259] He harbored benevolence toward that which the Chosen People had been, and he always had their conversion at heart. Inflexible in his principles but always merciful toward individuals, even before becoming pope, he had worked hard to gain their souls. It is surprising how an accurate historian like Stow overlooks an episode such as the conversion of Rabbi Corcos, which made a great stir in the Jewish community at the time.

Elia Corcos, chief rabbi of Rome and the richest of all the Jews in the ghetto, in order to get rid of the insistences of Cardinal Ghislieri, who desired his conversion, jokingly said to him, "I will become Christian when you are made Pope." The rabbi soon forgot his derisive phrase, but after the election of Pius V, he was invited by the pope to his palace and affectionately invited to keep his word. Corcos returned home sad and irresolute because of the difficult situation he found himself in, but

di Pietà e presenza ebraica in Italia (secoli XV-XVIII), edited by Daniele Montanari, Bulzoni, Rome, 1999.

[259] K. R. Stow, *More than Meets the Eye: Pius V and Jews*, in *Dominikaner und Juden/Dominicans and Jews*, edited by Elias H. Fullenbach and Gianfranco Miletto, De Gruyter, Berlin, 2014, pp. 375–394.

during the night the pope prayed ardently for his conversion, and the next day Elia and his three sons asked for the grace of Baptism. Pius V wanted to administer it personally. The ceremony took place in St. Peter's on June 20, 1566, in the presence of a multitude of people, and Elia received from the pope his same name, Michael, also taking the new surname Ghislieri.[260] The miraculous conversion of the rabbi led to other conversions among the Jews, so much so that it filled the Casa dei Catecumeni (house of catechumens) that had been constructed for them by Paul III.[261] As Renata Segre notes, the frequency and consistency of baptisms en masse that are recorded in the *Avvisi di Roma* for 1566–1567 are further confirmed by and are in continuity with the correspondence of Cardinal Sirleto for the years 1569–1571.[262]

This is an opportune point to recount the story of Sisto of Siena, which happened before Ghislieri's election as pope.[263] Born in Siena into the Jewish faith, as a youth he frequented the local synagogue and

[260] MAFFEI, *Vita di San Pio V*, pp. 339–340.

[261] Between 1542 and 1543, Paul III had established the Archconfraternity of the Hospital of the Neophytes, which later became the House of Catechumens, placing a cardinal "protector" over it. The growing influx of Jews to the baptismal font made the original seat of the House of Catechumens insufficient, and so it was moved in 1566 by Pius V (bull of November 29, 1566, in *Bullarium Romanum*, vol. 7, pp. 489–494). After a series of moves, the definitive seat of the house was established at Santa Maria dei Monti.

[262] RENATA SEGRE, *Il mondo ebraico nei cardinali della Controriforma*, in *Italia Judaica: gli ebrei in Italia tra Rinascimento ed età barocca*, Atti del convegno (1984), Ministero per i Beni Culturali e Ambientali, Rome, 1986, p. 127 (pp. 119–138). See also ATTILIO MILANO, *Battesimi di ebrei a Roma dal Cinquecento all'Ottocento*, in *Scritti in memoria di Enzo Sereni. Saggi sull'ebraismo romano*, edited by Daniele Carpi, Attilio Milano, and Umberto Nahon. Fondazione Sally Mayer, Jerusalem, 1970, pp. 140–147.

[263] FALLOUX, *Histoire de Saint Pie V*, vol. 1, pp. 35–37. On Sisto of Siena (1520–1569), see the views of VINCENZO LAVENIA, in DBI, vol. 93 (2018), pp. 12–15; and on his important erudite works JACQUES QUÉTIF, JACQUES ÉCHARD, *Scriptores Ordinis Praedicatorum recensiti*, II, Ballard et Simart, Paris, 1723, pp. 206–208.

there learned Hebrew. At the age of twenty he converted to Catholicism, entered the Franciscan Order, and thanks to his talents, became one of the greatest preachers of his time. But Sisto's success lured his pride, and he embraced heresy. In 1551 he was tried by the Holy Office and condemned to death. His judge, Michele Ghislieri, prayed to God to illuminate the heart of the heretic, and, exhorting him with fiery words, convinced him to retract his errors and to live in a spirit of penance and fidelity to the Church. And because only the authority of the pope could revoke a death sentence, Ghislieri threw himself at the feet of Julius III, imploring clemency for Sisto and guaranteeing his future life. Sisto of Siena was pardoned, welcomed into the Dominican Order, and employed in Cremona as a member of the Tribunal of the Inquisition. He is the author of *Bibliotheca Sancta ex Præcipuis Catholicae Ecclesiae Auctoribus Collecta*, published in Venice in 1566, which constitutes a monument of biblical erudition, still of great value for scholars today.

10. The Eternal City Is Reborn

Among the first acts of government of Pius V was, finally, the revision of the Carafa trial.[264] In 1560 Cardinal Ghislieri had been a member of the jury called to decide the fate of Paul IV's relatives, but when, despite Ghislieri's opposition, they were condemned, he was persuaded that the verdict had already been previously decided by Pius IV. Pius V ordered a new trial that lasted ten months, during which all of the documentation, testimonies, and defense briefs were meticulously scrutinized. The pope wanted to personally read all of the papers, study the results of the revision, and evaluate the evidence for conviction or acquittal.[265] The trial ended on September 26, 1567, with the annulment of the sentence that had been pronounced by Pius IV. The pope imposed the restitution of the confiscated goods to Carafa and the replacement of the family coat of arms in all the places where they had been removed.

[264] Pastor, *Storia dei Papi*, vol. 8, pp. 68–70.
[265] Aubert, *Paolo IV*, pp. 126–130.

The humanist Niccolò Franco,[266] who had written an infamous book against Paul IV and his family in 1561 entitled *Commentary on the Life and Customs of Gio. Pietro Carafa Who Was Paul IV*, was arrested and confessed that he had been commissioned to write the text by the then-governor of Rome, Alessandro Pallantieri. Franco was condemned to death and hanged on the Ponte Sant'Angelo on March 11, 1570, in conformity with a recent law that Pallantieri himself had strongly desired and promulgated.

Alessandro Pallantieri,[267] the fiscal prosecutor in the trial against Carafa, which he had carried out dishonestly, condemning the innocent to death, did not escape punishment. At the end of the rigorous trial to which he was subjected, he was beheaded on June 7, 1571, in the courtyard of the prison of Tor di Nona, the same place in which Giovanni Carafa had been beheaded. The pope thus forced the canons of St. Peter's to restore the bust of Paul IV to their sacristy, which they had removed in deference to Pius IV. A medal was minted with the image of the deceased Pope Paul IV, and his coffin was carried from the crypt of St. Peter's to the Church of the Minerva, to the Carafa Chapel, where his sepulchral monument was erected right in front of the magnificent fresco of Filippo Lippi, *The Triumph of Saint Thomas over the Heretics*. Pius V wanted this epigraph to be inscribed in Latin: "To Jesus Christ, the hope and way of the faithful; to Paul IV Supreme Pontiff, excellent in eloquence, in doctrine, and in knowledge; exemplary for innocence, liberality, and greatness of soul; an upright extirpator of every vice, and strenuous defender of the Catholic Church."

This fact made a great impression: on February 7, 1566, one month after his election, Pius V gave all of the ancient statues in the Belvedere

[266] Niccolò Franco (1515–1570) was a prolific writer of immoral works that attacked princes and ecclesiastics. Between 1559 and 1568 he lived in the "family" of Cardinal Morone. On his propaganda against Carafa, see AUBERT, *Paolo IV*, pp. 106–145.

[267] Alessandro Pallantieri (1505–1571) was the governor of Rome from April 26, 1563, to December 31, 1566, and governor of the Marche of Ancona from January 1, 1567, until August 1569.

garden in the Vatican to the Roman people. The reason was that he did not deem it appropriate for the successor of Peter to have "idols" and "pagan effigies" in his house.[268] In so doing, according to Cardinal Grente, he departed from the spirit of the Renaissance and revived the spirit of the Middle Ages.[269] However, Pius V asked a Renaissance artist whom he esteemed, Giorgio Vasari,[270] to paint the frescoes in the two chapels attached to the apartment where he used to pray. The pope wanted his private chapel to be dedicated to St. Peter Martyr,[271] the Dominican inquisitor who was assassinated by heretics and had become, along with St. Dominic, the patron of the Inquisition. Next to him there were male and female saints of the Order of St. Dominic, while on the vault there was painted the Triumph of the Faith surrounded by four Dominican saints and the theological virtues. For the altar, Vasari created an altarpiece showing the martyrdom of the saint.[272]

Daily Mass was the core of the spiritual life of the pope and his close entourage. It was accompanied by the Rosary and other prayers. At one point during his pontificate up to one hundred fifty people used to receive

[268] Sandro Benedetti, Giuseppe Zander, *L'arte in Roma nel secolo XVI*, Cappelli, Bologna, 1990, pp. 377–378.

[269] Grente, *Il Pontefice delle grandi battaglie*, p. 48.

[270] Giorgio Vasari (1511–1574) was a painter and architect in various Italian cities. He is known also for his work *Vite dei più eccellenti architetti pittori et scultori italiani da Cimabue insino a' tempi nostri* (1550). See Fulvio Cervini, *Pio V, Vasari e l'arte "medievale,"* in *Il tempo di Pio V. Pio V nel tempo. Atti del convegno internazionale di studi (Bosco Marengo, 11–13 March 2004)*, edited by Fulvio Cervini and Carla Enrica Spantigati, Edizioni dell'Orso, Alessandria, 2006, pp. 193–218.

[271] The Dominican Pietro da Verona, known as St. Peter Martyr and in the world as Pietro Rosini (1205–1252), appointed by Gregory IX as Inquisitor General for Lombardy, fought with his preaching against the Cathars, until he was killed at their hands, as he had predicted, on the road from Como to Milan. With his final effort, he wrote on the ground with his own blood: *Credo in Deum.* Eleven months later, on March 9, 1253, Pope Innocent IV canonized him, fixing the date of his feast on April 29.

[272] Maria Serlupi Crescenzi, *L'appartamento di San Pio V*, in *Il Palazzo Apostolico Vaticano*, edited by Carlo Pietrangeli, Nardini, Florence, 1992, pp. 147–149.

Holy Communion from his hands at the Mass celebrated in the pope's private apartment.[273]

Pius V did not content himself with praying in his private chapel, but with his external practices of piety he built up the city and made all of Rome marvel. One of his favorite devotions was the visit to the Seven Churches, a practice that St. Philip Neri had instituted in 1552 and that Pius V would make to some extent official.[274] The people, Cardinal Grente writes, "were moved to see the Holy Father go out without any apparatus and walk on foot, and they gradually became accustomed to the devotional exercises that were inspired by his example."[275]

One of the principal public devotions of the pope was, from the beginning, devotion to the Blessed Sacrament. In the first year of his reign, on the occasion of the Feast of Corpus Christi, he arrived so early for Mass that it was necessary to light lamps to be able to see. The preceding popes had followed the procession in a sedan chair, wearing on their head a jeweled tiara. Despite the length of the procession route, Pius V went on foot, carrying the Blessed Sacrament himself, with his head uncovered. The example of the pope, who carried the monstrance in such a devoted and recollected manner, contributed to reviving among the people that faith in the Real Presence of Jesus Christ in the Eucharist that Protestantism had sought to extinguish. "The Eternal City," wrote St. Francis Borgia on April 22, 1569, "looks very different from what it once was."[276]

[273] Sible de Blaauw, *Pio V e la liturgia*, in *Il tempo di Pio V. Pio V nel tempo*, cit., pp. 80–81.

[274] The visit to the Seven Churches is a practice that dates back to the Thursday of Shrovetide in 1552, when St. Philip Neri opposed the pagan celebrations of the Roman carnival with the devotion of going to the holiest places of Rome and meditating on the Passion. It involved a walking pilgrimage made on foot to the seven principal churches of the city: the basilicas of St. Peter in the Vatican, St. Paul outside the Walls, St. John in Lateran, St. Lawrence, St. Mary Major, Holy Cross in Jerusalem, and St. Sebastian. Cfr. A. Cistellini, *San Filippo Neri. L'Oratorio e la congregazione oratoriana*, cit. vol. 1, 96–97.

[275] Grente, *Il Pontefice delle grandi battaglie*, p. 55.

[276] Quoted in ibid., p. 56.

The new spirit that began to spread in the holy city under the pontificate of Pius V is well expressed by the inscription on the entrance of the Palazzo dei Conservatori, the seat of the city judiciary: "The Senate and the People of Rome now entrust the protection of the Campidoglio, at one time especially sacred to Jupiter, to the True God, to Jesus Christ the Author of all good, praying for the common good. The year of salvation 1568."[277]

[277] PASTOR, *Storia dei Papi*, vol. 8, p. 93.

3

Supreme and Perpetual Inquisitor

1. Faithfulness to the Dominican Spirit

There are popes for whom their ascent to the pontificate signifies a change in their life, as happened for example for Enea Silvio Piccolomini (Pius II, 1458–1464) or for Giovanni Maria Mastai Ferretti (Pius IX, 1846–1878). In the case of Michael Ghislieri, however, the pontificate was the crowning of a vocation embraced since his youth, when he received the Dominican habit that he wore underneath his pontifical vestments until his death. Hence his enemies said: "His Holiness wants all of Rome to become a Dominican monastery."[278]

Frà Michele Ghislieri displayed his fidelity to the spirit of St. Dominic above all in the coherence with which, over the span of thirty years, he carried out his role as Inquisitor of the Holy Roman Church. This assignment was fully part of the tradition of his order, to which Gregory IX had entrusted the nascent Inquisition in 1235, appointing St. Dominic di Guzmán, the first inquisitor "*in orbe toto christiano.*" In the Roman Inquisition the judges came from the Order of St. Dominic, except for in Florence and Venice, whose tribunals were traditionally run by the Franciscans. Moreover, beginning in the fifteenth century, a Dominican

[278] *Briefe von Andreas Masius und seinen Freunden 1538 bis 1573*, edited by Max Lossen, Alphons Dürr, Leipzig, 1886, p. 374. On the relationship between Ghislieri and the Dominican Order, see MICHELE MIELE, *Pio V e la presenza dei domenicani nel corso della sua vita*, in *Pio V nella società*, pp. 27–48.

was the *Magister Sacri Palatii*, who had the task of keeping watch over the orthodoxy of the papal court, and beginning in 1515, exercising the preventive censure of works that were to be printed in Rome. In the Roman congregation of the Holy Office, both the Master of the Sacred Palace as well as the superior general of the order regularly sat in meetings, in addition to one or two Dominican consultors.[279]

In the Spanish Chapel inside the Church of Santa Maria Novella in Florence, the ancient chapter room of the convent, a fresco depicts the *Via Veritas*, or rather the *Church Militant and Triumphant*, an allegory of the work and mission of the Dominicans. At the center are the figures of Pope Benedict XI, Emperor Charles IV, a cardinal, a Dominican bishop, and the king of France. Next to them are other religious men and women of every social condition, who represent the flock of Christians, guarded by piebald dogs: the *domini-canes*, that is, the dogs of the Lord, as they came to be called. Further to the right, one notes Sts. Dominic, Peter Martyr, and Thomas Aquinas, who confute heretics and invite them to abjure their errors, showing them the Wisdom books. Beneath this scene there is a scene of dogs chasing and tearing apart wolves and foxes.

The inquisitor fought against error because he loved the truth. A special virtue was required of him, as the Dominican Nicolas Eymerich explained in his celebrated *Directorium Inquisitorum*, expanded by the Spanish canonist Francisco Peña in 1578: "The inquisitor must be honest in his behavior, of extreme prudence, of persevering firmness, of perfect Catholic erudition and full of virtue."[280]

[279] See *The Dominicans and the Mediaeval Inquisition*, edited by Wolfram Hoyer, Angelicum University Press, Rome, 2004; Nikolaus Paulus, *Die deutschen Dominikaner im Kampfe gegen Luther (1518–1563)*, Herder, Freiburg, 1903; Michael Tavuzzi, *Renaissance Inquisitors. Dominican Inquisitors and Inquisitorial Districts in Northern Italy, 1474–1527*, Brill, Leiden-Boston, 2007; *Praedicatores, Inquisitores: I Domenicani e l'inquisizione romana*, Acts of the 3rd international seminar on "The Dominicans and the Inquisition" 15–18 February 2006, edited by Carlo Longo, Istituto Storico Domenicano, Rome, 2008.

[280] Nicolas Eymerich, Francisco Peña, *Il Manuale dell'inquisitore* (1376), Italian translation, Fanucci, Rome, 2000, p. 211. Nicolas Eymerich

The inquisitor's love of God was manifested in the abnegation with which he dedicated himself to defending the purity of faith, fighting against every heresy that compromised its integrity. For Frà Michele Ghislieri, his appointment as commissioner of the Inquisition and then as *Summus et Perpetuus Inquisitor* did not only involve the scrupulous conduct of an office, but was understood as an act of service to the Church in a moment in which she was gravely threatened.

In an interview with the Venetian ambassador Paolo Tiepolo[281] on the eve of his election, Pius V affirmed with pride that "nobody understood the matters of the Inquisition as well as we [Dominicans] do. . . . We have consumed our life and intellect in this practice."[282] On January 12, 1566, as soon as he was elected pope, he spelled out his program, affirming that he would not turn "his soul to anything other than maintaining as much peace and quiet as possible between Christian princes, while waiting to eradicate heresies."[283] The pope "sees every trial and reads all the writings," wrote Cardinal Girolamo da Correggio in 1567,[284] reporting how the new pontiff personally examined all of the imposing acts of the

(1320–1399), was the inquisitor general of the Crown of Aragon in the second half of the fourteenth century. Francisco Peña (1540–1612) was an Aragonese canonist who held important posts in the Roman Curia.

281 We owe to the Venetian ambassador Paolo Tiepolo (1523–1585) a famous comparison between the worldly Pius IV, "a prince who only looked after his own business" and who "paid very little attention to religion," and Pius V, completely full of "zeal and severity. . . . in the things of religion" (*Le relazioni degli ambasciatori veneti al Senato durante il secolo decimosesto*, edited by Eugenio Alberi, vol. 2, IV, Società editrice fiorentina, Florence, 1857, p. 171).

282 Aldo Stella, *Guido da Fano eretico del secolo XVI al servizio del re d'Inghilterra*, in "Rivista di storia della Chiesa in Italia," 13 (1959), p. 228 (pp. 196–238).

283 *Legazioni di Averardo Serristori ambasciatore di Cosimo I a Carlo Quinto e in corte di Roma (1537–1568) con un'appendice di documenti*, edited by Giuseppe Canestrini, Le Monnier, Florence, 1853, p. 420.

284 Quoted in Sergio Pagano, *Il processo di Endimio Calandra e l'inquisizione a Mantova nel 1567–1568*, Biblioteca Apostolica Vaticana, Vatican City, 1991, p. 36. Cardinal Girolamo da Correggio (1511–1572) was appointed archbishop of Taranto in 1569 and governor of Ancona in 1570 by Pius V.

inquisitorial trials in order to verify that they were carried out with the care and attention they deserved.

In October 1567 the imperial ambassador Prospero d'Arco[285] wrote that Pius V was truly more zealous against heretics than he was against the Turks.[286] In the six years of his pontificate, Pius V confronted error wherever it nestled, even when it thrived in the shadow of the courts of kings. He fought against the Lutherans in Germany, the Huguenots in France, the Anglicans in England, and he also did not hesitate to confront Philip II, when it seemed to him that the "Sword of the Counter-Reform" deviated from the path of being a faithful defender of orthodoxy. But the first and most subtle enemy that he opposed was the one that developed within the Catholic Church in Italy in order to conquer the highest levels of power.

Already in the aftermath of the posting of the theses of Wittenberg in 1517, the books of Luther were being read in Italy. In the space of a few decades, the circulation of heterodox books, which had their principal "port of entry" in Venice, extended throughout the entire peninsula and to all social levels, with the substantial support of the clergy.[287] But while in Europe Protestantism openly revolted against the Roman Church, in Italy the religious revolution sought to make the edifice collapse from within. In order to reach this end, the heretics developed a doctrine, or rather a strategy, called Nicodemism,[288] after Nicodemus, the man in the Gospel of St. John who went to visit Jesus Christ by night in order not to be recognized as a disciple. This strategy was based on the idea that a heretic of whatever sort could live in a Catholic country without having

[285] Count Prospero d'Arco (1522–1572) was the imperial ambassador in Rome from 1560 until his death, always defending the rights of the empire.

[286] PASTOR, *Storia dei Papi*, vol. 8, p. 234.

[287] See M. FIRPO, *Riforma protestante ed eresie nell'Italia del Cinquecento*, Laterza, Bari, 1993, pp. 11–28.

[288] CARLO GINZBURG, *Il nicodemismo. Simulazione e dissimulazione religiosa nell'Europa del '500*, Einaudi, Turin, 1970; ALBINO BIONDI, *La giustificazione della simulazione nel Cinquecento*, in *Eresia e riforma nell'Italia del Cinquecento*, vol. 1, Olschki, Florence-Chicago, 1974, pp. 7–68.

to openly profess his doctrine or flee to another country as many were doing. Instead, it was necessary to build up a secret web of relationships, hiding one's own opinions, until coming to the point, if possible, of occupying the throne of Peter. If this did not happen, it was thanks to a few intrepid defenders of the Faith, in particular three inquisitors destined to become popes: Gian Piero Carafa (Paul IV), Michele Ghislieri (Pius V), and Felice Peretti (Sixtus V). Of these three inquisitor popes, the one who is most identified with the institution of the Inquisition was, according to the historian Adriano Prosperi, St. Pius V.[289]

2. The Holy Roman Inquisition

The term *Inquisition* comes from the Latin word *inquisitio*, which means research or investigation.[290] The Inquisition, as a tribunal invested by the

[289] Adriano Prosperi, *Tribunali della coscienza. Inquisitori, confessori, missionari*, Einaudi, Turin, 2009, p. 146. Prosperi is a well-documented but tendentious author, like the majority of contemporary scholars of the heresies of the sixteenth century.

[290] The literature on the Inquisition is extremely vast, as may be found from the review of Emil van der Kené *Bibliographisches Verzeichnis der gedruckten Schriftsums zur Geschichte und Literatur der Inquisition*, 3 vol., 2 ed., Topos Verlag, Vaduz, 1982–1992. A useful tool, also for its extensive bibliography, is the *Dizionario Storico dell'Inquisizione*, 4 vol., edited by A. Prosperi, V. Lavenia, J. Tedeschi, Edizioni della Normale, Pisa, 2010, comprising 6,500 titles between essays and published sources. Worthy of mention in the field of historiography are the acts of the *Convegno internazionale sull'Inquisizione nei secoli XVI e XVII: metodologia delle fonti e prospettive storiografiche* organized by Armando Saitta in October 1981, found in the "Annuario dell'Istituto storico italiano per l'età moderna e contemporanea," vols. 35–36 (1983–84) and vol. 37–38 (1985–86); *L'inquisizione: atti del simposio internazionale*, Vatican City, 29–31 October 1998, edited by Agostino Borromeo, Vatican Apostolic Library, Vatican City, 2003; and *L'Inquisizione romana: metodologia delle fonti e storia istituzionale*, edited by Andrea Del Col and Giovanna Paolin, Edizioni Università di Trieste-Circolo Culturale Menocchio, Trieste, 2000. A useful bio-bibliography of two hundred members and collaborators of the Holy Office between 1542 and 1600 is offered by Herman H. Schwedt, *Die Anfänge der Römischen Inquisition. Kardinäle und Konsultoren 1542 bis 1600*, Herder, Freiburg, 2013.

pope with a special jurisdiction over crimes in matters of faith, originated in the Middle Ages in order to investigate heresies, which constituted a threat not only to the Church but also to Christian society as a whole. The French historian Jean-Baptiste Guiraud defines the medieval Inquisition as "a system of repressive measures, some of the spiritual order, others of the temporal order, which came simultaneously from ecclesiastical authority and civil power for the defense of orthodox religion and the social order, which was equally threatened by theological doctrines and social heresy."[291]

On November 1, 1478, the Catholic monarchs Ferdinand of Aragon and Isabella of Castile obtained from Pope Sixtus IV the institution of new tribunals of the Inquisition in order to investigate the problem of crypto-Judaism in their reign. The problem was not the Jews in themselves, who belonged to another religion and thus did not fall under the jurisdiction of the Inquisition, but rather of the *conversos* or *marrani*, the Jewish converts who continued to practice their religion in secret, despite having received Baptism.[292] The Portuguese Inquisition was instituted on May 23, 1536, for the same reasons.

The Roman Inquisition, established by Paul III with the bull *Licet ab Initio* of July 21, 1542, with the name *Sacra Congregatio Romanae et Universalis Inquisitionis seu Sancti Officii* (the Holy Office), was instead founded in order to address the new phenomenon of Catholics, above all in Italy, who embraced more or less secretly the doctrines of Protestantism.[293] Thus in the second half of the sixteenth century there were three active inquisitions: two on the Iberian Peninsula and one in Rome. The highest authority of the

[291] Jean-Baptiste Guiraud, *Inquisition*, in DAFC, vol. 2 (1924), col. 846 (cols. 823–857), then recast in *L'inquisition médiévale*, Bernard Grasset, Paris, 1929, Italian translation, *Elogio dell'Inquisizione*, Leonardo, Milan, 1994, p. 64.

[292] The official name was *conversos* or *cristianos nuevos*, and in 1380 a decree of the king of Castile forbade the use of the insulting term *marrano*. Later it was also used without being an insult, and it is now currently used in historical terminology.

[293] Silvana Seidel Menchi, *Origine e origini del Sant'Uffizio*, in *L'inquisizione. Atti del simposio internazionale*, pp. 291–322.

Inquisitions was the Roman Pontiff. But in actuality the pontiffs exercised their proper powers only over the Roman Inquisition, while the Spanish and Portuguese Inquisitions, while recognizing the supreme authority of the pope, were successful in achieving a certain autonomy.[294]

The procedure followed by various Inquisitions was substantially identical, because it was already defined in the canonical collections between the thirteenth and fourteenth centuries. The treatises of well-known inquisitors, such as Bernardo Gui[295] and Nicola Eymeric, and the acts of the trials, from the interrogations to the sentencings, offer us incontrovertible documentation on the work of the tribunals of the Inquisition. As the historian John Tedeschi emphasizes, "It was strict Holy Office practice to preserve detailed records of all its proceedings from the first summons to the final sentencing."[296]

Specialists have shown that the procedure of the Inquisition was in fact a step of progress in the history of law, because of the guarantees it granted to the accused and the seriousness with which the trial was carried out. The right to defend oneself could never be denied, because it is granted by natural law, and the guarantee of the right of defense, which was unusual for that time, went so far as to grant to the accused the right to freely choose a lawyer or a procurator whom he trusted and to have the court give him a copy of all the documentation gathered in his regard in order to set up a defense strategy.[297] Innocent IV, with the bull *Ad Extirpanda* (1252), had ordered that, according to Roman canon law, the accused could be subjected to moderate judicial torture. In the

[294] Borromeo, *Inquisizione*, in DSP, vol. 1, p. 816.

[295] The *Practica Inquisitionis haereticae pravitatis* of the Dominican Inquisitor Frà Bernard Guy (Bernardus Guidonis) (1261–1331) compiled around 1321, was published in a critical edition in Toulouse in 1886. See also Annette Pales-Gobilliard, *Le livre des sentences de l'inquisiteur Bernard Gui, 1308–1323*, CNRS, Paris, 2002, 2 vols.

[296] John Tedeschi, *The Prosecution of Heresy. Medieval & Renaissance Texts & Studies*, Binghamton, New York, 1991, p. 131.

[297] Andrea Errera, *Difesa*, in DSI, vol. 1, pp. 479–481. An accurate exposition of the organization and procedures of the Roman Inquisition is given by the historian John Tedeschi in his volume *The Prosecution of Heresy*.

sixteenth century torture was practiced by all European governments, and the Catholic Church allowed its use, under limited conditions, in order to obtain the *regina probarum*, the confession.[298] However, a confession extorted with torture, in order to be valid, had to be ratified by the accused. In fact, as Pope Nicholas I had already stated on November 13, 866, responding to a question of Bogoris, prince of the Bulgars: "One knows that he who professes with his mouth what he does not have in his heart, is not confessing, but only speaking!"[299]

In the judicial practice of the Roman Inquisition, torture required the existence of conditions that constituted a *semiplena* test ("half-proof"), and it could not be applied to minors under fourteen years old, to those older than sixty, to the mentally ill, or to pregnant women. It could not last longer than one hour, it could not lead to the death of the one tortured, and it had to be carried out in the presence of a doctor, without the shedding of blood or the fracturing of limbs. In practice it was generally limited to the so-called "stretch of rope."[300] Significantly, from the inquisitors' point of view, torture had to be moderate so that if the victim was innocent, he could return to enjoy his freedom, and if guilty he would be able to receive just punishment.

The hardest punishment was not detention in prison but condemnation to the galleys, that is, forced service at the oars of war boats.[301]

[298] On the liceity of torture under certain conditions, see the entry by Cardinal PIETRO PALAZZINI in EC, vol. 12 (1954), cols. 342–343.

[299] DENZ-H, n. 648.

[300] The "stretch of rope" consisted in lifting the victim off the ground by means of a pulley, with his hands tied behind his back. In this position, after the room had been cleared even of the jailers and only the inquisitor, the episcopal delegate, and the notary remained, the accused person was interrogated. The ordeal generally did not last longer than thirty minutes, and an hour was the maximum permitted. The practice of dropping the accused person to the floor in order to increase pain, which was widely used in the secular courts, was severely prohibited in Inquisition trials (see TEDESCHI, *The Prosecution of Heresy*, p. 145).

[301] The sentence to the oar was so widespread that in the Italian language the term *galera* (originally *galley*) became synonymous with *prigione* (prison). In reality this punishment often led to death, considering the conditions

Condemnation to capital punishment was rare. Burning at the stake was reserved for three main categories of offenders: the pertinacious, unwilling to reconcile with the Church in any way; the *relapsi* or recidivists, those who after having been condemned for formal heresy had fallen back into the same crime; and those who tried to subvert certain basic dogmas of the Christian faith such as the divinity of Jesus Christ and the virginity of Mary.[302]

Reconciliation with the Church was granted only once, on the condition that it was preceded by the abjuration of heresy, which had to be performed publicly. The Holy Roman Office often had recourse to private abjuration, which was not pronounced at the end of the trial but before it during the so-called "grace period," given to the accused in order to permit them a full and sincere confession.[303]

The creation of the Inquisition was in conformity with the teaching of the Roman Church, which has never imposed faith but always condemned the public manifestation of error. There is an essential distinction between the "*forum conscientiae*," or internal forum, and the "*forum exterioris iudicii*," or external forum.[304] The Church teaches the freedom of the act of faith in the internal forum, because no person may be forced to believe. But this interior liberty which, as such, no external force can coerce, does not imply religious freedom in the external forum, that is to say the right to publicly practice whatever form of worship or to propagate any sort of error.[305] The Catholic nation that professes the true Faith also has the duty to repress the social manifestation of error for the

---

of life to which the "*galeotti*" were subjected and the risks they faced during battle. See Luca Lo Basso, *Uomini da remo: galee e galeotti del Mediterraneo in età moderna*, Selene Edizioni, Milan, 2003.

302 Tedeschi, *The Prosecution of Heresy*, p. 151.

303 Elena Brambilla, *Abiura*, in DSI, vol. 1, pp. 5–6.

304 St. Thomas Aquinas, *In IV Sententiarum*, d. 18, q. 3, a. 2.

305 See Alfredo Ottaviani, *Institutiones Iuris Publici Ecclesiastici*, vol. 1, Typis Polyglottis Vaticanis, Vatican City, 1958, p. 302. On the theme of religious liberty, above all after the constitution *Dignitatis Humanae*, one of the most controversial texts of the Second Vatican Council, see *Dignitatis Humane Colloquium*, Dialogos Institute Proceedings, vol. 1 (2017), edited

public good. The handover of the culprit to the "secular arm" expressed the close collaboration that existed between the Church and Catholic nations, according to a teaching that was confirmed by the Church's uninterrupted Tradition, at least until Vatican II.[306] "God is not only Lord and Master of men considered individually, but also of nations and states; it is necessary, then, that the nations and those that govern them recognize Him, respect Him, and venerate Him publicly."[307]

The modern mentality shuns the death penalty and in particular burning at the stake. However, we need to recall that the former was practiced in the Papal States until 1870 and that it is not excluded by the new *Catechism of the Catholic Church*, approved by John Paul II on August 15, 1997.[308] However, the corporal punishments inflicted by the Inquisition were always milder than those inflicted by the governments of the time for crimes such as the *crimen laesae maiestatis* (crime against the sovereign's majesty). François Ravaillac, who murdered the king of France, Henri IV, on May 14, 1610, was condemned not by the Inquisition but by the secular tribunal of Paris, to be gripped on the breasts, arms,

---

by Fr. Thomas Crean, O.P., with an introduction by Cardinal Raymond Leo Burke.

306 See *Ecclesia et Status. Fontes selecti historiae iuris publici ecclesiastici*, edited by Giovanni Battista Lo Grasso, Apud Aedes Pontificiae Universitatis Gregorianae, Rome, 1952.

307 St. Pius X, Allocution to the Consistory, 21 February 1906, in *Les enseignements Pontificaux. La paix intérieure des nations*, edited by the Monks of Solesmes, Desclée, Paris, 1952, n. 393.

308 See *Catechism of the Catholic Church*, n. 2267. Pope Francis, departing from the teaching of the Church, modified article 2267 with the rescript *Ex audientia SSmi* of May 11, 2018, affirming that "the punishment of death is inadmissible because it attacks the inviolability and dignity of the human person," and he has committed himself with determination to its abolition across the whole world. On the legitimacy of the death penalty according to Catholic doctrine, see Edward Feser, Joseph M. Bessette, *By Man Shall His Blood Be Shed: A Catholic Defense of the Death Penalty*, Ignatius Press, San Francisco, 2017; J. M. Bessette, Michael Pakaluk, Brian W. Harrison, *Death Penalty*, in "First Things: A Monthly Journal of Religion and Public Life," 288 (December 2018).

thighs, and calves, on which was thrown molten lead, oil, and boiling pitch; his left hand, with which he had committed the crime, was burned with sulfurous fire; and finally his body was pulled and dismembered by four horses; his limbs and torso were burned and reduced to ashes, which were then thrown to the wind.[309]

3. Pius V and the Inquisition

In 1559, upon the death of Paul IV, the Palace of the Inquisition in the Via Ripetta was sacked and set on fire by a mob of troublemakers hired by the religious and political party opposed to Pope Carafa, causing irreparable damage to many important documents. When he ascended to the Chair of Peter, Pius V wanted above all to construct a new and more secure headquarters for the Roman Tribunal. On May 18, 1566, the pope purchased the palace located near the Teutonic Camposanto for 9,000 scudi from the heirs of the Florentine Cardinal Lorenzo to whom it had once belonged. This palace became the permanent seat of the Inquisition. On September 2, 1566, with great solemnity, the restored palace was rededicated, and Pius V arranged for all the records and documents of the Inquisition to be gathered and stored there. The palace, which was again restored in the first half of the twentieth century, is still the home of the Congregation for the Doctrine of the Faith.

One of the first acts of Pius V was the reform of the Holy Office, which he entrusted to four cardinals who were faithful to him: Bernardino Scotti, a former Theatine and collaborator of Paul IV; the Sicilian Scipione Rebiba,[310] who was also faithful to Paul IV and harshly persecuted by Pius

[309] See Pierre Chevallier, *Les Régicides: Clément, Ravaillac, Damiens*, Fayard, 1989. See also Mario Sbriccoli, Crimen laesae maiestatis. *Il problema del reato politico alle soglie della scienza penalistica moderna*, Giuffré, Milan, 1974; Bruno Neveu, *L'erreur et son juge: remarques sur les censures doctrinales à l'époque moderne*, Bibliopolis, Naples, 1993.

[310] Scipione Rebiba (1504–1577), appointed cardinal by Paul IV in 1555, was put on trial at the beginning of the pontificate of Pius IV for his ties to the Carafa family. Pius V restored him with full honors in the Congregation of the Holy Office and in 1573 Gregory XIII appointed him as Grand Inquisitor.

IV for his ties to the Carafa family; the Spaniard Francisco Pacheco;[311] and Gian Francesco Gambara[312] of Brescia. The pope also called Giulio Antonio Santori[313] to Rome to be his right hand in guiding the Holy Office. Santori had been his close collaborator in repressing heresy in the Kingdom of Naples.

The public ceremony in which a sentence decreed by the Inquisition was carried out was called *auto-da-fé*. Under Pius V there were twelve *autos-da-fé* carried out in six years, with greater solemnity than under preceding popes. The event was very public: cardinals participated in these ceremonies as well as the entire papal court, along with a great crowd of spectators, especially if a secret heretic who had hitherto been highly regarded and esteemed was being exposed.[314] Thus there was a great crowd on the occasion of the first *auto-da-fé* of 1567, which took place

[311] Francisco Pacheco de Villena (1508–1579), the nephew of Cardinal Pedro Pacheco, appointed cardinal by Pius IV in 1561, was the only member of the inquisitorial commission of Pius IV who was confirmed by Pius V, who appointed him bishop of Burgos (Spain) in 1567.

[312] Giovan Francesco Gambara (1533–1587), the nephew of Cardinal Umberto Gambara, was appointed cardinal by Pius IV in 1561. In the conclave of 1565 he was one of the supporters of the election of Pius V, who in 1566 appointed him as a member of Holy Office and bishop of the Diocese of Viterbo, which had been pervaded by heresy in the previous decades.

[313] Giulio Antonio Santori (1532–1602) was inquisitor at Caserta and Naples between 1559 and 1566 and was then transferred to Rome. Pius V appointed him archbishop of Santa Severina in Calabria, and gave him a key role within the Holy Office, first as a consultor (1566) and then as cardinal inquisitor (1570). He is the author of a celebrated *Autobiografia*, (published by the R. Società Romana di storia patria, Rome, 1890) and of a treatise against heresy *Pro confutatione articulorum et haeresum recentiorum Haereticorum et pseudo-apostolorum*, which remained a manuscript. See H. Jedin, *Die Autobiographie des Kardinals Giulio Antonio Santorio [gestorben 1602]*, Akademie der Wissenschaften und der Literatur, Mainz, 1969; Saverio Ricci, *Il Sommo Inquisitore. Giulio Antonio Santori tra autobiografia e storia (1532–1602)*, Salerno, Rome, 2002.

[314] Pastor, *Storia dei papi*, vol. 8, p. 206.

on February 24 at the Minerva, in which the preacher Basilio Zanchi[315] was condemned to imprisonment in his convent as a convicted heretic, and also on June 22 of that year, when the Neapolitan nobleman Mario Galeota[316] made public abjuration.

With an edict of June 6, 1566, the pope gave the Inquisition precedence over all other tribunals.[317] With the bull *Inter Multiplices Curas*[318] of December 21, 1566, Pius V solemnly declared that his first concern was to eliminate as much as possible heresies, false doctrines, and erroneous opinions in order to restore quiet and security to the Church, and he ordered the reopening of all the trials that had been underway during the pontificate of Paul IV.

This bull made clear the difference between the policy of Pius V and that of his predecessor. The pope appealed to his long experience as supreme inquisitor, which had taught him how many of those tried by the Holy Office presented false witnesses on their behalf and used artifice and deception to mislead their judges. The reference to what had happened under the preceding pontificate was obvious, and Pastor notes it: "It is clear to whom Pius V is referring when he deplores that even the popes have been duped by the heretics."[319]

Pius V, in fact, was not convinced by the biased, hasty way in which many trials were concluded under Pius IV, who had ordered the rehabilitation of all the prelates tried during the pontificate of Pope Carafa, among whom was the bishop of Modena, Egidio Foscarari; the bishop of Cheronissa, Giovan Francesco Verdura; the bishop of Cava de' Tirreni, Tommaso Sanfelice; the protonotary Pietro Carnesecchi; and above all

[315] Basilio Zanchi (1501–1558), one of the canons regular of the Lateran, was a theologian and scholar who was attracted, like many humanists, by the Lutheran theses. He probably died in prison.

[316] Mario Galeota (1499–1585) served, after his abjuration, the five-year prison sentence imposed on him by Pius V in 1567. See PASQUALE LOPEZ, *Il movimento valdesiano a Napoli. Mario Galeota e le sue vicende col Sant'Uffizio*, Fiorentino, Naples, 1976.

[317] Bull of June 6, 1566, in *Bullarium Romanum*, vol. 7, pp. 422–423.

[318] Bull of December 21, 1566, ibid., pp. 499–502.

[319] PASTOR, *Storia dei papi*, vol. 8, p. 203.

Cardinal Morone, whose absolution was the most explicit expression of the indulgent policy of Pius IV. The majority of the trials of these prelates had been personally followed by Cardinal Alessandrino, who was well aware of the existence of an organized party that was well-versed in the art of concealment and had reached the highest level of the Church even to the point of twice being within a hair's breadth of the papacy—once in 1550 with Cardinal Pole and again in 1565 with Cardinal Morone. Pius V had the intention of closing this painful chapter in the history of the Church by reopening the trials against those who had been acquitted of the charges of heresy brought against them by the Inquisition.

4. The "Spiritualist" Party

The strategy of dissimulation of one's own ideas had its most illustrious proponent in Erasmus of Rotterdam,[320] who exercised a cultural influence at the beginning of the sixteenth century similar to that of Voltaire two centuries later. Erasmus was a peculiar priest, one who did not celebrate Mass but dedicated all of his time to traveling and studying philology. With his criticism of the external works of the Church, his proclamation of the supreme liberty of the Christian, and his invitation to directly approach the text of Scripture without mediation, he prepared the way for Luther, although he did not follow him in his break from Rome.

One of the most ardent disciples of Erasmus was the Spaniard Juan de Valdés,[321] who, after leaving his native land to flee the Inquisition,

[320] Erasmus of Rotterdam (1466–1536), although remaining Catholic, subjected many aspects of Sacred Scripture and the Tradition of the Church to corrosive criticism. In 1557 the Inquisition condemned the works of Erasmus to be burned, while the indexes of Paul IV (1559), Pius IV (1564), and Sixtus V (1590) prohibited their reading. On the influence of Erasmus in Italy, see DELIO CANTIMORI, *Umanesimo e religione nel Rinascimento*, Einaudi, Turin, 1975; S. SEIDEL MENCHI, *Erasmo in Italia, 1520–1580*, Bollati Boringhieri, Turin, 1987. On the Iberian "Erasmists," see MARCELINO MENÉNDEZ Y PELAYO, *Historia de los Heterodoxos*, BAC, Madrid, 1956, pp. 655–782.

[321] Juan de Valdés (1509–1541), exiled from Spain, moved permanently to Naples around 1535. His mother was originally from a family of Jewish

formed a "spiritual circle" in his home on the island of Ischia, which was frequented by women of the aristocracy and other high ecclesiastical dignitaries. According to Friedrich Church, this group constituted the "first stone" in the construction of the Italian Reformation[322] and was the incubation ground for a truly crypto-heretical "party" called the "spiritualists" or also the "evangelicals,"[323] particularly influential in the Roman Curia until the early 1540s.

The "spiritualists" secretly professed the Lutheran doctrine of justification by faith alone, and, following the teaching of Erasmus, they despised the exterior rites and practices of the Church, to which they opposed the "interior illumination of the spirit" as a "rule of faith." This doctrine was the same as the *Alumbrados*,[324] a Spanish sect whose origins probably reach back to the Albigensians and other medieval heresies. For the pseudo-mysticism of the *Alumbrados*, as would be true later for the

---

converts to Christianity and his maternal uncle, the priest Fernando de Barreda, was burned at the stake in 1491 as a *relapso*. See M. FIRPO, *Juan de Valdés and the Italian Reformation*, Ashgate, Aldershot, 2015. MENENDEZ Y PELAYO, who dedicates a chapter to Valdés in his *Historia de los Heterodoxos* (vol. 1, pp. 783–832), documents his anti-trinitarianism (ibid., pp. 821–822).

322 FREDERIC E. CHURCH, *I Riformatori italiani*, Italian translation, Il Saggiatore, Milan, 1967, 2 vol. (1958), vol. 1, pp. 3ff. On Protestantism in Italy, see also D. CANTIMORI, *Eretici italiani del Cinquecento e altri scritti*, Einaudi, Turin, 1992 (1939); and the extensive review of the literature in *The Italian Reformation of the Sixteenth Century and the Diffusion of Renaissance Culture: A Bibliography of the Secondary Literature*, edited by J. Tedeschi, Panini, Modena, 2000.

323 The term *evangelicalism* was coined by the French historian PIERRE IMBART DE LA TOUR, in *Les origines de la Réforme*, vol. 3: *L'Evangelisme (1521–1538)*, Slatkine, Geneva, 1978 (1914). See PAOLO SIMONCELLI, *Evangelismo italiano nel Cinquecento*, Istituto storico italiano per l'età moderna e contemporanea, Rome, 1979.

324 On the *Alumbrados*, see ANTONIO MÁRQUEZ, *Los alumbrados: Orígenes y filosofía (1525–1559)*, Taurus, Madrid, 1980; STEFANIA PASTORE, *Alumbradismo*, in DSI, vol. 1, pp. 47–51 with bibliography; PASTORE, *Un' eresia spagnola. Spiritualità conversa, alumbradismo e Inquisizione (1449–1559)*, L. S. Olschki, Florence, 2004.

followers of quietism, the souls of the "elect" enter into contact with the divine essence, and by so doing are made incapable of sin. The spiritualists arrived at these same conclusions, which by implication negated the moral law of the Church, and consequently, all of them criticized the institutional dimension of the Church and thereby maintained the necessity of a policy of compromise with the Lutherans. Those who belonged to this party included, at different moments and in more or less explicit ways, many prominent cardinals such as Gasparo Contarini, Reginald Pole, Giovanni Morone, Jacopo Sadoleto,[325] and Girolamo Seripando;[326] bishops such as Vittore Soranzo and Pierpaolo Vergerio;[327] and ranking noblewomen such as Vittoria Colonna,[328] Caterina Cybo,[329] and Giulia Gonzaga.[330]

[325] Jacopo Sadoleto (1477–1547), secretary under Leo X and Clement VII, bishop of Carpentras in 1517, and appointed cardinal in 1536 by Paul III. His *Commentario sopra la lettera di San Paolo ai Romani* was condemned. See RICHARD M. DOUGLAS, *Jacopo Sadoleto. Humanist and Reformer*, Harvard University Press, Cambridge, Massachusetts, 1959.

[326] Girolamo Seripando (1493–1563), an Augustinian, held important positions within his order until he became general superior. He was then appointed archbishop of Salerno (1554) and created cardinal by Pius IV (1561). He presided over the sessions of the Council of Trent until his death. See H. JEDIN, *Girolamo Seripando: sein Leben und Denken im Geisteskampf des 16. Jahrhunderts*, Rita-Verlag u. Druckerei, Wurzburg, 1937.

[327] Pier Paolo Vergerio (1489–1565), papal nuncio and bishop of Capodistria, tried by the Inquisition because of his heretical ideas, fled from Italy in 1549 and apostasized from the Catholic Faith, publishing more than one hundred booklets against the Church. See ANNE SCHUTTE, *Pier Paolo Vergerio: The Making of an Italian Reformer*, Edition Dróz, Geneva, 1977.

[328] On the poetess Vittoria Colonna (1492–1547), married to Francesco d'Avalos, Marquis of Pescara, see CARLO DE FREDE, *Vittoria Colonna e il suo processo inquisitoriale postumo*, Giannini, Naples, 1989; FIRPO, *Inquisizione romana e controriforma*, pp. 119–176.

[329] On Caterina Cybo (1501–1557), see *Caterina Cybo, duchessa di Camerino (1501–1557)*, Acts of the convention of Camerino, 28–30 October 2004, edited by Pierluigi Moriconi, La nuova stampa, Camerino, 2005.

[330] Giulia Colonna Gonzaga (1513–1566) was married at the age of thirteen in 1526 to Vespasiano Gonzaga, and after his death in 1528, she governed

When Valdés died in July 1541, his disciples found their most authoritative point of reference in Cardinal Gasparo Contarini,[331] who had been the Venetian ambassador to Pope Clement VII. Following the recent Sack of Rome, Contarini rose to the head of the government of *La Serenissima*, but on May 21, 1535, Paul III, who was his admirer, gave him the episcopate of Belluno and made him a cardinal, later appointing him president of the commission charged with drawing up the *Consilium de Emendanda Ecclesia*. Notably, in 1541 Contarini participated in the Diet of Regensburg in which he worked for a compromise agreement between Catholics and Protestants. The two delegations reached an ambiguous agreement on justification, but the discussions about the sacraments failed, in particular on the concept of transubstantiation, which was entirely rejected by the Protestants. Contarini's compliant attitude toward these objections raised up protests from some cardinals, but Paul III ignored them, and when Contarini returned from Regensburg, he sent him as papal legate to Bologna. The elevation of Giovanni Morone, Tommaso Badia, and Gregorio Cortese to the cardinalate on June 2, 1542—all of whom were defenders of the theological and diplomatic efforts of Contarini in Regensburg—demonstrated that the influence of the spiritualist group was still substantial.

Contarini died in Bologna on August 24, 1542. A week before his death he met the superior general of the Capuchins, Bernardino Ochino,[332]

---

his estate by herself, transforming it into a cultural center open to heretical ideas. See Susanna Peyronel Rambaldi, *Una gentildonna irrequieta. Giulia Gonzaga fra reti familiari e relazioni eterodosse*, Viella, Rome, 2012.

331 On Gasparo Contarini (1483–1542), Venetian patrician, diplomat, and later cardinal, see Elisabeth G. Gleason, *Gasparo Contarini: Venice, Rome, and Reform*, University of California Press, Berkeley-Los Angeles, 1993; and Constance M. Furey, *Erasmus, Contarini, and the Religious Republic of Letters*, Cambridge University Press, Cambridge, 2005. The Inquisition reserved a mild posthumous treatment for him, purging his works from the formulation of the *duplex iustitia*.

332 Bernardino Tommassini, called Ochino (1487–1564), was, before his apostasy, a popular preacher and vicar general of the Capuchin Order. In Geneva he married a woman from Lucca with whom he had at least

who was a fervent disciple of Valdés and an acclaimed preacher. The great Italian cities fought over the honor of hearing Ochino's preaching, and rumors were rampant that the pope wanted to make him a cardinal. In 1536, however, the Capuchin got to know Valdés in Naples as well as the Augustinian religious Pietro "Martire" Vermigli.[333] He was introduced by them to the writings of Luther and Calvin, and his preaching soon showed a strong heretical influence. While Ochino received the applause of more worldly prelates, the Theatine religious, who were always vigilant in matters of doctrine, alerted the Inquisition to the danger of his defection from the Faith.

In July 1542, Ochino received a letter from Cardinal Farnese, who invited him to Rome to meet with the pope. The Capuchin was alarmed, and fearing an indictment for heresy by the new tribunal of the Holy Office, he decided to flee to Calvinist Geneva together with Vermigli. Ochino's apostasy caused a huge uproar,[334] but he maintained that it was Contarini himself who at their prior meeting encouraged him to flee. According to historians, the summer of 1542 was a pivotal moment in the religious history of the sixteenth century, since it witnessed the institution of the Holy Office, the death of Cardinal Contarini, and the flight of Ochino and Vermigli.[335]

---

five children. He died in Slavkov in Moravia, condemned as a heretic by all the churches of his time. See R. H. Bainton, *Bernardino Ochino. Esule e riformatore senese del cinquecento, 1487–1563*, Italian translation, Sansoni, Florence, 1940.

[333] Pietro Martire Vermigli (1499–1562), of the canons regular of the Lateran, a disciple of Valdés, fled to Strasbourg, where he married a former nun. He then fled with Ochino to England, and then to Zurich, where he died. See Mariano Di Gangi, *Peter Martyr Vermigli (1499–1562). Renaissance Man, Reformation Master*, University Press of America, Lanham, 1992; *Petrus Martyr Vermigli. Humanismus, Republikanismus, Reformation*, edited by Emidio Campi, Frank James, and Peter Opitz, Droz, Geneva, 2002; *Pietro Martire Vermigli (1499–1562), Umanista, riformatore, pastore*, edited by Achille Olivieri-Pietro Bolognesi, Herder, Rome, 2003.

[334] Cristiani, *La Chiesa al tempo del Concilio di Trento*, pp. 74–78.

[335] Firpo, *Inquisizione romana e controriforma*, p. 29.

5. Cardinal Reginald Pole

After the death of Valdés and Contarini, the spiritualists united around the English cardinal Reginald Pole, who formed a natural point of reference because of the nobility of his birth, the charisma of his person, and his abundant financial means. Although his mother and brother, faithful to the Roman Church, had been executed in London by order of Henry VIII because they were faithful to the Roman Church, Pole gathered a "cenacle" in his home in Viterbo, which included Marcantonio Flaminio, Pietro Carnesecchi, Bishop Vittore Soranzo, "and others suspected of and infected with heresy."[336] The Waldensians of Viterbo, as Apollonio Merenda, one of their number confessed, believed that works do not justify us but only the blood of Christ.[337] The manifesto of the spiritualists, the *Beneficio di Cristo* by Benedetto Fontanini, was reworked in Viterbo by Flaminio[338] and then published anonymously in Venice in 1543 through the initiative of Pole himself.[339] The booklet was greatly impacted by the

[336] *Processo Morone*, vol. 3, pp. 1363–1364.

[337] *Processo Carnesecchi*, vol. 1, pp. 28–29. Apollonio Merenda (1498–after 1566) was a Calabrian ecclesiastic, the secretary of Cardinal Pietro Bembo, and later chaplain of Cardinal Pole. Arrested in 1551, he revealed many details of the heretical circle, but he was released, apostatized from the Catholic Faith, and fled to Switzerland.

[338] Marcantonio Flaminio (1498–1550) frequented the circle of Valdés in Naples between 1538 and 1541. He accompanied Cardinal Pole to the Council of Trent and died in his Roman house on February 17, 1550. Before he died, he was interrogated by Cardinal Carafa who, when he became pope, in a conversation with the Venetian ambassador Bernardo Navagero (which took place on November 23, 1557), identified him as one of the greatest exponents, along with Pole and Morone, of the "accursed school" of Valdés that infected the Church from within. See *La corrispondenza di Bernardo Navagero, ambasciatore veneziano a Roma (1555–1558)*, edited by D. Santarelli, Aracne editrice, Rome, 2011, vol. 2, pp. 975–76. See also A. Pastore, *Marcantonio Flaminio. Fortune e sfortune di un chierico nell'Italia del Cinquecento*, Franco Angeli, Milan, 1981.

[339] Benedetto Fontanini, Marcantonio Flaminio, *Il beneficio di Cristo*, edited by Salvatore Caponetto, Claudiana, Turin, 2009. The Dominican Fr. Ambrogio Catarino Politi (1484–1553), in his *Compendio d'errori et*

influence of Luther, Melancthon, and Calvin, as well as the thought of Valdés, and thousands of copies were disseminated.

Between 1541 and 1545, the booklet and many other heretical works were at the center of the discussions of the cenacle that gathered around the English cardinal, who was considered an oracle by the disciples of Valdés such as Vittoria Colonna, who celebrated him as "the divine Pole, who shines alone and dignified above the stars."[340] At the end of September 1542, while he was on his way to Rome to receive the red hat as a cardinal, Giovanni Morone stopped for several days in Viterbo as a guest of the English cardinal, to Pole's "great content."[341] As determined at a subsequent inquisitorial trial, it was at this time that Cardinal Morone had radicalized his religious orientation, aligning himself with the positions of Pole and Flaminio.[342] And it was in this period that the hidden spiritualists, despite the suspicions of the Holy Office, began enjoying great political-cultural prestige, as is shown by the fact that even Paul III entrusted the presidency of the Council of Trent to Pole and Morone in the autumn of 1542.[343] The *ecclesia viterbensis* (the Church of Viterbo)

---

inganni luterani (1544), denounced the heretical nature of the work. See Giorgio Caravale, *Il* Beneficio di Cristo *e l'Inquisizione romana: un caso di censure tardive* in *Cinquant'anni di storiografia italiana sulla Riforma e i movimenti ereticali in Italia (1950–2000)*, edited by S. Peyronel Rambaldi, Claudiana, Turin, 2002, pp. 151–173.

340 Vittoria Colonna, *Rime*, edited by Alan Bullock, Laterza, Rome-Bari, 1982, p. 155. See *Nuovi documenti su Vittoria Colonna e Reginald Pole*, edited by Sergio M. Pagano, Concetta Ranieri, Archivio Vaticano, Vatican City, 1989.

341 *Processo Morone*, vol. 2, p. 469.

342 Ibid., p. 642. According to Vittorio Colonna, after the meeting with Pole, Morone "*erat conversus et habuerat istud lumen cognoscendi iustificationem nostram esse per solum sanguinem domini nostri Iesu Christi*" "(They said [and this is indeed true] that) he converted and he held the light of knowing our justification to be through only the blood of our Lord, Jesus Christ" (Ibid., p. 730).

343 Firpo, *Inquisizione romana e controriforma*, p. 113.

may be considered, according to Firpo,[344] the workbench on which the crypto-heretics tried to work out the points of their strategy to bring to Trent in order to find a compromise between Catholics and Lutherans after the failure of the colloquium of Regensburg.

Cardinal Pole followed the work of the Council in 1545–1546, but he abandoned the assembly on the vigil of the vote on the decree *De Iustificatione*, since he did not agree with the condemnation of the Lutheran principle of *sola fides*. "*Tenenda est via media, nec hoc neque illuc flectendum*":[345] the final words spoken by the English cardinal at the Council of Trent summarize his irenic and compromising ecclesiology. Pole was followed like a shadow by the Venetian Alvise Priuli,[346] whose name is mentioned several times in all the trials conducted for heresy during the middle of the sixteenth century. The preacher Lorenzo Davidico, who was interrogated by the Holy Office in 1556, testified that Priuli had said to him that the authentic vicar of Christ on earth was not the reigning Pope Julius III but Cardinal Pole, the "angelic pope" by whom there was finally being inaugurated the age of the spirit and the reform of the Church that was hoped for by the spiritualists.[347] Until then, the

[344] FIRPO, *Tra alumbrados e "spirituali." Studi su Juan de Valdés e il Valdesianesimo nella crisi religiosa del '500 italiano*, L. S. Olsckhi, Florence, 1990, pp. 155–184.

[345] "We should take the middle road, and not diverge from it." VITO MIGNOZZI, *"Tenenda est media via." L'ecclesiologia di Reginald Pole (1500–1558)*, Cittadella, Assisi, 2007, p. 539.

[346] Alvise Priuli (first decade of the 1500s–1560) belonged to an influential family of Venetian merchants. When in 1536, Paul III made Pole a cardinal, Priuli followed his English friend to Rome and he never left him, becoming his most trusted collaborator. Thomas D. Mayer, in the conclusion of his book dedicated to Cardinal Pole, affirms that Priuli was certainly homosexual and proposes the hypothesis, unproven and not taken up by other historians, that there was a bond of this nature between Priuli and Cardinal Pole (*Reginald Pole: Prince and Prophet*, pp. 442–451).

[347] FIRPO, *La presa di potere dell'Inquisizione romana*, p. 48.

Apostolic See was considered vacant and the Church like a "widow without a visible spouse."[348]

Later, when Mary Tudor rose to the throne, Pope Julius III sent Cardinal Pole to England, appointing him apostolic legate and archbishop of Canterbury in place of the schismatic Thomas Cranmer. In 1557, however, Paul IV revoked his appointment of Pole as legate and recalled him to Rome, with the intention of accusing him of heresy. Pole did not move from London, where he died on November 17, 1558, only a short distance from the queen. Before he died, he sent a document to the pope that may be considered his will, in which he reaffirms his full obedience to the Supreme Pontiff. However, as Carnesecchi, a member of Pole's inner circle, poignantly observed to Lady Giulia Gonzaga on February 13, 1559, because of the careful, conflicted ambiguity of his speech, Pole "remained in public opinion a Lutheran in Rome and a papist in Germany."[349] The Anabaptist Francesco Negri in turn accused Pole of wanting to reconcile Luther's ideas with the papacy, the Mass, and "a thousand other papist superstitions and impieties."[350] Negri interpreted Pole's Nicodemite strategy as cowardice and opportunism, yet among many Pole still enjoys to this day a reputation as a good Catholic prelate in the Anglo-Saxon countries.[351]

[348] Firpo-Marcatto, *I processi contro don Lorenzo Davidico*, Archivio Segreto Vaticano, Vatican City, 2011, pp. 215–216. Lorenzo Davidico (1513–1574), preacher and author of spiritual texts, was interrogated by the Holy Office, to which he denounced the crypto-heresy of Cardinals Pole and Morone.

[349] *Estratto del processo di Pietro Carnesecchi*, edited by Giacomo Manzoni, Stamperia Reale, Turin, 1870, p. 301.

[350] Quoted in Firpo, *Riforma protestante ed eresie nell'Italia del Cinquecento*, p. 131.

[351] See, for example, the benevolent judgment of an excellent historian like Warren H. Carroll in *The Cleaving of Christendom*, Christendom Press, Front Royal, Virginia, 2000, pp. 255–256, which draws from Martin Haile, *Life of Reginald Pole*, Pitman & Sons, London, 1910. The operation *ad memoriam* that sought to transform Pole into a champion of orthodoxy has conditioned other recent historians like Dermot Fenlon in *Heresy and*

6. The Carnesecchi Trial

Pius V long knew about the subversive maneuvers of the heretics, ever since he had investigated Bishop Vittore Soranzo in Bergamo. But for obvious reasons, what most concerned him was exposing the network of intrigues, plots, and complicities which heresy enjoyed at the top of the Church. In this regard, the one who was in his sights much more than Cardinals Contarini and Pole, both of whom by this time were deceased, was Cardinal Giovanni Morone, who by 1542 was co-opted into the spiritualist party and upon Pole's death had become its most authoritative proponent. Moreover, Morone had already undergone a prior inquisitorial trial of heresy under Pius IV, who had acquitted him and charged Cardinal Ghislieri with signing the acquittal. However, Pius V, who had personally interrogated Morone, was not convinced of the outcome of the trial; he had preserved the documentation and had exhibited it in the conclave in order to oppose the election of the Milanese cardinal.

Notably, a new opportunity to shed light on the spiritualists presented itself immediately after the election of Pius V when, on April 16, 1566, the princess Giulia Gonzaga died in Naples at the age of fifty-three. As soon as he received news of the death of this disciple of Valdés, the pope asked the viceroy of Naples to seize her papers and bring them to Rome. Gonzaga's Neapolitan home was searched, and over eight hundred documents fell into the hands of the Roman inquisitors. After examining them, Pius V said that if he had known about them while Gonzaga was still alive, "he would have burned her alive."[352] The documents showed the key role of the protonotary apostolic[353] Pietro Carnesecchi, who had

Obedience in Tridentine Italy: Cardinal Pole and the Counter Reformation, Cambridge University Press, Cambridge, 1972.

352 BRUTO AMANTE, *Giulia Gonzaga contessa di Fondi e il movimento religioso femminile nel secolo XVI*, Nicola Zanichelli, Bologna 1896, vol. 1, p. 182 n.

353 The protonotary apostolic is an honorary office of the Roman Curia that took on great importance in the pontifical court of the sixteenth century. See PETER PARTNER, *The Pope's Men: The Papal Civil Service in the Renaissance*, Oxford University Press, Oxford, 1990, pp. 56–60.

written more than 250 letters to Gonzaga and was one of the people who played the decisive role of liaison officer in the spread of heresies.

Born into a family of wealthy Florentine bankers, Pietro Carnesecchi[354] came to Rome when he was very young to begin a curial career under the aegis of his maternal uncle, Cardinal Bernardo Bibbiena. He was protected and cared for by Clement VII, who after appointing him protonotary, made him his first secretary. After the death of the pope, Carnesecchi moved to Florence and then to Naples, where he resided from 1539 to 1541 as a guest of Giulia Gonzaga, frequenting the circle of Valdés, whose ideas he came to agree with fully. Thanks to his capacity for relationships, the young Carnesecchi created a close network of friendships in those years, binding himself closely to declared heretics such as Ochino and Vermigli. Beginning in 1541, together with Marcantonio Flaminio, Carnesecchi did his utmost to secretly win over prelates and prestigious cardinals to the ideas of Valdés. One of the first followers was Cardinal Pole, who in October 1541 invited Flaminio and Carnesecchi to Viterbo to agree on a series of initiatives of heretical propaganda, such as the printing of two writings by Valdés and of the *Beneficio di Cristo*.

This frenetic activity did not escape the attentive eyes of the Holy Office. Between 1542 and 1546 Carnesecchi was in Venice, and during his time there, he underwent his first call to Rome to be examined by the Inquisition. The protonotary succeeded in escaping trial, but Paul IV, when he became pope, requested his extradition from the Republic of Venice. On April 6, 1559, the sentence was issued in Rome that declared Carnesecchi an impenitent heretic and condemned him to capital punishment. However, the subsequent election of Pius IV in January 1560 stopped the execution of the sentence. On June 4, 1561, the heretic was fully acquitted by Pius IV and was able to spend the last years of that

[354] Pietro Carnesecchi (1508–1567), a Florentine cleric and protonotary apostolic, particularly versed in intrigue, wandered to different Italian cities and remained for a long time at the French court. Concerning his life, see the entry by Antonio Rotondò in DBI, vol. 20 (1977), pp. 466–476; and, regarding his various trials: *Estratto del processo di Pietro Carnesecchi*, pp. 187–573, and *Processo Carnesecchi*.

pontificate in relative tranquility. After the death of the pope, Carnesecchi returned to live in Venice and later in Florence, where he continued to develop his secret network of relationships undisturbed.

The later discovery of the Carnesecchi-Gonzaga correspondence under Pius V, however, radically changed the situation. The bundles of letters confiscated from Gonzaga, Firpo observes, "handed the Holy Office an imposing amount of indicting material with which to nail down the responsibility of the Florentine heresiarch, who until then had succeeded in escaping the exemplary condemnation he deserved thanks only to the distraction of Paul III, the complicity of powerful cardinals, the protection of the duke of Florence, the stroke of fortune of the destruction of the inquisitorial archives, the thousand lies he had told as well as the insane blindness of Pope Pius IV."[355]

Pius V turned to the Duke of Florence, Cosimo de' Medici, who until then had protected Carnesecchi. The duke yielded to the insistence of the pope and ordered the arrest of the heretic. On June 26, 1566, Carnesecchi was handed over into the custody of the Master of the Sacred Palace Tommaso Manriquez and transferred to Rome.

The trial began a few days later. The judges were Cardinals Francisco Pacheco, Scipione Rebiba, Gian Francesco Gambara, and Bernardino Scotti. The interrogations were entrusted to Giulio Antonio Santori, an intelligent and capable inquisitor in whom Pius V placed the greatest trust.[356] Carnesecchi admitted the lies and falsifications to which he had had recourse during his prior trial of 1560–1561. For example, on January 25, 1561, in a letter that fell into the hands of the Holy Office, he boasted to his confidante Giulia Gonzaga that he had deceived the inquisitors so well that "whether they want to or not, they will have to drink it, because [Carnesecchi] has justified his positions so well that they cannot be challenged or reprobated by them if they do not want to be blamed for what they blame others."[357]

[355] *Processo Carnesecchi. Il processo sotto Pio V*, vol. 1, p. xiii.

[356] Ibid., pp. xxviii–xxix.

[357] Ibid., vol. 2, p. 921.

On the basis of the material now possessed by the inquisitors, the heretic was called to respond principally to three points: who were the "elect" to whom he referred in his letters to Gonzaga; why did he intend to flee to Geneva, a well-known den of heretics; and what were the reasons for his disapproval of the declaration of fidelity to the pope made by Cardinal Pole in his last will and testament? From that moment on, despite continuous attempts to evade the inquisitors' questions, Carnesecchi's compromising declarations followed one after another, and he admitted that he had approved, at least in part, of the doctrines of Luther and Calvin.[358]

In the first months of 1567 the interception of other messages that Carnesecchi wrote secretly from prison, in which he informed his friends and accomplices of the possible dangers that the findings of the interrogations from the trial could represent for them, confirmed his hypocrisy. Cosimo de' Medici was following the Carnesecchi affair from Florence, and he repeatedly appealed to the pope, asking him to lighten his position. But the trial took a turn in May, when Carnesecchi refused to sign a list renouncing thirty-four "heretical, reckless and scandalous opinions" drawn from trial interrogations. A few days later, on July 18, the protonotary sent to the tribunal a testimony in which he openly admitted "to have in effect assented not only to Valdés but also to Luther concerning the article on justification," as well as "to other articles connected to that one." He declared, finally, that he also had doubts about the divine origin of the sacraments and the primacy of the pope and that he "fell more on the heretical side than on the Catholic side" with regard to Confession and transubstantiation. Carnesecchi further confessed that he had read and appreciated the books of Luther "and others of his sect" in Viterbo.[359]

On September 21, 1567, during a solemn ceremony at the Minerva in the presence of the entire sacred college, there was a public reading

[358] Ibid., p. 922.

[359] Ibid., vol. 1, pp. 91–92.

of the long sentence that handed Pietro Carnesecchi over to the secular arm, declaring him an "unrepentant heretic" and a "fake convert."[360]

"The reading of the acts of the trial lasted two hours," Pastor relates. "With growing amazement, the listeners learned how a man, who had always appeared from the outside to be a minister of the Church and who apparently allowed himself to enjoy without remorse the richest ecclesiastical incomes, was at the same time secretly in relations with all sorts of heretics, adhered to a number of opinions contrary to the faith, and, brazenly denying it and prevaricating, had known how to deceive his judges."[361]

The sentence declared that Carnesecchi has confessed that he denied all the sacraments and the principal articles of the Faith, and that he had "very close intelligence with all the Lutherans of the world."[362] Since 1540, he had been "a heretic, a believer in the heretics, and respectively their advocate and receiver."[363] He professed the Lutheran doctrines of justification by faith alone and of *sola scriptura*, questioned the sacraments, denied transubstantiation, and wavered between the heresies of Luther and Calvin on the Mass. He rejected the primacy of the pope, the celibacy of priests, Purgatory, indulgences, and the cult of the saints, believing "in all the errors and heresies" contained in the book *Del beneficio de Christo* and "in the false doctrine and institutes taught by his master Giovanni Valdés."[364] After being acquitted in two trials of the Inquisition, he had not amended but had continued to the end to profess the Lutheran doctrine according to which one is saved by faith alone without works. There was therefore no hope of any correction from him, and the inquisitors judged him to be "an impenitent heretic and feignedly converted."[365]

[360] The entire text of the sentence is found in *Processo Carnesecchi. Il processo sotto Pio V*, vol. 3, pp. 1363–1379.

[361] Pastor, *Storia dei papi*, vol. 8, p. 206.

[362] *Processo Carnesecchi. Il processo sotto Pio V*, vol. 1, pp. cxxxii–cxxxiii.

[363] Ibid., vol. 3, p. 1378.

[364] Ibid., vol. 3, pp. 1371–1374.

[365] Ibid., vol. 3, p. 1378.

In his confession, Carnesecchi involved Cardinals Contarini, Pole, and Seripando, all of whom were deceased,[366] but he shrewdly sought in every way to exonerate Cardinal Morone, who was still living and represented perhaps the one hope for his own future and the future of his ideas.

Pius V delayed the execution of the sentence by ten days, hoping for Carnesecchi's repentance and for a complete confession, which would have saved his life. Michael Ghislieri, as the historian Dario Marcatto recalls, "knew to be hard on the unrepentant and pertinacious who sought by deception to deny errors past and present (like the protonotary Carnesecchi) and knew to be mild and open with those who showed they were repentant."[367] The Venetian ambassador Paolo Tiepolo wrote to his government that "if Carnesecchi had shown perfect repentance he would have saved his life, that such was the inclination of the pope and cardinals of the Inquisition;" but "he was so varied in what he said, and perhaps also in his belief, that in the end he himself confessed that he had satisfied neither the heretics nor the Catholics."[368]

There was no change of heart or mind. The sentence was thus executed on October 1, 1567, at Ponte Sant'Angelo. That same morning Pius V published the solemn rehabilitation of the nephews of Paul IV, who had been condemned to death by Pius IV during the same days on which the Medici pope had acquitted Pietro Carnesecchi.

7. Pius V and the Italian Anti-Trinitarianism

The Carnesecchi trial was the symbolic conclusion of a battle without quarter conducted by Pius V against heresy in Italy. The spiritualist party failed in its goal of conquering the Church from within, thanks to the vigorous workings of the Inquisition. For the Italian heretics, the only thing left for them was to emigrate, which had started among the most discerning of them in the 1540s. But with the emigration, all traces of

[366] Ibid., vol. 1, p. xxiv.

[367] D. Marcatto, *"Questo passo dell'heresia." Pietrantonio di Capua tra valdesiani, "spirituali" e "inquisizione,"* Bibliopolis, Naples, 2003, p. 97.

[368] *Processo Carnesecchi*, vol. 1, p. cxlix.

Nicodemism fell away, and the Italian Protestants openly renewed the anti-trinitarian heresies of the first Christian centuries.

The prior distinction between the "moderate" doctrinal position of the spiritualists and the "radical" position of the anti-trinitarians has fallen, as shown by documents that have come to light after the opening of the archives of the Inquisition in 1998.[369] Anti-trinitarianism, as Massimo Firpo[370] recalls, constituted the esoteric nucleus of a heretical group known to the inquisitors as the "Georgian sect," which took its name from its promoter, the Benedictine Giorgio Siculo.[371] Numerous personalities tied to the spiritualists were part of this sect, beginning with Benedetto Fontanini, the author of the first redaction of the *Beneficio di Cristo*.

When the Holy Office of Ferrara arrested Siculo in September 1550, the Roman Inquisition sent then-Brother Ghislieri to the Estense capital to follow the affair, but the heresiarch was strangled in prison before Ghislieri could interrogate him. The suspicion arose that the instigator of the killing, which took place in clear violation of the procedures of the Inquisition, was Duke Ercole II of Ferrara,[372] who was worried about the possibility that the investigations of the Alessandrian cardinal would reveal a network of heretical contacts that directly involved the Estense

[369] *L'apertura degli archivi del Sant'Uffizio romano* (Rome, 22 January 1998), Accademia Nazionale dei Lincei, Rome, 1998.

[370] Firpo, *Riforma protestante ed eresie nell'Italia del Cinquecento*, pp. 185–187.

[371] Giorgio Siculo (Giorgio Rioli, ca. 1517–1551), a religious of the Benedictine monastery of San Niccolò dell'Arena near Catania, gave hospitality between 1537 and 1543 to Benedetto Fontanini, who wrote the *Beneficio di Cristo*. See Firpo, *Riforma protestante ed eresie nell'Italia del Cinquecento*, p. 153. On Siculo, who was strangled in prison in Ferrara in 1551, see A. Prosperi, *L'eresia del libro Grande. Storia di Giorgio Siculo e della sua setta*, Feltrinelli, Milan, 2000.

[372] Ercole II d'Este (1508–1559) was the fourth Duke of Ferrara, Modena, and Reggio from 1534 until his death. He was married to Renata di Francia (1510–1575), the daughter of King Louis XII of France, who was tied to Calvin, with whom she regularly corresponded. See E. P. Rodocanachi, *Une protectrice de la Réforme en Italie et en France, Renée de France duchesse de Ferrare*, Ollendorff, Paris, 1896; Anne Puaux, *La huguenote Renée de France*, Hermann, Paris, 1997.

court and other Italian princes. Among the anti-trinitarian Europeans of the sixteenth century there existed in fact secret ties that permitted them to know each other, to help one another, and to secretly propagate their works.[373] At the center of this sectarian network were the *Collegia Vicentina*, the clandestine organization of Anabaptists whose history the Holy Office succeeded in documenting.[374] Frà Ghislieri had personally participated in this investigation.

It had all begun on October 17, 1551, when the priest Don Pietro Manelfi[375] from the Marche presented himself to the Bolognese inquisitor Leandro Alberti, to whom he had announced that he wanted to abandon the Anabaptist and anti-trinitarian doctrine that he had secretly professed until then. Manelfi revealed how, after he passed to "Lutheranism," he had known in Florence a certain Tiziano,[376] a mysterious person who had rebaptized him and introduced him into the ranks of the Anabaptists. He had then traveled as a "minister" to north-central Italy, participating in the Anabaptist synod in Venice in 1550. Finally, following a divine inspiration, he had decided to return to the Catholic Church.

The Father Inquisitor of Bologna sent Manelfi to Rome, where he was interrogated by Fr. Girolamo Muzzarelli,[377] assisted by the general

[373] STANISLAS KOT, *Le mouvement antitrinitaire au XVI et au XVII siècle*, G. Thone, Paris, 1937, p. 28.

[374] See WILLIAMS, *The Radical Reformation*, p. 561; and DE MATTEI, *A sinistra di Lutero, passim.*

[375] CARLO GINZBURG, *I costituti di Don Pietro Manelfi*, Sansoni, Florence, 1970. Pietro Manelfi (ca. 1519–after 1552) was a priest who, through reading the literature of Valdés, embraced the doctrines of Anabaptism, which he spread in Veneto.

[376] On Tiziano, the "apostle" of Anabaptism in the Italian Grisons and in northeastern Italy, see GINZBURG, *I costituti di Don Pietro Manelfi*, pp. 18–25; A. STELLA, *Dall'anabattismo al socinianesimo nel cinquecento veneto*, Liviana, Padua, 1967, pp. 37–38 *passim*; CESARE SANTUS, *sub voce*, in DSI, vol. 3, pp. 1575–1576.

[377] Girolamo Muzzarelli (1510–1561), a Dominican, was inquisitor in Bologna from 1550 to 1553, then archbishop of Conza in Campania (1553), Master of the Sacred Palace and a consultor of the Holy Office.

commissioner of the Holy Office, Frà Michele Ghislieri,[378] who thus had the possibility of ascertaining a detailed picture of the doctrinal characteristics and the geographical and social distribution of Italian Anabaptism. What emerged from the valuable testimony was not only the identity of a sectarian organization spread throughout the entire peninsula, but also the existence of irrefutable links between the disciples of Valdés and the most radical wing of Italian Protestantism.

The sect showed its consistency in the so-called Synod of Venice[379] of September 1550, a sort of heretical council, which was attended by about sixty Anabaptist "*ministri et episcopi*" from all over Italy. The dogmatic discussions led to openly anti-trinitarian conclusions: Christ is not God but a man filled with all the virtues of God; the angels of which the Bible speaks are men sent by God to carry out a specific mission; there is no devil other than human prudence, the enemy of God. Furthermore: "According to the Gospel it is not licit to baptize children if they do not first believe; magistrates cannot be Christian; the sacraments do not confer any grace whatsoever but are merely exterior signs; nothing should be held by the Church other than Sacred Scripture; no opinions of the doctors should be held; the Roman Church is held to be diabolical and anti-Christian; those who have been baptized are not Christians but need to be rebaptized."[380]

One of the participants in the Anabaptist synod, the Sicilian Camillo Renato,[381] probably a pseudonym of the Franciscan Paolo Ricci, also presented ideas of this kind: "The soul dies together with the body, or sleeps until the day of resurrection; the body will not resurrect in its substance; man was not created immortal and will die even if he has not

[378] GINZBURG, *I costituti di Don Pietro Manelfi*, p. 60.

[379] WILLIAMS, *The Radical Reformation*, p. 563; STELLA, *Dall'anabattismo al socinianesimo*, pp. 76–83.

[380] GINZBURG, *I costituti di Don Pietro Manelfi*, pp. 33–34.

[381] Camillo Renato (ca. 1500–ca. 1575), from Palermo, an apostate Franciscan friar, after being tried and condemned, succeeded in fleeing to Switzerland. Concerning him, see *Opere. Documenti e testimonianze*, edited by A. ROTONDÒ, Sansoni, Florence; The Newberry Library, Chicago, 1968.

sinned; there is no natural law that permits man to know what he should do and what he must avoid doing; the Decalogue is useless for those who believe; Scripture does not speak of the merits of Christ; Christ could have been a sinner; Christ was born in the curse, since he was conceived in original sin; justifying faith does not need confirmation of the sacraments, which are simple symbols that represent the past without any value of promise."[382]

According to the theory of the "sleep of souls" secretly professed by the Anabaptists, the souls of the deceased, definitively liberated from mortal bodies, are immersed in a sort of sleep, or even die, until the Last Judgment. Along with Purgatory, the resurrection of the body, which constitutes one of the foundations of the Christian faith, was also denied. One of the principal proponents of the Italian anti-trinitarians was the Piedmontese doctor Giorgio Biandrata,[383] the author of a work entitled *De vera et falsa unius Dei, Filii et Spiritus Sancti cognitione* (1568), which, according to the historian Antonio Rotondò,[384] constitutes one of the most important writings of the heretical European movement. In this work Biandrata maintained that the anti-trinitarian doctrine is the true Christian doctrine, which had been adulterated over the centuries with the definition of a "*tripersonatus*" God.

When the Italian heretics left Italy, spreading their doctrines throughout Europe, Biandrata was, along with Lelio Socino, the principal propagator of anti-trinitarianism in Poland, where Humanism had prepared the way and where a Calvinist church had been set up—which, however, was only of brief duration.[385]

[382] Emile Leonard, *Storia del Protestantesimo*, Il Saggiatore, Milan, 1971, vol. 2, pp. 69–70.

[383] On Giovanni Giorgio Biandrata (1516–1588), see the entry by A. Rotondò, in DBI, vol. 10 (1968), pp. 257–264. Biandrata died, so it seems, strangled by a nephew in the course of a scuffle (Louis Maimbourg, *Histoire de l'arianisme depuis sa naissance, jusqu'à sa fin. Avec l'origine et le progrès de l'hérésie des sociniens*, 3rd ed., Mabre-Camoisy, Paris, 1678, vol. 3, p. 513).

[384] Rotondò, *Biandrata Giorgio*, in DBI, p. 260.

[385] Profiting from the tolerance of Sigismund II (1520–1572), Biandrata and Socinus introduced in the Kingdom of Poland the principal exponents

8. From Lutheranism to Socinianism

Lelio Socini (or Sozzini) and his nephew Faustus,[386] of a noble family of Siena, were the organizers of a form of radical Protestantism in Italy in the sixteenth century. The apostasy of Socini occurred between 1540 and 1546, the year in which he played an influential role in the *Collegia Vicentina* (from the Italian town of Vicenza). In 1547, afraid of being identified by the Inquisition, he left Italy and traveled through Central Europe, visiting the main centers of Protestantism.

The writings of Lelio Socini were inherited by his nephew Faustus, who spread the ideas of his uncle throughout all of Europe.[387] He was also a native of Siena, and after a period of crypto-Protestantism, in 1575 he left Italy and went to Basel. He next went to Transylvania and then to Poland, where he established his residence in Krakow and welcomed emigrating Italian heretics. While not joining any of the sects or small groups that swarmed in the city, Faustus Socinus acquired great authority over various groups, enough to become the expressly recognized head of the anti-trinitarian community. On his tomb was written this epitaph: "*Alta ruet Babylon: destruxit tecta Lutherus, muros Calvinus, sed fundamenta*

---

of the *Collegia Vicentina*, among whom were Bernardino Ochino, Valentino Gentile (1515–1566), and Giovanni Paolo Alciati della Motta (ca. 1515–1573).

[386] On Lelio Socini (1525–1562) and Fausto Socini (1539–1604), see Valerio Marchetti, *Gruppi ereticali senesi del Cinquecento*, La Nuova Italia, Florence, 1975; Cantimori, *Eretici italiani*, pp. 214–222; Cristiani, *Socinianisme*, in DTC, vol. 14 (1941), cols. 2326–2334; Giovanni Pioli, *Fausto Socini. Vita, opera, fortuna*, Guanda, Modena, 1952; *Italian Reformation studies in honor of Laelius Socinus*, edited by J. A. Tedeschi, Le Monnier, Florence, 1965; *Faustus Socinus and His Heritage*, edited by Lech Szczucki, Polish Academy of Sciences, Krakow, 2005, pp. 29–51.

[387] Works of the Socinians in the first 2 vol. of the *Bibliotheca Fratrum Polonorum*, edited in 5 vol. by A. Wissowatius, Amsterdam, 1656; Italian translation, L. Socini, *Opere*, critical edition edited and with *Introduzione* by A. Rotondò, Olschki, Florence, 1986; to integrate with the texts gathered by D. Cantimori and Elisabeth Feist in *Per la storia degli eretici italiani del sec. XVI in Europa*, Reale Accademia d'Italia, Rome, 1937.

Socinus"[388] (Luther destroyed the roofs of old Babylon [that is, the Catholic Church], Calvin the walls, but Socini subverted the foundations).

For Socinianism, Scripture is the supreme authority, which however is not free from errors and must be interpreted according to reason. The divinity of Jesus Christ is contrary to Scripture and reason; it is doubted that man was immortal in the beginning and that Original Sin is hereditary. The necessity of grace for eternal life is denied (the ethical powers of man are considered sufficient for the observance of the commandments), and, along with this, predestination, the necessity of the redemption of Christ, and the application of his merits. The resurrection of the flesh is denied as are the eternal nature of the punishments of Hell; the sacraments are considered to be mere symbols, and the Last Supper has the simple significance of a commemorative ceremony of the death of Jesus.[389] The essence of Christianity is reduced to the principle of tolerance for all religions.

With these doctrines Protestantism completed its itinerary of apostasy, fully overturning the foundational premises from which it started. If Luther had proclaimed the principle of "faith alone," Socinus proclaimed the principle of "reason alone," subjecting Scripture to a rationalist desecration. The Lutheran and Calvinist doctrine was dissolved and only hatred for the Church of Rome survived as the unifying force for Protestantism.

Between the seventeenth and eighteenth centuries, Socinianism ultimately spread in Holland and England, not as a religious confession but as a mentality, contributing to the birth of Masonry. Voltaire was the great popularizer of Socinianism in France in the eighteenth century, and under this aspect it is not improper to affirm that Sociniansm represents the *trait d'union* between the Protestant Revolution and the French Revolution.[390]

[388] de Mattei, *A sinistra di Lutero*, p. 190.

[389] Kot, *Le mouvement antitrinitaire*, pp. 69ff.

[390] On the final phase of the history of Socinianism, see the volume of Fiorella de Michelis Pintacuda, *Socinianesimo e tolleranza nell'età del razionalismo*, La Nuova Italia, Florence, 1975. One of the first students of Masonry, the Eudist Fr. François Lefranc (1733–1792), a victim of

Pius V, presciently aware of the immediate dangers to the faithful posed by Socini and his followers, on March 29, 1566, issued the bull *Romanus Pontifex*,[391] renewing the constitution of Paul IV, *Cum Quorumdam*[392] of August 7, 1555, which condemned all those who denied the Trinity or the divinity of Jesus Christ, His conception by the Holy Spirit, and His death to redeem us from sin. The excommunication of the apostate Andrea Dudith-Sbardellati two years later was the last act of this battle against neo-Arianism.

9. The Excommunication of Andrea Dudith and the Trial of Aonio Paleario

The apostasy of Andrea Dudith-Sbardellati[393] constitutes a significant moment in the history of Protestant variations. Born to a Hungarian father and a Venetian mother, Dudith was a priest and personal secretary of Cardinal Pole, whom he had met in Verona. After leaving Italy for Austria, he became bishop of Knin in Croatia and then of Csanád in Hungary. In this capacity he participated in the Council of Trent in 1561, where he headed the Hungarian delegation. When he asked the assembly if the laity could receive Communion under both species and

the September massacres of the French Revolution, in *Voile levé (pour le curieux) ou l'histoire de la franc-maçonnerie depuis son origine jusqu'à nos jours* (Lepetit et Guillemard, Paris, 1792), hypothesized about a Masonic organisation, "the quintessence of all the heresies that divided Germany in the 16th century," that dated back to the *Collegia Vicentina* of 1546 and spread throughout Europe through the spread of Socinianism in Poland and England. This thesis was taken up and developed by Fr. NICOLAS DESCHAMPS in his work *Les sociétés secrètes et la société, ou philosophie de l'histoire contemporain*, Paris, 1874–1876, 3 vol., and by the Catholic scholar CLAUDE JANNET in *Les précurseurs de la Franc-Maçonnerie au XVI et XVII siècle*, Victor Palme, Paris, 1887.

391 *Bullarium Romanum*, vol. 7, pp. 722–723.

392 Ibid., pp. 500–502.

393 On Andrea Dudith-Sbardellati (1533–1589), see PIERRE COSTIL, *André Dudith, humaniste hongrois, 1553–1589*, Les Belles Lettres, Paris, 1935; DOMENICO CACCAMO, *Eretici italiani in Moravia, Polonia, Transilvania (1558–1611)*, Le Lettere, Florence, 1970, pp. 109–152.

spoke in favor of the marriage of priests, a large number of scandalized bishops asked the pope to remove him from the Council. Maximilian II, however, took him under his protection and in 1565 sent him as imperial ambassador to Sigismund Augustus in Poland, where Dudith fell in love with a lady of the queen's court and in the summer of 1567 married her and became Protestant. The historian of heresies Florimond de Roemond, commenting on the case of Dudith, writes about the marriage of priests: "It is the ordinary door for heresy."[394] However, the reverse is also true: heresy often leads religious to abandon their vow of chastity to embrace married life. In either case, the sixteenth-century heresiarchs flooded Christian Europe with wives and children.

On February 6, 1568, Pius V inflicted excommunication on the apostate bishop and requested his removal from Poland for the scandal he had caused on an official mission.[395] To justify his apostasy, Dudith wrote a theological booklet in defense of the marriage of priests, and then in 1574 he got married a second time, to Elzbieta Zborowski who was known as "the popess of anti-Trinitarianism," holding both Socinian and deist positions.[396]

The benevolence of King Sigismund of Poland saved Andrea Dudith-Sbardellati, who ended his life among the Arian and anti-trinitarian convents with which Poland was teeming.[397] More notable instead, for its tragic conclusion, is the case of Antonio della Paglia, called Aonio Paleario,[398] a heretical master of *belles lettres* in Siena and then in Milan beginning in 1555, and popularly considered by both Protestants and liberals as a "martyr" of freedom of thought.

[394] Florimond de Roemond, *L'Histoire de la naissance, progrès et décadence de l'hérésie de ce siècle*, Veuve Guillaume de la Noye, Paris, 1610, p. 477.

[395] Pastor, *Storia dei Papi*, vol. 8, p. 475.

[396] Costil, *André Dudith*, pp. 129–130; Kot, *Le mouvement antitrinitaire*, pp. 63–64.

[397] Maimbourg, *Histoire de l'arianisme*, p. 527; Costil, *André Dudith*, pp. 136–143.

[398] On Aonio Paleario (1503–1570), see Chiara Quaranta, *sub voce*, in DBI, vol. 80 (2014), pp. 412–417; Salvatore Caponetto, *Aonio Paleario (1503–1570) e la Riforma protestante in Toscana*, Claudiana, Turin, 1979.

Paleario was an ambitious humanist who, between 1534 and 1535, completed the *De animorum immortalitate*, a philosophical poem of neo-Platonic inspiration imbued with the ideas of Erasmus, Luther, and Melanchthon. In those years he met the heretic Flaminio in Padua and also Cardinal Pole through Alvise Priuli. In 1542, accused of heresy before the court of the Inquisition in Siena, he managed to escape the sentence, deceiving the judges, and on the advice of Cardinal Sadoleto he abstained for some time from theological discussions. But in 1559 he was again accused of heresy, this time before the Inquisition of Milan; he presented himself to the judge and obtained an acquittal in 1560. In this period he wrote his main work, the *Actio in Pontifices Romanos*, in which he denied the primacy of the Roman Pontiff and turned to secular princes to restore religious truth against the pope. The Milanese court in 1567 began an investigation against him, but the following year his trial was brought to Rome. The interrogations began in September 1568 and continued in 1569. Paleario considered faith in Purgatory, the veneration of relics, the celibacy of priests, and the doctrine of transubstantiation all to be superstitions. He also accused the papacy of being primarily responsible for misguiding the Church. After the inquisitorial phase, he was asked to recant his heresies. Faced with the refusal of the accused, the court had him locked up in the Tor di Nona prison and charged two theologians to try to convince him of the errors. On March 15, 1570, Paleario presented to the judges testimony in which he reaffirmed his positions. On June 14 the inquisitors asked him to formally recant and, upon his new refusal, he was handed over to the secular authorities. At dawn on July 3, Aonio Paleari was executed by burning at the stake as an unrepentant heretic in the square in front of Ponte Sant'Angelo, where Carnesecchi had already been executed.

The death by burning at the stake of Carnesecchi and Paleario may appear cruel to the mentality of modern man. Yet St. Thomas Aquinas says: "In heretics there is a sin for which they deserved not only to be separated from the Church with excommunication, but also to be removed from the world by death. In fact it is far more serious to corrupt the faith, in which the life of souls resides, than to falsify money, with which temporal life is provided. So, if counterfeiters and other evildoers are, rightly, immediately put to death by the authorities, with all the more reason and justly may heretics not only be excommunicated, but also killed, as soon as they are found guilty of heresy."[399]

On the other hand, the Angelic Doctor explains, the Church also uses mercy to convert the wanderer, admonishing him before punishment. The Inquisition, begun in order to seek the truth, did not punish for the sake of punishing, but rather to amend, correct, and convert the guilty. Zeal for souls was always the main characteristic of the inquisitor Michael Ghislieri, who visited heretics each day in prison, praying for their salvation.[400] When he became pope he continued to be inspired by this principle, as he demonstrated in the case of Michael Baius, a heretic who, although he was condemned, escaped the tribunal of the Inquisition.

10. The Condemnation of Baianism

Michael of Bay,[401] known as Baius, professor of philosophy and then exegesis in Leuven in the Netherlands, published a series of short treatises beginning in 1563 that were affected by Luther's influence on the doctrine of grace and freedom, which came to be known as "Baianism."

From 1564 to 1566, the main universities of Italy and Spain censored several errors present in his works. Pius V had these texts examined with utmost diligence and with the bull *Ex Omnibus Afflictionibus*[402] of October 10, 1567, he condemned seventy-nine propositions taken from

[399] St. Thomas Aquinas, *Summa Theologica*, II-II, q. 11, a. 3.

[400] Maffei, *Vita di S. Pio V*, p. 339.

[401] Michael Baius (1513–1589) studied and taught at Louvain, where he became *magister* in theology (1550), professor of Sacred Scripture (1551), and chancellor of the university (1575). In 1563 he was sent to the Council of Trent as royal theologian. After the condemnation of Pius V, he was again condemned in 1579 by Pope Gregory XIII. He submitted and became chancellor of the University of Louvain, a position that he held until his death in 1589. See Jean-Baptiste Du Chesne, *Histoire du Baianisme*, Jacques-François Willerval, à Douay [Douai], 1731; François-Xavier Jansen, *Baius et le Baianisme: Essai Théologique*, Museum Lessianum, Louvain, 1927.

[402] Denz-H, nn. 1901–1980.

the works of Baius as heretical, erroneous, and scandalous. The bull was not published but was communicated to the person concerned through the cardinal's vicar, who had to proceed mildly in carrying it out. Baius submitted, but a little more than a year later he addressed an *apologia* to the pope, defending, through an alleged fidelity to the thought of St. Augustine, only the thirty theses that he recognized as his own. On May 13, 1569, Pius V confirmed the condemnation and imposed the recantation on the theologian. Baius, then, relying on the deficient punctuation of the text of the bull and on the consequent interpretations of the sentence, appealed to the fact that he had not been censured for the literal sense of the propositions. Finally he succumbed and recanted the errors.

There is a close relationship between Baianism and seventeenth-century Jansenism.[403] According to the historian of Baianism Jean-Baptiste Du Chesne, Jansenius, in his book *Augustinus*, "gave body, constancy and color" to the heresy of Baius.[404] Urban VIII, as Fr. Henri de Lubac in turn affirms, "was correct when, through the bull *In Eminenti*, he condemned Augustinus as 'containing and renewing the articles, opinions, and feelings reproved' by Pius V."[405]

The heresy of Baius, like that of Jansenius, is based on an incorrect understanding of the relationship between the natural and supernatural order. According to the propositions of Baius that were censured by the Church, man was not created in a supernatural state but instead "the elevation and raising of human nature to the sharing of divine nature was due to the integrity of man's primitive condition and for this reason it must be said to be natural and not supernatural" (condemned proposition n. 21). All the gifts that we call supernatural and preternatural in Adam—the right to the beatific vision of God, exemption from pain and death, infused knowledge—are said to be gifts due to nature. It follows,

403 Jansenism is a heresy that takes its name from the Dutchman Cornelius Jansenius, bishop of Ypres (1585–1638), author of the book *Augustinus*, published in 1640, two years after his death, and condemned on June 19, 1643, by Pope Urban VIII's bull *In Eminenti Ecclesiae*.

404 Du Chesne, *Histoire du Baianisme*, p. 186.

405 Henri de Lubac, *Surnaturel. Etudes historiques*, Aubier, Paris, 1946, pp. 42–43.

according to Baius, that Original Sin was a corruption of nature itself and not the deprivation of supernatural and preternatural gifts. Ever since, man is incapable of any good without grace and is a slave to sin. For Baius there is no distinction between sin and concupiscence[406] (nn. 74, 75); "No sin is by its nature venial, but every sin is worthy of eternal punishment" (n. 20). Baius also says, "It is a Pelagian error to say that free will has the strength to avoid some sin" (n. 28); and the teaching of the Council of Trent, according to which "God has not ordained anything impossible to man" (n. 54), is Pelagian, and therefore heretical.

Baianism was a serious error that paved the way for subsequent heresies. As Fr. Agostino Trapè observes: "The Church walks safely between Pelagianism and Baianism, or, to speak according to the modern principles of philosophers, between rationalism and immanentism, following the middle path of truth. Against some she defends the possibility, at least negative, and the coexistence of the supernatural order, against the other the gratuitousness or transcendence of the supernatural order."[407]

It is not a question of abstract problems but of metaphysical questions that lie at the core of the faithful's spiritual life. Pius V, pastor of the universal Church, clearly understood their grave importance and wanted to remain, until the last day of his life, the *Summus Inquisitor* of Christianity, in order to prevent even one iota of the *Depositum Fidei* from being changed in the tradition of the Church (Matt. 5:18).

[406] Concupiscence (from *concupiscere*, "to crave") is a consequence of Original Sin, which consists essentially in a disordered inclination toward sensible pleasures against the order of reason (St. Thomas Aquinas, *Summa Theologica*, I-II, q. 9, art. 82, 3 etc.). Luther identified concupiscence with Original Sin and held that it is invincible. The Council of Trent, in the *Decree on Original Sin* of June 17, 1546, defined that concupiscence is not a sin and can be conquered with a good will and the help of divine grace (Denz-H, n. 1515).

[407] Agostino Trapè, *De gratuitate ordinis supernaturalis apud theologos augustinenses litteris encyclicis "Humani generis" praelucentibus*, in "Analecta Augustiniana," 21 (1951), pp. 217–265; Marie-Rosaire Gagnebet, *L'Enseignement du Magistère et le problème du surnaturel*, "Revue thomiste," 53 (1953), pp. 5–27.

4

Joined in Battle: Pius V and Philip II

1. The Strategic Vision of Pius V

Pius V did not belong to the ranks of the "political" or "diplomatic" popes who have often governed the Church. Like his predecessors St. Gregory the Great or St. Gregory VII, he lived his lofty mission in an eminently supernatural manner, with his gaze turned solely to the glory of God and the good of souls. The Church, however, lives in the world and, like every supreme pastor, Pius had to be concerned with his relations with the powers of the world, making use above all of apostolic nuncios,[408] papal representatives who constituted the hinge of the papacy's foreign policy after the Council of Trent. However, in an era in which the Machiavellian principle of "reasons of state"[409] triumphed, Pius V showed that he looked poorly on diplomatic

[408] *Nunzio apostolico*, in MORONI, *Dizionario di erudizione*, vol. 58, pp. 151–172; CLAUDIA DONADELLI, *Nunziature apostoliche*, in DSI, pp. 1119–1124, with bibliography.

[409] See FRIEDRICH MEINECKE, *L'idea della ragion di Stato nella storia moderna*, Italian translation, Vallecchi, Florence, 1942 (1924); ROMAN SCHNUR (editor), *Staatsräson: Studien zur Geschichte eines politischen Begriffs*, Duncker & Humblot, Berlin, 1975; RODOLFO DE MATTEI, *Il problema della Ragion di Stato nell'età della Controriforma*, R. Ricciardi, Naples, 1979; YVES CHARLES ZARKA (editor), *Raison et déraison d'Etat. Théoriciens et théories de la raison d'Etat aux XVI et XVII siècles*, P.U.F., Paris, 1994.

mediation, precisely because he did not accept the principle of reasons of state.[410] The Venetian ambassador recognized, however, that while Pope Pius IV had cultivated the temporal interests of his own family, stirring up unrest among the Italian princes, Pius V "showed a calm soul, and above all nothing ambitious against the interests of others, except that he truly desired a league of Catholic princes, first against heretics and then against the infidels."[411]

One fundamental idea dominated the pontificate of Pius V: the Supreme Pastor has the mission of defending the spiritual interests of the flock entrusted to him. He thus viewed Catholic sovereigns, in their capacity as rulers of their realms, to have a central duty of aiding the Church. As Charles Hirschauer observes, "the popes had never openly denied this principle, but for a long time they had no longer sought to put it into practice. Pius V, on the contrary, claimed it vigorously, and drew all the consequences with surprising logic."[412]

In order to attain this end, Pius V needed a system of alliances with the Catholic sovereigns of his time. But at that time both the emperor and the king of France were quite far from sharing a similar perspective, and the pope could only count on one man for the realization of his plans: the king of Spain, Philip II. According to Girolamo Catena, Pius V had so much affection for the Spanish sovereign "that God seemed to have wanted to join two similar souls in the closest friendship."[413] Once, when Philip II was sick, the pope raised his hands to Heaven and prayed, asking God to take some years away from his life and give them to the king, because they would be more useful to the king's life than to his own.[414]

[410] *Le relazioni degli ambasciatori veneti*, p. 179.

[411] Ibid., p. 180.

[412] Charles Hirschauer, *La politique de St Pie V en France (1566–1572)*, Fontemoing, Paris, 1922, p. 13.

[413] Catena, *Vita del gloriosissimo Papa Pio V*, p. 96.

[414] Ibid., reprinted by Leopold von Ranke, *Storia dei Papi*, Italian translation, Sansoni, Florence, 1959, p. 266.

2. Philip II, "Champion" of the Catholic Counter-Reform

For over seven centuries, between the coronation of Charlemagne in the year 800 and the Peace of Augsburg of 1555, Europe had formed a single Christendom under the spiritual authority of the papacy and the temporal authority of the Holy Roman Empire. During the reign of Emperor Charles V, Luther fractured this religious unity. This violent turn in Western history is sublimely captured in the celebrated portrait by Titian, who depicts Charles V on horseback after his victory against the Protestants at Mühlberg in 1547. The painting gives history the image of a victorious warrior, but the subtle expression on Charles V's face also expresses the idea of a defeat: the end of the illusion of having the power to find a peaceful solution to the religious conflict that had lacerated the empire. Luise Schorn-Schütte observes, "Charles appears exhausted, his face does not express joy for victory or a warrior spirit, but is marked by his efforts of the past years, by the effort expended to finish the ride."[415]

The agreement concluded on September 25, 1555, in the city of Augsburg between Charles's brother, Ferdinand I of Augsburg, and the representatives of the Schmalkaldic League officially sanctioned the division of Germany between Catholics and Protestants. The religious division of the empire was followed by the abdication of the sovereign. On January 16, 1556, Charles V gave the Kingdom of Spain to his son Philip, along with the Italian dominions as well as the Low Countries and the New Indies. On September 12 of the same year, he left the imperial crown to his brother, Ferdinand, along with the Habsburg dominions of east-central Europe. Immediately afterwards, Charles retired to the monastery of Yuste in Estremadura, Spain, where he died on September 21, 1558.

In his last letter to Philip, at the beginning of September 1558, Charles V had written to his son: "I address a prayer to you and I entrust you with a charge with all possible and necessary insistence and urgency; I order you as a loving father who asks of you dutiful obedience, that you see

[415] Luise Schorn-Schütte, *Carlo V*, Italian translation, Carocci, Rome, 2002, p. 22.

to it that heretics are annihilated and punished with all necessary force and to crush them, without exceptions and without mercy."[416] The role of *defensor fidei*, which Charles V had not succeeded in carrying out to the end, would now fall to the king of Spain, while the emperor now assumed the role of an ambiguous moderator between religious confessions that opposed each other in his dominions.

Philip II[417] inaugurated his reign with the spectacular victory of San Quentin against the French on August 10, 1557. The Peace of Cateau-Cambrésis of April 2–3, 1559, put an end to wars that had bloodied Italy in the first half of the sixteenth century and opened the era of Spain's European predominance. Philip II transferred the center of gravity of the empire from the Low Countries to Madrid, where he built El Escorial, an imposing architectural complex, simultaneously royal palace and monastery, in order to symbolize the religious and political unity of Spain. The design of El Escorial is in the form of a gridiron, in order to recall the martyrdom of St. Lawrence, whose feast day is on August 10, the day of the victory at San Quentin, which the sovereign attributed to the intercession of the saint.

Philip II was certainly, along with St. Pius V, the dominant figure of his age, but while the pontificate of Pope Ghislieri lasted only six years, the kingdom of the Spanish sovereign lasted for the entire second half of the sixteenth century. During this half-century, no great political decision

[416] Ibid., p. 21.

[417] There is an immense literature on Philip II Habsburg (1527–1598), king of Spain from 1556 until his death, king of Portugal beginning in 1581 and king of Sicily, Sardinia, and Naples beginning in 1554. Among modern works, see CHARLES PETRIE, *Philip II of Spain*, Eyre & Spottiswoode, London, 1963; HENRY KAMEN, *Philip of Spain*, Yale University Press, New Haven-London, 1997: GEOFFREY PARKER, *Philip II*, Little Brown, Boston-London, 1978, Italian translation, *Un solo re, un solo impero. Filippo II di Spagna*, il Mulino, Bologna, 2005; PARKER, *Imprudent King: A New Life of Philip II*, Yale University Press, New Haven-London, 2014; ANGELANTONIO SPAGNOLETTI, *Filippo II*, Salerno Editrice, Rome, 2018.

escaped his gaze and influence.[418] Pius V and Philip II both had in common the awareness of the dignity of their role, the conscience of their rights and duties, and the conviction that Catholic doctrine did not admit accommodations or compromises.[419] Philip II was convinced that his duty as king was above all that of favoring "the perfection and increase of the Christian religion,"[420] and, as one of his biographers wrote, "defending the Catholic religion, both from within and without, consumed all of the human and material resources of the monarchy."[421]

The unhappy experience of his father had convinced Philip II that religious unity was a condition of maintaining the peace and stability of his dominions. However, he was a convinced and devout Catholic who never considered religion an "*instrumentum regni*." For this reason Pius V saw in Philip II the political personification of the Counter-Reformation, the sword on which he could count to fight against heretics and the infidel Turks alike.[422]

The principal instrument of Philip II's religious policy was the Inquisition,[423] which had been introduced in Spain in 1478.[424] With the

[418] G. Parker, *The Grand Strategy of Philip II*, Yale University Press, New Haven–London, 1998.

[419] Bernard de Meester, *Le Saint Siège et les troubles des Pays Bas*, Bibliothèque de l'Université, Louvain, 1934, pp. 8–10.

[420] Luis Cabrera de Córdoba, *Historia de Felipe II Rey de España*, Impresores de Cámara de S. M., Madrid, 1876, vol. 2, p. 172.

[421] Spagnoletti, *Filippo II*, p. 143.

[422] R. García-Villoslada, *Felipe II y la Contrarreforma católica*, in García-Villoslada, *Historia de la Iglesia en España*, BAC, Madrid, 1979–1982, vol. 3 (bk. 2), pp. 3, 106.

[423] Parker, *Un solo re, un solo impero*, pp. 122–123.

[424] On the Spanish Inquisition, the literature is vast. See Henry Kamen, *L'Inquisizione spagnola*, Italian translation, Feltrinelli, Milan, 1973; Bartolomé Benassar, *Storia dell'Inquisizione spagnola dal XV al XIX secolo*, Italian translation, Rizzoli, Milan, 1985; and the important view of Roberto López Vela, *Inquisizione spagnola*, in DSI, pp. 827–845. For a picture of the institution from a Catholic point of view, see William Thomas Walsh, *Characters of the Inquisition*, P.J. Kenedy & Sons, New York, 1940; Tarcisio de Aczona *Isabel la Católica: Estudio crítico de su vida y su reinado*,

help of the Inquisitors General of the kingdom, Fernando de Valdés[425] (1547–1566) and Diego de Espinosa[426] (1566–1572), Philip increased the power of the Inquisition, increased its financial resources, and extended its jurisdiction to his American empire. The king personally attended five *autos-da-fé*, and at the one held in Valladolid on October 8, 1559, Philip II swore on his sword to defend the rights and prerogatives of the Inquisition and to work for the annihilation of heretics.[427] It was on this occasion that he pronounced the zealous words seized upon by all of his biographies. Carlo de Sesso,[428] a Venetian noble who had spread the works of Luther and Calvin in Spain, was condemned to death. On his way to the gallows, he asked the king why, given his social position, the king was allowing him to be burned at the stake, to which Philip II is said to have replied: "I would carry the wood to burn my own son if he was as wicked as you."[429]

Biblioteca de Autores Cristianos, Madrid, 1964; Jean Dumont, *Procès contradictoire de l'Inquisition espagnole*, Famot, Geneva, 1983.

425 Fernando de Valdés y Salas (1483–1568), archbishop of Seville, was appointed by Paul III in 1547 as inquisitor general of the Kingdom of Spain. See José Luis González Novalín, *El Inquisidor General Fernando de Valdés (1483–1568)*, vol. 1, *Su vida y su obra*, Universidad de Oviedo, Oviedo, 1968; and vol. 2, *Cartas y documentos*, 1971.

426 Diego Espinosa Arévalo (1513–1572), one of the closest collaborators of Philip II, was inquisitor general of Spain, superintendent for Italian affairs, head of the state council and also the private council of Philip II, bishop of Siguenza, and was made cardinal in 1568 by Pius V. See José Martínez Millán, *En busca de la ortodoxia: El Inquisidor General Diego de Espinosa*, in *La corte de Felipe II*, edited by José Martínez Millán, Alianza Editorial, Madrid, 1994, pp. 189–228.

427 Spagnoletti, *Filippo II*, p. 159.

428 Carlo Sesso, hispanized into Carlos de Sesso, born in Sandrigo near Vicenza, moved to Spain in 1532 and had a long association with Archbishop Carranza. He was in contact with the Anabaptist group of Francesco Negri in Verona. See Tomás Lopez Muñoz, *Sesso, Carlo di*, in DSI, vol. 3, pp. 1416–1417; José Ignacio Tellechea Idígoras, *Don Carlos de Seso y el arzobispo Carranza. Un veronés introductor del protestantismo en España*, in *Miscellanea Card. Giuseppe Siri*, edited by Raffaele Belvederi, Tilgher, Genoa, 1973, pp. 63–124.

429 Parker, *Imprudent King*, p. 133.

Nevertheless, Philip II's ecclesiastical policy was not immune to the jurisdictional tendencies of his time, and thereby his relations with Pius V also knew moments of strong tension when the king went beyond his sphere of competence and invaded the sphere of ecclesiastical competency.[430] One of the sharp points of dispute was the role of the Inquisition, which in Spain made itself autonomous from Rome, effectively passing under royal control.

3. The Religious Revolt in the Low Countries

Philip II reigned over a group of states that have been called an "empire," but in reality, as historian Henry Kamen notes, it was "more like a confederation."[431] The government of the seventeen provinces that constituted the Low Countries was entrusted to Philip II by his stepsister Margaret, the Duchess of Parma and Piacenza.[432] The Head of the General Estates and Inquisitor of these countries was, until 1563, Cardinal Antoine Perrenot de Granvelle.[433]

430 A. Borromeo, *Filippo II e il Papato*, in *Filippo II e il Mediterraneo*, edited by Luigi Lotti and Rosario Villari, Laterza, Bari, 2004, pp. 477–535. As Borromeo rightly observes, the expression "caesaropapism" used by Ludwig von Pastor to describe the ecclesiastical policy of Philip II appears to be inaccurate (p. 478).

431 Kamen, *Philip of Spain*, p. 108.

432 Margaret of Austria, or Parma (1522–1586), governess of the Spanish Low Countries from 1559 to 1566, was the natural daughter of Charles V. She married the Duke of Florence, Alessandro de' Medici, and then the Duke of Parma and Piacenza, Ottavio Farnese. See Renato Lefevre, *"Madama" Margarita d 'Austria (1522–1586)*, Newton Compton, Rome, 1986.

433 Antoine Perrenot de Granvelle (1517–1586) was bishop of Arras and then in 1561 became archbishop of Malines and primate of Belgium. Pius IV created him cardinal on February 8, 1561, and in 1566 Pius V appointed him a member of the Congregation of Princes, which was concerned with the relations of the papacy with European sovereigns. See Maurice Van Durme, *El cardenal Granvela (1517–1586). Imperio y revolución bajo Carlos V y Felipe II*, Teide, Barcelona, 1957.

The Spanish Low Countries, which Parker calls the "Great Bog of Europe,"[434] were a tranquil region, but one which had experienced religious and moral decadence, especially in the educated classes and the nobility. Pastor writes that " a large part of the Dutch aristocracy, confused and sluggish in terms of religion, led a sumptuous and immoral life and squandered their inherited goods on splendid parties, frenzied dice games, and orgies."[435] Philip had conferred important offices in the government of those provinces on the principal lords of Flanders as well as on the knights of the Golden Fleece,[436] but, as Ambassador Leonardo Donà[437] relates, they behaved insolently toward him, not accepting his authority.[438] Among the Dutch nobility, William of Nassau, Prince of Orange[439] held first place. Together with Emmanuele Filiberto of Savoy,

[434] PARKER, *The Grand Strategy of Philip II*, pp. 115–125. See LOUIS-PROSPER GACHARD, *Correspondance de Philippe II sur les affaires des Pays-Bas*, II, C. Muquardt, Brussels, 1858.

[435] PASTOR, *Storia dei Papi*, vol. 8, pp. 315–316.

[436] The Order of the Golden Fleece is an order of knights established on January 10, 1430, by Philip III of Bourgogne for the purpose of defending the Catholic religion. The order was restricted to a limited number of knights (fifty, after 1516) distinguished by their birth and their merits toward the Church and the crown. See ALASTAIR DUKE, *From King and Country to King or Country? Loyalty and Treason in the Revolt of the Netherlands*, in "Transactions of the Royal Historical Society," vol. 32 (1982), pp. 113–135.

[437] Leonardo Donà (1536–1612), Venetian patrician, was ambassador of the Republic of Venice to Philip II from 1569 to 1573. He was elected doge in 1606 and served in that capacity until his death. See GAETANO COZZI, *sub voce*, in DBI vol. 40 (1991), pp. 757–771.

[438] SPAGNOLETTI, *Filippo II*, p. 183.

[439] William I of Orange (1533–1584) was named stadtholder of the province of Holland, Zeeland, and Utrecht in 1559 by Philip II. On him, see MGR ALEXANDRE-JOSEPH NAMÈCHE, *Guillaume le Taciturne, prince d'Orange et la révolution des Pays-Bas au XVIme siècle*, C. Fonteyn, Louvain, 1890; CICELY V. WEDGWOOD, *William the Silent: William of Nassau, Prince of Orange, 1533–1584*, Yale University Press, New Haven, 1944. The French Catholic Balthasar Gérard, who killed him in Delft, was condemned to ferocious torture. The court decreed that Gérard's right hand should be burned with a burning iron, that his flesh should be

he had contributed to the victory of Spanish arms at San Quentin. His contemporaries named him the "*Taiseux*" or "the Silent," which did not simply mean "the one who spoke little" but rather he who, in order to deceive his interlocutor, knew how to be silent about his ideas and dissimulate.

The Low Countries were also the homeland of Erasmus, whose religious ideas had opened the path to the spread of the new Protestant doctrines. In East Frisia, where toward the end of 1530 Melchior Hoffman[440] had introduced Anabaptism, Hendryck Niclaes[441] gathered around him a clandestine community called the *Familia Caritatis* (Family of Love), in which ecumenical pantheism was professed and the sharing of goods in common and free love were practiced. The sect, like the *alumbrados*, was founded on the principle of mystical union with God, taken even to the point of the absolute identification of the creature with the Creator, and from this principle it was deduced that sin does not exist in the hearts of the so-called "regenerated." Similar to "familism" was "Davidism," which takes its name from the Dutch glass painter David Joris[442] of Delft. Joris too, like Niclaes and other Anabaptist "prophets,"

severed from his bones with pincers in six different parts of his body, that he was to be quartered and skinned alive, that his heart was to be ripped from his chest and thrown in his face, and finally that he was to be decapitated.

440 On Melchior Hoffman (1495–1543), see KLAUS DEPPERMANN, *Melchior Hoffman: soziale Unruhen und apokalyptische Visionen im Zeitalter der Reformation*, Vandenhoeck und Ruprecht, Göttingen, 1979, with ample bibliography; and CORNELIUS KRAHN, *Dutch Anabaptism: Origin, Spread, Life and Thought (1450–1600)*, M. Nijhoff, The Hague, 1968, pp. 80–117.

441 On Hendryck Niclaes (1502–ca. 1580) and the Family of Love, see WILLIAMS, *The Radical Reformation*, pp. 477–482; JEAN DIETZ MOSS, *"Godded with God": Hendryck Niclaes and His Family of Love*, The American Philosophical Society, Philadelphia, 1981; ALISTAIR HAMILTON, *The Family of Love*, The Attic Press, Greenwood, South Carolina, 1981.

442 In his ample biography of David Joris (1501–1556), GARY K. WAITE demonstrates the important role he played in the Radical Reformation, delineating his relations with the Anabaptists of the Low Countries

maintained that he was the "third David"—the first being the biblical king; the second Jesus Christ, Son of David; and the third he himself, David Joris.[443]

Until 1550, Anabaptism presented itself as the largest party of the "Reform" in the Low Countries. The catastrophe of the "city of God" of Münster,[444] where in 1535 the Anabaptists had been crushed by the combined forces of Catholic and Lutheran armies, provoked a fracture within the movement between a violent arm and a "pacifist" arm. The nonviolent group prevailed, thanks to the personality of Menno Simons,[445] an apostate parish priest of Witmarsum in Frisia, who gave a new organization to the Dutch Anabaptists.

His followers, who took the name "Mennonites," became divided among themselves, thus allowing the Calvinists to emerge as the most influential faction, beginning even to gather publicly, despite the bans made by the authorities.[446] As Joseph de Maistre observes, Protestantism "is not only a religious heresy but a civil heresy, because by freeing the people from the yoke of obedience and granting them religious sovereignty, it unleashes general pride against authority and puts discussion in place of obedience. Hence the terrible character that Protestantism

(*David Joris and Dutch Anabaptism 1524–1543*, W. Laurier University Press, Waterloo, Canada, 1990).

443 WILLIAMS, *The Radical Reformation*, p. 381.

444 See ERNEST BELFORT BAX, *Rise and Fall of the Anabaptist*, Sonneschein, London, 1903; KRAHN, *Dutch Anabaptism*, pp. 135–164; WILLIAMS, *The Radical Reformation*, pp. 362–388; and RICHARD VAN DULMEN, *Das Täuferreich zu Münster 1534–1535*, Deutscher Taschenbuch Verlag, Munich, 1974. FRIEDRICH RECK-MALLECZEWEN sees in the history of Münster the precursor of modern utopian revolutionaries (*Il re degli anabattisti*, Italian translation, Rusconi, Milan, 1971).

445 On Menno Simons (1496–1561), see C. KRAHN, *Menno Simons (1496–1561)*, H. Schneider, Karlsruhe, 1936; and HENDRIK WIEBES MEIHUIZEN, *Menno Simons*, T. Willink, Haarlem, 1961.

446 G. PARKER, *The Dutch Revolt*, Penguin, London, 1985, pp. 58–59; *La crisi religiosa del secolo XVI*, pp. 382–383.

displayed even from its cradle: it was born rebellious and insurrection is its habitual state."[447]

Within the Low Countries, Flanders, which was the heart of the empire of Charles V, was only a peripheral province of Philip II: a Catholic "island" pressed by the Protestant states that surrounded it: Holland, Prussia, and Hannover. Philip II foresaw that the revolt could start from there, and in 1559 he adopted civil legislation whose provisions on heresy were more rigid than the canonical ones. Word had also spread that Philip intended to introduce the Spanish Inquisition in Flanders, even if, as Kamen writes, "nothing could have been further from his mind."[448]

At the beginning of December 1565, a group of Calvinists, mainly belonging to the lesser nobility, united secretly to organize the revolt in the Low Countries. On the basis of this agreement or "compromise," on April 5, 1566, Count Louis of Nassau[449] and Count Hendrick van Brederode[450] presented themselves at the royal castle with three hundred armed nobles, to present a "supplication" to the regent, Duchess Margaret, in which it was asked that the Inquisition not be introduced and the edicts against heresy in the Low Countries be suspended. In addition to the Calvinist nobles, several Catholics who occupied prestigious posts joined them, such as Lamoral, Count of Egmont[451] and

[447] Joseph de Maistre, *Sur le protestantisme* (1798), in *Oeuvres*, Robert Laffont, Paris, 2007, p. 312.

[448] Kamen, *Philip of Spain*, p. 112.

[449] Louis, Count of Nassau (1538–1574), the brother of William the Taciturn, was one of the promoters of the Calvinist revolution in Flanders. He died, together with his brother Henry, in the Battle of Mook, on the Meuse, in which the Calvinist army was annihilated by Spanish troops commanded by Luis de Requesens.

[450] Hendrick Count van Brederode (1531–1567) embraced Protestantism around 1560, after having been one of the promoters of the revolution, was banished from the Low Countries by the Duke of Alba, and died shortly afterward in exile at the age of thirty-six.

[451] Lamoral, Count of Egmont (1522–1568), after being among the architects of the Spanish victory at San Quentin, was appointed stadtholder of Flanders and Artois in 1559, and a member of the council of state, who

stadtholder[452] of Flanders, and Philip of Montmorency,[453] Count of Horn, stadtholder of Gelderland.

Margaret, without any forewarning to Philip II, accepted the insurgents' request and pushed two of them, the Marquis of Berghes[454] and the Baron of Montigny,[455] to go to Madrid to plead their cause directly with the sovereign. Predictably, their request for freedom of worship in the Low Countries was clearly unacceptable. Philip II and Pius V agreed on the fact that the peace and political unity of a country were unattainable without religious unity, as events in the Kingdom of France had demonstrated, where the concessions granted by Catherine de' Medici had increased the audacity of the Huguenots.

One of the regent's councilors, Count Charles de Berlaymont,[456] contemptuously defined the demonstrating Calvinists as "beggars" [*gueux*], a title that they henceforth took as their badge. In their protest, political demands mixed with religious ones. "Roman idolatry" was attacked publicly, as Protestant exiles flocked from France, England, Germany, and Geneva, stirring up the people to revolt. William of Orange placed

---

was to assist Margaret of Parma in the government of the Low Countries, after the departure of Philip II for Spain.

452 The term *stadtholder* (in Dutch: *Stadhouder*) defines a position that existed from the middle of the fifteenth century until 1795 in the Low Countries, which designated the civil lieutenant of the king of Spain and, with the independence of the Republic of the Seven United Provinces, the lieutenant of the General States.

453 Philippe de Montmorency, Count of Horn (ca. 1518–1568) was stadtholder of Gelderland, then admiral of Flanders and cavalier of the Order of the Golden Fleece.

454 Marquis John of Glymes, marquis of Berghes (1528–1567), Grand Huntsman of Brabant, Knight of the Golden Fleece, was stadtholder of Henegouwen beginning in 1560.

455 Floris de Montmorency, Baron Montigny (1527–1570), stadtholder of Tournais and Knight of the Golden Fleece, was the brother of the Count of Horn.

456 Count Charles de Berlaymont (1510–1578), head of the financial administration of the Low Countries, was councilor of Regent Margaret of Parma and the Duke of Alba. From 1553 to 1577 he was stadtholder of Namur.

himself at the head of the rebels, allowing Philip II to believe that he was Catholic while he told the Protestants that he was on their side. As Cardinal Hergenrother writes, William was a "man without faith or religion, but an expert in deceiving and uprooting peoples."[457]

In two letters written to Pius V on May 13 and June 8, 1566, Orange had assured the pope that he wanted to preserve the Catholic religion in his principality, but in November 1566, in a confidential letter to the Lutheran William of Hesse, he wrote that in his heart he had "always held and professed" Protestantism.[458] In reality he believed in nothing. As Cardinal Grente observes, "Cautious, a good speaker, popular, he diminished religion, reducing it to a political venture; burdened with debts due to his lavishness and married to the Protestant princess Anne of Saxony, by waging war on Catholicism he obtained a double advantage. With the confiscation of his ecclesiastical assets, he filled his empty coffers, and in the meantime he succeeded in making other princes recognize his authority."[459]

4. The Iconoclastic Fury of the Huguenots

Concerned by the news that reached him from Rome, in March 1566 Pius V entrusted the Archbishop of Sorrento, Giulio Pavesi,[460] with the task of giving him an assessment of the religious situation in the Low Countries. Pavesi carried out his mission scrupulously, visiting Antwerp, Brussels, Louvain, Namur, and Liege. When Pius V received his reports and those of other informers, he immediately informed the Spanish ambassador Requesens with the greatest energy that the situation was much

[457] HERGENROTHER, *Storia universale della Chiesa*, vol. 6, p. 359.

[458] PASTOR, *Storia dei Papi*, vol. 18, p. 317.

[459] GRENTE, *Il pontefice delle grandi battaglie*, p. 133.

[460] Giulio Pavesi (1510–1571), Dominican, archbishop of Sorrento, was commissioner of the Roman Inquisition in Naples from 1557 to 1562. From March to July 1566 he received the charge from the pope of legate *a latere* in the Low Countries, with the mandate of gathering information on the political-religious situation then in ferment. On his mission in the Low Countries, see DE MEESTER, *Le Saint Siège et les troubles des Pays Bas*, pp. 10–16.

more dangerous than was believed in Madrid and that the king needed to go to the Low Countries. On July 16 Pius V addressed a resolute letter to the sovereign[461] and on August 13 he wrote to the Spanish nuncio that Philip II would one day have to render an account for the loss of so many souls, since only his personal presence could help to pacify souls.[462]

Philip II, who was naturally of a hesitant character, vacillated, without making a decision, but he also wanted to reassure the pope of his Catholic sentiments, writing to his ambassador in Rome: "You can assure His Holiness that rather than suffer the least injury to religion and the service of God, I would lose my states and a hundred thousand lives if I had them, for I do not intend to rule over heretics."[463]

But as Pius V had foreseen, immediately the situation worsened. In August 1566 a wave of violence struck the Low Countries. Calvinists, Anabaptists, and Mennonites began to sack hundreds of churches and Catholic monasteries. With the cry of "Long live the *gueux*," bands of ruffians destroyed statues, stained-glass windows, chalices, monstrances, sacred images, and altars in the main cities. Within just a few weeks more than four hundred churches and monasteries were destroyed,[464] Catholic worship ceased in a large part of the country, and the Calvinists began to hold their services in many of the churches they had "purified."[465] The iconoclastic fury swept through Antwerp, Amsterdam, Leuven, Delft, and Utrecht. In the Antwerp cathedral the Calvinists destroyed the statue of the Virgin, trampled the Sacred Hosts, scattered the relics, tore the vestments to shreds, and burned altars, statues, and paintings.[466] The Jesuit Fr. Cleysson was indignant at the cowardice of the magistrates of

461 *Philippo Hispaniarum regi: admonitio ut se conferat in Flandram. "Saepe cum dilecto"* (*Epistolae ad principes*, n. 3537).

462 *Epistolae ad principes*, nn. 3562–3563; Pastor, *Storia dei Papi*, vol. 8, p. 26.

463 Philip II to the ambassador Luis de Requesens, in *Correspondencia diplomatica entre España y la Santa Sede*, edited by Luciano Serrano, Impr. of the Instituto Pio IX, Madrid, 1914, vol. 1, pp. 316–317.

464 Kamen, *Philip II of Spain*, p. 116.

465 Parker, *Imprudent King*, p. 149.

466 *La crisi religiosa*, p. 385; Parker, *Dutch Revolt*, pp. 74–75.

the city, who tolerated everything. He wrote to his brother Jesuit Juan Alfonso Polanco, "They impose silence on Catholics, *ne forte tumultus fiat in populo* [lest there arise uproar among the people]. In the meantime, the heretics raise their heads, preach in public, and even in St. George Church, where they brazenly celebrate the Lord's Supper. Look at how the hypocrisy and tyranny of the enemies of the Cross and the timidity and cowardice of the good have reduced us."[467]

As soon as he heard of the open violence, looting, and profanations, Pius V asked Philip II to return to the Low Countries at the head of a powerful army in order to take immediate and decisive action against the rebels. For the pope, the personal intervention of the king of Spain in the Low Countries was the only remedy for a situation that was at risk of being aggravated and of having dramatic consequences in all of Europe.[468] The pope understood clearly how catastrophic a victory of the rebels would be for the Church, and he was convinced that Philip II needed to show the world his power. The iconoclastic fury of 1566 should have opened the sovereign's eyes, but he limited himself to vague promises. Even a contemporary historian like Parker observes: "Events would soon show that Philip's decision to delay his journey to the Netherlands was a critical error: only his return to Brussels could have stabilized the situation."[469]

5. The Hesitation of Philip II

On October 4, 1566, Pius V sent the bishop of Fiesole, Pietro Camajani[470] as extraordinary nuncio to Spain, with the primary purpose of persuading the king of the urgent necessity of going to the Low Countries. Camajani

[467] ALFRED PONCELET, *Histoire de la Compagnie de Jésus dans les anciens Pays Bas*, Marcel Hayez, Brussels, 1927, p. 274.

[468] Pius V to Philip II, February 24, 1566; Bonelli to Castagna, 8 and 29 May 1566, quoted in DE MEESTER, *Le Saint Siège et les troubles des Pays Bas*, p. 26.

[469] PARKER, *Imprudent King*, p. 153.

[470] Pietro Camajani (1519–1579), bishop of Fiesole (1552–1566), promoted to bishop of Ascoli Piceno on October 7, 1566, while he was traveling to Madrid, was extraordinary nuncio to Spain until February 12, 1567.

accompanied Giovanni Battista Castagna,[471] who had been appointed nuncio to Madrid by Pius IV in September 1565. In his instructions to Camajani, the pope directed him to "expound to His Catholic Majesty, with the most effective reasons and words that the Lord God will place in your mind, the loss of so many thousands of souls redeemed by the Most Precious Blood of Our Lord Jesus Christ" because of the seditious masters of error, whose work however has been born and has grown "through the carelessness and negligence of those who govern."[472]

Subsequently, with a brief given to Camajani on January 17, 1567, Pius V proposed to Philip II that he at least come to Milan, "where Your Majesty will be able to decide with greater ease about a possible expedition to Flanders, and in the meantime the mere rumor of your arrival will disconcert the seditious and encourage the faithful. May it please God that Your Majesty may clearly know our predictions and our concerns, when we consider, given the surprising nature of what has already happened before our eyes, the ruin, the ruin that is imminent, unless you act to prevent such a great danger."[473]

In March 1567, again hoping to convince Philip II to go personally to the Low Countries to quell the ongoing revolts that had broken out there, Pius V sent a document to him through the nuncio Castagna that expressed with great richness of argument the papal point of view, favoring a massive and direct intervention aimed at reestablishing orthodoxy as the only source of "firm peace and tranquility of the states." In addition, on the basis of "political reasons" or "reasons of state," the missive listed the reasons why the king ought to decisively use force and renounce every

[471] Giovanni Battista Castagna (1521–1590), nuncio to Spain from 1565 to 1572, later cardinal (1583) and Inquisitor General of the Holy Office (1585), was elected pope on September 15, 1590, taking the name Urban VII, but he died just twelve days later on September 27. His pontificate is remembered as the shortest in history.

[472] Pius V to Camajani, September 1566, quoted in DE MEESTER, *Le Saint Siège et les troubles des Pays Bas*, p. 33.

[473] *Philippo Hispaniarum Regi: adhortatio ad succurrendum rebus Flandrine et venendum in Italiam*. "Cogit nos" (*Epistolae ad principes*, n. 3726).

form of moderation. For Pius V there was a need to act without further hesitation or delay, since what was at stake was the Catholic Faith itself. In a long instruction to the nuncio in Madrid, the pope indicated to the king the path he ought to follow in order to combat heresy and conquer it. In his opinion, two methods of pacification were possible. The first was to reduce the rebels to obedience, suppressing the preaching and meetings of heretics. The second possibility was to tolerate freedom in religious matters until a more opportune time. In the latter case, the pope stated that it would be impossible to reach a true peace. The example of Charles V confirmed his view, given how few states remained subject to him and how precarious the peace was that held sway in the empire.

To the objections that came to him from those who wanted him to fight in the name of national interests rather than the interest of the Catholic Faith, Pius V responded that tolerating the meetings and preaching of the reformers in order to obtain religious peace actually meant feeding the flames. For this pope, the hour had come for Christian princes to understand that it was impossible to save their own nations while permitting the practice of heresy.

To whomever affirmed the necessity of not irritating the nations that were their neighbors, Pius V shrewdly responded that in the present situation there was nothing to fear. France had no political interest in protecting a movement of revolt that constituted, even for France itself, a grave danger. The German princes had been ruined in their war against the Turks. The queen of England, busy maintaining peace in her own kingdom, had spent so much money on the Huguenots in France that she no longer wanted to intervene. The king of Denmark was occupied with making war on Sweden and was thereby short on resources to intervene.

The final reason adopted by the "*politiques*" was that the dissimulation of religious motives would have allowed the recruiting of heretical German soldiers to join the revolt. The pope responded, however, by affirming that the soldier would remain loyal to whoever feeds and pays him best. As a result, Pius V asked Philip II to intervene without further delay, to suppress meetings and preaching, and to reestablish Catholic worship everywhere, without dissembling the cause of religion.

The king, with his political and theological advisers, continued to ponder what to do. On the other hand, as Parker observes, no other sovereign of the sixteenth century could have tolerated the challenge to authority that was expressed in the "Compromise of Brussels" and the iconoclastic fury.[474] On September 22 and October 22, 1566, Philip II presided over two meetings of the council of state to discuss the problems of the Low Countries. Within the council of state there was a difference of opinion as to how the sovereign ought to reestablish his authority, but all the counselors agreed on the necessity of using force to reestablish order.[475] The decision of Philip II was to send the Duke of Alba,[476] Fernando Alvarez of Toledo, to the Low Countries, who together with the Inquisitor General Diego de Espinose supported taking a hard line against the rebels.

6. The Duke of Alba Enters the Scene

As Henry Kamen recalls, "Surprisingly for a world power, Spain had no standing army or navy."[477] In the case of war, the soldiers were recruited from among the Spanish domains and organized into *tercios*, combat units formed by three thousand men (hence the name *tercio*), which were feared throughout Europe for their iron discipline and their combative spirit. For such an elite regiment there could be no better commander than the Duke of Alba, who combined a character of steel with knowledge of the most modern military techniques.

474 PARKER, *Un solo re, un solo impero*, p. 97.

475 Bonelli to Castagna March 6, 1567, quoted in DE MEESTER, *Le Saint Siège et les troubles des Pays Bas*, pp. 50–51.

476 Fernando Álvarez de Toledo y Pimentel, third Duke of Alba (1507–1582), was governor of the Duchy of Milan in 1555, viceroy of the Kingdom of Naples in 1556, and governor of the Spanish Netherlands from 1567 to 1573. See WILLIAM S. MALTBY, *Biography of Fernando Alvarez de Toledo, Third Duke of Alba, 1507–82*, University of California, Berkeley-Los Angeles-London, 1983; H. KAMEN, *The Duke of Alba*, Yale University Press, New Haven-London, 2004.

477 KAMEN, *Philip of Spain*, p. 109.

The duke gathered his army in northern Italy. It was composed of *tercios* coming from Spain, Naples, and Sicily, and from Lombardy it began *El Camino de las Flandas*, which went through Savoy, Bourgogne, Lorraine, and the German principalities along the Rhine.

Pius V asked of Philip II that, during his march toward the Low Countries, the Duke of Alba would make a detour toward Geneva, from where, even after the death of Calvin, his heresy continued to spread throughout Europe. Pius V was convinced that this was an extraordinary opportunity to strike the evil at its roots. Without the support of Geneva, the Huguenots would not be able to resist in France, and likewise the same rebellion in the Low Countries would be destined to fail if it was deprived of support. Philip II, however, rejected the proposal, responding to the pope that it did not seem to him like the right moment to attack Geneva.[478] In an overall strategic sense, one may well credibly argue in retrospect that the king of Spain missed a golden opportunity. If the army of the Duke of Alba had annihilated the center of world Calvinism, it would have spared Europe decades of wars of religion.

On August 28, 1567, the Duke of Alba entered Brussels at the head of his ten thousand veterans, at the end of a march that, as Spagnoletti writes, "was a real strategic and logistical feat for those times."[479] Philip II had given him full military powers and the task of arresting and punishing the rebels. On September 9 the duke instituted the so-called "Council of Troubles" (*Tribunal de los Tumultos* or *Conseil de Troubles*), to suppress the civil and religious unrest that was shaking the region, while the regent Margaret left Flanders.

At the beginning of Lent in 1568, many rebels and their accomplices were arrested on the same day in every part of the Low Countries. The documents that were seized indisputably proved the existence of a conspiracy against the king involving the Counts of Egmont and Horn, who were summoned before the court and arrested for treason. They were

478 Pastor, *Storia dei Papi*, vol. 8, p. 330; de Meester, *Le Saint Siège et les troubles des Pays Bas*, p. 56.

479 Spagnoletti, *Filippo II*, p. 185.

beheaded in the Grand Place of Brussels on June 5, 1568, after receiving the sacraments. Notably, William of Orange managed to escape Alba's clutches, taking refuge in Germany.

Like Philip II, Pius V also welcomed the news of the arrest of the rebels with great satisfaction, and he approved the rigorous sentences given them by the Duke of Alba, considering that such punishment was a necessary evil and that clemency could only be admitted in favor of a very small number of them.[480] Before the news of the execution of Counts Egmont and Horn had reached Rome, the ambassador of the Venetian Republic permitted himself one day to say to Pius V that enough blood had been shed in the Low Countries, and since everyone knew the services rendered by Count Egmont, it was only right that they would also know what his offenses were that made him merit condemnation. The pope responded with vivacity that these offenses must have been very serious if Philip had decided to punish him so severely, and a few days later he had the text of the sentence brought to the ambassador, asking him to examine it and see if the punishment was disproportionate to the crimes committed.[481] For Pius V, the fact that two such preeminent people had supported the rebellion of the heretics was a sufficient reason to justify their condemnation.

The judgment of Ludwig von Pastor and other Catholic historians on the repression of the Duke of Alba is excessively severe. Sir Charles Petrie is one of the few modern historians who has written a reasonable account of the role of the duke in the Low Countries.[482] He followed the orders that he had received from the king, and the first of these was that of punishing the leader of the rebellion against him. Egmont and Horn were knights of the Golden Fleece; they had sworn fidelity to Philip II and they were put to death as traitors to their legitimate sovereign. Even the Baron of Montigny and the Marquis of Bergen, who in Spain had

[480] de Meester, *Le Saint Siège et les troubles des Pays Bas*, p. 61. *Epistolae ad principes*, n. 3840.

[481] de Meester, *Le Saint Siège et les troubles des Pays Bas*, p. 64.

[482] Petrie, *Philip II of Spain*, pp. 228–233.

secretly attempted to win over Philip's son, Don Carlos, to their cause, were indicted for felony. While the Marquis of Bergen died during the trial, Baron Montigny, who was imprisoned in the castle of Simanca, was secretly strangled by order of the king on October 16, 1570. Philip had it announced to the baron that he was condemned to death, but that he would be permitted to receive the sacraments. Montigny thus went to Confession and received Holy Communion, and although he protested his innocence a final time, he thanked the king for having decided "that he should be executed in private and not in public," as had happened to his brother, the Count of Horn.[483]

Like Philip II, the Duke of Alba maintained that the war in the Low Countries should not be conducted in the name of the Catholic Faith against the heretics, but rather in the name of the interests of the crown against rebellious subjects. Pius V was convinced of the contrary: that there was a need to put religion in the first place, and that divine assistance would be granted much more easily the more publicly the war was fought in defense of the Faith. The nuncio Castagna, in a colloquium with the Duke of Alba, reminded him that Charles V, after he had conquered the Protestants in the name of purely political reasons, had not obtained the desired results from the religious point of view because he had shown himself to be accommodating in the area of faith. The response of the Duke of Alba was that, since the pope and the king were in agreement on the end, it was up to the duke, being in the service of the king, to decide on the means.

Pius V still held in great esteem the Duke of Alba,[484] on whom he counted to bring the war to Protestant England.[485] Every time he faced an enemy, the Duke of Alba defeated him without being rash. "One characteristic he had in common with Philip, and that was caution,"[486] Sir Charles Petrie writes, recalling that "caution was the keynote of his strategy." Alba was convinced that the best way to attain a definitive

[483] PARKER, *Imprudent King*, pp. 198–199; KAMEN, *Philip II of Spain*, pp. 127–128.

[484] DE MEESTER, *Le Saint Siège et les troubles des Pays Bas*, pp. 57–58.

[485] *Epistolae ad principes*, nn. 4445, 4504, 4539.

[486] PETRIE, *Philip II of Spain*, p. 43.

victory against the rebels in the Low Countries was to let the enemy army unravel itself, as it did.

When the Duke of Alba annihilated the army of Luigi of Nassau on July 21, 1568, at Jemingen, he wanted to communicate news of the victory personally to the pope. The Spanish ambassador Zúñiga relates that he gave Alba's letter to Pius V, who ordered three days of solemn processions to thank God and pray together for further divine assistance.[487] "I believe," the ambassador testified, "that the interior satisfaction that the Holy Father felt was even greater than that which was demonstrated with these exterior demonstrations, because in my entire life I have never seen a man more contented than he was, when I went to kiss his feet to thank him."[488]

On August 29, Pius V made the Seven Churches pilgrimage, imploring God for the defense of religion in the Low Countries. William of Orange, who led the resistance, gathered his forces for a final offensive against the Spaniards, but he was once more defeated. This victory of the Duke of Alba, news of which reached Rome on December 7, 1568, was considered to be a miracle thanks to the prayers and exhortations of the holy pontiff, who had fasted and distributed abundant alms, and on October 29 he again visited the Seven Churches, imploring the Lord for the victory of the Catholic army.

St. Pius V had the *Te Deum* sung in St. Peter's, and he sent a hat decorated with gems to the Duke of Alba along with a golden sword with this inscription: "*Accipe sanctum gladium, munus a Deo, in quo dejicies adversarios populi mei Israel*": Receive the holy sword, gift of God with which you will drive out the adversaries of my people Israel.[489]

7. The Bull *In Coena Domini*

The nuncio to Spain, Giovanni Battista Castagna, knew how to protect the interests of the Holy See in the face of disagreements with Philip

[487] Pastor, *Storia dei Papi*, vol. 8, pp. 333–334. The pope responded with a brief on August 26, 1568 (*Epistolae ad principes*, n. 4155).

[488] de Meester, *Le Saint Siège et les troubles des Pays Bas*, p. 66.

[489] Grente, *Il pontefice delle grandi battaglie*, p. 137; Pastor, *Storia dei Papi*, vol. 8, p. 335; de Meester, *Le Saint Siège et les troubles des Pays Bas*, p. 68.

II, but he also succeeded in remaining in the good graces of the king, despite his frequent lively discussions with him.[490] The directives that Pius V sent him concerned violations of canon law above all else, following the so-called "*recurso de fuerza*," with which the Spanish government sought control of all acts of ecclesiastical jurisdiction. By means of the *recurso*, any person, whether cleric or lay, could appeal to the Spanish Royal Council against the decisions of bulls or other pontifical documents that seemed unjust.[491] If the council accepted the *recurso*, the ecclesiastical directive was suspended. Furthermore, with the *retención de bulas*, the crown reserved to itself the prerogative of subjecting all bulls and other pontifical documents sent from Rome to the judgment of the Royal Council, even to the point of suspending their execution.[492] This simmering conflict over papal authority in Spain exploded upon Pius V's issuance of the bull *In Coena Domini*.

The bull *In Coena Domini*[493] was a solemn papal act that announced a series of universal and general excommunications related to certain crimes for which the pope reserved absolution to himself. The bull was solemnly proclaimed from the loggia of the Vatican basilica in the presence of the pope and cardinals, and it was affixed to the doors of St. John in Lateran, while in other dioceses it was proclaimed by the bishops in the cathedral churches. On April 15, 1568, Pius V introduced an

[490] Pastor, *Storia dei Papi*, vol. 8, pp. 263–264.

[491] Ibid., p. 265. On the *recursos de fuerza*, see Borromeo, *Filippo II e il Papato*, pp. 501–502.

[492] Vicente de la Fuente, *La retención de Bulas en España ante la Historia y el Derecho*, Impr. A. Perez Dubrull, Madrid, 1865; Borromeo, *Filippo II e il Papato*, pp. 501–503.

[493] Fernand Claeys-Bouuaert, *Bulle In Coena Domini*, in DDC, vol. 2 (1937), cols. 1132–1136; S. Pastore, *In Coena Domini*, in DSI, vol. 2, pp. 774–775; M. C. Giannini, *Tra politica, fiscalità e religione: Filippo II di Spagna e la pubblicazione della bolla In Coena Domini (1567–1570)*, in "Annali dell'Istituto storico italo-germanico in Trento," XXIII (1997), pp. 83–152; M. C. Giannini, *El martillo sobre el anima: Filippo II e la bolla In Coena Domini nell'Italia spagnola tra religione e sovranità (1568–1570)*, in *Felipe II (1527–1598). Europa y la Monarquía Católica*, edited by J. Martínez Millán, Ed. Parteluz, Madrid 1998, vol. 3, pp. 251–270.

important innovation. Until then the validity of the censures was tied to the condition that the bull would be solemnly proclaimed each year on Holy Thursday, the day on which the solemn reconciliation of sinners was performed in Rome.[494] The pope established instead that bulls would remain the permanent law of the Church until the publication of a new bull, and that what it established was to remain in force until its express revocation by the popes themselves. The bull contained a series of injunctions aimed directly against the abuses and usurpations of the civil authorities in the ecclesiastical field. For example, all those who appealed against the pope to an ecumenical council, whatever their condition, were explicitly excommunicated.[495]

The bull *In Coena Domini* was based on the maxims of Gregory VII's *Dictatus Papae*,[496] which affirmed the superiority of the Roman Pontiff over every earthly power and condemned so-called caesaropapism, or regalism, that is, the ancient pretense of temporal authority to hold supreme power over spiritual authority. The regalism of the sixteenth century expressed itself above all by means of the institutions of the *placet* and the *exequatur regi*, by which sovereigns subordinated the introduction of papal resolutions in their reigns to their approval. In Spain the bishops thus refused to publish the bull, in deference to the will of the sovereign, who did not agree with the censures it contained against lay abuses in ecclesiastical matters.

When the nuncio Castagna received the document in May 1568, he duly sent it to the Spanish bishops for publication in their dioceses. However, as noted, not a single prelate dared to promulgate it out of fear of Philip II, who had no intention of renouncing what he considered his

[494] In Italy the bull *In Coena Domini* was published almost everywhere until the end of the eighteenth century. In the bull *Apostolicae Sedis Moderationi* of October 12, 1869, Pius IX revised the list of censures imposed on transgressors *latae sententiae*.

[495] PASTOR, *Storia dei Papi*, vol. 8, pp. 287–288.

[496] On the *Dictatus Papae* of Gregory VII (1073–1085), see the fundamental work of KARL HOFMANN, *Der "Dictatus Papae" Gregors VII. Eine rechtsgeschichtliche Erklärung*, F. Schöningh, Paderborn, 1933.

proper rights. As early as July 11, the nuncio Castagna warned that the Spanish government would set up every possible obstacle to the diffusion of the bull. At the beginning of October 1568 Philip II declared that he was ready to renounce the crown rather than allow himself to be stripped of what his ancestors had possessed. The insistence with which Pius V endeavored to eliminate the doubts of Philip II and reach an understanding with him appears again in an instruction he sent to Castagna on August 17, 1568, which explained that the bull did not in any way intend an innovation or to diminish the jurisdiction of the king, but only to preserve the authority of the Holy See for the overall good of the Church.[497]

If Pius V demanded that the king of Spain recognize the rights of the Church, he also did not miss any opportunity to show him his benevolence. Pius V did not want to enter into conflict with the one monarch who supported the Faith just when Catholics were being gravely threatened throughout Europe, most notably in France, England, and Germany. At the beginning of November 1568 he instituted a special commission of cardinals to examine the objections raised against the bull. The fruit of this work was a note in which the pope reaffirmed that the bull, even though published in Rome, had an obligatory character for all of Christianity, as was also apparent from the fact that it had been promulgated on one of the most solemn days of the ecclesiastical year. The pope felt the duty to demand its publication not only in Spain but in all countries, even in Germany, and to insist that all the clergy become aware of it. In the final part of the bull, it ordered all bishops to solemnly publish it each year in their churches.[498]

At the end of the note, Pius V stressed that he had no other aim than to preserve the authority of the Church and to eliminate indubitable abuses. The pope concluded by energetically recalling the distinction between temporal power and spiritual power according to the words of Christ: "Give to Caesar what belongs to Caesar and to God what belongs

[497] PASTOR, *Storia dei Papi*, vol. 8, p. 291.
[498] Ibid., pp. 297–300.

to God." Despite the continued objections of Spain and Venice, Pius V did not change the form of the bull, which was republished in 1569 and 1570 with the same tone.

8. The *Annus Horribilis* of Philip II

The year 1568 was, as Manuel Fernández Álvarez observes, the *annus horribilis*[499] of Philip II, not only because of the tormented affairs of the Low Countries, but also because of a family drama whose theater was El Escorial Palace. Before he rose to the throne, Philip had married the princess Maria Manuela of Portugal, who, on July 8, 1545, bore him a son, Don Carlos, and who died four days after his birth. In 1554 the king then married Mary Tudor, queen of England, and again became a widower, without any children by her; he had two sons with his third wife, Elisabeth of Valois; and finally, he had five children with Anne of Austria, four of whom died before they were seven years old.[500]

Sadly, Don Carlos,[501] who had caused the death of his mother during childbirth, had shown signs of mental imbalance from his youth because of his violent and unpredictable temperament. One of the causes of this imbalance can be traced back to what Fernández Álvarez calls "a malignant genetic circle."[502] The parents of the prince, Philip of Spain and Maria Manuela of Portugal were in fact first cousins both on the paternal as well as the maternal side, and Don Carlos was on both sides

[499] Manuel Fernández Álvarez, *Felipe II y su tiempo*, Espasa, Madrid 1999, pp. 395–416.

[500] Marcel Dhanis, *Les quatres femmes de Philippe II*, Alcan, Paris, 1933. The four wives of Philip II were Maria, infante of Portugal (1527–1545); Mary Tudor, queen of England (1516–1558); Elisabeth of Valois, princess of France (1545–1568), and Anne of Austria (1549–1580).

[501] On Don Carlos, prince of Asturias (1545–1568), see the fundamental work of Louis-Prosper Gachard, *Don Carlos et Philippe II*, E. Devroye impr. du Roi, Brusells, 1863; Parker offers us a synthesis of the question in the chapter dedicated to "The Enigma of Don Carlos" in *Imprudent King*, pp. 175–191. A precise reconstruction of the events is also offered by Carroll in *The Cleaving of Christendom*, pp. 326–331.

[502] Fernández Álvarez, *Felipe II y su tiempo*, pp. 398–399.

the great-grandson of Joanna the Mad (Juana la Loca), who was sequestered for most of her life because of her altered mental state. In 1562, following a fall down the steps of the palace of Alcalá di Henares where he was studying, Don Carlos had his head drilled by the acclaimed doctor Andrea Vesalio. His ailments worsened, leading him to acts of cruelty toward his servants and those who were near him. Once he nearly killed his horses with the mistreatment to which he subjected them; another time he threw a page who had bumped into him out the window; still another time he made a shoemaker who had brought him a pair of boots that did not suit him eat the boots in punishment.[503]

The most concerning aspects of Don Carlos's comportment, however, regarded political affairs. In 1567 he got the bizarre idea into his head that he needed to go to the Low Countries that were in revolt and attack both the Duke of Alba as well as his father, who sought to dissuade him from the insane idea. Eventually he made a plan to escape, but his half-brother Don Juan, in whom he confided, told King Philip of the plan. Don Carlos's support for the Calvinists would have been disastrous for the monarchy that at that moment was facing the revolt of the Low Countries. Philip II ordered that public prayers be offered in the monasteries and churches to ask God for the grace of enlightening him, without specifying the reason. Finally, after a meeting with his closest counselors and some theologians, he made the painful decision to place his son in prison. On January 18, 1568, the sovereign gave the order to lock him up in the Alcázar Tower in Madrid.

Imagining that Pius V would not have understood such a measure, on January 20 Philip wrote to him, addressing these words to the pontiff:

> As a most obedient son, out of the profound respect that I nourish towards the Holy See, I must notify Your Holiness of my decision to imprison the Most Serene Prince Carlos, my son. ... Your Holiness and all of Europe know enough about my system of government to be convinced that if I induced myself to such a

[503] Parker, *Un solo re, un solo impero*, p. 111.

> decision, I did not take it except after mature examination, due to the deplorable conduct of the prince, whose evil character has rendered vain the education he received from his masters and the care that was taken for his education. I have employed all sorts of means to correct his vicious inclinations and to repress his excesses. I tried the paths of sweetness; and on seeing, with that pain that Your Holiness may imagine, that all these remedies were unable to inspire in him any feeling of piety towards God, and nor even one of the qualities necessary for a prince, I found myself obligated to assure myself of his person, to see if this path of rigor can lead him back to his duty. I am informing Your Holiness, and I hope that from my way of acting you may judge how I prefer the glory of God, the interests of my State, and the peace of my people to the tenderness that nature inspires in me for my son.[504]

The king did not enter into the details of the faults of Don Carlos, but among the news that came to Rome in these months was that of Don Carlos's adherence to Protestant ideas. According to an account sent by Cardinal Zaccaria Dolfin to Emperor Maximilian II on March 6, 1568, on receiving the news Pius V exclaimed, as he threw his arms up toward Heaven: "God! God! There is only too much reason to believe it, as we knew that this prince had no regard either for priests or monks and did not show respect to any ecclesiastical dignitary."[505]

However, when the pope insisted on asking the sovereign the true reasons for the detention of the prince, Philip II responded to him on May 9, 1568, stating that Don Carlos had been guilty of neither rebellion nor heresy, but his incarceration had appeared necessary because there did not seem to be any hope of avoiding future evils: "As a punishment for my sins, it has pleased God to burden the prince with so many serious defects, partly of prudence, partly of character, that make him unsuitable for government and cause fear for the future if the inheritance falls to

[504] Catena, *Vita del gloriosissimo Papa Pio V*, pp. 94–95; Fernández Álvarez, *Felipe II y su tiempo*, pp. 416–417.
[505] Pastor, *Storia dei Papi*, vol. 8, p. 29.

him, the worst dangers for the stability of the kingdom."[506] We know the response of one of his counselors, the theologian and canonist Martín de Azpilcueta, who said to him: "If Don Carlos fled from Spain, the dangers to Spain and to all Christendom would be serious: the greatest of them the possibility of a civil war on a grand scale, not merely in Flanders but even in Spain, with the king on one side and his own son set up as a leader on the other."[507]

Don Carlos did not accept the confinement and tried to kill himself, refusing food, gulping down ice water, and swallowing a large diamond ring. Eventually he fell ill and died at the age of twenty-three, on July 24, 1568, after six months of imprisonment. Less than three months later, on October 3, the second wife of the king also died as she was bringing into the world a daughter who also died prematurely, aggravating the family tragedy.

The Calvinists spread the rumor that Don Carlos had been killed by his father for his pro-Protestant ideas and because of an insane passion for his stepmother, Elisabeth of Valois. In fact, while it cannot be ruled out that the prince may have made contact with the Dutch rebels, it is impossible that inappropriate moral conduct could have taken place in a palace where, as Parker observes, the queen lived surrounded by her "chambermaids," headed by the austere Duchess of Alba.[508] The dark legend originated with the *Apologia* of William of Orange, a vulgar pamphlet that accused the king of assassinating his son and wife. Ever since then, through Protestant and liberal literature, "Don Carlos became the hero of the *Leyenda Negra*, that is, of the most colossal operation of propaganda ever orchestrated in history. Not unlike the United States in recent times, the Spanish superpower was accused of all negligence. The Inquisition, the *autos-da-fé*, the atrocities against the Indians, the raid of

[506] Ibid., p. 294.

[507] WALSH, *Philip II*, pp. 435–436, quoted in CARROLL, *The Cleaving of Christendom*, p. 330. On Martín de Azpilcueta, "Doctor Navarrus" (1491–1586), see MARIANO ARGITA Y LASA, *El Doctor Navarro Don Martín de Azpilcueta y sus obras, Estudio histórico-crítico*, Analecta Editorial, Pamplona, 1998.

[508] PARKER, *Un solo re, un solo impero*, p. 116.

the infamous *Tercios*. . . . Thus was created the Hispanophobic cliché of a fanatic and ferocious people."[509]

The literature, along with Vittorio Alfieri and Friedrich Schiller, who inspired Giuseppe Verdi's melodrama in 1865, contributed to nurturing a myth that, historically, lacks any foundation.[510]

The pope was immediately informed of the death of Don Carlos, but he thought that his disappearance was a relief for everyone, and he never endorsed the legend that Philip II was a heartless father.[511] As Cardinal Grente writes, referring to the king of Spain, "the man who held the memory of his own father in veneration to the point of conferring the highest dignities on his natural brother, Don Juan of Austria, and who wrote letters to his own daughters that breathed paternal simplicity and true affection, could not have been inexorable with his son unless he had first exhausted all of the goodness of his heart toward the guilty one."[512]

9. The Carranza Case

A thorny problem accompanied the entire span of the pontificate of Pius V, placing him in opposition to Philip II: the "Carranza case."

The Spanish Inquisition followed the spread of Protestantism in the Iberian Peninsula with great concern. In 1559, the Inquisitor General Fernando de Valdés began to harbor suspicions toward Bartolomé Carranza,[513]

[509] Marco Cicala, *L'Affaire don Carlos. Leggenda nera arrivata fino a Verdi*, in *La Repubblica*, 1 February 2017.

[510] See Virginia Cisotti, *Schiller e il melodramma*, La Nuova Italia, Florence, 1975; Elena Liverani, *Don Carlos nel teatro spagnolo del XIX secolo*, La Nuova Italia, Florence, 1995.

[511] Letter to King Philip on the death of the prince, his son, *Abbiamo ricevuto*, in *Epistolae ad Principes*, n. 4009.

[512] Grente, *Il Pontefice delle grandi battaglie*, p. 74.

[513] Bartolomé de Carranza (1503–1576), Dominican, imperial representative in 1545 at the Council of Trent, consecrated archbishop of Toledo in 1558, was arrested by the Inquisition on August 22, 1559, and brought to the prison of the tribunal of the Holy Office in Valladolid, where he remained until he was transferred to Rome. Condemned in 1576 as

a Dominican bishop, who at the time was at the height of popularity, in part because after participating in the Council of Trent he was among the principal architects of the re-Catholicization of England under Mary Tudor. To reward him for his services, Philip II had nominated him to be archbishop of Toledo, the primatial see of Spain. On August 22, 1559, Carranza was arrested at the request of Inquisitor Valdés and taken to the prison of the Holy Office in Valladolid. News of his arrest left Spain and all of Europe astonished.

As background to the arrest, from 1557 to 1558, the Inquisition had discovered the existence of a network of Protestant circles in Seville and Valladolid. In the *Relación* of September 9, 1558, sent to Pope Paul IV, Inquisitor Valdés established a direct connection between the *alumbrados* and these circles. Carranza was accused of crypto-Lutheranism for his relations with the circle operating in Valladolid. The cardinal's *Comentarios Sobre El Catechismo Christiano*, published in 1558, were moreover judged heretical by his fellow Dominican brothers Melchor Cano[514] and Domingo de Soto.[515] Today, as the historian Michel Boeglin observes,

---

"strongly suspected of heresy," he abjured sixteen propositions taken from his writings. He was thus set free and retired to the convent of Santa Maria Sopra Minerva, where he died. MENENDEZ PELAYO is convinced that Carranza "wrote, taught, and dogmatized propositions of a Protestant flavor" (*Historia de los heterodoxos*, vol. 2, p. 50 and, more fully, pp. 3–52); JOSÉ IGNACIO TELLECHEA IDIGORAS, *Fray Bartolomé Carranza. Documentos históricos*, vols. 1–7, Real Academia de la Historia, Madrid, 1962–1994; TELLECHEA IDIGORAS, *Fray Bartolomé Carranza de Miranda (Investigaciones históricas)* (Gobierno de Navarra, Pamplona, 2002) instead supports the orthodoxy of Carranza's doctrine.

514 Melchor Cano (1509–1560), Dominican, was professor at Alcalá and Salamanca and played an important role at the Council of Trent. In 1559 he became provincial of Spain for his order. See the entry by PIERRE MANDONNET, in DTC, vol. 2, cols. 1537–1540.

515 Domingo de Soto (1494–1560), Dominican, participated in the Council of Trent as the theologian of Charles V and was one of the major exponents of the School of Salamanca. See MERIO SCATTOLA, *Domingo de Soto e la fondazione della scuola di Salamanca*, in *Veritas. Revista de filosofía*, vol. 54, n. 3 (2009), pp. 52–70.

scholars recognize that the majority of those individuals who were judged for "Lutheranism" had truly adhered to Protestant doctrines.[516]

Carranza prepared a meticulous defense, accusing Inquisitor Valdés and his Dominican brothers of harboring a preconceived hatred against him. The king probably realized that there were some prejudices in the accusations against Carranza, but he confirmed his confidence in the Spanish Inquisition. Pope Paul IV authorized that the instruction of the trial take place in Spain, but he asked that the accused then be transferred to Rome for the conclusive judgment. The decision of Paul IV to reserve the final sentence to himself was further confirmed by his successor, Pius IV, but Philip II considered this a violation of his sovereignty. Thus an extended and fierce tug-of-war broke out between Rome and Madrid over the jurisdiction in which the prisoner would be tried. In July 1565, Pius IV sent Cardinal Ugo Boncompagni,[517] the future Pope Gregory XIII, as his legate to Philip II. The death of the pope interrupted the mission, and Boncompagni returned to Rome to participate at the conclave.

By the time Pius V was elected, due to the ongoing dispute, Carranza had languished as a prisoner of the Spanish Inquisition for seven years. One of the first acts of the new pope was to ask Philip II to comply with the decision of the Holy See. Since the king continued to balk, on July 30, 1566, Pius V sent a brief to the nuncio Castagna with the following content: Archbishop Carranza has been held prisoner for seven years, but the pope still does not know exactly what the accusations are; thus the pope orders the members of the Spanish Inquisition, under pain of excommunication and suspension, to immediately send Carranza to Rome and to send the acts of the process against him to the Holy Office. With sharp words, Pius V explained to the king that the Supreme Pontiff was above the Spanish Inquisition, that it received its jurisdiction from the

[516] Michel Boeglin, *Valdés Ferdinando de*, in DSI, vol. 3, p. 1623.

[517] Ugo Boncompagni (1501–1585), was pope with the name of Gregory XIII from 1572 until his death in 1585. He was created cardinal in 1565 by Pius IV, who sent him as papal legate to Spain (1565). Pius V named him Secretary of Briefs.

pope, and that respecting the rights of the pope was in the interests of the Spanish tribunal.[518]

Following the insistences of Pius V, Pastor writes, "the unbelievable came true: the almighty Spaniard adapted himself."[519] To the wonder of all of Spain, on December 1, 1566, Archbishop Carranza was released from prison, and on December 5 he went to Valladolid in the litter that was to take him to Rome, where he was held in decent accommodations in Castel Sant'Angelo, receiving permission to go out occasionally.

In Rome, the archbishop was considered innocent by everyone, and it was said that the trial would be finished in a few weeks and that Carranza would return to Spain as a cardinal. The pope himself judged the opinions of the Spanish theologians unfavorably, and many of the archbishop's theological propositions that were judged heretical or suspicious in Spain were instead considered orthodox by Roman theologians. However, Cardinal Gian Paolo della Chiesa,[520] whose judgment held much weight with Pius V, was of the opinion that a strong suspicion of heresy remained attached to Carranza. The Jesuit theologian Francisco de Toledo,[521] who had a great reputation in Rome for his doctrine, expressed the same opinion, and thus in January 1570 he was called to take part in the debates and often discussed the matter with the pope.[522]

The pope appointed a tribunal, giving every regard to Philip II in its composition, but it was clear that if the Apostolic See decided in a

[518] *Epistolae ad principes*, n. 3552.

[519] PASTOR, *Storia dei Papi*, vol. 8, p. 235.

[520] Gian Paolo della Chiesa (1521–1575) was a lay jurist, who after the death of his wife entered the service of the Holy See. Pius V appreciated his skills, and after appointing him cardinal, at the end of 1568 he named him as the fourth cardinal inquisitor, replacing the deceased Cardinal Bernardino Scotti. Cardinal della Chiesa considered the Spanish archbishop to be suspect "*de vehementi*" of heresy; however, he declared that juridically he could not be deposed but only suspended for a certain time.

[521] Francisco de Toledo Herrera (1532–1596) entered the Society of Jesus in 1558, was rector of the German-Hungarian college in Rome, a theologian of the Sacred Penitentiary, and consultor of the Roman Inquisition.

[522] PASTOR, *Storia dei Papi*, vol. 8, pp. 237–238.

contrary manner to the Spanish Inquisition and Carranza resumed his post in Toledo as Primate of Spain, the prestige of the Spanish institution would have diminished considerably. The controversy between Madrid and Rome thus was not only theological but also political. Philip II continued to show his concern, both with a letter to the pope that he personally signed on July 28, 1568, as well as a letter to his ambassador in Rome on October 26, 1569, that was really directed to the pope. St. Pius V assured the king that Archbishop Carranza would be treated with absolute justice, but the Spanish ambassador insisted that the final sentence be submitted to the king prior to its publication; otherwise the sovereign would be "forced," in order to protect the universal good, to remedy the situation "with the best means capable of avoiding a scandal."[523]

Pius V was above all displeased by the fact that King Philip was persuaded that he was prejudiced in favor of Carranza. In a letter to Philip II on August 12, 1571, referring to Philip's own words in which he said that his actions were guided by zeal for the Faith, the Church, and religion, the pope made the astute observation that "one cannot fight for the Church against the Church, nor for religion against religion, nor for the faith against the faith."[524]

10. The Foresight and Balance of Pius V

In view of the high stakes, Pius V treated the Carranza case with supreme diligence. The pope wanted to be present at the reading of the acts of the trial, and when it was determined that in Spain the archbishop was not sufficiently examined, he established commissions of Spanish and Italian theologians who diligently interrogated Carranza on all the principal points for more than two months.

The tireless perseverance with which Pius V intervened in person in the interminable discussions aroused the wonder of his contemporaries, as Pastor observes.[525] This was also a source of serious effort and fatigue

[523] Ibid., p. 243.

[524] *Epistolae ad principes* n. 4936.

[525] Pastor, *Storia dei Papi*, vol. 8, p. 249.

for him. Galeazza Cusano, the imperial agent in Rome, judged that the trial was one of the things that caused the hastening of the pope's death. On the one hand, according to Cusano, Pius V was convinced of the archbishop's innocence and considered it his duty to absolve him; on the other hand, he feared a rupture with Spain if he overturned the sentence of the Spanish Inquisition. The pope, who sought nothing other than the truth, was perplexed and postponed the judgment. In July 1571 the Spanish ambassador to Rome, Zúñiga,[526] learned from the pope's own mouth that he still did not know how to decide the case, and when in October 1571 the diplomat insisted on knowing when the matter would be decided, Pius V assured him under oath that he did not know.[527] Thus the entire year of 1571 passed. In the first months of 1572, poor health conditions did not permit the pope to address the case, and when Pius V died on May 1, 1572, the Carranza trial was still not concluded. According to Pastor, "only one resolution remained firm in the conscientious judge among the vicissitudes of the discussions: the resolution not to pronounce Pilate's sentence but to decide according to justice, even if it should ruin the world."[528]

On April 14, 1576, Pius V's successor, Gregory XIII, pronounced the sentence in which Carranza was considered "*vehementer suspectus de haeresi*" and was obliged to retract seventeen propositions. The pope absolved the archbishop from censures, suspended him for five years from the administration of the archdiocese, imposed various penitential practices on him, and awarded him a thousand gold crowns for his

[526] Juan de Requeséns y Zúñiga (1539–1586) was sent to Rome by King Philip II of Spain as ambassador to the Holy See, replacing his brother Luis, who was appointed governor of Milan. Later he was viceroy of Naples (1579) and tutor of the future King Philip III (1585).

[527] Pastor, *Storia dei Papi*, vol. 8, p. 249.

[528] Ibid., p. 249. Pius V, at the time of his death, was said to have come to the conclusion that Carranza was innocent and had already had the draft of the sentence of acquittal drawn up. See J. I. Telechoa Idígoras, *Sondeo en el proceso romano del arzobispo Carranza*, in "Archivium Historiae Pontificiae," 3 (1965), pp. 193–238.

livelihood.[529] "It was a very just sentence," comments the Church historian Monsignor Cristiani. In the end Carranza was recognized as having written some heretical propositions, but the other accusations against him were dismantled, showing how Pius V had acted with far-sightedness in removing his case from the jurisdiction of the Spanish Inquisition.[530]

Two other interventions of Pope Pius V in Spanish affairs deserve to be remembered for his firm balance. In both cases, the image that the pope offers is quite different from that of a cold and cruel man that a certain anti-Catholic historiography has attempted to convey. With an edict of November 1, 1567, Pius V issued a general prohibition on bullfights, which had already been forbidden in the Papal States:

> Considering that these shows in which bulls and beasts run in the circus or in the public square have nothing to do with piety and Christian charity, and wanting to abolish such bloody and shameful spectacles, which are proper not to men but to the devil, and in order to look after the salvation of souls to the extent of our abilities and with the help of God, by this constitution we definitively prohibit the participation of any Christian in these spectacles in perpetuity, under the penalty of excommunication and anathema *ipso facto*, whatever dignity they may hold, whether ecclesiastical or civil, even if imperial or royal.[531]

Lastly, on January 25, 1568, the pope wrote to the nuncio in Madrid:

> It has been told to us that in Spain secular judges forbid the Sacrament of the Eucharist after Confession duly made to a priest to those condemned to death. However, we think that it should not be refused to them. In fact, it is more conformed to Christian

[529] See J. I. Tellechea Idígoras, *El final de un proceso. Sentencia original de Gregorio XIII y abjuración del arzobispo Carranza (14 de abril de 1576)*, in "Scriptorium Victoriense," 23 (1976), pp. 202–232.

[530] L. Cristiani, *La Chiesa al tempo del Concilio di Trento*, Editrice S. A. I. E., Turin, 1977, p. 264.

[531] *Bullarium Romanum*, vol. 7, pp. 630–631.

> solicitude that they be strengthened by Holy Communion, so that in this terrible passage they can resist with greater courage the temptations of despair, so that if the body must perish, at least as far as possible the health of the soul may be obtained. Wherefore, wishing to make this abuse disappear, which is contrary to the sacred canons, we desire that you address this matter with our beloved son in Jesus Christ, the Catholic King, and that you communicate our request to him. You will exhort him to be vigilant that this may be done from now on in all of Spain and the other provinces of his dominion, as befits his piety.[532]

Those condemned to death may be guilty of the worst crimes, but Jesus Christ shed His blood for each of them, and the fate of the Good Thief teaches how much mercy should be shown to each of them until the moment of death. Inflexible in his application of justice, Pius V wanted to show, even in this case, his zeal for the salvation of souls.

[532] "*De concedenda sacra Communione iis, qui capite damnati fuerint*. "*Relatum est*." *Epistolae ad principes*, n. 3964.

5

The Defender of the Faith and of Christianity

1. Pius V and Maximilian II

When Pius V rose to the papal throne, Christian Europe offered a spectacle of tragic religious division. The Scandinavian countries, England, Switzerland, and parts of Germany and the Netherlands had all turned their backs on Catholicism and proposed to completely Protestantize Europe. Philip II's Spain represented the backbone of Catholic Europe, but the Holy Roman Empire and the Catholic kingdoms of France and Poland wavered under the offensive of the Lutherans and Calvinists. Pius V, pastor and supreme defender of the Roman Faith, intervened with energy both on the diplomatic level as well as militarily. If he found an ally in Philip II, he found the greatest obstacle to his apostolic plan in Holy Roman Emperor Maximilian II and above all in two queens, Catherine of France and Elizabeth of England.

There was a close political and dynastic connection between the Habsburg courts of Madrid and Vienna. But Maximilian II[533] had a very different religious sensibility from that of his cousin Philip II and the

[533] Maximilian II (1527–1576), the son of Ferdinand I and Anna Jagiellon, rose to the imperial throne in 1564 after having been elected king of Germany and Bohemia in 1562 and of Hungary in 1563. On his deathbed he refused to receive the last rites of the Church. On his life, cf. among others PAULA SUTTER FICHTNER, *Emperor Maximilian II*, Yale University Press, New Haven, 2001.

reigning Pope Pius V. As Pastor observes, "the Pope, with clear and sharp ideas, the sworn enemy of all pretense and treachery, and also profoundly penetrated by the truth of the Catholic faith, saw salvation only in the faith, and thus he kept watch with inflexible rigor over the conservation of the purity of this supreme good. For him, a convicted Catholic, any compromise on dogmatic questions was excluded. The emperor instead was a skilled politician and an expert in all the arts of double diplomacy. In religious matters he had supremely confused ideas; he was hesitant and equivocal."[534]

The policy of Maximilian, like that of Charles V, tended toward compromise, but he went much further than his predecessor on the imperial throne, maintaining that a political combination of Lutheranism and Catholicism was possible. The pretext was the pressure placed on the eastern borders of the empire by the Turks, who, after taking over Hungary, made no secret of their plans to conquer Vienna. The convocation of an imperial diet became urgent, and Maximilian set the date for the spring of 1566 in Augsburg. The pope was not ignorant of the fact that a group of Protestant princes intended to use this assembly to wrest new privileges from the emperor and to push him to break relations with Rome. Their first enemy was not the Turks but the Roman Pontiff.

The Diet of Augsburg took place from March to September of 1566. Pius V chose Cardinal Giovanni Francesco Commendone[535] to represent him, a capable and resolved man who knew the German situation perfectly. On January 23, 1566, the pope appointed Cardinal Commendone

[534] Pastor, *Storia dei Papi*, vol. 8, p. 434.

[535] Francesco Giovanni Commendone (1524–1584), secretary of Julius III (1550), was sent to England during the Catholic restoration of Queen Mary, took part in the Council of Trent, and was then sent on other difficult diplomatic missions in Flanders, England, and Portugal. Pius IV made him cardinal on March 12, 1565, at the suggestion of his cardinal nephew Charles Borromeo. See Antonii Mariae Gratiani, *De Vita Joannis Francisci Commendoni*, Typis Petri Mariae Frambotti, Patavii, 1685, and the views of Lucienne Van Meerbeeck, in DHGE, vol. 13 (1956), pp. 367–378; and D. Caccamo, in DBI, vol. 27 (1982), pp. 606–613.

as his legate to the Imperial Diet (*Reichstag*).[536] According to Pastor, "[he] was the first cardinal of the Roman court and the one in whom Pope Pius V placed the most faith,"[537] as demonstrated by the numerous and delicate assignments entrusted to him. Cardinal Grente observed that the character of this cardinal was in many ways different from Pius V: "While Pius V loved to keep himself, so to speak, in the mountains, Commendone willingly descended to lesser heights, seeking conciliatory measures. Moreover, both agile and noble at the same time, he did not get entangled in any affair, and he felt at ease in all the courts, where, immediately gaining the affection of princes, he left on his departure a good reputation for integrity, ability, and dignified affability. It is the duty of justice to render homage to this savvy collaborator of Pius V, and it should be recognized that papal diplomacy had in him a precious helper.[538]"

The pope shared the concern of Maximilian for the Turkish threat,[539] but he feared that the diet, instead of limiting itself to political questions, would attempt to intervene in religious matters. Therefore he had recommended to his representative that he should abandon the assembly, protesting vigorously if any decision was made contrary to the decisions of the Council of Trent and if the religious peace of 1555 was recognized, which Pius V flatly condemned, just like his predecessor Paul IV.

Cardinal Commendone arrived in Augsburg on February 17, 1566, accompanied by the canonist Scipione Lancellotti[540] and by experienced

[536] *Epistolae ad principes*, n. 3251. The Imperial Diet (*Reichstag*) was the main legislative organ of the Holy Roman Empire. It was composed of the seven prince-electors of the empire and the college of princes (about one hundred, including ecclesiastics). The diet was presided over by the archbishop of Mainz.

[537] PASTOR, *Storia dei Papi*, vol. 8, p. 75.

[538] GRENTE, *Il Pontefice delle grandi battaglie*, p. 73.

[539] *Epistolae ad principes*, n. 3278.

[540] Scipione Lancellotti (1527–1598), papal jurist, carried out numerous missions over the course of the Council of Trent. He was created cardinal by Gregory XIII on December 12, 1583. See RAISSA TEODORI, *Lancellotti Scipione*, in DBI, vol. 63 (2004), pp. 305–306.

theologians: the Englishman Nicholas Sanders[541] and the Jesuits Jeronimo Nadal, Peter Canisius, and Diego Ledesma. Along the way he stopped in Bavaria to secure the collaboration of Duke Albert of Wittelsbach,[542] who had married Anne of Austria, the daughter of Emperor Ferdinand, and who was thus the brother-in-law of Maximilian II, on whom he had a salutary influence.

Through numerous personal meetings, Commendone notified the archbishop electors of Trier and Mainz, the bishop of Constance, and the Dukes of Cleves, Bavaria, and Brunswick, that the Holy Father had prohibited, under the pain of incurring censures, that the diet would address doctrinal questions. Thanks to the cardinal's intense diplomatic activity, the maneuver of the Protestant princes was thwarted and religious arguments were not addressed by the diet.

Recognition of the Peace of Augsburg seemed unavoidable, however, and there was a difference of opinion among Cardinal Commendone's advisers on this point. Lancellotti was decisively against accepting any form of recognition, while Sanders and the Jesuits showed more flexibility. Fr. Peter Canisius[543] composed a memorandum for Commendone, whose purpose was proving that there was no formal opposition between the

[541] Nicholas Sanders (1530–1581) was an English theologian, ordained a priest in Italy after Elizabeth I ascended to the throne. In 1565 he was appointed professor of theology at Louvain, where he published his work *De visibili Monarchia Ecclesiae*, in which he defended the doctrine of the Roman primacy, and the great unfinished work *De origine et progressu schismatis Anglicani* (1585). He died in Ireland, participating in the armed resistance of Catholics against Elizabeth I.

[542] Albert of Wittelsbach (1528–1579) was Duke of Bavaria from 1550 until his death. In 1547 he married Anne Habsburg, one of the daughters of emperor Ferdinand I. He was a patron of the arts and made Munich one of the propulsive centers of Catholic Counter-Reformation.

[543] On Peter Canisius, S.J. (1521–1597), proclaimed a saint and doctor of the Church by Pius XI in 1925, see L. CRISTIANI, *Le Bienheureux Pierre Canisius second apôtre de l'Allemagne (1521–1597)*, J. Gabalda, Paris, 1925, pp. 121–125; JAMES BRODRICK, S.J., *Saint Peter Canisius*, Geoffrey Chapman, London, 1963.

peace of 1555 and the definitions of the Council of Trent, maintaining that it was necessary to distinguish between a dogmatic definition, which did not admit any compromises, and a political treaty, which could be provisionally accepted.

Pius V, for his part, consulted the Congregation of the Inquisition and Fr. Francis Borgia, superior general of the Jesuits. Their opinion was that a generic reference to the Peace of Augsburg would not prejudice the rights of the Holy See. The pope, at this point, authorized Commendone to act with full liberty and the cardinal decided not to protest.

The diet closed with a reinforcing of the Catholic positions. According to the German historian Karl Maria von Aretin: "This was the first Reichstag at which the Reformation Party quite incontestably lost ground. Hitherto the assailants, they now become the assailed and were obliged to look to their defenses."[544]

Cardinal Commendone thus shifted his concern to the other task given him by Pius V: that of obliging Catholic states to eliminate ecclesiastical abuses and to conform themselves expressly to the decrees of the Council of Trent. All the German Catholic princes accepted the conciliar decrees in whatever regarded dogma and divine worship, limiting themselves to asking for some facilitations in disciplinary matters.[545] The result obtained from Commendone's mission was a decisive advance from the time of Pius IV, who had never received a satisfactory response from the German princes.

When Commendone reached Rome, Pius V wanted to confer outstanding honors on his diplomatic representative, and he commissioned a deputation of the sacred college to accompany him in triumph to the Vatican. Sitting on his throne, Pius V received Cardinal Commendone with great signs of esteem and declared him worthy of the Apostolic See and of God.[546]

[544] Karl Maria von Aretin, *Geschichte des Bayerischen Herzogs und Kurfursten Maximilian des Ersten*, vol. 1, Pleuger, Passau, 1842, p. 185.

[545] Pastor, *Storia dei Papi*, vol. 8, pp. 441–442.

[546] Grente, *Il Pontefice delle grandi battaglie*, p. 105.

The second mission of Commendone took place in the fall of 1568, after the news reached Rome that Maximilian II had conceded to the Protestants of Lower Austria the free exercise of their religious faith. Pastor states that the sorrow of Pius V was so great that he could not hold back his tears.[547] Commendone was sent to the emperor to express the protests of the Holy See. The papal representative had more than just a meeting with the emperor, insisting on the necessity of maintaining the Catholic Faith in all of its purity, without concessions to the heretics. Maximilian asked the cardinal to assure the pope that he was one of his devoted sons, committed to serving God and the Catholic Faith. The facts, however, were not in accord with these words, and the cardinal had to face another controversy between Pius V and Maximilian II that broke out in August 1569: the elevation of Cosimo I de' Medici[548] to Grand Duke of Tuscany.

2. Pius V and the Grand Duke Cosimo of Tuscany

The de' Medici family held *de facto* power over Florence, which had its moment of greatest splendor under Lorenzo the Magnificent. After a succession of various Medici and anti-Medici governments, in 1537 Cosimo I assumed power. After he conquered the city of Siena, he asked the pope to make official the position of preeminence assumed by his duchy.

On August 27, 1569, Pius V published a bull[549] in which he conceded the title of Grand Duke of Tuscany to Cosimo I, explaining all the reasons

[547] Pastor, *Storia dei Papi*, vol. 8, p. 448.

[548] Cosimo I de' Medici (1519–1574), son of the commander Giovanni delle Bande Nere, was Duke of Florence beginning in 1537 and Grand Duke of Tuscany from 1569. The Grand Duchy of Tuscany was a confederal state made up of the Duchy of Florence (called the "Old State") and the "New State" of Siena, governed by the Medici dynasty until the death of Gian Gastone (1737), when, lacking a legitimate direct heir, it passed to Francesco Stefano, Duke of Lorraine, the consort of Maria Theresa of Austria. See Vennocchio Maffei, *Dal titolo di duca di Firenze e di Siena a granduca di Toscana. Contributo alla storia della politica di Cosimo I*, Bernardo Seeber, Florence, 1905; Roberto Cantagalli, *Cosimo I de' Medici granduca di Toscana*, Mursia, Milan, 1985.

[549] *Bullarium Romanum*, vol. 7, pp. 763–767.

for his decision: the Duke of Florence had opposed the spread of the Protestant heresy in Tuscany, and religion and justice were flourishing in his kingdom; Cosimo, upon hearing the pope's request, had sent his soldiers into France, contributing also to the expenses of the war against the Huguenots; he had instituted an order of knights under the patronage of St. Stephen to defend religion and fight against the Turks, and he fought against the corsairs who were sacking the Italian coast; his state occupied a very important place in Italy both in terms of size as well as wealth, with populous cities, metropolitan churches, cathedrals, universities, ports, fortresses, and many people distinguished in letters, the sciences, the arts, and war; and finally the Medici family, which was related to the emperor and the king of France, had entered into the family of Christian princes and counted as members of its family tree three popes, many cardinals, many famous personalities, in such a way as to place themselves among the rank of sovereigns.[550]

After he received the delivery of the papal bull at the Palazzo Vecchio in Florence on February 18, 1570, the duke arrived with great pomp in Rome, where he was received by the pope and cardinals in consistory. On March 5, 1570, during the pontifical Mass celebrated in the Sistine Chapel, Cosimo knelt before the altar and swore an oath of fidelity to the Catholic Apostolic Roman religion. The pope placed on his head a golden crown on which he had inscribed these words: "Given by Pius V Supreme Pontiff in recognition of the esteemed affection and zeal for the Catholic religion and of the distinct love of justice."[551]

The pontifical concession of the title of Grand Duke to Cosimo seemed to Emperor Maximilian, however, to be a violation of his sovereign rights. The nuncio Cardinal Commendone reminded the emperor, however, that the source and legitimacy of his imperial sovereignty came directly from the Church as well, dating back to the crown that Charlemagne

[550] PASTOR, *Storia dei Papi*, vol. 8, p. 454.

[551] "*Pius V Pontifex Maximus, ob eximiam dilectionem ac catholicae religionis zelum praecipuumque iustitiae studium, donavit.*" See FALLOUX, *Histoire de St Pie V*, vol. 2, p. 169.

had received on the night of Christmas in the year 800 from Pope St. Leo III. And likewise, popes had granted royal titles elsewhere: Benedict IX had made Casimir king of Poland, despite the opposition of Germany; Gregory IX had given Demetrios the realm of Croatia; and Innocent IV had called Alphonse de Boulogne to the throne of Portugal. Therefore, Maximilian could not but admit that Cosimo's title was valid for the same reasons.

Pius V intended not only to reward Cosimo I for his loyal service to the Church, but also to reaffirm the supreme right of the pope in temporal matters, as his medieval predecessors had done. To those who criticized him for this decision, the Holy Father would respond: "If a pope gave Charlemagne the title of Emperor, all the more can I bestow the title of Grand Duke on a meritorious prince of the Church."[552]

3. Pius V and Sigismund II of Poland

Pius V wanted to utilize the diplomatic capacities of Cardinal Commendone in another thorny matter, and so he appointed him as his legate to the court of Sigismund II Augustus,[553] king of Poland. Sigismund, married to Catherine, the sister of Maximilian, intended to dissolve his marriage, under the pretext of the lack of heirs. Pius V was afraid that Sigismund might follow the path of Henry VIII, all the more so since the archbishop of Gnesen, Jakub Uchański,[554] instead of dissuading the king, encouraged him on the path of divorce, and Sigismund seemed favorable to the idea of a national Polish Church, emancipated from Rome.

[552] Pastor, *Storia dei Papi*, vol. 8, p. 453.

[553] Sigismund II Augustus (1520–1572), King of Poland and Grand Duke of Lithuania, was the last of the Jagiellonian line, which had governed Poland since 1388.

[554] Jakub Uchański (1502–1581) was archbishop of Gniezno and primate of Poland from 1562 until his death. He was suspected of heresy, just like the bishop of Krakow, Filip Padniewski (1510–1572), but, despite the interventions of Rome, he succeeded in maintaining the governance of the archdiocese.

Commendone, however, found support in Cardinal Hosio,[555] the bishop of Ermland, very eminent for his wisdom, theological knowledge, and virtue, and highly regarded by the pope, who called him "the pillar of the Church." Thanks to his intervention and that of Commendone, Archbishop Uchański was impelled to convoke the episcopate. The nuncio presented himself to this assembly where, with great eloquence, he recalled that the doctrine of the Church on the indissolubility of marriage does not admit exceptions, even for a sovereign, describing the evils that England endured because of the divorce of Henry VIII. The strength of his arguments convinced the bishops, and Pius V, satisfied by the result, then sent Commendone back to Germany to resume the difficult negotiations that he had interrupted. The novelties of Uchański and Sigismund, however, continued in Catholic Poland: they attempted to introduce Communion under both species for lay people, marriage for priests, the free exercise of Lutheran worship, and access for Protestants to public offices.

At the beginning of 1568, the nuncio in Poland, Giulio Ruggieri, sent Pius V a detailed report on the situation of the kingdom.[556] The nuncio compared the colorful mixture of sects in Poland to the confusion of tongues at Babel. All the errors of the whole world, he wrote, were preached there. Lutherans and Calvinists, but above all Anabaptists and anti-Trinitarians, all found refuge there.[557] Furthermore, he wrote, a bishop there had become Lutheran,[558] thanks to the complacency of the

[555] Stanislao Hosio (1504–1579), bishop-prince of Ermland, created cardinal by Pius IV in 1561, was the great promoter of the defense of the Catholic Faith in Poland against Protestantism.

[556] Giulio Ruggieri (who died in 1568) was nuncio to Poland from March 2, 1566, to February 18, 1568. See his *Relatione al Santissimo Signor Nostro Papa Pio Quinto da Monsignor Giulio Ruggieri Protonotario Apostolico ritornato Nuntio di Sua Santità dal Serenissimo Re di Polonia nell'anno 1568*, in *Acta Nuntiaturae Polonae*, vol. 6, Iulius Ruggieri (1565–1568), edited by Thaddaeus Glemma and Stanislaus Bogaczewicz, Institutum Historicum Polonicum, Rome, 1991, pp. 146–198.

[557] Pastor, *Storia dei Papi*, vol. 8, p. 476.

[558] Mikolaj Pac (1527–1589) was named bishop of Kiev in 1564 without papal authorization. In 1566 he married and officially announced his adherence

sovereign, who now illegitimately occupied the see of Kiev. In a letter of March 26, 1568, he wrote to Sigismund:

> Your Majesty shows that you are blind when you pretend to bring peace to your states by making concessions that are unworthy of a Christian prince. ... Your allusion to doctrine and to the conduct of our Divine Savior carries no greater weight; because, when Your Majesty quotes the words [of the Gospel] that forbid the weeds to be eradicated in order not to destroy the good grain, you do not quote them in the sense that they are meant to be understood. We would like Your Majesty to remember the clear expressions with which the Divine Savior speaks of kingdoms that are divided among themselves. Now, is there a greater incentive to division than religious disputes? If the disorders are now multiplied to the point that Your Majesty finds himself powerless to repress them altogether, Your Majesty should at least put an end to the disorder caused by the impostor bishop of Kiev. We ask you with paternal affection, beloved son, to take shelter in the name of your dignity, the glory of God and the salvation of souls. If you delay in remedying it, we will be constrained to act against the false bishop with the rigor of the sacred canons, in order not to seem complicit in your inaction, rendering us guilty before God and men.[559]

The pope thus asked Cardinal Commendone to return to Poland. Commendone immediately left Vienna and arrived in Krakow, where he found support in Cardinal Hosio, and especially in the Jesuits who had been invited to Poland by this bishop. It is thanks to them and Commendone that Poland did not fall into schism and heresy but maintained the strong Catholic identity that it still preserves today.

---

to Lutheranism. See DAINORA POCIŪTĖ, *L'arginamento dell'eterodossia riformata nel Granducato di Lituania e in Polonia: il trattato Orthodoxa fidei confessio di Mikołaj Pac*, pl.it/rassegna italiana di argomenti polacchi, 8 (2017), pp. 5–21.

[559] *Sigismundus Augustus Poloniae regi*: "*Maiestatis tuae*," in *Epistolae ad Principes*, n. 4022; FALLOUX, *Histoire de St Pie V*, vol. 2, pp. 132–134.

Meanwhile, on February 28, 1572, his wife Queen Catherine died, and Sigismund, who had done everything to repudiate her, flaunted an exaggerated mourning; he never spoke of a new marriage, perhaps aware of his imminent end, which came after just a few months, on July 7 of the same year. With his death the Jagiellonian dynasty, which had governed Poland for three centuries, came to an end.

4. The Huguenots Storm the Throne of France

On July 10, 1559, the king of France, Henry II,[560] died as a result of wounds sustained in a jousting tournament. His son François II succeeded him, but his reign was short-lived: the young sovereign died on December 5, 1560, of a brain aneurysm, and his brother Charles IX ascended the throne. The new king was only ten years old, and the council of state entrusted the regency to the queen mother, Catherine de' Medici,[561] who from this moment on effectively governed France, inheriting the burdensome legacy of the Peace of Cateau-Cambrésis.

Catherine was the sole direct and legitimate descendant of Lorenzo the Magnificent, and she embodied in her person all of the famed intrigues and ambiguities of the Medici dynasty, which in the sixteenth century radiated its power over all of Europe. Her true talent, according to Jean Orieux, was lying and the ability of using all sorts of manipulation and

560 Henry II Valois (1519–1559), the son of Francis I, was king of France from 1547 to 1559. In 1533 he married Catherine de' Medici. Three of his sons succeeded him on the throne of France: Francis II (1559–1560), Charles IX (1560–1574) and Henry III (1574–1589). During the celebrations following the marriage of his daughter Elizabeth with King Philip II of Spain, he was wounded in a jousting tournament by Count Gabriel of Montgomery (1530–1574), and he died after ten days of agony.

561 Catherine de' Medici (1519–1589), the daughter of Lorenzo II de' Medici, the Duke of Urbino, was queen consort of France as the wife of Henry II, from 1547 to 1559, and regent from 1560 to 1563, but she exercised a *de facto* regency at least until 1580. See Ivan Cloulas, *Catherine de Médicis: Le destin d'une reine*, Tallandier, Paris, 2007; Matthieu Gellard, *Une reine épistolaire. Lettres et pouvoirs au temps de Catherine de Médicis*, Garnier, Paris, 2015; Jean Orieux, *Un'italiana sul trono di Francia*, Italian translation, Mondadori, Milan, 2018.

intrigue to attain her purposes.[562] Catherine had *The Prince* of Machiavelli in her blood, but since her childhood she was also fascinated with the occult sciences, and she could not live far from her astrologers, Cosimo Ruggieri[563] and the more famous Nostradamus.[564] According to her biographer, "the true pope of Catherine's authentic, strange religion was Ruggieri, not the pope of the Vatican,"[565] who was no less than her own uncle, Clement VII.

The religious division between Catholics and Huguenots (from the Swiss term for conspirator, *eudguenot*) spread across the royal court and the three estates of the Kingdom of France: the clergy, the nobility, and the third estate. The Dukes of Guise, Francis[566] and his brother Charles,[567] cardinal of Lorraine, were the heads of a powerful family that led the Catholic party, whose influence increased after Francis reconquered Calais in 1558, thus completing after a century the work of Joan of Arc. The Guises were opposed by the Huguenots Anthony de Bourbon, the

562 ORIEUX, *Un'italiana sul trono di Francia*, p. 286.

563 Cosimo Ruggieri (who died in 1615), the son of a doctor and the astrologer of Lorenzo II de' Medici, was adviser of Catherine and then of Maria de' Medici, participating in many intrigues of the time. See EUGÈNE DEFRANCE, *Catherine de Médicis, ses astrologues et ses magiciens envoûteurs. Documents inédits sur la diplomatie et les sciences occultes du XVIe siècle*, Mercure de France, Paris, 1911.

564 ORIEUX, *Un'italiana sul trono di Francia*, pp. 248–250. Nostradamus, the pseudonym of Michel de Nostredame (1503–1566), was celebrated for his books *Centuries et prophéties* (Avignon, 1566).

565 Ibid., p. 104.

566 Francis I of Lorraine (1519–1563), the second Duke of Guise, Count and then Duke of Aumale, married Anna d'Este on April 29, 1548, the daughter of Ercole II d'Este and Renate of France. He was killed on February 18, 1563, by a pistol shot fired by Jean de Poltrot de Méré on the order of the admiral of Coligny. See STUART CARROLL, *Martyrs and Murderers: The Guise Family and the Making of Europe*, Oxford University Press, Oxford, 2009.

567 Charles of Lorraine and of Guise (1524–1574) was archbishop of Rheims and bishop of Metz. Created cardinal by Pope Paul III in 1547, he headed the French delegation at the Council of Trent, where however he maintained the superiority of the Council over the pope.

first prince by blood, who became king of Navarre by his marriage with the Calvinist Jeanne d'Albret;[568] by Bourbon's brother Prince Louis de Condé,[569] and by the three Coligny-Châtillon brothers: Cardinal Odet,[570] François,[571] commander of the infantry, and Gaspard,[572] the admiral.

The Huguenots enjoyed overt religious and political organization, and on May 26, 1559, openly held the first national synod for three days in Paris, discussing two texts especially written for the occasion by Calvin.[573] Calvin himself approved a plan for a *coup d'état*, in order to seize adolescent King François II and thereby assume power in France. The attempt, known as the "Conspiracy of Amboise,"[574] failed, however,

[568] Jeanne d'Albret (1528–1572), the daughter of Henry II of Navarre and Margaret of Valois, the sister of Francis I, was queen of Navarre from 1555 to 1572. Under the influence of Théodore de Bèze she became Protestant around 1560 and introduced Calvinism in her realm.

[569] Louis I de Bourbon-Condé (1530–1569) married the Calvinist Eleanor de Roucy. He was the progenitor of the dynastic branch of Bourbon-Condé.

[570] Odet de Coligny, called Cardinal Châtillon (1517–1571), received the red hat from Clement VII in 1533 when he was sixteen. Around the year 1560 he apostatized from the Catholic Faith and became Calvinist. He died in England, where he represented the Huguenots at the court of Elizabeth I—poisoned, according to rumors, by his personal servant.

[571] François d'Andelot de Coligny (1521–1569), colonel general of the infantry, was the first of the Châtillon family to adhere to Protestantism, later participating in many military clashes. He was defeated, together with his brother Gaspard, in the Battle of Jarnac on March 13, 1569.

[572] Admiral Gaspard de Coligny (1519–1572) was the military commander of the Huguenots in the French wars of religion until his murder on August 24, 1572. See Antoine César Becquerel, *Souvenirs historiques sur l'amiral Coligny: sa famille et sa seigneurie de Châtillon-Sur-Loing*, Firmin-Didot, Paris, 1876; Nicola M. Sutherland, *The Assassination of François duc de Guise, February 1563*; and *The Role of Coligny in the French Wars of Religion*, in *Princes, Politics and Religion 1547–1589*, The Hambledon Press, London, 1984.

[573] Menna Prestwich, *International Calvinism 1541–1715*, Clarendon Press, Oxford, 1985, pp. 87–91.

[574] See Lucien Romier, *La conjuration d'Amboise*, Perrin, Paris, 1923; and Corrado Vivanti, *La congiura d'Amboise*, in *Complots et conjurations dans l'Europe moderne. Actes du colloque international organisé à Rome*,

and Duke François of Guise was royally appointed lieutenant general of France in response.

Catherine, who relied on the counsel of chancellor of France Michel de L'Hôpital,[575] a supporter of the "Third Party" of *politiques*,[576] opted to convoke a meeting between Catholics and Huguenots in an effort to overcome the religious division by means of a theological compromise. "Skeptical and astute," according to Cardinal Grente, "she would have easily adapted herself to a species of Anglicanism if this would have served to increase her influence."[577]

The interreligious meeting opened on September 9, 1559, in the refectory of the Dominican friary of Poissy. François II attended with his royal family in order to give a greater solemnity to the ceremony. The participants included, on opposing sides, Théodore de Bèze, with a delegation of Calvinist ministers, and the cardinal of Lorraine, with a group of cardinals and French bishops. The conversation came to nothing; indeed, it only brought out all the religious differences in all their sharpness—above all on the question of the Eucharist, which the Calvinists considered as a purely symbolic sacrament.

After this failure, Catherine had young Charles IX promulgate the Edict of Saint-Germain-en-Laye on January 17, 1562, which granted the Huguenots the right to practice their religion, obliging the Parliament of Paris, which opposed it, to register the edict. Orieux states that for a

---

30 septembre–2 octobre 1993, edited by Yves M. Bercé and Elena Fasano Guarini, École Française de Rome, 1996, pp. 439–450.

575 Michel de L'Hôspital (1505–1573) was councilor to the Parliament of Paris, superintendent of finances, and finally chancellor of France. See Albert Buisson, *Michel de L'Hospital: 1503–1573*, Hachette, Paris, 1950; Denis Crouzet, *La sagesse et le malheur. Michel de L'Hôspital, Chancellier de France*, Ed. Champ Vallon, Ceyzérieu, 1998.

576 The group of *politiques*, known also as the *moyenneurs* (mediators) was an ideological movement composed of both Catholics and Huguenots, who were often members of the judiciary and the nobles of the gown (*noblesse de robe*), and who subordinated religious questions to the political interests of the French monarchy.

577 Grente, *Il Pontefice delle grandi battaglie*, pp. 112–113.

French Catholic of this time, this Florentine princess, who was educated in a humanistic environment, simply could not be considered Catholic. "In reality, we must not fear to say this, Catherine was pagan. This was the secret of her policy towards the Huguenots in the years 1561 and 1562. Because she did not profess any faith, she tolerated every religious creed."[578]

5. Pius V and Catherine de' Medici

Despite Calvinism being officially recognized by the king for the first time as a religious confession within a Catholic monarchy, the Huguenots were discontented and became ever more audacious and violent. They began to attack priests and desecrate tombs and churches, throwing consecrated hosts to dogs and swine in order to emphasize their denial of the Real Presence of Christ in the Sacrament of the Altar. The Catholic reaction was led by Duke François of Guise, one of the most esteemed knights of France. This movement of resistance was the first nucleus of the celebrated "League," which opposed Calvinism with courage in the following decades, defending the honor of Catholic France.[579]

On March 1, 1562, in the village of Wassy, where Francis of Guise was staying and where a Huguenot community was gathered, a riot broke out that ended with twenty dead and one hundred Huguenots wounded.[580]

[578] ORIEUX, *Un'italiana sul trono di Francia*, p. 282.

[579] The "Catholic League" or the "Holy League" was created in France in 1576 by Henry of Guise (1550–1588), with the support of Sixtus V, for the purpose of defending Catholic identity in France against the violations of Protestantism. It did not dissolve until Henry Bourbon abjured Protestantism to return to the Catholic Faith and was crowned as Henry IV of France. Charles of Guise, the Duke of Mayenne (1554–1611), the second-born son of Francis of Guise, was its last head after the assassination of his brother. See JEAN-MARIE CONSTANT, *La Ligue*, Fayard, Paris, 1996.

[580] On the supposed "massacre" of Wassy, see JEAN GUIRAUD, *Histoire partiale. Histoire vraie*, II. *Moyen âge, Renaissance, Réforme*, Beauchesne, Paris, 1912, which explains how it was a "*bagarre sanglante*" (bloody brawl), with dead and wounded on both sides (p. 103).

Immediately there was an outcry against the "massacre," declaring that the slaughter was desired and ordered by the duke himself. It marked the beginning of the first war of religion in which Guise was opposed by the Prince of Condé as head of the Huguenots. Many important cities, such as La Rochelle, Poitiers, Le Havre, Dieppe, and Caen, fell into the hands of the Calvinists. Every conquest was accompanied by destruction and massacres. Priests and religious were thrown alive into wells, altars were sacked, the relics of the saints were thrown to the wind, and tombs were profaned, as happened at Plessis-les-Tours, where on April 13, 1562, the Huguenots opened the tomb of St. Francis of Paola, found his body incorrupt, and set it on fire.[581] On November 23, 1563, the cardinal of Lorraine presented the first accounting of the massacres of the Huguenots: about three thousand martyrs in France.[582] The Catholics defended themselves vigorously, and in the Battle of Dreux on December 19, 1562, Francis of Guise defeated the troops of Condé and Coligny. On February 18, 1563, however, beneath the walls of the city of Orléans, the duke was killed by a Huguenot, at the order of Gaspard de Coligny. On March 19, 1563, Catherine imposed the Treaty of Amboise, which accorded amnesty to the Calvinists but restricted Protestant worship to taking place outside the cities and on the lands of certain nobles.

The edict did not satisfy either Catholics or Calvinists, and the four years that followed were years of only a surface truce. Catherine was confident in her diplomatic ability, but the widening scope of the Protestant revolt, now spilling over into the Netherlands in August 1566, with all of its consequences in Europe, revealed how fragile the religious

[581] See Richard Verstegan, *Theatrum Crudelitatum hæreticorum nostri temporis*, Adrianus Hubertus, Antwerp, 1587 (the French translation was reprinted by Franck Lestringant: *Théatre des cruautés des hérétiques de notre temps*, Chandeigne, Paris, 1995); Olivier Christin, *Une révolution symbolique. L'iconoclasme huguenot et la reconstruction catholique*, Les Editions de Minuit, Paris, 1991; Louis de Reau, *Histoire du vandalisme. Les monuments détruits de l'art français*, Hachette, Paris, 1994; Christian Biet, Marie-Madeleine Fragonard, *Tragédies et récits de martyres en France*, Garnier, Paris, 2009.

[582] *Concilium Tridentinum*, vol. 9 (1924), p. 1044.

peace was that the queen believed that she had guaranteed in France. In fact, her concessions never brought peace but instead gave rise to the bloodiest of civil wars.

It was against this background that Pius V entered the scene, sending detailed instructions to his representative in France, the new nuncio, Michele della Torre.[583] The Abbé Victor Martin, a historian of moderation and wisdom, has made an attentive analysis of this document, bringing to light its moderation and wisdom.[584] The principles are set out there with limpid clarity, but their application had to be made with all possible prudence, as also shown by a brief that the pope sent to Charles IX on June 20.[585]

If the pope sought to maintain more cordial relations with the French court, in private he did not refrain from frankly expressing his grave concerns.[586] Between June and August 1566, Pius V wrote briefs encouraging Catherine, but he considered her policy to be tortuous and considered her to be in large part responsible for the progress of heresy in her kingdom. In a letter sent on August 17 to the nuncio della Torre, the pope lamented the fact that Catherine surrounded herself almost exclusively with heretics and bestowed ecclesiastical benefits on them.[587]

[583] The Count Michele della Torre (1511–1586) was appointed bishop of Ceneda (the present Vittorio Veneto) in 1547 by Paul III and sent as nuncio to France. On April 17, 1566, Pius V entrusted him with a second nunciature in France. Gregory XIII made him a cardinal on December 12, 1583. See MARCO PENZI, *La politica francese di Pio V: tra riforma cattolica e guerra contro l'eresia*, in *Pio V nella società e nella politica del suo tempo*, pp. 251–276.

[584] VICTOR MARTIN, *Le gallicanisme et la réforme catholique*, Librairie Alphonse Picard, Paris, 1919, pp. 90–93. "*L'on est presque étonné de trouver chez cet ancien inquisiteur si peu d'intransigeance, un sens si juste de l'opportunité*" (One is almost astonished to find in this former inquisitor such little intransigence, such a just sense of expediency), (p. 91).

[585] *Carolo Francorum regi: ut auxilio sit episcopis regni sui ad reformandos cleri mores. "Inter plurimas"* (*Epistolae ad principes*, n. 3512).

[586] PASTOR, *Storia dei Papi*, vol. 8, pp. 337–338.

[587] *Epistolae ad principes*, n. 3565.

Cardinal Odet de Châtillon, excommunicated by Pius IV, was married wearing the cardinalatial robes and continued to wear red. Through the nuncio, Pius V asked Charles IX to distance himself from the royal council under pain of no longer conferring the cardinal's hat on any French prelate. The nuncio communicated to the sovereign that the Holy Father, resuming the process already initiated under Pius IV against the eight French bishops suspected of heresy, was taking the matter under his personal oversight. In the consistory of December 11, 1566, Pius V, with the consent of the sacred college, promulgated the definitive sentence, declaring that the archbishop of Aix and the bishops of Troyes, Uzès, Valenza, Leschar, Chartres, Oloron, and Dax "were by name deprived and stripped of all their episcopal titles, rights, and honors both in the spiritual order as well as the temporal."[588] Only the bishop of Aix, Jean de Chaumont, actually lost his office. For the others the sentence remained without effect due to the protection that Catherine gave to the Huguenot and pro-Huguenot prelates.

6. The Wars of Religion in France

In September 1567 the Huguenots attempted to repeat the *coup d'état* of 1560, to seize the young Catholic king and royal family, neutralize the Guises, and convoke the Estates General. The plan had been meticulously prepared in secret by Coligny and Condé, but the action known as the "*surprise de Meaux*" failed. Thus began the second war of religion, which had one of its most heinous episodes in Nîmes, where on September 29 the Calvinists massacred eighty Catholic nobles, throwing them in a well. Catherine and Charles IX miraculously succeeded in fleeing and reaching Paris, escorted by the faithful Swiss Ludwig Pfyffer,[589] who himself faced and defeated the Huguenots at Saint-Denis at the gates of Paris. In the

[588] Pastor, *Storia dei Papi*, vol. 8, pp. 339–340.

[589] Ludwig Pfyffer (1524–1594), after fighting against the Huguenots in France, returned to Switzerland in 1569, where he made Lucerne the stronghold of Catholicism against the Calvinists. See Anton Philipp, *Ludwig Pfyffer und seine Zeit. Ein Stück französischer und schweizerischer Geschichte im 16. Jahrhundert*, Wyss, Bern, 1880–1881.

battle among the combatants there fell one of the most prominent leaders of the Catholic party, Anne de Montmorency.[590]

Pius V, who followed the affairs of France with apprehension, decreed a universal jubilee, which opened in Rome during the final week of October in 1567 with three great processions, in which he participated on foot. But the pope also worked to support French Catholics materially, and to raise money he imposed a general tax for the entire papal state.[591] On October 17 he sent a dispatch to the doge of Venice, Girolamo Priuli, urging him "to help the Most Christian King with every effort in this critical moment, in order to avert the storm by which you are equally threatened."[592]

The pope continued to distrust Catherine, and on December 25 he wrote to the nuncio in Paris about his fear of a reconciliation with the rebels, because the queen never acted loyally toward God and the Catholic religion, and she trusted more in her own cunning than in divine help.[593] Pius V's fears were confirmed by the peace between Catholics and Huguenots stipulated at Longjumeau on March 23, 1568. Catherine renewed the unhappy Edict of Amboise, preventing a decisive victory for the Catholic party. Thanks to the new treaty, the Protestants preserved all that they had previously acquired, including their strongholds. However, the Catholic reaction did not take long to show itself once again, and Catherine was forced to sacrifice Chancellor Michel de l'Hôpital, whose religious policy of compromise had definitively failed.

[590] Anne de Montmorency (1493–1567), marshal and constable of France in 1498, accompanied Charles VIII, when he was nineteen, on his expedition to Italy, and was covered in glory in the Battles of Marignano, Pavia, San Quentin, and Dreux. Together with Francis of Guise and Jacques d'Albon de Saint-André (1505–1562), he was part of the "Catholic triumvirate" that led resistance against the Huguenots prior to the birth of the "League."

[591] Pastor, *Storia dei Papi*, vol. 8, pp. 343–344.

[592] *Epistolae ad principes*, n. 3858. Girolamo Priuli (1486–1567) was the eighty-third doge of the Republic of Venice from 1559 until his death in 1567.

[593] Pastor, *Storia dei Papi*, vol. 8, p. 344.

On August 15, 1568, Pius V recalled della Torre and announced to the French court that the new nuncio would be the bishop of Caiazzo, Fabio Mirto Frangipani.[594] In his instructions to Frangipani, the pope recommended that he inform Catherine de' Medici and Charles IX of "our good will and the great desire we have to free that kingdom from the rebels against God and their Majesties' Crown."[595]

On March 6, 1569, Pius V wrote to Charles IX to announce the sending of Count Sforza di Santa Fiora[596] with a contingent of four thousand papal soldiers to fight the Calvinists. "We send to Your Majesty, in the name of the Omnipotent God, infantry troops and cavalry for the war stirred up by the Huguenots your subjects, who are declared enemies of God and of His Church. We pray to God that the God of armies and the King of Kings, who governs all things with his infinite wisdom, to mercifully grant to Your Majesty a full victory over all your enemies, so that you can reestablish tranquility in your kingdom."[597] Pius V then exhorted the sovereign, once he should obtain victory, "to punish with the most extreme rigor the heretics and their leaders, because they are enemies of God, and to legitimately avenge on them, not only your own injuries

[594] Fabio Mirto Frangipani (1514–1587) was the titular archbishop of Nazareth and bishop of Caiazzo. During his term as nuncio to France (1568–1572), he acted in close contact with Castagna, who had replaced him as governor of Umbria in 1559. See Stefano Andretta, *Frangipani Ottavio Mirto*, in DBI, vol. 50 (1998), pp. 249–252. See also *Correspondance du nonce en France Fabio Mirto Frangipani*, edited by A. Lynn Martin, École Française de Rome, Pontificia Università Gregoriana, Rome, 1984.

[595] *Correspondance du nonce en France Fabio Mirto Frangipani*, p. 61 (pp. 61–65).

[596] Guido Sforza, Count of Santa Fiora (1520–1575), was the general captain of the papal and Spanish cavalry, then head of the papal militia sent by Pius V in support of Charles IX of France in his battle against the Huguenots. He was then general of the Spanish infantry and fought alongside Don Juan of Austria in the Battle of Lepanto.

[597] De Potter, *Lettres de Saint Pie V*, Letter XI, p. 34 (pp. 32–33). Louis de Potter (1786–1859), was a Belgian journalist and the author of revolutionary works, but he rendered a service to history by publishing thirty-nine letters of St. Pius V related to the religious wars in France.

but also those of Almighty God." And the pope wrote to Catherine on March 28, 1569, that she should "seek only the honor of Almighty God and fight openly and ardently against the enemies of the Catholic religion until they are all destroyed," because "it is only by means of the total extermination of the heretics that the King will be able to render to the noble kingdom of France the ancient cult of the Catholic religion."[598]

In the third war of religion, the royal troops achieved two brilliant victories: on March 13, 1569, at Jarnac, and on October 3 of the same year at Montcontour. The victory of Montcontour was attributed to Pius V, because the pontifical soldiers, who were the first to attack and the last to retreat, played a decisive role. It is said that when the Count of Santa Fiora gave the order to raise the banner of the Church, the Huguenots saw warriors in the heavens with bloody swords who fought against them, so that one of their captains instantly converted to the Catholic Faith.[599] The news of the victory so moved Pius V that for three days he had all the bells of Rome rung, while cannons were fired from Castel Sant'Angelo as a sign of celebration. The Count of Santa Fiora received three of the thirty-seven flags torn from his enemies as a gift from the French sovereign, which he placed as a votive offering in the Basilica of St. John Lateran. Already in April of that year, Charles IX had sent the pope twelve Hugenot flags captured in Jarnac. Pius V, surrounded by the entire college of cardinals, received these trophies in the Hall of Constantine as he wept, declaring that the gift of the Most Christian King was the most precious he had ever given to religion, to the Holy See, and to himself personally.[600]

The pope was not satisfied with these military victories, but instead exhorted the king of France to continue the war until the Huguenots were annihilated, declaring that it was his duty to eradicate the roots, even "the slightest fiber of the roots of such a terrible and strongly established evil."[601]

598 Ibid., Letter XIII, p. 45 (pp. 41–45).

599 Catena, *Vita del gloriosissimo Papa Pio V*, p. 84.

600 Pastor, *Storia dei Papi*, vol. 8, p. 348.

601 De Potter, *Lettres de Saint Pie V*, Letter XII, p. 37 (pp. 36–40).

In letters sent to the sovereign and other Catholic princes, Pius V repeatedly admonished them not to follow the biblical example of King Saul, who despite God's command spared the Amalekites and thus was stripped of his kingdom by Samuel and ultimately lost his life. "By this example God wanted to teach all kings that being negligent in the vindication of outrages done against Him means provoking his anger and indignation."[602]

In the letter of congratulations that he sent to Charles IX on October 20, 1569, Pius V warned that he should not allow himself to be taken by false compassion, because there was nothing crueler than compassion for the wicked and those who deserved the death penalty.[603] In another letter to the king on January 29, 1570, the pope recalled that it was not possible to have any accommodation between Catholics and heretics that was not actually a trap. "If we judged that between Your Majesty and your enemies there could be an understanding suitable to serving religion or procuring the tranquility of your kingdom that has been exhausted by so many wars, we would certainly not forget our sacred character, nor would we be so negligent as to not intervene with all zeal and our authority in order to hasten the conclusion of this treaty. But we personally know that the only possible agreement would be fictitious and full of pitfalls."[604] On the same day, the pope wrote in analogous terms to Queen Catherine[605] and the Duke of Anjou,[606] the brother of Charles IX, reiterating to both, as he had written to the sovereign, that "there can be nothing in common between light and darkness; no agreement is possible between Catholics and heretics."[607]

Unfortunately, the king of France did not exploit these victories, and on August 8, 1570, he laid down his arms, granting the Huguenots the

602 Ibid., p. 39 (pp. 39–40). The same example of Amalekites is cited in the letter to the Duke of Anjou of April 26, 1569, ibid., Letter XVIII, p. 64 (pp. 62–65).

603 *Epistolae ad principes*, n. 4441; text in De Potter, *Lettres de Saint Pie V*, Letter XXIV, pp. 84–88.

604 De Potter, *Lettres de Saint Pie V*, Letter XXVIII, pp. 97–100.

605 Ibid., Letter XXIX, pp. 101–104.

606 Ibid., Letter XXX, pp. 105–107.

607 Ibid., Letter XXVIII, p. 98.

Peace of Saint-Germain-en-Laye, which renewed the provisions of the Edict of Amboise, granting Protestants four strategic "*places de sûreté*" for a period of two years. On September 22, 1570, in a long audience with the sovereigns, Nuncio Frangipani protested vigorously against the Peace of Saint-Germain-en-Laye, pointing out the risks for the monarchy of France and for the Catholic religion of an agreement that granted much more to the Huguenots than they had possessed prior to the defeats of the preceding year.

Pius V was convinced that this "shameful peace dictated to the French king by the vanquished enemies of God" would provoke an even worse disturbance in France than in the past, and so in November 1570 he secretly sent the papal notary, Francesco Bramante, to France to protest against the Treaty of Saint-Germain and draw France into the league against the Turks.[608] Meanwhile, Catherine, pursuing her policy of national reconciliation, had conceived a plan to marry her daughter Margaret with the Calvinist Henry of Navarre. Pius V however made it known that as long as the prince of Navarre was Huguenot, he would not grant under any treaty a dispensation for Princess Margaret to marry, which was necessary for her union with Henry, "even if he had to lose not only the obedience of France but also his own head, unless the Prince of Navarre first became Catholic."[609]

On the night of August 23–24, 1572, the leader of the Huguenots, Gaspard de Coligny, and several other Protestant aristocrats were killed in Paris. Then the massacre was extended to other Huguenots present in the city, with the death of thousands of people in Paris and in other French cities over the following days.[610] The so-called "St. Bartholomew's Day Massacre" of August 24, 1572, in Paris has been attributed to St. Pius V,

[608] PASTOR, *Storia dei Papi*, vol. 8, p. 355; MARTIN, *Le gallicanisme et la réforme*, pp. 8–9.

[609] GRENTE, *Pio V, il pontefice delle grandi battaglie*, p. 124.

[610] See the syntheiss of STEFANO TABACCHI, *La strage di San Bartolomeo. Una notte di sangue a Parigi*, Salerno Editrice, Rome, 2018; see also DENIS CROUZET, *La nuit de Saint-Barthélemy. Un rêve perdu de la Renaissance*, Fayard, Paris, 1994.

even though he died before it happened. In reality the one responsible for the massacre was Catherine de' Medici, who in order to reach her political goals, was ready to utilize assassination and betrayal. Pius V, as Hirschauer recalls, "never hid his desire to destroy Protestantism in France, and he pursued his goal relentlessly; for example, through his counsel he succeeded in entreating the majority of Catholic princes to come to the French battlefield in support of the cause of the Church."[611] However, the pope hated subterfuges and dissimulation, and he always set out to annihilate heresy only by fair combat in the open field. Because of this he could not hide his disgust when he learned that the court of France had ordered the assassination of Coligny and the prince of Condé. On March 10, 1567, the Spanish ambassador Zúñiga wrote to Philip II: "Pope Pius V has told me a great secret: Those French gentlemen are considering doing something that I can neither advise nor approve, because my conscience will not let me. They want to use secret means to take the lives of Condé and the Admiral."[612]

While Catherine never renounced the Catholic Faith, she detested the uncompromising Catholics of her time more than she disliked the Calvinists, without ever understanding the deeply religious nature of the conflict that divided her kingdom. The attack against Coligny, which was agreed on by Catherine and the Duke of Anjou, was to take place after the wedding of Henry of Navarre and Margaret de Valois. The plan was to eliminate the Protestant leadership, placing responsibility for the massacre on the Guises, in order to unleash the revenge of the Huguenots against them. But the attempt on Coligny's life failed, because he was only lightly wounded, and the Huguenot nobility asked Charles IX, who was unaware of the background of the attack, for the severe punishment of those who were guilty. At this point, Catherine succeeded in convincing the king

[611] Hirschauer, *La politique de St Pie V en France*, p. 94.

[612] Grente, *Pio V, il pontefice delle grandi battaglie*, p. 119. Juan de Requensens y Zúñiga (1539–1586) succeeded his brother Luis as ambassador to the Holy See from January 1568 to November 1579, during the pontificates of Pius V and Gregory XIII. He was then viceroy of Naples (1579–1582) and, beginning in 1583, president of the council of state in Madrid.

of the existence of a plot against the royal family, and she obtained full authority to carry out a preventive action against the Huguenots, who were gathered in Paris for the royal wedding. The result of the massacre was the escalation of the religious conflict,[613] which in the years to follow saw the assassination of Henry of Guise, the head of the Catholic party, who was treacherously killed by Henry III on December 23, 1588, in the royal castle of Blois, and in the killing of Henry III himself, who was stabbed on August 1, 1589, by the young third-order Dominican Jacques Clément in the royal castle of Saint-Cloud.

7. England between Elizabeth and Mary Stuart

No less dramatic than the events in the Kingdom of France were those that unfolded before the eyes of Pius V in the Kingdom of England, where in 1558 Elizabeth I[614] ascended to the throne after the brief five-year reign of the Catholic Mary who died without an heir.[615] Since 1555 the imperial

[613] On May 30, 1574, Charles IX died when he was not yet twenty-four years old, and the throne passed to Henry, Duke of Anjou (Henry III), who had become king of Poland the previous year. Between 1577 and 1594, years in which Henry IV Bourbon rose to the throne after he had abjured Protestantism, France was torn apart by new wars of religion, culminating in the assassination of Henry of Guise and Henry III. Henry IV promulgated the Edict of Nantes on April 30, 1598, which recognized Huguenot control of some forty cities. The edict eliminated the risk of a civil war but did not end the Huguenot problem. (Tabacchi, *La strage di San Bartolomeo*, pp. 126–127).

[614] Elizabeth I Tudor (1533–1603), illegitimate daughter of Henry VIII and Anne Boleyn, was queen of England and Ireland from November 17, 1558, until her death. Among the most recent works, see Williams Neville, *The Life and Times of Elizabeth the First*, Weidenfeld and Nicolson, London, 1972; Christopher Haigh, *Elizabeth I*, Longman, London, 1988; Maria Perry, *The World of a Prince. A Life of Elizabeth I from Contemporary Documents*, Boydell Press, Rochester, New York, 1990; Elisabetta Sala, *Elisabetta la sanguinaria. La creazione di un mito. La persecuzione di un popolo*, Ares, Milan, 2010.

[615] Mary Tudor (1516–1558), the daughter of Henry VIII and Catherine of Aragon, the only legitimate heir to the English throne, was the queen of England and Ireland from July 19, 1553, until her death, and, after

ambassador Simon Renard had predicted: "If Elizabeth succeeds to the throne, it is certain that the kingdom will return to heresy."[616] The new parliament that opened on January 25, 1559, proclaimed the spiritual "supremacy" of the sovereign, with the abolition of "every foreign power contrary to this jurisdiction." The Law of Uniformity, approved by the House of Lords in June 1559 by a three-vote majority, made the *Book of Common Prayer* obligatory for religious services, and the queen assumed the supreme title of Head of the Church of England. A declared Calvinist, Matthew Parker, who was the former chaplain of Anne Boleyn, was promoted to the primatial see as archbishop of Canterbury. He was consecrated according to the Ordinal of Edward VI, considered invalid by the Catholic Church, and he in turn consecrated all new bishops according to the same ceremonial.[617]

If in 1559 Parliament reintroduced the cult of Edward VI, in 1563 it reintroduced the "Creed," reducing the Forty-two Articles of the Anglican Church to thirty-nine. Every person who assumed a public office in England had to recognize that the monarch was the supreme governor "in all spiritual and ecclesiastical things and causes." Those who refused to take the oath were charged with treason. Catholics had three alternatives.[618]

---

her marriage to Philip II, the queen consort of Spain. In her brief reign she sought to restore Catholicism in England, but she died without any children, to the great disappointment of the English. See LINDA PORTER, *Mary Tudor*, Piakts Books, London, 2007; EAMON DUFFY, *Fires of Faith: Catholic England under Mary Tudor*, Yale University Press, New Haven, 2009.

[616] JOSEPH CONSTANT, *Angleterre*, in DHGE, vol. 3 (1924), col. 204.

[617] Matthew Parker (1504–1575), former chaplain of Anne Boleyn, was archbishop of Canterbury from 1559 until his death. He was one of the authors of the Thirty-nine Articles of the Anglican Church. Leo XIII, after a scrupulous historical and theological examination, declared Anglican ordinations invalid with the bull *Apostolicae Curae* of September 13, 1896, because of the defect of form as well as the defect of intention. See CAMILLO CRIVELLI, *Anglicane, Ordinazioni*, in EC, vol. 1 (1948), cols. 1271–1273.

[618] SALA, *Elisabetta la sanguinària*, pp. 80–81. See also MARY H. ALLIES, *History of the Church in England from the Accession of Henry VIII to the Death of*

The first was to submit to the decrees of the queen and abjure Catholicism. The second was to refuse to participate in Anglican religious services, thereby breaking the law, which meant risking the confiscation of their goods, life in prison, or being condemned to death. The third option was to feign adherence to the Anglican Church, privately maintaining the Catholic Faith, in hope of better times. Those Catholics who refused any compromise were called recusants, while those who collaborated were known as "Church-papists."[619]

At first, Pius V pursued a policy of conciliation with the queen, but he soon realized that he was facing a woman even more cynical and dissimulating than Catherine de' Medici herself. His gaze then turned to a Catholic princess who could possibly occupy the throne more worthily than Elizabeth. Mary Stuart[620] had grown up at the French court, where her mother, Marie of Guise, was from. She was imbued with the spirit of great faithfulness to Rome that characterized the Guise family and incarnated in her person the *Auld Alliance*,[621] the ancient agreement of

---

Queen Elizabeth, Burns & Oates, London, 1895; JOHN HUNGERFORD POLLEN, S.J., *The English Catholics in the Reign of Queen Elizabeth, 1558–1580: A Study of Their Politics, Civil Life, and Government*, Longmans, Green & Co., London, 1920; PHILIP CARAMAN, *The Other Face: Catholic Life under Elizabeth I*, Longman, London, 1960.

619 See BRIAN MAGEE, *The English Recusants: A Study of the Post-reformation Catholic Survival and the Operation of the Recusancy Laws*, Burns, Oates & Washbourne, London, 1938; ALEXANDRA WALSHAM, *Church Papists: Catholicism, Conformity, and Confessional Polemic in Early Modern England*, Boydell Press, Rochester, New York, 1993.

620 Mary Stuart (1542–1587), daughter of James V of Scotland and Marie of Guise, was queen consort of France from July 10, 1559, until December 5, 1560, and queen of Scotland from December 14, 1542, until July 24, 1567. Among the numerous biographies, see FRANCIS EDWARDS, S.J., *The Dangerous Queen*, Geoffrey Chapman, London, 1964; and ANTONIA FRASER, *Mary Queen of Scots*, Phoenix, London, 1988. See also CHARLES PETRIE, *Gli Stuart*, Dall'Oglio, Varese, 1964.

621 The *Auld Alliance*, a historic alliance between the Kingdom of Scotland and the Kingdom of France against England dates back to a treaty signed in Paris on October 23, 1295, and ratified in February 1296 at Dunfermline under the reigns of John of Scotland and Philip IV of France.

friendship between France and Catholic Scotland. However, she was very young and her character was not without frailty. The Count of Falloux sums up Mary's antagonism toward Elizabeth in these words:

> Daughter of the Guises, pupil of the Valois, noble in her instincts, blind in her passions, mobile in her will, invincible in her faith, fragile, imprudent, and above all slandered, served with ardor by her friends and constantly betrayed by fortune, Mary Stuart faced the woman most ably disposed to profit from all of her faults, from all of the fatalities of a rival. Elizabeth knew no passions other than the one that excludes them all, ambition, and she had no defects other than those that served her. . . . She had meditated on the vices that make one ascend to an uncertain throne and she had made them her virtues; she had studied the levities that discredited her rival and made these her prudence.[622]

The two kingdoms of England and Scotland were at the center of an implacable religious antagonism for thirty years.

When Elizabeth took power in England, Mary had just married the dauphin, who in 1559 became Francis II of France. He died a few months later and Mary returned to Scotland, where she found a country dominated by the Calvinist party headed by John Knox,[623] whose violent preaching had stirred up revolt throughout the country.

With the Treaty of Edinburgh of July 6, 1560, the Scottish Parliament approved the withdrawal of the French troops from its territory, and on August 17, 1560, it adopted a Calvinist confession of faith. Mary never ratified the treaty, and she proposed to restore Catholic worship while keeping Calvinism as the state religion. In 1565 she married a Scottish

[622] Falloux, *Histoire de St Pie V*, vol. 1, p. 266.

[623] John Knox (1505–1572) organized the Calvinist Church of Scotland on the Huguenot model. He was one of the biggest opponents of Mary Stuart and by his preaching he assured the victory of Protestantism in Scotland.

Catholic nobleman, Henry Darnley,[624] the Count of Lennox, but she did not find in him the support she desired and found herself in an extremely difficult situation. Her marriage to a Catholic had in fact incited the Count of Moray,[625] the illegitimate son of James I and therefore the half-brother of Mary Stuart, to unite himself with other Protestant nobles in a rebellion against the queen. On the evening of March 9, 1566, some of these entered the royal palace of Holyrood by force of arms and killed Mary's secretary and confidant, David Riccio, [626] to whom the queen's anti-Protestant approach was attributed, right before her eyes.

Mary Stuart was now being sorely tried, and on June 6, 1566, Pius V wrote to her in his own hand to encourage her, sending her 20,000 gold scudis to supply for her needs, with the promise of sending her more when he had the opportunity. After having assured her of his prayers, the pope added, "For fear that our sins make us unworthy of being heard, we have had recourse to the prayers of many religious and priests. We would be willing to sacrifice our lives for you. ... Since we are unable to go to Scotland due to our advanced age and our innumerable concerns, we send you as nuncio the bishop of Mondovi, virtuous, learned, prudent, worthy of your esteem and ready to serve you."[627]

[624] Henry Stuart, Lord Darnley (1545–1567), oldest son of the Count of Lennox, a descendant through his father from the king of Scotland and through his mother from the king of England, was king consort of Scotland as the second husband of Mary Stuart, whom he married on July 29, 1565.

[625] James Stuart, first Earl of Moray (ca. 1531–1570), illegitimate son of king James V and Margaret Erskine, was regent of Scotland from 1567 until his assassination in 1570.

[626] David Riccio or Rizzio (1533–1566) was a Piedmontese musician who, following the ambassador Carlo Emmanuele of Savoy, moved to Scotland, where he became secretary to Mary Stuart. He was killed in front of the queen, who unsuccessfully tried to save his life. Eric Frattini says that Riccio may have been an agent of Pius V (*Le spie del papa. Dal Cinquecento a oggi, venti vite di assassini e sicofanti al servizio di Dio*, Ponte alle Grazie, Milan, 2009, p. 18) taking up a thesis that Pastor finds unlikely (*Storia dei Papi*, vol. 8, p. 373).

[627] Grente, *Pio V, il pontefice delle grandi battaglie*, p. 129.

Mary Stuart thanked Pius V with all her heart, and informed him of the birth of her son, the future James I of England,[628] who was baptized in the castle of Stirling on December 10, 1566, with a splendid Catholic ceremony. Meanwhile, the promised nuncio arrived, Vincenzo Lauro,[629] who in the name of the pope suggested to the queen to proceed with severe justice against the leaders of the rebellion. Mary did not take his advice, declaring that she did not want to stain her hands with the blood of her subjects. The nuncio, a man of great political experience, insisted, convinced that the events of recent months had proven him right. He wrote to the pope that because of her excessive goodness and indulgence, the queen had placed herself in danger of becoming the prey of heretics and losing her life.[630]

Events now unfolded. Lord Darnley, who had participated in the murder of Riccio, was assassinated in his own turn on February 10, 1567, and on May 15 of the same year, in a fit of inexplicable rashness, Mary Stuart married James Hepburn, Count of Bothwell,[631] in a Protestant rite. Hepburn was suspected of being the material author of the homicide of the queen's prior husband.

The marriage of Mary Stuart was certainly, as Pastor writes, "a tremendous error,"[632] the source of all the misfortunes of the unhappy princess. A bitter conflict opened up between Moray and Bothwell, and the latter was forced to leave Scotland. Mary passed from Bothwell's prison to Moray's and was relegated to Lochleven Castle, where she was forced to

[628] James I Stuart (1566–1625) reigned over Scotland from July 24, 1567, until his death. On March 24, 1603, he succeeded Elizabeth I to the English throne, with the name of James I.

[629] Vincenzo Lauro (1523–1592) was appointed bishop of Mondovi by Pius V on January 20, 1566, and sent as nuncio to the queen of Scotland and then to Piedmont (1568–1573).

[630] Pastor, *Storia dei Papi*, vol. 8, p. 379.

[631] James Hepburn, Count of Bothwell (1534–1578), was lord grand admiral of Scotland and prince consort of Scotland as the third husband of Queen Mary Stuart. Fleeing from England, he spent the last ten years of his life as a prisoner of King Frederick of Denmark.

[632] Pastor, *Storia dei Papi*, vol. 8, p. 386.

sign her abdication in favor of her son, James, who was then only one year old. After ten months in prison, in early May 1568 Mary escaped, heading west to the country of the Hamiltons,[633] among the strongest of her remaining supporters, with the determination to restore her rights as queen. The Battle of Langside was fought on May 13, 1568, between forces loyal to her and forces acting in the name of her infant son, James I. Mary was defeated, but she committed another fatal error. Instead of going to France under the protection of the Guises, she took refuge with her cousin Elizabeth, who from that moment on held her prisoner. Moray was assassinated in Linlithgow (Scotland) on January 23, 1570, by James Hamilton of Bothwellhaug, a faithful supporter of Mary.[634]

8. Pius V and "Ridolfi's Plot"

Pius V did not remain inactive in the face of this persecution. A Florentine banker, Roberto Ridolfi,[635] was the pope's trusted agent in England. Ridolfi lived in London for many years, and his financial activity made

[633] The Hamilton Clan, or House of Hamilton, is a Lowland Scottish clan. The clans are family communities of noble origin recognized by the Scottish sovereigns. The present Duke of Hamilton is the head of both the Hamilton and Douglas clans.

[634] James Hamilton fatally wounded Moray with a carbine shot from a window of his uncle Archbishop Hamilton's house in Linlithgow. Moray was the first head of government to be assassinated by a firearm. After killing Moray, Hamilton fled to France, where he died in 1581.

[635] Roberto Ridolfi (1531–1612), of a noble Florentine family, transferred to London in 1562, carrying out—alongside his activity as a financier—the role of "secret nuncio" of Pius V (Catena, *Vita del gloriosissimo papa Pio V*, p. 113). Finding himself abroad when the plot was discovered, Ridolfi never returned to England. He was governor of Pisa and Pistoia and became a Florentine senator in 1600. On his life, see the entry by Lucinda Byatt, *Ridolfi*, in DBI, vol. 87 (2016), pp. 478–482, with bibliography. The judgments of English historians on his "conspiracies" are excessively severe: Pollen, *The English Catholics*, pp. 160–184; Edwards, *The Dangerous Queen*, pp. 297–356; G. Parker, *The Place of Tudor England in the Messianic Vision of Philip II of Spain*, in "Transaction of the Royal Historical Society," vol. 13 (2002), pp.187–221; Cyril Hamshere, *The Ridolfi Plot 1571*, in "History Today," pp. 32–39.

his frequency of travel and the variety of his relationships natural. The pope gave him the mission of working to restore the Catholic Church in England, ensuring him adequate financial support. In the course of 1568, Ridolfi made contact with Mary's chief counselor, John Leslie,[636] the bishop of Ross, with the Spanish ambassador, Guerau de Spes,[637] and with the principal Catholic nobles of the kingdoms of England and Scotland. When he sent the blessed tuck [swordsman] to the Duke of Alba on March 21, 1569, Pius V made him inquire at the same time whether through an alliance between France and Spain it would not be possible to carry out an armed naval landing to invade England. Alba responded that there was no chance of hoping for the cooperation of France, and that the only way would be either for Philip II to conquer England himself or else to confer the kingdom on a Catholic nobleman who would marry Mary Stuart.[638] Ridolfi elaborated a plan according to which Mary Stuart, the widow of three husbands,[639] after having married the Duke of Norfolk,[640] who was Anglican but open to Catholicism, could resume

[636] John Lesley (or Leslie) (1527–1596), became bishop of Ross in 1565. After being imprisoned in the Tower of London from 1571 to 1572, he was then exiled to the Netherlands and France where in 1593 he became bishop of Coutances. He died in Brussels, leaving an important historical work dedicated to *De origine moribus et rebus gestis Scotorum* in ten books, which goes up to 1562.

[637] Guerau de Espés del Valle (1524–1572) was the representative in London of Philip II from 1518 to 1571. See Julio Retamal Favereau, *Anglo-Spanish Relations, 1566–1572: The Mission of Don Guerau de Spes at London*, University of Oxford, Oxford, 1972.

[638] Pastor, *Storia dei Papi*, vol. 8, p. 402.

[639] The three husbands were Francis II, who died in 1560, Lord Darnley, assassinated in 1567, and the Count of Bothwell, who was assassinated in 1570. See Claudina Fumagalli, *Maria Stuarda: tre mariti, due corone, un patibolo*, De Vecchi, Milan, 1967.

[640] Thomas Howard, fourth Duke of Norfolk (1536–1572), supported the Catholic cause while continuing to declare himself a Protestant. His father, Henry Howard, Count of Surrey (1517–1547), was beheaded on January 19, 1547, on the charge of treason, the last victim of Henry VIII. His firstborn son, Philip Howard, Count of Arundel (1557–1595), was

her place as the legitimate queen of Scotland and the heir to Elizabeth on the English throne.

Meanwhile, Elizabeth had assembled an efficient mechanism of espionage, led by her ruthless secretary William Cecil[641]—later Lord Burghley—and by Sir Francis Walsingham,[642] who joined him in December 1568. The torturer Richard Topcliffe[643] worked alongside them, tireless in his determination to eradicate Catholicism from England. Thanks to her spies, the queen learned of Ridolfi's plot and furiously opposed it. The English ports were closed and Mary was transferred to the remote Tutbury Castle, while the Duke of Norfolk was imprisoned in the Tower of London. Ridolfi and a few accomplices were promptly arrested for treason. Ridolfi was interrogated by Sir Francis Walsingham on twenty-five counts of treason, but despite Elizabeth's suspicions, no evidence was found against him and he was released on bail of a thousand pounds. Some historians propose the hypothesis that Ridolfi agreed to act as a double agent on behalf of the British. In reality, the clever Florentine mocked Walsingham, as astute as he was presumptuous, to the point of pretending to interrogate him in the Italian language, which he knew

---

martyred and in 1970 was canonized by Paul VI. See NEVILLE WILLIAMS, *Thomas Howard, Fourth Duke of Norfolk*, Dutton, New York, 1965.

641 William Cecil (1520–1598), Baron Burghley, was chief adviser of Queen Elizabeth I, twice served as secretary of state, and was lord high treasurer. See STEPHEN ALFORD, *Burghley: William Cecil at the Court of Elizabeth I*, Yale University Press, New Haven, 2008.

642 On the spy network organized by Sir Francis Walsingham (1532–1590), see ALAN HAYNES, *The Elizabethan Secret Services*, Sutton, Stroud, 2011; HAYNES, *Walsingham: Elizabethan Spymaster and Statesman*, Sutton, Stroud, 2007; ROBERT HUTCHINSON, *Elizabeth Spymaster*, Phoenix, London, 2006. Walsingham and Cecil, together with the Count of Leicester, Robert Dudley (1532–1588), formed the "triumvirate" of the most powerful men during the reign of Queen Elizabeth.

643 Richard Topcliffe (1531–1604) was an agent of the English government who persecuted, captured, and even personally tortured numerous Catholics. See MARK RANKIN, *Richard Topcliffe and the Book Culture of the Elizabethan Catholic Underground*, in "Renaissance Quarterly" (Summer 2019), pp. 492–536.

poorly. The esteem that Ridolfi continued to enjoy in the following years from Pius V, Philip II, and Cosimo de' Medici, confirmed his loyalty and devotion to the Catholic cause.

Ridolfi had made contacts with the Counts of Northumberland[644] and Westmoreland,[645] for whom, with the agreement of Pius V, he had assured consistent financial help for their projects of relieving Catholics in England and freeing Mary Stuart. [646] A subsequent insurrection broke out in Durham and Ripon on November 16, 1569. The banner of the insurgents, representing the Savior with the Five Bleeding Wounds, like that of the Pilgrimage of Grace of 1536, was carried by an old white-haired gentleman named Norton, to whom, writes Falloux, "zeal and faith seemed to restore his youth."[647] Responding to a message of the Catholic nobles who led the insurgency, on February 26, 1570, Pius V sent them a brief that was full of praise, in which among other things he wrote:

> We are sorry that it is reserved for the times of our pontificate to see the venom of so many and such abominable heresies bring

[644] Thomas Percy (1528–1572), the seventh Count of Northumberland, led the Catholic insurgence against Elizabeth and was decapitated on August 22, 1572. Before offering his neck to the executioner, he turned to the people and declared that he was dying as a Catholic and would never recognize the new church of England. Leo XIII beatified him on May 13, 1895.

[645] Charles Neville (1543–1601) was the sixth Count of Westmoreland. After the effort to liberate Queen Mary Stuart failed, he was forced to live in exile in the Netherlands, enjoying a pension provided by Philip II until his death.

[646] See KRISTA KESSELRING, *The Northern Rebellion of 1569: Faith, Politics and Protest in Elizabethan England*, Palgrave McMillan, London, 2007. On the Catholic revolt against Henry VIII in Yorkshire in 1536, see RICHARD W. HOYLE, *The Pilgrimage of Grace and the Politics of the 1530s*, Oxford University Press, Oxford, 2001.

[647] FALLOUX, *Histoire de St Pie V*, vol. 1, p. 304. Richard Conyers Norton ("Old Norton"), a member of the first noble family of Yorkshire, was considered the "Patriarch of the Rebellion" of English Catholics. He fled to Flanders, where he died in poverty in 1585 at the age of about ninety. His seventh son, Christopher, and his brother Thomas were quartered at Tyburn on May 27, 1570.

> mortal blows to the Christian republic in such great numbers. But nevertheless we recall the efficacy of the prayer of the one who prayed for blessed Peter that his faith would not fail, and that by spreading his church even in the midst of tribulation, he governs it even more admirably, through the secret counsels of Providence, the more he sees it shaken and battered by the waves. ... Even if you have to face death and shed your blood for the freedom of the Catholic faith and the authority of the Holy See, it is far more advantageous for you to gain eternal life for the short journey of a glorious death, than to live in shame and serve the passion of an impious woman with danger to your soul.[648]

The pope concluded his letter by assuring the English nobles that he was working on their behalf with Christian princes and promised other subsidies "more copious than those that the poverty of his finances could offer for the moment," entrusting his agent Ridolfi to explain his projects clearly and in more detail.

Northumberland and Westmoreland at first triumphed and had the joy of assisting at Mass in Durham Cathedral; but when they came to Tutbury Castle, they found that Mary Stuart was no longer there but had been transferred by her captors to Coventry, where Elizabeth's army was gathering. There was also a lack of the decisive help that Philip II and Charles IX had promised. The aid of the Duke of Alba did not appear, while the southern counties of England gathered an army of twelve thousand men under the orders of the Count of Warwick. The insurgents were thus dispersed, and the entire north of England, which had widely rebelled against the queen, was devastated and sacked by Warwick's army. The Duke of Norfolk, who had not openly taken part in the rebellion, was arrested. Westmoreland escaped to continental Europe while Northumberland was captured and confined in the same Lochleven Castle in which Mary Stuart had been imprisoned. The last battle was fought

[648] Letter of February 20, 1570. See FALLOUX, *Histoire de St Pie V*, vol. 1, pp. 300–304.

near Naworth Castle, Cumberland, on February 20, 1570, by Leonard Dacre.[649] Dacre was defeated and returned to Scotland. Five days later, Pius V published the bull of excommunication of Elizabeth.

9. The Excommunication of Elizabeth Tudor

The auditor of the Rota, Alessandro Riario,[650] who had been instructed by Pius V to prepare the dossier for the trial, had already warned the queen that he would proceed against her according to the canons of the Church. On February 5, 1570, the trial was opened, in which twelve English witnesses were heard, "*viri docti et promoti in facultatibus eius*," and the accusation against the queen was formulated in seventeen articles.[651] Once the trial was over, the pope spent several days in fasting and prayer, and then on February 25, 1570, he signed and promulgated in consistory the bull *Regnans in Excelsis*, with which he pronounced a sentence of excommunication against Queen Elizabeth I, declaring her to have lapsed from her claimed right to the English crown; her subjects were not bound to their oath of fidelity toward her, and under pain of excommunication they could not show her obedience.[652]

> Therefore, resting upon the authority of him whose pleasure it was to place us (though unequal to such a burden) upon this supreme justice-seat, we do out of the fullness of our apostolic power declare the aforesaid Elizabeth to be a heretic and a favorer of heretics, and her adherents in the matters aforesaid to have incurred the sentence of anathema and to be cut off from the unity of the body of Christ. And moreover, we declare her to be deprived of her pretended title

[649] Leonard Dacre (1533–1573), second-born son of William Dacre, third Baron of Gisland, emigrated to Brussels after the defeat and died there on August 12, 1573.

[650] Alessandro Riario Sforza (1543–1585), auditor of the Apostolic Camera, was appointed the patriarch of Alexandria in Egypt (1570) by Pius V, and made a cardinal by Gregory XIII on February 21, 1578. He was later legate to Perugia and Umbria and prefect of the Apostolic Signatura (see M.T. FATTORI, *Riario Alessandro*, in DBI, vol. 87 [2016], pp. 90–92).

[651] POLLEN, *The English Catholics*, pp. 147–149.

[652] *Bullarium Romanum*, vol. 7, 810ff.

> to the aforesaid kingdom, and of all dominion, dignity and privilege whatsoever. And we also declare the nobles, subjects and people of the said realm and all others who have in any way sworn oaths unto her, to be forever absolved from any such oath and from any duty arising from duty, lordship, allegiance and obedience; and we do, by authority of these here present so absolve them, and so deprive the same Elizabeth of her pretended title to the crown and all the other matters stated above. We charge and command all and each of the nobles, subjects, peoples and others aforesaid that they do not dare obey her orders, mandates and laws. Those who shall act to the contrary we include in the like sentence of excommunication.

With this official act, Pius V dispelled all misunderstanding and made known to all the position of the Church of Rome toward Elizabeth Tudor: the queen of England was a heretic and schismatic. Without such a declaration the pope would have endorsed the idea that the English state church was still part of the Catholic Church. The bull resoundingly condemned the "third party" of the Church-papists and encouraged the recusants to resistance, not necessarily armed.

Philip II and the Duke of Alba made known to the pope their perplexity over the negative consequences that the bull would have, but as Fr. Pollen observes, "against this must be set the inestimable advantage of making it evident to all the world that Elizabeth and her followers were cut off from the Catholic Church, that to accept and submit to her was to reject that Church."[653] Thus, "in regard to England, Pius's chief work was the excommunication, a stroke of incomparably greater importance than any made before."[654]

Pius V referred to the Magisterium of the Church and to the behavior of the great popes of the Middle Ages, like St. Gregory VII, Innocent III, Innocent IV, and Boniface VIII,[655] up to Paul III, who in 1535 had declared

[653] Ibid., p. 15.

[654] POLLEN, *The English Catholics*, p. 142.

[655] ALFONSO MARIA STICKLER, *Sacerdozio e regno nelle nuove ricerche attorno ai secoli XII e XIII nei decreti e decretalisti fino alle decretali di Gregorio IX*, in

King Henry VIII of England[656] to be deprived of his reign, excommunicated by Clement VII. This position would be considered that of the Magisterium of the Church by two jurists of the twentieth century, Fr. Luigi Cappello and Cardinal Alfredo Ottaviani, in their manuals of ecclesiastical public law, which was the basis for forming clergy up until recent times.[657]

Elizabeth tried in every way to prevent the bull from being introduced and known in her realm, but on the night of March 25, 1570, a gentleman from Southwark, John Felton,[658] affixed a copy of the papal bull on the door of the house of the schismatic bishop of London, next to St. Paul's Anglican cathedral.

The next morning the news spread among the people of London, who gathered excitedly at the bishop's palace. Elizabeth went into a rage and ordered that torture be used to discover who posted it. Felton, instead of fleeing, claimed the honor of the undertaking, and declared that many copies of the bull were already circulating in the hands of the faithful of the city. On August 4, 1570, Felton, led before the tribunal, publicly denied the spiritual supremacy of Elizabeth, declaring himself ready to die for the Catholic Faith. Then, in order to show that he harbored no personal hatred against the queen, he took from his finger a ring in which a precious diamond was cast, and gave it to the Count of Sussex, so that he could give it to the queen. He was hanged and drawn and quartered on August 8, 1570, and as his daughter Frances testifies, while

---

Sacerdozio e regno da Gregorio VII a Bonifacio VIII, Pontifical Gregorian University, Rome, 1954, pp. 1–26; Othmar Hageneder, *Il potere di deposizione del principe: i fondamenti canonistici*, in *Il sole e la luna. Papato, Impero e regni nella teoria e nella prassi dei secoli XII e XIII*, Italian translation, Vita e Pensiero, Milan, 2000, pp. 165–211.

656 Joannes B. Lo Grasso, S.J., *Ecclesia et Status. Fontes selecti iuris publici ecclesiastici*, Pontifical Gregorian University, Rome, 1952, pp. 250–254.

657 A. Ottaviani, *Institutiones Iuris Publici Ecclesiastici*; Felice Cappello, S.J., *Summa Iuris pubblici Ecclesiastici*, editio sexta, Apud Aedes Universitatis Gregoriana, Rome, 1954.

658 John Felton was beatified by Leo XIII on December 29, 1886. See J. F. Pollen, *Acts of English Martyrs*, Burns and Oates, London, 1905, pp. 209–212. His son Thomas became a priest and underwent the same torture in 1588.

the executioner was already holding his heart, which had been torn from his chest, he was still heard to invoke twice the name of Jesus.[659]

His martyrdom was followed by that of John Storey,[660] an elderly jurist who was a member of Parliament in the final years of Henry VIII. Storey had returned to England under Mary Tudor, and after her death had taken refuge in Flanders, where he had taken Spanish citizenship, placing himself under the protection of Philip II. In the summer of 1570, he was lured into a trap onboard an English vessel, chained, and taken to London, where he was held in the Tower prison and sentenced to death. The Spanish ambassador interceded for him to Philip II, but Elizabeth replied with mocking ferocity: "If the King of Spain wants his head, I will send it to him voluntarily, but Storey's body must remain in England."[661] On May 26, 1571, he was quartered at Tyburn, where today the Marble Arch rises in the center of London.

Storey's torture was similar to that of Felton and many Catholics who were "hanged, drawn and quartered" at Tyburn. The condemned person was led on a cart to the place of execution, stripped naked, with his hands bound, and hung in such a way that his neck would not break. Before death came, the condemned was taken to the quartering table and hideously mutilated, while still living and conscious. The torture began with the total castration of the condemned man. While the assistants held his legs and arms still, the executioner tied a tight rope around the base of the testicles of the one being tortured and using a very sharp blade, severed them completely at their root in the body. After having torn off the genitals, the executioner cut open the belly, extracting the intestines, which

[659] Celestino Testore, *Felton Giovanni*, in BSS, vol. 10 (1991), cols. 614–615.

[660] John Storey (1504–1571) was professor of law at Oxford. First arrested from 1548 to 1549, he took refuge at Louvain, but upon Mary Tudor's return to England, he was appointed chancellor of the diocese of Oxford and London. He was arrested again at the beginning of the reign of Elizabeth and managed to escape again, taking refuge once more at Louvain. He was beatified by Leo XIII in 1886. See Niccolò Del Re, *Storey*, in BSS, vol. 12 (1990), cols. 36–38.

[661] Sala, *Elisabetta la sanguinaria*, pp. 113–114.

he placed in a box. The executioner was careful not to damage the vital organs, so that the condemned man remained alive until the end of the torture. Near the dismembering table there was a brazier where every piece of the organs was placed to be burned before the eyes of the tortured one. When the entrails were completely torn from the one being tortured while he was still alive, the executioner cut off his head and finally proceeded to the dismemberment of the body. With an axe he divided it into four parts, first cutting it vertically and then horizontally. The four quarters of the body were hung in different corners of the city. Thus died many English Catholic martyrs under Elizabeth the Bloody.[662]

10. The Last Attempts at Catholic Rebellion

When the northern rebellion failed, Pius V convinced himself of the necessity of a foreign intervention to remove Elizabeth and place Mary Stuart on the throne. Writing to the pope on September 1, 1570, Ridolfi proposed the idea that the Duke of Alba, commander of the Spanish army in the Netherlands, would invade England in support of a new Catholic rebellion. Elizabeth I was to be killed, perhaps by the daring Gian Luigi Vitelli,[663] sent to London by the Duke of Alba to negotiate with the queen for the restitution of several Spanish ships that had to take refuge in English ports because of a storm.

On March 25, 1571, Ridolfi left England and met the Duke of Alba in Brussels, who however received him coldly; then he went to Rome,

[662] See JOHN H. CHAPMAN, *The Persecution under Elizabeth*, in "Transactions of the Royal Historical Society," vol. 9 (1881) pp. 21–43; RAFAEL E. TARRAGO, *Bloody Bess: The Persecution of Catholics in Elizabethan England*, in "Logos: A Journal of Catholic Thought and Culture," vol. 7, 1 (Winter 2004), pp. 117–133; SALA, *Elisabetta la sanguinaria, passim*.

[663] The text of the letter of Ridolfi to Pius V, in POLLEN, *The English Catholics*, pp. 162–163. Gian Luigi Vitelli (1519–1575), better known as Chiappino Vitelli, was not a "mercenary" as some English historians define him, but one of the best Italian generals of his time, in the service of Cosimo I de' Medici, who appointed him marquis of Cetona and grand constable of the Order of St. Stephen. He participated in the war in Flanders alongside the Duke of Alba, who esteemed him for his valor.

where he explained his plan to Pius V. The pope gave his support to the initiative, and on May 5, 1571, he gave Ridolfi a letter for Philip II,[664] in which he invited the Spanish sovereign to provide the necessary means for the execution of the enterprise. Pius V was enthusiastic for the project but, as he wrote to Mary Stuart, he left its implementation to the prudence of the Spanish sovereign.[665] At the end of June, Ridolfi went to Madrid, where he found a supporter for his plans in the nuncio Castagna, who had insistently called for Philip's intervention in English matters. The Spanish sovereign also seemed enthusiastic about the plan, but left the last word to the Duke of Alba, who was instead skeptical about the undertaking. On August 29, 1571, Alba wrote to Philip II that the plans made by Ridolfi, who had no military experience whatsoever, seemed impossible to him: "Wherefore, Sir, in the case of men of such little balance as those who treat these topics, and have such little comprehension of what is practicable, nothing at all should be risked upon their words; but only on their deeds, when their part is actually executed."[666] The Duke of Alba, who was always more pragmatic, had written to Philip II on December 5, 1569, making a sarcastic point, that the pope "was so zealous that he thought everything could be accomplished without using ordinary human means."[667] This observation could be turned around to mean that the Duke of Alba was so pragmatic that he thought that everything could be accomplished without using supernatural means. Less than two years later, the Battle of Lepanto would demonstrate the results of the supernatural zeal of Pius V.

However, the decisive help of the king of Spain, which the pope and Ridolfi counted on, failed. The bishop of Ross, Leslie, was arrested

664 Text of the letter of Pius V to Philip II in J. I. TELLECHEA IDÍGORAS, *El papado y Felipe II: colección de breves pontificios*, Fundación Universitaria Española, Madrid, 1999, vol. 1, pp. 243–244.

665 PASTOR, *Storia dei Papi*, vol. VIII, p. 425.

666 Letter of the Duke of Alba to Philip II of August 29, 1571, in POLLEN, *The English Catholics*, p. 164.

667 See *Coleccion de Documentos Ineditos para la Historia de Espana*, edited by Fernandez Navarrete, La Viuda de Calero, Madrid, 1844, vol. 4, p. 519.

and admitted the existence of the conspiracy, revealing the details. The Spanish ambassador was expelled, and Ridolfi, who was in Italy, never set foot in England again. The Duke of Norfolk, arrested at the beginning of September 1571, was tried for high treason and beheaded on June 2, 1572, without obtaining martyrdom because he proclaimed himself a Protestant.

The insurgency failed, but under Pius V the great movement of Catholic rebirth in England began, sealed by the blood of hundreds of martyrs.[668] Among these was Mary Stuart, publicly beheaded by order of Elizabeth I on February 8, 1584. Before her execution, the queen of Scotland knelt down and offered a final, fervent prayer to Heaven, declaring that she firmly hoped for the salvation of her soul through the merits of Jesus Christ, for whom she was ready to shed her blood.

Pius VI proclaimed the martyrdom of Mary Stuart, recalling what Benedict XIV wrote in the third book of the *Beatificazione dei Servi di Dio*:

> If we examine the true cause of her death, which is summed up in hatred of the Catholic religion which she alone, the only survivor, professed in England; if we examine the invincible constancy with which she rejected the proposals to abjure the Catholic religion; if we observe the admirable strength with which she underwent her death; if we take into account, as we should, that she protested prior to her beheading, and at the moment of execution itself, that she had always lived as a Catholic and that she died willingly for the Catholic faith; if we do not omit, as ought not to be omitted, the very evident reasons from which emerge not only the falsity of the crimes attributed to Queen Mary by her opponents, but also the unjust sentence of death, based on slanders inspired by hatred against the Catholic Religion, so that the heretical dogmas would remain immutable in the kingdom of England; then we will understand that none of the necessary conditions are lacking to affirm that hers was a true martyrdom.[669]

668 Pollen, *The English Catholics*, pp. 244–289.

669 Pius VI, Allocution *Quare Lacrimae* of June 17, 1793, in *Bullarii Romani Continuatio*, vol. 6, part 3, Tipografia Aldina, Prato, 1849, pp. 2627–2637.

Helped by the pope and Philip II, William Allen,[670] the future cardinal, founded a college at Douai in 1568 where priests were prepared for trials and martyrdom and were secretly introduced into England to carry out a daring apostolate.[671] The bull of excommunication of Elizabeth I, criticized by "political" Catholics, constituted the foundation and presupposition of this missionary epic and represents one of the high points of the pontificate of St. Pius V. On April 17, 1580, two of these priests, Frs. Edmund Campion and Robert Parsons, along with thirteen students of the English College, departed and went to labor for the conversion of their homeland. Entering England was like pronouncing their own death sentence, but this was the price to pay to prevent the Catholic Faith from dying out in their native country.[672]

670 William Allen (1532–1594) founded the seminary at Douai and the English College in Rome. He was created cardinal on August 7, 1587. In 1588, before the "Invincible Armada" of Philip II set sail, he issued a proclamation to the nobility and the English and Irish people calling on them to support Philip II's attempt. See *The Letters and Memorials of William Cardinal Allen*, edited by the Fathers of the Congregation of the London Oratory, with a historical introduction by Thomas Francis Knox, Nutt, London, 1882; and J. CONSTANT, in DHGE, vol. 2, cols. 599–607, with ample bibliography.

671 By the end of 1610, 135 of them had already shed their blood for the Faith, and the news of their deaths was received at Douai with the celebration of a solemn Mass. See C. TESTORE, S.J., *Il primato spirituale di Pietro difeso dal sangue dei martiri inglesi*, Tip. Macioce & Pisani, Isola del Liri, 1929.

672 Gregory XIII wanted to facilitate the task of Frs. Edmund Campion (1540–1581) and Robert Persons (1546–1610), later known as Robert Parsons, and gave the two Jesuits the faculty to permit English Catholics to recognize Elizabeth as their queen "under present circumstances" (MARY H. ALLIES, *History of the Church in England from the Accession of Henry VIII to the Death of Queen Elizabeth*, Burns & Oates, London, 1895, p. 205). Edmund Campion, together with Frs. Ralph Sherwin and Alexander Briant, was hanged, drawn, and quartered at Tyburn on December 1, 1581. The three Jesuits are among the *Forty Martyrs of England and Wales*, canonized on October 25, 1970, by Pope Paul VI.

6

The Victor of Lepanto

1. Islam against Christianity

In addition to the fight against heresy, the defense of Christianity against the Turks constituted a dominant theme of the pontificate of Pius V. In the second half of the sixteenth century, Islam had reached the apex of its expansion from the Red Sea to Gibraltar, from Baghdad to Budapest, reaching the gates of Vienna. The architect of this expansion was Suleiman I,[673] called "the Magnificent," who throughout his forty-five-year reign threatened the capital of the empire and thus all of Europe. The Italian coasts were devastated by the raids of Barbary pirates, who sought women for the harems of the viziers and men to sell as slaves or to be enlisted in the Janissaries, the elite private army of the sultan.[674] The

[673] Suleiman I (1494–1566), called "the Magnificent" or *Kanuni*, or "the Lawmaker," was sultan of the Ottoman Empire from 1520 until his death. Among the numerous works on the Ottoman Empire, see JUSTIN MCCARTIS, *The Ottoman Turks: An Introductory History to 1923*, Longman, New York, 1997; LORD PATRICK KINROSS, *The Ottoman Centuries: The Rise and Fall of the Turkish Empire*, Perennial, New York, 2002 (1977); DANIEL GOFFMAN, *The Ottoman Empire and Early Modern Europe*, Cambridge University Press, Cambridge, 2007 (2002).

[674] See SALVATORE BONO, *I corsari barbareschi*, ERI, Turin, 1964; and JACQUES HEERS, *Les Barbaresques: La course et la guerre en Méditerranée, XIVe–XVIe siècle*, Perrin, Paris, 2001. The Janissaries were a chosen militia, composed above all of Christian children taken from their families and forcefully

statement of the historian Jason Goodwin, who wrote that the Ottoman Empire "lived for war," is not false.[675] From its foundation to its fall, it was a state dedicated to expanding the Islamic faith by means of arms.[676]

The ultimate objective of the Turkish conquests was called the "Red Apple" (*Kizil-Elma*). This was the name given to the golden globe surmounted by the cross that stood atop the statue of the emperor in Constantinople. After the conquest of Constantinople in 1453, the sultan looked further west to Rome, the heart of Christianity and the most-prized "Red Apple," symbol of Islam's final and ultimate triumph over Christianity.[677] Pius V was aware of this.

Suleiman's plans for expansion found an obstacle in the island of Malta, in the heart of the Mediterranean, the stronghold of the Order of Hospitallers of St. John, later called the Knights of Malta.[678] "If you will not decide to take it quickly," one of his advisers wrote, "it will in a short time interrupt all communications between Africa and Asia and the Islands of the Archipelago."[679]

---

converted to Islam, of which they became fanatical adherents. The militia was formed during the reign of Murad I (1362–1389) and dissolved in 1826. See DAVID NICOLLE, *The Janissaries*, Osprey Publishing, London, 1995.

[675] JASON GOODWIN, *Lords of the Horizons: A History of the Ottoman Empire*, Vintage, London, 1998, p. 65.

[676] BERNARD LEWIS, *The Emergence of Modern Turkey*, Oxford University Press, New York, 2002 (1961), p. 13.

[677] See MASSIMO VIGLIONE, *La conquista della "Mela d'oro." Islam ottomano e Cristianità tra guerre di religione, politica e interessi commerciali (1299–1739)*, Solfanelli, Chieti, 2018.

[678] Among the vast literature on the history of the Order of Malta, see JONATHAN RILEY-SMITH, *Hospitallers: The History of the Order of St. John*, The Hambledon Press, London, 1999; ERNLE BRADFORD, *The Shield and the Sword: The Knights of St. John*, Penguin Books, London, 2002 (1973).

[679] E. BRADFORD, *The Great Siege: Malta 1965*, Penguin Books, London, 1964 (1961), p. 14. The same author published a diary of an arquebusier who fought in Malta: Francesco Balbi di Correggio (1505–1589) in *The Siege of Malta 1565*, Penguin Books, London, 2003 (1965). On the siege of Malta, see also ANNE BROGINI, *1565. Malte dans la tourmente. Le grand siege de l'île par le turcs*, Bouchène, Saint-Denis, 2011.

Malta was not only a strategic objective but also had great symbolic importance, because of the presence on the island of a handful of monk-knights who, in addition to the three traditional vows, took a fourth vow of fidelity to the insignia of Holy Religion, even to the shedding of their blood.

The Order of Knights of St. John had played a decisive role in all of the military events that concerned the life of Christendom, even after the fall of the Latin Kingdom of Jerusalem.[680] After a brief sojourn in Cyprus, the Knights of St. John settled on the island of Rhodes until, in 1533, it too was forced to succumb to the imposing forces of Suleiman. Charles V gave the knights the island of Malta, and in its new seat the order solidified its role as the "maritime police" of the Mediterranean.[681] Jonathan Riley-Smith, the historian of the English crusades, observes how in the five centuries between the fall of St. John of Acre in 1291 and the Napoleonic occupation of Malta in 1798, the knights played an important role on the sea in almost all of the principal campaigns against the Turks.[682] Suleiman decided to prepare an expedition to attack them at their base.

In 1565, the grand master of the order was Jean Parisot de La Valette,[683] whose forefathers had participated in the Crusades with St. Louis. At the end of March that year, he received news that the Ottoman fleet,

[680] On the persistence of warrior activity by the Knights of Rhodes (later of Malta) after the fall of Acre, see JOSEPH MARIE ANTOINE DELAVILLE LE ROULX, *Les Hospitaliers à Rodhes jusqu'à la mort de Philibert de Naillac (1310–1421)*, Leroux, Paris, 1913; ELISABETH W. SCHERMERHORN, *Malta of the Knights*, AMS Press, New York, 1978 (1929).

[681] See ETTORE ROSSI, *Storia della marina dell'Ordine militare di San Giovanni di Gerusalemme, di Rodi e di Malta*, Società Editrice d'Arte, Milan, 1936; UBALDINO MORI UBALDINI, *La Marina del Sovrano Militare Ordine di S. Giovanni di Gerusalemme, di Rodi, di Malta*, Regionale Editrice, Rome, 1971.

[682] J. RILEY-SMITH, *Breve storia delle Crociate*, Oscar Mondadori, Milan, 1994, p. 326.

[683] Jean "Parisot" de Valette (1495–1568) was the forty-ninth grand master of the Knights of the Order of Malta from August 21, 1557, until his death in 1568 while he was directing the reconstruction of the city. On the

composed of 180 boats, including 103 galleys, had left the port of the Golden Horn at Constantinople and were headed toward the island of Malta. The grand master ordered the elderly, women, and children to embark for Sicily, and he recalled all the knights who at that moment were in Europe to return to Malta. The only ones who remained on Malta were those ready to fight to the bitter end. La Valette had only seven hundred knights at his disposal, but they were perfectly equipped and above all they were animated by an extraordinary fighting spirit. On May 18, 1565, the day on which the imposing Turkish fleet was first seen on the horizon, he gathered his knights and said to them: "We must defend our faith, in order to prevent the Koran from supplanting the Gospels. God asks our life of us, which we have already vowed to his service. Blessed are those who are the first to consume the sacrifice."[684]

The fortress of St. Elmo was the first goal of the Turks. It took thirty-one days of siege before they managed to break into the fortress, where the few surviving knights were slaughtered. La Valette, in the other fort of Sant'Angelo, brilliantly defending the bastion island with his greatly outnumbered forces and dwindling supplies, waited in vain for the rescue of relief forces, but the galleys of Philip II had still not yet arrived when on August 7 the Turks attacked the castle. The knights' resistance was so indomitable that that when the Spanish galleys did finally arrive, the Turks, exhausted by the loss of over thirty thousand men, had already decided to abandon the island. It was September 12, 1565. Two hundred fifty Knights of Malta had died in the siege and almost all of the rest were incapacitated from their wounds, but Suleiman had been defeated. La Valette, disappointed by the lack of help from the Christian princes, thought of abandoning the island, but Pius V, who had only been reigning for two months, wrote him on March 22, 1566, and ordered him to remain on Malta:

---

siege of Malta, see Bradford, *The Great Siege*; Roger Crowley, *Empires of the Sea*, Random House, New York, 2008, pp. 85–190.

684 Jack Beeching, *La battaglia di Lepanto*, Italian translation, Rusconi, Milan, 1989, p. 92.

> Do you not understand that your departure would immediately cause the ruin of the island, and Sicily, Italy, and all the Christian nations would encounter even greater dangers?... Without mentioning that you would compromise your reputation, don't you think the destiny of your Order is at stake? And how can it be believed, that, whichever of the Knights of Malta would go forward with the idea of no longer obeying anything but their own will, that you could one day call them to be docile to your commands?... You need, dear son, to stand firm at your post!... We will not abandon you; even less will God abandon you.[685]

Consistent with this commitment, the pope sent 15,000 ducats to Malta and sent the architect Francesco Laparelli to direct the reconstruction of the city. On March 28, 1566, amidst the greatest enthusiasm, the grand master laid the first stone of the new capital of Malta, which, in his honor, was called "*humilissima civitas Valettae*," today La Valletta. Pius V offered La Valette the cardinal's hat, but the grand master tactfully and humbly refused the honor.

Meanwhile, the pontiff began to put pressure on Philip II, to convince him to organize an expedition against the Turks. With a bull of March 9, 1566,[686] addressed to all of Christendom, Pius V described the threat of Islam with heartfelt words and decreed a jubilee indulgence for the defense of the *Respublica Christiana*. Then, in the consistory of April 2, he announced that he intended to use all his strength for the protection of Christendom.[687] On July 21 the jubilee was announced for the success of the war against the Turks, and eight days later, on July 28, the pope personally took part in the first procession that was done in Rome to drive away the danger of Islam. On July 31 the second procession took place, and the third on August 2, with the participation of forty thousand

[685] Grente, *Il Pontefice delle grandi battaglie*, p. 146; *Epistolae ad principes*, nn. 3347–3348.

[686] Bull *Cum gravissima*, in *Bullarium Romanum*, vol. 7, p. 431.

[687] Pastor, *Storia dei Papi*, vol. 8, pp. 512–513.

people. At the end of the year Pius V instituted a commission of cardinals to examine the possibility of a great military coalition against the Turks.

2. The New Sultan Selim II

In the same year 1566, Suleiman had reopened the conflict with the Austrian empire on the western border of his empire. The sultan, assisted by the grand vizier, Sokollu Mehmet Pascià,[688] advanced toward Budapest, but he wanted to divert to destroy the imperial stronghold of Szigetvár, from where Count Nikola Šubić Zrinski[689] challenged the Muslims with his forays into their camps. Suleiman surrounded the fortress, which was defended by 2,300 Croatians, with his army of 90,000 men and 300 cannons. The siege of Szigetvár lasted from August 5 to September 8, 1566, when the count, holding up his sword inlaid with gold, exhorted the six hundred surviving men to make the last sortie with him and to die in combat rather than surrender: "With this sword," he said, "I have reaped my first honor and first glory, and I wish to present myself again with it before the eternal throne to hear my sentence."[690] Then the defenders of the fortress opened the great gate and with a large mortar fired all their shot against the mass of Turks who crowded around the castle. Then Count Zriny led the final charge at the head of his men. The count, who had attacked without helmet or armor so as to be on the same level

[688] Mehmet Pascià (ca. 1506–1579) was the son of a Serbian Orthodox priest named Sokolovic, from whom came the name Sokollu by which he was known. After being kidnapped in his village in 1516, he abjured his religion to pass to Islam. He was grand vizier under three sultans and opposed Selim's decision to make war on Venice.

[689] Count Nikola Šubić Zrinski (1508–1566), of ancient Croatian nobility, after distinguishing himself during the first siege of Vienna in 1529, saved the imperial army in 1542 at Pest, attacking the enemy with four hundred Croats. He was *bano* of Croatia and Slavonia (1542–1557) and commander of the square of Szigetvár. He is considered a national hero of Croatia and Hungary. See KENNETH MEYER SETTON, *The Papacy and the Levant, 1204–1571*, vol. 4, The Sixteenth Century from Julius III to Pius V, The American Philosophical Society, Philadelphia, 1984, pp. 845–846; and BEECHING, *La battaglia di Lepanto*, pp. 162–166.

[690] BEECHING, *La battaglia di Lepanto*, p. 165.

as the last of his soldiers, was struck by two musket shots in the chest and killed shortly after by an arrow in the head. All the defenders of the fortress were massacred. Suleiman, however, did not have the satisfaction of seeing Szigetvár capitulate: two days prior to the final assault he died in his tent of dysentery. Grand Vizier Sokollu hid the death of the sultan from the Turkish soldiers, killed those who had witnessed it, and sent a messenger to Suleiman's son, Prince Selim, to tell him to hurry up and reach Belgrade, where the army would recognize him as the new sultan.

Selim II,[691] known to history as *Sarhoş* (the drunkard), was the son of Suleiman and a slave of the harem. He was "very ugly looking, having ruined and roasted his face both from excessive wine and from the large amount of brandy he used to drink to digest."[692] He listened to his advisers, however, and when Sokollu suggested to him to renounce the conflict with Emperor Maximilian, the sultan signed the Treaty of Adrianople on February 17, 1568, which essentially ended the Habsburg-Ottoman conflict by doing nothing.

Selim's shadow-man was, however, the rich and powerful Portuguese Jew, Josef Nassì,[693] driven by deep hatred of Philip II and the Republic of

[691] Selim II (1524–1574), the son of Suleiman and a slave of his harem, was sultan of the Ottoman Empire from 1566 until his death. From the time of Mahomet II every son that the sultan had with one of his concubines was in mortal danger. Only one of the sons born from the harem could survive and become the sultan; the others had to be killed. See Leslie P. Peirce, *The Imperial Harem: Women and Sovereignty in the Ottoman Empire*, Oxford University Press, Oxford, 1993.

[692] Andrea Badoero, *Relazione al Senato veneziano del 1573*, in *Relazioni degli ambasciatori veneti*, series 3, vol. 1, pp. 360–361.

[693] João Miguez (alias Josef Nassi, or Giuseppe Micas), was a Castilian Marrano who had been banished from Venice in 1555 and took refuge in Constantinople, returning to the Jewish religion. A precursor of Zionism, he cherished the dream of giving a homeland to the Jews. He had received the fief of the island of Naxos in the Cyclades from Sultan Selim. See Paul Grunebaum-Ballin, *Joseph Naci, Duc de Naxos*, Mouton, Paris, 1968; Anna Levi, Cecil Roth, *Joseph Nassì, duca di Nasso, e i Savoia*, "La Rassegna Mensile di Israel," 34, 8 (August 1968), pp. 464–474; Paolo Preto, *La guerra segreta: spionaggio, sabotaggi, attentati in Venezia e la difesa*

Venice, who pushed the sultan to conquer all of the islands of the Aegean, and thus draw his foes to battle. The war was destined to shift to the sea.

3. Philip II and the Revolt of the Moriscos

At that moment Philip II was enduring one of the most difficult moments of his reign. In addition to the rebellion in Flanders, there was the rebellion of the Moriscos,[694] the Iberian Muslims who had feigned to renounce their religion after the fall of Granada in 1492. They remained faithful to the Koran, raised their children in their religious faith, and harbored a profound aversion against the Christian conquerors. The majority of them were not Arabs but Berbers, inhabitants of North Africa, called Moors in Europe. In the provinces where the Moors lived, such as Andalusia, there was also a significant relaxation of Christian customs as a result of the influence of the sensual habits of Islam. Philip II issued a decree that obliged the Moors to learn the Castilian language within three years, to dress as Christians, permitting their women to go out with uncovered faces, to abandon their Muslim names and surnames to take Christian ones, and to have their children educated exclusively by Catholic priests. These measures provoked rebellion in southern Spain.

On Christmas Day 1568, the revolt exploded in the former Kingdom of Granada, with uprisings in many of the communities of Moriscos. The rebels repudiated Christianity and chose their king, the caliph of Cordova, Hernando de Cordoba y Valor, who returned to his Islamic name of Abu Humeya and took possession of several of the small ports of southern Spain, from which they made political and military ties with

---

del Levante. Da Lepanto a Candia, Arsenale, Venice, 1986, pp. 101–102; CECIL ROTH, *The Duke of Naxos of the House of Nasi*, The Jewish Publication Society, Philadelphia, 1992.

[694] See JULIO CARO BAROJA, *Los Moriscos del Reino de Granada*, Instituto de estudios politicos, Madrid, 1957; BERNARD VINCENT, *La guerre des Alpujarras et l'Islam méditerranéen*, in *Felipe II y el mediterráneo*, edited by Ernest Belenguer Cebria, vol. 4, *La monarquía y los reinos*, Sociedad Estatal para la Conmemoración de los Centenarios de Felipe II y Carlos V, Madrid, 1999, pp. 267–276.

the Islamic states of North Africa. The Moriscos did not succeed in conquering the city of Granada and concentrated on the mountains of Alpujarras, where they sustained a bloody guerilla war. Captured priests were mutilated or burned alive, and women were sent to be slaves in the harem. The rebels awaited the help of the sultan, and the Christians waited for the help of Philip II, but at that moment Selim was aiming for the conquest of Cyprus rather than a return to Andalusia, while the king of Spain found himself deprived of his best soldiers because of the revolt in the Netherlands. Several months passed until Philip, ever more worried, entrusted the task of quelling the revolt to his stepbrother, Don Juan of Austria,[695] who was twenty-three years old and desirous of glory. In April he reached Granada with an army of Spanish troops and Italian veterans. Don Juan had received orders from Philip not to expose himself, but the young prince replied to him: "I know that Your Majesty's interests require that the soldiers, if called to fight or to any other undertaking, should see me at their head."[696]

It took almost a year to put down the revolt. At the end of January 1570, Don Juan personally led the attack against the rebels barricaded in the fortress of Galera, which fell on February 15 after nine hours of bloody combat. The city was then razed to the ground and sprinkled with salt. Philip II then ordered the dispersion of eighty thousand Moriscos in Granada to other areas of Spain. Profiting from the situation, the new

[695] John or Don Juan of Austria (1547–1578), the natural son of Emperor Charles V and Barbara Blomberg, was recognized by Philip II as his stepbrother. After the victory of Lepanto, the king named him vicar general in Italy (1574) and governor of the Netherlands (1576). C. Petrie, *Don John of Austria*, Norton, New York, 1967; Eugenio Sotillos, *Juan de Austria: el vencedor de Lepanto*, Torray, Barcelona, 1978; B. Bennassar, *Don Juan de Austria un héroe para un imperio*, Temas de Hoy, Madrid, 2000. See also P. O. de Törne, *Don Juan d'Autriche et les projets de conquête de l'Angleterre. Étude historique sur dix années du xvie siècle, 1568-1578*, 2 vols., Helsingfors Bokhandel, Helsinki, 1915, 1928; and the novel by Louis de Wohl, *The Last Crusader: A Novel about Don Juan of Austria*, Ignatius Press, San Francisco, 2010 (1957).

[696] Beeching, *La battaglia di Lepanto*, p. 134.

bey of Algeria, a renegade corsair known as Occhialì,[697] conquered Tunis, which Charles V had taken from Islam, and made it a new base for his raids in the Mediterranean.

4. Venice Threatened by the Turks

The Arsenal of Venice, which occupied an area of almost twenty-four hectares, was the heart of the military power of Venice.[698] One hundred blacksmiths worked there incessantly, while four hundred women wove the sails of the galleys. A permanent order established that at the first alarm eighty-five galleys were put into the sea, one after the other, ready for combat.[699] The ordinary galley was a boat forty-one meters long and five or six meters wide, with two lateen sails. Its principal propulsive force was the rowers, who sat on twenty-four or twenty-six benches on each side of the ship. With full sails the galley reached a maximum speed of nine or ten knots. In the shipyards of the Arsenal the construction of a new type of ship had begun: the galeazza, which was bigger than the standard galley, about fifty meters long, equipped with thirty-six guns installed mainly along the sides of the ship. They would make their first appearance, and play a decisive role, in the Battle of Lepanto.

[697] Giovan Dionigi Galeni (1519–1587), born in Le Castella in Calabria, renounced the Christian faith and took the Turkish name Uluç Alì, which was probably the origin of the nickname Occhialì, or Uccialì, by which the Christians knew him. He was the only Turkish commander at the Battle of Lepanto to survive the fight, and in 1574 he again conquered Tunisia. See GINO BENZONI, *Galeni*, in DBI, vol. 51 (1998), pp. 409–415; BARTOLOMÉ e LUCILE BENNASSAR, *I cristiani di Allah*, Italian translation, Rizzoli, Milan, 1991, pp. 359ff.

[698] See ENNIO CONCINA, *L' Arsenale della Repubblica di Venezia; tecniche e istituzioni dal medioevo all'età moderna*, Electa, Milan, 1984; and GIOVANNI BATTISTA RUBIN DE CERVIN, *La flotta di Venezia: Navi e barche della Serenissima*, Automobilia, Milan, 1985. On the "technology" of the Venetian Republic, see also NICCOLÒ CAPPONI, *Lepanto 1571. La lega santa contro l'Impero ottomano*, Italian translation, Il Saggiatore, Milan, 2008, pp. 162–190.

[699] BEECHING, *La battaglia di Lepanto*, p. 134. See also JOHN FRANCIS GUILMARTIN JR., *Galleons and Galleys*, Cassel, London, 2002.

On the night of September 13–14, 1569, a tremendous roar shook Venice when the gigantic ammunition depot of the Arsenal blew up. The Senate of the Republic attributed responsibility to saboteurs hired by Nassi, the sworn enemy of the Venetian Republic.[700] What is certain is that Nassi personally brought the news to the sultan, explaining to him that the damage had greatly weakened Venice's military capacity. Selim II decided to break the peace that had been made with Venice in 1540, claiming alleged rights on the island of Cyprus,[701] a Venetian colony that was of great importance from a strategic and commercial point of view. At the time it was held by the Republic of Venice, and along with Malta it was the one Christian enclave in a predominantly Ottoman sea.

The authorities of the Serenissima were faced with a dilemma: either to abandon the island of Cyprus or else to challenge the Ottoman power, renouncing the policy of conciliation toward the Turks that Venice had adopted in recent decades. If they chose the latter, the Venetians would need help to confront the Turkish power, but their relations with Spain, the only other naval power of the Mediterranean, were tense because of their rivalry as great maritime powers. They could only count on the support of Pope Pius V.

From the time of his election, Pius V said that he was convinced that no Christian power could face the clash with the Ottoman Empire

[700] ALVISE ZORZI, *La Repubblica del Leone. Storia di Venezia*, Rusconi, Milan, 1979, p. 343.

[701] The best-documented history of the siege of Cyprus is that of GUIDO ANTONIO QUARTI, *La guerra contro il Turco a Cipro e a Lepanto: 1570-1571: storia documentata*, Bellini, Venice, 1935. See also JURIEN DE LA GRAVIÈRE, *La Guerre de Chypre et la bataille de Lépante*, Plon, Paris, 1887; KENNETH MEYER SETTON, *The Papacy and the Levant, 1204–1571*, vol. 4; VERA COSTANTINI, *Il sultano e l'isola contesa. Cipro tra eredità veneziana e potere ottomano*, UTET, Turin, 2009; and the collective volumes *Il Mediterraneo nella seconda metà del '500 alla luce di Lepanto*, edited by G. Benzoni, Leo S. Olschki, Florence, 1974; *Venezia e la difesa del Levante: da Lepanto a Candia 1570–1670*, edited by Maddalena Redolfi, Arsenale, Venice, 1986.

alone, but that, on the contrary, a global alliance was necessary.[702] The pope had explicitly requested of Philip II, by means of a brief of July 15, 1567, the active participation of the Kingdom of Spain in the defense of Christendom, emphasizing how Turkish expansionism threatened not only Venice but also the Spanish kingdoms of Naples and Sicily.

On February 27, 1570, Pius V had gathered the cardinals in consistory to examine the possibility of helping Venice, including on the military level. Cardinal Granvelle, the emissary in Rome on behalf of Philip II, spoke against giving such help, imploring the pope and the college of cardinals not to throw the Church into such a dangerous enterprise.[703] In his opinion, the treacherous Republic of St. Mark did not deserve help, and it could be helped later after its pride had been humiliated. In His judgment God had exposed that proud power to the invasion of the infidels to punish it for its selfishness and to convince Venice that even she herself could be reduced to humility, imploring help and protection. However, Granvelle's declaration was opposed decisively by Cardinal Commendone. He recalled the merits of Venice toward Christendom and the Holy See and sought to defend the Serenissima from accusations of infidelity and selfishness. His argument was approved by the pope: what was at stake was not only the interests of Venice but the interests of all of Italy and indeed all of Christendom. The majority of cardinals also expressed themselves in favor of this view.

On March 6, 1570, Pius V entrusted the cleric of the Apostolic Camera, Luys de Torres,[704] with an extraordinary nunciature to the courts of Spain and Portugal, with the principal task of negotiating the establish-

[702] Maurizio Gattoni, *Pio V e la politica iberica dello stato pontificio (1566–1572)*, Studium, Rome, 2006, pp. 86–87.

[703] Pastor, *Storia dei Papi*, vol. 8, p. 522.

[704] Luys de Torres (1533–1584) was originally from Malaga. After the mission given him by Pius V, in 1573 he was appointed archbishop of Monreale by Gregory XIII. See Pietro Messina, *De Torres, Ludovico*, in DBI, vol. 39 (1991), pp. 478–483; Alonso Dragonetti de Torres, *La Lega di Lepanto nel carteggio inedito di don Luys de Torres, nunzio straordinario di S. Pio V a Filippo II*, Fratelli Bocca, Turin, 1931.

ment of a league against the Turks between the Holy See, Spain, and Venice. In a bold stroke of statecraft, and seeking to find common ground in Spain and Venice's complex rivalry, Pius V implored the king to entrust the negotiations to him personally and send to Rome a person endowed with full powers for the conclusion of the treaty, which was to be drawn up with the maximum justice so that no one could feel harmed. On March 8, 1570, the pope wrote a vibrant letter[705] to Philip II that was a true manifesto and that deserves to be quoted extensively:

> God, who never leaves guilt unpunished, seeing that instead of appeasing his anger we irritate him every day with new offenses, is sending us new causes of affliction. Selim II, succeeding his father Emperor Suleiman in hatred as well as on the throne, is preparing to wage a bloody war against Christians. He has already launched a powerful fleet and raised numerous troops of infantry and cavalry.... Have we therefore been preserved in this world only to be spectators of such a bloody tragedy? Are we to witness the evils that oppress Christendom without bringing it any remedy? But what could we do alone, as our forces are so unequal and unable to oppose such powerful enemies? The empire of the Turks has extended itself so much through our cowardice, that they are no longer in a position to oppose their usurpation, unless the Christian princes make considerable efforts and unite together against their common enemy, and oppose them with powerful forces on land and on sea.
>
> At present, in order to repay the duties of our office, we cannot do anything other than follow the counsel of the prophet, that is, God having placed us as his sentinel to keep watch with pastoral attention over the conservation of the Church and of Christians who are his children, we announce to the King and to the peoples of the earth that we already see the sword of divine vengeance. In

[705] Letter *Cum praesentem*, in *Epistolae ad Principes*, n. 4519; FALLOUX, *Histoire de St. Pie V*, vol. 2, pp. 236–243.

> order not to be guilty of the blood of those who perish, we therefore warn you, and from now on we will raise our voice, so that it may be a trumpet that warns Christians of the terrible disasters they are threatened with.

After invoking the God of vengeance, the pope exhorted the king to trust in the God of mercy:

> He will certainly be with us to protect us, if we defend the interests of His Church. Yes, it is in Him and through Him that we fight, and since His hand has not become shortened, we must be certain that He will confound our enemies. Although our sins make us unworthy of His protection, He can be appeased by penance, since He is always willing to receive us if we return to Him with a contrite heart.

At this point the pope addressed Philip II directly, asking him to place the most powerful fleet that he could muster at sea without delay and send it to Sicily.

> The greatness of the danger by which all of Christendom is threatened and the preservation of your own lands must determine you. Recall the promises that you have made in Holy Baptism, think of the obligations that you have towards God and His Church: to God, who created you and redeemed you by the adorable Blood of his Only-Begotten Son and made you sovereign of many kingdoms; of the Church, since Your Majesty's ancestors, sovereigns of happy memory, have often received signal favors from the Holy Apostolic See and the glorious name of Catholic kings. This holy Mother is now immersed in sadness; She weeps, groans, and sighs; She implores your help. If the son does not listen to the prayers of his mother, by whom can she hope to be heard?

On March 28, 1570, Selim sent one of his ambassadors to Venice to give an ultimatum: either surrender the island of Cyprus or suffer war. The conversation between the ambassador and Doge Pietro Loredan lasted only a few minutes. "The Republic will defend herself, trusting in the help of God and in the strength of his weapons," the old doge declared. On Easter Monday, in the Basilica of St. Mark, the standard of battle was given to Girolamo Zane,[706] "general sea captain" of the fleet of the Serenissima. Venice prepared for war.[707] Pius V rejoiced; it would be a great opportunity to achieve his goal: a league of Christian princes against the age-old enemy of the Catholic Faith.[708]

Luys de Torres arrived in Spain in the beginning of April 1570 and met with Philip II while the Spanish council of state pondered the pros and cons of the pope's proposal. Philip seemed disposed to mobilize, but would have preferred to commit himself against the Barbary States of North Africa rather than against the Turks, and he distrusted the Republic of Venice, suspecting that it was acting under the table with the Sublime Porte and that Spain would end up finding itself exposed to Turkish attack. In the meantime Torres left the Spanish court to go to Portugal, where he was supposed to push the Lusitanian Kingdom, which already had a presence on the Atlantic, to also be present in the Mediterranean, participating in the Holy League against the Turks.[709]

5. The Difficulties of Arming a Fleet

Pius V wanted to draw into the war against the Turks not only Spain and Portugal but also France, which, however, balked. The pope wrote to Charles IX, begging him to participate in the Holy League, and he replied to his cold response on June 18 with a very serious letter, in which he warned him that he was on a completely false path and exhorted him

[706] Girolamo Zane, who died in 1572, was general sea captain of the Venetian fleet during the War of Cyprus. When he returned to Venice he was arrested for alleged failures in the management of the fleet during the mission in the east and he died in prison.

[707] See ALESSANDRO BARBERO, *Lepanto. La battaglia dei tre imperi*, Laterza, Rome-Bari, 2010, pp. 85–89.

[708] See LUCIANO SERRANO, *La liga de Lepanto entre España, Venecia y la Santa Sede (1570–1573): ensayo historico a base de documentos diplomaticos*, Editorial Órbigo, Madrid, 1918, p. 31.

[709] GATTONI, *Pio V e la politica iberica dello stato pontificio*, pp. 93–105.

to follow the example that France had given in the time of its glory and greatness.[710] As Pastor observes, Pius V was preaching to the deaf.[711] French diplomacy came to the point of directly opposing the league, attempting to effect a treaty between Venice and the Turks. The historian John Dumont says that "militant Islam had France, the eldest daughter of the Church, for its accomplice."[712]

The pope's attempts to draw Catholic Poland and Eastern Orthodox Russia into the common cause against the Ottomans came to the same end. In this case too, ancient antagonisms between these two powers prevailed. Pius V believed in the possibility of the return of Russia to the Catholic Faith, and also knew that Czar Ivan IV was an enemy of the Lutherans and thus thought he would not be averse to a union with Rome, at least on the military level, to oppose Turkish expansion. The nuncio in Poland, Del Portico, was sent to Moscow with the purpose of drawing the czar into an anti-Turk league, without entering into religious controversies, unless Ivan himself touched on them. Pius V's plan was that the czar would oppose the Turks together with the emperor and the king of Poland and that this attack on land would support the Christian fleet in the Mediterranean.[713]

At the end of May a courier sent from Torres arrived in Rome with the news that Philip II was willing to help Venice immediately and enter negotiations with the league. Philip wrote to the pope that the interests of the Church were superior to his own particular interests, and "seeing the holy purpose and intention by which Your Holiness is moved, because of the great desire I have to satisfy and correspond to what Your Holiness

[710] Lettera *Accepimus Litteras*, in *Epistolae ad Principes*, n. 4624.

[711] PASTOR, *Storia dei Papi*, vol. 8, p. 527.

[712] JEAN DUMONT, *Lépante. L'Histoire étouffé*, Criterion, Paris, 1997, p. 25. According to Dumont, the treaty of the "Capitulations," signed on February 4, 1536, between Francois I and Suleiman, masked a "secret alliance" against Christianity (pp. 30–31). See also CLARENCE DANA ROUILLARD, *The Turk in French History, Thought and Literature (1520–1660)*, Boivin, Paris, 1940; ALBERTO TENENTI, *La Francia, Venezia e la Sacra Lega*, in *Il mediterraneo nella seconda metà del 500*, pp. 393–408.

[713] PASTOR, *Storia dei Papi*, vol. 8, p. 529.

proposes to me, I have resolved to agree and condescend everything that touches this League."[714] The letter was accompanied by ample instructions that conferred on Cardinal Granvelle, Cardinal Pacheco, and Ambassador Zúñiga the power of concluding an immediate alliance.

Pius V felt immense joy and wept with consolation. Within the Senate of Venice, however, there still existed some resistance, but it was defeated by the firmness of the new doge, Alvise Mocenigo, and by the young patricians of the Serenissima. Giovanni Soranzo went to Rome on an extraordinary mission to join Ambassador Michele Surian,[715] while Sebastiano Venier[716] replaced Zane at the command of the Venetian fleet. On June 11, 1570, Pius V appointed Marcantonio Colonna,[717] duke of Paliano and grand constable of the Crown of Naples, as general captain of the papal forces under the forming Holy League. On that day the duke, who was thirty-five, went from his ancient palace in the Piazza Santi Apostoli toward the Vatican, dressed in magnificent armor and

[714] Letter of Philip II to Pius V of May 16, 1570, in CATENA, *Vita del gloriosissimo Papa Pio V*, p. 264 (pp. 263–265).

[715] Michele Surian (1519–1574) was the Venetian ambassador to Rome from 1568 to 1571. See *Relazione di Roma del clariss. Sig. Michel Soriano, tornato ambasciatore da Papa Pio V l'anno 1571*, in STEPHANI BALUZII - JOHANNIS DOMINICI MANSI, *Miscellanea*, vol. 4, Apud Vincentium Junctinium, Lucae, 1764, pp. 168–178.

[716] Sebastiano Venier (1496–1578), podesta of Brescia in 1562 and of Verona in 1566, later procurator of San Marco, was appointed *Capitano General da mar* of the Venetian fleet on December 13, 1570. On June 11, 1577, he was elected doge of the Venetian Republic. See POMPEO MOLMENTI, *Sebastiano Veniero alla battaglia di Lepanto*, Barbera, Florence, 1899.

[717] Marcantonio Colonna (1535–1584), of the ancient Roman family, had been deprived by Paul IV of the Duchy of Paliano, which was attributed to Pope Giovanni Carafa's nephew, but regained possession of the fief under Pius IV. Pius V, with whom he always had good relations, elevated the fiefdom to a principality after the Battle of Lepanto. Philip II appointed Colonna constable and then lieutenant of the Kingdom of Naples and viceroy of Sicily in 1577. See FRANCA PETRUCCI, *Colonna, Marcantonio*, in DBI, vol. 27 (1982), pp. 371–383; ALBERTO GUGLIELMOTTI, *Marcantonio Colonna alla battaglia di Lepanto*, Le Monnier, Florence, 1862; NICOLETTA BAZZANO, *Marco Antonio Colonna*, Salerno Editrice, Rome, 2003.

followed by a procession of nobles and knights. The pope received him in the papal chapel and, after the celebration of Mass, invested him with the insignia of the command of the fleet, entrusting him with the banner he had just blessed, "which was made of red damask with the image of the Crucifix flanked by St. Peter and St. Paul, with the motto *IN HOC SIGNO VINCES*."[718]

Marcantonio Colonna, taking the banner in his hands, swore that he wanted to be the faithful defender of the Roman Church against the enemies that threatened Europe and the Church. On June 21 the duke weighed anchor with the pontifical galleys from Civitavecchia, and the following day he landed at Gaeta, where, going to the cathedral amidst the cheers of the people, he made a vow to offer the standard entrusted to him by St. Pius V as a gift to that church if the enterprise was successful.

On June 12 Pius V wrote to Fra Mathurin Lescaut,[719] called Romegas, the Knight of Malta who was considered the greatest sea fighter of that era, inviting him to join the fleet. Ten days later Romegas was aboard Marcantonio Colonna's flagship with the rank of superintendent of the papal galleys.[720]

On July 2 the pope handed the representatives of Spain and the ambassador of Venice a draft of a treaty of alliance for discussion with a commission of cardinals. The meetings were held secretly each day in the presence of the pope.

[718] Catena, *Vita del gloriosissimo Papa Pio V*, p. 170; Pietro Fedele, *Lo stendardo di Marco Antonio Colonna a Lepanto*, Unione Tipografica Cooperativa, Perugia, 1903. The words *In hoc signo vinces* ("under this sign you will conquer") appeared in the sky to the Emperor Constantine, next to a luminous cross-shaped trophy, on the eve of the victory at Saxa Rubra (Battle of the Milvian Bridge) on October 28, 312.

[719] Mathurin Lescaut, called Romegas (1528–1581), belonging to a cadet branch of the Armagnacs, entered the Knights of Malta in 1546 and, after having fought the Huguenots in France, became the terror of the Muslim Corsairs who infested the Mediterranean. At Lepanto he fought as captain of the pontifical fleet and left an account of the battle. See Carmel Testa, *Romegas*, Midsea Books, Malta, 2002.

[720] Testa, *Romegas*, p. 126.

Meanwhile, on July 3, 1570, the troops of Lala Mustafa Pashà[721] landed on Cyprus and laid siege to Nicosia, the capital of the island. The approximately 6,000 men of the Venetian garrison were vastly outnumbered by the Sultan's 100,000 soldiers equipped with 1,500 cannons and supported by about 150 ships, which formed a blockade to choke off any relief to the Venetians. Despite a heroic defense, Nicosia ultimately fell after two months, the garrison was massacred, and more than two thousand inhabitants were captured and sold as slaves. Famagusta, the main stronghold of the island, remained under Venetian control.

On July 27, a courier brought the pope welcome news that the Spanish naval forces commanded by Gianandrea Doria[722] would join the Venetian fleet under the command of Girolamo Zane and the pontifical fleet led by Marcantonio Colonna. The now-combined Christian fleet assembled on the eastern coast of Candia, the present island of Crete, and on September 17 they set out jointly toward Cyprus. The directions that Gianandrea Doria had received from Philip II were to move with extreme prudence and, if possible, to take his time. The ships were stopped by a storm when they received news of the fall of Nicosia and this news, instead of causing them to hurry since Famagusta was still resisting, made them desist from the enterprise. On October 10, Doria decided to wholly abandon the combined fleet and return his Spanish ships to Italy. The papal and Venetian fleets remained together until Corfù, where they separated. The expedition had thus been concluded without any result, and the Genovese admiral was considered the one

[721] Lala Mustafa Pashà (ca. 1500–1580), of Bosnian origin, after the conquest of Cyprus was grand vizier of the Ottoman Empire for a brief time.

[722] Gianandrea Doria (1539–1606), Marquis of Tursi and then Prince of Melfi, commanded the right arm of the Christian fleet at Lepanto and was the most-discussed figure of the battle because of his comportment. See BENEDETTO VEROGGIO, *Gianandrea Doria alla battaglia di Lepanto*, Tip. del R. Istituto Sordo-Muti, Genoa, 1886; A. STELLA, *Gian Andrea Doria e la "sacra Lega" prima della battaglia di Lepanto*, Herder, Rome, 1965; *Vita del Principe Giovanni Andrea Doria scritta da lui medesimo*, edited by Vilma Borghesi, Ed. Compagnia dei Librai, Genoa, 1997.

mainly responsible for the failure.[723] At Famagusta the Venetians, led by the civil governor Marcantonio Bragadin[724] and the military commander Astorre Baglioni,[725] were reduced to five hundred men but continued to resist. In January 1571, the daring and indefatigable Venetian commander Marco Querini,[726] departing from Crete, breached the Turkish blockade with his galleys, carried civilians away from Famagusta, and reinforced the small garrison with munitions, food, and 1,600 men. He spent the winter there and in spring renewed the attacks with increasing fury, while Pius V, as French historian Fernand Braudel writes, painstakingly recomposed the fragments of the Holy League. "Nothing resisted his zeal, neither the ulterior motives of one or the other, nor their divergent calculations, nor their prudence."[727]

6. The Formation of the Holy League

To speed things up, Pius V decided to send Marcantonio Colonna to Venice. Colonna left on April 6, 1571. He did not have an easy task, because eight months of negotiations had only brought out the differences between the Venetians and the Spaniards. Furthermore, in addition to the party of war in the City of Canals, there was also a party that wanted

[723] Capponi, *Lepanto 1571*, pp. 141–142.

[724] Marcantonio Bragadin (1523–1571) was appointed governor general (rector) of Famagusta in 1569. On his life, see Angelo Ventura, *Bragadin Marcantonio*, in DBI, vol. 13 (1971), pp. 686–689. On the events of Famagusta, see the account of one of the survivors, Nestore Martinengo, *Relatione di tutto il successo di Famagosta*, Giorgio Angelieri, Venice, 1572, which is the principal source of Gigi Monello, *Accadde a Famagosta - L'assedio turco ad una fortezza veneziana ed il suo sconvolgente finale*, Scepsi & Mattana Editori, Cagliari, 2006.

[725] Astorre Baglioni (1526–1571), Count of Spello and of Bettona, received the charge of governor of Cyprus in 1569. See Gaspare De Caro, *Baglioni Astorre*, in DBI, vol. 5 (1963), pp. 197–199.

[726] Marco Querini (1515–1577), Venetian general administrator in Crete, was vice-commander of the Venetian fleet at Lepanto. See Barbero, *Lepanto*, pp. 311–314.

[727] Fernand Braudel, *Bilan d'une bataille*, in *Il mediterraneo nella seconda metà del 500*, p. 114.

a treaty with the Turks. By the end of April, however, the duke succeeded in getting the Senate to approve the continuation of negotiations. The Venetian accessions conquered the hesitations of Philip II. Finally, on May 20, 1571, the treaty constituting the league was officially signed, and in a consistory on May 25, the articles of the alliance were approved by the pope and the cardinals, and then by Cardinal Pacheco and Juan de Zúñiga, representing Spain, and by Michele Surian and Giovanni Soranzo on behalf of Venice.

The clauses established that Pope Pius V, King Philip II of Spain, and the Republic of Venice constituted "a perpetual League, both offensive and defensive, against the Turks," in order to recover all the places usurped by them from the Christians, including Tunis, Algeria, and Tripoli; the Christian forces would arm a fleet of 200 galleys and 100 ships, with 50,000 soldiers, 4,500 knights, and 9,000 horses. The cost of the expedition would be divided into six, with three-sixths being paid by Spain, two-sixths by Venice, and one-sixth by the pope. Don Juan of Austria would have supreme command of the armada, with Marcantonio Colonna as lieutenant; all of the strategic decisions were to be made by the commanders of the three fleets, but approved and executed by Don Juan; the division of spoils would be made in proportion to the expenses incurred; Pius V was chosen to arbitrate future disputes. Of the twenty-four articles that composed the text of the treaty, articles 19 and 20 were an invitation to the kings of France, Poland, and Portugal to adhere to the league, together with all Christian princes.[728]

The pope was finally seeing the realization of his dream. Luciano Serrano, in his documented study of the origin of the treaty, says that Pius V was the true author of the Holy League: "He proposed it, he stipulated it and gave it consistency, dedicating the deepest energies of his spirit and the sacrifices and prayers of his most holy life."[729] The coalition against the Turks was not only defensive in nature but also offensive, as Catholic

[728] Catena, *Vita del gloriosissimo Papa Pio V*, pp. 178–184; Pastor, *Storia dei Papi*, vol. 8, pp. 548–549.

[729] Serrano, *La liga de Lepanto*, p. 31.

morality permits.[730] Pius V renewed the Bull of the Crusade to the king of Spain.[731] The pontiff knew that there would be no possible truce with Islam until the Ottoman Empire was definitely annihilated.

The solemn promulgation of the treaty took place on May 27, 1571, in St. Peter's Basilica. In the presence of all the ambassadors, Pius V announced to the Roman people the conclusion of the treaty and promulgated a universal jubilee in order to call down the blessing of God on the battles of the Christian army. The pope personally participated in the processions, which took place on May 28 and 30 and on the first of June.[732] That same day the pope wrote to Philip II, expressing his hope that "His Majesty Caesar (Maximilian II), His Most Christian Majesty, his son-in-law (Charles IX), the King of Portugal (Sebastian I) and the King of Poland (Sigismund II)" would enter the league.[733]

Pius V insisted that the Holy League be extended and strengthened with the adherence of other Christian powers. To this end, beginning on May 30, he addressed special letters to the emperor and the kings of France and Poland. In a secret consistory of June 18, he appointed Cardinal Commendone as legate to the emperor, the German Catholic princes, and the king of Poland, with the mission of pushing them to join the league. At the same time Cardinal Bonelli was appointed legate *a latere* in Spain and Portugal. Accompanying him were the young

[730] Roberto de Mattei, *Holy War, Just War: Islam and Christendom at War*, Chronicles Press, Rockford, Illinois, 2007. The compatibility between the Crusades and just war theory is at the center of the volume by J. Riley-Smith, *What Were the Crusades?*, Palgrave, London, 2002 (1997).

[731] Catena, *Vita del gloriosissimo Papa Pio V*, p. 184. The Bull of the Crusade was granted by Pope Julius II to the king of Spain in 1509 and then extended to the Spanish dominions in America by means of Gregory XIII's apostolic constitution *Cum alias felicis* of July 10, 1573. The bull granted indulgences and privileges, including financial ones, to those who committed to serve the Church with arms. See José Goñi Gaztambide, *Historia de la Bula de Cruzada en España*, Editorial del Seminario, Vitoria, 1958; Gattoni, *Pio V e la politica iberica*, pp. 135–137.

[732] Pastor, *Storia dei Papi*, vol. 8, 549.

[733] The text of the letter is in Tellechea Idígoras, *El papado y Felipe II*, pp. 243–244.

auditor of the Rota, Ippolito Aldobrandini,[734] the future Clement VIII, and the general of the Society of Jesus, Francis Borgia, who despite his old age and his illnesses, willingly accepted, saying that "the obedience that I owe to the Vicar of Christ requires that I remain silent; it even brings me a certain pleasure in my efforts."[735]

The two cardinals set off at the end of June: Commendone from Verona and Bonelli from Rome. The instructions given to Bonelli about his behavior on the journey and in foreign courts were significant. Neither the cardinal nor his entourage were to accept gifts, nor participate in banquets, hunts, or plays; they were to dress and eat simply and comport themselves in an edifying manner.[736]

King Sebastian of Portugal,[737] without rejecting the Holy See's proposals, expressed his desire to fight against the Turks alone. In effect, however, this was a craftily diplomatic "no" to the league. Cardinal Bonelli did not have any better reception at the French court. To the proposals made to him by the pope's nephew, Charles IX responded that he had already renewed relations of both alliance and trade with the Ottoman Empire.

734 Ippolito Aldobrandini (1536–1605), created cardinal on December 18, 1585, by Sixtus V, was elected pope in 1592 with the name of Clement VIII.

735 Grente, *Il Pontefice delle grandi battaglie*, p. 154. Francesco Borgia (1510–1572), fourth Duke of Gandia, recovered the office of viceroy of Catalogna. He became a widower and entered the Society of Jesus and in 1565 was elected superior general. He was proclaimed a saint by Pope Clement X in 1670. See Suau, *San Francesco Borgia*; Enrique García Hernán, *Francisco de Borja, grande de España*, Institució Alfons el Magnànim, Valencia, 1999; and Hernán, *La acción diplomática de. Francisco de Borja al servicio del Pontificado, 1571–1572*, Organismo Público de Investigación, Valencia, 2000.

736 Pastor, *Storia dei Papi*, vol. 8, p. 552.

737 Sebastian I of Aviz (1554–1578), king of Portugal, did not participate in the Holy League but was killed and his army defeated in the great battle against the Moors at Alcacer-Quibir in Morocco in 1578. His demise provoked a dynastic crisis that ended the Aviz dynasty and the union, until 1668, of the Portuguese crown with the Spanish crown. See António Villacorta Baños-Garcia, *Don Sebastián, Rey de Portugal*, Ed. Ariel, Barcelona, 2001.

The king then wrote a letter to Rome that was so ambiguous that the pope responded to him in these terms:

> We easily believe what Your Majesty writes to us regarding the sorrow you feel, both for the Church in general and for the Republic of Venice in particular. To which of the Catholic kings should belong the feelings of most heartfelt sorrow for the misfortune that strikes all of Christianity, if not to the one who by long tradition has been given the title "Most Christian King," acquired and merited by your predecessors by their glorious exploits against the infidels?
>
> Now in your letter there is a phrase that causes us to marvel and moves us to disdain; and our duty demands that we manifest our displeasure with all the liberty that befits our character. Your Majesty does not have any difficulty in designating with the name of Emperor of the Turks an inhuman tyrant and a declared enemy of Our Lord Jesus Christ, as if he who does not know the true God was not already usurping the imperial dignity on his behalf! ... As for the close alliance that you express you wish to maintain between Your Majesty and the kings, your illustrious ancestors, in the interests of Christianity, we say to you that this is only a strange illusion and a grave error. It is a forgetting that one must never do evil for the sake of good. Your Majesty will certainly not escape blame if for the sake of personal advantage or an imaginary thing you persist in having friendly relations with the infidels. ... The wrongs of your ancestors do not justify yours. At times the Lord punishes the sins of parents in their children. How much more will God exercise his justice on those who want to perpetuate the errors of their fathers![738]

Charles IX and Catherine de' Medici, not content to simply not participate in the Holy League, attempted to stop the Venetians, and pushed

[738] FALLOUX, *Histoire de St. Pie V*, vol. 2, pp. 256–257; GRENTE, *Il Pontefice delle grandi battaglie*, pp. 154–155.

Elizabeth and the Lutheran princes of Germany against Rome, saying that the pope was concerned more about the destruction of Protestantism than victory over the Turks. The Emperor Maximilian contented himself with promising a land attack against the Turks in support of the Christian fleet, on the condition that the diet grant him a new contingent of twenty thousand men. On June 15 the pope wrote him that there were two reasons why His Imperial Majesty should have entered the league as soon as possible to make war on the enemy: "the first zeal for Christ and His Holy Church," and "the other love of neighbor"; and also because "it is obvious that after the Vicar of Christ, the burden of defending Christianity rests above all on the shoulders of the Roman Emperor."[739] These words too fell on deaf ears.

Meanwhile Don Juan of Austria moved from Barcelona to Genoa, where he was welcomed as a guest in the palace of Gianandrea Doria and sent Hernando de Carillo to Rome to inform the pope that he would soon be in Messina with his fleet. On August 7 Carillo was received by Pius V, who charged him to remind Don Juan that he had departed to wage war for the Catholic Faith and that God would certainly give him the victory. On August 14, in the Church of Santa Chiara in Naples, Cardinal Granvelle gave Don Juan the captain's staff and the sacred banner of the Holy League in the name of the pope. The standard had a red field of blue silk, with the image of the Crucified Savior, at whose feet were the arms of Pius V, at the right the arms of Spain, and at the left the arms of Venice.

During those very same days, at Famagusta, after supplies and ammunition ran out, Bragadin had been forced to decree the surrender of the city. Lala Mustafa had formally promised, with a signed document, to allow survivors to leave the island, embarking on their ships "to the beat of the drum, with banners unfurled, artillery, weapons and luggage, wife and children."[740] Accordingly, on August 2 Bragadin, accompanied by Astorre Baglioni, went to Lala Mustafa's tent to give him the keys of

[739] CATENA, *Vita del gloriosissimo Papa Pio V*, pp. 278–281.

[740] ZORZI, *La Repubblica del Leone*, p. 348.

the city, but the two Venetian commanders were instead immediately arrested. Baglioni was beheaded on the spot, while a far worse fate awaited Bragadin, who had his ears and nose cut off and was locked up for twelve days in an open cage exposed to the sun, with very little water and food. On the fourth day the Turks offered him freedom if he would convert to Islam, but Bragadin refused.[741] On August 17 he was hung from the mast of his own ship and scourged with over one hundred lashes, then he was forced to carry a heavy basket full of stones and sand on his shoulders through the streets of Famagusta until he collapsed. He was then brought back to the main square of the city and chained to a column, upon which a Genoese renegade began to slowly flay him alive from the shoulders down.[742] The Venetian commander endured the martyrdom with heroic courage, continuing to recite the *Miserere* and to invoke the name of Christ until, after his arms and torso had been skinned, he cried out: "*In manus tuas Domine commendo spirituum meum*," and expired.[743] It was three in the afternoon on August 17, 1571. Bragadin's body was then quartered, and with his flayed skin stuffed with straw and cotton and clothed with the garments and insignia of command, was carried in a macabre procession through the streets of Famagusta and then hung from the mast of a galley, which carried him to Constantinople as a trophy, together with the heads of the other Christian leaders.

7. The Two Opposing Fleets

On August 24 Don Juan arrived in Messina, where the admirals of the pope and Venice, Marcantonio Colonna and Sebastiano Venier, were waiting for him. On September 2 the fleet was reinforced by sixty Venetian ships commanded by Overseers Antonio da Canal and Marco Querini. On September 3, with the arrival of twelve galleys under the command of Gianandrea Doria, the Christian armada was now complete. The papal

[741] ZORZI, *La Repubblica del Leone*, p. 350.

[742] CATENA, *Vita del gloriosissimo Papa Pio V*, pp. 242–255.

[743] VENTURA, *Bragadin*, p. 689; CAPPONI, *Lepanto 1571*, p. 202. On the martyrdom of Bragadin, see MONELLO, *Accadde a Famagosta*, pp. 111–120.

fleet was composed of twelve galleys of the Grand Duke of Tuscany, three galleys of the Duke of Savoy, and four galleys of the Knights of Malta. On September 16 the boats slowly began to leave port, blessed one by one by Nuncio Giulio Maria Odescalchi, sent by Pius V. The spectacle of the Christian fleet under the Sicilian sun was imposing. The armada sailed for twenty days, heading toward the east. On September 26 the fleet skirted Corfù and stopped in the port of Igoumenitza, where some Spanish sailors provoked a tumult on one of the Venetian ships. Venier did not hesitate to have three of them hanged, arousing such indignation in the Spanish commander, Don Juan of Austria, that only with difficulty did Agostino Barbarigo and Marcantonio Colonna succeed in avoiding a rupture of the alliance. On that day the terrible news of the massacre of Famagusta arrived, which aroused the Christians to seek revenge. Pius V prayed day and night, recommending the Christian fleet to the protection of the Most High. On September 26, 1571, the Spanish ambassador reported that His Holiness was fasting three days per week and dedicated many hours to prayer each day.[744] On October 5 the Christian armada arrived at the island of Kefalonia. From there the ships of the league sailed toward the waters of Lepanto in the order of battle.[745] Gianandrea Doria, conveying the wishes of the king of Spain, asked Don Juan to reflect on the risks of the clash: if the Christian fleet were defeated so far from their base, a catastrophe for Europe would be inevitable. The Venetians and Marcantonio Colonna insisted on the attack against the enemy. "My Lords," Don Juan responded, courteously but decisively, "the time for discussion is over, the moment has come to fight."[746]

At dawn on October 7, at the entrance of the Gulf of Patras, the Christian armada found itself face to face with the Ottoman fleet. About 270 galleys with numerous small fighting vessels formed an enormous

[744] Pastor, *Storia dei Papi*, vol. 8, p. 561.

[745] On the arrangement of the Christian fleet at Lepanto, see Catena, *Vita del gloriosissimo San Pio V*, pp. 355–367; Eric Glatre, *Lépante 1571*, Socomer, Paris, 1991, pp. 100–109; Barbero, *Lepanto*, Appendix 2, pp. 623–647.

[746] Pierre de Brantôme, *Oeuvres*, Aux Dépens du Libraire, London, 1779, vol. 2, pp. 126–127 (pp. 123–155).

and menacing crescent moon that occupied all of the waters from the coast of Albania on the north to the shallows of Morea on the south. The supreme Turkish commander, Müezzinzade Alì Pashà,[747] was at the center of the crescent moon, in command of ninety-six ships. At the right extremity were fifty-six galleys that were almost all from Egypt, under the command of Mohammed Scirocco,[748] the governor of Alexandria; on the left extremity were ninety-four galleys and galeottas commanded by Pasha Occhialì of Algiers. Smaller boats with other soldiers were ready to lend reinforcements, for a total of about three hundred boats.[749] On the mainmast of the *Sultana*, Alì Pashà's flagship galley, there was flying a green banner that came from Mecca, which bore the name of Allah embroidered in gold letters 28,900 times.

The Christian armada was divided into three squadrons in the form of a cross. In the vanguard, six galleys led the way toward the enemy, two in front of each squadron, equipped with a new type of cannon whose firepower was superior to all the others. These were under the command of Admiral Francesco Duodo[750] and had the task of breaking the momentum of the enemy's first attack with their force.

In the center was Don Juan of Austria, with sixty-one galleys. On his flanks were Marcantonio Colonna, admiral of the papal fleet, and Sebastiano Venier, commander of the Venetian fleet. At the left horn

[747] Müezzinzade Alì Pashà replaced Vizier Piyale Pashà (1515–1578) in 1567 as admiral (*Kapudan deryà*) of the Ottoman fleet. He was killed on his galley at Lepanto.

[748] Mehmet Sulik Pashà, (1525–1571), known as Mohammed Scirocco, was viceroy of Egypt and governor of Alexandria. He commanded the right flank of the Ottoman fleet at Lepanto, where he was killed and beheaded by Giovanni Contarini.

[749] Capponi, *Lepanto 1571*, p. 219.

[750] Francesco Duodo (1518–1592), member of the Council of Ten, commanded the six galleys that led the Christian fleet. Following the Battle of Lepanto, he was governor of Brescia. The armor with which he fought at Lepanto was preserved by his descendants in the armory of the Arsenal in Venice, where it is still preserved. See Giuseppe Gullino, *Duodo Francesco*, in DBI, vol. 42 (1993), pp. 30–32.

was the Venetian overseer Agostino Barbarigo,[751] in command of fifty-one galleys; on the right horn was the Genoese admiral Gianandrea Doria with fifty-three galleys. The fleet of the rearguard, which flew the white banner in honor of the Immaculate Conception, was composed of thirty-seven galleys commanded by Don Alvaro of Bazan, Marquis of Santa Cruz.[752] The plan was that this fleet would enter the action at the moment when the battle was fiercest.

Don Juan wore the insignia of the Golden Fleece on his breastplate and around his neck he wore a relic of a fragment of the True Cross given to him by the pope. The decks of the galleys were full of men kneeling in worship at Mass and receiving general absolution from the chaplains. Pius V wanted the combatants to be assisted by Jesuits aboard the Spanish ships, Dominican and Franciscans aboard the Genoese, Savoian, and Venetian ships, and Capuchins on the papal ships.[753] The theme of all the preaching that morning was: "no heaven for cowards." Then the papal bull that proclaimed a plenary indulgence for all those who would fall fighting the infidels was read aloud on each boat of the league.

The trumpets sounded on the flagship, and on the mainmast of Don Juan's *Reale* there was hoisted the great standard of the Holy League that bore the impressed image of the crucifix. A mighty cry of "*Vittoria!*" exploded and ran through the entire deployment, repeating itself like an echo from one ship to the other.

[751] Agostino Barbarigo (1516–1571) held various administrative positions in the Venetian Republic prior to receiving the rank of general overseer, with authority equal to that of the general captain in his absence. See FRANCO GAETA, *Barbarigo Agostino*, in DBI, vol. 6 (1964), pp. 50–52.

[752] Alvaro di Bazan (1526–1588), Marquis of Santa Cruz. After Lepanto he won the battle of Ponta Delgada (1582) in the Azores, during the War of the Portuguese Succession, and was the initial commander of the "Invincible Armada" formed by Philip II against Elizabeth I's England. See ANGEL DE ALTOLAGUIRRE Y DUVALE, *Don Alvaro de Bazán, primer marqués de Santa Cruz de Mudela*, Editora Nacional, Madrid, 1971.

[753] G. CASTELLANI, *L'assistenza religiosa nell'armata di Lepanto (1570–1572). Con documenti inediti*, in "Civiltà Cattolica," 4 (1936), pp. 470–481; 1 (1937), pp. 39–49 and 433–443; 2 (1937), pp. 259–269 and 538–547.

Although the Ottoman fleet was numerically superior in ships arrayed for battle, the league prevailed in terms of overall firepower. Furthermore, the Christian infantry was composed almost entirely of arquebusiers, who after firing on the enemy dropped their muskets and took up swords.[754] The Turks made extensive use of curved bows, but the breastplates and helmets worn by Christians provided considerable protection against arrows. It is difficult to calculate the number of combatants, but an estimated thirty thousand on each side took part in the battle. According to Niccolò Capponi, the two fleets were more or less equal in terms of soldiers, even if there were probably more expert veterans among the Ottomans.[755]

Suddenly and miraculously, the wind shifted. The sails of the Turks suddenly collapsed, while along Don Juan's array the lateen sails unfolded on the masts, inflated by the wind. Among the Christian fleet the gunsmiths blew up the shackles of the Christian convicts and gave them their weapons. The prisoners took up swords and small halberds, ready to gain their liberty with weapons.

Among the Turkish fleet more than fourteen thousand Christian prisoners were handcuffed to the oars. Alì Pashà ordered death for anyone who raised his head from the oars to look at the Christian fleet that was advancing.

8. The Battle of Lepanto

The beginning of the battle was signaled by the opposing fleet admirals, who exchanged a few rounds of cannon fire. The first collision, however, occurred on the left front of the Christian fleet, where Barbarigo had to

[754] BARBERO, *Lepanto*, pp. 575. The arquebus was operated by a fuse and fired a lead bullet of about fifteen grams, capable of killing an unprotected man at a distance of two hundred meters, even if in practice it took an excellent marksman to hit a target at more than sixty meters (CAPPONI, *Lepanto 1571*, p. 186).

[755] CAPPONI, *Lepanto 1571*, p. 223. The fleet of Don Juan of Austria, according to Barbero, had more than thirty-six thousand armed men on board, to which must also be added the rowers (BARBERO, *Lepanto*, p. 576).

resist the simultaneous assault of six Turkish galleys. Having removed the protection of his helmet from his face in order to be better able to give orders, the Venetian admiral was hit by an arrow in his left eye, but he continued to fight until he had no more strength and then he was replaced in command by Federico Nani.

Suddenly, on the Turkish ships a large group of Christian convicts rose up at a predetermined sign and, spinning their broken chains, they rushed against the backs of the unsuspecting Turks. The mutiny turned the tide of battle on the left front. Mohammed Scirocco was killed in close combat, and the sight of his corpse floating on the sea was a severe blow to the Turks.

On the right flank, Occhialì tried to outflank the Genoese fleet, but in order to avoid the maneuver, Gianandrea Doria extended his flank by spreading his ships southward into the open sea. The corsair took advantage of this to wedge himself between Dorian and the center of the Christian flotilla. The connection between the center and the right of the Christian fleet was held by three galleys of the Knights of Malta commanded by the Grand Prior of Messina, Pietro Giustiniani,[756] and by a small squadron of Spanish and Venetian galleys commanded by Giovanni Cardona.[757] With a numerical superiority of ten to one, Occhialì succeeded in overwhelming them, using seven galleys to attack the *Capitana*, the flagship of the hated Knights of Malta. At the end of a terrible battle, thirty Knights of Malta lay on the deck of the *Capitana* under the bodies of three hundred Turks.

[756] Pietro Giustiniani (ca. 1510–1572), professed knight of the Order of Malta and Prior of Messina, commanded the contingent of the Knights of Malta at Lepanto. He survived the fight with Occhialì with grave wounds.

[757] Giovanni Cardona (1530–early 1600s), commanded *La Capitana di Sicilia* at Lepanto. He was later nominated to command the Spanish fleet. He was then appointed captain general of the Kingdom of Naples to replace the Marquis of Santa Cruz, who was called to command the Spanish fleet. See Giuseppe Arenaprimo, *La Sicilia nella battaglia di Lepanto*, EDAS, Messina, 2011 (1892) *ad indicem*.

The battle was decided, however, in the center of the flotilla, where the *Reale* of Don Juan and the *Sultana* of Alì Pashà thrust themselves against each other. The spur of the *Sultana* penetrated deeply into the hull of the *Reale*, while Marcantonio Colonna's galley in turn rammed the *Sultana*. A floating battlefield had now been formed, in which attacks and counterattacks followed one upon another. The four hundred Janissaries of Alì Pashà burst onto the deck of the *Reale*, but the three hundred arquebusiers from the *tercio* of Sardinia under the guidance of the *maestro de campo* Lope de Figueroa,[758] pushed them back and threw them in turn onto the Turkish deck. Twice the Turks were pushed back against the mast, and twice they drove the Sardinians back to the bow.

Among the Christian fighters who were covered in valor[759] were the twenty-six-year-old Alessandro Farnese,[760] hereditary prince of Parma, and the twenty-two-year-old Francesco Maria della Rovere,[761] hereditary prince of Urbino. Both of them were descendants of Pope Paul III and nephews of Charles V and had been educated along with Don Juan of Austria at the Spanish Court.

[758] Lope de Figueroa (ca. 1541–1585), Knight of Santiago and *Maestro di Campo* (colonel) of the Spanish *Tercios*, had been a longtime slave of the Turks after the defeat at Djerba.

[759] Regarding the Italian combatants at Lepanto, see ALFONSO SALIMEI, *Gli italiani a Lepanto. Riassunto storico della Lega contro i Turchi: 1570–1573, con nuovi documenti sull'Armata cristiana dagli Archivi vaticani*, Lega Navale Italiana, Rome, 1931; and GIUSEPPE PORFIRI, *Gli ordini equestri italiani alla battaglia di Lepanto*, In proprio, Rome, 1976.

[760] Alessandro Farnese (1545–1592), the third Duke of Parma and Piacenza, was the son of Ottavio Farnese and Margaret of Austria, the sister of Charles V. He was one of the greatest generals of his time, in the service of Philip II as a commander of the Army of Flanders. See ANTONELLO PIETROMARCHI, *Alessandro Farnese l'eroe italiano delle Fiandre*, Gangemi, Rome, 1998.

[761] Francesco Maria II della Rovere (1549–1631), Duke of Urbino, was the son of Guidobaldo II of Urbino and of Vittoria Farnese, the daughter of Pierluigi Farnese. The Duchy of Urbino was annexed at his death to the Papal States of Urban VIII. See G. BENZONI, *Francesco Maria II*, in DBI, vol. 50 (1998), pp. 55–60.

Other valiant fighters included: Count Francesco of Savoy, killed on his galley with all the Piedmontese volunteers; the Romans Paolo Giordano Orsini, son-in-law of Cosimo de' Medici; Alessandro Negroni; and Onorato Caetani, who captured two galleys with the *Grifona*;[762] the Neapolitan Giulio Carafa who, when taken prisoner, freed himself and took possession of the enemy brig; Sforza di Santa Fiora; Ascanio della Corgna; Desiderio and Sigismondo Montecuccoli; Silvio di Porcía; Gabrio Serbelloni, master of the artillery; and the Knight of St. Stephen Bernardino Antinori of Florence. A Frenchman also distinguished himself among the combatants, Duke Louis des Balbes de Crillon,[763] and an Englishman, Sir Thomas Stukeley.[764] On the captured galleys, both men and women who had been reduced to slavery following Muslim raids were set free. Girolamo Diedo also tells of a monk, Anselmo of Pietramolara, who, finding himself surrounded by the Turks, abandoned the cross with which he had fought until then and "inflamed with the zeal of faith, like

[762] Onorato Caetani (1542–1592), Duke of Sermoneta, general of the papal infantry, participated in the Battle of Lepanto aboard the galley *La Grifona*, the first Christian ship attacked by the governor of Valona, Kara Khodja. See ONORATO CAETANI, GIROLAMO DIEDO, *La battaglia di Lepanto (1571)*, edited by Salvatore Mazzarella, Sellerio, Palermo, 1995, with a collection of his letters, pp. 75–174; G. DE CARO, *Caetani Onorato*, in DBI, vol. 16 (1973), pp. 205–209.

[763] Louis des Balbes de Berton de Crillon (1541–1645), called by other soldiers "*l'hommes sans peur*" (the man without fear) and by Henry IV "*le brave des braves*," after covering himself with valor against the Huguenots in Dreux, St. Denis, Jarnac, and Moncontour, fought as a volunteer at Lepanto. On his return he wrote an account of the battle. See MARGUERITE DE LUSSAN, *Vie de Louis Balbe-Berton de Crillon, surnommé le Brave et Mémoires des règnes de Henri II, François II, Charles IX, Henri III et Henri IV pour servir à l'histoire de son temps*, Pissot, Paris, 1757.

[764] Sir Thomas Stukeley (1520–1578) was a soldier of fortune, who after having fought in France, Ireland, and at Lepanto, died fighting against the Moors in the battle of Alcazar on August 4, 1578. See BEECHING, *La battaglia di Lepanto*, pp. 152–156; and *The Stukeley Plays: "The Battle of Alcazar" by George Peele and "the Famous History of the Life and Death of Captain Thomas Stukeley,"* edited by Charles Edelman, Manchester University Press, Manchester, 2011.

another Maccabeus, clasped a sword with both hands and threw himself against the enemies with such ardor and force that he left seven of them at his feet and forced the others to retreat and flee."[765] There was even a woman who received permission to participate in the battle on Don Juan's flagship, Maria la Bailadora, who wore the uniform of a Spanish arquebusier.[766] There was also a thirty-three-year-old volunteer on one of Doria's galleys, the *Marquesa*. He lost his left hand in the battle, "to the glory of his right," as he said, and he defined the battle as "*la más alta ocasión que vieron los siglos pasados, los presentes ni esperan ver los venideros*" (*the highest occasion that past ages have ever seen, and which neither present nor future ages will ever hope to see*).[767]

On his flagship, the seventy-five-year-old Sebastiano Venier fought with uncovered head and wearing slippers. When asked why, he replied that they had a better grip on the deck.[768] He held a crossbow, assisted by a sailor who helped him to load the weapon because he no longer had the strength to do so. Unshakeable amid the cloud of arrows, he aimed and hit the enemies one by one. Overwhelmed by their great number, he was helped by the galleys of Giovanni Loredan and Caterino Malipiero, who both died in the battle. With equal force of soul, the twelve-year-old Filippo Pasqualigo held his brother Antonio, who had been struck down by the Turks, as he took his last breath. Antonio Pasqualigo was the commander of the galley *Il Crocifisso*. He had brought his younger

765 CAETANI, DIEDO, *La battaglia di Lepanto*, p. 62.

766 CROWLEY, *Empires of the Sea*, p. 262.

767 Miguel de Cervantes Saavedra (1547–1616), Prologue to *Novelas Ejemplares*, Castalia, Madrid, 1972 (1613). The author of *Don Quijote de la Mancha* participated in the Battle of Lepanto, receiving two gunshot wounds in the chest and one on the left hand. In 1572, having recovered from his wounds, he joined the Lope de Figueroa regiment, in which he fought at Navarino, Tunis, and Goletta. In 1575, while he was sailing from Naples to Spain, his ship was assailed by Muslim corsairs, and he spent five years in prison in Algiers, until he was rescued by the Trinitarian Brothers.

768 BEECHING, *La battaglia di Lepanto*, p. 257.

brother with him so that he could learn how the Venetian patricians served their country.[769]

The battle ended when Don Juan of Austria's men succeeded in launching a third attack. Alì was struck by a bullet from an arquebus. An armed convict from Malaga was on top of him and cut off his head, taking it to the stern deck of the *Reale*. A group of knights and Sardinian soldiers lowered the crescent and hoisted the Christian banner over the *Sultana*.

The battled ended after five hours. An eyewitness, Ferrante Caracciolo, described the spectacle of that afternoon in his *Commentaries* as follows:

> The sea was full of dead men, tables, clothes, some Turks who fled swimming, others who drowned, many smashed fragments of vessels, and because of the many killings the sea was mostly bright red; vessels were seen burning, and others sinking to the bottom of the sea, the rocky coast was full of Turks fleeing, and our galleys that were nearby fired cannonades on them with great fury, the sight of so many enemies stranded clinging to pieces of wood was a horrible and frightful spectacle for the losers, but for us it was a happy and delightful sight.[770]

The league had lost more than 7,000 men, including 4,800 Venetians, 2,000 Spaniards, and 800 of the papal forces, with an additional 20,000 wounded; the Turks counted more than 25,000 casualties and 3,000 prisoners, in addition to the 15,000 slaves who were released.[771] For the first time in a century the Mediterranean was free. From that day forward the Ottoman Empire began its long decline.[772]

[769] G. A. Quarti, *La battaglia di Lepanto nei canti popolari dell'epoca*, Istituto Editoriale Avionavale, Milan, 1930, p. 56.

[770] Ferrante Caracciolo, *I Commentari delle guerre fatte coi Turchi da don Giovanni d'Austria dopo che venne in Italia*, Giorgio Marescotti, Florence, 1581, p. 42.

[771] Capponi, *Lepanto 1571*, p. 243.

[772] See Michel Lesure, *La crise de l'Empire ottoman, Lépante*, Gallimard, Paris, 1973.

9. Triumph at Rome

When the battle was over it was about five in the evening on Sunday, October 7, 1571. At the very same hour, Pius V was examining the accounts with his treasurer general, Bartolomeo Bussotti.[773] All of a sudden, as if moved by an irresistible impulse, he got up, opened the window, and fixed his gaze toward the east as if absorbed in contemplation; then, he turned back, his eyes shining with a divine light: "Let's not concern ourselves with business anymore," he exclaimed, "but let's go and thank God, because at this very moment our armada has obtained victory."[774] He dismissed the prelates and went immediately to the chapel, where a cardinal who rushed in on hearing the good news found the pope immersed in tears of joy. Bussotti and the prelates who were nearby, amazed at this sudden affirmation, duly noted the day and hour in which the pope had made it, and hastened to make it known to various cardinals and other people, who also made note of the date. But after fifteen days, no confirmation had yet come to reassure their souls.

Finally, on the night of October 21–22, a courier arrived, sent by the nuncio to Venice, Facchinetti, with news of the great victory. The pope, woken up in the middle of the night, broke out in tears of joy, pronouncing the words of old Simeon: *Nunc dimittis servum tuum Domine . . . quia viderunt oculi mei salutare tuum* (Now, Master, you may let your servant go in peace, ... for my eyes have seen your salvation) (Luke 2:29–30, NABRE).[775] At dawn the next morning the bells rang out, and the singing of the *Te Deum* announced the victory to the Roman people.

[773] Bartolomeo Bussotti (1520–1576) was appointed treasurer general of the Church by Pius V on January 17, 1566, replacing Donato Matteo Minali, and maintained his charge until May 1572, when he was replaced by the Bolognese Tommaso Gigli.

[774] Catena, *Vita del gloriosissimo papa Pio V*, pp. 215–216; Pastor, *Storia dei Papi*, vol. 8, p. 579. The vision took place in the summer residence of the Pontiff, which he had constructed not far from the Vatican, which was later known by the name of Casale San Pio V [Saint Pius V Farmhouse] (today a private university).

[775] Pastor, *Storia dei Papi*, vol. 8, p. 562.

Philip II reacted in the phlegmatic manner that was typical of him. He was attending Vespers when a gentleman of the royal household approached him to tell him in a quiet voice that a courier had just arrived, bringing news of the victory. The king of Spain remained unmoved on his kneeler and continued to pray until the end of the Divine Office. Then he announced the news to those present, ordering that a Mass be offered the next morning for the souls of those who had died in the battle.[776] In the following days celebrations resounded from one end of Spain to another, just as in Rome and Venice. Paolo Veronese dedicated two magnificent representations to the Battle of Lepanto, one in the Accademia in Venice, the other in the Doges' Palace. Titian, who was then ninety-five years old, created an allegory of the memorable event for Philip II. A celebrated altarpiece, *Allegory of the Holy League*, was commissioned by Philip II to the painter El Greco.[777]

As early as October 22, the pontifical chancery began to notify all parts of the world of the great event. Pius V went to St. Peter's Basilica for a solemn prayer of thanksgiving; then he received the ambassadors and cardinals to whom he said that it was now necessary to multiply the efforts to annihilate the Turks. The three admirals of the Christian fleet received enthusiastic letters of congratulations, while by the express order of the pope, the Catholic powers were urged insistently to exploit "the greatest victory that had ever been reported against the infidels."[778]

Duke Marcantonio Colonna was welcomed in Rome by the pope in triumph. On December 4, 1571, thousands of people flocked to the Appian Way to receive the duke, who came from his palace in Marino. The

[776] William Thomas Walsh, *Philip II*, Sheed & Ward, London, 1938, pp. 523–524.

[777] Antony Blunt, *El Greco's "Dream of Philip II": An allegory of the Holy League*, "Journal of the Warburg and Courtauld Institutes," 3 (1939/40), pp. 58–69; Ernst H. Gombrich, *Celebrations in Venice of the Holy League and of the Victory of Lepanto*, in *Studies in Renaissance and Baroque Art presented to Anthony Blunt*, Phaidon, London-New York, 1967, pp. 62–68; Cecilia Gibellini, *L'immagine di Lepanto: la celebrazione della vittoria nella letteratura e nell'arte veneziana*, Marsilio, Venice, 2008.

[778] Pastor, *Storia dei Papi*, vol. 8, p. 563.

people were attracted above all by the 170 Turkish prisoners, clothed in their red and yellow liveries, chained and guarded by halberdiers. In front of them rode a Roman man wearing Turkish clothes, who dragged the sultan's banner in the dust. The Knight of Malta Romegas carried the banner of the Holy Church, and Giovan Giorgio Cesarini carried the banner of the city of Rome. Next to him rode Pompeo Colonna and Onorato Caetani, with two of the pope's nephews, Michele and Girolamo Bonelli. Finally there came Duke Marcantonio Colonna, followed by the senators of Rome and the protectors of the city. He was mounted a white horse given to him by the pope; a mantle of black silk surrounded by fur covered his jacket made of golden cloth; on his head he wore a black hat, from which a white feather extended, held by a clasp made of pearls. At the rear of the procession came the pope's light cavalry.[779]

Marcantonio Colonna entered through the Porta San Sebastiano, which was decorated with the arms of the Roman people and the pontiff, passed in front of the Baths of Caracalla and through the triumphal arches of Constantine and Titus, ascended to the Campidoglio, and from there went by the Via Papale to Ponte Sant'Angelo and then to St. Peter's Basilica. After he had prayed at the tomb of the Prince of the Apostles, the victor of Lepanto went to the Vatican, where the Holy Father, surrounded by twenty-five cardinals, received him with every honor in the Sala Regia, exhorting him to give glory to God. There were no banquets, because the pope wanted the money to be used for the support of young orphans.

The churches of all the Catholic countries resounded with the *Te Deum* of thanksgiving. On the commemorative medals that he had made, Pius V placed the words of the psalmist: "The right hand of the LORD does valiantly; the right hand of the LORD is exalted" (Psalm 118:15–16).

The Venetian Senate also wanted to attribute the principal merit for the victory to the Blessed Virgin, and on the picture it had painted in its meeting chamber, it had these words written: "*Non virtus, non arma,*

[779] PASTOR, *Storia dei Papi*, vol. 8, p. 567.

non duces, sed Maria Rosarii, victores nos fecit" ("Not valor, not weapons, not leaders, but Our Lady of the Rosary made us victors").

Pius V attributed the triumph of Lepanto to the intercession of the Virgin and ordered that the invocation "*Auxilium Christianorum, ora pro nobis*" be added to the Litany of Loreto, and made October 7 a feast day in honor of Our Lady of Victory. Gregory XIII, his successor, instituted the Feast of Our Lady of the Rosary, and Clement XI extended the feast to the entire Church in 1716, after the victory of Prince Eugene of Savoy against the Turks at Petrovaradin.[780]

10. An Unfinished Crusade

Hubert Jedin dedicated an ample study to the Holy League and Pius V's idea of a crusade.[781] According to the German historian, for the pope the league was not just another treaty between states: it was supposed to renew one of the greatest ideas of the medieval papacy. Although Pius V never used the term "crusade," perhaps because by his time it was reserved for the indulgence valid in Spain, there is no doubt that the *santissima expeditio* he conceived and promoted in 1570 fully corresponded to the traditional concept of the crusade. Pius V's conception was an "offensive" one that "principally distinguished itself from that of the Republic of St. Mark as well as from the Spanish concept, which were both based on the *defense* of their own territorial and maritime possessions." Christendom was still a reality for Pius V. The goal of the Holy League was not political but religious—"*el bien de la Cristianidad,*" said Pius V to the Spanish ambassador Zúñiga, on December 18, 1570—and he demanded the creation of the league "for the service of Christendom."[782] Although he did not send a papal legate with the Christian fleet, Pius V was considered the

[780] Emilio Campana, *Maria nel culto cattolico*, Marietti, Turin-Rome, 1933, pp. 407–410.

[781] Hubert Jedin, *Papa Pio V, la Lega Santa e l'idea di crociata*, in *Chiesa della fede. Chiesa della storia*, Morcelliana, Brescia, 1972, pp. 703–722. The same text is found in German in *Il Mediterraneo nella seconda metà del Cinquecento*, pp. 193–213.

[782] Serrano, *Correspondencia diplomatica*, vol. 4, p. 139.

true head of the Holy League, since he still felt himself to be the head of Christendom and was considered to be such. "The League of 1571," Jedin repeats, "was conceived by the Pope as the beginning of the undertaking of a crusade; it was posited under the idea of a crusade."[783]

The crusade therefore is a concept that did not cease after the loss of the Holy Places and the Kingdom of Jerusalem in 1291.[784] The banner raised by Marcantonio Colonna over the waters of Lepanto was the same *Vexillum Sancti Petri* that flew over the fields of the Crusades: the flag of the Church, whose shape varied but whose color was always red and which always bore the image of the Crucified or the Keys of St. Peter.[785] "If the medieval insignia, indicating sovereignty, expresses many of the ideal characteristics of medieval sovereignty," Jedin continues,

> this also holds for the banners that the League fought under at Lepanto. When Marcantonio Colonna took the oath in the papal chapel on June 11, 1570, he received from the hands of the pope, in addition to the staff of command, a red silk flag. On this flag was imprinted Christ Crucified between the Princes of the Apostles Peter and Paul; beneath them was the coat of arms of Pius V and the words "*In Hoc Signo Vinces*" as a motto. The Crucified Christ was not a simple image of Christ but the Cross of the Crusades: Peter and Paul symbolized not only that Colonna commanded the papal contingent but that the Roman Church and its head, the Pope, identified itself with the undertaking.

[783] Serrano, *Correspondencia diplomatica*, vol. 4, p. 718.

[784] On the survival of the idea of crusade, see Norman Housley, *The Later Crusades, 1274–1580: From Lyons to Alcazar*, Oxford University Press, Oxford, 1992; Riley-Smith, *Breve storia delle crociate*, pp. 275–328; M. Viglione, *Il problema della crociata dal II Concilio di Lione alla morte di Pio II (1274–1464)*, with relevant bibliography in "Ricerche di Storia sociale e religiosa," 27, 54 (1998), pp. 201–263.

[785] Moroni, *Bandiera*, in *Dizionario di erudizione*, vol. 3, pp. 86–90; Nicolò Del Re, *Vessillo e Vessillifero di Santa Romana Chiesa*, in *Mondo Vaticano*, Libreria Editrice Vaticana, Vatican City, 1995, pp. 1077–1078.

The motto *In Hoc Signo Vinces* showed how the war was a war of faith.[786]

On October 25, 1571, the pope wrote to Philip II that the victory had gladdened his heart "with incredible joy and happiness." This was the work of God, who is admirable in everything he does, "through whom Kings reign and princes command."[787] The victory of Lepanto was not enough for the holy pontiff. He saw the way open for a new attack against the Ottoman Empire.

On November 17 Pius V thus informed the king of Portugal that he intended to extend the war against the Turks to the kings of Ethiopia and Persia and the other princes of that area.[788] The pope wrote to Shah Tahmāsp I,[789] to Seriph Mutahar, king of *Arabia Felix*,[790] and to Menna, king of Ethiopia,[791] exhorting them to take up arms. This decision demonstrates the breadth of the pontiff's vision, willing to ally himself not only with the Orthodox czar of Moscow but even with the Shiite Muslims of Arabia against the Sunni Ottomans, for the good of Christianity.

[786] JEDIN, *Papa Pio V*, p. 715. The ceremony to which Jedin refers did not take place in 1571 but in 1570.

[787] SERRANO, *Correspondencia diplomatica*, vol. 4, n. 235, p. 492.

[788] SUTTON, *The Papacy and the Levant*, p. 1063.

[789] CATENA, *Vita del gloriosissimo Papa Pio V*, pp. 282–285. Shah Tahmāsp I (1514–1576) belonged to the Safavid dynasty that reigned in Persia from 1501 to 1736. See GUGLIELMO BERCHET, *La Repubblica di Venezia e la Persia*, Paravia, Turin, 1865, pp. 29–38; ROGER SAVORY, *Iran under the Safavids*, Cambridge University Press, Cambridge, 2007 (1980), pp. 96–100.

[790] CATENA, *Vita del gloriosissimo Papa Pio V*, pp. 285–288. *Arabia Felix* included the most southern regions of the Arabian Peninsula, which are today the nations of Yemen and Oman.

[791] CATENA, *Vita del gloriosissimo Papa Pio V*, pp. 288–290; OSVALDO RAINERI, *Lettere tra i pontefici romani e i principi etiopici (secc. XII–XX)*, Archivio Segreto Vaticano, Vatican City, 2005: Letter of Pius V to King Miñas (November 17, 1571), pp. 114–115. The Solomonis dynasty, which was descended from the queen of Sheba, governed Ethiopia almost uninterruptedly from the thirteenth century until 1974. The pope was not aware, however, that the king had been dead for eight years.

On December 16, 1571, writing to Giannotto Lomellini, doge of the Republic of Genoa, Pius V wrote that he was convinced that the enemy, irritated by the disaster, "thinks day and night of new opportunities to spew the venom of his implacable rage on Christians"; thus it was necessary for Christians to remain strictly united, focusing their efforts.[792] On February 10, 1572, the Holy League was renewed in the Vatican. Philip II was represented by Cardinal Pacheco, Don Juan de Zúñiga, and Luis de Requesens, who had just been appointed governor of Milan. Paolo Tiepolo and Giovanni Soranzo represented Venice. Pius V was represented by Cardinals Giovanni Morone, Gianpaolo della Chiesa, Giovanni Aldobrandini, and Girolamo Rusticucci. The pope confided to Cardinal Santori that war must be waged against the Turks by land and sea for ten years.[793] In a long brief sent on March 12, 1572, to all of Christendom (*universis et singulis Christifidelibus*), Pius V called for the continuation of the war against the Turks, and he granted to all those who took up arms or contributed money to the war the same indulgences that in the past the crusaders had acquired; the goods of those who departed for the war remained under the protection of the Church.[794] However, during those very same days the bishop of Dax, François de Noailles,[795] arrived in Istanbul as the ambassador of Charles IX, with the mission of obtaining peace between Venice and the Ottoman Empire, so as to isolate Spain.

[792] FALLOUX, *Histoire de St. Pie V*, vol. 2, pp. 312–313.

[793] PASTOR, *Storia dei Papi*, vol. 8, p. 573.

[794] *Breve di Pio V col quale si concedono privilegi e grazie a coloro che forniranno aiuti per la guerra contro i Turchi*, Archivio Vaticano, ar. IV, t. 1, p. 165.

[795] François de Noailles (1519–1585), bishop of Dax, was ambassador to Constantinople from 1572 to 1575, where he worked in favor of a political alliance between France and Turkey. During his stay he cultivated the peace between Venice and the Ottoman Empire signed on March 7, 1573. See ERNEST CHARRIÈRE, *Négociations de la France dans le Levant*, Imprimerie Nationale de France, Paris, 1850, vol. 2, pp. 252–254; A. DEGERT, *Une ambassade périlleuse de François de Noailles en Turquie*, "Revue Historique," 159, 2 (1929), pp. 225–260; M. LESURE, *Notes et documents sur les relations vénéto-ottomanes 1570-1573*, in "Turcica" 15 (1972), pp. 134–164, 8 (1976), pp. 117–156.

The "nefarious peace" between Venice and the Turks marked the end of the Holy League.[796]

The efforts of Pius V's successor, Pope Gregory XIII, to keep the spirit of Lepanto alive were vain.[797] The great dream of Pius V was to restore religious and political peace to Christendom, destroying its internal and external enemies. Divine Providence had ordained that the project of the victor of Lepanto would remain unfinished.

[796] BEECHING, *La battaglia di Lepanto*, pp. 274–276; IVONE CACCIAVILLANI, *Lepanto*, Corbo e Fiore Editori, Venice, 2003, pp. 190–194.

[797] VIGLIONE, *La conquista della "Mela d'oro,"* pp. 223–224.

7

The Moral Reformer

1. The Implementation of the Council of Trent

Among the relics of St. Pius V that are preserved in the Basilica of St. Mary Major, there is the text of the decrees of the Council of Trent that he used. The religious ideal of the Tridentine Council was, in fact, always at the center of the pontiff's concerns, in order to purify the Church of the abuses and corruptions that she suffered during this time.[798] The goal of the diligent application of the decrees of Trent is already present in the directives that Pius V sent to the bishops of France and Spain only one month after his election. On July 1, 1566, he wrote to the Republic of Genoa that he wanted to reform everything in the Church of God that was in need of reform,[799] and the Venetian ambassador Tiepolo wrote to his government on October 19, 1566, that the pope "does nothing but reform."[800] The papal will to implement the Tridentine ideal was communicated with an encyclical to the French and Spanish bishops, and

[798] MAFFEI, *Vita di S. Pio V*, pp. 56–57; FALLOUX, *Histoire de St. Pie V*, vol. 2, p. 115; See also GIOVANNI GIUDICI, *La tensione riformatrice di Pio V nella Chiesa del suo tempo*, in *San Pio V nella Storia*. Symposium on the occasion of the third centenary of the canonization of Pope Pius V, edited by Carlo Bernasconi, Ibis, Pavia, 2012, pp. 33–37; PIERRE BLET, *Pio V e la riforma tridentina per mezzo dei nunzi apostolici*, in *San Pio V e la problematica del suo tempo*, pp. 33–46.

[799] PASTOR, *Storia dei Papi*, vol. 8, p. 93.

[800] PASTOR, *Storia dei Papi*, vol. 8, p. 117.

the conciliar text was also sent to the mission countries of Mexico, Guatemala, Venezuela, the Congo, and Goa, along with the announcement of his election.[801] If it is true, as Church historian Jedin writes, that "the Council of Trent is the reforming council *par excellence* in the history of the Church,"[802] then Pope Ghislieri, who carried out these reforms with dispatch and zeal, would thus be the reforming pope *par excellence* in the entire history of the Church. Pius V, followed by his successors, Gregory XIII and Sixtus V, along with the great saints Philip Neri, Peter Canisius, and Charles Borromeo, infused life into the Tridentine decrees, ensuring that they did not remain a dead letter. And this is the essential characteristic of every true reform: infusing new life into an immutable truth.

For this reason, the person among the collaborators of Pius V who probably was most appreciated by the pope was St. Charles Borromeo, whom St. Pius X in his encyclical *Editae Saepe* of May 26, 1910,[803] identifies as a model of an authentic reformer of the Church. He in fact was a "tireless advocate and advisor of the true Catholic reform against those recent innovators, whose intention was not reintegration but above all the deformation and destruction of faith and morals."[804] Indeed, true reformers, Pope Sarto recalled, "do not suffocate the shoot in order to save the root, that is, they do not separate faith from sanctity of life, but they nourish and warm both of them with the breath of charity, which is the 'bond of perfection' (Col 3:14)."[805]

In order to accomplish his pastoral plan, Pius V wanted the archbishop of Milan at his side, of whom he said: "There is no cardinal more pious

[801] See CONSTANTIN BAYLE, *El Concilio de Trento en las Indias Españolas*, "Razón y Fe," 564 (1945), pp. 257–284; JUAN DE VILLEGAS, *Aplicación del Concilio de Trento en hispanoamerica 1564–1600*, Instituto Teologico del Uruguay, Montevideo, 1975.

[802] H. JEDIN, *Riforma cattolica o Controriforma?*, Italian translation, Morcelliana, Brescia, 1974, p. 80.

[803] ST. PIUS X, Encyclical *Editae Saepe, De S. Caroli Borromaei apostolica activitate et doctrina*, in EE, 4 (1998), pp. 369–411.

[804] ST. PIUS X, Encyclical *Editae Saepe*, in EE, 4 (1998), p. 375.

[805] ST. PIUS X, Encyclical *Editae Saepe*, in EE, 4 (1998), p. 395.

than him, and no one speaks the truth to me more openly."[806] However, the pope had given Borromeo authorization to retake possession of his archdiocese in June 1566, and so he called Nicolò Ormaneto,[807] who had been the vicar of the cardinal during his absence from Milan, to join him in Rome. Borromeo reluctantly let him go. "I feel," Borromeo wrote, "as if I have been asked to give up my right hand."[808]

Formed in the school of Bishop Matteo Giberti,[809] Ormaneto had extensive diplomatic experience, including accompanying Cardinal Pole as legate to England, but he had never abandoned his parish of Bovolone in the Diocese of Verona, where he continued to concern himself with his flock. The charge that Pius V gave him was to reform the clergy and the people of Rome, beginning with the cardinal and the papal court. Ormaneto waited to take radical measures; then, in June 1567, he began the renewal of the papal court, dismissing 150 gentlemen and minor servants. Out of six doctors, only three were retained, and out of thirty-seven stable employees only eighteen were kept. All of the employees had to have their habitation in the papal palace, whose doors were all closed at night except for one.[810] Ormaneto, Cardinal Alciati and the Jesuit Toledo were charged by Pius V with examining all the confessors of the churches of Rome. The pope then directed that no one could be ordained a priest without first undergoing an examination before his

[806] Pastor, *Storia dei Papi*, vol. 8, p. 95.

[807] Nicolò Ormaneto (1515–1570), parish priest of Bovolone, was later vicar general for Charles Borromeo during his absence from Milan (1564–65). In 1570 he was appointed by bishop of Padua, and in 1572 he was sent to Spain as the nuncio of Pope Gregory XIII. See Carlo Marcora, *Nicolò Ormaneto Vicario di san Carlo*, in *Memorie storiche della Diocesi di Milano*, 8 (1961), pp. 209–590; A. Stella, *L'età postridentina* in *Diocesi di Padova*, edited by Pierantonio Gios, Editrice Gregoriana, Padua, 1996, pp. 221–225, with bibliography on pages 241–242.

[808] Pastor, *Storia dei Papi*, vol. 8, p. 96.

[809] Antonio Filipazzi, *L' influsso di Gian Matteo Giberti attraverso l'azione di Nicolò Ormaneto*, in *Atti del Convegno di studi Gian Matteo Giberti*, pp. 73–87.

[810] Pastor, *Storia dei Papi*, vol. 8, pp. 97–98.

vicar. In order to remedy the bad custom of priests wearing lay clothes, the pope obliged all clerics to wear ecclesiastical dress.[811] The reform of the Roman Curia followed the same lines as the reform carried out by St. Charles Borromeo in the Diocese of Milan.

As early as 1567, the father general of the Jesuits, Francis Borgia, wrote: "The Pope works very hard. He is always fixed in his purpose of working for reform, and every day he attains something in this regard. He has many projects that in due time will prove very useful for the Church and pleasing to God, although not everyone likes them. Here in Rome he concerns himself only with making reforms, and so everyone resents him, ecclesiastics and laity alike."[812] Among the first reforms were those of the ecclesiastical organs such as the Datary[813] and the Penitentiary,[814] in order to avoid the continuous scandals of simoniacal intrigues. The pope applied the same policies that he took with regard to Rome and the Papal States to the universal Church.

Hundreds of documents attest to Pope Ghislieri's commitment to reform. Cardinal Grente rightly observes: "There is nothing that better demonstrates his industriousness and vigilance than these writings, often considerably lengthy, always expressed amply and properly, always energetic and precise in their conclusions, and inspired by an intense piety. Through the reasonings of the theologian and the orders of the head of the Church one feels the soul of the saint resound, and this is what gives his apostolate and all his acts a sacred greatness."[815]

The papal desire to fulfill the Tridentine ideal affected the entire Church, far beyond Rome. Twenty days after his coronation, Pius V

[811] Pastor, *Storia dei Papi*, vol. 8, pp. 128–129.

[812] Grente, *Pio V, il Pontefice delle grandi battaglie*, p. 176.

[813] The Apostolic Datary was an ancient and important dicastery of the Roman Curia. It was suppressed in 1967. It was responsible for the acceptance and examination of petitions and the granting of graces.

[814] The Apostolic Penitentiary is the supreme tribunal of the Church for the internal forum. Pius V suppressed it on April 23, 1569, in order reconstitute it, completely transformed, on the following May 18.

[815] Grente, *Pio V, il Pontefice delle grandi battaglie*, p. 176.

wrote to the archbishop of Krakow: "Since it is most certain that bad priests are the ruin of the people, and that the detestable heresies that are established with fire and sword have no other purpose than the corruption of the faithful, we implore you to work with true pastoral zeal to reform your clergy, since this is the most suitable way to restore the Church to her dignity."[816]

2. The *Cura Animarum* of the Shepherds of the Church

Among the words that are repeated most often in the Tridentine reform decrees are "*cura animarum.*" Bishops and clergy are essentially defined by their pastoral care and the service of souls. Thus the care of souls constituted the distinctive feature of the "ideal type" of the Tridentine bishop.[817] As early as January 13, 1547, the Council had approved a decree on the residence of bishops, in five chapters,[818] affirming that in order to "begin to re-establish much-decayed ecclesiastical discipline and to correct the corrupt morals of the clergy and the Christian people,"[819] it was necessary to begin with those in charge of the major churches: "The integrity of those who preside is in fact the salvation of their subjects."[820] The first point was the obligation of all pastors to reside with their flock. After ample discussion, which touched also on the nature of this obligation, the Council Fathers returned to it with the decrees *De Reformatione* of March 3, 1547,[821] and of

[816] FALLOUX, *Histoire de St. Pie V*, vol. 2, p 80.

[817] See H. JEDIN, *Il tipo ideale di vescovo secondo la riforma cattolica*, Morcelliana, Brescia, 1950; BRUNO MARIA BOSATRA, *Ancora sul "vescovo ideale" della riforma cattolica. I lineamenti del pastore tridentino-borromaico*, in "La Scuola Cattolica," 112 (1984), pp. 517–579; GIANLUIGI PANZERI, *Carlo Borromeo e la figura del Vescovo della Chiesa tridentina*, in "La Scuola Cattolica," 124 (1996), pp. 685–731.

[818] CONCILIO DI TRENTO, Sessione VI, *De residentia episcoporum et aliorum inferiorum*, in COD, pp. 681–683.

[819] CONCILIO DI TRENTO, Sessione VI, *De residentia episcoporum et aliorum inferiorum*, in COD, p. 681.

[820] ST. LEO I in *Epistola* 12, c. 1, in PL, vol. 54, col. 647.

[821] COUNCIL OF TRENT, Session 7, *Super reformatione*, in COD, pp. 685–689.

July 15, 1563,[822] which dealt with the requirements for a candidate for the episcopate, the obligation of bishops with pastoral responsibility to reside in their own dioceses, and the "visitations" they should make to their flock. Pastoral visits in a bishop's own diocese, which were to be carried out on the basis of a precise questionnaire, were a form of investigation for bishops to correct abuses and to stimulate progress in charity in their dioceses.[823] The Council of Trent required bishops to make these visits personally each year. Borromeo went to the most remote alpine valleys of his diocese, even finding time to visit Milan's suffragan dioceses such as Bergamo.

Lastly, the care of souls required that bishops and all clergy preach on Sundays and feast days.[824] In canon 4 of the decree *De Reformatione* it is repeated that preaching is the *munus* of the bishop *par excellence* and that the bishop must thus preach as frequently as possible in his own church, either personally or delegating someone else if he is unable.[825] Pius V therefore required that all those who were responsible for episcopal and patriarchal sees, as well as cardinals, archbishops, and bishops, should reside in their diocese and parishes and carry out their proper duties, according to the decrees of the Council of Trent. In conformity with these decrees, in the secret consistory of April 18, 1567, the pope further prescribed that every bishop in Italy should be examined in Rome by a commission.[826] Pastoral activity was followed by apostolic visitators both inside and outside the peninsula: Tommaso Orsini[827] inspected the

[822] COUNCIL OF TRENT, Session 7, *Super reformatione*, in COD, pp. 743–753.

[823] See *Le visite pastorali. Analisi di una fonte*, edited by Umberto Mazzone and Angelo Turchini, in "Annali dell'Istituto Storico Italo-Germanico," 18, Il Mulino, Bologna, 1985.

[824] ROBERTO RUSCONI, *Predicazione e vita religiosa nella società italiana (da Carlo Magno alla Controriforma)*, Loescher, Turin, 1981; ANNA CALAPA, *Le indicazioni del Concilio di Trento circa la predicazione e la loro incidenza nella prassi*, in *L'omelia. Atti della XXXVIII settimana di studio dell'APL. CLV*, Edizioni liturgiche, Rome, 2012, pp. 46–69.

[825] COUNCIL OF TRENT, Session 24, *De reformatione*, canon 4, in COD, p. 763.

[826] PASTOR, *Storia dei Papi*, vol. 8, pp. 151–152.

[827] Tommaso Orsini (1511–1576), not "Orfini," as almost all historians write, of an ancient Roman family, was appointed bishop of Strongoli in Calabria

churches of the Kingdom of Naples, while Leonardo Marini did the same for south-central Italy; Bartolomeo of Porcia[828] visited the patriarchate in Aquileia; Giulio Pavesi was charged with investigating the state of the Church and the clergy in the Low Countries; and Giovanni Francesco Commendone was sent to the convents of southern Germany. Almost all the visitators came from the circle of Cardinal Borromeo.

One of the most important prescriptions of the Council of Trent was the erection of seminaries in every diocese for the education of the clergy.[829] These subsequently became a permanent structure in the Church, entrusted to the bishop and intended for the spiritual and cultural formation of aspirants to the ecclesiastical state. Pius V wrote many times that among all the prescriptions of the Council none was as beneficial and in keeping with the times than the decree on seminaries.[830]

Until that time, these houses to prepare clerics for the priesthood in an atmosphere conducive to piety and study did not exist. In its twenty-third session on July 15, 1563, the Council of Trent decreed that it wished that in every diocese a *perpetuum Seminarium* be founded in which the bishop could "maintain, religiously educate, and instruct a certain number of

---

by Pius V on August 24, 1566, and was charged with the visitation of the southern Italian dioceses. He was then bishop of Foligno from 1568 until his death. See PASQUALE VILLANI, *La visita apostolica di Tommaso Orfini* [sic] *nel Regno di Napoli (1566–1568). Documenti per la storia dell'applicazione del Concilio di Trento*, in "Annuario dell'Istituto storico italiano per l'età moderna e contemporanea," 8 (1956), pp. 5–79.

828 Bartolomeo di Porcia (1540–1578), of a noble family of Friuli, succeeded Cardinal Borromeo as commendatory abbot of Moggio, and was then nuncio to southeastern Germany. During the pontificate of Gregory XIII he became one of the key figures in the foreign policy of the Holy See. See ALEXANDER KOLLER, *Porcia, Bartolomeo*, in DBI, vol. 85, (2016), pp. 27–30.

829 MAURILIO GUASCO, *La formazione del clero: i seminari*, in *Storia d'Italia, Annali*, IX, *La Chiesa e il potere politico dal Medioevo all'età contemporanea*, edited by Giorgio Chittolini and Giovanni Miccoli, Einaudi, Turin, 1986, pp. 629–715.

830 PASTOR, *Storia dei Papi*, vol. 8, pp. 145–146.

young boys from the same city or diocese in ecclesiastical disciplines."[831] The Council established who could be admitted to seminaries: "boys at least twelve years old, born from legitimate marriage, sufficiently capable of reading and writing, and whose disposition and will cause hope for their perpetual fidelity to the ecclesiastical ministry. The council desires that children of the poor be chosen above all, without however excluding the children of the rich, so long as they provide for themselves and demonstrate their commitment to the service of God and the Church."[832]

After the Council, new seminaries were instituted in Milan, Modena, Vicenza, Nola, Naples, and Avellino. Hundreds of letters were sent from Pius V to diocesan bishops still lacking seminaries, admonishing them to erect them without further delay: "You should have taken this decision on your own initiative, already prior to the council. Now that the Fathers have revealed their thought on this point, in addition to the reasons for which a seminary already should have been erected a formal order is now being added."[833]

On February 11, 1566, Pius V sent a letter along these lines to the primate of Hungary;[834] in 1569 he congratulated the synods held in Germany for the decision they made to establish seminaries in Salzburg, Freising, Regensburg, and Brixen; and he established one himself in Lucerne, Switzerland.

In this area as well, the great protagonist of the implementation of this decree of the Council of Trent was Archbishop Borromeo of Milan,

[831] COUNCIL OF TRENT, Session 23, *De Reformatione*, canon 18, in COD, p. 750. On the text of the decree and related sources, see JAMES O' DONOHOE, *The Seminary Legislation of the Council of Trent*, in *Il Concilio di Trento e la Riforma tridentina*, I, Herder, Rome-Freiburg, 1963, pp. 157–172; O'DONOHOE, *Tridentine Seminary Legislation: Its Sources and Its Formation*, Publications universitaires de Louvain, Louvain, 1957; H. JEDIN, *L'importanza del decreto tridentino sui seminari nella vita della Chiesa*, in "*Seminarium*," 3 (1963), pp. 396–412.

[832] COUNCIL OF TRENT, Session 23, *De Reformatione*, canon 18, in COD, p. 750.

[833] GRENTE, *Pio V, il Pontefice delle grandi battaglie*, p. 187.

[834] *Epistolae ad principes*, n. 3276.

who not only established a seminary in Milan along with several minor seminaries but also offered his personal assistance to several neighboring dioceses.

The concern for a rigorous cultural formation of clerics and laity required, along with seminaries, the creation of colleges where university studies could be undertaken. Pius V knew very well the Collegio Capranica, which had been established in the fifteenth century by Cardinals Domenico Capranica and Stefano Nardini, and he reformed it with the motu proprio *Accepimus Quod* in 1566.[835] He also knew the colleges that St. Ignatius of Loyola founded: in 1551, the Roman College[836] for the education of teachers, and in 1552 the Germanicum[837] for the education of students. When Pius V thought of instituting a college, however, he took as his model the *Almo Collegio Borromeo*, founded in Pavia in 1561 by the archbishop of Milan. Pavia was an important center of university formation and Pius V wanted to create another college[838] in this city, which like the *Borromeo* would bear his name of *Ghislieri*, with the purpose of hosting and sponsoring both lay and ecclesiastical students. The laying of the first stone of the *Collegio Ghislieri*,[839] which was founded in 1567, took place on July 17, 1571, by the bishop of Pavia. With the bull

[835] *Bullarium Romanum*, vol. 7, pp. 722–724.

[836] See Luca Testa, *Fondazione e primo sviluppo del collegio romano (1565–1608)*, Pontificia Università Gregoriana, Rome, 2002.

[837] See Peter Schmidt, *Das Collegium Germanicum in Rom und die Germaniker. Zur Funktion eines römischen Ausländerseminars (1552–1914)*, Niemeyer, Tubingen, 1984.

[838] Simona Negruzzo, *I collegi della controriforma: il caso pavese*, in *Dai collegi medievali alle residenze universitarie*, Clueb, Bologna, 2010, pp. 43–54.

[839] Massimo Marcocchi, *La personalità di Pio V e le direttive religiose, disciplinari e culturali delle Costituzioni del collegio Ghislieri*, in *Il Collegio universitario Ghislieri*, Giuffrè, Milan, 1966–1970, pp. 93–129; *Il collegio Ghislieri: 1567–1967*, edited by Associazione alunni, Lacroix, Milan, 1967; S. Negruzzo, *Pio V e la formazione dei giovani*, in *San Pio V nella storia*, pp. 23–32; Luciano Musselli, *Il Collegio Ghislieri*, in *Almum Studium Papiense. Storia del l'Università di Pavia*, edited by Dario Mantovani, vol. 1, *Dalle origini all'età Spagnola*, vol. 2, Monduzzi Editore, Bologna, 2013, pp. 947–959.

Copiosus in Misericordia Dominus of January 10, 1569, Pius V wanted to make the new institute directly dependent on the Holy See, exempting it from any other jurisdiction or authority, either ecclesiastical or secular. The text of this bull, Simona Negruzzo observes, "may be understood as the pedagogical manifesto of Pope Ghislieri: after having affirmed that the harmonious synthesis of *sapientia* and *probitas morum* is the goal of every educational activity, it is addressed to young people, so that they may be formed in letters and good morals through their experience at the nascent college in Pavia."[840]

Collegio Ghislieri has endured for over 450 years, being in continuous operation up to the present time.

3. The Reform of Religious Orders

With regard to religious orders, Pius V imposed the cloister, the choral office, and solemn profession on all orders, addressed age limits, and banned living outside of the convent or passing from one order to another. He recommended the virtue of obedience, exhorting all religious to promptly obey their superiors. He reestablished the vow of poverty, forbidding all religious from owning any private property and requiring them not to keep anything in their cell without the permission of their superiors. He reduced the authority of the superiors to a reasonable length of time, recalling that one day they would have to render an account of their governance before the Tribunal of God.[841] The deliberations of Trent, in addition to insisting on the importance of freedom in the choice of entering an order, had also strongly insisted on the cloister for female monasteries. Pius V, at the request of Borromeo and Ormaneto, rigorously applied the cloister to all female convents[842] and promulgated the first universally obligatory pontifical law that prohibited women from entering male monasteries.

[840] Negruzzo, *Pio V e la formazione dei giovani*, p. 31.

[841] Maffei, *Vita di S. Pio V*, pp. 67–71.

[842] Bull *Circa Pastoralis Officii* of 1 February 1566, apud Antonium Bladum, Rome, 1566.

There were those who believed that a remedy to the religious crisis could be found in the abandonment of ecclesiastical celibacy. Maximilian II himself had proposed this to Pius IV. From his very first audience with the German ambassador, Pius V, wanting to prevent any new effort in this direction, said: "I ask your Sovereign to not wish to renew the motion already made to my predecessor; I absolutely would not be able to accept it." The letter sent by him to the archbishop of Salzburg, Johann Jacob von Kuehn-Belasy, with which he exhorted him to act with energy, shattered the hopes of the innovators seeking to relax strict celibacy. "Inform yourself immediately by making a canonical visitation of your clergy, and extirpate evil without any regard, proceeding according to the rigor of the canons. Punish not only those who are your subjects, but also those who try to remove themselves from your jurisdiction as Ordinary. We grant you all authority and we charge you to transmit our apostolic letters to your suffragan bishops, so that they too may act with the same vigor."[843]

Action to address laxness in the orders was swift and decisive. Beginning in November 1566, the conventual branches of the mendicant orders were suppressed and reunited with the observant branches or a similar order. With the bull *Superna Dispositione* of February 18, 1566, Pius V approved all of the privileges, indulgences, and graces granted to the Carmelite Order, including the Sabbatine Privilege.[844] The group of the "Brothers of John of God" or of Mercy was erected on August 8, 1571, with the brief *Salvatoris Nostri*, and it was established as a Religious-Hospitaler Congregation under the Rule of St. Augustine on January 1, 1572, by the bull *Licet ex debito*.[845] The Barnabites, of whom Cardinal Ghislieri was the protector, replaced the Humiliati at Cremona and Monza. Finally, with the

[843] GRENTE *Pio V, il Pontefice delle grandi battaglie*, p. 178.

[844] The privilege is called "sabbatine" because, according to tradition, on the Saturday following their death the Blessed Virgin Mary frees those souls from Purgatory who in life honored her under the title of Our Lady of Mount Carmel by wearing the scapular. See CAMPANA, *Maria nel culto cattolico*, vol. 2, pp. 415–423.

[845] *Bullarium Romanum*, vol. 7, pp. 959–962.

bull *Quantum animus noster*[846] of December 10, 1569, Pius V entrusted to the Camaldolese the historic abbey of Fonte Avvelana, where St. Peter Damian had been prior and wrote his *Regula vitae eremiticae*.

On the day he took possession of the Lateran Basilica, passing in front of the house of professed Jesuits and seeing their superior general, Francis Borgia, surrounded by his community, Pius V ordered the procession to stop and embraced Borgia warmly, encouraging his apostolate. On January 17, 1566, the Society of Jesus obtained a decree from Pius V, *Confirmatio ed extentio privilegii Societatis contra apostatas*, which restated the ban on passing to another order, with exceptions made for certain situations. The pope however did not look kindly on religious with only simple vows, while St. Ignatius and his first companions thought that, prior to solemn vows, it was necessary to have a long training to demonstrate the capacity of the candidates. Furthermore, St. Ignatius had obtained a dispensation for the Jesuits from reciting the choral office, in order not to sacrifice time from the active life of the order. When Pius V asked the Jesuits in 1567 to abolish the law that dispensed them from the choir, St. Francis Borgia presented the pope with a long testimony defending the Jesuit practice.[847] The pontiff, however, in 1568, introduced choral prayer and imposed solemn vows prior to priestly ordination. The Jesuits accepted the requirement of choir (which was later revoked), and with regard to the second point they resorted to the expedient of having the three solemn religious vows made prior to priestly ordination, reserving the right to participate in the general congregation to those who later were admitted to the fourth vow of obedience to the pope. On July 17, 1571, Pius V, who had conceded various privileges to the Society, admitted them among the mendicant orders, that is, among those religious orders that lived on almsgiving, professing evangelical poverty in its perfection.[848] Among the mendicants, which included the Dominicans, the Franciscans,

[846] *Bullarium Romanum*, vol. 7, pp. 788–792.

[847] Jacques Crétineau-Joly, *Histoire religieuse de la Compagnie de Jésus*, Paul Mellier Frères, Paris, 1846, vol. 2, pp. 25–35.

[848] Enrico Rosa, S.J., *I gesuiti. Dalle origini ai nostri giorni*, La Civiltà Cattolica, Rome, 1957, p. 160.

the hermits of St. Augustine, the Carmelites, the Servants of Mary, and the Minims, he gave precedence to the Dominicans.[849]

A very different destiny awaited the Humiliati, a form of Benedictine Third Order founded in the eleventh century, which had become quite rich by dedicating itself to the textile industry, from processing wool to making clothes.[850] The order was protected by many noble families of Milan, who used it as a place of employment for their relatives, and its members lived in magnificent palaces, consuming their rich patrimony in banquets and worldliness.

In 1567, Pius V charged Cardinal Borromeo, who was the cardinal protector of the Humiliati, with overseeing a radical reform of the order in line with the directives of the Council of Trent. The archbishop of Milan, complying with the pope's orders, declared the election of the new general superior of the order that had just taken place invalid, and in virtue of his full pontifical powers, he conferred the office on someone more worthy.[851]

The Humiliati opposed this reform with armed resistance and organized a conspiracy that, in their plans, would have culminated with killing the cardinal of Milan. St. Charles usually prayed each evening, after sunset, in his private chapel inside the archbishop's palace, along with his household and devout people. On the evening of October 26, 1569, as the words were being sung, "*Non turbetur cor vestrum neque formidet*" (don't let your heart be troubled and don't tremble), an assassin fired a shot at the cardinal from a musket at close range.[852] The musketball went through Borromeo's clothing, hitting him in the back, but miraculously left him unharmed. The cardinal remained unshaken and ordered the

849 *Bullarium Romanum*, vol. 7, p. 700.

850 Domenico Maselli, *Saggi di storia ereticale lombarda al tempo di S. Carlo*, Società editrice napoletana, Naples, 1979; *Sulle tracce degli Umiliati*, edited by Maria Pia Alberzoni, Anna Maria Ambrosioni, Alfredo Lucioni, Vita e pensiero, Milan, 1997.

851 Pastor, *Storia dei Papi*, vol. 8, p. 169.

852 Carlo Pirovano, *Sotto il cielo di Lombardia. Breve storia degli umiliati*, Marna, Barzago, Lc, 2007, pp. 21–25.

singing of the Divine Office to continue. When he heard of the attack, Pius V asked Philip II to punish the culprit, and he delegated the bishop of Lodi, Antonio Scarampi, to make a search for the assailant in his name. It was discovered that the shot had been fired by a member of the Humiliati, Gerolamo Donato, known as Farina,[853] and that the attack had been planned by three dignitaries of the order. Pius V gathered accurate information about the Humiliati, and although St. Charles begged him to show mercy, on February 7, 1571, he signed, along with forty-three cardinals, a bull suppressing the order.[854] This act served to restore the constitution of Boniface VIII against the killers of cardinals.

In Episcopalis dignitatis excelsa sede collocati sumus (The episcopal dignity places bishops on a high seat). As one of his biographers observes, the sense of episcopal dignity and of the hierarchy given by the Catholic tradition to Borromeo's meditation on the figure of the ideal bishop must certainly be counted among the reasons that were at the origin of this struggle that St. Charles waged in order to affirm his own authority as bishop against the interference of the Spanish governors, the Milanese Senate, and the requests for exemptions and autonomy made by the religious orders.[855]

4. Pius V and St. Charles Borromeo

The Spanish government was represented in Italy by a governor in Milan and two viceroys, one in Naples and the other in Palermo. In the state of Milan, the king's representative had the duty of applying the orders of the crown, even though his orders and appointments had to obtain the approval of the Milanese Senate in order to have legal value. At that moment the governor of Milan representing Philip II was Gabriel de Cueva,[856] the Duke of Albuquerque. Desirous of defending the

[853] Oreste Clizio, *Gerolamo Donato detto IL FARINA l'uomo che sparò a san Carlo*, Edizioni La Baronata, Lugano and Carrara, 1998.

[854] *Bullarium Romanum*, vol. 7, pp. 885–888.

[855] Panzeri, *Carlo Borromeo*, p. 26.

[856] Gabriel de Cueva, Duke of Albuquerque (1515–1571), viceroy of Navarra, was, until his death, governor and commander general of Milan.

prestige of his sovereign, he clashed with the reforming work of Cardinal Borromeo.[857]

Cardinal Borromeo, in full harmony with Pius V, introduced a special Congregation of the Inquisition in his own archepiscopal curia, closely tied to the Holy Office in Rome. The congregation, composed of theologians and canonists, met weekly and was presided over by the archbishop himself, who followed its work attentively, following the example of what the pope did in Rome. The archbishop of Milan dedicated all of his energies to preserving his diocese from heretical infiltration—especially from Calvinists—from Switzerland and Piedmont as well as the Republic of Venice, and "he made the extirpation of heresy an integral part of his diocesan reform and the reorganization of the Church."[858]

In the government of the diocese that had been entrusted to him, Charles Borromeo did not limit himself to mere words, but he put those words into action, using all the means at his disposal, including force. The cardinal had his own police force, his "armed family," which by ancient custom was tasked with executing the sentences of the episcopal

---

See ROMANO CANOSA, *Storia di Milano nell'età di Filippo II*, Sapere, Rome, 2000.

857 MARIO BENDISCIOLI, *L'inizio della controversia giurisdizionale a Milano tra l'arcivescovo Carlo Borromeo e il Senato milanese (1566–1568)*, in "Archivio storico lombardo," 53 (1926), pp. 241–280; 409–462; BENDISCIOLI, *La Bolla "In coena Domini" e la sua pubblicazione a Milano nel 1568*, in "Archivio storico lombardo," 54 (1927), pp. 381–400; A. BORROMEO, *Archbishop Carlo Borromeo and the Ecclesiastical Policy of Philip II in the State of Milan*, in *San Carlo Borromeo, Catholic Reform and Ecclesiastical Policy in the Second Half of the Sixteenth Century*, edited by John M. Headley and John B. Tomaro, Folger Books, Washington, D.C.-London-Toronto, 1988, pp. 85–111; *L'arcivescovo Carlo Borromeo, la Corona spagnola e le controversie giurisdizionali a Milano*, in *Carlo Borromeo e l'opera della "Grande riforma." Cultura, religione e arti del governo nella Milano del pieno Cinquecento*, edited by Franco Buzzi and Danilo Zardin, Silvana Editoriale, Milan, 1997, pp. 257–272.

858 WIETSE DE BOER, *Carlo Borromeo*, in DSI, vol. 1, p. 280; DE BOER, *The Conquest of the Soul: Confession, Discipline and Public Order in Counter-Reformation Milan*, Brill, Leiden, 2001.

tribunal—a right that was contested by the Milanese Senate. He was also made head of the *crocesignati*, a Milanese congregation of forty nobles dedicated to fighting heresy, to which Pius V granted numerous privileges.[859]

When the cardinal ordered the captain of his police to incarcerate certain suspicious and dangerous individuals, a true sedition broke out. The senate, under the pretext that the captain had been carrying forbidden weapons, had him arrested at the door of the cathedral, imposed "three sections of rope" on him as a public punishment, and exiled him from Milan with the threat of sending him to the galleys. The archbishop, seeing that his jurisdiction had been violated, excommunicated the authors of these measures, but the senate had the excommunication removed from the door of the church. The Duke of Albuquerque, governor of the city, informed Philip II of what had happened, communicating his impression that Borromeo was an ambitious man, and that underneath the mantle of devotion he was hiding purely human ambitions. The canons of La Scala blew on the fire in order to be free of Borromeo, invoking its exemption from episcopal jurisdiction. When Borromeo announced to the canons that he would make a pastoral visit to their collegiate church, the canons went furiously to the governor to enlist his support. But Cardinal Borromeo did not retreat, and went at the head of a solemn procession and presented himself at the door of the church. The canons barricaded themselves inside, posting armed men, who fired a few gunshots. Faced with such violence, the archbishop of Milan dismounted from his mule, raised up the cross, and pronounced the excommunication of the entire chapter.

[859] *Confimatio privilegiorum et gratiarum societatis Cruce Signatorum pro sanctae Inquisitionis contra haereticos praesidio antiquitus institutae*, Bull of October 1, 1568, in *Bullarium Romanum*, vol. 7, pp. 860–861. Founded in 1255 under the patronage of St. Peter Martyr, the Congregation of Crocesignati was a lay association at the service of Inquisition, residing in the Dominican Church of Sant'Eustorgio in Milan. It was composed of forty members, elected from the most noble families of the city. See DENNJ SOLERA, *I crocesignati e le origini della famiglia del Sant'Uffizio romano*, in "Studi Storici" (January–March 2019), pp. 71–102.

The Duke of Albuquerque accused Borromeo of fomenting disorder and wrote to the pope that there would be no peace in Milan until the archbishop was sent away.[860] Having been advised on the conflict, on September 10, 1569, Pius V wrote a brief to the Duke of Albuquerque in which he defended the cardinal and warned the governor of the consequences that would result from any violent acts against him:

> Every affront made against such an eminent dignitary of the Church is also made against us and against the Holy See. Your Lordship wishes us to judge Cardinal Borromeo as an impetuous and obstinate man; but, although we have respect for your words, we are constrained by equity not to accept your opinion. We remember very well the admirable conduct of this worthy archbishop when, under the pontificate of Pius IV, his uncle and our illustrious predecessor, he wonderfully discharged the affairs of the Church. If he truly merited all that you reprove him for, why has he not left any trace of the nature for which you reproach him during the entire time of his administration of a more important and more difficult charge like that of Milan? We therefore feel great pain at seeing a bishop, manifestly given by God to your city, so pure, so zealous, so attentive to the extirpation of abuses, being persecuted by those who ought to defend him and shower him with praise, made the victim of such unjust recriminations, since there is no shadow of any shortcoming in him.[861]

On October 8, 1569, Pius V wrote to Philip II:

> If we did not know Cardinal Borromeo, we would be deeply impressed by the bad information that you enclose regarding his habits, his goals, and his way of proceeding. But the personal esteem that we have for him, confirmed by accurate reports about what he thinks, his conduct, his household, and his administration,

[860] Pastor, *Storia dei Papi*, vol. 8, p. 280.

[861] *Epistolae ad principes*, n. 4405; Grente, *Pio V, il Pontefice delle grandi battaglie*, pp. 68–69.

> incline us to believe that the enemy of the human race, judging the good relations between Your Highness and the cardinal to be fatal to his projects, is doing everything he can to make such a holy prelate lose esteem. . . . You say that in order to assure royal jurisdiction you are constrained to make him leave the city and the state. While we have no difficulty in responding to your threats according to justice, we do warn you, however, out of pure benevolence, to reflect well about what you want to do, so as not to regret too late to have put yourself in an embarrassing situation that could harm you. We have no apprehension for the cardinal. What greater glory could there be for him than to be banished for having defended the freedom and rights of the Church? Even if he were to seal his interdicts with his blood, should he not consider himself as one who is privileged by God? It is therefore in your interest to avoid any imprudent measure, since while you would obtain imperishable glory for the cardinal, you would draw down the condemnation of the Christian world upon your head, and you would cover your name with an indelible stain.[862]

The pope thus sent two future cardinals to Madrid as extraordinary ambassadors: Vincenzo Giustiniani,[863] superior general of the Dominicans, and Giulio Acquaviva,[864] an official of the Signatura. The two envoys managed to dispel the king's prejudices, obtaining his disapproval of the Duke of Albuquerque's way of acting and accepting the reasoning of the archbishop of Milan. But since the attack had been public and the violence of the governor and the canons continued to agitate the city,

[862] Grente, *Pio V, il Pontefice delle grandi battaglie*, pp. 69–70.

[863] Vincenzo Giustiniani (1519–1582), master general of the Order of Preachers from 1558 to 1570, was sent as nuncio to Philip II, and when he was about to go to Flanders in 1570 he was informed of his appointment as cardinal.

[864] Giulio Acquaviva d'Aragona (1546–1574) was the nephew of the superior general of the Society of Jesus, Claudio Acquaviva, and brother of Blessed Rodolfo Acquaviva, martyred in the Orient in 1583. He died when he was only twenty-eight years old.

the pope wanted there to be solemn reparation. On December 22, 1569, Borromeo received a letter from the king, sent through the governor, in which Philip II disapproved of the conduct of the canons of La Scala and demanded that they make amends to the archbishop, accompanying him in procession to their collegiate church, where they were to pay him the homage of their obedience. This was a new confirmation of the close bond that united St. Pius and St. Charles Borromeo, who gave this significant testimony: "In the disturbances provoked against my ministry I received help from the Holy Father that I would not have dared to hope for even from my uncle, Pius IV."[865]

5. The Inquisitional Activity of Borromeo

Collaboration between Pius V and Cardinal Borromeo was also seen in the case of the heretics of Modena. In 1567 a grave conflict arose between Guglielmo Gonzaga, the Duke of Mantua, and Camillo Campeggi,[866] the inquisitor of the city, which culminated with the killing of two Dominican friars in the street. Pius V was not satisfied with the duke's generic apologies and decided to send the archbishop of Milan to Mantua to settle the question definitively. The seriousness with which the cardinal took his task, Pastor recalls, is demonstrated by the fact he ordered numerous hours of prayer to be held in all the churches and convents of Milan asking for a good outcome, arranged in such a way that when an hour of prayer ended in one church, another hour would begin at a different church.[867] The presence of the cardinal in Mantua, which lasted four months, constrained the duke to abandon all opposition, permitting the

[865] GRENTE, *Pio V, il Pontefice delle grandi battaglie*, p. 70.

[866] Camillo Campeggi (1500–1569), Dominican, was inquisitor at Pavia, vicar general of the Inquisition, and inquisitor general in the Duchy of Ferrara and Mantua. Pius V appointed him bishop of Sutri and Nepi in 1569, but he died shortly after taking possession of his see. Campeggi also edited one of the fundamental texts of the medieval inquisition, the *De haereticis tractatus aureus* of Ugolino Zanchini (Rome, 1568). See V. MARCHETTI, *Campeggi Camillo*, in DBI, vol. 17 (1974), pp. 439–440; A. PROSPERI, *Campeggi*, in DSI, vol. 1, pp. 252–253.

[867] PASTOR, *Storia dei Papi*, vol. 8, p. 222.

Inquisition to continue its work. The heretic Endimio Calandra, arrested in Mantua in March 1568, was subjected to a trial, which concluded with his abjuration of heresy, which he pronounced on October 12, 1568.[868]

Cardinal Borromeo, in collaboration with the inquisitor Campeggi, finally took care of flushing out the last followers of the "Georgian sect," which took its name from Giorgio Siculo. His followers nested in the Mantuan monastery of San Benedetto Po of the congregation of Benedictines of Monte Cassino. Some of these monks had turned to the Holy Office to denounce the heresies that were circulating within the monastery where Benedetto Fontanini, the author of the infamous book *Beneficio di Cristo*, had made his profession in 1511. Fontanini, denounced as a heretic in 1548 when he was in Venetian territory, was imprisoned and then confined to the Paduan monastery of Santa Giustina, but following this he returned to the convent of St. Benedict, where he died around 1555–1556, leaving a group of followers. Fontanini had held to the theory of dissimulation along with the Benedictine Giorgio Rioli, known as "the Sicilian." He underwent the inquisition in Ferrara in 1551 and had survived his brother monk. In the monasteries of San Benedetto Po and Santa Giustina the doctrine of Siculo was secretly professed, the most extreme point of which was the denial of the dogma of the Trinity.[869] The arrest of the last followers of Siculo and Fontanini closed a page of which the inquisitor Michael Ghislieri had been the protagonist eighteen years earlier. The investigation uncovered the ramifications of the sect and confirmed the need for extreme vigilance against heresy.

6. The Index of Forbidden Books

Fighting against heresy, Friar Michael Ghislieri had played a primary role in the preparation and application of the first Index of Forbidden Books, which was issued in December 1558 under Paul IV. It is thus no surprise that Pius V committed himself not only to updating and renewing the

[868] Sergio Pagano, *Il processo di Endimio Calandra e l'inquisizione a Mantova nel 1567–1568*, Biblioteca Apostolica Vaticana, Vatican City, 1991.

[869] A. Prosperi, *L'eresia del Libro grande*, pp. 262–266.

Index but also to creating a special congregation that would promote its work.

The composition of lists of prohibited books is a traditional practice of the Church.[870] In 325 the Council of Nicea prohibited Arius's book *Thalia*; in 400 Pope Anastasius condemned the works of Origen, because they are more harmful to the ignorant than useful to the wise; Pope Gelasius I (492–496), in the *Decretum* which promulgates the list of canonical books of the Bible, proscribes a list of apocryphal texts. But it was only after the invention of the printing press that the lists of forbidden books became more frequent,[871] given added impetus because the spread of Protestantism took place above all by means of books.

In 1515 Leo X published the bull *Inter Sollicitudines*,[872] with which he stipulated that every text destined to be printed had to first receive the approbation of religious authority. When he established the Congregation of the Inquisition in 1542, Paul II ordered it to proscribe bad books, and Paul IV requested that the congregation form a list of these books. In those same years the theologians of the University of Paris and the University of Louvain published various lists of prohibited books. In Italy, the first index of forbidden books is considered to be the one published by the city of Lucca in 1545. It was followed by a *Catalog* of prohibited

[870] Jesus Martinez de Bujanda, *Indici dei libri proibiti*, in DSI, vol. 2, pp. 775–780; Martinez de Bujanda (edited by), *Index des livres interdits*, 10 vols., Centre d'Études de la Renaissance-Librairie-Droz, Sherbrooke and Geneva, 1984–1996; Franz Heinrich Reusch, *Der Index der verbotenen Bücher: Ein Beitrag zur Kirchen- und Literaturgeschichte*, Cohen, Bonn, 1883–1885, reprint Scientia Verlag, Aalen, 1967. See also Abbé Louis Petit, *L'Index, son histoire, ses lois, sa force obligatoire*, Lethielleux, Paris, 1888; Lucien Choupin, *Valeur des Décisions Doctrinales et Disciplinares du Saint-Siège*, Beauchesne, Paris, 1928; and Bruno Neveu, *L'erreur et son juge: remarques sur les censures doctrinales à l'époque moderne*. Bibliopolis, Naples, 1993.

[871] Lucien Febvre - Henri-Jean Martin, *La nascita del libro*, Laterza, Rome-Bari 1977; *La Réforme et le livre. L'Europe de l'imprimé (1517–v.1570)*, edited by Jean-François Gilmont, Les Editions du Cerf, Paris, 1990.

[872] *Bullarium Romanum*, vol. 5, pp. 623–624.

books by Monsignor Giovanni della Casa published in Venice in 1549.[873] Other indexes appeared in Florence in 1552 and in Milan and Venice in 1554. All were abolished when the Index of Paul IV was published, printed with a decree of the Inquisition on December 30, 1558.[874]

In the Index, for every letter of the alphabet there were three groups of prohibited works: those by authors who were condemned *a priori* (*in odium auctoris*); those condemned because of the danger that their content represented for faith and morals; and anonymous writings or those signed by pseudonyms. A clause condemned all the anonymous writings that had appeared since 1519. In addition to the writings of the heretics of the sixteenth century, the works of Valla, Erasmus, Machiavelli, and Guicciardini were all banned. A list of printers was also drawn up whose entire corpora were considered dangerous.[875]

Following the request of the Council of Trent, Pius IV directed that the Index be revised and updated with the constitution *Dominici Gregis Custodiae*, issued on March 24, 1564.[876] This Index, which became the model for all successive revisions, consisted of two parts. The first contained ten rules that established the categories of books prohibited either by natural law or by general law. The second gave a list in alphabetical order of those books prohibited by special decree. The first five

[873] *Catalogo di diverse opere, compositioni et libri, li quali come eretici, sospetti, impii et scandalosi si dichiarano dannati et prohibiti in questa inclita città di Vinegia*, Vincenzo Valgruisi, Venice, 1549. The author, Msgr. Giovanni Della Casa (1503–1556), author of the celebrated *Galateo* (1553), was appointed bishop of Benevento and the pontifical nunciature of Venice was entrusted to him, where he published the pamphlet that aroused the opposition of the Senate and was taken out of circulation (only one copy exists today, in the Biblioteca Marciana [Library of St. Mark]).

[874] *Index auctorum, et librorum, qui ab Officio Sanctae Rom. et universalis Inquisitionis caveri ab omnibus et singulis in universa Christiana Republica mandantur, sub censuris contra legentes, veltenentes libros prohibitos in bulla, quae lecta est in Coena Domini expressis, et sub aliis poenis in decreto eiusdem sacri officii contentis*, Antonio Blado, Rome, 1558.

[875] Mario Scaduto, S.J., *Laìnez e l'indice del 1559. Lullo, Sabunde, Savonarola, Erasmo*, in "Archivum Historicum Societatis Iesu," 24 (1955), pp. 3–32.

[876] *Bullarium Romanum*, vol. 7, pp. 281–282.

rules concerned books stained by heresy. Luther, Zwingli, and Calvin were specifically named, but also the radical Anabaptist and Socinian authors. The vernacular version of the Bible, which the Lutherans had so insistently promoted, was also condemned. Catholics were able to read an authorized version of it only after receiving the permission of their parish priest or their confessor. The last five rules were concerned with the banning of obscene and immoral books, with an exception made for the classical books of antiquity, which were forbidden only to the very young. Books of magic, necromancy, judicial astrology, and the Jewish Kabbalah were also condemned.

Pius V confirmed these rules and established a special Congregation of the Index, which was destined to become a permanent organ of the government of the Church.[877] The task of the congregation was to evaluate all books that had been published recently (or not so recently); to periodically draw up an index of prohibited books, and to monitor its application. The congregation was composed of cardinals created by Pius V, all of whom belonged to the regular clergy: two Dominicans, Arcangelo de' Bianchi and the general of the order, Vincenzo Giustiniani; the general of the Cistercians, Jérôme Souchier; and the Minor Conventual Felice Peretti, the future Sixtus V. The congregation held its first session on March 27, 1571. Pius V consulted it continually about questions and theological difficulties that originated above all in the battle against Protestantism.

The legislation of the Index was extended to all Catholic countries and to all the baptized, including the highest levels of the hierarchy, except obviously the members of the Congregation of the Inquisition and the Congregation of the Index.

7. Old and New Cardinals

One of the causes of the crisis in the Church in the century preceding the pontificate of Pius V was the appointment of cardinals who were morally

[877] Gigliola Fragnito, *Pio V e la censura*, in *Pio V nella società e nella politica del suo tempo*, pp. 129–158.

bankrupt, who in turn elected popes who were not worthy of carrying out their supreme mission. An example of this evil practice, which caused severe pain to Pius V, was the affair of Cardinal Innocenzo Ciocchi del Monte,[878] who had been a dissolute man since his youth but was elevated to the cardinalate by Julius III. After he killed one of his servants in 1559, the following year, during a trip to Venice and Rome, Cardinal del Monte killed an innkeeper and his son in Nocera Umbra for trivial reasons. On May 27, 1560, he was imprisoned in Castel Sant'Angelo on the orders of Pius IV, but he was set free after little more than a year after paying a restitution of 100,000 scudi. His disordered life did not cease, and then in 1566, during the conclave that elected Pius V, he sought illegally to communicate with the outside. In December 1567 he committed a more serious crime in Tuscany, when he kidnapped two women of humble origins in Sienese territory, keeping them locked up in his villa for several days. Pius V sought to investigate the matter, but Cosimo I protected the cardinal, who was able to remain in Tuscany. When he returned to Rome towards the end of 1568, the cardinal was forbidden to return to Florence, and he was assigned a room in the Vatican with two Theatine monks who sought to make him repent. But in May 1569 Cardinal del Monte was once again placed on trial after two prostitutes were discovered in his carriage and it was found that they had frequented his house for all of Lent and Holy Week. When he was in prison the cardinal confessed not only the murder of 1559 but also that he frequented various prostitutes and kept them in his house as concubines. The commission of cardinals

[878] Innocenzo Ciocchi del Monte (1532–1577), of humble origins, took this name because Cardinal Giovanni Ciocchi del Monte adopted him from his brother and, immediately after his election as pope, he created him cardinal on May 30, 1550, despite the fact that the nomination of the seventeen-year-old caused scandal throughout all of Rome. By the order of Pius V, he was not able to participate in the next conclave in 1572, but the new pope Gregory XIII wanted to rehabilitate him and recalled him to Rome. See Pietro Messina, *Del Monte Innocenzo*, in DBI, vol. 38 (1990), pp. 138–141; Francis A. Burkle Young, Michael Leopoldo Doerrer, *The Life of Cardinal Innocenzo del Monte: A Scandal in Scarlet*, E. Mellen Press, Lewiston, 1997.

that was created to judge him condemned him to remain enclosed in the monastery of Monte Cassino, guarded by two Jesuits. The cardinal seemed to repent and left the Papal States.

The affair of Cardinal del Monte naturally was an extreme case, but it was the expression of that tendency to violence and immorality that formed the inheritance of the Renaissance Church. For this reason, the Council of Trent had recommended in the first canon of the decree *De Reformatione* that the Roman Pontiff should "show that solicitude which, in virtue of his office, he ought to have for the universal Church, especially in choosing only excellent cardinals and in placing excellent and suitable pastors in charge of individual churches, and all the more so since the Lord Jesus Christ will ask him to give an account for the blood of his sheep who perish because of the wicked governance of negligent pastors who are forgetful of their duty."[879]

Pius V, aware of his responsibility as Supreme Pastor of the Church, wanted to examine the clergy around him, and in the first consistory that was held shortly after his election on March 6, 1566, he limited himself to appointing only one cardinal, his first nephew Michele Ghislieri-Bonelli, whose righteousness was known to all.

Two years passed before the creation of more new cardinals. This time four were very carefully chosen for the consistory of March 24, 1568. They were the Spaniard Diego de Espinosa, the president of the Royal Council of Castile, the Frenchman Jérôme Souchier, the superior general of the Cistercians, and two Italians: Antonio Carafa, the nephew of Pope Paul IV, and Gian Paolo della Chiesa, referendary of the Apostolic Signatura.

After two more years, on May 17, 1570, Pius V created sixteen new cardinals: the Frenchmen Charles d'Angennes de Rambouillet, bishop of Le Mans, and Nicolas de Pellevé, the archbishop of Reims; and the Spaniards Gaspar de Zúñiga y Avellaneda, archbishop of Seville, and Gaspare Cervantes, archbishop of Tarragona. The other twelve were Italians: the master general of the Dominicans, Vincenzo Giustiniani; the Dominican

[879] COUNCIL OF TRENT, Session 25, *De reformatione*, canon 1, in COD, p. 761.

Arcangelo Bianchi, the pope's regular confessor; Girolamo Rusticucci, who had been his secretary for nine years; the general of the Capuchin Order, Felice Peretti da Montalto (the future Sixtus V); the Theatine Paolo Burali, bishop of Piacenza; the inquisitor Giulio Antonio Santori, archbishop of Santa Severina; Giovanni Girolamo Albani, the governor of the Marches, who had helped Friar Ghislieri against the heretics in Bergamo; Giovanni Aldobrandini, the bishop of Imola; Marcantonio Maffei, the archbishop of Chieti; Carlo Grassi, the bishop of Montefiascone; Donato Cesi, the apostolic administrator of Narni; and the young Giulio Acquaviva d'Aragona, referendary of the Apostolic Signatura, whose brother Rodolfo would die as a martyr in India.

The appointments were the fruit of a careful evaluation of the candidates and aimed at the conclave that would choose the successor of Pius V. The pope wanted to make sure that the possibility of scandals and intrigues was minimized, and he chose zealous men, but also men who were scholars in the ecclesiastical sciences, such as Zúñiga, who had been a professor in Salamanca, or Giustiniani, who had edited the works of St. Thomas Aquinas. Some had notable juridical experience, such as Albani, Burali, and Santori. For this reason, Pastor comments, "the renewal of the College of Cardinals in 1570 was an *act of reform* in the most beautiful sense of the word."[880] How much the pope had the spiritual life of his collaborators at heart is confirmed by the praises that he lavished on those who shone by reason of the purity of their faith and morals. When, for example, he honored Juan de Ribera,[881] who had been archbishop of Valencia since 1569, with the title of Patriarch of Antioch, he celebrated him as "the light of all of Spain" because of his holiness of life.[882]

[880] Pastor, *Storia dei Papi*, vol. 8, p. 117. On the list of cardinals, see also Catena, *Vita del gloriosissimo San Pio V*, pp. 348–353.

[881] Juan de Ribera (1532–1611), son of Pedro Afán de Ribera, first Duke of Alcalá, was viceroy and archbishop of Valencia and founder of the order of the Discalced Augustinian Nuns. In 1960 he was proclaimed a saint by Pope John XXIII.

[882] Pastor, *Storia dei Papi*, vol. 8, p. 153.

Among the new cardinals, a prominent figure, who was destined to be beatified, was the Theatine Paolo Burali,[883] whom Pius V had appointed as bishop of Piacenza. The new bishop revealed in his diocese all of his greatness as an organizer and as a spiritual teacher. His apostolic activity took place during eight years of intense apostolate in which he applied the Tridentine decrees by making two pastoral visits to the entire diocese, by holding two synods, by constantly preaching to the faithful with the help of the Theatines, Somascans, and Capuchins, and by founding a seminary, to whose leadership he called another future saint, the Theatine Andrea Avellino.[884]

8. The Condemnation of Sodomy

In the age of Humanism and the Renaissance, homosexuality and sodomy, which since antiquity had been considered an opprobrious vice, were widespread, even in the Church. The cities of Sodom and Gomorrah, which were immersed in this sin against nature, were condemned to destruction by God, as St. Peter recalls (2 Pet. 2:6–9), so that throughout the ages they would be a divine warning. St. Peter Damian, Doctor of the Church, in his *Liber Gomorrhanus*, written in 1051 by Pope St. Leo IX, vigorously denounces the grave consequences caused by this vice that "kills the body, ruins the soul, contaminates the flesh, extinguishes the light of the intellect, drives the Holy Spirit out of the temple of the soul

[883] *Scipione Burali* (1511–1578), took the name Paolo d'Arezzo, after entering the Theatine Clerics Regular. Pius V appointed him bishop of Piacenza on July 23, 1568, and cardinal on May 17, 1570. In 1576 Pope Gregory XIII transferred him to be archbishop of Naples, where he is buried in the Basilica of San Paolo Maggiore. Clement XIV proclaimed him Blessed on May 13, 1772. See Gaspare De Caro, *Burali, Scipione*, in DBI, vol. 15 (1972), pp. 370–376; Francesco Andreu, *Burali*, in BSS, vol. 3 (1962), cols. 602–604; Franco Molinari, *Il cardinale teatino Paolo Burali e la riforma tridentina a Piacenza*, Pontificia Università Gregoriana, Rome, 1957.

[884] Lancellotto Avellino (152–1608) took the name of Andrew after taking the habit of the Theatine Clerics Regular. He was canonized together with Pius V by Clement XII on May 22, 1712. One of his disciples was the Venerable Lorenzo Scupoli (1530–1610), the author of the celebrated treatise, *The Spiritual Combat*.

and introduces the demon there." Those who are guilty of sodomy, he affirms, ought to be inexorably deprived in a definitive manner of their offices, qualifications, and ecclesiastical dignities. It would be better for the community to be without priests or dioceses without bishops than to be led by sodomites.[885]

St. Bernardine of Siena had denounced this moral scourge in the fifteenth century with fiery words: "God always turns his wrath against this sin more than any other. The great flood for the whole world and the fire and brimstone for Sodom and Gomorrah."[886]

For the Inquisition, sodomy, more than just a sin, was a heresy, because it violated both the natural and divine law.[887] In fact, according to St. Thomas Aquinas, if the order of reason comes from man, the order of nature comes from God himself. Therefore, "in sins against nature in which the natural order is violated, God himself is offended in his quality as the one who orders nature."[888]

On November 25, 1557, by the decision of Paul IV, sodomy was formally numbered among crimes against the Faith. Cardinal Ghislieri had countersigned the decree, and once he was elected pope he reinforced it. According to Count Arco,[889] from his very first year of government two purposes kept the pope especially busy: taking care of the Inquisition and the struggle against sodomy, "the horrible sin, for which the terrible judgment of God makes cities that are stained with it burn."[890]

In the bull *Cum Primum Apostolatus Officium*,[891] of April 1, 1566, Pius V condemned those who did not respect divine worship and those who blasphemed or sinned by simony, but also those who stained themselves

[885] St. Peter Damian, *Liber Gomorrhianus*, in PL, vol. 145, cols. 159–190, Italian translation, *Liber Gomorrhianus*, Edizioni Fiducia, Rome, 2015.

[886] St. Bernardine of Siena, *Del peccato contro natura*, in *Le prediche volgari*, Libreria Editrice Fiorentina, Florence, p. 277.

[887] P. Scaramella, *Sodomia*, in DSI, vol. 3, pp. 1445–1450.

[888] St. Thomas Aquinas, *Summa Theologica*, II-IIae, q. 154, a. 12.

[889] Pastor, *Storia dei Papi*, vol. 8, p. 227.

[890] *Bullarium Romanum*, vol. 7, p. 702.

[891] *Bullarium Romanum*, vol. 7, pp. 434–440.

with the sin of sodomy. For these, the pontiff intensified the penalties: even ecclesiastics would have to be consigned to the secular arm for the execution of the sentence, which was generally understood as *ultimum supplicium*, the death penalty. In the document the pope affirms,

> Having turned our minds to remove everything that can offend the divine majesty in some way, we have decided to punish first of all and without delay those things that, both with the authority of the Sacred Scriptures and with very serious examples, are shown to be more displeasing to God than any other thing and which spur him to wrath; that is, the neglect of divine worship, ruinous simony, the crime of blasphemy, and the execrable libidinous vice against nature, sins for which people and nations are scourged by God, with just condemnation, with disasters, wars, famines, and plagues. . . . The magistrates know that if even after this constitution they are negligent in punishing these delicts, they will be guilty when they stand before divine judgment and will also incur our indignation. . . . If anyone commits the nefarious crime against nature, because of which divine anger fell on the sons of iniquity, he shall be consigned to the secular arm for punishment, and if he is a cleric, he shall be subjected to a similar penalty, after having been deprived of every degree.

In a second document, the bull *Horrendum Illud* of August 30, 1569,[892] Pius V wrote that

> that horrible crime, because of which corrupt and impure cities were destroyed with fire by divine judgment, provokes in us a bitter pain and shakes our minds, pushing us to such a crime with the greatest zeal possible. With good reason, the Lateran Council established by a decree that every member of the clergy caught in that vice against nature, since the wrath of God falls on the children of perfidy, must be removed from the clerical order or

[892] *Bullarium Romanum*, vol. 7, p. 33.

> forced to do penance in a monastery; so that the contagion of such a grave offense may not progress with greater audacity because of impunity, which is the greatest incitement to sin, and in such a way as to punish more severely clerics who are guilty of this heinous crime and are not frightened by the death of their souls, we decide that they shall be consigned to the severity of the secular authority, which applies the civil law. Therefore, desiring to pursue more rigorously that which we have exercised since the beginning of our pontificate, we establish that any priest or member of the clergy, whether secular or regular, who commits such an execrable crime shall by the authority of the present canon be deprived of every clerical privilege, every post, dignity, and ecclesiastical benefice. And after being degraded by the ecclesiastical judge, he shall be immediately consigned to the secular authority so that he may be destined for that sentence foreseen by the law as an opportune punishment inflicted upon the laity who have fallen into such an abyss.

The severe measures taken by Pius V against sodomites, common to all governments of that time, must naturally be understood by bearing in mind that, in addition to his role as head of the Church, he was also the temporal sovereign of the Papal States. However, even after the fall of the Papal States (September 20, 1870), the condemnation of homosexuality was restated in the twentieth century by John Paul II[893] and by Cardinal Ratzinger, who became Pope Benedict XVI,[894] thus constituting part of the ordinary Magisterium of the Church.

[893] John Paul II, Angelus Address, 20 February 1994, in *L'Osservatore Romano*, 22 February 1994.

[894] Congregation for the Doctrine of the Faith, *"Persona Humana" Declaration on Certain Questions Concerning Sexual Ethics*, 29 December 1975, in AAS, vol. 68 (1976), pp. 77–96, and Congregation for the Doctrine of the Faith, *Letter on the Pastoral Care of Homosexual Persons*, 1 October 1986, in AAS, vol. 79 (1987), pp. 543–554.

9. The Condemnation of Necromancy

During the period of Humanism, along with sodomy, the plague of occultism and magic, known also as necromancy, was widespread. The term necromancy means, in a strict sense, the evocation of spirits of the dead and of demons by means of determined magic formulas, but in the sixteenth centrury it was applied to any form of the occult sciences.[895] In the *Directorium Inquisitorum*, Nicolas Eymerich makes explicit reference to several magic texts, such as the *Clavicula Salomonis* and the *Tesoro Della Negromanzia*, explaining that "the heretical diviners or seers are those who, in order to predict the future or penetrate the secrets of hearts, render a cult of *latria* or *dulia* to the devil, rebaptizing children, etc." These "are clearly heretical and ought to be considered as such by the Inquisition."[896] The intervention of an exorcist was very often needed against the malefices of necromancers. The essential difference between the exorcist and the necromancer was—as has been observed—that "the exorcist's intent was to dispel the demons, while the conjurer's was to summon them."[897]

The historian of philosophy Frances A. Yates has traced the history of this "occult philosophy" in the Renaissance and Reformation through such figures as the Florentine humanist Pico della Mirandola, the German humanist Johannes Reuchlin, and the Kabbalist friar of Venice Francesco Giorgi, up to Heinrich Cornelius Agrippa, who in his *De occulta philosophia* united the hermetic magic of Ficino with the Kabbalistic magic of Pico della Mirandola.[898] Their heir would be the English Kabbalist John Dee,

[895] LYNN THORNDIKE, *The History of Magic and Experimental Science*, Columbia University Press, New York, 1932; DANIEL P. WALKER, *Spiritual and Demonic Magic from Ficino to Campanella*, The Warburg Institute, London, 1958 (Italian translation, *Magia spirituale e magia demoniaca da Ficino a Campanella*, Aragno, Turin, 2002); OSCAR DI SIMPLICIO, *Autunno della stregoneria. Maleficio e magia nell'Italia moderna*, Il Mulino, Bologna, 2005.

[896] EYMERICH, PEÑA, *Il Manuale dell'inquisitore*, p. 76.

[897] RICHARD KIECKHEFER, *Forbidden Rites: A Necromancer's Manual of the Fifteenth Century*, Tamesis Books, London, 1997, p. 14.

[898] Heinrich Cornelius Agrippa von Nettesheim (1486–1536), nicknamed "the archmagus," wrote *De occulta philosophia*. See THORNDIKE, *The History*

the necromancer-magician of Queen Elizabeth Tudor.[899] In 1564 the *Magia Naturalis* of Giovanni Battista della Porta[900] was also published, which tried to distinguish demonic magic from natural magic, which sought to concern itself with the powers hidden in nature, hidden from the senses. In reality, in both cases the magic formula is set in opposition to prayer, as an instrument to obtain determined ends without having recourse to the help of God, and also an emancipation from Divine Wisdom.

Isidore of Seville had already affirmed, in book 8 of his *Etymologiae*, dedicated to the Church and to heresies, that

> the magi are those who are popularly called sorcerers or witches due to the magnitude of their crimes. They agitate the elements, disturb men's minds, and kill by the power of spells alone without a sip of poison. Necromancy is linked on the one hand to divination techniques, and on the other hand to magic both as something that produces illusions and as a harmful art. It was invented by the evil angels, along with other forms of technical and inspired divination. Magic arts upset the natural elements and the human mind, provoking death simply by the power of the magic formulas without the ingestion of poison. Their rites are composed of evocations of demons, blood sacrifices, and contact with corpses.[901]

---

of Magic, pp. 127–139. Walker emphasizes the "overtly demonic" character of Agrippa's magic, (*Spiritual and Demonic Magic*, p. 75). Marlowe's *Doctor Faustus* expressly states that it is modeled on Agrippa, while the monologue that opens Goethe's *Faust* is a summary of another work by Agrippa, *De vanitate scientiarum*.

[899] Frances A. Yates, *The Occult Philosophy in the Elizabethan Age*, Routledge & Kegan Paul, London, 1979.

[900] Giovanni Battista Della Porta (1535–1615) was a magus and an alchemist, and also the author of *De humana physiognomonia* in four books (1586). See Donato Verardi, *La scienza e i segreti della natura a Napoli nel Rinascimento*, Firenze University Press, Florence, 2018.

[901] Isidore of Seville, *Etymologiae*, VIII, 9, 11. See William E. Klingshirn, *Isidore of Seville's Taxonomy of Magicians and Diviners*, in "Traditio," 58 (2003), pp. 59–90; Valerio Neri, *Magia e divinazione in Isidoro di Siviglia (Etym. VIII, 9)*, in *Ravenna Capitale Uno sguardo ad Occidente Romani e*

The occult sciences were practiced by humanists and from them they spread to the authors of the Protestant Revolution. Philip Melancthon,[902] for example, was interested in Kabbalah, astrology, and divination. He affirmed that after the fall of Constantinople into the hands of the Turks, the scholars of Byzantium, who guarded the core and most precious essence of the knowledge of antiquity, had transmitted it to the Florentines, and from Florence it passed to the "reformers" of the sixteenth century.[903] This explains the severity with which the Inquisition pursued the spread of necromancy. Like the Roman Inquisition, the Milanese Inquisition was also concerned with it. In the course of the first provincial council called in 1568 by Charles Borromeo, the decree *De magicis artibus, veneficiis divinationibusque prohibitis* was approved, which attacked necromancers, astrologers, diviners, and alchemists.[904] For Borromeo the magic arts fell into the category of crimes of apostasy and heresy, as was demonstrated by the use of the Eucharist, the crucifix, and sacred images for the purposes of spells and curses. On this point too, the ideas of the archbishop of Milan were in accord with those of the Roman Pontiff, who attributed above all to the Jews the false arts of "divination, conjuring, magic, and sorcery."[905]

10. The Condemnation of Simony and the Economic Reform

Simony was an ancient evil, which Pius V condemned by comparing it to sodomy. New decrees against the act of selling Church offices and

---

Goti - Isidoro di Siviglia, Maggioli, Santarcangelo di Romagna, 2012, pp. 147–160.

[902] On Philip Melancthon (1497–1560), see Wilhelm Maurer, *Der Junge Melanchthon*, 2 vols., Vandenhoeck and Ruprecht, Göttingen, 2001; *Melanchthon in Europe: His Work and Influence beyond Wittenberg*, edited by K. Maag, Baker Books, Grand Rapids, 1999. Melancthon was the nephew of Johannes Reuchlin (1455–1522), a friend of Luther, and his teacher and tutor in Greek and Hebrew.

[903] Cantimori, *Umanesimo e religione*, pp. 265–267.

[904] *Acta Ecclesiae Mediolanensis a S. Carolo Card: Archiep. Condita ...*, Paulo Pagnonio, Mediolani, 1843, p. 11.

[905] *Bullarium Romanum*, vol. 7, p. 74. See Marina Caffiero, *Legami pericolosi. Ebrei e cristiani tra eresia, libri proibiti e stregoneria*, Einaudi, Turin, 2012.

roles had been issued by the Council of Trent.[906] With the constitution *Intollerabilis* of June 1, 1569, Pius V not only confirmed these decrees under the pain of excommunication, loss of the right to benefice, and corporal punishment, but he also desired that even its appearance would be eliminated, forbidding so-called "confidential" simony, by which the transfer of benefices to relatives took place by means of contract and inheritance.[907] Some popes and bishops had made use of simoniacal maneuvers to finance their initiatives, but when Pius V was told that because of his measures papal income was diminishing, he responded with disdain: "Better poverty than disorder; the patrimony of the Church must no longer be the prey of avarice and ambition."[908]

The ecclesiastical reform of Pius V was also expressed by means of economic instruments. Monsignor Bartolomeo Bussotti, who held the position of treasurer general throughout the entire pontificate, was the faithful and capable executor of papal directives in this area. The pope wanted above all to base his economic policy on great thriftiness regarding the pomp of the papal court, which would also lighten the tax burden that weighed upon the population.[909] Among the first acts of Pius V was the abolition, in Rome, of the tax on wine and the abolition of the tax on coffee in the Patrimony of St. Peter, replacing it with a monetary fee that was to be paid only one time. The pope further issued severe prescriptions against those officials of the administration who accepted gifts as bribes. The important bull *Admonet nos*[910] of March 29, 1567, prohibited the alienation of property belonging to the Apostolic See.

[906] COUNCIL OF TRENT, Session 24, *De reformatione*, canon 14, in COD, p. 768.

[907] *Bullarium romanum*, vol. 7, pp. 157–160. Simony is called "confidential" when it involves the temporary transfer of an ecclesiastical benefice to a third person, provided however that, at a later time, it is restored to the person who obtained it or to a family member (INNOCENZO PARISELLO, *Simonia*, in EC, vol. 2 [1953], col. 643 [642–646]).

[908] GRENTE, *Pio V, il Pontefice delle grandi battaglie*, p. 177.

[909] See M. C. GIANNINI, *L'oro e la tiara. La costruzione dello spazio fiscale italiano della Santa Sede (1560–1620)*, il Mulino, Bologna, 2003.

[910] *Bullarium romanum*, vol. 7, p. 560ff.

The intention was to prevent future pontiffs from any action that could prejudice the Church's patrimony, bringing an end to the era of so-called "great nepotism," with which major jurisdictions had been devolved to relatives of the popes up until that time.[911]

On the other hand, the multiple activities of Pius V required a considerable financial effort, not only for the governance of the Papal States but also to support his great religious and diplomatic objectives on the international level. The financial policy of the pope was aimed at increasing income and recovering ecclesiastical income that was enjoyed by private individuals. In 1569, as the need to help French Catholics became more and more pressing, Bussotti suggested to the pope the imposition of an extraordinary tax in the amount of 500,000 scudi. In June of the same year, in order to create new income for the Apostolic Camera, the papal treasurer proposed the selling of the Papal State notariates, which yielded a revenue of 70,000 scudi. Such measures undoubtedly had their effect, for when Pius V died, despite the help he gave to the king of France against the Huguenots, the expenses incurred on behalf of the Holy League and sending the papal naval contingent to Lepanto, the state treasury of the Church amounted to one million scudi, plus a 500,000 scudi loan collectible after three months, in addition to the substantial amounts that were found in Castel Sant'Angelo and in the pope's private rooms.

The papal treasury had also supported Mary Stuart with 20,000 gold scudi and the English Catholics who were victims of Protestant persecutions with 50,000 gold scudi. Although he was thrifty, Pius V had also exercised grandiose beneficence in the Papal States, giving the treasurer Bussotti a mandate to subsidize the hospitals, especially Santo Spirito, to which he gave 20,000 scudi; to increase the establishments for poor girls at the Minerva; and to make a donation of 10,000 scudi to the Monte di

[911] Federico Alessandro Goria, *La bolla De non infeudando del 1567: politica antinepotistica e tutela del demanio ecclesiastico*, in Aa. Vv., *Le Carte del Diritto e della Fede*, Atti del convegno di studi, Alessandria, 16–17 June 2006, edited by Elisa Mongiano, Gian Maria Panizza, Società di Storia e di Archeologia, Alessandria, 2008, pp. 93–105.

Pietà in order to place the institution in a position to lend to the poor more freely, ordering at the same time that the pawns could not be sold for eighteen months.

One of the last acts of Pius V was to give Bussotti a box containing 13,000 scudi, from which he used to draw money for his private almsgiving, recommending that he donate the money toward the war against the Turks.[912] This confirms what the dominant concerns of Pope Pius V were.

[912] Luisa Bertoni Argentini, *Bussotti Bartolomeo*, in DBI, vol. 15 (1972), p. 589.

8

The Pope of the Catechism, the Breviary, and the Mass

1. The Roman Catechism

In its last session, the Council of Trent gave a mandate to Pope Pius IV to proceed to the publication of the Roman Catechism, the Roman Breviary, and the Roman Missal.[913] It was his successor, Pius V, who promulgated three documents: the catechism in 1566, the breviary in 1568, and the missal in 1570.

The choice of these three actions was not casual: the intention of the Council was to actuate a true reform, beginning with what the clergy taught, prayed, and celebrated.[914] From the beginning of the Church, faith and liturgy were intimately tied together. The formula that states the way in which the rule of prayer corresponds to the rule of faith goes back to the fifth century: "*Lex orandi, lex credendi.*" St. Prosper of Aquitaine attributes this sentence to Pope St. Celestine I, said to have been

[913] COUNCIL OF TRENT, Session 25 of December 4, 1563, Decree *De indice librorum et catechismo, breviario et missali*, in COD, p. 797.

[914] DAVIDE RIGHI, *Dall' Ordo Missae di Pio V all' Ordo Missae di Paolo VI. Contesti storici e prospettive teologico-liturgiche*, in "Rivista di teologia dell'evangelizzazione," 13 (2009), p. 15 (pp. 9–37).

the first to affirm that "the order of supplication determines the rule of faith" (*Legem credendi lex statuat supplicandi*).[915]

The relationship between the doctrine of the Faith and liturgical cult may be compared to that between the body and the soul, between the thought and the word.[916] Therefore, in its formulas, rites, and symbols, Catholic liturgy ought to reflect its dogma, and so also its pastoral application should be coherent with doctrine. "The liturgy in other words could not have formulated its prayers and celebrated its mysteries if faith in those same truths and mysteries did not exist. It is thus not the liturgy that creates faith or dogma, but vice versa: from faith and dogma, there arises the liturgical celebration of this or that mystery with those determined formulas."[917]

In this sense, the Roman Missal promulgated by Pius V expresses the truth that the catechism had summarized and that the Council of Trent had defined against the Protestant innovators. The catechism, missal, and breviary are thus different but complementary expressions of the same Tradition of the Church.

The term *catechism* means a compendium of the principal truths of Christian faith and moral teaching, laid out in a clear and comprehensive way, preferably in a dialogical format.[918] The sixteenth century may be called the century of catechisms because of the opposition that it saw between those who, by means of catechisms, wanted to either distort the Catholic Faith or reaffirm it. However, it is not true that catechisms were invented by Protestants. In the Middle Ages, up until the thirteenth century, the *Disputatio per Interrogationes et Responsiones*,[919] attributed to

915 The aphorism is taken from the *Capitula Celestini* of 431, quoted by Prosper of Aquitaine (See PL, 50, 535, now in DENZ-H, n. 246).

916 Msgr. Mario Righetti, *Manuale di storia liturgica*, Editrice Ancora, Milan, 1964, vol. 1, p. 30.

917 Giuseppe Löw, *Liturgia*, in EC, vol. 7 (1951), cols. 1443–1444.

918 C. Testore, *Catechismo*, in EC, vol. 3 (1949), cols. 1118–1125; Eugène Mangenot, *Catéchisme*, in DTC, vol. 2 (1932), cols. 1895–1968.

919 Alcuin, *Disputatio per interrogationes et responsiones*, PL, vol. 101, cols. 1097–1144c. The text was commissioned to Blessed Alcuin of York (735–804) by the Emperor Charlemagne. See Claudio Leonardi, *Alcuino e la*

Alcuin, which summarizes Christian doctrine in a dialogue form, was widely disseminated. In the fifteenth century, the *Libretto della doctrina christiana* of St. Antonino of Florence,[920] which preceded Luther's catechism by sixty years, may be considered a true and proper catechism in the modern sense of the term. It is true, however, that Martin Luther published a *Little Catechism* for children in 1528 in order to spread his ideas, and a *Large Catechism* the following year, with which he intended to give pastors a greater explanation of his doctrines. Calvin also published a catechism in 1538 that summarized his new doctrine (*Instruction et confession de foi dont on use dans l'Église de Genève*).

Many Catholic catechisms appeared during the same years to fight the Protestant heresy, written at the initiative of individual theologians or religious institutes.[921] The most widespread catechism of the sixteenth century was the one written by St. Peter Canisius: *Summa Doctrinae Christianae per Quaestiones Tradita* (1554), followed in 1556 by *Catechismus Minimus* and in 1557 by *Catechismus Major*.[922]

The Council of Trent, at the suggestion of Cardinal Borromeo, addressed the question of books "to finally restore the Catholic faith, polluted

---

scuola palatina: le ambizioni di una cultura unitaria, in Medioevo latino. *La cultura dell'Europa cristiana*, edited by Francesco Santi, Sismel-Edizioni del Galluzzo, Florence, 2004, pp. 191–217.

920 Antonino Pierozzi (1389–1459), archbishop of Florence, was proclaimed a saint by Pope Adrian VI on May 31, 1523, and is known as St. Antonino of Florence. His work has been reprinted, edited by Gilberto Aranci: *Libretto della dottrina cristiana attribuito a s. Antonino arcivescovo di Firenze*, Pontecorboli Editore, Florence, 1996. See also G. ARANCI, *I 'Confessionali' di S. Antonino Pierozzi e la tradizione catechistica del '400*, in "Vivens Homo," 3 (1992), pp. 273–292.

921 See JEAN-CLAUDE DHOTEL, *Les origines du catéchisme moderne d'après les premiers manuels imprimés en France*, Aubier, Paris, 1967.

922 The theologian and Jesuit controversialist, in the *Summa Doctrina Christiana*, written for educated people, "expounds all of Catholic doctrine with exactness and lucidity in 211 questions and answers (later expanded to 222), emphasizing those Catholic truths and customs that were most opposed and fought against" (ARNOLDO M. LANZ, *Canisio Pietro*, in EC, vol. 9, col. 1453 [cols. 1451–1453]).

and tarnished in many places, to its ancient purity and splendor"[923] in its nineteenth session on February 26, 1562.

In the concluding decrees of December 4, 1563,[924] the Council Fathers emphasized the need for a compilation of the doctrine of the Faith, and they sent the material that had already been collected to Pius IV, including a popular catechism on the truths of the Faith in the Creed, the Commandments, the sacraments, and prayer. Thus, as is written in the preface of the Roman Catechism, "they did not limit themselves to clarifying by their definitions the principal points of Catholic doctrine against all the heresies of our time, but they also decreed to propose a certain formula and a determined method for instructing the Christian people in the rudiments of the faith, to be adopted in all the churches by those who hold the office of legitimate pastors and teachers."[925]

Pius IV appointed a commission to examine this material, composed of Leonardo Marini,[926] the archbishop of Lanciano; Egidio Foscarari,[927] the bishop of Modena; Muzio Calini,[928] the bishop of Trent;

[923] Council of Trent, Session 28 of 26 February 1562, in COD, p. 723.

[924] Council of Trent, Session 25 of 4 December 1563, in COD, p. 797.

[925] Preface of the *Roman Catechism*, n. 4.

[926] Leonardo Marini (1509–1573), a Dominican from the Island of Chios in Greece, administrator of the Diocese of Mantua, appointed archbishop of Lanciano by Pius IV, was appointed apostolic visitator of twenty-five dioceses after the redaction of the catechism. See Paolo Cherubelli, *Il contributo degli Ordini religiosi al Concilio di Trento*, Vallecchi, Florence, 1946, pp. 19–55.

[927] Egidio Foscarari (1512–1564), Master of the Sacred Palace in 1546, then bishop of Modena; suspected of heresy under Paul IV; he was later completely acquitted. See S. Feci, *Foscarari Egidio*, in DBI, vol. 49 (1997), pp. 280–283; Michelle M. Fontaine, *For the Good of the City: The Bishop and the Ruling Elite in Tridentine Modena*, in "Sixteenth Century Journal," 28, 1 (1997), pp. 29–43; Matteo Al Kalak, *Riformare la Chiesa. Egidio Foscarari tra inquisizione, concilio e governo pastorale (1512–1564)*, Il Mulino, Bologna, 2016.

[928] Muzio Calini (1509–1573) was archbishop of Zara in Dalmatia. See Victor Ivo Comparato, *Calini Muzio*, in DBI, 16 (1973), pp. 725–727. For more on him, see *Lettere conciliari (1561–1563)*, edited by Alberto Marani, Geroldi, Brescia, 1963.

and Francesco Foreiro,[929] the theologian of the king of Portugal, the last three of whom were Dominicans. Cardinal Borromeo assumed the direction of this commission and appointed the humanist Giulio Pogiani[930] as its secretary.

The work of the commission thus passed into the hands of Cardinal Sirleto for a final revision. In the meantime, Pius IV died on December 9, 1565. When Pius V succeeded him, he immediately took an interest in the publication of the catechism, but he wanted a further revision by theologians whom he trusted: the Master of the Sacred Palace, Tomás Manrique,[931] and the procurator of the Dominicans, Eustachio Locatelli.[932] Msgr. Pogiani was charged with placing the text into literary Latin. The work was finally completed in April 1566. The catechism was thus not "a compilation of materials gathered at Trent, but a work of Thomistic theologians, with a unitary structure extraneous to theological controversies, which thanks to the humanist Pogiani received a splendid linguistic form. The Roman Catechism, as it is often called, was compiled on the basis of the decree of session XXV, but it was not the work of the Council."[933]

[929] Francesco Foreiro (1523–1581) held the office of secretary of the conciliar commissions for the Index, the reform of the missal and breviary, and the redaction of the catechism of the council. See RAUL DE ALMEIDA ROLO, *Foreiro*, in DHGE, 17 (1971), cols. 1030–1032; RAÚL LANZETTI, *Francisco Foreiro, o la continuidad entre el Concilio de Trento y el catecismo romano*, in "Scripta Theologica," 16, 1–2 (1984), pp. 451–458.

[930] Giulio Pogiani (1522–1568), secretary of Charles Borromeo, compiled many theological texts of the Council of Trent and edited the catechism commonly called "*ad Parochos*."

[931] Tomás Manrique, Spanish Dominican, was the procurator general of his order in Rome (1533–1560) and Master of the Sacred Palace from 1565 to 1573, the year in which he died. In 1570 Pius V entrusted him with the chair of the Doctrine of St. Thomas at the Vatican.

[932] Eustachio Locatelli (ca. 1518–1575), Dominican, inquisitor, and consultor of the Holy Office, was appointed bishop of Reggio Emilia by Pius V on April 15, 1569.

[933] JEDIN, *Storia del Concilio di Trento*, pp. 343–344.

Pius V promulgated the Roman Catechism on September 25, 1566, with the title *Catechismus ex decreto Concilii Tridentini, ad parochos, Pii Quinti Pont. Max. iussu editus*[934] and entrusted the printing of the volume to the famous printer Paolo Manuzio. The Italian translation was published immediately after the Latin text by the Dominican Alessio Figliucci.

The Roman Catechism opens with an introduction that emphasizes the necessity of revelation so that man can attain "that supernatural salvation for which he was created, out of nothing, in the image and likeness of God." Divine revelation reaches us by means of the Son of God, Jesus Christ, whose teaching is transmitted by the apostles and their successors. For this reason, Jesus said, addressing them: "Whoever listens to you listens to me, and whoever rejects you rejects me" (Luke 10:16).

[934] See the critical edition directed by Pedro Rodriguez, accompanied by rich documentation; *Catechismus Romanus seu Catechismus ex decreto Concilii Tridentini, ad parochos, Pii Quinti Pont. Max. iussu editus*, Libreria Editrice Vaticana/Ediciones Universidad de Navarra, Vatican City/ Pamplona, 1989, Italian translation by L. Andrianopoli, *Il Catechismo romano del Concilio di Trento*, Libreria Editrice Vaticana, Vatican City, 1946; Andrianopoli, *Il Catechismo Romano commentato, con note di aggiornamento teologico pastorale*, Ares, Milan, 1983. On its history, see the synthesis by Pio Paschini, *Il Catechismo Romano del Concilio di Trento*, Pontificio Seminario Romano Maggiore, Rome, 1923. See also Gerhard J. Bellinger, *Der Catechismus Romanus und die Reformation. Die katechetische Antwort des Trienter Konzils auf die Haupt-Katechismen der Reformatoren*, Bonifacius-Druckerei, Paderborn, 1970; Bellinger, *Bibliographie des Catechismus Romanus. Ex Decreto Concilii Tridentini ad Parochos 1566–1978*, Valentin Koerner, Baden-Baden, 1983; P. Rodriguez-R. Lanzetti, *El Catecismo Romano: fuentes e historia del texto y de la redacción. Bases críticas para el estudio teológico del Catecismo del Concilio de Trento (1566)*, Ed. Universidad de Navarra, Pamplona, 1982; P. Rodríguez García, *La cuestión histórico-doctrinal del Catecismo Romano*, in "Scripta Theologica," 17 (2), (1985), pp. 467–486; M. Al Kalak, *La nascita del Catechismo Romano*, in "Revue d'histoire écclesiastique," 112 (2017), pp. 126–168.

The introduction goes on to say that the teaching of revealed truth, which is an essential and perennial task of the Church, in times of heresy "is an urgent necessity to which all intelligence and fervor must be dedicated." "The world," it says,

> knows today too many teachers of error, false prophets of whom God once said: "I did not send them, and yet they speak; I said nothing to them and they pretend to prophesy in my name" (Jer. 23:21). They poison souls with "strange and false doctrines" (Heb. 13:9). And the propaganda of their impiety, in whose service they have employed diabolical arts, has penetrated so much everywhere that it cannot be circumscribed. And if we could not lean upon the luminous promise of the Savior, which states that he has given the Church such a solid foundation that the gates of hell will never prevail against it (Matt. 16:18), we would be afraid that in our days the Church, besieged on every side, assailed and attacked by so many machinations, would be on the point of succumbing.[935]

The catechism expounds the truths of the faith of the Church in four parts, which are: the Apostolic Symbol or Creed, the seven sacraments, the Decalogue, and the Lord's Prayer or Our Father.

> In fact, everything that according to the norm of Christian faith must be held and known about God, creation and the government of the world, the redemption of the human race, the reward of the good and the punishment of the wicked, is contained in the teaching of the Symbol. That which concerns the signs and instruments by which we procure divine grace is contained in the teaching on the seven Sacraments. What refers to the Law, whose purpose is charity, is described in the Decalogue. Finally, all that men can salutarily desire, hope for, and ask for, is contained in the Lord's Prayer. This is why by explaining these four formulas, which constitute, as it were, common points of reference of Sacred

[935] Preface of the *Roman Catechism*, n. 3.

Scripture, there remains almost nothing else to teach about the things that the Christian is bound to learn and desire.[936]

There are forty-six chapters, and every point is addressed with simplicity, in a logical order, not dialogical. "The doctrinal structure is clearly a function of pastoral action and of a fervent and enlightened Christian commitment. … The Catechism takes account of the historical situation of the Christian of all time and today. True wisdom and holiness is a gift of God, and faith which is grace requires 'the work and ministry of those who teach legitimately and faithfully' as executors of a mandate received from Christ, the Word of God."[937]

The Roman Catechism was followed by many others, including the famous one of St. Robert Bellarmine published in 1598 with the title *Dottrina Cristiana Breve*,[938] but it retains its dogmatic primacy over all of them.[939] Its success is revealed by the number of its editions and translations.[940] The popes have often intervened to recommend its diffusion. Gregory XIII in 1583 and Clement XIII in 1761 renewed the approval of the catechism for its reprintings. Leo XIII recommended "that all seminarians hold in

[936] Preface of the *Roman Catechism*, n. 8.

[937] PIETRO BRAIDO, *Lineamenti di storia della catechesi e di catechismi. Dal "tempo delle riforme" all'età degli imperialismi (1450–1870)*, Editrice ElleDiCi, Turin, 1991, p. 73.

[938] See FRANCESCO GUSTA, *Sui catechismi moderni. Saggio critico-teologico.* Ferrara, heirs of G. Rinaldi, 1788, pp. 337; new enlarged edition, G. Tomassini, Foligno, 1793. Tradivox, an ambitious editorial project (*Catholic Catechism Index*, Sophia Institute Press, Manchester, New Hampshire, 2019), is compiling the publication of several of the most important catechisms published in recent centuries, beginning with those of Edmund Bonner, *An Honest Godlye Instruction* (London, 1556); Laurence Vaux, *A Catechism of Christian Doctrine* (Louvain, 1583); and Diego Ledesma, *The Christian Doctrine* (English Secret Press, 1597).

[939] JOHANNES BAPTISTA DE TOTH, *De auctoritate theologica Catechismi Romani*, Pustel, Budapest, 1941.

[940] G. B. BELLINGER in *Bibliographie*, lists 499 Latin editions, 75 Italian, 1 Romanian, 93 French, 38 Spanish, 40 English, 48 German, 10 Polish, 2 Czech, 1 Croatian, 1 Ukrainian, 2 Hungarian, 1 Armenian, 1 Chaldean, 2 Arabian, 2 Japanese, and 1 Mexican.

their hand and reread often the golden book known by the name of the Catechism of Holy Council of Trent or the Roman Catechism, dedicated to all priests charged with pastoral care (*Catechismus ad parochos*). Remarkable for the richness and exactness of its doctrine as well as its elegance of style, this catechism is a precious summary of all dogmatic and moral theology."[941]

The Major Catechism[942] of St. Pius X, published in 1905, is a compendium of the Roman Catechism of St. Pius V containing 993 questions and answers, to which Pope Sarto expressly refers in the encyclical *Acerbo Nimis*.[943]

John Paul II, who approved a new *Catechism of the Catholic Church*[944] in 1997, said that the Roman or Tridentine Catechism "is a work of the first rank as a summary of Christian teaching and traditional theology for use by priests. It gave rise to a remarkable organization of catechesis in the Church. It aroused the clergy to their duty of giving catechetical instruction. Thanks to the work of holy theologians such as St. Charles Borromeo, St. Robert Bellarmine and St. Peter Canisius, it involved the publication of catechisms that were real models for that period."[945]

2. The Sacred Order of the Liturgy

The liturgy is the public worship that the Church offers to God.[946] It dates back to the Old Testament, but Jesus Christ, in his earthly life,

941 Leo XIII, Encyclical *Depuis le jour* of 8 September 1899, in EE, *Leone XIII*, p. 1159 (pp. 1143–1183).

942 Pius X, *Compendio della Dottrina Cristiana*, Tipografia Vaticana, Rome, 1905. Among the numerous reprintings, see *Catechismo Maggiore*, Edizioni Ares, Milan, 2006.

943 Pius X, Encyclical *Acerbo Nimis* of 15 April 1905, in EE, *Pio X, Benedetto XV*, p. 117 (pp. 106–129).

944 John Paul II, Apostolic Letter *Laetamur Magnopere* of 15 August 1997, promulgating the *Catechism of the Catholic Church*, in *Insegnamenti*, 20, 2 (1997), pp. 120–126.

945 John Paul II, Apostolic Exhortation *Catechesi Tradendae*, 16 October 1979, n. 13, in *Insegnamenti*, 2, 2, 1979, p. 919.

946 Pius XII, Encyclical *Mediator Dei*, 20 November 1947, in Discorsi e Radiomessaggi, vol. IX, 2, pp. 493–561.

completed and perfected the Old Law and also instituted Christian worship, which began in an unbloody manner in the Last Supper and was consummated in the blood of Calvary. In addition to instituting the Eucharist and the other sacraments during the forty days between the Resurrection and the Ascension, Jesus entrusted to his disciples "a norm of believing and praying" that is at the origin of the liturgy of the Church and the various rites that flourished within her, both in the East and in the West.[947]

The history of the Western rites hinges on the Roman Rite, destined to become the rite *par excellence* of the Catholic Church. Pope St. Damasus I (366–384), a Spaniard by birth, gave the Church of his time its definitive "Roman" note.[948] Two aspects unite in his "*Romanitas*," which ever since then have been inextricably united: *Petrinitas*, that is, the affirmation of the primacy of the Roman Pontiff; and *Latinitas*, as the expression of this same *Romanitas*, in the governance, Magisterium, and worship of the Church. It was Damasus who asked St. Jerome to translate the Bible into Latin, the so-called *Vulgate* translation, and it was he who adopted Latin as the universal language of the Church. Ever since then the order of prayer, like the norm of faith, has been defined by the Apostolic Tradition.[949] Innocent I (401–417), in his letter to Decentius, bishop of Gubbio, on March 19, 416,[950] condemns the liturgical innovations of his time, arguing that the priests, out of eagerness for novelty, had distanced themselves from the teaching transmitted by Christ himself to the apostles, and calls for the observance of the liturgical rule guarded by the Roman Pontiff. St. Celestine I (422–432) and Pope Vigilius (537–555) confirm that

[947] MADRE M. FRANCESCA DELL'IMMACOLATA, *Le origini apostolico-patristiche della Messa cosiddetta "tridentina,"* in *Il Motu Proprio "Summorum Pontificum" di S.S. Benedetto XVI. Una speranza per tutta la chiesa*, edited by P. Vincenzo M. Nuara, O.P., Fede e Cultura, Verona, 2013, vol. 3, pp. 93–131.

[948] See CHARLES PIETRI, *Damase évêque de Rome*, in *Saecularia Damasiana*, Libreria Editrice Vaticana, Vatican City, 1986, pp. 29–58.

[949] MONS. ATHANASIUS SCHNEIDER, *Il significato degli ordini minori nella Sacra Liturgia*, in *Il Motu Proprio "Summorum Pontificum" di S.S. Benedetto XVI. Una speranza per tutta la chiesa*, pp. 54–70.

[950] DENZ-H, nn. 215–216.

the liturgy celebrated then was not created between the fourth and fifth centuries but was the same one handed down by the apostles.[951] This work was completed by the pope whose name would remain forever linked to the Sacred Liturgy: St. Gregory the Great[952] (590–604), who worked to ensure that the new peoples of Europe would receive both the Catholic Faith as well as the treasures of worship and culture accumulated by the Romans in the preceding centuries. He commanded that the form of the Sacred Liturgy regarding both the Sacrifice of the Mass as well as the Divine Office be defined and preserved in the way in which it was celebrated in the city of Rome.

In this sense, Christianity originated around a liturgical order that during the seventh, eighth, and above all the ninth centuries, was expressed by *Sacramentaria*, books containing all the formulas that together contribute to the consecration of the Eucharist.[953] Christopher Dawson observes that, after the fall of the Western Roman Empire, the sacred order of the liturgy remained intact in the chaos, and the liturgy

[951] See MONS. FRANCESCO MAGNANI, *L'antica liturgia romana*, 2 vols., Tip. Pontificia S. Giuseppe, Milan, 1897, vol. 1, pp. 19–26.

[952] Gregory I (540–604), or Gregory the Great, was pope from September 3, 590, until his death. The Catholic Church venerates him as a saint and Doctor of the Church. See ANDREAS HEINZ, *Gregorio Magno e la liturgia romana*, in *Gregorio Magno nel XIV centenario della morte*, (Rome, 22–25 October 2003), Accademia Nazionale dei Lincei, Rome, 2004, pp. 282–290; *Liturgie e culture tra l'età di Gregorio Magno e il pontificato di Leone III. Aspetti rituali, ecclesiologici e istituzionali*, edited by Renata Salvarani, Libreria Vaticana, Vatican City, 2012.

[953] On the formation of the first liturgical books: MICHEL ANDRIEU, *Les "Ordines Romani" du Haut Moyen-âge*, Spicilegium Sacrum Lovaniense, Louvain, 1931; EMMANUEL BOURQUE, Étude sur les Sacramentaires Romains, Pontifical Institute of Christian Archaeology, Vatican City, 1949; BERNARD BOTTE, *Le Canon de la messe romaine*. Édition critique. introduction et notes, Mont César, Louvain, 1935; JEAN DESHUSSES, *Le Sacramentaire Grégorien*, Editions Universitaires, Fribourg, 1982; GUY NICHOLLS, *Historique des prières du canon romain*, in *Aspects historiques et théologiques du missel romain. Actes du cinquième colloque d'études historiques, théologiques et canoniques sur le rite romain* (Versailles, November 1999), Centre International d'Etudes Liturgiques, Paris, 2000, pp. 129–158.

formed society's principal bond of interior unity.[954] The liturgy of the Abbey of Cluny wrapped medieval Christianity's theocentric vision of the world with majesty and splendor.[955]

3. The Roman Breviary and the Revolution of the Humanists

The official prayer of the Church of the Roman Rite was designated from the beginning as the *Officium Divinum*,[956] a term that was replaced with *Breviarium*[957] beginning in the thirteenth century. The breviary is the liturgical book that contains the Divine Office of the Church, ordered according to the canonical hours of the day or the night by priests, religious, and clerics who are obliged by their vocation to perform this duty.[958] The breviary does not include Mass and other liturgical ceremonies. It includes some variable parts that are recited according to the different liturgical seasons, and other fixed parts that are said identically every day.

The internal crisis of the Church due to the great Western Schism and the development of Humanism led to a decadence of the liturgy and a chaotic proliferation of breviaries and particular rites. The humanists ridiculed the medieval Latin of the breviary and proposed modifications on a purely aesthetic basis. Marsilio Ficino and Pietro Pomponazzi, for

954 Christopher Dawson, *Il Cristianesimo e la formazione della civiltà occidentale*, Italian translation, BUR, Milan, 1997, pp. 53–57.

955 See Joan Evans, *Monastic Life at Cluny 910–1157*, Oxford University Press, Oxford, 1968; Herbert Edward John Cowdrey, *The Cluniacs and the Gregorian Reform*, Oxford Clarendon Press, Oxford, 1970; Marcel Pacaut, *L'Ordre de Cluny (909–1789)*, Fayard, Paris, 1986.

956 Dom Pierre Salmon, *L'Office divin au Moyen âge: histoire de la formation du bréviaire du IXe au XVIe siècle*, Éditions du Cerf, Paris, 1967.

957 The last edition of the Roman Breviary was issued in 1961. With the liturgical reform introduced by Paul VI, the Divine Office contained in the *Breviarium Romanum* was renamed *Liturgia Horarum*.

958 See Dom Fernand Cabrol, *Breviary*, in *The Catholic Encyclopedia*, vol. 2, pp. 768–777. See Dom Henri Leclercq, *Bréviaire romaine*, in DACL, vol. 2 (1910), cols. 126–1316; Dom Suibert Bäumer, *Histoire du Bréviaire*, Letouzey et Ané, Paris, 1905, 2 vols.; Jules Baudot, *Le bréviaire romain: ses origines, son histoire*, Paris, 1907; Hans Bohatta, *Bibliographie der Breviere: 1501–1850*, Karl W. Hiersemann, Stuttgart, 1937.

example, suggested that the clergy should read classical authors instead of the breviary. Others proposed translating the breviary into Ciceronian Latin. Among the corrections that were suggested: the forgiveness of sins became "*superosque manesque placare* [To placate the supernal gods and the souls of mortals]"; the eternal generation of the Word was "*Minerva Jovis capite orta*"; and the Holy Spirit was "*Aura Zephyri coelestis*."[959] Pope Leo X made himself the interpreter of these trends and entrusted to Monsignor Zaccaria Ferreri a reform of the breviary, which fortunately never saw the light of day.[960]

Among the reforms that were by contrast actually implemented, there was that of the Spanish Cardinal Francisco Quiñones,[961] who on behalf of Clement VII produced a *Breviarium Sanctae Crucis*, named after his cardinalatial titular church, Santa Croce in Gerusalemme. Quiñones's breviary was approved on July 3, 1536, and within thirty-two years more than one hundred editions were printed, but it stirred up strong criticism of his idea of creating a "new" breviary in discontinuity with preceding tradition. The greatest opposition came from the Theatines, who proposed their own reform of the breviary as an alternative to that proposed by the Spanish cardinal. In 1558, after the Theatine Cardinal Carafa became Pope Paul IV, Quiñones's breviary was abolished, but one year later, after the pope died, it was approved once more by Pius IV, until in 1568 it was definitively prohibited by Pius V. This shows that a document of the

[959] Bäumer, *Histoire du Bréviaire*, pp. 114–115.

[960] H. Jedin, *Il Concilio di Trento e la riforma dei libri liturgici*, in *Chiesa della fede*, p. 396 (pp. 390–425). Zaccaria Ferreri (1479–1524), bishop of Guarda Alfieri in the Kingdom of Naples, was a humanist, Italian monk, and papal legate.

[961] Francisco de los Ángeles Quiñones, in secular life Enrique de Quiñones (1475–1540), was the minister general of the entire Order of Friars Minor (1523–1528), and was created cardinal (1527) and then bishop (1530) by Clement VII. On his breviary, see Bäumer, *Histoire du Bréviaire*, pp. 126–150. Many of his innovations were included again in the liturgical reform of Paul VI. See Silvestro Gorczyca, *Significato del Breviario di Quiñones alla luce della liturgia delle ore di Paolo VI*, Università Gregoriana, Rome, 1992.

Church, even though it is officially promulgated by one or more popes, does not enjoy infallibility when the proper conditions are not present, and may be suppressed or condemned by later popes.

Pius IV, despite his approval of Quiñones's breviary, was obliged to form a commission composed of many of the same cardinals charged with reviewing the catechism. "The commission had adopted wise and reasonable principles: not to invent a new Breviary and a new Liturgy; to stand by tradition; to keep all that was worth keeping, but at the same time to correct the multitude of errors of which had crept into the Breviaries and to weigh just demands and complaints. Following these lines, they corrected the lessons, or legends, of the saints and revised the Calendar; and while respecting ancient liturgical formularies such as the collects, they introduced needful changes in certain details."[962]

Pius V resumed the position of Paul IV, and two years after his election he promulgated the new breviary with the bull *Quod a Nobis* of July 9, 1568.[963] In this document the pope lays out the reasons for the reform and the principles that inspired him, dating back to the origins of the breviary, saying:

> This form of the Divine Office was established at other times with piety and wisdom by the Supreme Pontiffs Gelasius I and Gregory I, later reformed by Saint Gregory VII. Since with the passage of time it has diverted from its ancient institution, it has become necessary to make it newly conformed to the ancient rule of prayer. Some have in fact deformed the harmonious whole of the ancient Breviary, mutilating it in many places and altering it with the addition of many uncertain and new things. Others, in large numbers, attracted by the greatest comfort, have adopted with eagerness the Breviary that has been newly compiled and composed by Francesco Quiñones, Cardinal Priest with the title

[962] CABROL, *Breviary*, p. 775.

[963] *Bullarium Romanum*, vol. 7, pp. 685–688. See *Breviarium Romanum: Editio Princeps (1568)*, Edizione anastatica edited by Manlio Sodi, Achille Maria Triacca, Libreria Editrice Vaticana, Vatican City, 1999.

> of Santa Croce in Gerusalemme. Furthermore, this detestable custom has crept into the provinces, that in the churches which from their origin had the custom of saying and reciting the canonical hours according to the ancient Roman usage, each bishop instead has made his own particular breviary, thereby tearing apart, by means of these new offices that are different from each other and, so to speak, proper to each bishopric, that communion which consists in offering to the same God prayers and praises in one and the same form (*uni Deo et una formula*). From there came disorder in divine worship in a great number of places; from there came the ignorance of the clergy of the ceremonies and ecclesiastical rites, in such a way that many ministers of the churches carried out their functions with indecencies, causing great scandal to devout people. We have today the fortune, through the great Mercy of God (as we think so) to finally see this Roman Breviary completed.

The dominant idea of the breviary of Pius V is diametrically opposed to the breviary of Quiñones: "Nothing essential must be taken out of the ancient Roman Breviary. A new Breviary must not be created, but rather what it already possesses must be restored to its primitive state, taking changed circumstances into account."[964] The future Cardinal Newman, when he was still a Protestant pastor (1836), offered this homage to the Tridentine breviary: "There is so much of excellence and beauty in the services of the Breviary, that were it skillfully set before the Protestant by Roman controversialists as the book of devotions received in their communion, it would undoubtedly raise a prejudice in their favour, if he were ignorant of the circumstances of the case, and but ordinarily candid and unprejudiced."[965]

[964] Giulio Baudot, *Il Breviario Romano. Origini e storia*, Italian translation, Desclée, Rome, 1909, pp. 108–109.

[965] John Henry Newman, *Tracts for the Time*, n. 75. *On the Roman Breviary as embodying the substance of the devotional services of the Church Catholic*, J.G. & F. Rivington, Oxford, 1836, p. 1.

The breviary composed by Cardinal Quiñones was abolished by Pius V in any church, monastery, or religious order, just as he abolished any other form of Office, with the exception of those rites that had existed for more than two hundred years. The majority of dioceses and religious orders accepted the new breviary, except for the Benedictines, the Dominicans, the Carmelites, the Premonstratensians, and the dioceses of Milan, Aquileia, Toledo, and Paris, which maintained their own usages. The Tridentine breviary adopted the Vulgate as the text for the psalms and the daily readings of Sacred Scripture, and in general preserved the antiphons and responsories of the eighth century, introducing modifications, however, in the readings for the feast days and the saints. Furthermore, for the first time the four principal Greek Doctors of the Church—Athanasius, Basil, Gregory of Nazianzus, and John Chrysostom—were honored with public worship as teachers of the universal Church alongside the four Western Doctors—Ambrose, Augustine, Jerome, and Gregory the Great. The pope added a fifth name to this list, Thomas Aquinas, whom he had raised to such a dignity the previous year.

4. St. Thomas, Doctor of the Church

On April 11, 1567, after having requested and obtained the advice and unanimous consent of the cardinals, Pius V declared St. Thomas Aquinas a Doctor of the Church with the bull *Mirabilis Deus*.[966] The pope made explicit reference to the presence of the doctrine of St. Thomas in the Council of Trent. In *Mirabilis Deus* St. Thomas is called and praised as both the *doctor angelicus* and as *doctor sanctus*. The bull does not make an explicit and direct declaration that proclaims St. Thomas as a Doctor of the Church, but does so by means of the liturgical celebration, that is, in an equivalent manner. "However the sense is clear: from now on St. Thomas Aquinas is in the choir of holy doctors of the universal Church and is celebrated as such."[967]

[966] *Bullarium Romanum*, vol. 7, pp. 564–565.

[967] Angelo Walz, O.P., *San Tommaso d'Aquino dichiarato dottore della Chiesa nel 1567*, in "Angelicum," 55 (1967), p. 157 (pp. 145–173).

The first edition of the *Opera Omnia* of the angelic doctor[968] is entitled with the name of Pius V. The edition was edited by Fr. Tommaso Manrique, and its year of publication is 1570. "From this moment onward, Thomas's destiny would be ever more intimately linked with that of the Church of Rome, and so with the Catholic tradition, making Thomas the polemical target not only of the Reformers within the Christian confessions, but also of all philosophers outside the Roman Church."[969]

On August 4, 1879, Leo XIII addressed the encyclical *Aeterni Patris*[970] to the Catholic world, with which he proposed the doctrine of St. Thomas as the foundation of higher studies of philosophy, indicating Thomism as the first and necessary response to the philosophical errors that threatened both the Catholic Faith and the natural moral law itself. With the apostolic letter *Cum Hoc Sit*[971] of August 4, 1880, Pope Pecci added the title of "*Patronus caelestis studiorum optimorum*" to those of "*Doctor ecclesiae*" and "*Doctor angelicus*," which had been given to him by St. Pius V.

In the long document *Doctoris Angelici* issued by Pope St. Pius X on June 29, 1914, two months before his death, Pope Sarto expressly ordered the placing of "scholastic philosophy as the foundation of the sacred sciences," specifying once again that he meant the philosophy of St. Thomas Aquinas.[972] John Paul II dedicated ample space to "the perennial novelty

968 St. Thomas Aquinas, *Opera omnia gratiis privilegisque Pii V pont. max. typis excusa*, Romae, 1570, 7 vols. The *Editio Piana* was re-edited by the Dominican College of Ottawa, with the confirmation of quotations, between 1941 and 1945.

969 Pasquale Porro, *Thomas Aquinas: A Historical and Philosophical Profile*, Catholic University of America Press, Washington, D.C., 2016, p. 403. See also Cornelio Fabro, *Breve introduzione al tomismo*, Edivi, Rome, 2007, pp. 67–71. A compendium of the fundamental documents of the Magisterium up until 1952, with ample commentary, in Santiago Ramirez, O.P., *De auctoritate doctrinali S. Thomae Aquitanatis*, Apud Sanctum Stephanum, Salamanca, 1952.

970 Leo XIII, Encyclical *Aeterni Patris* of August 4, 1879, in EE, *Leone XIII*, pp. 53–93.

971 Leo XIII, *Acta*, vol. 2, pp. 108–113.

972 St. Pius X, *Doctoris Angelici* of June 29, 1914, in AAS, 6 (1914), p. 338.

of the thought of St. Thomas Aquinas"[973] in his encyclical *Fides et Ratio* of September 14, 1998, and in his speech to the Pontifical Athenaeum of the Angelicum on November 17, 1979, he recalled the titles of *Doctor ecclesiae* and *Doctor angelicus* that St. Pius X attributed to Aquinas.[974]

5. The Liturgical Revolution of the Sixteenth Century

The Protestant Revolution of the sixteenth century was also a liturgical revolution. In the first book of the *Institutions Liturgiques*, Dom Guéranger characterizes the anti-liturgical spirit in its various manifestations by speaking of heresy. With this term, the Abbot of Solesmes does not mean the denial or refutation of truths relevant to the Faith. Under the name of anti-liturgical heresy, Dom Guéranger describes a spirit, an approach that "goes against the forms of worship," stating that hatred for the Catholic liturgy is a common denominator of the various "innovators" who have succeeded each other over the centuries, who in order to attack Catholic dogma began their ferocious work of the destruction of the liturgy. "The first characteristic of the anti-liturgical heresy," he writes,

> is hatred of the Tradition in the formulas of divine worship. One cannot contest the presence of such a specific character in all of the heretics, from Vigilantius to Calvin, and the reason is easy to explain. Every sectarian who wants to introduce a new doctrine finds himself necessarily in the presence of the Liturgy, which is the Tradition in its highest power, and he cannot find rest before silencing this voice, before having torn up these pages that give shelter to the faith of past centuries. Indeed, how have Lutheranism, Calvinism, and Anglicanism become established and maintained among the masses? In order to obtain this all that had to

[973] John Paul II, Encyclical *Fides et Ratio* of September 14, 1998, in EE, pp. 1886–1891.

[974] John Paul II, Speech of November 17, 1979, in *Insegnamenti*, vol. 3/2 (1979), pp. 1177–1189.

be done was to replace the old books and formulas with new ones, and everything was complete.[975]

The attack by the so-called reformers of the liturgy was not only aimed against abuses but stemmed from dogma. Luther, in *De Captivitate Babylonica* (1520), reduced the significance of the Mass to a simple promise and testimony.[976] The attacks continued in *De Abroganda Missa Privata* (1521) and in *Contra Henricum Regem Angliae* (1522), as well as in the pamphlet on *The Abomination of the Canon of the Mass* (1525), and were then translated into the practical aspects of the "reformed" liturgies of 1523 and 1526, in which the sacrificial expressions in the Eucharistic Rite were suppressed.[977] Karlstadt, one of Luther's first companions, followed the principles of the German heresiarch to their ultimate consequences: on Christmas Day 1521 he celebrated the first "Evangelical Mass" of the Reformation in civilian clothes in Wittenberg, omitting the elevation of the host and every reference to sacrifice, allowing the participants to take Communion on their own under both species according to the

975 GUÉRANGER, *Institutions liturgiques*, Victor Palmé, Paris, 1878, p. 397. The first volume of the *Institutions Liturgiques* of Dom Guéranger offers us a thorough reconstruction of the Catholic liturgy and its enemies from the time of the apostles down to the seventeenth century. See WOLFGANG WALDSTEIN, *Le mouvement liturgique de Dom Guéranger à la veille du Concile Vatican II*, in Centre International d'Études Liturgiques, *La Liturgie: Trésor de l'Eglise*, Paris, 1995, pp. 163–182.

976 M. LUTHER, *De Captivitate Babylonia*, WA, vol. 6, pp. 512, 514–518, 523.

977 See ABBÈ MARIUS LEPIN, *L'idée du sacrifice de la Messe d'après les théologiens depuis l'origine jusqu'à nos jours*, Beauchesne, Paris, 1926; HANS GRASS, *Die Abendmahlslehre bei Luther und Calvin*, C. Bertelmann, Gütersloh, 1954; GRASS, *Die evangelische Lehre vom Abendmahl*, Heliand, Lüneburg, 1961; FRANCIS CLARK, S.J., *Eucharistic Sacrifice and the Reformation*, Darton, Longmann & Todd, London, 1960; ALBRECHT PETERS, *Realpräsenz. Luthers Zeugnis von Christi Gegenwart in Abendmahl*, Lutherisches Verlagshaus, Berlin and Hamburg, 1966; JOSÉ ANTONIO DE ALDAMA, S.J., *La doctrina de Lutero sobre la transubstanciación, segun los teólogos del Concilio de Trento*, in "Archivio Teologico Granadino," 42 (1979), pp. 49–59.

principles of the "utraquists."[978] Karlstadt's Mass, with all of its innovations, became the prototype of the liturgical reform of the various sects and the first radical actuation of Luther's program: "*Triumphata vero Missa, puto nos totum Papam triumphare*": Having defeated the Mass, I think we will totally triumph over the Pope.[979]

Luther however did not reach the point of repudiating the Real Presence of Jesus Christ in the Sacrament of the Altar. Such a radical denial is due above all to Zwingli,[980] whose sacramental theories were destined to exercise a profound influence on Calvin, who reduced the sacrament of the Eucharist to a "spiritual supper."[981] In England, Thomas Cranmer[982] adhered to the Zwinglian-Calvinist interpretation of the Eucharist, under the influence of Bullinger and Vermigli. Cranmer conceived an unscrupulous plan of radical modification of the faith of the English people through the changing of the liturgy.[983] He was in fact convinced

[978] WILLIAMS, *The Radical Reformation*, p. 40. Andreas Bodenstein (ca. 1480–1541), called "Karlstadt" after his native city in Bavaria, had been the archdeacon of the Church of All Saints, and was among the first followers of Luther. See HERMANN BARGE, *Andreas Bodenstein von Karlstadt*, B. de Graaf, Nieuwkoop, 1968, 2 vols.

[979] M. LUTHER, *Contra Henricum Regem Angliae* (1522), in WA, vol. 10b, p. 220.

[980] See ULRICH ZWINGLI, *De vera et falsa religione commentarius* (1525); *Subsidium sive coronis de Eucharistia* (1525); *Eine Klare Unterrichtung von Nachmal Christi* (1526); *Dass diese Worte: "Das ist mein Leib," etc. ewiglich den alten Sinn haben werden* (1527).

[981] JOHN CALVIN, *Institutio christianae religionis* (1559), bk. 4, chap. 17. See WILHELM NIESEL, *Calvin's Lehre vom Abendmahl*, Kaiser Verlag, Munich, 1935.

[982] Thomas Cranmer (1489–1556), whose name is linked to the redaction of the first edition of the *Book of Common Prayer* (1549), was archbishop of Canterbury under the reigns of the English sovereigns Henry VIII and Edward VI. He was condemned to the stake for heresy under the reign of Mary the Catholic. See PHILIP HUGHES, *Faith and Works: Cranmer and Hooker on Justification*, Morehouse-Barlow, Wilton, Connecticut, 1982.

[983] DOM GREGORY DIX, *The Shape of Liturgy*, Dacre Press, London, 1945 (reprinted by Continuum, London, 2005); P. HUGHES, *The Reformation in England*, Macmillan, New York, 1951.

that daily liturgical practice would transform the ideas and mentality of the people better than any book or speech. The history of the English Reformation is that of a design that, albeit at alternating moments, ended up succeeding thanks to the profoundly equivocal character of the 1549 *Common Book of Prayer*, which sought to give liturgical expression to the doctrine of "justification by faith alone."[984] In the name of the "politics of compromise, the English Catholic clergy accepted the *Book of Prayer*,[985] but in the Anglican supper, "the priest is transformed into a minister of worship, the altar into a table, and the Eucharist into a commemoration."[986]

6. The Council of Trent and the Liturgy

In the face of the Protestant liturgical anarchy, the Council of Trent expressed the vow to return to the traditional conception of the liturgy. In the eighteenth session, the Council charged a commission with the task of examining the missal, reviewing it, and restoring it "according to the custom and rite of the holy Fathers." "It was not to make a new missal, but to restore the existing one 'according to the custom and rite of holy Fathers' using for that purpose the best manuscripts and other documents."[987]

The restoration of the Sacrifice of the Mass was one of the central points of the Council, which in the twenty-second session on September 17, 1562, reiterated that "in this divine sacrifice, which is accomplished

[984] Hugo Ross Williamson, *Breve cenno storico sulla instaurazione del protestantesimo in Inghilterra*, Italian translation, Una Voce, Rome, 1971, pp. 12–13.

[985] Michael Davies, however, renders justice to eleven bishops who died in prison between 1559 and 1578 and were venerated as martyrs since the sixteenth century (*La Riforma anglicana. La distruzione del cattolicesimo attraverso la rivoluzione liturgica*, Editrice Ichthys, Albano, 2019. See also Eamon Duffy, *The Stripping of the Altars*, Yale University Press, New Haven-London, 1992, pp. 377–593.

[986] Bainton, *La riforma protestante*, p. 188.

[987] Adrian Fortescue, *The Mass: A Study of the Roman Liturgy*, Longmans, Green & Co., London, New York, 1950 (1912), p. 206.

in the Mass, there is contained and immolated in an unbloody manner the same Christ who offered himself a single time in a bloody manner on the altar of the Cross," anathematizing not only those who deny the sacrificial character of the Mass but also those who say "that the rite of the Roman Church, in which part of the Canon and the words of consecration is offered in a low voice is to be condemned; or that the Mass should be celebrated only in the language of the people; or that in offering the chalice water should not be mixed with wine, because this would be against the institution of Christ."[988]

Furthermore, addressing the ceremonies of the Holy Sacrifice of the Mass, the Council declared that it is necessary to relate to the apostolic institution the mystical blessings, the lit candles, the incensations, the sacred vestments, and generally all of the particular acts that reveal the majesty of this great action, and to bring the souls of the faithful to contemplation of the sublime things hidden in this profound mystery by means of these visible signs of religion and piety.

Cardinal Alfons M. Stickler has emphasized the importance—in the context of councils in general—of the difference between two types of conciliar declarations and decisions: those that concern doctrine and those that instead concern discipline. "The majority of the Councils," says the cardinal, "have issued declarations and decisions that are both doctrinal as well as disciplinary. But others have issued either only doctrinal decisions or only disciplinary decisions. ... We find both dispositions explicitly in the Council of Trent: chapters and canons that first address problems of faith exclusively, and afterwards, in almost all the Sessions, arguments exclusively concerning disciplinary order. This distinction is important: all of the theological canons affirm that anyone who opposes the decisions of the Council is excommunicated: *anathema sit*. But the Council never imposes anathemas for opposition against purely disciplinary dispositions."[989]

[988] Denz-H, nn. 1743, 1759.

[989] A. M. Stickler, *L'attrattiva teologica della Messa tridentina*, Casa Editrice La Magione, Poggibonsi, 1996.

Cardinal Stickler offers several examples. In chapter 5 of the Decree on the Sacrifice of the Mass, the Council of Trent states:

> Whereas such is the nature of man that he is not easily drawn to meditation on divine things without small external helps, therefore the Church, as a pious Mother, has established certain rites, and so it is that certain things in the Mass are pronounced in a low voice, and others in a louder voice. She has likewise established ceremonies, such as mystical benedictions, she uses lights, incensations, vestments, and many other elements transmitted from the teaching of the apostolic tradition, which serve to manifest the majesty of such a great sacrifice, and the minds of the faithful are drawn by these visible signs of religion and piety to the contemplation of the highest things, which are hidden in this sacrifice.

It subsequently says, in canon 7, that "If anyone says that the ceremonies, vestments, and other outward signs which the Catholic Church makes use of in the celebration of Masses, are elements that favor impiety rather than manifestations of piety, let him be anathema."

Chapter 8 of the Decree on the Sacrifice of the Mass is dedicated to the language to be used in the worship of the Mass. "The Council Fathers," Cardinal Stickler observes,

> knew perfectly that the majority of the faithful who assisted at the Mass did not know Latin, nor could they read the translation, since they were generally unlettered and illiterate. But they also knew that the Mass contains many parts that give instruction to the faithful. However, they did not approve the opinion of the Protestants that it was indispensable to celebrate the Mass only in the vernacular. For the purpose of favoring the instruction of the faithful, the Council ordered that there be maintained everywhere the ancient tradition approved by the Holy Roman Church, which is the mother and teacher of all the churches, that is, to take care and explain to souls the central mystery of the Mass. Canon 9 thus

imposes excommunication on those who say that the language of the Mass should be only the vernacular.

For these same reasons, canon 9 imposes excommunication on those who say that the rite of the Roman Church, in which a part of the Canon and the words of Consecration are pronounced silently, must be condemned.

These anathemas reveal that, for the Council Fathers, the transgressions of the innovators were not purely disciplinary but involved doctrine and theology and, in the end, the Faith itself.

7. The Bull *Quo Primum*

The Roman Missal desired by the Council of Trent was promulgated by Pius V with the bull *Quo Primum* of July 19, 1570.[990] The expressions "Tridentine Mass" or "Mass of St. Pius V" by which the rite codified by Pius V is known are improper, because the pope did nothing else than wisely fix and set limitations on a rite that had already been in use in Rome for centuries.[991] In its essential elements it dates back to St. Gregory the Great, from which it is also called the *Gregorian* rite,[992] a more correct but not exhaustive name, because the rite dates back even before Gregory the Great to apostolic times. From the account of the Acts of the Apostles we can deduce the existence of a simple but fixed ritual that was essentially complete and that was followed uniformly by the apostles and their collaborators.

These apostolic prescriptions had the authority of law, since in the first half of the second century the apologist St. Justin attests to the fidelity with which it was followed in the description he gave of the Mass of his

[990] *Bullarium Romanum*, vol. 7, pp. 839–845; *Missale Romanum: Editio Princeps (1570)*, anastatic edition edited by Manlio Sodi, Achille Maria Triacca, Libreria Editrice Vaticana, Vatican City, 1998.

[991] See M. FRANCESCA DELL'IMMACOLATA, *Le origini apostolico-patristiche della Messa*, p. 92.

[992] For a general overview, see FORTESCUE, *The Mass*, and, more recently, the accurate synthesis of Abbé CLAUDE BARTHE, *Storia del Messale tridentino*, Italian translation, Solfanelli, Chieti, 2018; and MICHAEL FIEDROWICZ, *The Traditional Mass: History, Form, and Theology of the Classical Roman Rite*, Angelico, Brooklyn, 2020.

time.[993] "The description of the Mass left us by Justin is the first that we encounter in liturgical history, and it is for us a very precious source of information, both for its antiquity as well as for the criteria with which it was written. But it is even more precious because of the fact that it attests to the ritual practice of the Roman Church, in which, as St. Irenaeus († 202) writes 'the tradition that has come from the apostles is faithfully guarded.'"[994]

Blessed Alfredo Ildefonso Schuster writes,

> It is a Roman tradition that in the fifth century we note it to be in full possession, undisputed, reverently accepted in all of the papal patriarchate, attributing an apostolic origin to the Canon. In harmony with this belief, Roman historians believed that they could account in the *Liber Pontificalis* even for the slightest modifications made to the text of this traditional *Eucharistia* made by the ancient pontiffs; the popes and the writers who deal with it do so as an unaltered and untouchable prayer which requires acceptance by all the Churches. The documentation of the individual parts of our Canon dates back to at least the fifth century, and obliges us to identify it in its broad outlines with what the ancients held to be of apostolic tradition. The direct and intimate examination of the document, far from weakening our argument, does nothing but reinforce it, giving our Roman *Eucharistia* the halo of such an ancient origin that, repeating the consecratory prayer in the Mass today after so many centuries, we can be certain to be praying not only with the faith of Damasus, Innocent, and Leo the Great,

993 St. Justin, *Apologia*, 1, 65–67. Latin text in *Prex Eucharistica. Textus e variis liturgiis antiquioribus selecti*, edited by Anton Hänggi, Irmgard Pahl, Fribourg, 1968 (Spicilegium Friburgense, 12), pp. 71–72. Justin Martyr (100–162/168) was one of the first Christian apologists and was probably instructed in the Faith by someone who had learned it directly from the apostles.

994 Righetti, *Manuale di storia liturgica*, Ancora, Milan, 1963 (anastatic edition, Milan, 1998), vol. 3, p. 68.

but with the very same words that they repeated at the altar and which indeed sanctified the primeval age of the Doctors, Confessors, and Martyrs.[995]

But if the apostles ought to be incontestably considered as the fathers of all the universal liturgical forms, the rite was adapted, in its changeable parts, to the customs of the nations and to the genius of the various peoples, in order to facilitate the spread of the gospel. This is the origin of the differences that exist between the various Eastern liturgies, which are the more or less direct work of one or more of the apostles, and the Western liturgy, of which one — that of Rome — must recognize St. Peter as its principal author.

"There is moreover a constant tradition that St. Gregory was the last to touch the essential part of the Mass, namely the Canon. Benedict XIV (1740–1758) says: 'No Pope has added to or changed the Canon since St. Gregory.'"[996] Even if the rite of the Mass continued to develop in its nonessential parts after the era of St. Gregory, Fr. Fortescue explains that "all later modifications were fitted into the old arrangement and the most important parts were not touched. From, roughly, the time of St. Gregory we have the text of the Mass, its order and arrangement, as a sacred tradition that no one ventured to touch except in unimportant details."[997]

The Roman Rite then spread rapidly, and in the eleventh and twelfth centuries it practically supplanted all other rites in the West, except those of Milan and Toledo. This should not be surprising, after all: if the Church of Rome was universally considered as the guide in faith and morals, this primatial role also played a role in liturgical matters. The Mass in the High Middle Ages was already considered an inviolable inheritance.

[995] Blessed Ildefonse Schuster, *Liber sacramentorum: note storiche e liturgiche sul messale Romano*, Marietti, Turin-Rome, 1923–1926, vol. 2, pp. 106–107.

[996] Fortescue, *The Mass*, pp. 172–173.

[997] Fortescue, *The Mass*, p. 173.

Even more, it was commonly held that it dated back to the apostles and that it was written by St. Peter himself.[998]

Among the many plenary missals in use by the thirteenth century, the one used by the Curia or the papal chapel was destined to become universal. The type of this missal was definitively fixed at the time and through the interest of Innocent III (1198–1216). The Missal of the Curia was among the first to be printed. The *editio princeps* was published in Milan on December 6, 1474, using the types of Antonio Zaccaria.[999]

8. The Missal of the Tradition

All of the doctrine on the Mass of the Council of Trent is contained in the bull *Quo Primum* of Pius V, which did not introduce anything new but restored the worship of the Church to its integrity, after being disfigured by Protestants and humanists in the preceding fifty years.

"Since the time of Our elevation to the highest summit of the Apostolate," the pope explains,

> we have turned Our soul, Our thoughts, and all Our strength to things concerning the cult of the Church, in order to keep it pure, and, to this end, we have applied ourself with all possible zeal to prepare opportune provisions and, with the help of God, to put them into effect. And since, among the other Decrees of the Sacred Council of Trent, it was incumbent upon us to carry out those concerning the care of the amended edition of the Holy Books, the Missal, the Breviary, and the Catechism, having already, with divine approbation, published the Catechism destined for the instruction of the people, and corrected the Breviary so that the praises which are due to God might be given to him, it was now absolutely necessary for us to think as soon as possible about what still remained to be done on this matter, namely, to publish the

[998] M. Francesca dell'Immacolata, *Le origini apostolico-patristiche della Messa*, p. 116.

[999] Amato Pietro Frutaz, *Messale*, in EC, vol. 8 (1952), col. 836 (cols. 831–840).

Missal, and in such a way that it would correspond to the Breviary: a timely and convenient thing, since just as in the Church of God there is only one way of chanting the psalms, so also it is supremely fitting that there be only one rite for celebrating the Mass.

Pius V states that he has entrusted this difficult task to "men of chosen doctrine." "And these, indeed, after having diligently collected all of the codices recommended for their chastity and integrity—the old ones from Our Vatican Library and others sought out from every place—and having further consulted the writings of ancient and proven authors who have left us testimonies about the sacred ordering of the same rites, they have finally restored the Missal in its ancient form according to the norm and rite of the holy Fathers." Therefore, Pius V orders that

> in the churches of all the Provinces of the Christian world ... in the future and without any time limitations, the Mass, both the Conventual Mass sung with the choir as well as the Mass that is simply read in a low voice, shall not be sung or recited in any other way than that prescribed by the order of the Missal published by Us; and this is so, even if the aforementioned Churches, however exempt, enjoyed a special indult of the Apostolic See, a legitimate custom, a privilege based on a sworn and confirmed declaration of the Apostolic Authority, or any other faculty.
>
> Instead, while with this Our present Constitution, to be valid in perpetuity, we deprive all of the aforementioned Churches of the use of their Missals, which we repudiate in a total and absolute way, we establish and command, under the penalty of Our indignation, that nothing may ever be added to, detracted from, or changed in this Our Missal, recently published. Therefore, we order each and all of the Patriarchs and Administrators of the aforementioned Churches, and all ecclesiastics, invested with whatsoever dignity, degree, and preeminence, not excluding Cardinals of the Holy Roman Church, imposing on them a severe obligation in virtue of holy obedience, that in the future they shall totally abandon and completely reject all of the other

> orders and rites contained in other Missals, without any exception, no matter how ancient they may be or how commonly used until now, and they shall sing and read the Mass according to the rite, form, and norm that We have prescribed in the present Missal; and, therefore, they shall not have the audacity to add other ceremonies or recite other prayers than those contained in this Missal.... In fact, in virtue of our Apostolic Authority, We grant to all priests, in accord with the present decree, the perpetual Indult to be able to follow this same Missal, in a general way, in whatever Church, without any scruple of conscience or danger of incurring any penalty, judgment, or censure, and that therefore they shall have the full faculty to use this Missal freely and licitly: so that Prelates, Administrators, Canons, Chaplains, and all other secular Priests, of whatever rank, and Regular priests, belonging to any Order, are not bound to celebrate the Mass in a manner different from that which We have prescribed, nor, on the other hand, may they be constrained or pressured by anyone to change this Missal. ... Similarly, we decree and declare that the present Letters may not be revoked or diminished at any time, but they ought to retain their force, ever stable and valid.

The Holy Father concludes with these words: "Therefore, no one, in any way, is permitted with rash temerity to violate and transgress this Our document, faculty, statute, order, mandate, precept, concession, indult, declaration, will, decree, and inhibition. And if anyone shall have the audacity to attack it, know that he shall incur the indignation of Almighty God and of His Blessed Apostles Peter and Paul."

The missal promulgated by St. Pius V is not simply a personal decree of the Sovereign Pontiff but an act of the Council of Trent, whose official title is *Missale Romanum ex decreto sacrosancti Concilii Tridentini restitutum* (Roman Missal restored according to the decrees of the sacrosanct Council of Trent).

Pius V made this missal obligatory in all of the churches that could not prove an antiquity of two hundred years for their particular usage, as he had already done for the breviary. In fact, Abbé Barthe observes, the majority of dioceses and congregations could prove that their specific usages, texts, and ceremonies, especially in the cathedrals, dated to before the fourteenth century, but despite this, the vast majority of bishops and chapters preferred to fall in line with the missal and the other Roman books, which thus became the ones commonly used.[1000]

The missal published by Pius V included precise directions for the ritual: the *Rubricae Generales* and an introduction entitled *Ritus servandus in celebratione missae* that explained in detail the performance of the gestures and ceremonies, which together constituted a true and proper modern *Ordo Romanus*. This *Ritus servandus* was in continuity with the *Ordo servandus per sacerdotem in celebratione missae* of Giovanni Burcardo, master of ceremonies of the papal chapel under five popes.[1001] The reform of Pius V consisted in "restoring the Roman Mass to its original purity, purging it of all its profane elements and things from the Renaissance that have invaded it in recent centuries."[1002]

Since the time of the reform of St. Pius V, there have been revisions, but never substantial ones. Sometimes those revisions which today are referred to as "reforms" were nothing other than restorations of the missal to the form codified by St. Pius V. This is particularly true of the "reforms" of Clement VIII, established in the instruction *Cum Sanctissimum* of July 7, 1604, and those of Urban VIII in the instruction *Si Quid Est*, of September 2, 1634. Thus in 1929 Cardinal Schuster was able to write:

[1000] BARTHE, *Storia del Messale tridentino*, p. 100.

[1001] Giovanni Burcardo (ca. 1450–1506) assumed the office of master of papal ceremonies, which he maintained even after his election as bishop of Orte and Civita Castellana (1503). He published the first edition of the *Liber Pontificalis* (1485), edited the revision of the Roman ceremonial (*Rituum ecclesiasticorum sive sacrarum caeremoniarum libri tres*, 1516), and is the author of an *Ordo Missae secundum consuetudinem Sanctae Romanae Ecclesiae* (1498). See WALTER INGEBORG, *Burckard Johannes*, in DBI, vol. 15 (1972), pp. 405–408.

[1002] GIUGNI, *San Pio V*, p. 85.

Comparing the present Missal which we have now after the Tridentine reform with the medieval Missal and the Gregorian Sacramentary, the difference does not appear to be substantial. Ours is more rich and varied in that which concerns the hagiographical cycle; but the Stational Masses of the Sundays, of Advent, of Lent, of the Feasts of the Saints included in the Sacramentary of Saint Gregory, except for a few differences, are almost the same. In short, we may say that our Eucharistic codex, even taking into account the development achieved with the passing of the centuries, is substantially the same as that used by the great Doctors of the Church in the Middle Ages, which bore the name of Gregory the Great on its cover.[1003]

"Our Missal is still that of Pius V," Fr. Fortescue reiterates. "We may be very thankful that his commission was so scrupulous to keep or restore the old Roman tradition. Essentially the Missal of Pius V is the Gregorian Sacramentary; that again is formed from the Gelasian book, which depends on the Leonine collection. ... In spite of unsolved problems, in spite of later changes, there is not in Christendom another rite so venerable as ours."[1004] He then adds, "Since the Council of Trent the history of the Mass is hardly anything but that of the composition and approval of new Masses. The scheme and all the fundamental parts remain the same. No one has thought of touching the venerable liturgy of the Roman Mass, except by adding to it new Propers."[1005]

The essence of the reform of St. Pius V was, like that of St. Gregory the Great, respect for tradition. In 1912 Fr. Fortescue could comment with satisfaction:

Pius V's restoration was on the whole eminently satisfactory. The standard of commission was antiquity. They abolished later ornate features and made for simplicity, yet without destroying all those

[1003] SCHUSTER, *Liber sacramentorum* 1, p. 8.
[1004] FORTESCUE, *The Mass*, p. 213.
[1005] FORTESCUE, *The Mass*, p. 213.

> picturesque elements that add poetic beauty to the severe Roman Mass. They expelled the host of long sequences that crowded Mass continually, but kept what are undoubtedly the five best ones; they reduced processions and elaborate ceremonial, yet kept the really pregnant ceremonies, candles, ashes, palms and the beautiful Holy Week rites. Certainly we in the West may be very glad that we have the Roman Rite in the form of Pius V's missal.[1006]

Monsignor Amato Pietro Frutaz says that the commission charged with reforming the missal "did not create a new Missal, but retouched and updated the Missal of the Curia, which had been printed many times after 1474. In general the essential parts of the Missal of Saint Pius V differed little from those of the 1474 edition, indeed at times there are the exact same variants in the Scriptural texts."[1007]

Rightly does Abbé Barthe affirm: "The distinctive character of the Tridentine liturgy is in its regulated nature: it is a mirror of the *regula fidei* of Rome in the law of prayer. The manuscripts of the Vatican Library gave the Tridentine drafters the ability to establish the best text corresponding to those that were in force."[1008]

9. The Tridentine Mass after St. Pius V

After the promulgation of the Roman Missal in 1570, the ancient Roman Rite remained substantially unchanged for almost four centuries, until the reform of Holy Week in 1955–1956, which the future cardinal Ferdinando Antonelli defined as "the most important act in the history of the liturgy from Saint Pius V to today."[1009] This reform was made,

[1006] Fortescue, *The Mass*, p. 208.

[1007] Frutaz, *Messale*, col. 836

[1008] Barthe, *Storia del Messale tridentino*, p. 98.

[1009] F. Antonelli, *La riforma liturgica della Settimana Santa: importanza attualità prospettive*, in *La Restaurazione liturgica nell'opera di Pio XII. Atti del primo Congresso Internazionale di Liturgia Pastorale, Assisi-Roma, 12–22 settembre 1956*, Centro di Azione liturgica, Genoa, 1957, pp. 179–197, cit. in Carlo Braga, *"Maxima Redemptionis Nostrae Mysteria" 50 anni dopo (1955–2005)*, in "Ecclesia Orans," n. 23 (2006), p. 34 (pp. 11–36).

under Pius XII, by a commission whose members included Monsignor Giovanni Battista Montini, the future Paul VI, and Monsignor Annibale Bugnini.[1010] They are the ones responsible for the liturgical reform that culminated in 1969 with the radical transformation of the Roman Rite.

On April 3, 1969, Paul VI published the apostolic constitution *Missale Romanum*, which promulgated the new *Ordo Missae*, "renewed by order of the Second Vatican Ecumenical Council." The new missal was promulgated by Paul VI in the consistory of April 28, 1969.[1011] It was, as the Jesuit historian Giacomo Martina has observed, "an authentic liturgical revolution, much greater than that of Trent."[1012] In fact, observes Pietro Leone, in following this reform the Tridentine Missal "underwent a series of changes so far-reaching and so profound as to completely destroy the rite and replace it with another."[1013]

When the new *Ordo Missae* came into force in 1969, some eminent members of the hierarchy, as well as many theologians and lay persons,

[1010] Annibale Bugnini (1912–1982), a member of the Congregation of the Mission (the Lazarists or Vincentians), was the secretary of the Congregation for Divine Worship (1969–1976), titular archbishop of Diocletiana (1972), and apostolic pro-nuncio to Iran (1976–1982). See NICOLA GIAMPIETRO, O.F.M., *Il Card. Ferdinando Antonelli e gli sviluppi della riforma liturgica dal 1948 al 1970*, Pontifical Atheneum S. Anselmo, Rome, 1998; GIAMPIETRO, *A cinquant'anni dalla riforma liturgica della Settimana Santa*, in "Ephemerides liturgicae," 3 (2006), pp. 293–332. On the work of the commission, see also C. BRAGA, *La riforma liturgica di Pio XII. Documenti. I. La "memoria sulla riforma liturgica,"* Edizioni Liturgiche, Rome, 2003.

[1011] On April 3, 1969, the apostolic constitution *Missale Romanum* appeared, which consisted of two documents: the *Institutio Generalis Missalis Romani* (General Instruction of the Roman Missal) and the new *Ordo Missae* properly so-called, that is, the new text of the Mass and the rubrics that accompanied it (See AAS, 61 (1969), pp. 217–226). The breviary received its new form on February 2, 1971, with the *Institutio Generalis de Liturgia Horarum* (General Instruction of the Liturgy of the Hours); see AAS, 63/2 (1971), pp. 527–535.

[1012] G. MARTINA, *Storia della Chiesa*, Morcelliana, Brescia, 1995, vol. 3, p. 359.

[1013] PIETRO LEONE, *Come è cambiato il Rito romano antico*, Solfanelli, Chieti, 2018, p. 15.

made a sharp criticism of the new liturgy of the Mass.[1014] In October 1969, Cardinals Alfredo Ottaviani and Antonio Bacci presented Paul VI with a *Brief Critical Examination of the Novus Ordo Missae* written by a select group of theologians of various nationalities. Their letter addressed to the pontiff said that "the *Novus Ordo Missae* ... represents, both as a whole and in detail, a stunning departure from the Catholic theology of the Holy Mass that was formulated in the 22nd session of the Tridentine Council, which by definitively fixing the 'canons' of the rite erected an insurmountable barrier against any heresy that would affect the integrity of the mystery."[1015]

An eminent canonist, Abbé Raymond Dulac,[1016] has examined the juridical implications of St. Pius V's bull *Quo Primum*, affirming that this bull is not only a personal act of the Sovereign Pontiff but a decree in which the pope refers explicitly to the norms of the Council of Trent. Pius V also does not introduce anything new but restores an ancient law, conferring in perpetuity to every priest the privilege of celebrating

[1014] Among the numerous critical studies of the "New Mass" and the liturgical reform: A. Vidigal Xavier da Silveira, *La nouvelle Messe de Paul VI qu'en penser?*, Diffusion de la Penséé Française, Chiré-en-Montreuil, 1975; Louis Salleron, *La Nouvelle Messe*, Nouvelles Editions Latines, Paris, 1976 (1971); Wolfgang Waldstein, *Hirtensorge und Liturgiereform*, Lumen Gentium, Schaan, Fl, 1977; Mons. Klaus Gamber, *Die Reform der Römischen Liturgie*, F. Pustet, Regensburg, 1979 (the French translation of this work contains prefaces by Cardinals Silvio Oddi, Joseph Ratzinger, and A. M. Stickler); Michael Davies, *Pope Paul's New Mass*, The Angelus Press, Dickinson, Texas, 1980; Claude Barthe, *La Messe de Vatican II*, Via Romana, Paris, 2018; Leone, *Come è cambiato il Rito romano antico*; Peter Kwasniewski, *Noble Beauty, Transcendent Holiness*, Angelico Press, Kettering, 2017; Peter Kwasniewski, *Reclaiming Our Roman Catholic Birthright: The Genius and Timeliness of the Traditional Latin Mass*, Angelico, Brooklyn, 2020.

[1015] The study, promoted by "Una Voce Italia," has been republished by the same association together with a *Nuovo esame critico del "Novus Ordo Missae,"* the work of French liturgists and theologians (*Il Novus Ordo Missae: due esami critici*, "Una Voce," found at n. 48–49 of the January–July 1979 newsletter).

[1016] Fr. Raymond Dulac, *In Defence of Roman Mass*, Te Deum Press, 2020, pp. 287–297.

it, a privilege that no one, not even a pope, may legitimately abrogate without betraying the deposit of the Faith.

In the opening address given to the international symposium that took place at the Abbey of Fontgombault from July 22 to 24, 2001, Cardinal Joseph Ratzinger noted how, after the Second Vatican Council, the idea of sacrifice is becoming extraneous to the modern liturgy, aligning the latter with Lutheran belief. "A not insignificant number of Catholic liturgies," Ratzinger said, "seem to have practically come to the point that one must conclude that Luther was substantially right against Trent in the debate of the 16th century; and one can also widely see that the same holds true for post-conciliar discussions about the priesthood."[1017]

When Cardinal Ratzinger became Pope Benedict XVI, he restored the full right of citizenship to the ancient Roman Rite with the motu proprio *Summorum Pontificum*[1018] of July 7, 2007, promulgated with the purpose of satisfying "the just aspirations" of the faithful of the traditional rite and in order to "reach a reconciliation within the Church." The ancient Roman Rite had never been abrogated but was *de facto* "interdicted" for forty years.[1019]

10. Pius V and the Restoration of Sacred Music

Among all the arts, the ones that have most contributed to the sacrality of the liturgical rite have been architecture, painting/sculpture, and

[1017] *Autour de la question liturgique avec le cardinal Ratzinger*, 22–24 July 2001, Abbaye-Notre Dame de Fontgombault, 2001, pp. 15–16.

[1018] See BENEDICT XVI, Apostolic Letter *Summorum Pontificum* of July 7, 2007, giving the motu proprio, in *Insegnamenti di Benedetto XVI*, 3, 2 (2007), pp. 20–24.

[1019] Jean Madiran tells the story of this interdiction in France, beginning in November 1969, when Cardinal Marty (1904–1994), the president of the French Bishops' Conference, established that, beginning on January 1, 1970, the new *Ordo Missae* would be obligatory and was to be used only in the French language (see J. MADIRAN, *Histoire de la messe interdite*, Via Romana, Versailles, 2007 and 2009, 2 vols.).

above all music. Of these three, the one that has most elevated the soul of the faithful has been music.[1020] The liturgy, in fact, has gradually taken a ritual form in union with the art of chant. Sacred music thus participates in and contributes to the general purpose of the liturgy, which is the glory of God and the sanctification of the faithful. The most rich and ancient musical patrimony of Christian civilization is contained in Gregorian chant, which was later joined by popular religious chant and polyphonic chant.[1021]

In the encyclical *Musicae Sacrae Disciplina* of December 25, 1955, Pius XII recalls the role of St. Gregory the Great, who "according to tradition carefully gathered what had been handed down and gave it a wise organization, providing appropriate laws and norms to assure the purity and integrity of sacred chant."[1022] The same choral chant, "which began to be called 'Gregorian' beginning in the 8th and 9th centuries in almost all regions of Christian Europe, acquired new splendor with the accompaniment of the musical instrument called the organ. Beginning in the 9th century, little by little this choral chant was joined by polyphonic chant, whose theory and practice became more and more precise in the succeeding centuries and which, above all in the 15th and 16th centuries, reached admirable perfection through the work of supreme artists."[1023]

In the sixteenth century, however, the craving for profane music had invaded the Church and had become a theatrical genre.[1024] The churches

[1020] See on this point GIOVANNI TEBALDINI, *La musica sacra in Italia*, Giuseppe Palma, Milan, 1893. On Giovanni Tebaldini (1864–1952), maestro of music and composer, see *Giovanni Tebaldini (1864–1952) e la restituzione della musica antica*, Atti della Giornata di Studio (November 16, 2015), edited by Paola Dessi, Antonio Lovato, Centro di Studi Antoniani, Padova, 2017.

[1021] FIORENZO ROMITO, *Musica sacra*, in EC (1952), col. 1552.

[1022] PIUS XII, Encyclical *Musicae Sacrae Disciplina* of December 25, 1955, in *Discorsi e Radiomessaggi*, vol. 17, p. 573 (pp. 571–588).

[1023] PIUS XII, Encyclical *Musicae Sacrae Disciplina*, in *Discorsi e Radiomessaggi*, vol. 17, p. 573 (pp. 571–588).

[1024] CLAUDE V. PALISCA, *Humanism in Italian Renaissance Musical Thought*, Yale University Press, New Haven-London, 1985; PALISCA, *Baroque Music*,

had become concert halls in which virtuoso singing was performed. As a result of these abuses, Marcellus II even thought about prohibiting music in the churches during his brief pontificate of only twenty-one days (April 9–May 1, 1555). In his coronation ceremony, which took place on April 12, 1555, Good Friday, the musicians of the papal chapel, among whom was Giovanni da Palestrina, felt that they had to show off their most brilliant repertory in order to make a good impression on the new pope. The effect, however, was just the opposite: the pope called them to an audience and reproved them for having sung too bombastically: "Especially in these days which recall the Passion of Our Lord, we should be sad and wash away our sins with our tears, and even more in this place in which the highest leaders of the Church and the cornerstone of the Christian world gather together, the singers should express supreme joy with their voices and musical devices."[1025]

The Council of Trent seemed to embrace this rigor, and some bishops proposed returning liturgical chant to exclusive Gregorian monody, but the Council limited itself to giving some directives of a general character. In September 1562, the twenty-second session decreed concerning sacred music that: "The bishops shall ban from the churches any music which, either with organ or singing, mixes in something lascivious or impure ... so that the house of God may seem to be and may truly be called a house of prayer."[1026]

Pius V created an ad hoc commission that included Cardinal Borromeo and Cardinal Vitellozzo Vitelli.[1027] The two cardinals convened various composers, including Pierluigi da Palestrina,[1028] lamenting with

---

Prentice Hall, Englewood Cliffs, New Jersey, 1991.

[1025] Fabio Avolio, *La musica sacra nel Concilio di Trento e lo stile contrappuntistico di Giovanni Pierluigi da Palestrina*, Aracne, Rome, 2008, p. 1.

[1026] Council of Trent, Session 22 of September 17, 1562, in COD, p. 737.

[1027] Vitellozzo Vitelli (1532–1568), bishop of Florence in 1554, was created cardinal by Paul IV in 1557. He was camerlengo of the Holy Roman Church from 1564 until his death.

[1028] Giovanni Pierluigi da Palestrina (ca. 1525–1594) was choirmaster of the Cappella Giulia (1551–1554), of the Cappella Pia Lateranense

them the profane and confused character of the sacred music that had been executed up until then. In the course of the meeting, Palestrina was charged with writing a Mass in which neither the measures nor the melodies contained anything lascivious or worldly, and in which the words and the meaning of the phrases were clear. Palestrina set to work with fervor, and on April 28, 1565, the *Missa Papae Marcelli* (*Mass of Pope Marcellus*) was performed in the presence of the cardinals, a polyphonic Mass for six voices composed in honor of the deceased pontiff. Cardinal Borromeo and Cardinal Ghislieri, two of the most austere princes of the Church who were present, judged Palestrina's composition to be admirable both for its simplicity as well as for its sacredness, and from that time on Palestrina established himself as the "prince" of the Roman musical school.[1029]

Along with the restoration of the Mass, Pius V is responsible for the rebirth of Gregorian chant in its ancient splendor,[1030] and also for the strong impulse given to polyphonic chant with the appointment of Pierluigi da Palestrina as maestro of the Cappella Giulia in April 1571.[1031] We can apply the words which Abbé Barthe dedicated to the liturgy to the musical restoration of Pius V: "The art that is proper to the

(1555–1560), and again of the Cappella Giulia from 1571 until his death. See GIUSEPPE BAINI, *Memorie storico-critiche della vita e delle opere di Giovanni Pierluigi da Palestrina*, Società tipografica, Rome, 1828; LINO BIANCHI, *Giovanni Pierluigi da Palestrina nella vita, nelle opere, nel suo tempo*, Fondazione Giovanni Pierluigi da Palestrina, Rome, 1995; CLARA MARVIN, *Giovanni Pierluigi da Palestrina: A Research Guide*, Routlege Publishing, New York–London, 2002.

[1029] DOM GUÉRANGER, *Institutions Liturgiques*, pp. 458–459.

[1030] ENRICO DE MARIA, *Il canto gregoriano nelle scelte e nei corali di Pio V*, in *Il tempo di Pio V*, pp. 255–287.

[1031] The motu proprio of St. Pius X of November 22, 1903, *Tra le sollecitudini*, on sacred music, restates that Gregorian chant is the model of sacred music and that, along with it, classical polyphony is also to be renewed, "especially of the Roman school, which in the 16th century obtained the highest level of perfection through the work of Pierluigi da Palestrina" (ASS, 36 [1903–1904], pp. 329–359).

Counter-Reformation, Baroque art, continued the traditionally astonishing aspect of divine worship and its decorum, but also favored a more direct and sensible access to sacred things on the part of the faithful; it displayed the mystery in its striking power and its sensible proximity."[1032]

[1032] BARTHE, *Storia del Messale tridentino*, p. 106. The departure, also aesthetically, from the traditional liturgy of the Church restored by St. Pius V has been well illustrated by Martin Mosebach in his book *Häresie der Formlosigkeit, Die römische Liturgie und ihr Feind*, Karolinger, Vienna-Leipzig, 2003. See also PETER KWASNIEWSKI, *Resurgent in the Midst of Crisis: Sacred Liturgy, the Traditional Mass, and Renewal in the Church*, Angelico Press, Kettering, Ohio, 2015.

9

From Earth to the Glory of Heaven

1. Pius V Concludes His Earthly Mission

During the six years of his pontificate, Pius V worked tirelessly, without giving any regard to the care of his body. Nothing could stop him, and the eyewitnesses agree in telling us how energetic the pope was during the tempestuous years of 1570 and 1571.[1033] "His activity appears wonderful and unheard of. He sought rest only by changing his activities, and only in prayer did he find a bit of distraction from his affairs and from study. There was in him a superabundance of energy that animated him and drove him to work. There was no sign of softness in him: he was neither melancholic nor too sweet, nor simply resigned to the course of events. He was a force that advances relentlessly, without respite or comfort, for the glory of God and the honor of the Church."[1034]

The supernatural spirit that animated the activity of the pontiff emerges from the moving words with which he wrote to the grand master of Malta, Pietro de Monte,[1035] on December 8, 1570, exhorting him not to abandon his post, because "it would be against the divine will of the One who, by His special Providence, has called you to this place

[1033] Pastor, *Storia dei Papi*, vol. 8, pp. 580–581.

[1034] Grente, *Il Pontefice delle grandi battaglie*, pp. 206–207.

[1035] Pietro del Monte (1495 or 1496–1572) succeeded Jean de La Valette as grand master of the Order of Malta from 1568 to 1572. See Pietro Messina, *Del Monte Pietro*, in DBI, vol. 38 (1990), pp. 146–148.

and who will help you to carry the burden that he has placed upon your shoulders." Pius then exhorted the grand master to not allow himself to become discouraged "neither because of your age nor because of your weakness, indeed to rouse yourself ever more to joyfully carry your cross and follow Our Lord, who carried his cross for our sins."[1036]

The pope continued thus:

> You will know without a doubt that my cross is heavier than yours, that I am now lacking strength, and that there are many who try to make me succumb. I would certainly have failed and would have already renounced my dignity (which I have thought of doing more than once), if I did not trust, not in my own strength, but in the One who has said: "Whoever wants to come after me, let him take up his cross and follow me." Therefore we cast our thoughts on Christ Our Lord, and we conform our will to his, repeating not only with the mouth but with the heart, *non mea sed tua voluntas fiat*.

He had written to the archbishop of Goa, Gaspar de Leão Pereira,[1037] in similar words on October 7, 1567. The elderly prelate, sick and tormented by many burdens, had begged the pope to free him from his office. But Pius V replied to him that as a good soldier he ought to die on the battlefield, and in order to encourage him he confided in him about his own sufferings: "We fraternally pity you that you feel, old as you are, fatigue from so many efforts, in the midst of so many dangers; but recall that tribulation is the normal path that leads to heaven, and that we must not abandon the place assigned to us by Providence. Do you believe perhaps that we too, among so many concerns full of responsibility, are not also at times tired of living? And that we desire to return to our former state as a simple religious? Nevertheless, we are resolved not to

[1036] CATENA, *Vita del gloriosissimo papa Pio V*, p. 214.

[1037] Gaspar de Leão Pereira, from Portugal, was bishop of Goa from 1560 until his death in 1576. He is the author of *Carta do primeiro Arcebispo de Goa, ao Povo de Israel, seguidor ainda da ley de Moyses e do Talmud, por engano e malicia dos seus Rabbis* (1565).

shake off our yoke but to carry it courageously until God shall call us to himself. Therefore, renounce any hope of being able to retire to a more quiet life."[1038]

At the center of Pius V's worries during the last months of his life was the defense of Christendom against Islam. The victory of Lepanto was not for him a point of arrival but the beginning of a possible reconquest of the Christian East. Thus he wanted to immortalize the great naval battle at the Vatican in the Sala Regia, where sovereigns and ambassadors are received, entrusting the work to Giorgio Vasari, on whom he had conferred the honor of Knight of the Golden Spur and of St. Peter on June 25, 1571.[1039] The artist from Arezzo reached Rome on February 23, 1572, and finished the frescoes on May 2, the day after the death of the pope. On the west wall of the Sala Regia, in the space between the door that leads to the Sistine Chapel and the door that opens to the Sala Regia, Vasari depicted the preparatory phrase of the Battle of Lepanto. On the same wall, between the door that leads to the Papal Sacristy and the door that leads into the Sala Regia, the painter depicted the encounter between the Christian and Ottoman fleet. The battle is also shown taking place in Heaven, with Christ with a lightning bolt in hand, followed by St. Peter and St. Paul. On the left side of Christ appear St. Mark, the patron of Venice, and St. James, the patron of Spain, and around them is a host of angels with darts and bolts of lightning.[1040]

[1038] *Epistolae ad principes*, n. 3847; GRENTE, *Pio V, il Pontefice delle grandi battaglie*, p. 181.

[1039] JAN L. DE JONG, *The painted decoration of the Sala Regia in the Vatican. Intention and reception*, in *Functions and Decorations: Art and Ritual at the Vatican Palace in the Middle Ages and the Renaissance*, edited by Tristan Weddigen, S. de Blaauw, Bram Kempers, Brepols-Biblioteca Apostolica Vaticana, Tournhout and Vatican City, 2003, pp. 153–168; RICK SCORZA, *Vasari's Lepanto frescoes: apparati, medals, prints and the celebration of victory*, in "Journal of the Warburg and Courtauld Institutes," 75 (2012), pp. 141–200; ALESSIO CELLETTI, *Autorappresentazione papale ed età della Riforma: gli affreschi della Sala Regia Vaticana*, Eurostudium, Rome, 2013.

[1040] In the same Sala Regia, in the space to the right of the door that leads to the Sistine Chapel, Giorgio Vasari was commissioned by Pope

Toward the end of 1571, the chronic kidney and bladder disease that afflicted Pius V intensified. After a crisis during the month of January, which was soon overcome, in the middle of March 1572 the pain became excruciating,[1041] but the pope preferred to suffer still more rather than to be operated on and have other people's hands touch his body.[1042] Pius sought to mitigate the illness by means of a treatment of donkey milk, but this remedy, which in the past had often benefited him, now made his digestion more difficult. The Holy Father worsened in a rapid and unexpected manner, until at the end of March most of his doctors believed that he would live at most only a few more months.[1043]

It was in these days that the Lord revealed to him the day and hour of his death,[1044] and he "concentrated solely on leaving mortal life in a holy manner, setting aside all other thoughts."[1045] Violent pains tormented him, but the pope wanted these sufferings to increase so that he could increase the merit of his patience by enduring them. "He was frequently heard to sigh, lying prostrate before his Jesus crucified, kissing him and lovingly looking at him and saying to him: "*Domine adauge dolores, sed adauge etiam patientiam*" (Lord, increase the sufferings if you like, but also increase my patience).[1046]

On April 3, 1572, Holy Thursday, Pius V received Holy Viaticum from Cardinal Bonelli, who had heard about his uncle's grave illness when he was in Lyons and had hastened to return to Rome. On Good Friday the Holy Father ordered a cross to be brought to him, and getting out of bed,

---

Gregory XIII to paint the wounding of the Huguenot leader Gaspard de Coligny; then, on the north wall, to the right of the papal throne, the massacre of the French Calvinists and the killing of Coligny; finally, to the left of the papal seat, King Charles IX of France was portrayed in Parliament in the act of assuming responsibility for the massacre.

[1041] During the embalming of the body, "three black stones in the bladder" were found (Maffei, *Vita di S. Pio V*, p. 272).

[1042] Maffei, *Vita di S. Pio V*, p. 264.

[1043] Pastor, *Storia dei Papi*, vol. 8, p. 581.

[1044] Maffei, *Vita di S. Pio V*, p. 398.

[1045] Minorelli, *Vita di S. Pio V*, p. 103.

[1046] Maffei, *Vita di S. Pio V*, p. 272.

he adored it in his bare feet. On Easter Sunday, April 6, the pope was unable to offer the Pontifical Mass, but although he was in great pain he wanted to impart the solemn Easter blessing to the Roman people. At this news, an incalculable crowd gathered that wanted to see Pius's face one last time. On hearing his faint voice, many wept for joy and prayed for his life to be preserved for a long time. The pope felt better, and there was great hope that he could recover his health, but in the following days his illness worsened. His stomach refused food and his pain from kidney stones increased. Pastor recalls that in addition to his physical pains Pius V also had great spiritual suffering, above all due to the behavior of the great Catholic powers, which had not accepted his exhortation to unite themselves once more against the Turks.[1047] Pius V had hoped to live to see the destruction of the Ottoman Empire, but now, through the mysterious designs of God, he saw the historical hour of the triumph of Christianity, which he had believed was drawing near, grow distant.

Despite his sufferings, on April 21, with a final surge of strength, the Holy Father made known his desire to visit the seven basilicas of Rome. In vain, cardinals, doctors, and family members sought to dissuade him. He went out on foot, supported by two servants, so pale and weak that Marco Colonna, meeting him on the street, begged him to return on a litter to the Vatican Palace. Pius politely refused and continued his walk. When he came to the Scala Santa, he kissed the last step three times. Upon his return, at the threshold of the Vatican he met a group of English Catholics who had been forced into exile. He spoke with them paternally, ordered Cardinal Bonelli to take care of them, and then exclaimed: "My God, you know that I have always been ready to shed my blood for the salvation of their nation."[1048] He had once promised that for an expedition against Protestant England he would not only have committed the goods of the Church but would also have personally gone to lead it.[1049]

[1047] PASTOR, *Storia dei Papi*, vol. 8, p. 582.
[1048] MAFFEI, *Vita di S. Pio V*, p. 338.
[1049] CATENA, *Vita del gloriosissimo papa Pio V*, p. 17.

In the following days Pius was no longer able to handle current affairs, but he showed himself to be absolutely calm, trying to comfort the affliction of those who surrounded him. Among the prayers that he had read without interruption, even at night, he preferred the seven penitential psalms and the account of the Passion.[1050] On April 30 the pope felt that his end was drawing near. In order to die as a simple religious, he put on the habit of St. Dominic, and he asked the bishop of Segni, Giuseppe Pamfili, the sacristan of St. Peter's Basilica, to administer Extreme Unction to him. To the other prelates near him, such as Cardinals Bonelli and Rusticucci, who assisted him, Pius V said:

> My dearest sons, the hour has come to pay the final debt to nature as a man, by means of death, so that my flesh may return to the dust from which it was formed and my soul may return to God who created it. If you have loved my mortal life, full of an infinite number of miseries, you should love even more the immutable and happy life that the Mercy of God, as I hope, shall soon grant to me in Heaven, among the angels and saints. You know with how much zeal I have labored for the happy success of the Christian armadas opened by the victory of Lepanto, through which I trusted to see the Ottoman Empire destroyed; but my sins have not made me worthy to see this triumph, and they deprive me of the great consolation that I would have had in seeing religion restored in those places from which it had been banned. I humbly adore the divine judgments and I accept the Lord's will. I commend to you, however, the Holy Church, which I have loved so much. Do your best to elect a zealous successor, who will seek only the glory of the Savior and who will not have any other desire than the good of the Church and the honor of the Apostolic See.[1051]

On his deathbed, casting a final glance toward the Church on earth, which he was leaving for the Church of Heaven, he recited with a faltering

[1050] Pastor, *Storia dei Papi*, vol. 8, p. 583.
[1051] Maffei, *Vita di S. Pio V*, p. 271.

voice the verse of one of the hymns of the Easter season: "*Quaesumus, autor hominum, in hoc paschali gaudio, ab omni mortis impetu tuum defende populum*" (Creator of men, grant that in these days filled with the joy of Easter, you may preserve your people from all the assaults of death).[1052] "Finally, as the Gospel account of the Passion of Our Lord Jesus Christ was being read, he extended his hands in the form of a cross, and without making any movement or noise, he sweetly breathed forth his soul and restored it to the Creator."[1053]

It was the evening of May 1, 1572. Pius V had reached the age of sixty-eight and had held the Chair of Peter for six years, seven months, and twenty-three days. That same day, Teresa of Ávila had a vision of the pope, who from Heaven encouraged her to continue her work, promising that he would assist her.[1054]

The inhabitants of the Eternal City flocked by the thousands to come and see the body of the pope exposed in St. Peter's Basilica. Everyone tried to obtain something connected to the deceased as a precious relic.[1055] Thus was realized the prophecy spoken by Pope Ghislieri as soon he was elected, when he said that the Roman people would grieve even more over his death than they grieved over his election.[1056] After a very short conclave that lasted only two days, on May 13, 1572, Cardinal Ugo Boncompagni was elected pope, taking the name of Gregory XIII (1572–1585).

The Protestant historian Leopold von Ranke writes: "It is certain that his attitude and character exercised an immeasurable influence over his contemporaries and on the entire evolution of the Church."[1057] Ranke

[1052] Maffei, *Vita di S. Pio V*, p. 270.

[1053] Benedetto XIV, *La beatificazione dei Servi di Dio e la canonizzazione dei Beati*, Libreria Editrice Vaticana, Vatican City, 2011, p. 567.

[1054] P. Federico di S. Antonio, *Vita di S. Teresa di Gesù fondatrice degli scalzi e scalze dell'Ordine di N. S. del Carmine*, Tip. Marini, Rome, 1837, vol. 2, p. 437.

[1055] Pastor, *Storia dei Papi*, vol. 8, pp. 584–585.

[1056] Maffei, *Vita di S. Pio V*, p. 49.

[1057] Ranke, *Storia dei Papi*, p. 260.

cites a report by the Venetian ambassador Paolo Tiepolo, written four years after Pope Ghislieri's death:

> The fact that there have been, one after another, numerous popes of irreproachable life, has contributed infinitely to the good of the Church. As a result all of the other ones became better, or at least appeared to do so. Cardinals and prelates assist diligently at the Mass: in their tenor of life they make an effort to avoid everything which could give scandal; the entire city has ceased being as wild as it once was: in its customs and manner of living it is much more Christian than it was before. One may say that in the things of religion Rome is by no means far from the perfection that human nature is able to achieve.[1058]

2. The Burial in the Sistine Chapel

Pius V was provisionally buried in St. Peter's Basilica, in the chapel of St. Andrew, close to the tomb of Pius III. With the Bull *Praeclarum Quidem Opus*, issued on August 1, 1566, Pope Ghislieri had approved the construction of a Dominican convent and church dedicated to the Holy Cross (Santa Croce) in Bosco Marengo, his birthplace, where he wanted to be permanently buried.[1059] The pope had commissioned the main altar of the church to Vasari, who had painted a triumphal Last Judgment there.[1060] The tomb, built in 1571, was engraved with an epigraph, dictated by the pope himself, which recalled his family origins,

[1058] RANKE, *Storia dei Papi*, p. 366

[1059] The monumental complex of Santa Croce, composed of a church and a convent, represents one of the first examples of Post-Tridentine architecture. Its construction was completed by Cardinal Bonelli after the death of Pius V, and the Dominicans celebrated the Divine Office there until 1854, when the edifice was expropriated by the Piedmontese State. See *I luoghi di San Pio V. Itinerari turistico-culturali*, Anthelios, Milan, 2006, pp. 38–53.

[1060] DAVIDE ARECCO, ALESSANDRO LANTERO, *Due lavori del Vasari nel complesso monumentale di Santa Croce in Bosco Marengo*, "Novinostra," 1 (March 1999), pp. 77–85.

his Dominican profession, and the hope of the resurrection.[1061] Gregory XIII, however, did not authorize the translation of the body to Bosco Marengo, and his successor, Sixtus V,[1062] decided to transfer the body of Pius V to the Basilica of St. Mary Major, in the same chapel in which he had begun to build his own funerary monument and which had been named after him the "Sistine Chapel."[1063]

The construction of the sumptuous chapel, designed by Domenico Fontana,[1064] had begun in 1585, three months before the election of Felice Peretti as Roman Pontiff, and it was initially envisaged that the

[1061] GIULIO IENI, *"Una superbissima sepoltura": il mausoleo di Pio V*, in *Pio V e Santa Croce di Bosco. Aspetti di una committenza papale*, edited by Carlenrica Spantigati, G. Ieni, Edizioni dell'Orso, Alessandria, 1985, pp. 31–48.

[1062] Sixtus V (Felice Peretti: 1521–1590), of the Order of Friars Minor Conventual, was made bishop, vicar general of the Conventuals and then cardinal (1570) by St. Pius V. He was elected pope on April 24, 1585. See the view of SILVANO GIORDANO, in EP (2000) pp. 202–222; and the classic text of JOSEPH ALEXANDER VON HÜBNER, *Sixte-Quint par M. le Baron de Hübner ancient Ambassadeur d'Autriche à Paris et à Rome. D'après des correspondances diplomatiques inédites tirées des archives d'état du Vatican, de Simancas, Venise, Paris, Vienne et Florence*, Librairie A. Franck, Paris, 1870.

[1063] See ALEXANDRA HERZ, *The Sixtine and Pauline Tombs in Santa Maria Maggiore: An Iconographical Study*, Institute of Fine Arts, New York University, New York, 1974; ENZO BORSELLINO, *Il monumento di Pio V in S. Maria Maggiore*, in *Sisto V. Roma e il Lazio*, edited by Marcello Fagiolo and Maria Luisa Madonna, Istituto Poligrafico e Zecca dello Stato, Rome, 1992, pp. 837–850; STEVEN F. OSTROW, *Art and Spirituality in Counter-Reformation Rome: The Sistine and Pauline Chapels in S. Maria Maggiore*, Cambridge University Press, Cambridge, 1996. See also SIMON DITCHFELD, *Il Papa come pastore? Pio V e la liturgia*, in *Pio V nella società e nella politica*, pp. 164–165 (pp. 159–178).

[1064] Domenico Fontana (1543–1607) was an architect from Ticino, to whom Sixtus V entrusted the development of the new master plan of Rome. In 1586 he erected the obelisk in St. Peter's Square that he relates in the book *Della transportatione dell'obelisco Vaticano e delle fabriche di Sisto V* (Rome, 1590). See ALESSANDRO IPPOLITI, *Fontana, Domenico*, in DBI, vol. 48 (1997), pp. 638–643; LEROS PITTONI, GABRIELLE LAUTENBERG, *Roma felix. La città di Sisto V e Domenico Fontana*, Viviani, Rome, 2002.

funerary monument of his Franciscan brother Sixtus IV (1471–1484), whose name Pope Peretti took, would be placed in front of his own monument. Instead, in July 1586, Sixtus V publicly announced his intention to erect the sepulchral monument of Pius V in the chapel.[1065] Sixtus V had strictly collaborated as an inquisitor with Pope Ghislieri, who had made him a bishop and cardinal, and Sixtus believed that he had an affinity of character and vision of his pontificate with Pius. Moreover, the people venerated Pius V as a saint. It is therefore not surprising that Sixtus V wanted to have him resting in front of him, awaiting the final resurrection, in the most important Marian basilica of Rome.

In June 1587 an imposing statue of Pius V, the work of Leonardo Sormani, was placed in the center of the monument in St. Mary Major, and the following autumn the sculptor Giovanni Antonio Paracca, known as "the Valsoldo," began the statue of Sixtus V to be placed on the opposite side of the chapel. The translation of the body of Pius V from the Vatican basilica to St. Mary Major took place with a solemn ceremony on January 9, 1588. Maffei writes that "there has never been a more pompous, magnificent and devout event" in Rome.[1066] The following day, Sunday, January 10, the streets were filled with countless people of every class and condition who went to pay their homage to Pius V. On Monday, January 11, Sixtus V paid his respects, accompanied by forty-four cardinals and the entire papal court.

The decoration of the grandiose tomb in the Sistine Chapel exalts the image of the pope as the conqueror of Lepanto and of heretics. The mausoleum that encloses his body includes, in addition to the statue, five bas-relief sculptures. On the left, Pius V, seated on a throne in pontifical robes and tiara, hands the standard of the fleet to Don Juan of Austria, alongside Marcantonio Colonna; on the right he hands the captain's staff to Count Sforza of Santa Fiora, the conqueror of the Huguenots in France. In the center, above the statue, the coronation of the pope is

[1065] R. Rusconi, *Santo Padre. La santità del Papa da san Pietro a Giovanni Paolo II*, Viella, Rome, 2010, pp. 250–252.

[1066] Maffei, *Vita di S. Pio V*, p. 425.

portrayed, while the two smaller squares, on the sides, show the victory of Lepanto and the victory over the Huguenots.[1067] On the tomb of Pius V one reads the words: "Pope Sixtus V, Franciscan, placed this expression of gratitude for Pope Pius V, Dominican."

3. The Beatification and the Canonization

Sixtus V, the first pope to pay great honors to Pius V, was also the one who initiated his process of canonization. In 1616–1617, Paul V (1605–1621) authorized the investigation by the ordinary authority in Rome and other places in Italy. In 1624, Urban VIII (1623–1644) authorized the apostolic authorities to initiate the canonical investigations that were held in Rome, Osimo, Urbino, Fano Bologna, Milan, Cortona, Bergamo, and Madrid. On February 1, 1625, the Sacred Congregation of Rites authorized the Order of Friars Preachers, of which Michael Ghislieri had been a member, to celebrate the Mass of the Holy Trinity on the anniversary of his death. However, considerable time had to pass before the beatification occurred, the first step in the recognition of holiness. This happened by means of a brief of Pope Clement X (1670–1676) on April 27, 1672.[1068]

In the investigations that take place in the processes of beatification and canonization, the scrupulous investigation of men is not sufficient.[1069] The Church requires an indubitable confirmation from Heaven. Therefore, since the earliest centuries of the Church, the proclamation of a saint was tied to the recognition of miracles worked by the saint[1070]—not

[1067] These bas-reliefs are attributed to Niccolò Fiammingo, also known as Niccolò Pippi or of Arras (his native city), the pseudonym of Nicolaus Mostaert (1530–1604), who was also responsible for the monument to Sixtus V. Another Flemish sculptor collaborated with him, Egidio della Riviera (Gillis van den Vliete), who died in Rome in 1602. The creator of the depiction of the coronation is perhaps Silla Giacomo Longhi (1569–1622).

[1068] *Bullarium Romanum*, vol. 18, pp. 304–306.

[1069] See the large entry by G. Löw dedicated to the canonization, in EC, vol. 3 (1949), cols. 571–607.

[1070] Yves Chiron, *Enquête sur les béatifications et les canonisations*, Tempus, Paris, 2011, pp. 129–150. A miracle is an extraordinary event that happens

necessarily the miracles worked during his or her life, but certainly those done postmortem. Paolo Alessandro Maffei offers an accurate account of the miracles done by Pope Ghislieri during his life (fourteen cases),[1071] those done after his death (thirty-four cases),[1072] those done by means of the so-called *Agnus Dei*[1073] blessed by him (eight cases),[1074] and finally those that occurred after the beatification and considered prior to the canonization (twenty-four cases).[1075] "But if we were to tell in detail how many times he chased the devil from the body of many people, how many people close to death he unexpectedly called back to life, how many sick people he healed and restored to health out of the blue, how many fires he put out, how many times he averted shipwrecks and how many other marvels of this nature he worked, the story would be destined to have practically no end."[1076]

From the time of Urban VIII until that of Paul VI, the process of canonization required two miracles for beatification and another two for canonization. On the basis of the documents received by the Congregation of Rites, the three oldest auditors of the Rota recognized the formal correctness of the procedural files, the common opinion of the holiness of the pope and eight miracles, two of which were performed during his life. The auditors of the Rota, having examined 146 witnesses, reported under oath that Pius V had died a virgin, that he had never committed a single mortal sin in all of his life, that he had possessed all of the virtues in a heroic degree, that the gift of prophecy had been communicated to

---

outside of, or contrary to, the normal course of nature. See A. Michel, *Miracle*, DTC, vol. 10 (1929), cols. 1789–1859.

[1071] Maffei, *Vita di S. Pio V*, pp. 399–401.

[1072] Maffei, *Vita di S. Pio V*, pp. 401–408.

[1073] The *Agnus Dei* are wax disks bearing the impression of the Lamb of God on one side and the image of a saint on the other. The custom of blessing them at Easter is very ancient; traces of them are believed to have been found in liturgical monuments since the fifth century.

[1074] Maffei, *Vita di S. Pio V*, pp. 408–411.

[1075] Maffei, *Vita di S. Pio V*, pp. 411–420.

[1076] Minorelli, *Vita di S. Pio V*, p. 113.

him by God, and that he had worked many miracles.[1077] The congregation confirmed the juridical validity of the acts of recognition of his virtues in a heroic degree.[1078]

Two other miracles of Pius V were also approved,

> the first of which was that two images of the pope, one made of paper and the other of canvas, were completely spared from fire as they hung on the wall in the chapel of Don Antonio, the Duke of Cardona and of Sessa, even though the fire raged with such fury throughout the whole house that even silver statues were melted by the force of the flames, and the altar stone was reduced to baked pumice, and all of the sacred furnishings of that chapel (excepting only these two images and that part of the stone floor where one of them had fallen) were reduced to dust and ashes.
>
> The other miracle was the instantaneous healing of Tiburzia Fiorenza, a seventy-year-old woman from Osimo. She was overwhelmed by an acute and malignant fever and oppressed by other ailments all at the same time, so that according to her doctors it was believed that she would die within three hours, when a garment of Blessed Pius was devoutly applied to her sick body, and she immediately got up from the bed alive and well, and she lived happily for many more years.[1079]

On March 8, 1672, the Congregation of Rites approved two other miracles:

[1077] FALLOUX, *Histoire de St. Pie V*, vol. 2, p. 355.

[1078] On the heroic virtues required for elevation to the altars, see AMBROGIO ESZER, O.P., *Il concetto della virtù eroica nella storia*, in *Sacramenti, liturgia, cause dei santi. Studi in onore del cardinale Giuseppe Casoria*, Editoriale Comunicazioni Sociali, Naples, 1992, pp. 605–636. See also ROMEO DE MAIO, *L'ideale eroico nei processi di canonizzazione della Controriforma*, in *Riforme e miti nella Chiesa del Cinquecento*, Guida, Naples, 1973, pp. 257–278.

[1079] BENEDETTO XIV, *La beatificazione dei Servi di Dio*, p. 568.

The first was the copious multiplication of wheat flour that took place in the monastery of the sisters of Saint Dominic near Prato in Tuscany. The second was the divine knowledge infused in Blessed Pius, by which on the very same day at the very same hour Pius V was given knowledge of the victory that had been won by the Christians and which he made known to those who were with him, who noted the month, day, and hour when it happened, and then, when the certain news arrived of the victory, openly recognized that it had happened just as Pius had previously said to them.[1080]

Dom Guéranger describes two other miracles as follows:

One day, as [Pius V] was walking with the Polish ambassador across the Vatican square, which extends over the area that was once the Circus of Nero, he became filled with enthusiasm for the glory and courage of the martyrs who had suffered in that same place during the first persecution. He bent down and collected a handful of dust from that field of torments, walked over by so many generations of the faithful ever since the peace of Constantine. He poured the dust into a white cloth given him by the ambassador; but when the ambassador returned home and was about to open it, he found that it was filled with crimson blood, as if it had been spilled that very instant: the dust was gone. The faith of the Pontiff had evoked the blood of the martyrs, and this same blood reappeared at his call to attest, in the face of heresy, that the Roman Church, still in the 16th century, was the same Church for which those heroes, at the time of Nero, had given their life.[1081]

Guéranger continues:

[1080] Benedetto XIV, *La beatificazione dei Servi di Dio*, p. 569.

[1081] Dom Guéranger, *L'anno liturgico*, vol. 4, *Proprio dei Santi (11 aprile–11 novembre)*, Italian translation, Fede e Cultura, Verona, 2018, p. 78.

> The perfidy of the heretics tried more than once to put an end to a life that left their plans for the conquest of Italy without any hope of success. By means of a stratagem, as vile as it was sacrilegious, supported by a hateful betrayal, they filled the feet of the Crucifix that the holy Pontiff had in his oratory, which he often kissed with his lips, with a subtle poison. Pius V, in the fervor of his prayer, was preparing to give this sign of his love to the Savior of men through this holy image; but suddenly, O prodigy! The feet of the Crucifix separated from the Cross and seemed to flee from the respectful kisses of the elderly man. Pius V then understood that the wickedness of his enemies had wanted to transform even the wood that had given us life into an instrument of death.[1082]

We have numerous representations of the miracle of the crucifix.[1083] Among the most notable, we recall the one that is preserved in the Church of Santa Maria in Castello in Genoa, one in the museum next to the Convent of Santa Sabina in Rome, and another placed in the Chapel of the Collegio Ghislieri in Pavia.

The echo of this miracle further inspired the composer Giovanni Antonio Costa in the composition of the oratorio *L'Empietà Delusa* on the libretto of Carlo Giuseppe Cornacchia, staged in the Chapel of the Collegio Ghislieri in Pavia in 1713. The oratorio tells the story of the miracle of the crucifix: Impiety, the assassin of the Devil, attempts to take Pius V's life by sprinkling poison on the feet of the crucifix that Pius would usually kiss during his prayers, but in response to the prayers of the Church, a divine intervention takes place by Christ, who miraculously makes the feet of the crucifix fall off and saves the pope from death.

[1082] Dom Guéranger, *L'anno liturgico*, vol. 4, p. 78.

[1083] M. Firpo, *San Pio V e il miracolo del crocefisso*, in M. Firpo, *Storie di immagini. Immagini di storia. Studi di iconografia cinquecentesca*, Edizioni di storia e letteratura, Rome, 2010, pp. 219–230.

The beatification ceremony took place in St. Peter's Basilica on May 1, 1672.[1084] The painting by Lazzaro Baldi[1085] exhibited in the gallery of the Vatican basilica depicted the scene of the angel who revealed to Pius V the naval victory of Lepanto.[1086] Between 1672 and 1673 five other canvases were painted for the Collegio Ghislieri of Pavia to celebrate the beatification.[1087] In front of the same college, an imposing bronze statue was created in 1691 by Francesco Nuvolone,[1088] considered one of the masters of sculpture of the time.[1089]

The superior general of the Dominican Order, Antonin Cloche,[1090] who was greatly devoted to Pope Ghislieri, obtained permission to place a magnificent marble sarcophagus, the work of Pierre le Gros, in the Sistine Chapel of St. Mary Major. On September 11, 1697, the body of

[1084] GIUSEPPE ELMI, *Breve relatione delle cerimonie et apparato della basilica di San Pietro nella beatificazione del Glorioso beato Pio V dell'ordine dei predicatori*, Stamperia del Mancini, Rome, 1672; MARIA TERESA MAZZILLI SAVINI, *Da Papa Pio V all'iconografia di San Pio V: come è espressa la sua canonizzazione*, in *San Pio V nella storia*. Symposium on the occasion of the third centenary of the canonization of Pope Pius V Ghislieri, edited by C. Bernasconi, Collegio Ghislieri, Pavia, 2012, pp. 81–110; VITTORIO CASALE, *L'arte per le canonizzazioni. L'attività artistica intorno alle canonizzazioni e alle beatificazioni del Seicento*, Allemandi, Turin, 2011.

[1085] Lazzaro Baldi (ca. 1624–1703) was a painter who was a student of Pietro da Cortona, who worked principally in Rome. See EVELINA BOREA, in DBI, vol. 5 (1963), pp. 469–470.

[1086] RUSCONI, *Santo Padre*, p. 259.

[1087] The canvases include the *Battle of Lepanto* by Giovanni Battista Del Sole: *Saint Pius Freeing the Possessed from Demons* by Giovanni Peruzzini; *The Crucifix Pulls Back Its Feet from the Kiss of Saint Pius* and *The Portrait of the Saint Extinguishes a Fire* by Giovanni Scaramuccia; and finally the *Vision of Pius V of the Battle of Lepanto* by Lazzaro Baldi.

[1088] Francesco Nuvolone, not to be confused with his contemporary Carlo *Francesco Nuvolone* (1609–1662), was an artist from Ticino, known above all for his monumental statue of Pius V in Pavia. See CRISTIANO GIOMETTI, *Nuvolone Francesco*, in DBI, vol. 79 (2013), pp. 23–25.

[1089] SILLI, *San Pio V*, p. 41.

[1090] Jean François Antonin Cloche (1628–1720) was superior general of the Dominicans from 1686 until his death.

the saint was translated from the crypt of St. Peter's and exposed for the veneration of the faithful.

The ceremony took place by torchlight at seven o'clock in the evening. From the Vatican basilica to the Church of Santa Cecilia in Trastevere, the coffin was carried by the canons of St. Peter's; then by the canons of San Marcello to their church in the Via Flaminia (today the Via del Corso); and from there the canons of St. Mary Major carried it to their basilica. Two long lines of Swiss Guards, armed with halberds, were arrayed around the body of Pius V in order to contain the crowd. Behind the coffin, Pope Sixtus V followed with the entire papal "family" and the cardinals, bishops, and prelates of the Roman Court, each wearing their own characteristic garments.[1091] In these solemn ceremonies in which the Church expressed all her majesty, the infinite distance that separates earth from Heaven seemed to be reduced.

During the pontificate of Clement XI (1700–1721), the process that led to the proclamation of sanctity of Pius V reached its conclusion, and two other miracles were examined and approved by the Congregation of Rites in the presence of the Supreme Pontiff.

The first concerned the sudden healing of Margherita Massia, a ten-year-old girl, who had suffered from paralysis for a long time; the second, the instantaneous expulsion of a fetus that had already been dead for many days from its mother's womb without any pain to her, while the mother, Isabella Riccio, was preserved from the apparent danger of death.[1092]

After hearing the votes of the cardinals and consultors of the sacred congregation, the pope gave his approval, and Pius V was canonized on May 22, 1712, the Feast of the Most Holy Trinity, along with three other saints: the Theatine Andrea Avellino, the Claretian Catherine of Bologna, and the Capuchin Felice da Cantalice. The latter two were contemporaries of Pope Ghislieri. For eight days in the month of August, Rome resounded with liturgical celebrations and with sumptuous

[1091] Maffei, *Vita di S. Pio V*, pp. 429–431.
[1092] Benedetto XIV, *La beatificazione dei Servi di Dio*, p. 570.

representations in the Piazza della Minerva and Piazza Navona, where six galleys were set up to represent the Battle of Lepanto.[1093]

The Roman painter Andrea Procaccini[1094] created the altarpiece for the chapel of St. Pius V[1095] in Santa Maria Sopra Minerva, depicting *St. Pius V Raising the Crucifix over the Defeated Turk*, in which the Turkish enemy is thrown to the ground by St. Michael the Archangel, who represents the pontiff. In the same chapel there is the canvas of Lorenzo Baldi depicting *St. Pius V Praying*, which was used as a standard in St. Peter's Basilica during the beatification ceremony. In the same year of the canonization, the almost five-hundred-page long *Life of Saint Pius V* by Paolo Alessandro Maffei was published, as well as the short *Vita S. Pii V Summi Pontificis*, written in Latin by the Dominican Tommaso Maria Minorelli.[1096]

It had been four centuries since the canonization of a pope, Celestine V, and it would be another two before there was another sainted pope, Pius X, canonized by Pius XII on May 19, 1954.[1097] The Church fixed the celebration of the liturgical feast of Pius V on May 5. The new liturgical calendar of Paul VI moved it to April 30.

In March 1904, on the fifth centenary of Pius V's birth, by the will of St. Pius X, the canonical recognition of the remains of Pius V was carried out. The remains were solemnly returned to the urn, covering

[1093] Rusconi, *Santo Padre*, p. 264.

[1094] Andrea Procaccini (1671–1734) was a Roman painter of the Baroque era, who also worked in Spain, where he painted for the royal family of Philip V for over a decade.

[1095] The Chapel of St. Pius V belonged to the Millini family and then to the Braschi family. On the left side of chapel are the sepulchral monuments of Cardinal Michele Bonelli (who died in 1598) and Cardinal Carlo Bonelli (who died in 1676).

[1096] See Fulvio Gasti, *L'immagine di Pio V negli scritti biografici del 1712*, in *San Pio V nella storia*, edited by C. Bernasconi, Ibis, Pavia, 2012, pp. 59–79.

[1097] Between the year 1000 and the Second Vatican Council, the Church canonized five popes: Leo IX (1049–1054); Gregory VII (1073–1085); Celestine V (1294); Pius V (1566–1572); and Pius X (1903–1914).

the skull with a silver mask.[1098] Today the remains of St. Pius V rest in the Sistine Chapel of St. Mary Major, on the opposite side from the Borghese Chapel, where the icon of Our Lady of St. Mary Major, *Salus Populi Romani*, is venerated—she to whom Pius V was greatly devoted and who accompanied his entire pontificate.

4. The Pope of the Rosary

The victory of Lepanto, of which St. Pius V was the architect, is inextricably linked to the Holy Rosary, of which he was "the Pope *par excellence*."[1099] The Roman Breviary defines the Rosary thus: "It is a fixed prayer in honor of the Most Holy Virgin consisting of the recitation of 150 'Ave Marias' separated by 15 'Pater Nosters' which divide it into 15 decades, in each one of which one meditates piously on one of the mysteries of our Redemption."[1100] This form was given to the Rosary by St. Pius V.

Since childhood, Michele Ghislieri venerated the Blessed Mother with exceptional devotion by means of the practice of the Holy Rosary. In 1539, Fr. Ghislieri promoted a Company of the Rosary in his home parish, and also as pope he wanted the Rosary to be recited each day in the Vatican palace, according to a practice that until that time was unusual.[1101] In 1568, when he promulgated the new breviary, the pope obliged all priests to begin each hour of the Divine Office not only with the Pater Noster but also with the Ave Maria, completed with its second part which begins with the *Sancta Maria*.[1102] In 1212 St. Dominic di Guzman, during his stay in Toulouse, saw the Virgin Mary, who gave him

[1098] Rusconi, *Santo Padre*, p. 267.

[1099] Venchi, O.P., *San Pio V*, p. 144. See also Catherine Mary Antony, *Saint Pius V: Pope of the Holy Rosary*, Longmans, Green and Company, London, 1911.

[1100] *Breviarium romanum ex decreto Sacrosancti Concilii Tridentini restitutum*, Les Amis de Sant-François de Sales, Seduni, 2007, *Die 7 Oct.*, vol. 2, pp. 615–616.

[1101] Alberto Carlo Scolari, *Le cappelle delle Reliquie e del Rosario nella chiesa del convento di S. Croce in Bosco Marengo*, in *Pio V e Santa Croce di Bosco*, pp. 63–83.

[1102] Campana, *Maria nel culto cattolico*, p. 563.

the Rosary, as a response to the prayer he made to her asking to know how to combat the Albigensian heresy. It was thus that the Holy Rosary became the most widespread prayer to oppose heresies. Later, the disciples of St. Dominic, above all Blessed Alàn de la Roche, spread the practice of the Rosary, that is, the recitation of 150 Ave Marias, with the help of the crown formed by beads held together by a cord or chain which was to be used to count the Ave Marias. But between the fifth and fifteenth centuries the Ave Maria was limited to the first part, which at that time went up to the words "*fructus ventris tui*." Pius V approved the complete form of the Ave Maria, codifying the prayer "*Sancta Maria, Mater Dei*," added to the first part. It took about a century before the directives of Pope Ghislieiri were universally adopted, and it was only toward the middle of the seventeenth century that the Ave Maria in its present form entered universally into popular use.

In the bull *Consueverunt Romani Pontifices*,[1103] of September 17, 1569, which is considered the *magna carta* of the Rosary because it gave an official form to the practice, Pius V explained the origin of the Rosary, its name, its essential elements, its effects, its spiritual fruitfulness, and the best way to spread it. The document, after recalling the link between this religious practice and the Order of Preachers, especially in reference to the extirpation of the Albigensian heresy, affirms that

> Dominic identified an easy, accessible to all, and extremely pious way of praying and imploring God, that is, the Rosary or the Psalter of the Blessed Virgin Mary, through which the same Blessed Virgin Mary is venerated with the *Salutatio Angelica* 150 times according to the number of the Psalter of David, interposing a Pater Noster after each decade with determined meditations illustrating the entire life of Our Lord Jesus Christ. Following the example of our predecessors, seeing that the Church militant, which God has placed in our hands, is agitated at present by so many heresies

[1103] Pius V, Apostolic Letter *Consueverunt Romani Pontifices* of September 17, 1569, in *Bullarium Ord. Praed.*, vol. 5, p. 223.

and gravely disturbed and afflicted by so many wars and the moral deprivation of men, we lift our eyes full of tears, but also of hope, towards that same mountain (Mary), from whom descends all help [cf. Ps. 121:1–2], and we invite all the faithful, admonishing them benevolently in the Lord, to do likewise.

The victory of Lepanto, which the pope attributed to the power of the Rosary, seemed like a heavenly seal to the practice of this devotion. The institution of the Feast of Our Lady of Victory or of the Rosary was the last relevant action of the pontificate of St. Pius V, who added to this the title of *Auxilium Christianorum* (Help of Christians). On March 5, 1572, he published another bull, *Salvatoris Domini*,[1104] to commemorate "the victory, unforgettable for all time, won against the Turks, the enemies of the Catholic faith through the merits and pious intercession of the glorious and ever Virgin Mary Mother of God." In this bull he grants a plenary indulgence to all those who on October 7 visit the Chapel of the Rosary erected in Martorell (Catalonia), by Luis de Requeséns y Zúñiga, the lord of that city, who had participated in the Battle of Lepanto. In the consistory of March 17, 1572, Pius expressed finally his desire to institute a "*Commemoratio Sanctae Mariae de Victoria*" to be celebrated on October 7 in memory of the victory of Lepanto. In the 1597 painting on the altar of the Chapel of the Rosary in his native Bosco, as in many other famous paintings, Our Lady of the Rosary stands above the banner of the great victory.[1105]

Leo XIII, in his encyclical *Supremi Apostolatus* of September 1, 1883, affirms that

the efficacy and power of the Rosary were wonderfully experienced in the 16th century, when the imposing forces of the Turks threatened to impose on almost all of Europe the yoke of superstition

[1104] *Bullarium Ordinis FF. Praedicatorum: Ab Anno 1550 ad 1621*, vol. 5, pp. 295–298.

[1105] The painting by Grazio Cossali (1562–1629) preserved in the Church of Santa Croce in Bosco Marengo shows St. Pius V attributing to Our Lady of the Rosary the merit of the victory of Lepanto.

> and barbarism. In that circumstance the Pontiff Saint Pius V, after having exhorted the Christian princes to the defense of a cause that was the cause of all, directed all of his zeal above all to obtain the help of the most powerful Mother of God for the Christian people, invoked with the prayers of the Rosary. And the answer was the marvelous spectacle which was then offered to heaven and earth, that captured the minds and hearts of everyone. On the one hand, the faithful ready to give their life and shed their blood for the salvation of their religion and homeland, intrepidly awaited the enemy not far from the Gulf of Corinth; on the other hand, unarmed men in pious and pleading ranks invoked Mary, and with the formula of the Rosary repeatedly saluted Mary, asking her to assist the combatants even unto victory. And the Blessed Mother, moved by this prayer, assisted them. In fact, allowing the Christian fleet to be attacked in battle near the Echinades in the Ionian Sea, she fought and killed the enemies without grave losses and won a splendid victory. For this reason the Most Holy Pontiff, in order to eternalize the grace that had been obtained, decreed that the anniversary day of this great battle was to be considered a feast day in honor of Mary the Victor, and later Gregory XIII consecrated this feast with the title of the Rosary.[1106]

Paul VI, in his apostolic exhortation *Recurrens Mensis October* of October 7, 1969, in which he commemorates the fourth centenary of the apostolic letter *Consueverunt Romani Pontifices*, recalls that with this document "Saint Pius V defined the form of the Rosary still in use today, in an era of turmoil for the Church and the world. Faithful to this very holy inheritance, from which the Christian people have never ceased to draw strength and courage, we exhort the clergy and the faithful to insistently ask from God through the intercession of the Virgin Mary peace and reconciliation between all men and between all peoples."[1107]

[1106] LEO XIII, Encyclical *Supremi Apostolatus* of September 1, 1883, in EE, pp. 258–259.

[1107] PAUL VI, *Insegnamenti*, vol. 7 (1969), p. 659.

In his subsequent apostolic exhortation *Marialis Culto* of February 2, 1974, Paul VI reiterated that "Saint Pius V illustrated and, in some way, defined the traditional form of the Rosary." To the Rosary, he explains, "Our Predecessors dedicated vigilant attention and solicitous concern: they have repeatedly recommended its frequent recitation, favored its diffusion, illustrated its nature, recognized its aptitude for developing contemplative prayer, which is both praise and supplication, recalling its connatural effectiveness in promoting the Christian life and apostolic commitment."

5. Dominican Spirituality: *Caritas primae veritatis*

Secular historiography is unable to understand the connection between a military event like the Battle of Lepanto and a spiritual devotion such as the Rosary. Even modern Catholic historiography often tends to separate the spiritual life of the popes from their public action, with the result that the significance of the mission of the Vicar of Christ is impoverished. We need to recall that every soul has a vocation that is proper to it. "In time and space there is a wonderful reciprocity between souls and vocations. . . . A special form corresponds to a special destiny."[1108] Every human being thus has a specific mission to fulfill on earth. There are private missions, limited to the sphere of one's own family or one's own religious order, but there also exist public missions, and among these the government of the Church of Christ is the highest that a man can carry out. The Congregation of Rites that evaluated the sanctity of Pius V judged first of all the heroic virtues with which Michele Ghislieri had carried out his role as Supreme Pastor of the Church.

The Holy Spirit knows the needs of the Church and prepares men to carry out the mission destined for them. In an era like the sixteenth century, in which heresy was spreading, the spiritual life of St. Pius V had its foundation in the defense of the truth of the Faith. He defined

[1108] Joseph Tissot, *The Interior Life Simplified and Reduced to Its Fundamental Principle*, R. & T. Washbourne, London, 1916, pp. 167–168.

himself as a "sentinel of the Church,"[1109] conscious that the primary duty of the Vicar of Christ was to guard and defend from the wolves the flock that had been entrusted to him.

Like Paul IV and Sixtus V, St. Pius V was a pope of the sixteenth century formed in the school of the Roman Inquisition and animated by horror for every deviation from the doctrine of the Faith. In this he was a perfect Dominican. The characteristic of Dominican spirituality is in fact that of contemplating God above all as Divine Truth. "The supreme and primary divine attribute is *Veritas*, to whose explicit and conscious cult the Dominican consecrates his entire life," writes Fr. Innocenzo Colosio.[1110] Therefore, "the soul, the guiding and informing principle, of the Dominican is *caritas primae veritatis*;"[1111] "the cult of God as *Veritas*; love for God, the first *Veritas*: behold the substance, the soul of Dominican spirituality."[1112]

The words that the Lord addressed to St. Catherine of Siena[1113] in the *Dialogue of Divine Providence* help us to understand the Dominican soul of Pius V:

> Each order shines through some particular virtue ... although all virtues have life from charity ... your father Dominic wanted his

[1109] MAFFEI, *Vita di S. Pio V*, p. 243.

[1110] I. COLOSIO, *Appunti sulla spiritualità domenicana*, in *Saggi sulla spiritualità domenicana*, Libreria Editrice Fiorentina, Florence, 1961, p. 26 (pp. 25–33).

[1111] COLOSIO, *Appunti sulla spiritualità domenicana*, p. 27.

[1112] COLOSIO, *Appunti sulla spiritualità domenicana*, p. 31.

[1113] Catherine of Siena (1347–1380), third order Dominican, was canonized by Pius II in 1461 and proclaimed a Doctor of the Church by Paul VI in 1970. Her famous *Dialogue*, known as the *Book of Divine Revelation* or the *Dialogue of Divine Providence*, "is a sort of apocalypse in which God is supposed to speak through the mouth of Catherine in ecstasy, in order to reproach the worldly for their vices and the pastors of the Church for their disorders. ... The *Summa* of St. Thomas Aquinas is there, in certain chapters, transparent" (POURRAT, *La spiritualité chrétienne*, vol. 2, 313–314). On Catherine, see among others the important views of, with bibliography, MAXIME GORCE, in DSp, vol. 2 (1953), cols. 327–348; EUGENIO DUPRÉ THESEIDER, in DBI, vol. 22 (1979), pp. 361–379; ADRIANA CARTOTTI ODDASSO, in BSS, vol. 3 (1962), pp. 996–1044.

> friars to have no other thought than my honor and the salvation of souls, through the light of wisdom. And it is in this light that he made the primary purpose of his Order to be the extirpation of the errors that were widespread in his time. He assumed the office of the Word, my Only-Begotten Son. In the world he appeared as an apostle; such was the truth and the light with which he sowed my word, removing the shadows from the world and giving it light.[1114]

"The history of the Order," Fr. Colosio writes, "may be summarized in the history of our cult of the Truth, and its protagonists are precisely the great *diffusers* of the truth (theologians, preachers, missionaries, etc.), the *defenders* of the same (apologists, inquisitors, etc.), the *victims* for the truth (the martyrs, and not only those who shed their blood, but also those who consummated their life, expending all of their vital energy for the increase and deepening of revelation)."[1115]

Caritas veritatis (the charity of truth) was the mother idea that guided the entire life of St. Pius V and constituted the first specific note of his spirituality as a son of St. Dominic, as inquisitor, and as Supreme Pontiff. "Upon becoming pope in 1566, Michel Ghislieri continued to wear his religious habit, but above all he preserved and continued the grace of his religious profession. This was the source of his government, his spirit of faith, his simplicity of gaze, his rectitude of judgment, his loyalty and strength."[1116]

6. An Ascetic and Combative Spirituality

The conquest of the truth is tiring and implies an ascetic effort of the will. Ascesis is above all a battle against self and the disordered movements of one's soul. All historians agree that one of the main characteristics of Italian spirituality in the sixteenth century is the theme of ascesis and

[1114] St. Catherine of Siena, *Dialogue of Divine Providence*, Tan Books, Gastonia, North Carolina, 1991, chap. 15.

[1115] Colosio, *Appunti sulla spiritualità domenicana*, p. 32.

[1116] Roger T. Calmel, *Nous sommes fils de Saints*, Nouvelles Editions Latines, Paris, 2011, pp. 105–106.

"spiritual combat."[1117] One famous expression of this spiritual approach is the book *The Spiritual Combat* by the Theatine Lorenzo Scupoli:[1118] it is a true course in "spiritual strategy,"[1119] dedicated to the "Supreme and Most Glorious Captain Jesus Christ," in which one breathes on almost every page — as has been noted — the atmosphere of the Ignatian meditation of the two standards.[1120] For Scupoli, the weapons of the Christian are as follows: distrust of ourselves, because with our own strength we can do nothing; faith in God, through whose help we can do all things; the good use of the faculties of our soul and body, beginning with reason and the will; and finally, the practice of prayer.[1121]

A notable difference separates this spirituality from that of Erasmus of Rotterdam's *Enchiridion Militis Christiani*, which appeared in 1503. "For Erasmus, the spiritual life has for its purpose not so much conformity to the divine will, the increase of grace, union with Christ, and divine filiation, as much as the peace and tranquility of the soul. The supreme good, happiness *par excellence*, is for Erasmus tranquility of soul. Holiness is reduced to wisdom, prudence, and moderation: from these stem the ethical character of his piety."[1122]

The humanistic spirituality of Erasmus prefigured that which Plinio Corrêa de Oliveira has called "white heresy."[1123] The characteristic of "white heresy" is the refusal of any vigorous and open opposition to evil and the extinction of the more noble passions that can guide a

[1117] Colosio, *I mistici italiani*, p. 2174.

[1118] Lorenzo Scupoli (1530–1610) was an ascetical writer of the Theatine Order. His book *The Spirtual Combat* (G. e P. Gioliti de' Ferrari, Venice, 1589) had an extraordinary diffusion in the seventeenth and eighteenth centuries.

[1119] Pierre Pourrat, *La spiritualité chrétienne*, Lecoffre, Paris, 1935, vol. 3, p. 360 (pp. 358–368).

[1120] Pierre Pourrat, *La spiritualité chrétienne*, p. 363.

[1121] Pierre Pourrat, *La spiritualité chrétienne*, pp. 360–361.

[1122] R. García-Villoslada, *Erasme*, in DSp, vol. 4 (1960), col. 933; García-Villoslada, *Loyola y Erasmo*, Taurus, Madrid, 1965.

[1123] R. de Mattei, *Plinio Corrêa de Oliveira, Profeta del Regno di Maria*, Edizioni Fiducia, Rome, 2017, pp. 145–150.

Christian, such as an ardent love for justice in itself, hatred for sin, and indignation against the enemies of the Church. "Spiritual combat" was instead a distinctive note of St. Pius V's Dominican spirituality, which was also richly influenced by Ignatian and Theatine spirituality. Pius V waged a continuous battle against himself first and foremost, in order to seek always and above all else the greater glory of God. The strength with which he fought against the internal enemies of his soul explains the vigor and passion with which he confronted the external enemies of the Church. In his classic work *The Liturgical Year*, Dom Guéranger begins the section in the "Proper of Saints" dedicated to "Saint Pius V, Pope and confessor," with these words: "Pius V's entire life was a battle."

St. Pius V was a resolute and combative pope who personally involved himself in military matters. According to his biographer Catena, he loved good soldiers no less than holy men, and he had the intention of constructing "a militia of nine thousand chosen soldiers, three thousand of whom would serve, in the name of the Church, wherever was necessary."[1124] His pontificate constitutes, according to a contemporary historian, "the laboratory of an ambitious project of political and religious culture: the construction of the figure of the Christian soldier."[1125] In 1567 there appeared a treatise on Christian military life, *Le pédagogue d'armes*[1126] by the Jesuit Edmond Auger,[1127] who distinguished himself

[1124] CATENA, *Vita del gloriosissimo papa Pio V*, p. 155.

[1125] GIAMPIERO BRUNELLI, *Soldati del papa: Politica militare e nobiltà nello Stato della Chiesa (1560–1644)*, Carocci, Rome, 2003.

[1126] EDMOND AUGER, *Le Pédagogue d'Armes pour instruire un prince chrétien à bien entreprendre et heureusement achever une bonne guerre*, chez Sebastian Nivelle, Paris, 1568. See GIANCLAUDIO CIVALE, *Religione e mestiere delle armi nella Franca dei primi torbidi religiosi. Il "Pedagogue d'armes" del gesuita Emond Auger (1568)*, in "Bibliothèque d'Humanisme et Renaissance," 74 (2012), pp. 505–533.

[1127] Edmond Auger (1530–1591) was a Jesuit controversialist who dedicated himself to preaching against Calvinism in France; taken prisoner by the Huguenots in Valence (1562), he succeeded in fleeing to Lyons, and he was a preacher at the French court (1569–1588). He lived his final years in Italy and died in Como. See JEAN DORIGNY, *La vie du Père Edmond*

in the battle against the Huguenots alongside the Duke of Anjou. Pius V asked another Jesuit, Fr. Antonio Possevino,[1128] to draw up a booklet to distribute to the pontifical and Medici army corps that came together in Turin under the command of the Count of Santa Fiora. The work, entitled *Il Soldato Christiano*, appeared in 1569.[1129] It explains the difference between the profane character of the valor of the ancient Romans and the perfection of those who pursue the glory of God by fighting. Upon meeting the representatives of Spain and Venice during the negotiations for the Holy League, Pius V said to them: "I affirm to you that if my person could be useful to the present enterprise, I would be content not only to expose myself to dangers and shed my blood, but also to go and die among the first for the glory of God and the benefit of the Christian Republic."[1130]

The solemn ceremony promoted by Pius V in Rome in December 1571 to celebrate the victory of Marcantonio Colonna at Lepanto expresses this militant vision, in which Catholic triumph is freed from every paganizing element and the glory of the Church on earth prefigures its triumph in Heaven.[1131]

Auger, de la Compagnie de Jésus, confesseur et prédicateur de Henri III, roy de France et de Pologne, A. Laurens, Lyon, 1616.

1128 Antonio Possevino (1533–1611) entered the Jesuit order in 1559, was secretary general of the order between 1573 and 1577, and was apostolic nuncio in Sweden, Russia, Poland, Lithuania, Moravia, and Transylvania at the mandate of Gregory XIII. See V. LAVENIA, *Tra Cristo e Marte. Disciplina e catechesi del soldato cristiano in epoca moderna*, in *Dai cantieri alla storia. Liber amicorum per Paolo Prodi*, Il Mulino, Bologna, 2007, pp. 37–54.

1129 ANTONIO POSSEVINO, Il *soldato christiano con l'instruttione dei capi dello esercito cattolico*, Eredi di V. e L. Dorico, Rome, 1569. See JEAN DORIGNY, *La vie du Père Antoine Possevin de la Compagnie de Jésus, où l'on voit l'histoire des importantes négociations auxquelles il a été employé en qualité de Nonce de Sa Sainteté, en Suède, en Pologne et en Moscovie*, E. Ganeau, Paris, 1612.

1130 CATENA, *Vita del gloriosissimo papa Pio V*, pp. 174–175.

1131 M. A. VISCEGLIA, *La città rituale. Roma e le sue cerimonie in età moderna*, Viella, Rome, 2002, pp. 220–225; BRUNELLI, *Soldati del papa*, p. 17.

7. A Public and Triumphal Spirituality

The ascetical spirit, which presupposed a life of abnegation, sacrifice, and spiritual battle, in full abandonment to Divine Providence, is diametrically opposed to the humanistic spirit that is based on the search for material and spiritual pleasure. This explains the permanent anti-Humanism of the great Italian spiritual writers, especially in the fifteenth and sixteenth centuries,[1132] expressed by saints such as Blessed Giovanni Dominici, St. Antonino of Florence, St. Francis of Paola, and St. Bernardine of Siena, all the way up to St. Charles Borromeo and St. Pius V himself.

The life of Pius V was spent in continual prayer. The pope used to say that prayer is necessary for popes to be able to carry the burden of the pontificate.[1133] He was convinced that the principal obligation of a Supreme Pontiff was to pray uninterruptedly for the needs of the Christian people entrusted to his care.[1134] Philip II affirmed that he had obtained three great graces from God through the prayers of Pius V: the victory against the Turks, an heir to the throne, and rain after a very long drought.[1135]

In addition to his personal prayer, the pope added his public prayer, in which he addressed himself to God as the Vicar of Christ and the Head of the Church. This public prayer was expressed not only in the great liturgical ceremonies in the Roman basilicas, but also in manifestations of public devotion like solemn processions in which the clergy and the faithful united their voice to invoke the Lord following auspicious or inauspicious events for the Church. The center of the Church's life, as the Council of Trent had confirmed, is the worship of the Eucharist. "Everything in the Church radiates out from the Blessed Sacrament,"[1136] as Fr.

[1132] I. Colosio, *Alcuni dei principali punti teorici, pratici, metodologici, storici difesi su questa Rivista nei suoi primi quattordici anni*, in "Rivista di ascetica e mistica," 5–6 (December 1969), pp. 448–450 (pp. 416–456).

[1133] Maffei, *Vita di S. Pio V*, p. 316.

[1134] Maffei, *Vita di S. Pio V*, p. 316.

[1135] Maffei, *Vita di S. Pio V*, p. 317.

[1136] Frederick William Faber, *All for Jesus: or, The Easy Ways of Divine Love*, Thomas Richardson and Son, London, 1853, p. 213.

Faber explains, and the procession of the Most Blessed Sacrament is "the highest culminating point of ecclesiastical and Catholic ceremony."[1137] It expresses the triumph of the Church against all of her enemies past and present, and in this sense it is "a compendium of Church History."[1138]

Pius V wanted to increase the cult of the Eucharist with triumphal processions of the Blessed Sacrament through the streets of Rome. The pope had processions held at important political and religious moments in order to pray for victory over the enemies of the Faith, or to give thanksgiving for having obtained it. The processions were often *triduanae*, that is, they were held for three consecutive days with the participation of the pontiff. On July 28, 1566, the first of three processions was held in Rome to drive away the danger of the Turks. The victory of Jemingen against the rebels of the Low Countries on July 21, 1568, was celebrated for three days with solemn public processions to thank God. There were numerous processions to pray for the Holy League against the Turks, and the pope also always participated personally in them.

For the most solemn of the processions, that of *Corpus Domini*, Pius V gave up the *sedia* and tiara and passed through the boroughs on foot with his head uncovered, carrying the Blessed Sacrament in his own hands. In processions, despite the length of the path and pain caused by the kidney stones which he suffered, Pius V never wanted to use the *sedia gestatoria*. The pope appeared on foot, as a shepherd in the midst of his flock, defying fatigue and often bad weather. During the procession against the Calvinist heresy of the Low Countries in August 1568, the pope was almost the only participant to persevere despite a torrential downpour.[1139] When the Blessed Sacrament was carried through the streets of Rome to a sick person, by order of the pope, even cardinals that met it had to descend from their carriage and accompany it, as did the king of Spain and other princes.[1140] With his public cult of

[1137] FABER, *The Blessed Sacrament: or, the Works and Ways of God*, Burns & Oates, London, 1855, p. 513.

[1138] FABER, *The Blessed Sacrament: or, the Works and Ways of God*, p. 14.

[1139] DE BLAAUW, *Pio V e la liturgia*, pp. 83–85.

[1140] PASTOR, *Storia dei Papi*, vol. 8, pp. 155–156.

the Blessed Sacrament, St. Pius V fought against what Fr. Calmel has called "a double kingdom of absence"[1141] which at that time extended over the world. Wherever the Protestant heresy triumphed, the Real Presence of the Eucharist disappeared, the tabernacle remained empty, and the priest, without the Blessed Sacrament, ceased to be such. With even greater reason, the Blessed Sacrament was absent in the lands of Islam, where it was forbidden under pain of death to profess faith in the Most Holy Trinity and in Jesus Christ the Incarnate Word. St. Pius V publicly restored the honor to the cult of the Eucharist which the Council of Trent had bestowed on it in its dogmatic decrees. "The Blessed Sacrament is God in His mysterious miraculous veils. ... It is this possession of her God which is of necessity the lifelong triumph of the Church."[1142]

8. A Conquering Spirituality

Pius V's spirituality was not defensive but conquering, and the instrument *par excellence* of this strategy of conquest was the missions. The holy pontiff felt the obligation of expanding the Church of Jesus Christ throughout the world,[1143] and "he dedicated an incomparably more lively activity to the missions than his immediate predecessors."[1144]

The mission is not a generic work of apostolate undertaken to save individual souls of non-believers, but rather has a specific and institutional goal: to extend the Kingdom of God to all peoples by means of the so-called *plantatio Ecclesiae*. It is a matter of both a sacramental and institutional work, not so much the conversion of individual souls as much as the sanctification of peoples by bringing the Faith to those who do not yet know it and incorporating them into the visible Church.[1145]

[1141] Calmel, *Nous sommes fils de Saints*, pp. 107–108.

[1142] Faber, *The Blessed Sacrament*, p. 18.

[1143] Maffei, *Vita di S. Pio V*, p. 332.

[1144] Pastor, *Storia dei Papi*, vol. 8, p. 208.

[1145] This missionary vocation of the Church has been restated by John Paul II, who states: "the mission *ad gentes* has this objective: to found Christian communities, develop churches to their complete maturation.... The

In 1552 St. Francis Xavier died, the "Apostle of the Indies." According to the most accurate calculations, at least thirty thousand conversions are attributed to him, from India to Japan. But it would be a mistake to imagine that Catholic missionary expansion began with him. Before Francis Xavier, all of the ancient orders—Franciscans, Dominicans, Augustinians, Hieronymites, and so on—had embarked on daring missionary undertakings in the Congo, India, the Philippines, Japan, and above all in the Americas. The first black African bishop is not from our time but from 1518, right after Luther's revolt, and he was a native of the Congo.[1146]

In a letter of August 18, 1568, the Holy Father wrote to Cardinal Espinosa, the minister of Philip II: "Do well to lead the wisdom of His Majesty to understand that these people should be freed from burdens that are too heavy and treated in such a way that they will rejoice more and more each day to have abandoned the worship of idols in order to embrace the sweet law of Jesus Christ. Keep watch scrupulously so that the customs and life of Christians, who have departed from our districts, may be of edification to those of the provinces. Thus some will be strengthened in the faith, and others will be sweetly led to recognize the truth."[1147]

In no field did St. Pius V manifest that trait of his spirituality that has been called "practical spirituality" so much as he did in the missions.[1148]

---

phase of ecclesial history called *plantatio Ecclesiae* is not over, indeed in many human groupings it has yet to begin" (JOHN PAUL II, Encyclical *Redemptoris Missio*, 7 December 1990, in *Insegnamenti*, XIII/2 (1990), pp. 1487–1557).

[1146] The conversion of the king Mbemba Nzinga ("Dom Afonso") marked the beginning of the great Christian Kingdom of the Congo. In 1518, Henrique, the son of Dom Afonso, became the first bishop from black Africa (and the last for the following four centuries). See TEOBALDO FILESI, *Enrico, figlio del re del Congo, primo vescovo dell'Africa Nera*, "*Euntes Docete*: Commentaria Urbaniana," 19 (1966), pp. 365–385.

[1147] FALLOUX, *Histoire de St. Pie V*, vol. 2, pp. 47–48.

[1148] LEON LOPETEGUI, *San Francisco de Borja y el plan misionel de san Pio V. Primeros pasos de una Congregación de Propaganda Fide*, in "Archivum Historicum

Prudence and daring were admirably balanced in his directives. "While no one appreciated courage and fortitude more than Pius did, he exhorted his missionaries not to risk their lives recklessly in their desire to achieve martyrdom."[1149] Pius V's principal collaborator in his missionary plan was St. Francis Borgia.[1150] The Jesuits made a fourth vow of special obedience to the pope for being sent to mission lands, and from his very first visit to Pius V in January 1566, the general of the Society of Jesus placed himself at the service of the pope. At the end of Lent that same year, Borgia received a request from Philip II for twenty-four Jesuits for the West Indies. Pius V blessed the undertaking, granting a plenary indulgence *in articulo mortis* (at the point of death) for those who were preparing to leave.[1151] At the end of August 1566, thirty-five Jesuit missionaries who were leaving for Germany, France, and other places received the personal blessing of the pope. In November of that same year it was the superior of the Jesuit College of Loreto's turn, Fr.

Societatis Iesu," 11, (1942), pp. 1–26; PEDRO DE LETURIA, *Relaciones entre la Santa Sede e Hispanoamérica. 1493–1835*, Caracas-Rome, 1959–1960; ERNEST JOSEPH BURRUS, *Pius V and Francisco Borgia: Their Efforts on Behalf of the American Indians*, in "Archivum Historicum Societatis Iesu," 41 (1972), pp. 207–226; JOSEF WICKI, *Nuovi documenti attorno ai piani missionari di Pio V nel 1568*, in "Archivum Historicum Societatis Iesu," 37 (1968), pp. 408–417.

[1149] BROWNE, *The Sword of St. Michael*, pp. 226–227.

[1150] Francis Borgia (Francisco de Borja y Aragón: 1510–1572), fourth Duke of Gandia, was the great-grandson of Rodrigo Borgia (who became Pope Alexander VI). At the age of twenty, he married Eleonora de Castro of Portugal, who gave him eight children in ten years. In 1530, Charles V made him the Marquis of Lombai and in 1539 the viceroy of Catalonia. After he became a widower, he entered the Society of Jesus and was elected its superior general in 1565. He was proclaimed a saint by Pope Clement X on April 12, 1671. See ENRIQUE GARCÍA HERNÁN, *Francisco de Borja, Grande de España*, Institució Alfons el Magnanim, Valencia, 1999; GARCÍA HERNÁN, *La acción diplomática de Francisco de Borja al servicio del Pontificado, 1571–1572*, Institució Alfons el Magnanim, Valencia, 1999.

[1151] LOPETEGUI, *San Francisco de Borja*, p. 3.

Gnecchi Soldo Organtino,[1152] who was destined to carry out his apostolate in Japan.

In the same year 1566, Francis Borgia sent the Portuguese Jesuit Ignazio de Azevedo[1153] across the ocean as a visitator in the mission of Brazil, where the Society of Jesus had established several houses. In 1569, Azevedo returned to Rome to report on the situation and ask the superior general to send new and numerous missionaries. The pope thanked God, because he had raised up such men for the glory of his Church and encouraged the new mission in Brazil. Sixty-nine youth responded to the appeal. Forty of these, thirty-one of whom were Portuguese, led by Fr. Azevedo, embarked on the boat *Santiago*, one of the six vessels of the little fleet commanded by the viceroy-elect, Fernando de Vasconcellos. On July 15, 1570, when the boat reached the archipelago of the Canary Islands, it was attacked by five corsair ships captained by Jacques Sourie, a Huguenot corsair in the service of the queen of Navarre, Jeanne d'Albret, famous for her anti-Catholic fanaticism.

The young Jesuits gathered around the mainmast of the *Santiago*, along with their superior, who held up an image of the *Salus Populi Romani* from St. Mary Major. They then intoned the Litany of Loreto and offered their lives to God in a loud voice. Fr. Azevedo designated a group to proclaim the Catholic Faith during the battle and to succor the wounded combatants, while the others would remain in unceasing prayer. He remained standing at the foot of the mainmast until it fell, crying out: "I call in witness the Angels and the men who have died for the Holy Roman Church and the defense of her dogmas!"[1154] The Huguenots massacred the Jesuits with blows of the sword and the lance, and then they threw

[1152] Gnecchi Soldo Organtino (1533–1609) was a Jesuit missionary who lived for about thirty years in Mikayo, the imperial capital of Japan, and died in Nagasaki. See Giuliano Bertuccioli, in DBI, vol. 57 (2001), *ad vocem*.

[1153] On the martyr of the Society of Jesus Ignazio de Azevedo (1526–1570), see C. Testore, in BSS, vol. 3 (1963), cols. 388–389. Pius IX proclaimed Ignazio Azevedo and thirty-eight companions Blessed on May 11, 1854.

[1154] Falloux, *Histoire de St. Pie V*, vol. 2, p. 56.

them in the sea, whether dead or still alive. Only one of them was saved, spared by the heretics to be a cook, and he was able to testify to what had happened.

In far off Spain, at that moment, St. Teresa of Ávila received a vision of all that had taken place on the *Santiago* and of the triumph of the glorious martyrs.[1155] When Pius V was told the news that Fr. Azevedo and his brothers had been killed by the Huguenots, he exclaimed: "Instead of praying for them, let us recommend ourselves to their prayers because they are truly martyrs."[1156]

In those same years, in the Spanish colony of Nuova Granada and in the Caribbean islands, the Dominican Luis Beltrán[1157] preached the gospel to the native peoples with extraordinary success. Armed only with Sacred Scripture and his breviary, barefoot and without provisions, at times even without guides, he made his long missionary journeys through impassable forests, enjoying fame as a great preacher and a worker of miracles. In 1569 he returned to his homeland and continued to dedicate himself to the home missions. He was among the most trusted advisers and collaborators of the bishop of Valencia, Juan de Ribera, and one of the fruits of sanctity of the pontificate of St. Pius V.

9. Pius V and the Communion of Saints

Because the humanistic and pagan spirit had penetrated to the interior of the Church, it was necessary to bring to a conclusion the spiritual reform

[1155] Enrique Jorge, *Santa Teresa de Jesús y el B. Ignacio de Azevedo. Martirio y profecía*, in "Manresa," 43 (1971), pp. 79–90.

[1156] *Relazione della vita e martirio del venerabile Padre Ignazio de Azevedo*, Stamperia Antonio de' Rossi, Rome, 1743, p. 186.

[1157] Luis Beltrán (1526–1581), entered the Order of St. Dominic in 1544 and became a priest in 1547; in 1562 he left as a missionary for America and arrived in the Spanish colony of New Granada (the present Colombia), where he converted more than twenty thousand native people. He returned to his homeland in 1569 and was among the faithful collaborators of the bishop of Valencia, Juan de Ribera. He was beatified by Paul V in 1608 and canonized by Clement X on April 12, 1671.

that Adrian VI had attempted to initiate during his brief pontificate (1522–1523) but whose rules had been codified only by the Council of Trent with its decrees and canons. St. Pius V was the great accomplisher of the Tridentine reform, and he felt especially close to those souls who offered their life for the reform of the Church. Among these, two who merit particular mention are the great reformer of Carmel St. Teresa of Ávila and the Dominican mystic St. Catherine de' Ricci.

On August 24, 1562, Teresa of Jesus[1158] founded a Carmel in Ávila with the purpose of beginning a reform of the Carmelite Order, restoring it to the observance of its ancient rule. In 1566 the saint obtained from Fr. Giovanni Battista Rossi,[1159] the prior general of the Carmelites who had received the charge of reforming the order from Pius V, authorization to found two male monasteries of brothers called "reformed" or "discalced."[1160] On November 28, 1568, three Observant Carmelites assumed the primitive rule as it had been corrected and approved by Innocent IV. They are the first three "contemplative apostolic Carmelites," according to the permission granted by Giovanni Battista Rossi on August 10, 1567. They adopted, in imitation of the discalced

[1158] The literature on Teresa of Jesus, baptized Teresa Sánchez de Cepeda Dávila y Ahumada (1515–1582), beatified on April 24, 1614, by Paul V and canonized March 12, 1622, by Gregory XV, is immense. See Valentino di S. Maria, *Teresa, santa*, in BSS, vol. 12, pp. 395–419; and Tomas de la Cruz-Jesus, *Santa Teresa de Jesús. Actualidad. Panorama editorial. Estudios biográficos. Estudios doctrinales*, in "Ephemerides Carmeliticae," 19 (1968), pp. 9–44.

[1159] Giovanni Battista Rossi, baptized Bartolomeo Rossi (1507–1578), was prior general of the Order of the Blessed Virgin of Mount Carmel from 1564 until his death. Pius V appointed him apostolic commissioner of the entire Order of the Blessed Virgin of Mount Carmel from 1564 until his death, with the purpose of applying the decrees of reform of the Council of Trent to the Carmelites. See *Documenta Primigenia ab Instituto Historico Teresiano edita*, vol. 1 (1560–1571), Teresianum, Rome, 1973, vol. 1, pp. 39–43.

[1160] *Documenta Primigenia ab Instituto Historico Teresiano edita*, vol. 1, pp. 39–43.

Carmelites, new surnames: Anthony of Jesus, John of the Cross, and Joseph of Christ.

On April 16, 1567, with the brief *Superioribus Mensibus* dedicated to the reform of the various religious orders, Pius V subjected the Carmelites to bishops who were to be assisted in their work by a small group of Dominicans. Two years later, in accord with the desires of Philip II, Pope Pius V appointed as apostolic visitators with full powers Frs. Pietro Fernandez for Castile and Francisco Vargas for Andalusia.[1161] Shortly afterward, Vargas appointed Fr. Baldassarre Nieto as his delegate in the visits. Nieto, in turn, delegated his faculties to Fr. Jerónimo Gracián,[1162] the closest collaborator of St. Teresa, as apostolic visitator of the Carmelites of Castile and Andalusia. A period of conflict began within the order, in which Pius V always supported the reforming wing.

The spiritual reformer St. Catherine de' Ricci was substantially no different from great reformer St. Teresa of Ávila. When Pius V sent his nephew, Cardinal Michele Bonelli, to Philip II of Spain, with the purpose of concluding the agreement for the league between Spain and Venice, Pius instructed him to stop in Prato in order to undertake a delicate diplomatic mission to the stigmatist Catherine de' Ricci,[1163] who lived

[1161] Otger Steggink, *La reforma del Carmelo español. La visita canónica del general Rubeo y su encuentro con Santa Teresa (1566–1567)*, Teresianum, Rome, 1965; José García Oro, *Observantes, recoletos, descalzos: la monarquía católica y el reformismo religioso del siglo xvi*, in *Actas del Congreso Internacional Sanjuanista*, Avila, 23–28 September 1991, *Junta de Castilla y León*, Valladolid, 1993, pp. 53–97.

[1162] Jerónimo Gracián Dantisco (1545–1614), a Carmelite religious brother, was the first inspector of the Discalced Carmelites and spiritual director of St. Teresa of Ávila. See Carlos Ros Caballar, *Jerónimo Gracián, el amigo de Teresa de Jesús*, Editorial Monte Carmelo, 2014.

[1163] Catherine de' Ricci, baptized Alessandra Lucrezia Romola (1522–1590), was a Dominican religious in the monastery of San Vincenzo in Prato, where she was elected prioress many times. Under her governance the community flourished to the point of having 160 sisters and became a model of regular observance. Catherine was beatified by Clement XII on November 23, 1732, and declared a saint by Benedict XIV on June 29, 1746. See *Compendio della vita, virtù e miracoli della beata Caterina de' Ricci*

in that small town in the Monastery of San Vincenzo.[1164] In his meeting with Catherine, the cardinal had such light and consolations that, as the saint's biographer tells us, he wanted to pass through Prato on his return trip to thank her for her efficacious intercession.[1165] "The victory of Lepanto," Fr. Domenico Silli observes, "stands as testimony of how God directed the efforts of the holy pontiff and the valid prayer of the Florentine saint."[1166]

St. Catherine de' Ricci was a mystic who conceived the spiritual life as a battle of the soul. "With St. Philip Neri, her fellow citizen who like her was a disciple of the Dominicans of Saint-Marc, she recommends peace and joy, acquired through a 'vigorous combat' against ourselves."[1167] Her spirituality, centered on the theme of the reform of the Church, was not understood by her fellow sisters, but it was greatly appreciated by the great saints of the era, such as Pius V, Charles Borromeo, and Philip Neri.

Within the communion of saints that unites all the members of the Mystical Body of the Church, there exist mysterious affinities. Among these, Charles Borromeo was perhaps the saint closest to Pius V. Their

---

[. . .] cavato dai processi fatti per la sua beatificazione e canonizzazione [. . .], Mainardi, Rome, 1732; Guglielmo Di Agresti, *Santa Caterina de' Ricci. Bibliografia, fonti, indici*, Olschki, Florence, 1973, and edited by the same, the *Epistolario* in 5 vols. (Florence, 1973–1975); Renzo Ristori, in DBI, vol. 22 (1979), pp. 359–361 with bibliography. Patrick Preston, *St Pius V (1504–72) and Sta Caterina De' Ricci (1523–90): Two Ways of Being a Saint in Counter-Reformation Italy*, in *Studies in Church History*, vol. 47 (*Saints and Sanctity*), Cambridge University Press online, 2011, pp. 208–227.

1164 The Monastery of San Vincenzo had been founded in 1503 by nine ladies who had been followers of Savonarola. The foundation was under the jurisdiction of the vicar general of the Congregation of San Marco, at that time Fra Francesco Salviati. The monastery became a library of Savonarola's works and a memorial chapel to his memory, where his relics were kept. See Giuseppe Scalia, *Girolamo Savonarola e santa Caterina de'Ricci*, Libreria Editrice Fiorentina, Florence, 1924.

1165 Giacinto Bayonne, *Vita della santa Caterina de'Ricci*, Italian translation, Ranieri Guasti, Prato, 1874, p. 184.

1166 Silli, *San Pio V*, p. 52.

1167 Raffaele Cai, O.P., *Cathérine de' Ricci*, in DSp, vol. 2 (1961), col. 326.

friendship and collaboration, which began during the days of the conclave, developed in the following years up until the death of the pontiff. One can say that St. Charles, who outlived Pius V by twelve years, was the person who most continued his Tridentine spirit. A lesser affinity tied Pius V to Philip Neri, even if responsibility for the attacks that Philip's oratory underwent during Pius's pontificate must be traced back to certain circles of his Curia more than to the pope personally. The Curia did not approve of Philip's walks with his disciples through the streets of Rome, the sermons given by laypeople, and singing in the vernacular.[1168] The Curia was on the point of decreeing the closure of the oratory in 1567, when Borromeo's resolute intervention averted this extreme measure.

In addition to St. Charles Borromeo there is certainly St. Francis Borgia, the Jesuit superior general, who seemed to Pius V like the incarnation of the perfect *miles Christi* (soldier of Christ): "a great man of the earth who, translating the Ignatian contemplation of the 'two standards' into reality, had renounced worldly fame, power, and honors in order to lead a life dedicated to penance, ascetical rigor and evangelical perfection."[1169] The Spain of his time "does not offer another figure of a gentleman like Francis Borgia, who was so familiar with his Emperor (Charles V) but walked before God with the humility of his servants."[1170] The generalate of Francis Borgia coincided with the pontificate of Michele Ghislieri and, as one of his biographers writes, "his entire life is summarized" in this diplomatic activity in the service of Pius V.[1171] St. Francis Borgia poured out all of his energies in the service of Pope Ghislieri, and he

[1168] Between 1568 and 1569 Philip was denounced to Pius V over the orthodoxy of sermons and oratory "done by simple persons of little education." See VITTORIO FRAJESE, *Filippo Neri, santo*, in DBI, vol. 47 (1997), pp. 741–750.

[1169] GIANCLAUDIO CIVALE, *Francesco Borgia e gli esordi della pastorale gesuitica nei confronti dei soldati*, in *Francisco de Borja y su tiempo: Política, religión y cultura en la Edad Moderna*, edited by Hernán and María del Pilar Ryan, Albatros Ediciones, Valencia and Rome, 2011, p. 210.

[1170] MARIO SCADUTO, S.J., *Storia della Compagnia di Gesù*, vol. V, *L'opera di Francisco Borgia*, Edizioni "La Civiltà Cattolica," Rome, 1992, p. 29.

[1171] GARCÍA HERNÁN, *Francisco de Borja*, p. 234.

died, exhausted by fatigue, on September 30, 1572, four months after the holy pontiff.

Pius V did not know St. Cajetan of Thiene, who died in 1547, but he deeply knew Theatine spirituality through the co-founder of the order, Gian Pietro Carafa, with whom he closely collaborated, appreciating his austere and disinterested service of the Church. Among the bishops whom he personally chose, based on their apostolic spirit, were the Theatine Blessed Paolo Burali, whom he appointed bishop of Piacenza, and the Barnabite St. Alessandro Sauli,[1172] whom he appointed bishop of Aleria, the largest diocese of Corsica. Paolo Burali was beatified by Clement XIV in 1772; Alessandro Sauli was canonized by St. Pius X in 1904. We may thus say that a crown of saints surrounded the brief pontificate of Pope Ghislieri, like a halo.

There is a final question to ask: May Pius V, whom the Church recognizes as a saint, be defined as a mystic? We must understand what is meant by this term. Mysticism is often understood to mean the presence of visions, revelations, and extraordinary phenomena. A great theologian like Fr. Garrigou-Lagrange explains however, that up until the seventeenth and eighteenth centuries, the single title of mystical theology included not only infused contemplation and the extraordinary graces that accompany it, but also Christian perfection in general, in all states of life.[1173]

If the definition of a mystic were to exclude any form of active life so that one could limit oneself to extraordinary graces, very few would be able to reach this threshold, much less a pope forced to live a "practical" spirituality due to his duties of state. But it would be paradoxical if the Vicar of Christ were denied the possibility of reaching that contemplative

[1172] Alessandro Sauli (1534–1592) of the Order of Clerics Regular of St. Paul (Barnabites), was elected its superior general in 1567, and was appointed bishop of Aleria by St. Pius V on February 10, 1570, at the suggestion of St. Charles Borromeo. He was proclaimed a saint by Pope Pius X on December 11, 1904.

[1173] Réginald Garrigou-Lagrange, *Perfezione cristiana e contemplazione secondo S. Tommaso d'Aquino e S. Giovanni della Croce*, Italian translation, Edizioni Vivere In, Rome, 2011, vol. 2, pp. 35–58.

state of life that is granted to the simplest of the faithful when he ascends in the way of perfection. In reality, contemplation is not incompatible with any state of life: all souls are called to it as the perfection that disposes one to eternal life.[1174] The mystical life is nothing other than a perfect conformity to the will of God in fulfilling one's duties of state and in abandoning oneself to God's will of good pleasure.[1175] God is no more present in prayer than in work, no more present in contemplation than in action. He is wherever His will is. Michele Ghislieri had the gift of supernatural prophecies, such as the vision of the victory of Lepanto, but this is not what makes a soul mystical. He lived immersed in contemplation because he fulfilled his duties as pope with perfection and he conformed his will to the divine will in all the events of his pontificate, even the adverse ones. In this sense, Pius V is an example of a contemplative and mystical soul, but above all he is a model Roman Pontiff for all the successors of Peter until the end of time.

10. A Final Prayer to St. Pius V

As we close the pages of this book, we turn our gaze to St. Pius V, the Pope of the Rosary, the Pope of Lepanto, the Pope of the Tridentine reform and liturgical restoration, the indomitable defender of the Catholic Faith. We are aware of the inadequacy of our work, which would have needed additional skills in order to be exhaustive. But to him we offer that which we have been able to accomplish, with our poor strength, at a historical moment when everything is extremely difficult, including examining the life of a saint.

Paintings of the Battle of Lepanto always show the figure of St. Pius V praying, along with the Blessed Mother and the angels who assist the combatants of the Christian armada from Heaven. Today another battle is unfolding, more dramatic and uncertain, and it seems as if the

[1174] Garrigou-Lagrange, *Perfezione cristiana e contemplazione*, p. 226.

[1175] "This conformity consists in submitting oneself to all providential events willed or allowed by God for our greater good, and chiefly for our sanctification" (Tanqueray, *The Spiritual Life*, p. 236).

enemies have conquered the flagship of Christ's fleet. However, St. Pius V continues to assist the Church Militant from Heaven, whose destiny was entrusted into his hands for six brief yet momentous years. His mission is not over, and he appears as a model of the Pastor of the Church that the Christian people urgently need. And so we ask him to continue to exercise this paternal mission by means of his intercession, repeating the words of the Roman Breviary: "*Deus qui ad conterendos Ecclesiae tuae hostes, et ad divinum cultum reparandum, beatum Pium Pontificem maximum eligere dignatus est: fac nos ipsius defendi praesidiis, et ita tuis inhaerere obsequiis; ut, omnium hostium superatis insidiis, perpetua pace laetemur*": O God, who deigned to choose blessed Pius, pope, to break the enemies of thy Church and to repair divine worship: grant that we, by his watchful care, may adhere to thy service, so that, having overcome the snares of the enemy, we may rejoice in perpetual peace.[1176]

[1176] *Die 5 Maii, Sancti Pii V*, in *Breviarum Romanum*, Les Amis de Sant-François de Sales, Seduni, 2007, vol. 1, p. 667.

Abbreviations

AAS (ASS prior to 1909): *Acta Apostolicae Sedis*, Typis Vaticana, Vatican City, 1909ff.

ASV: Vatican Secret Archive.

Benedict XVI, *Insegnamenti*: *Insegnamenti di Benedetto XVI*, Libreria Editrice Vaticana, Vatican City, 2006–2014, 9 vols.

Bss: *Bibliotheca Sanctorum*, John XXIII Institute of the Pontifical Lateran University, Città Nuova, Rome, 1961.

Bullarium Romanum: *Bullarium Diplomatum et Privilegiorum Sanctorum Romanorum Pontificum*, S. and H. Dalmezzo, Turin, 1860.

Catholic Encyclopedia: *The Catholic Encyclopedia: An International Work of Reference on the Constitution, Doctrine, Discipline, and History of the Catholic Church*, Encyclopedia Press, New York, 1907–1914.

COD: *Conciliorum Oecumenicorum Decreta*, edited by the Istituto per le Scienze Religiose, bilingual edition, EDB, Bologna, 2002.

DACL: *Dictionnaire d'Archéologie Chrétienne et de Liturgie*, Paris, Letauzey et Ané, 1907–1953, 15 vols.

DAFC: *Dictionnaire Apologétique de la Foi Catholique*, Beauchesne, Paris, 1911–1928, 4 vols.

DBI: *Dizionario Biografico degli Italiani*, Istituto dell'Enciclopedia Italiana, Rome, 1960ff.

DDC: *Dictionnaire de Droit Canonique*, Letouzey et Ané, Paris, 1935–1958, 7 vols.

Denz-H: Heinrich Denzinger, *Enchiridion Symbolorum definitionum et declarationum de rebus fidei et morum*, edited by Peter Hünermann, bilingual edition, EDB, Bologna, 1995.

DHGE: *Dictionnaire d'Histoire et de Géographie Ecclésiastiques*, Letouzey et Ané, Paris, 1912ff.

DIP: *Dizionario degli Istituti di Perfezione*, Paoline, Rome, 1965, 10 vols.

DSI: *Dizionario Storico dell'Inquisizione*, edited by A. PROSPERI, V. LAVENIA, J. TEDESCHI, Edizioni della Normale, Pisa 2010, 4 vols.

DSp: *Dictionnaire de Spiritualité*, Beauchesne, Paris, 1937–1994, 16 vols.

DSP: *Dizionario Storico del Papato*, Bompiani, Milan, 1996, 2 vols.

DTC: *Dictionnaire de Théologie Catholique*, edited by A. VACANT and E. MANGENOT, Letouzey et Ané, Paris, 1909–1972, 33 vols.

EC: *Enciclopedia Cattolica*, Sansoni, Florence, 1949–1954, 12 vols.

EE: *Enchiridion delle Encicliche*, bilingual edition, EDB, Bologna, 1995–1999.

EI: *Enciclopedia Italiana*, Istituto della Enciclopedia Italiana, Rome, 1949–1952, 36 vols.

EP: *Enciclopedia dei Papi*, Istituto della Enciclopedia Italiana, Rome, 2000, 3 vols.

Epistolae ad principes: *Epistolae ad principes*, vol. 2, *S. Pius V–Gregorius XIII (1566–1585)*, edited by TOMISLAV MRKONJIĆ, Vatican Secret Archive, Vatican City, 1994.

FLICHE-MARTIN: AUGUSTIN FLICHE, VICTOR MARTIN, *Storia della Chiesa*, Italian translation, S.A.I.E., Turin, 1977.

GAF: *Grande Antologia Filosofica*, edited by UMBERTO ANTONIO PADOVANI, Marzorati, Milan, 1954.

HERGENRÖTHER: JOSEPH HERGENRÖTHER, *Storia universale della Chiesa*, fourth edition compiled by Msgr. G. P. Kirsch, first Italian translation by Fr. Enrico Rosa, S.J., Libreria editrice Fiorentina, Florence, 1907–1911, 7 vols.

JOHN XXIII, *Insegnamenti*: *Discorsi messaggi colloqui di Sua Santità Giovanni XXIII*, Libreria Editrice Vaticana, Vatican City, 1960–1967, 5 vols.

JOHN PAUL II, *Insegnamenti*: *Insegnamenti di Giovanni Paolo II*, Libreria Editrice Vaticana, Vatican City, 1980–2006, 28 vols.

LTK: *Lexikon für Theologie und Kirche*, Herder, Freiburg im Breisgau, 1957–1965, 10 vols.

MANSI: GIOVANNI DOMENICO MANSI, *Sacrorum conciliorum nova et amplissima Collectio*, edited by LOUIS PETIT, JEAN-BAPTISTE MARTIN, Paris-Arnhem-Leipzig, 1901–1927.

MORONI, *Dizionario di erudizione*: GAETANO MORONI, *Dizionario di erudizione storico-ecclesiastica*, Tipografia Emiliana, Venice, 1840–1879.

NCE: *New Catholic Encyclopedia*, Catholic University of America, Washington, D.C., 1967, 15 vols.

PASTOR: LUDWIG VON PASTOR, *Storia dei Papi dalla fine del Medioevo*, Desclée, Rome, 1926–1963, 16 vols.

PAUL VI, *Insegnamenti*: PAUL VI, *Insegnamenti*, Tipografia Poliglotta Vaticana, Vatican City, 1963–1978, 16 vols.

PIUS XII, *Discorsi e Radiomessaggi*, Tipografia Poliglotta Vaticana, Vatican Vity, 1959, 21 vols.

PL: *Patrologiae Cursus Completus, Series Latina*, edited by JEAN-PAUL MIGNE, Paris, 1844–1864, 226 vols.

POTTER: LOUIS DE POTTER, *Lettres de Saint Pie V, sur les affaires réligieuses de son temps, en France: suivi d'un cathéchisme catholique romain, comprennant la législation pénale ecclesiastique en matière d'hérésie*, H. Tarlier, Brussels, 1827.

Processo Carnesecchi: MASSIMO FIRPO - DARIO MARCATTO, *I processi inquisitoriali di Pietro Carnesecchi*, Archivio Segreto Vaticano, Rome, 2000, 3 vols.

Processo Morone: MASSIMO FIRPO - DARIO MARCATTO, *Il processo inquisitoriale del cardinal Giovanni Morone. Edizione critica*, Istituto Storico Italiano per l'Età Moderna e Contemporanea, Rome, 1981–1995, 6 vols.

VILLOSLADA RICARDO GARCÍA - LLORCA BERNARDINO, *Historia de la Iglesia Católica*, vol. 3, *Edad Nueva (1306–1648). La Iglesia en la época del Renacimiento y de la reforma Católica*, BAC, Madrid, 1967.

WA: MARTIN LUTERO, *Werke. Kritische Gesamtausgabe*, Böhlau, Weimar, 1883–1985.

ZW: HULDRICI ZWINGLI, *Opera*, M. Schuler et J. Shulthess Fratres, Parisiis, 1844–1890.

Bibliography

Acta Ecclesiae Mediolanensis a S. Carolo Card: Archiep. Condita, Paulo Pagnonio, Mediolani, 1843.

Acta Ecclesiae Mediolanensis, edited by Achille Ratti, III, ex Typographia Pontificia Sancti Iosephi, Mediolani, 1897.

ACZONA (DE) TARCISIO, *Isabel la Católica: Estudio crítico de su vida y su reinado*, Biblioteca de Autores Cristianos, Madrid, 1964.

AL KALAK MATTEO, *Riformare la Chiesa. Egidio Foscarari tra inquisizione, concilio e governo pastorale (1512–1564)*, Il Mulino, Bologna, 2016.

ALBERZONI MARIA PIA - AMBROSIONI ANNA MARIA - LUCIONI ALFREDO (edited by), *Sulle tracce degli Umiliati*, Vita e Pensiero, Milan, 1997.

ALFORD STEPHEN, *Burghley: William Cecil at the Court of Elizabeth I*, Yale University Press, New Haven, 2008.

ALLIES MARY H., *History of the Church in England from the Accession of Henry VIII to the Death of Queen Elizabeth*, Burns & Oates, London, 1895.

ALTOLAGUIRRE Y DUVALE (DE) ANGEL, *Don Alvaro de Bazán, primer marqués de Santa Cruz de Mudela*, Editora Nacional, Madrid, 1971.

AMANTE BRUTO, *Giulia Gonzaga contessa di Fondi e il movimento religioso femminile nel secolo XVI*, Nicola Zanichelli, Bologna, 1896.

ANDRIEU MICHEL, *Les "Ordines Romani" du Haut Moyen-âge*, Spicilegium Sacrum Lovaniense, Louvain, 1931.

ANTONY CATHERINE MARY, *Saint Pius V: Pope of the Holy Rosary*, Longmans, Green and Company, London, 1911.

Apertura degli archivi del Sant'Uffizio romano (Rome, 22 January 1998), Accademia Nazionale dei Lincei, Rome, 1998.

Arenaprimo Giuseppe, *La Sicilia nella battaglia di Lepanto*, EDAS, Messina, 2011 (1892).

Aretin (von) Karl Maria, *Geschichte des Bayerischen Herzogs und Kurfusten Maximilian des Ersten*, Pleuger, Passau, 1842.

Argita y Lasa Mariano, *El Doctor Navarro Don Martín de Azpilcueta y sus obras, Estudio histórico-crítico*, Analecta Editorial, Pamplona, 1998.

Aubert Alberto, *Paolo IV, Politica inquisizione e storiografia*, Le Lettere, Rome, 1999.

Auger Edmond, *Le Pédagogue d'Armes pour instruire un prince chrétien à bien entreprendre et heureusement achever une bonne guerre*, chez Sebastian Nivelle, Paris, 1568.

Avolio Fabio, *La musica sacra nel Concilio di Trento e lo stile contrappuntistico di Giovanni Pierluigi da Palestrina*, Aracne, Rome, 2008.

Baini Giuseppe, *Memorie storico-critiche della vita e delle opere di Giovanni Pierluigi da Palestrina*, Società tipografica, Rome, 1828.

Bainton Roland H., *Bernardino Ochino. Esule e riformatore senese del cinquecento, 1487–1563*, Italian translation, Sansoni, Florence, 1940.

Bainton Roland H., *La riforma protestante*, Italian translation, Einaudi, Turin, 1964.

Barbero alessandro, *Lepanto. La battaglia dei tre imperi*, Laterza, Rome-Bari, 2010.

Barge Hermann, *Andreas Andreas Bodenstein von Karlstadt*, B. de Graaf, Nieuwkoop 1968, 2 vols.

Barthe Claude, *La Messe de Vatican II*, Via Romana, Paris, 2018.

Barthe Claude, *Storia del Messale tridentino*, Italian translation, Solfanelli, Chieti, 2018.

Baudot Giulio, *Il Breviario Romano. Origini e storia*, Italian translation, Desclée, Rome, 1909.

Bäumer Suibert, *Histoire du Bréviaire*, Letouzey et Ané, Paris, 1905, 2 vols.

Baumgartner Frederic J., *Behind Locked Doors: A History of the Papal Elections*, Palgrave Macmillan, New York, 2003.

Bayonne Giacinto, *Vita della santa Caterina de' Ricci*, Italian translation, Ranieri Guasti, Prato, 1874.

Bazzano Nicoletta, *Marco Antonio Colonna*, Salerno Editrice, Rome, 2003.

Beeching Jack, *La battaglia di Lepanto*, Italian translation, Rusconi, Milan, 1989.

Belfort Bax Ernest, *Rise and Fall of the Anabaptists*, Sonneschein, London, 1903.

BELLINGER GERHARD J., *Der Catechismus Romanus und die Reformation. Die katechetische Antwort des Trienter Konzils auf die Haupt-Katechismen der Reformatoren*, Bonifacius-Druckerei, Paderborn, 1970.

BELLINGER GERHARD J., *Bibliographie des Catechismus Romanus. Ex Decreto Concilii Tridentini ad Parochos 1566–1978*, Valentin Koerner, Baden-Baden, 1983.

BENEDICT XIV, *La beatificazione dei Servi di Dio e la canonizzazione dei Beati*, Libreria Editrice Vaticana, Vatican City, 2011.

BENNASSAR BARTOLOMÉ, *Storia dell'Inquisizione spagnola dal XV al XIX secolo*, Italian translation, Rizzoli, Milan, 1985.

BENNASSAR BARTOLOMÉ, *Don Juan de Austria un héroe para un imperio*, Temas de Hoy, Madrid, 2000.

BENNASSAR BARTOLOMÉ and LUCILE, *I cristiani di Allah*, Italian translation, Rizzoli, Milan, 1991.

BENZONI GINO (edited by), *Il Mediterraneo nella seconda metà del '500 alla luce di Lepanto*, Olschki, Florence, 1974.

BERCHET GUGLIELMO, *La Repubblica di Venezia e la Persia*, Paravia, Turin, 1865.

BERLINER ABRAHAM, *Storia degli ebrei a Roma*, Rusconi, Milan, 1992.

BERNARDINE OF SIENA, SAINT, *Le prediche volgari*, Libreria Editrice Fiorentina, Florence, 1934.

BERNASCONI CARLO (edited by), *San Pio V nella storia*, Symposium on the occasion of the third centenary of the canonization of Pope Pius V, Ibis, Pavia, 2012.

BESSE (DA) LODOVICO, *Il beato Bernardino da Feltre e la sua opera*, Tip. Pontificia S. Bernardino, Siena, 1905, 2 vols.

BIANCHI LINO, *Giovanni Pierluigi da Palestrina nella vita, nelle opere, nel suo tempo*, Fondazione Giovanni Pierluigi da Palestrina, Rome, 1995.

Bibliotheca Fratrum Polonorum, A. Wissowatius, Amsterdam, 1656, 5 vols.

BIET CHRISTIAN - FRAGONARD MARIE-MADELEINE, *Tragédies et récits de martyres en France*, Garnier, Paris, 2009.

BOGLIOLO LUIGI, *Battista da Crema. Nuovi studi sopra la sua vita, i suoi scritti, la sua dottrina*, SEI, Turin, 1952.

BOHATTA HANS, *Bibliographie der Breviere: 1501–1850*, Karl W. Hiersemann, Stuttgart, 1937.

BONCOMPAGNI LUDOVISI UGO, *Il Sacco di Roma*, Fratelli Strini, Albano Laziale, 1928.

BONO SALVATORE, *I corsari barbareschi*, ERI, Turin, 1964.

BONORA ELENA, *Giudicare i vescovi. La definizione dei poteri nella Chiesa postridentina*, Laterza, Bari, 2007.

BORGHESI VILMA (edited by), *Vita del Principe Giovanni Andrea Doria scritta da lui medesimo*, Ed. Compagnia dei Librai, Genoa, 1997.

BORROMEO AGOSTINO (edited by), *L'inquisizione: atti del simposio internazionale*, Vatican City, 29–31 October 1998, Vatican Apostolic Library, Vatican City, 2003.

BOSSUET JACQUES-BÉNIGNE, *Histoire des variations des Eglises protestantes*, Veuve Sebastien Marbre-Cramoisy, Paris, 1688.

BOTTE BERNARD, *Le Canon de la messe romaine*. Édition critique. Introduction et notes, Mont César, Louvain, 1935.

BOURQUE EMMANUEL, Étude sur les Sacramentaires Romains, Pontifical Institute of Christian Archaeology, Vatican City, 1949.

BRADFORD ERNLE, *The Great Siege: Malta 1965*, Penguin Books, London, 1964 (1961).

BRADFORD ERNLE, *The Shield and the Sword: The Knights of St. John*, Penguin Books, London, 2002 (1973).

BRAIDO PIETRO, *Lineamenti di storia della catechesi e di catechismi. Dal "tempo delle riforme" all'età degli imperialismi (1450–1870)*, Editrice ElleDiCi, Turin, 1991.

BRAGA CARLO, *La riforma liturgica di Pio XII. Documenti. I. La "memoria sulla riforma liturgica,"* Edizioni Liturgiche, Rome 2003.

BRANDI KARL, *Carlo V*, Italian translation, Einaudi, Turin, 2008.

BRANTÔME (DE) PIERRE, *Oeuvres*, Aux Dépens du Libraire, London, 1779.

Breviarium Romanum: Editio Princeps (1568), Edizione anastatica edited by Manlio Sodi, Achille Maria Triacca, Libreria Editrice Vaticana, Vatican City, 1999.

Breviarum Romanum, Les Amis de Sant-François de Sales, Seduni, 2007.

BRIGANTI BARBARA - CRESCENTINI CLAUDIO - MIGLIO MASSIMO - STRINATI CLAUDIO - VIALLON MARIE, *Les Borgia et leur temps: de Léonard de Vinci à Michel-Ange*, Gallimard, Paris, 2014.

BRODRICK JAMES, S.J., *Saint Peter Canisius*, Geoffrey Chapman, London, 1963.

BROGINI ANNE, *1565. Malte dans la tourmente. Le grand siege de l'île par le turcs*, Bouchène, Saint-Denis, 2011.

BROMATO CARLO, *Storia di Paolo IV*, Anton Maria Landi, Ravenna, 1748–1753, 2 vols.

BRUNELLI GIAMPIERO, *Soldati del papa: Politica militare e nobiltà nello Stato della Chiesa (1560–1644)*, Carocci, Rome, 2003.

BUISSON ALBERT, *Michel de L'Hospital: 1503–1573*, Hachette, Paris, 1950.

BUJANDA (DE) JESUS MARTINEZ (edited by), *Index des livres interdits*, Centre d'Études de la Renaissance-Librairie-Droz, Sherbrooke-Geneva, 1984–1996, 10 vols.

BURCKHARDT JAKOB, *La civiltà del Rinascimento in Italia*, Italian translation, Avanzini e Torraca, Rome, 1967.

BURKLE YOUNG FRANCIS A. - DOERRER MICHAEL LEOPOLDO, *The Life of Cardinal Innocenzo del Monte: A Scandal in Scarlet*, E. Mellen Press, Lewiston, 1997.

CABRERA DE CÓRDOBA LUIS, *Historia de Felipe II Rey de España*, Impresores de Cámara de S. M., Madrid, 1876.

CACCAMO DOMENICO, *Eretici italiani in Moravia, Polonia, Transilvania (1558–1611)*, Le Lettere, Florence, 1970.

CACCIAVILLANI IVONE, *Lepanto*, Corbo e Fiore Editori, Venice, 2003.

CAETANI ONORATO - DIEDO GEROLAMO, *La battaglia di Lepanto (1571)*, edited by Salvatore Mazzarella, Sellerio, Palermo, 1995.

CAFFIERO MARINA, *Legami pericolosi. Ebrei e cristiani tra eresia, libri proibiti e stregoneria*, Einaudi, Turin, 2012.

CALINI MUZIO, *Lettere conciliari (1561–1563)*, edited by Alberto Marani, Geroldi, Brescia, 1963.

CALLAEY FREDEGANDO, *Praelectiones historiae ecclesiasticae mediae et modernae*, Pontificium Urbanum de Propaganda Fide, Rome, 1950.

CALMEL ROGER T., O.P., *Nous sommes fils de Saints*, Nouvelles Editions Latines, Paris, 2011.

CAMPANA EMILIO, *Maria nel culto cattolico*, Marietti, Turin-Rome, 1933.

CAMPI EMIDIO (edited by), *Petrus Martyr Vermigli. Humanismus, Republikanismus, Reformation*, Frank James and Peter Opitz, Droz, Geneva, 2002.

The Canons and Decrees of the Council of Trent, edited by Henry-Joseph Schröder, TAN Books and Publishers, Rockford, Illinois, 1978.

CANOSA ROMANO, *Storia di Milano nell'età di Filippo II*, Sapere, Rome, 2000.

CANTAGALLI ROBERTO, *Cosimo I de' Medici granduca di Toscana*, Mursia, Milan, 1985.

CANTIMORI DELIO, *Umanesimo e religione nel Rinascimento*, Einaudi, Turin, 1980.

CANTIMORI DELIO, *Eretici italiani del Cinquecento e altri scritti*, Einaudi, Turin, 1992 (1939).

CANTIMORI DELIO - FEIST ELISABETH, *Per la storia degli eretici italiani del sec. XVI in Europa*, Reale Accademia d'Italia, Rome, 1937.

CAPONETTO SALVATORE, *Aonio Paleario (1503–1570) e la Riforma protestante in Toscana*, Claudiana, Turin, 1979.

CAPPELLO FELICE, S.J., *Summa Iuris pubblici Ecclesiastici*, editio sexta, Apud Aedes Universitatis Gregoriana, Rome, 1954.

CAPPONI NICCOLÒ, *Lepanto 1571. La lega santa contro l'Impero ottomano*, Italian translation, Il Saggiatore, Milan, 2008.

CARACCIOLO ANTONIO, *De vita Pauli IV Pont. Max. Collectanea Historica*, Johann Kinckius, Colonia, 1612.

CARACCIOLO FERRANTE, *I Commentari delle guerre fatte coi Turchi da don Giovanni d'Austria dopo che venne in Italia*, Giorgio Marescotti, Florence, 1581.

CARAMAN PHILIP, *The Other Face: Catholic Life under Elizabeth I*, Longman, London, 1960.

CARAVALE MARIO - CARACCIOLO ALBERTO, *Lo Stato pontificio da Martino V a Pio IX*, UTET, Turin, 1978.

CARO BAROJA JULIO, *Los Moriscos del Reino de Granada*, Instituto de estudios politicos, Madrid, 1957.

CARROLL STUART, *Martyrs and Murderers: The Guise Family and the Making of Europe*, Oxford University Press, Oxford, 2009.

CARROLL WARREN H., *The Cleaving of Christendom*, Christendom Press, Front Royal, Virginia, 2000.

CASALE VITTORIO, *L'arte per le canonizzazioni. L'attività artistica intorno alle canonizzazioni e alle beatificazioni del Seicento*, Allemandi, Turin, 2011.

Catechismus Romanus seu Catechismus ex decreto Concilii Tridentini, ad parochos, Pii Quinti Pont. Max. iussu editus, Libreria Editrice Vaticana/Ediciones Universidad de Navarra, Vatican City/Pamplona, 1989.

CATENA GIOVANNI GIROLAMO, *Vita del gloriosissimo papa Pio Quinto: con una raccolta di lettere di Pio V & le risposte*, Filippo de' Rossi, Rome, 1647.

CATHERINE OF SIENA, SAINT, *Dialogue of Divine Providence* (1378), Tan Books, Gastonia, North Carolina, 1991.

Catholic Catechism Index, Sophia Institute Press, Manchester, New Hampshire, 2019.

CELLETTI ALESSIO, *Autorappresentazione papale ed età della Riforma: gli affreschi della Sala Regia Vaticana*, Eurostudium, Rome, 2013.

CERVINI FULVIO - SPANTIGATI CARLA ENRICA (edited by), *Il tempo di Pio V. Pio V nel tempo. Atti del convegno internazionale di studi (Bosco Marengo, 11–13 marzo 2004)*, Edizioni dell'Orso, Alessandria, 2006.

CÉSAR BECQUEREL ANTOINE, *Souvenirs historiques sur l'amiral Coligny: sa famille et sa seigneurie de Châtillon-Sur-Loing*, Firmin-Didot, Paris, 1876.

CESTARO ANTONIO (edited by), *Geronimo Seripando e la Chiesa del suo tempo nel V centenario della nascita*, Acts of the convention at Salerno, October 14–16, 1994.

CHASTEL ANDRÉ, *Il Sacco di Roma*, Italian translation, Einaudi, Turin, 1983.

CHERUBELLI PAOLO, *Il contributo degli Ordini religiosi al Concilio di Trento*, Vallecchi, Florence, 1946.

CHEVALLIER PIERRE, *Les Régicides: Clément, Ravaillac, Damiens*, Fayard, 1989.

CHIAPPINI LUCIANO, *Gli Estensi. Storia di mille anni*, Corbo Editore, Ferrara, 2001.

CHIRON YVES, *Enquête sur les béatifications et les canonisations*, Tempus, Paris, 2011.

CHITTOLINI GIORGIO - MICCOLI GIOVANNI (edited by), *Storia d'Italia. Annali*, IX, *La Chiesa e il potere politico dal Medioevo all'età contemporanea*, Einaudi, Turin, 1986.

CHOUPIN LUCIEN, *Valeur des Décisions Doctrinales et Disciplinares du Saint-Siège*, Beauchesne, Paris, 1928.

CHRISTIN OLIVIER, *Une révolution symbolique. L'iconoclasme huguenot et la reconstruction catholique*, Les Editions de Minuit, Paris, 1991.

CHURCH FREDERIC E., *I Riformatori italiani*, Italian translation, Il Saggiatore, Milan, 1967, 2 vols.

CISTELLINI ANTONIO, *San Filippo Neri, l'Oratorio e la Congregazione oratoriana, storia e spiritualità*, Morcelliana, Brescia, 1989, 3 vols.

CLARK FRANCIS, *Eucharistic Sacrifice and the Reformation*, Darton, Longmann & Todd, London, 1960.

CLIZIO ORESTE, *Gerolamo Donato detto IL FARINA l'uomo che sparò a san Carlo*, Edizioni La Baronata, Lugano-Carrara, 1998.

CLOULAS IVAN, *Jules II*, Librairie Arthème Fayard, Paris, 1990.

CLOULAS IVAN, *Catherine de Médicis: Le destin d'une reine*, Tallandier, Paris, 2007.

Collecion de Documentos Ineditos para la Historia de Espana, edited by Fernandez Navarrete, La Viuda de Calero, Madrid, 1844.

COLONNA VITTORIA, *Rime*, edited by Alan Bullock, Laterza, Rome-Bari, 1982.

Compendio della vita, virtù e miracoli della beata Caterina de' Ricci . . . cavato dai processi fatti per la sua beatificazione e canonizzazione . . ., Mainardi, Rome, 1732.

Concili Tridentini Tractatum, Ed. Vincentius Schweitzer, vol. 12, Herder, Freiburg im Breisgau, 1930.

CONCINA ENNIO, *L' Arsenale della Repubblica di Venezia; tecniche e istituzioni dal medioevo all'età moderna*, Electa, Milan, 1984.

CONGREGATION FOR THE DOCTRINE OF THE FAITH, *Dichiarazione "Persona Humana." Alcune questioni di etica sessuale*, of 29 December 1975, in AAS, vol. 68 (1976), pp. 77–96.

CONGREGATION FOR THE DOCTRINE OF THE FAITH, *Lettera sulla cura pastorale delle persone omosessuali*, of 1 October 1986, in AAS, vol. 79 (1987), pp. 543–554.

CONSTANT JEAN-MARIE, *La Ligue*, Fayard, Paris, 1996.

CORRÊA DE OLIVEIRA PLINIO, *Rivoluzione e Contro-Rivoluzione*, Italian translation, Sugarco, Milan, 2009.

Correspondance du nonce en France Fabio Mirto Frangipani, edited by A. Lynn Martin, École Française de Rome, Pontificia Università Gegoriana, Rome, 1984.

COSTANTINI VERA, *Il sultano e l'isola contesa. Cipro tra eredità veneziana e potere ottomano*, UTET, Turin, 2009.

COSTIL PIERRE, *André Dudith, humaniste hongrois, 1553–1589*, Les Belles Lettres, Paris, 1935.

COWDREY HERBERT EDWARD JOHN, *The Cluniacs and the Gregorian Reform*, Oxford Clarendon Press, Oxford, 1970.

CREAN THOMAS, O.P. (edited by), *Dignitatis Humane Colloquium*, Dialogos Institute Proceedings, 2017.

CRÉTINEAU-JOLY JACQUES, *Histoire religieuse, politique et littéraire de la Compagnie de Jésus, composée sur les documents inédits et authentiques*, Mellier, Paris, 1844–1846.

CRISTIANI LÉON, *Le Bienheureux Pierre Canisius second apotre de l'Allemagne (1521–1597)*, J. Gabalda, Paris, 1925.

CRISTIANI LÉON, *L'insurrection protestante. L'Eglise de 1450 à 1623*, Librairie Fayard, Paris, 1961.

CRISTIANI LÉON, *La Chiesa al tempo del Concilio di Trento*, Italian translation, Editrice S.A.I.E., Turin, 1977.

CROUZET DENIS, *La nuit de Saint-Barthélemy. Un rêve perdu de la Renaissance*, Fayard, Paris, 1994.

CROUZET DENIS, *La sagesse et le malheur. Michel de L'Hôspital, Chancellier de France*, Ed. Champ Vallon, Ceyzérieu, 1998.

CROWLEY ROGER, *Empires of the Sea*, Random House, New York, 2008.

DANIEL ROPS HENRI, *L'Eglise de la Renaissance et de la Réforme*, Fayard, Paris, 1955.

DAVIES MICHAEL, *Pope Paul's New Mass*, The Angelus Press, Dickinson, Texas, 1980.

DAWSON CHRISTOPHER, *Il Cristianesimo e la formazione della civiltà occidentale*, Italian translation, BUR, Milan, 1997, pp. 53–57.

DE BOER WIETSE, *The Conquest of the Soul: Confession, Discipline and Public Order in Counter-Reformation Milan*, Brill, Leiden, 2001.

DE FREDE CARLO, *Vittoria Colonna e il suo processo inquisitoriale postumo*, Giannini, Naples, 1989.

DE MAIO ROMEO, *Alfonso Carafa cardinale di Napoli*, Libreria Editrice Vaticana, Vatican City, 1961.

DE MAIO ROMEO, *L'ideale eroico nei processi di canonizzazione della Controriforma*, in *Riforme e miti nella Chiesa del Cinquecento*, Guida, Naples, 1973.

DE MATTEI ROBERTO, *Holy War, Just War: Islam and Christendom at War*, Chronicles Press, Rockford, Illinois, 2007.

DE MATTEI ROBERTO, *A sinistra di Lutero*, Solfanelli, Chieti, 2017.

DE MATTEI ROBERTO, *Plinio Corrêa de Oliveira, Profeta del Regno di Maria*, Edizioni Fiducia, Rome, 2017.

DE MATTEI RODOLFO, *Il problema della Ragion di Stato nell'età della Controriforma*, R. Ricciardi, Naples, 1979.

DE MICHELIS PINTACUDA FIORELLA, *Socinianesimo e tolleranza nell'età del razionalismo*, La Nuova Italia, Florence, 1975.

DE TÖRNE, *Don Juan d'Autriche et les projets de conquête de l'Angleterre. Étude historique sur dix années du xvie siècle, 1568–1578*, Helsingfors Bokhandel, Helsinki, 1915, 2 vols.

DE TOTH JOHANNES BAPTISTA, *De auctoritate theologica Catechismi Romani*, Pustel, Budapest, 1941.

DE WOHL LOUIS, *The Last Crusader: A Novel about Don Juan of Austria*, Ignatius Press, San Francisco, 2010 (1957).

DEFRANCE EUGÈNE, *Catherine de Médicis, ses astrologues et ses magiciens envoûteurs. Documents inédits sur la diplomatie et les sciences occultes du XVIe siècle*, Mercure de France, Paris, 1911.

DEL COL ANDREA - PAOLIN GIOVANNA (edited by), *L'Inquisizione romana: metodologia delle fonti e storia istituzionale*, Edizioni Università di Trieste-Circolo Culturale Menocchio, Trieste, 2000.

DEL VECCHIO EDOARDO, *I Farnese*, Istituto di Studi Romani editore, Rome, 1972.

DELAVILLE LE ROULX JOSEPH MARIE ANTOINE, *Les Hospitaliers à Rodhes jusqu'à la mort de Philibert de Naillac (1310–1421)*, Leroux, Paris, 1913.

DELLA CASA GIOVANNI, *Catalogo di diverse opere, compositioni et libri, li quali come eretici, sospetti, impii et scandalosi si dichiarano dannati et prohibiti in questa inclita città di Vinegia*, Vincenzo Valgruisi, Venice, 1549.

DENIFLE FRIEDRICH HEINRICH, *Luther und Luthertum in der Ersten Entwickelung*, Franz Kirchheim, Mainz, 1905–1906, 3 vols.

DEPPERMANN KLAUS, *Melchior Hoffman: soziale Unruhen und apokalyptische Visionen im Zeitalter der Reformation*, Vandenhoeck und Ruprecht, Göttingen, 1979.

DESCHAMPS NICOLAS, *Les sociétés secrètes et la société, ou philosophie de l'histoire contemporain*, Fr. Seguin Ainé, Avignon, 1876.

DESHUSSES JEAN, *Le Sacramentaire Grégorien*, Editions Universitaires, Fribourg, 1982.

DESSI PAOLA - LOVATO ANTONIO (edited by), *Giovanni Tebaldini (1864–1952) e la restituzione della musica antica*. Atti della Giornata di Studio (November 16, 2015), Centro di Studi Antoniani, Padova, 2017.

DHANIS MARCEL, *Les quatres femmes de Philippe II*, Alcan, Paris, 1933.

DHOTEL JEAN-CLAUDE, *Les origines du catéchisme moderne d'après les premiers manuels imprimés en France*, Aubier, Paris, 1967.

DI AGRESTI GUGLIELMO, *Santa Caterina de' Ricci. Bibliografia, fonti, indici*, Olschki, Florence, 1973.

DI GANGI MARIANO, *Peter Martyr Vermigli (1499–1562). Renaissance Man, Reformation Master*, University Press of America, Lanham, 1992.

DI SIMPLICIO OSCAR, *Autunno della stregoneria. Maleficio e magia nell'Italia moderna*, Il Mulino, Bologna, 2005.

DIETZ MOSS JEAN, *"Godded with God," Hendryck Niclaes and His Family of Love*, The American Philosophical Society, Philadelphia, 1981.

DITTRICH FRANZ, *Nuntiaturberichte aus Deutschland*, Perthes, Gotha-Berlin, 1892–1981, IV.

DIX GREGORY, *The Shape of Liturgy*, Dacre Press, London, 1945 (reprinted by Continuum, London, 2005).

Documenta Primigenia ab Instituto Historico Teresiano edita, vol. 1 (1560–1571); vol. 2 (1578–1581), (*Monumenta Historica Carmeli Teresiani* 1–2), Teresianum, Rome, 1973.

DOMINICI GIOVANNI, *Lucula noctis*, edited by Edmund Hunt, University of Notre Dame Press, Notre Dame, Indiana, 1940.

DORIGNY JEAN, *La vie du Père Edmond Auger, de la Compagnie de Jésus, confesseur et prédicateur de Henri III, roy de France et de Pologne*, A. Laurens, Lyon, 1616.

DOUGLAS RICHARD M., *Jacopo Sadoleto. Humanist and Reformer*, Harvard University Press, Cambridge, Massachusetts, 1959.

DRAGONETTI DE TORRES ALONSO, *La Lega di Lepanto nel carteggio inedito di don Luys de Torres, nunzio straordinario di S. Pio V a Filippo II*, Fratelli Bocca, Turin, 1931.

DUFFY EAMON, *The Stripping of the Altars*, Yale University Press, New Haven and London, 1992.

DUFFY EAMON, *Fires of Faith: Catholic England under Mary Tudor*, Yale University Press, New Haven, 2009.

DULAC RAYMOND, *In Defence of Roman Mass*, Te Deum Press, 2020.

DUMONT JEAN, *Procès contradictoire de l'Inquisition espagnole*, Famot, Geneva, 1983.

DUMONT JEAN, *Lépante. L'Histoire étouffé*, Criterion, Paris, 1997.

EDELMAN CHARLES (edited by), *The Stukeley Plays: "The Battle of Alcazar" by George Peele and "The Famous History of the Life and Death of Captain Thomas Stukeley,"* Manchester University Press, Manchester, 2011.

EDWARDS FRANCIS, *The Dangerous Queen*, Geoffrey Chapman, London, 1964.

ELMI GIUSEPPE, *Breve relatione delle cerimonie et apparato della basilica di San Pietro nella beatificazione del Glorioso beato Pio V dell'ordine dei predicatori*, Stamperia del Mancini, Rome, 1672.

EVANS JOAN, *Monastic Life at Cluny 910–1157*, Oxford University Press, Oxford, 1968.

EYMERICH NICOLAS - PEÑA FRANCISCO, *Il Manuale dell'inquisitore*, (1376) Italian translation, Fanucci, Rome, 2000.

FABER FREDERICK WILLIAM, *All for Jesus: or, The Easy Ways of Divine Love*, Thomas Richardson and Son, London, 1853.

FABER FREDERICK WILLIAM, *The Blessed Sacrament; or, The Works and Ways of God*, Burns & Oates, London, 1855.

FABRO CORNELIO, *Breve introduzione al tomismo*, Edivi, Rome, 2007.

FALLOUX (DE) ALFRED, *Histoire de Saint Pie V, Pape de l'ordre des Frères Precheurs*, Sagnier et Bray, Paris, 1844.

FEBVRE LUCIEN - MARTIN HENRI-JEAN, *La nascita del libro*, Laterza, Rome-Bari, 1977.

FEDELE PIETRO, *Lo stendardo di Marco Antonio Colonna a Lepanto*, Unione Tipografica Cooperativa, Perugia, 1903.

FEDERICO DI S. ANTONIO, *Vita di S. Teresa di Gesù fondatrice degli scalzi e scalze dell'Ordine di N. S. del Carmine*, Tip. Marini, Rome, 1837, 2 vols.

FENLON DERMOT, *Heresy and Obedience in Tridentine Italy: Cardinal Pole and the Counter Reformation*, Cambridge University Press, Cambridge, 1972.

FERGUSON WALLACE K., *The Renaissance in Historical Thought*, Houghton Mifflin Company, Cambridge, Massachusetts, 1948.

FERNÁNDEZ ÁLVAREZ MANUEL, *Felipe II y su tiempo*, Espasa, Madrid, 1999.

FESER EDWARD - BESSETTE JOSEPH N., *By Man Shall His Blood Be Shed: A Catholic Defense of the Death Penalty*, Ignatius Press, San Francisco, 2017.

FESTA GIANNI - RAININI MARCO (edited by), *L'ordine dei predicatori. I domenicani: storia, figure e istituzioni* (1216–2016), Laterza, Rome-Bari, 2016.

FIEDEBURG (VON) ROBERT, *Luther's Legacy: The Thirty Years War and the Modern Notion of "State" in the Empire, 1530s to 1790s*, Cambridge University Press, New York, 2016.

FIEDROWICZ MICHAEL, *The Traditional Mass: History, Form, and Theology of the Classical Roman Rite*, Angelico, Brooklyn, 2020.

FIRPO MASSIMO, *Tra alumbrados e "spirituali." Studi su Juan de Valdés e il Valdesianesimo nella crisi religiosa del '500 italiano*, L. S. Olsckhi, Florence, 1990.

FIRPO MASSIMO, *Inquisizione romana e Controriforma. Studi sul cardinal Giovanni Morone (1509–1580) e il suo processo d'eresia*, Morcelliana, Brescia, 2005 (1992).

FIRPO MASSIMO, *Riforma protestante ed eresie nell'Italia del Cinquecento*, Laterza, Bari, 1993.

FIRPO MASSIMO, *I processi inquisitoriali di Vittore Soranzo (1550–1558). Edizione critica* (in collaboration with Sergio Pagano), Vatican Secret Archive, Vatican City, 2004, 2 vols.

FIRPO MASSIMO, *Storie di immagini. Immagini di storia. Studi di iconografia cinquecentesca*, Edizioni di storia e letteratura, Rome, 2010.

FIRPO MASSIMO, *La presa di potere dell'Inquisizione romana 1550–1553*, Laterza, Bari, 2014.

FIRPO MASSIMO, *Juan de Valdés and the Italian Reformation*, Ashgate, Aldershot, 2015.

FIRPO MASSIMO, *Giovanni Morone. L'eretico che salvò la Chiesa*, Einaudi, Turin, 2019.

FIRPO MASSIMO - MARCATTO DARIO, *I processi contro don Lorenzo Davidico*, Archivio Segreto Vaticano, Vatican City, 2011.

FLEURY CLAUDE, *Storia religiosa*, Italian translation, Vincenzo Pazzini Carli, Siena, 1782.

FONTANINI BENEDETTO - FLAMINIO MARCANTONIO, *Il beneficio di Cristo*, edited by Salvatore Caponetto, Claudiana, Turin, 2009.

FORTESCUE ADRIAN, *The Mass: A Study of the Roman Liturgy*, Longmans, Green & Co., London - New York, 1950 (1912).

FRASER ANTONIA, *Mary Queen of Scots*, Phoenix, London, 1988.

FUMAGALLI CLAUDINA, *Maria Stuarda: tre mariti, due corone, un patibolo*, De Vecchi, Milan, 1967.

FUREY CONSTANCE M., *Erasmus, Contarini, and the Religious Republic of Letters*, Cambridge University Press, Cambridge, 2005.

GACHARD LOUIS-PROSPER, *Correspondance de Philippe II sur les affaires des Pays-Bas*, II, C. Muquardt, Brussels, 1858.

GACHARD LOUIS-PROSPER, *Don Carlos et Philippe II*, E. Devroye impr. du Roi, Brussels, 1863.

GALLONIO ANTONIO, *Vita beati p. Philippi Neri Florentini Congregatione Oratorio fondatoris in annos digesta*, Aloysium Zannettum, Rome, 1600.

GAMBER KLAUS, *Die Reform der Römischen Liturgie*, F. Pustet, Regensburg, 1979.

GARCÍA HERNÁN ENRIQUE, *Francisco de Borja, Grande de España*, Institució Alfons el Magnanim, Valencia, 1999.

GARCÍA HERNÁN ENRIQUE, *La acción diplomática de Francisco de Borja al servicio del Pontificado, 1571–1572*, Institució Alfons el Magnanim, Valencia, 1999.

GARCÍA-VILLOSLADA RICARDO, *Loyola y Erasmo*, Taurus, Madrid, 1965.

GARIN EUGENIO, *L'umanesimo italiano*, 3rd ed., Laterza, Rome-Bari, 2000.

GARRIGOU-LAGRANGE RÉGINALD, *Perfezione cristiana e contemplazione secondo S. Tommaso d'Aquino e S. Giovanni della Croce*, Italian translation, Edizioni Vivere In, Rome, 2011, 2 vols.

GASTALDI UGO, *Storia dell'anabattismo*, Claudiana, Turin, 1972–1981, 2 vols.

GATTONI MAURIZIO, *Pio V e la politica iberica dello stato pontificio (1566–1572)*, Studium, Rome, 2006.

GAUME JEAN-JOSEPH, *La Révolution. Recherches historiques sur l'origine et la propagation du mal en Europe depuis la Renaissance jusqu'à nos jours*, Gaume frères, Paris, 1856, 12 vols.

GELLARD MATTHIEU, *Une reine épistolaire. Lettres et pouvoirs au temps de Catherine de Médicis*, Garnier, Paris, 2015.

GIAMPIETRO NICOLA, *Il Card. Ferdinando Antonelli e gli sviluppi della riforma liturgica dal 1948 al 1970*, Pontificio Ateneo S. Anselmo, Rome, 1998.

GIANNINI MASSIMO CARLO, *L'oro e la tiara. La costruzione dello spazio fiscale italiano della Santa Sede (1560–1620)*, il Mulino, Bologna, 2003.

GIANNINI MASSIMO CARLO, *I domenicani*, il Mulino, Bologna, 2016.

GIBELLINI CECILIA, *L'immagine di Lepanto: la celebrazione della vittoria nella letteratura e nell'arte veneziana*, Marsilio, Venice, 2008.

GILMONT JEAN-FRANÇOIS (edited by), *La Réforme et le livre. L'Europe de l'imprimé (1517–v.1570)*, Les Editions du Cerf, Paris, 1990.

GINZBURG CARLO, *Il nicodemismo. Simulazione e dissimulazione religiosa nell'Europa del '500*, Einaudi, Turin, 1970.

GINZBURG CARLO, *I costituti di Don Pietro Manelfi*, Sansoni, Florence, 1970.

GIRARDI FELICE, *Diario delle cose più illustri seguite nel mondo. Diviso in quattro libri*, Presso Roberto Mello, Naples, 1653.

GIUGNI UGOLINO, *San Pio V*, Centro Librario Sodalitium, Verrua Savoia, 2004.

GIUSSANO GIOVANNI PIETRO, *Vita di S. Carlo Borromeo*, Tip. Gaetano Motta, Milan, 1821.

GLATRE ERIC, *Lépante 1571*, Socomer, Paris, 1991.

GLEASON ELISABETH G., *Gasparo Contarini: Venice, Rome, and Reform*, University of California Press, Berkeley - Los Angeles, 1993.

GOFFMAN DANIEL, *The Ottoman Empire and Early Modern Europe*, Cambridge University Press, Cambridge, 2007 (2002).

GOODWIN JASON, *Lords of the Horizons: A History of the Ottoman Empire*, Vintage, London, 1998.

GORCZYCA SILVESTRO, *Significato del Breviario di Quiñones alla luce della liturgia delle ore di Paolo VI*, Università Gregoriana, Rome, 1992.

GRASS HANS, *Die Abendmahlslehre bei Luther und Calvin*, C. Bertelmann, Gütersloh, 1954.

GRASS HANS, *Die evangelische Lehre vom Abendmahl*, Heliand, Lüneburg, 1961.

GRATIANI ANTONII MARIAE, *De Vita Joannis Francisci Commendoni*, Typis Petri Mariae Frambotti, Patavii, 1685.

GRAVIÈRE (DE LA) JURIEN, *La Guerre de Chypre et la bataille de Lépante*, Plon, Paris, 1887.

GRENTE GIORGIO, *Il Pontefice delle grandi battaglie*, Italian translation, Paoline, Rome, 1937.

GRISAR HARTMANN, *Luther*, Herder, Freiburg im Breisgau, 1921–1930, 3 vols.

GRUNEBAUM-BALLIN PAUL, *Joseph Naci, Duc de Naxos*, Mouton, Paris, 1968.

GUASCO MAURILIO - TORRE ANGELO (edited by), *Pio V nella società e nella politica del suo tempo*, Il Mulino, Bologna, 2005.

GUÉRANGER PROSPER, *Institutions liturgiques*, Victor Palmé, Paris, 1878.

GUÉRANGER PROSPER, *Jésus-Christ roi de l'histoire*, Association Saint-Jérôme, Saint-Macaire, 2005.

GUÉRANGER PROSPER, *L'anno liturgico*, vol. 4, *Proprio dei Santi (11 aprile–11 novembre)*, Italian translation, Fede e Cultura, Verona, 2018.

GUGLIELMOTTI ALBERTO, *Marcantonio Colonna alla battaglia di Lepanto*, Le Monnier, Florence, 1862.

GUIBERT JOSEPH (DE), *La spiritualità della Compagnia di Gesù*, Italian translation, Città Nuova, Rome, 1992.

GUILMARTIN JOHN FRANCIS, *Galleons and Galleys*, Cassel & Co., London, 2002.

GUIRAUD JEAN, *Histoire partiale. Histoire vraie. II. Moyen âge, Renaissance, Réforme*, Beauchesne, Paris, 1912.

GUIRAUD JEAN-BAPTISTE, *L'inquisition médiévale*, Bernard Grasset, Paris, 1929, Italian translation, *Elogio dell'Inquisizione*, Leonardo, Milan, 1994.

GUSTA FRANCESCO, *Sui catechismi moderni. Saggio critico-teologico*, Heirs of G. Rinaldi, Ferrara, 1788, new enlarged edition, G. Tomassini, Foligno, 1793.

HAAR STEPHEN, *Simon Magus: The First Gnostic?*, Walter de Gruyter, Berlin, 2003.

HAIGH CHRISTOPHER, *Elisabeth I*, Longman, London, 1988.

HAILE MARTIN, *Life of Reginald Pole*, Pitman & Sons, London, 1910.

HAMILTON ALISTAIR, *The Family of Love*, The Attic Press, Greenwood, South Carolina, 1981.

HAY DENYS, *The Church in Italy in the Fifteenth Century*, Cambridge University Press, New York, 1971.

HAYNES ALAN, *Walsingham: Elizabethan Spymaster and Statesman*, Sutton, Stroud, 2007.

HAYNES ALAN, *The Elizabethan Secret Services*, Sutton, Stroud, 2011.

HEERS JACQUES, *Les Barbaresques: La course et la guerre en Méditerranée, XIVe-XVIe siècle*, Perrin, Paris, 2001.

HEERS JACQUES, *La vita quotidiana nella Roma pontificia ai tempi dei Borgia e dei Medici*, Italian translation, BUR, Milan, 2017.

HERZ ALEXANDRA, *The Sixtine and Pauline Tombs in Santa Maria Maggiore: An Iconographical Study*, Institute of Fine Arts, New York University, New York, 1974.

HIRSCHAUER CHARLES, *La politique de St Pie V en France (1566–1572)*, Fontemoing, Paris, 1922.

HOFMANN KARL, *Der "Dictatus Papae" Gregors VII. Eine rechtsgeschichtliche Erklärung*, F. Schöningh, Paderborn, 1933.

HOUSLEY NORMAN, *The Later Crusades, 1274–1580. From Lyons to Alcazar*, Oxford University Press, Oxford, 1992.

HOYER WOLFRAM (edited by), *The Dominicans and the Mediaeval Inquisition*, Angelicum University Press, Rome, 2004.

HÜBNER (VON) JOSEPH ALEXANDER, *Sixte-Quint par M. le Baron de Hübner ancient Ambassadeur d'Autriche à Paris et à Rome. D'après des correspondances diplomatiques inédites tirées des archives d'état du Vatican, de Simancas, Venise, Paris, Vienne et Florence*, Librairie A. Franck, Paris, 1870.

HUDON WILLIAM V., *Marcello Cervini and Ecclesiastical Government in Tridentine Italy*, Northern Illinois University Press, De Kalb, 1992.

HUGHES PHILIP, *The Reformation in England*, Macmillan, New York, 1951.

HUGHES PHILIP, *Faith and Works: Cranmer and Hooker on Justification*, Morehouse-Barlow, Wilton, Connecticut, 1982.

HUTCHINSON ROBERT, *Elizabeth's Spymaster*, Phoenix, London, 2006.

IACOBILLI LUDOVICO, *Vite del Ss. S.P. Pio V, del B. Bonaparte, etc.*, Vincenzo Galeffi, Todi, 1661.

Index auctorum, et librorum, qui ab Officio Sanctae Rom. et universalis Inquisitionis caveri ab omnibus et singulis in universa Christiana Republica mandantur, sub censuris contra legentes, veltenentes libros prohibitos in bulla, quae lecta est in Coena Domini expressis, et sub aliis poenis in decreto eiusdem sacri officii contentis, Antonio Blado, Rome, 1558.

IPARRAGUIRRE IGNACIO - RUIZ JURADO MANUEL, *Orientaciones bibliograficas sobre S. Ignacio de Loyola*, Institutum Historicum S. I., Rome, 1965–1989, 3 vols.

ISIDORO OF SEVILLE, SAINT, *Etymologiae*, Italian translation, UTET, Turin, 2004, 2 vols.

JANNET CLAUDE in *Les précurseurs de la Franc-Maçonnerie au XVI et XVII siècle*, Victor Palme, Paris, 1887.

JANSEN F. X., *Baius et le Baianisme: Essai Théologique*, Museum Lessianum, Louvain, 1927.

JEDIN HUBERT, *Girolamo Seripando: sein Leben und Denken im Geisteskampf des 16. Jahrhunderts*, Rita-Verlag u. Druckerei, Wurzburg, 1937.

JEDIN HUBERT, *Katholische Reformation oder Gegenreformation?*, Josef Stocker, Lucerne, 1946.

JEDIN HUBERT, *Geschichte des Konzils von Trient*, Herder, Freiburg im Breisgau, 1949–1975, 4 vols.

JEDIN HUBERT, *Il tipo ideale di vescovo secondo la riforma cattolica*, Italian translation, Morcelliana, Brescia, 1950.

JEDIN HUBERT, *A History of the Council of Trent*, Herder, London, 1957 and 1961, 2 vols.

JEDIN HUBERT, *Carlo Borromeo*, Istituto della Enciclopedia Italiana, Rome, 1971.

JEDIN HUBERT, *Chiesa della fede. Chiesa della storia*, Italian translation, Morcelliana, Brescia, 1972.

JEDIN HUBERT, *Riforma cattolica o Controriforma?*, Italian translation, Morcelliana, Brescia, 1974.

JOHN PAUL II, Esortazione Apostolica *Catechesi tradendae*, 16 October 1979, n. 13, in *Insegnamenti*, vol. 2/2, 1979.

JOHN PAUL II, Encyclical *Redemptoris Missio*, of 7 December 1990, in *Insegnamenti*, vol. 13/2 (1990), pp. 1487–1557.

JOHN PAUL II, Apostolic Letter *Latamur Magnopere* of 15 August 1997, promulgating the *Catechism of the Catholic Church*, in *Insegnamenti*, vol. 20, 2 (1997), pp. 120–126.

JOHN PAUL II, Encyclical *Fides et Ratio*, of 14 September 1998, in EE, pp. 1886–1891.

JOURNET CHARLES, *L'Eglise du Verbe incarné*, 2 vols., Desclée de Brouwer, Paris, 1941.

KAMEN HENRY, *L'Inquisizione spagnola*, Italian translation, Feltrinelli, Milan, 1973.

KAMEN HENRY, *Philip of Spain*, Yale University Press, New Haven - London 1997.

KIECKHEFER RICHARD, *Forbidden Rites: A Necromancer's Manual of the Fifteenth Century*, Tamesis Books, London, 1997.

KINROSS PATRICK, *The Ottoman Centuries: The Rise and Fall of the Turkish Empire*, Perennial, New York, 2002 (1977).

KOHLER ALFRED, *Carlo V*, Italian translation, Salerno, Rome, 2005.

KOT STANISLAS, *Le mouvement antitrinitaire au XVI et au XVII siècle*, G. Thone, Paris, 1937.

KRAHN CORNELIUS, *Menno Simons (1496–1561)*, H. Schneider, Karlsruhe, 1936.

KRAHN CORNELIUS, *Dutch Anabaptism: Origin, Spread, Life and Thought (1450–1600)*, M. Nijhoff, The Hague, 1968.

KRISTELLER OSKAR, *Il pensiero filosofico di Marsilio Ficino*, Le Lettere, Florence, 2005.

KWASNIEWSKI PETER, *Noble Beauty, Transcendent Holiness*, Angelico Press, Kettering, Ohio, 2017.

KWASNIEWSKI PETER, *Reclaiming Our Roman Catholic Birthright: The Genius and Timeliness of the Traditional Latin Mass*, Angelico Press, Brooklyn, 2020.

KWASNIEWSKI PETER, *Resurgent in the Midst of Crisis: Sacred Liturgy, the Traditional Mass, and Renewal in the Church*, Angelico Press, Kettering 2015.

LANDINI GIUSEPPE, *S. Girolamo Miani. Dalle testimonianze processuali, dai biografi, dai documenti editi e inediti fino ad oggi*, Ordine dei Chierici Regolari Comaschi, Rome, 1947.

LAUGENI BERNARDO, *Una vita per la Chiesa: Gian Pietro Carafa – Paolo IV, il Pontefice della riforma cattolica*, Curia dei Chierici Regolari teatini, Morlupo, 1995.

LEFEVRE RENATO, *"Madama" Margarita d'Austria (1522–1586)*, Newton Compton, Rome, 1986.

LEFRANC FRANÇOIS, *Voile levé (pour le curieux) ou l'histoire de la franc-maçonnerie depuis son origine jusqu'à nos jours*, Lepetit et Guillemard, Paris, 1792.

Legazioni di Averardo Serristori ambasciatore di Cosimo I a Carlo Quinto e in corte di Roma (1537–1568) con un'appendice di documenti, edited by Giuseppe Canestrini, Le Monnier, Florence, 1853.

LEO XIII, Encyclical *Aeterni Patris* of August 4, 1879, in EE, *Leone XIII*, pp. 53–93.

LEO XIII, Encyclical *Supremi Apostolatus* of September 1, 1883, in EE, pp. 258–259.

LEO XIII, Encyclical *Depuis le jour* of September 8, 1899, in EE, *Leone XIII*, 1143–1183.

LEONARD EMILE, *Storia del Protestantesimo*, 3 vols., Italian translation, Il Saggiatore, Milan, 1971.

LEONE PIETRO, *Come è cambiato il Rito romano antico*, Solfanelli, Chieti, 2018.

LEPIN MARIUS, *L'idée du sacrifice de la Messe d'après les théologiens depuis l'origine jusqu'à nos jours*, Beauchesne, Paris, 1926.

LESTRINGANT FRANCK, *Théatre des cruautés des hérétiques de notre temps*, Chandeigne, Paris, 1995.

LESURE MICHEL, *La crise de l'Empire ottoman, Lépante*, Gallimard, Paris, 1973.

LETURIA (DE) PEDRO, *Relaciones entre la Santa Sede e Hispanoamérica. 1493–1835*, Caracas-Rome, 1959–1960.

LEWIS BERNARD, *The Emergence of Modern Turkey*, Oxford University Press, New York, 2002 (1961).

Lo Grasso Joannes B., *Ecclesia et Status. Fontes selecti iuris publici ecclesiastici*, Pontifical Gregorian University, Rome, 1952.

Lopez Pasquale, *Il movimento valdesiano a Napoli. Mario Galeota e le sue vicende col Sant'Uffizio*, Fiorentino, Naples, 1976.

Lossen Max (edited by), *Briefe von Andreas Masius und seinen Freunden 1538 bis 1573*, Alphons Dürr, Leipzig, 1886.

Luoghi di San Pio V. Itinerari turistico-culturali, Anthelios, Milan, 2006.

Lussan (de) Marguerite, *Vie de Louis Balbe-Berton de Crillon, surnommé le Brave et Mémoires des règnes de Henri II, François II, Charles IX, Henri III et Henri IV pour servir à l'histoire de son temps*, Pissot, Paris, 1757.

Maag K. (edited by), *Melanchthon in Europe: His Work and Influence beyond Wittenberg*, Baker Books, Grand Rapids, 1999.

Madiran Jean, *Histoire de la messe interdite*, Via Romana, Versailles, 2007–2009, 2 vols.

Maffei Paolo Alessandro, *Vita di S. Pio V*, Giacomo Tummassini, Venice, 1712.

Maffei Vennocchio, *Dal titolo di duca di Firenze e di Siena a granduca di Toscana. Contributo alla storia della politica di Cosimo I*, Bernardo Seeber, Florence, 1905.

Magee Brian, *The English Recusants: A Study of the Post-reformation Catholic Survival and the Operation of the Recusancy Laws*, Burns, Oates & Washbourne, London, 1938.

Magnani Francesco, *L'antica liturgia romana*, 2 vols., Tip. Pontificia S. Giuseppe, Milan, 1897.

Maimbourg Louis, *Histoire de l'arianisme depuis sa naissance, jusqu'à sa fin. Avec l'origine et le progrès de l'hérésie des sociniens*, 3rd ed., Mabre-Camoisy, Paris, 1678.

Manzoni Giacomo (edited by), *Estratto del processo di Pietro Carnesecchi*, Stamperia Reale, Turin, 1870.

Marcatto Dario, *"Questo passo dell'heresia." Pietrantonio di Capua tra "valdesiani," "spirituali" e "inquisizione,"* Bibliopolis, Naples, 2003.

Marchetti Valerio, *Gruppi ereticali senesi del Cinquecento*, La Nuova Italia, Florence, 1975.

Marcocchi Massimo, *Il collegio Ghislieri: 1567–1967*, Associazione alunni, Lacroix, Milan, 1967.

Márquez Antonio, *Los alumbrados: Orígenes y filosofía (1525–1559)*, Taurus, Madrid, 1980.

MARTIN VICTOR, *Le gallicanisme et la réforme catholique*, Librairie Alphonse Picard, Paris, 1919.

MARTINA GIACOMO, *Storia della Chiesa*, "Ut Unum Sint," Rome, 1980.

MARTINA GIACOMO, *Storia della Chiesa*, Morcelliana, Brescia, 1995.

MARTINENGO NESTORE, *Relatione di tutto il successo di Famagosta*, Giorgio Angelieri, Venice, 1572.

MARTINES LAURO, *Savonarola. Moralità e politica a Firenze nel Quattrocento*, Mondadori, Milan, 2008.

MARTÍNEZ GIL JOSÉ LUIS, *San Juan de Dios fundador de la Fraternidad Hospitalaria*, Biblioteca Autores Cristianos, Madrid, 2002.

MARVIN CLARA, *Giovanni Pierluigi da Palestrina: A Research Guide*, Routledge Publishing, New York and London, 2002.

MASELLI DOMENICO, *Saggi di storia ereticale lombarda al tempo di S. Carlo*, Società editrice napoletana, Naples, 1979.

MAULDE (DE) LA CLAVIÈRE RENÉ, *San Gaetano di Thiene e la Riforma cattolica italiana*, Italian translation edited by G. Salvadori, Desclée, Rome, 1911.

MAURER WILHELM, *Der Junge Melanchthon*, Vandenhoeck and Ruprecht, Göttingen, 2001, 2 vols.

MAYER THOMAS F., *Cardinal Pole in European Context: A Via Media in the Reformation*, Ashgate, Aldershot, 2000.

MAYER THOMAS F., *Cardinal Pole, Prince & Prophet*, Cambridge University Press, Cambridge-New York, 2000.

MCCARTIS JUSTIN, *The Ottoman Turks: An Introductory History to 1923*, Longman, New York, 1997.

MEESTER (DE) BERNARD, *Le Saint Siège et les troubles des Pays Bas*, Bibliothèque de l'Université, Louvain, 1934.

MEINECKE FRIEDRICH, *L'idea della ragion di Stato nella storia moderna*, Italian translation, Vallecchi, Florence, 1942 (1924).

MELLONI ALBERTO, *Il conclave*, Il Mulino, Bologna, 2001.

MENCHI SEIDEL, *Erasmo in Italia, 1520–1580*, Bollati Boringhieri, Turin, 1987.

MENÉNDEZ Y PELAYO MARCELINO, *Historia de los Heterodoxos*, BAC, Madrid, 1956.

MEYER SETTON KENNETH, *The Papacy and the Levant, 1204–1571: The Sixteenth Century*, vol. 4, The American Philosophical Society, Philadelphia, 1984.

MICHEL ALBERT, *Les décrets du Concile de Trente*, Letouzey et Ané, Paris, 1938.

MIGNOZZI VITO, *"Tenenda est media via." L'ecclesiologia di Reginald Pole (1500–1558)*, Cittadella, Assisi, 2007.

MINORELLI TOMMASO MARIA, *Vita di San Pio V*, (1712), edited by Fabio Gasti, Ibis, Pavia, 2012.

Missale Romanum: Editio Princeps (1570), anastatic edition edited by Manlio Sodi - Achille Maria Triacca, Libreria Editrice Vaticana, Vatican City, 1998.

MITCHELL BONNER, *Rome in the High Renaissance: The Age of Leo X*, University of Oklahoma Press, Norman, 1973.

MOLINARI FRANCO, *Il cardinale teatino Paolo Burali e la riforma tridentina a Piacenza*, Pontificia Università Gregoriana, Rome, 1957.

MÖLLER BERND, *Imperial Cities and the Reformation*, Fortress Press, Philadelphia, 1972.

MOLMENTI POMPEO, *Sebastiano Veniero alla battaglia di Lepanto*, Barbera, Florence, 1899.

MONELLO GIGI, *Accadde a Famagosta – L'assedio turco ad una fortezza veneziana ed il suo sconvolgente finale*, Scepsi & Mattana Editori, Cagliari, 2006.

MONTAIGNE (DE) MICHEL, *Journal de voyage en Italie par la Suisse et l'Allemagne en 1580 et 1581*, Les Belles Lettres, Paris, 1946.

MORI UBALDINI UBALDINO, *La Marina del Sovrano Militare Ordine di S. Giovanni di Gerusalemme, di Rodi, di Malta*, Regionale Editrice, Rome, 1971.

MORICONI PIERLUIGI (edited by), *Caterina Cybo, duchessa di Camerino (1501–1557)*, Acts of the convention of Camerino, 28–30 October 2004, La Nuova Stampa, Camerino, 2005.

MOSEBACH MARTIN, *Häresie der Formlosigkeit, Die römische Liturgie und ihr Feind*, Karolinger, Vienna-Leipzig, 2003.

NAMÈCHE ALEXANDRE-JOSEPH, *Guillaume le Taciturne, prince d'Orange et la révolution des Pays-Bas au XVIme siècle*, C. Fonteyn, Louvain, 1890.

NEVEU BRUNO, *L'erreur et son juge: remarques sur les censures doctrinales à l'époque moderne*, Bibliopolis, Naples, 1993.

NEWMAN JOHN HENRY, *Tracts for the Time* n. 75. *On the Roman Breviary as embodying the substance of the devotional services of the Church Catholic*, J.G. & F. Rivington, Oxford, 1836.

NICOLLE DAVID, *The Janissaries*, Osprey Publishing, London, 1995.

NIESEL WILHELM, *Calvin's Lehre vom Abendmahl*, Kaiser Verlag, Munich, 1935.

NOVALÍN JOSÉ LUIS GONZÁLEZ, *El Inquisidor General Fernando de Valdés (1483–1568)*, 2 vols., Universidad de Oviedo, Oviedo, 1968–1971.

NUARA VINCENZO M., O.P. (edited by), *Il Motu Proprio "Summorum Pontificum" di S.S. Benedetto XVI. Una speranza per tutta la chiesa*, Fede e Cultura, Verona, 2013.

O'Donohoe James, *Tridentine Seminary Legislation: Its Sources and Its Formation*, Publications universitaires de Louvain, Louvain, 1957.

Olivieri Achille - Bolognese Pietro (edited by), *Pietro Martire Vermigli (1499–1562), Umanista, riformatore, pastore*, Herder, Rome, 2003.

O'Malley John W., *Trent: What Happened at the Council*, The Belknap Press of Harvard University Press, Cambridge, Massachusetts, 2013.

Orieux Jean, *Un'italiana sul trono di Francia*, Italian translation, Mondadori, Milan, 2018.

Ostrow Steven F., *Art and Spirituality in Counter-Reformation Rome: The Sistine and Pauline Chapels in S. Maria Maggiore*, Cambridge University Press, Cambridge, 1996.

Pacaut Marcel, *L'Ordre de Cluny (909–1789)*, Fayard, Paris, 1986.

Pacifici Vincenzo, *Ippolito II d'Este, Cardinal di Ferrara*, Società di Storia e d'Arte in Villa d'Este, Tivoli, 1984 (1923).

Pagano Sergio, *Il processo di Endimio Calandra e l'inquisizione a Mantova nel 1567–1568*, Biblioteca Apostolica Vaticana, Vatican City, 1991.

Pagano Sergio - Ranieri Concetta (edited by), *Nuovi documenti su Vittoria Colonna e Reginald Pole*, Archivio Vaticano, Vatican City, 1989.

Pales-Gobilliard Annette, *Le livre des sentences de l'inquisiteur Bernard Gui, 1308–1323*, CNRS, Paris, 2002, 2 vols.

Palisca Claude V., *Humanism in Italian Renaissance Musical Thought*, Yale University Press, New Haven-London, 1985.

Palisca Claude V., *Baroque Music*, Prentice Hall, Englewood Cliffs, New Jersey, 1991.

Paravicini Bagliani Agostino - Visceglia Maria Antonietta, *Il Conclave. Continuità e mutamenti dal Medioevo ad oggi*, Viella, Rome, 2018.

Parker Geoffrey, *The Grand Strategy of Philip II*, Yale University Press, New Haven-London, 1998.

Parker Geoffrey, *Un solo re, un solo impero. Filippo II di Spagna*, Italian translation, il Mulino, Bologna, 2005.

Parker Geoffrey, *Imprudent King: A New Life of Philip II*, Yale University Press, New Haven-London, 2014.

Partner Peter, *The Pope's Men. The Papal Civil Service in the Renaissance*, Clarendon Press, Oxford, 1990.

PASCHINI PIO, *Il Catechismo Romano del Concilio di Trento*, Pontificio Seminario Romano Maggiore, Rome, 1923.

PASCHINI PIO, *San Gaetano di Thiene, Gian Pietro Carafa e le origini dei chierici regolari teatini*, Storia e Letteratura, Rome, 1926.

PASTORE ALESSANDRO, *Marcantonio Flaminio. Fortune e sfortune di un chierico nell'Italia del Cinquecento*, Franco Angeli, Milan, 1981.

PASTORE STEFANIA, *Un'eresia spagnola. Spiritualità conversa, alumbradismo e Inquisizione (1449–1559)*, L. S. Olschki, Florence, 2004.

PATTENDEN MILES, *Pius IV and the Fall of the Carafa: Nepotism and Papal Authority in Counter-Reformation Rome*, Oxford University Press, Oxford, 2013.

PATTENDEN MILES, *Electing the Pope in Early Modern Italy, 1450–1700*, Oxford University Press, Oxford, 2017.

PAULUS NIKOLAUS, *Die deutschen Dominikanerim Kampfe gegen Luther (1518–1563)*, Herder, Freiburg, 1903.

PEIRCE LESLIE P., *The Imperial Harem: Women and Sovereignty in the Ottoman Empire*, Oxford University Press, Oxford, 1993.

PELLEGRINI MARCO, *Il papato nel Rinascimento*, Il Mulino, Bologna, 2010.

PERRIMEZZI GIUSEPPE MARIA, *La vita di S. Francesco da Paola, fondatore dell'ordine de'Minimi*, Tipografia Francesco de Angelis, Naples, 1842.

PERRONE GIOVANNI, *Il protestantesimo e la regola della fede*, La Civiltà Cattolica, Rome, 1853, 2 vol.

PERRY MARIA, *The Word of a Prince. A Life of Elizabeth I from Contemporary Documents*, Boydell Press, Rochester, New York, 1990.

PETERS ALBRECHT, *Realpräsenz. Luthers Zeugnis von Christi Gegenwart in Abendmahl*, Lutherisches Verlagshaus, Berlin-Hamburg, 1966.

PETIT LOUIS, *L'Index, son histoire, ses lois, sa force obligatoire*, Lethielleux, Paris, 1888.

PETRIE CHARLES, *Philip II of Spain*, Eyre & Spottiswoode, London, 1963.

PETRIE CHARLES, *Gli Stuart*, Italian translation, Dall'Oglio, Varese, 1964.

PETRIE CHARLES, *Don John of Austria*, Norton, New York, 1967.

PHILIPP ANTON, *Ludwig Pfyffer und seine Zeit. Ein Stück französischer und schweizerischer Geschichte im 16. Jahrhundert*, Wyss, Bern, 1880–1881.

PIETROMARCHI ANTONELLO, *Alessandro Farnese l'eroe italiano delle Fiandre*, Gangemi, Rome, 1998.

PIOLI GIOVANNI, *Fausto Socini. Vita, opera, fortuna*, Guanda, Modena, 1952.

PIROVANO CARLO, *Sotto il cielo di Lombardia. Breve storia degli Umiliati*, Marna, Barzago, Lc, 2007.

PITTONI LEROS - LAUTENBERG GABRIELLE, *Roma felix. La città di Sisto V e Domenico Fontana*, Viviani, Rome, 2002.

PIUS X, *Compendio della Dottrina Cristiana*, Tipografia Vaticana, Rome, 1905.

PIUS X, Encyclical *Acerbo Nimis* of 15 April 1905, in EE, *Pio X, Benedetto XV*, pp. 106–129.

PIUS X, Allocution to the Consistory, 21 February 1906, in *Les enseignements Pontificaux. La paix intérieure des nations*, edited by the Monks of Solesmes, Desclée, Paris, 1952.

PIUS X, Encyclical *Editae Saepe. De S. Caroli Borromaei apostolica activitate et doctrina*, of 26 May 1910, in EE, IV (1998), pp. 369–411.

PIUS X, *Doctoris Angelici* of 29 June 1914, in AAS, 6 (1914).

PIUS XII, Encyclical *Mediator Dei*, 20 November 1947, in *Discorsi e Radiomessaggi*, vol. 9, 2, pp. 493–561.

PIUS XII, Encyclical *Musicae Sacrae Disciplina*, 25 December 1955, in *Discorsi e Radiomessaggi*, vol. 17, pp. 571–588.

POLLEN JOHN HUNGERFORD, *Acts of English Martyrs*, Burns and Oates, London, 1905.

POLLEN JOHN HUNGERFORD, *The English Catholics in the Reign of Queen Elizabeth, 1558–1580. A Study of Their Politics, Civil Life, and Government*, Longmans, Green & Co., London, 1920.

PONCELET ALFRED, *Histoire de la Compagnie de Jésus dans les anciens Pays Bas*, Marcel Hayez, Brussels, 1927.

PONNELLE LOUÎS-BORDET LOUIS, *Saint Philippe Néri et la société romaine de son temps*, Bloud et Gay, Paris, 1928.

PORFIRI GIUSEPPE, *Gli ordini equestri italiani alla battaglia di Lepanto*, In proprio, Rome, 1976.

PORRO PASQUALE, *Thomas Aquinas: A Historical and Philosophical Profile*, Catholic University of America Press, Washington, D.C., 2016.

PORTER LINDA, *Mary Tudor*, Piatkus Books, London, 2007.

POSSEVINO ANTONIO, Il *soldato christiano con l'instruttione dei capi dello esercito cattolico*, Eredi di V. e L. Dorico, Rome, 1569.

POURRAT PIERRE, *La spiritualité chrétienne*, Lecoffre, Paris, 1935, 3 vols.

PRESTWICH MENNA, *International Calvinism 1541–1715*, Clarendon Press, Oxford, 1985.

PRETO PAOLO, *La guerra segreta: spionaggio, sabotaggi, attentati in Venezia e la difesa del Levante. Da Lepanto a Candia*, Arsenale, Venice, 1986.

PREZZOLINI CARLA - NOVEMBRI VALERIO *(edited by)*, *Papa Marcello II Cervini e la Chiesa della prima metà del '500*, Le Balze, Montepulciano, 2003.

PROSPERI ADRIANO, *L'eresia del libro Grande. Storia di Giorgio Siculo e della sua setta*, Feltrinelli, Milan, 2000.

PROSPERI ADRIANO, *Tribunali della coscienza. Inquisitori, confessori, missionari*, Einaudi, Turin, 2009.

PROSPERI ADRIANO, *Tra evangelismo e controriforma: Gian Matteo Giberti (1495–1543)*, Edizioni di Storia e Letteratura, Rome, 2011.

PUAUX ANNE, *La huguenote Renée de France*, Hermann, Paris, 1997.

QUARANTA CHIARA, *Marcello II Cervini (1501–1555). Riforma della Chiesa, concilio, Inquisizione*, Il Mulino, Bologna, 2010.

QUARTI GUIDO ANTONIO, *La battaglia di Lepanto nei canti popolari dell'epoca*, Istituto Editoriale Avionavale, Milan, 1930.

QUARTI GUIDO ANTONIO, *La guerra contro il Turco a Cipro e a Lepanto: 1570–1571: storia documentata*, Bellini, Venice, 1935.

QUÉTIF JACQUES-ÉCHARD JACQUES, *Scriptores Ordinis Praedicatorum recensiti*, II, Ballard et Simart, Paris, 1723.

RAINERI OSVALDO, *Lettere tra i pontefici romani e i principi etiopici (secc. XII–XX)*, Archivio Segreto Vaticano, Vatican City, 2005.

RAMBALDI S. PEYRONEL, *Una gentildonna irrequieta. Giulia Gonzaga fra reti familiari e relazioni eterodosse*, Viella, Rome, 2012.

RAMIREZ SANTIAGO, *De auctoritate doctrinali S. Thomae Aquitanatis*, Apud Sanctum Stephanum, Salamanca, 1952.

RANKE (VON) LEOPOLD, *Storia dei Papi*, Italian translation, Sansoni, Florence, 1959.

REAU (DE) LOUIS, *Histoire du vandalisme. Les monuments détruits de l'art français*, Hachette, Paris, 1994.

RECK-MALLECZEWEN FRIEDRICH, *Il re degli anabattisti*, Italian translation, Rusconi, Milan, 1971.

REDOLFI MADDALENA (edited by), *Venezia e la difesa del Levante: da Lepanto a Candia 1570–1670*, Arsenale, Venice, 1986.

Le relazioni degli ambasciatori veneti al Senato durante il secolo decimosesto, edited by Eugenio Alberi, Società editrice fiorentina, Florence, 1857, 2 vols.

Relazione della vita e martirio del venerabile Padre Ignazio de Azevedo, Stamperia Antonio de' Rossi, Rome, 1743.

RENATO CAMILLO, *Opere. Documenti e testimonianze*, edited by Antonio Rotondò, Sansoni, Florence - The Newberry Library, Chicago, 1968.

RETAMAL FAVEREAU JULIO, *Anglo-Spanish Relations, 1566–1572: The Mission of Don Guerau de Spes at London*, University of Oxford, Oxford, 1972.

REUSCH FRANZ HEINRICH, *Der Index der verbotenen Bücher: Ein Beitrag zur Kirchen- und Literaturgeschichte*, Cohen, Bonn, 1883–1885, reprint Scientia Verlag, Aalen, 1967.

RICCI SAVERIO, *Il Sommo Inquisitore. Giulio Antonio Santori tra autobiografia e storia (1532–1602)*, Salerno, Rome, 2002.

RIDOLFI ROBERTO, *Vita di Girolamo Savonarola*, 4th enhanced edition, Sansoni, Florence, 1974.

RIES JULIEN, *Gnostici e manicheismo. Gli gnostici. Storia e dottrina*, Italian translation, Jaca Book, Milan, 2010.

RIGHETTI MARIO, *Manuale di storia liturgica*, 3 vols., Ancora, Milan, 1963–1964 (anastatic edition, Milan, 1998).

RILEY-SMITH JONATHAN, *Breve storia delle Crociate*, Oscar Mondadori, Milan, 1994.

RILEY-SMITH JONATHAN, *What Were the Crusades?*, Palgrave, London, 2002 (1997).

RILEY-SMITH JONATHAN, *Hospitallers: The History of the Order of St. John*, The Hambledon Press, London, 1999.

ROBERT BELLARMINE, SAINT, *Conciones habitae*, Coloniae Agrippinae, Lovanii, 1615.

ROBERTI GIUSEPPE, *S. Francesco di Paola*, Curia Generalizia dei Minimi, Rome, 1963.

ROBERTSON CLARE, *Il Gran Cardinale Alessandro Farnese: Patron of the Arts*, Yale University Press, New Haven, 1992.

RODOCANACHI EMMANUEL P., *Une protectrice de la Réforme en Italie et en France, Renée de France duchesse de Ferrare*, Ollendorff, Paris, 1896.

RODOCANACHI EMMANUEL P., *La première renaissance: Rome au temps de Jules II et de Léon X*, Librairie Hachette & Cie, Rome, 1912.

RODRIGUEZ PEDRO - LANZETTI RAOUL, *El Catecismo Romano: fuentes e historia del texto y de la redacción. Bases críticas para el estudio teológico del Catecismo del Concilio de Trento (1566)*, Ed. Universidad de Navarra, Pamplona, 1982.

ROEMOND (DE) FLORIMOND, *L'Histoire de la naissance, progrés et decadence de l'hérésie de ce siècle*, Veuve Guillaume de la Noye, Paris, 1610.

ROHRBACHER RENÉ FRANÇOIS, *Storia universale della Chiesa cattolica*, Italian translation, Giacinto Marietti, Turin, 1969.

ROMIER LUCIEN, *La conjuration d'Amboise*, Perrin, Paris, 1923.

ROS CABALLAR CARLOS, *Jerónimo Gracián, el amigo de Teresa de Jesús*, Editorial Monte Carmelo, 2014.

ROSA ENRICO, *I gesuiti. Dalle origini ai nostri giorni*, La Civiltà Cattolica, Rome, 1957.

ROSCOE GUGLIELMO, *Vita e pontificato di Leone X*, Sonzogno, Milan, 1805, 12 vols.

ROSINI PATRIZIA, *Clelia Farnese la figlia del Gran cardinale*, Sette Città, Viterbo, 2010.

ROSS WILLIAMSON HUGO, *Breve cenno storico sulla instaurazione del protestantesimo in Inghilterra*, Italian translation, Una Voce, Rome, 1971.

ROSSI ETTORE, *Storia della marina dell'Ordine militare di San Giovanni di Gerusalemme, di Rodi e di Malta*, Società Editrice d'Arte, Milan, 1936.

ROTH CECIL, *The Duke of Naxos of the House of Nasi*, The Jewish Publication Society, Philadelphia, 1992.

ROUILLARD CLARENCE DANA, *The Turk in French History, Thought and Literature (1520–1660)*, Boivin, Paris, 1940.

RUBIN DE CERVIN GIOVANNI BATTISTA, *La flotta di Venezia: Navi e barche della Serenissima*, Automobilia, Milan, 1985.

RUGGIERI GIULIO, *Relatione al Santissimo Signor Nostro Papa Pio Quinto da Monsignor Giulio Ruggieri Protonotario Apostolico ritornato Nuntio di Sua Santità dal Serenissimo Re di Polonia nell'anno 1568*, in *Acta Nuntiaturae Polonae*, vol. 6, Iulius Ruggieri (1565–1568), edited by Thaddaeus Glemma and Stanislaus Bogaczewicz, Institutum Historicum Polonicum, Rome, 1991, pp. 146–198.

RUIZ JURADO MANUEL, *Storia della spiritualità: secoli XV–XVI*, Pontificia Università Gregoriana, Rome, 2000.

RUSCONI ROBERTO, *Predicazione e vita religiosa nella società italiana (da Carlo Magno alla Controriforma)*, Loescher, Turin, 1981.

RUSCONI ROBERTO, *Santo Padre. La santità del Papa da san Pietro a Giovanni Paolo II*, Viella, Rome, 2010.

RUSSELL CHAMBERLIN ERIC, *The Sack of Rome*, Dorset, New York, 1979.

SABA AGOSTINO, *Storia della Chiesa*, UTET, Turin, 1938–1940.

SALA ELISABETTA, *Elisabetta la sanguinaria. La creazione di un mito. La persecuzione di un popolo*, Ares, Milan, 2010.

SALIMEI ALFONSO, *Gli italiani a Lepanto. Riassunto storico della Lega contro i Turchi: 1570–1573, con nuovi documenti sull'Armata cristiana dagli Archivi vaticani*, Lega Navale Italiana, Rome, 1931.

SALLERON LOUIS, *La Nouvelle Messe*, Nouvelles Editions Latines, Paris, 1976 (1971).

SALMON PIERRE, *L'Office divin au Moyen âge: histoire de la formation du bréviaire du IXe au XVIe siècle*, Éditions du Cerf, Paris, 1967.

SALVARANI RENATA, *I Gonzaga e i papi. Roma e le corti padane fra Umanesimo e Rinascimento (1418–1620)*, Libreria Editrice Vaticana, Rome, 2014.

SANTARELLI DANIELE (edited by), *Corrispondenza di Bernardo Navagero*, Aracne editrice, Rome, 2011.

SAVORY ROGER, *Iran under the Safavids*, Cambridge University Press, Cambridge 2007 (1980).

SBRICCOLI MARIO, *Crimen laesae maiestatis. Il problema del reato politico alle soglie della scienza penalistica moderna*, Giuffré, Milan, 1974.

SCADUTO MARIO, *Storia della Compagnia di Gesù*, vol. 5, *L'opera di Francisco Borgia*, Edizioni "La Civiltà Cattolica," Rome, 1992.

SCALIA GIUSEPPE, *Girolamo Savonarola e santa Caterina de' Ricci*, Libreria Editrice Fiorentina, Florence, 1924.

SCHERMERHORN ELISABETH W., *Malta of the Knights*, AMS Press, New York, 1978 (1929).

SCHMIDT PETER, *Das Collegium Germanicum in Rom und die Germaniker. Zur Funktion eines römischen Ausländerseminars (1552–1914)*, Niemeyer, Tübingen, 1984.

SCHNUR ROMAN (edited by), *Staatsräson: Studien zur Geschichte eines politischen Begriffs*, Duncker & Humblot, Berlin, 1975.

SCHORN-SCHÜTTE LUISE, *Carlo V*, Italian translation, Carocci, Rome, 2002.

SCHUSTER ILDEFONSE, *Liber sacramentorum: note storiche e liturgiche sul messale Romano*, Marietti, Turin-Rome, 1923–1926.

SCHUTTE ANNE, *Pier Paolo Vergerio: The Making of an Italian Reformer*, Edition Dróz, Geneva, 1977.

SCHWEDT HERMAN H., *Die Anfänge der Römischen Inquisition. Kardinäle und Konsultoren 1542 bis 1600*, Herder, Freiburg, 2013.

Scupoli Lorenzo, *Il combattimento spirituale*, G. e P. Gioliti de' Ferrari, Venice, 1589.

Serrano Luciano, *La liga de Lepanto entre España, Venecia y la Santa Sede (1570–1573): ensayo historico a base de documentos diplomaticos*, Editorial Órbigo, Madrid, 1918.

Sforza Pallavicino Francesco, *Storia del concilio di Trento*, Angelo Bernabò, Rome, 1656–1657, 6 vols.

Shaw Christine, *Julius II: The Warrior Pope*, Blackwell Publishing, Oxford, 1996.

Shaw Christine - Mallett Michael, *The Italian Wars, 1494–1559: War, State and Society in Early Modern Europe*, Pearson Education Limited, Harlow, 2012.

Silli Antonino, O.P., *San Pio V. Note agiografiche ed iconografiche*, Biblioteca B. Angelico, Rome, 1979.

Silveira Vidigal (da) Arnaldo Xavier, *La nouvelle Messe de Paul VI qu'en penser*, Diffusion de la Penséé Française, Chiré-en-Montreuil, 1975.

Simoncelli Paolo, *Il caso Reginald Pole. Eresia e santità nelle polemiche religiose del cinquecento*, Edizioni di Storia e Letteratura, Rome, 1977.

Simoncelli Paolo, *Evangelismo italiano nel Cinquecento*, Istituto storico italiano per l'età moderna e contemporanea, Rome, 1979.

Socini Lelio, *Opere*, edited by Antonio Rotondò, Olschki, Florence, 1986.

Solfaroli Camillocci Daniela, *I devoti della carità. Le confraternite del Divino Amore nell'Italia del primo Cinquecento*, La Città del Sole, Naples, 2002.

Sotillos Eugenio, *Juan de Austria: el vencedor de Lepanto*, Torray, Barcelona, 1978.

Spagnoletti Angelantonio, *Filippo II*, Salerno Editrice, Rome, 2018.

Steggink Otger, *La reforma del Carmelo español. La visita canónica del general Rubeo y su encuentro con Santa Teresa (1566–1567)*, Teresianum, Rome, 1965.

Stella Aldo, *Gian Andrea Doria e la "sacra Lega" prima della battaglia di Lepanto*, Herder, Rome, 1965.

Stella Aldo, *Dall'anabattismo al socinianesimo nel cinquecento veneto*, Liviana, Padua, 1967.

Stickler Alfonso Maria, *L'attrattiva teologica della Messa tridentina*, Casa Editrice La Magione, Poggibonsi, 1996.

Stow Kenneth R., *Theater of Acculturation. The Roman Ghetto in the Sixteenth Century*, University of Washington Press, Seattle-London, 2001.

Suau Pierre, *San Francesco Borgia (1510–1572)*, Desclée, Rome, 1909.

Šusta Josef, *Die römische Kurie und das Koncil von Trient unter Pius IV*, Hölder, Vienna, 1901–1914, 4 vols.

SUTHERLAND NICOLA M. (edited by), *Princes, Politics and Religion 1547–1589*, The Hambledon Press, London, 1984.

SUTTER FICHTNER PAULA, *Emperor Maximilian II*, Yale University Press, New Haven, 2001.

SZCZUCKI LECH (edited by), *Faustus Socinus and His Heritage*, Polish Academy of Sciences, Krakow, 2005.

TABACCHI STEFANO, *La strage di San Bartolomeo. Una notte di sangue a Parigi*, Salerno Editrice, Rome, 2018.

TACCHI VENTURI PIETRO, *Storia della Compagnia di Gesù in Italia. La vita religiosa in Italia durante la prima età della Compagnia di Gesù*, Civiltà Cattolica, Rome, 1930.

TALLON ALAIN, *Le concile de Trente*, Editions du Cerf, Paris, 2000.

TANQUERAY ADOLPHE, *The Spiritual Life: A Treatise on Ascetical and Mystical Theology*, Society of St. John the Evangelist, Tournai, 1930.

TAVUZZI MICHAEL, *Renaissance Inquisitors: Dominican Inquisitors and Inquisitorial Districts in Northern Italy, 1474–1527*, Brill, Leiden-Boston, 2007.

TEBALDINI GIOVANNI, *La musica sacra in Italia*, Giuseppe Palma, Milan, 1893.

TEDESCHI JOHN (edited by), *Italian Reformation Studies in Honor of Laelius Socinus*, Le Monnier, Florence, 1965.

TEDESCHI JOHN, *The Prosecution of Heresy: Collected Studies on the Inquisition in Early Modern Italy*, Binghamton, New York, 1991.

TEDESCHI JOHN (edited by), *The Italian Reformation of the Sixteenth Century and the Diffusion of Renaissance Culture: A Bibliography of the Secondary Literature*, Italian translation, Panini, Modena, 2000.

TELLECHEA IDIGORAS JOSÉ IGNACIO, *Fray Bartolomé Carranza. Documentos históricos*, vols. 1–7, Real Academia de la Historia, Madrid, 1962–1994.

TELLECHEA IDIGORAS JOSÉ IGNACIO, *Fray Bartolomé Carranza de Miranda (Investigaciones históricas)*, Gobierno de Navarra, Pamplona, 2002.

TESTA CARMEL, *Romegas*, Midsea Books, Malta, 2002.

TESTA LUCA, *Fondazione e primo sviluppo del collegio romano (1565–1608)*, Pontificia Università Gregoriana, Rome, 2002.

TESTORE CELESTINO, *Il primato spirituale di Pietro difeso dal sangue dei martiri inglesi*, Tip. Macioce & Pisani, Isola del Liri, 1929.

THOMAS AQUINAS, SAINT, *Opera omnia gratiis privilegisque Pii V pont. max. typis excusa*, Rome, 1570, 7 vols.

THORNDIKE LYNN, *The History of Magic and Experimental Science*, Columbia University Press, New York, 1932.

TISSOT JOSEPH (DOM FRANÇOIS DE SALES POLLIEN), *The Interior Life Simplified and Reduced to Its Fundamental Principle*, R. & T. Washbourne, London, 1916.

TODESCHINI GIACOMO, *La banca e il ghetto. Una storia italiana (secoli XIV–XVI)*, Laterza, Bari, 2016.

TRANQUILLINO MOLTEDO FRANCESCO, *Vita di S. Antonio Maria Zaccaria fondatore de' Barnabiti e delle Angeliche*, Tipografia M. Ricci, Florence, 1897.

VAN DER KENÉ EMILE, *Bibliographisches Verzeichnis der gedruckten Schriftsums zur Geschichte und Literatur der Inquisition*, 2nd ed., Topos Verlag, Vaduz, 1982–1992, 3 vols.

VAN DULMEN RICHARD, *Das Täuferreich zu Münster 1534–1535*, Deutscher Taschenbuch Verlag, Munich, 1974.

VAN DURME MAURICE, *El cardenal Granvela (1517–1586). Imperio y revolución bajo Carlos V y Felipe II*, Teide, Barcelona, 1957.

VANNI ANDREA, *"Fare diligente inquisitione": Gian Pietro Carafa e le origini dei chierici regolari teatini*, Viella, Rome, 2010.

VENCHI INNOCENZO, *San Pio V. Il pontefice di Lepanto, del rosario e della liturgia tridentina*, Edizioni Studio Domenicano, Rome, 1997.

VERARDI DONATO, *La scienza e i segreti della natura a Napoli nel Rinascimento*, Florence University Press, Florence, 2018.

VEROGGIO BENEDETTO, *Gianandrea Doria alla battaglia di Lepanto*, Tip. del R. Istituto Sordo-Muti, Genoa, 1886.

VERSTEGAN RICHARD, *Theatrum Crudelitatum hæreticorum nostri temporis*, Adrianus Hubertus, Antwerp, 1587.

VIGLIONE MASSIMO, *La conquista della "Mela d'oro." Islam ottomano e Cristianità tra guerre di religione, politica e interessi commerciali (1299–1739)*, Solfanelli, Chieti, 2018.

VILLA GIUSEPPE - BENEDICENTI PAOLO, *I domenicani della 'Lombardia Superiore' dalle origini al 1891*, Editore Valerio Ferrua, Turin, 2002.

VILLACORTA BAÑOS - GARCIA ANTÓNIO, *Don Sebastián, Rey de Portugal*, Ed. Ariel, Barcelona, 2001.

VILLEGAS (DE) JUAN, *Aplicación del Concilio de Trento en hispanoamerica 1564–1600*, Instituto Teologico del Uruguay, Montevideo, 1975.

VILLOSLADA RICARDO GARCIA, *Martin Lutero*, IPL, Milan, 1985.

VISCEGLIA MARIA ANTONIETTA, *La città rituale. Roma e le sue cerimonie in età moderna*, Viella, Rome, 2002.

VISCEGLIA MARIA ANTONIETTA, *Morte e elezione del papa. Norme, riti e conflitti. L'Età moderna*, Viella, Rome, 2013.

WAITE GARY K., *David Joris and Dutch Anabaptism 1524–1543*, W. Laurier University Press, Waterloo, Canada, 1990.

WALDSTEIN WOLFGANG, *Hirtensorge und Liturgiereform*, Lumen Gentium, Schaan, Fl, 1977.

WALKER DANIEL P., *Spiritual and Demonic Magic from Ficino to Campanella*, The Warburg Institute, London, 1958.

WALSH WILLIAM THOMAS, *Philip II*, Sheed & Ward, London, 1938.

WALSH WILLIAM THOMAS, *Characters of the Inquisition*, P.J. Kenedy & Sons, New York, 1940.

WALSHAM ALEXANDRA, *Church Papists: Catholicism, Conformity, and Confessional Polemic in Early Modern England*, Boydell Press, Rochester, New York, 1993.

WARBURG ABY, *The Renewal of Pagan Antiquity*, Getty Research Institute for the History of Art and the Humanities, Los Angeles, 1999.

WEDGWOOD CICELY V., *William the Silent: William of Nassau, Prince of Orange, 1533–1584*, Yale University Press, New Haven, 1944.

WIEBES MEIHUIZEN HENDRIK, *Menno Simons*, T. Willink, Haarlem, 1961.

WILLIAMS GEORGE H., *The Radical Reformation*, Westminster Press, Philadelphia, 1962.

WILLIAMS NEVILLE, *Thomas Howard, Fourth Duke of Norfolk*, Dutton, New York, 1965.

WILLIAMS NEVILLE, *The Life and Times of Elizabeth the First*, Weidenfeld and Nicolson, London, 1972.

XAVIER ADRO, *Luis de Requesens en la Europa del siglo XVI*, Vassallo de Mumbert, Madrid, 1984.

YATES FRANCES A., *The Occult Philosophy in the Elizabethan Age*, Routledge & Kegan Paul, London, 1979.

ZARKA YVES CHARLES (edited by), *Raison et déraison d'Etat. Théoriciens et théories de la raison d'Etat aux XVI et XVII siècles*, P. U. F., Paris, 1994.

ZORZI ALVISE, *La Repubblica del Leone. Storia di Venezia*, Rusconi, Milan, 1979.

Items from Dictionaries and Articles in Magazines and Collective Works

ABAD CAMILO, *Ascetas y místicos españoles del siglo de oro anteriores y contemporáneos al V.P. Luis de la Puente*, in "Miscelánea Comillas," 10 (1948), pp. 27–127.

AL KALAK MATTEO, *La nascita del Catechismo Romano*, in "Revue d'histoire écclesiastique," 112 (2017), pp. 126–168.

ALCUIN OF YORK, *Disputatio per interrogationes et responsiones*, in PL, vol. 101, cols. 1097–1144.

ALDAMA (DE) JOSÉ ANTONIO, *La doctrina de Lutero sobre la transubstanciación, segun los teólogos del Concilio de Trento*, in "Archivio Teologico Granadino," 42 (1979), pp. 49–59.

ALMEIDA (DE) ROLO RAUL, *Foreiro*, in DHGE, 17 (1971), cols. 1030–1032.

ANCEL RENÉ, *La disgrace et le procès des Carafa d'après des documents inèdits, 1559–1567*, in "Revue Bénédictine," 22 (1905), pp. 525–535; 24 (1907), pp. 224–253, 479–509; 25 (1908), pp. 194–224; 26 (1909), pp. 52–80, 189–220, 301–324.

ANDRETTA STEFANO, *Frangipani Ottavio Mirto*, in DBI, vol. 50 (1998), pp. 249–252.

ANDREU FRANCESCO, *Burali*, in BSS, vol. 3 (1962), cols. 602–604.

ANTONELLI FERDINANDO, *La riforma liturgica della Settimana Santa: importanza attualità prospettive*, in *La Restaurazione liturgica nell'opera di Pio XII. Atti del primo Congresso Internazionale di Liturgia Pastorale, Assisi-Roma, 12–22 settembre 1956*, Centro di Azione liturgica, Genova, 1957, pp. 179–197.

ARANCI GILBERTO, *I 'Confessionali' di S. Antonino Pierozzi e la tradizione catechistica del '400*, in "Vivens Homo," 3 (1992), pp. 273–292.

Arecco Davide - Lantero Alessandro, *Due lavori del Vasari nel complesso monumentale di Santa Croce in Bosco Marengo*, "Novinostra," 1 (March 1999), pp. 77–85.

Badoero Andrea, *Relazione al Senato veneziano del 1573*, in Alberi, *Relazioni degli ambasciatori veneti*, vol. 1, pp. 360–361.

Bayle Constantin, *El Concilio de Trento en las Indias Españolas*, in "*Razón y Fe*," 564 (1945), pp. 257–284.

Bendiscioli Mario, *L'inizio della controversia giurisdizionale a Milano tra l'arcivescovo Carlo Borromeo e il Senato milanese (1566–1568)*, in "Archivio storico lombardo," 53 (1926), pp. 241–280; 409–462.

Bendiscioli Mario, *La Bolla "In coena Domini" e la sua pubblicazione a Milano nel 1568*, 54 (1927), pp. 381–400.

Benedict XVI, Apostolic Letter *Summorum Pontificum* of July 7, 2007, giving the motu proprio, in *Insegnamenti di Benedetto XVI*, 3, 2 (2007), pp. 20–24.

Benzoni Gino, *Francesco Maria II*, in DBI, vol. 50 (1998), pp. 55–60.

Benzoni Gino, *Galene Giovan Dionigi*, in DBI, vol. 51 (1998), pp. 409–415.

Bernard Vincent, *La guerre des Alpujarras et l'Islam méditerranéen*, in *Felipe II y el mediterráneo*, a cura di Ernest Belenguer Cebria, vol. 4, *La monarquía y los reinos*, Sociedad Estatal para la Conmemoración de los Centenarios de Felipe II y Carlos V, Madrid, 1999, pp. 267–276.

Bertuccioli Giuliano, *Soldi Gnecchi Organtino*, in DBI, vol. 57 (2001).

Biondi Albino, *La giustificazione della simulazione nel Cinquecento*, in *Eresia e riforma nell'Italia del Cinquecento*, vol. 1, Olschki, Florence-Chicago, 1974, pp. 7–68.

Blet Pierre, *Pio V e la riforma tridentina per mezzo dei nunzi apostolici*, in *San Pio V e la problematica del suo tempo*, pp. 33–46.

Blunt Antony, *El Greco's "Dream of Philip II": an allegory of the Holy League*, in "Journal of the Warburg and Courtauld Institutes," 3 (1939/40), pp. 58–69.

Boeglin Michel, *Valdés Ferdinando de*, in DSI, vol. 3, pp. 1622–1625.

Bonora Elena, *Inquisizione e Papato tra Pio IV e Pio V*, in M. Guasco - A. Torre (edited by), *Pio V nella società e nella politica del suo tempo*, pp. 33–67.

Bonzi da Genova Umile, *Catherine de Gênes*, in DSp, vol. 2 (1953), cols. 290–325.

Borea Evelina, in DBI, vol. 5 (1963), pp. 469–470.

Borean Linda, *I cardinali Francesco e Alvise Pisani: ascesa al potere, magnificenza e vanagloria*, in Furlan Caterina - Tosini Patrizia (edited by), *I cardinali della*

Serenissima. Arte e committenza tra Venezia e Roma (1523–1605), Silvana, Cinisello Balsamo, 2015, pp. 105–127.

BORROMEO AGOSTINO, *Archbishop Carlo Borromeo and the Ecclesiastical Policy of Philip II in the State of Milan*, in *San Carlo Borromeo, Catholic Reform and Ecclesiastical Policy in the Second Half of the Sixteenth Century*, edited by John M. Headley and J. B. Tomaro, Folger Books, Washington. D.C.-London-Toronto, 1988;

BORROMEO AGOSTINO, *L'arcivescovo Carlo Borromeo, la Corona spagnola e le controversie giurisdizionali a Milano*, in *Carlo Borromeo e l'opera della "Grande riforma." Cultura, religione e arti del governo nella Milano del pieno Cinquecento*, edited by Franco Buzzi and Danilo Zardin, Silvana Editoriale, Milan, 1997.

BORROMEO AGOSTINO, *Inquisizione*, in DSP, vol. 1, pp. 815–818.

BORSELLINO ENZO, *Il monumento di Pio V in S. Maria Maggiore*, in *Sisto V. Roma e il Lazio*, edited by Marcello Fagiolo and Maria Luisa Madonna, Istituto Poligrafico e Zecca dello Stato, Rome, 1992.

BOSATRA BRUNO MARIA, *Ancora sul "vescovo ideale" della riforma cattolica. I lineamenti del pastore tridentino-borromaico*, in "La Scuola Cattolica," 112 (1984), pp. 517–579.

BRAGA CARLO, *"Maxima Redemptionis Nostrae Mysteria" 50 anni dopo (1955–2005)*, in "Ecclesia Orans," n. 23 (2006), pp. 11–36.

BRAMBILLA ELENA, *Abiura*, in DSI, vol. 1, pp. 5–6.

BRAUDEL FERNAND, *Bilan d'une bataille*, in G. BENZONI (edited by), *Il Mediterraneo nella seconda metà del '500*, pp. 109–120.

BRUNELLI GIAMPIERO, *Rusticucci Girolamo*, in DBI, 89 (2017), pp. 360–362.

BUJANDA (DE) JESUS MARTINEZ, *Indici dei libri proibiti*, in DSI, vol. 2, pp. 775–780.

BURRUS ERNEST JOSEPH, *Pius V and Francisco Borgia: Their Efforts on Behalf of the American Indians*, in "Archivum Historicum Societatis Iesu," 41 (1972), pp. 207–226.

BYATT LUCINDA, *Este, Ippolito d'*, in DBI, vol. 43 (1993), pp. 367–374.

BYATT LUCINDA, *Ridolfi*, in DBI, vol. 87 (2016), pp. 478–482.

CABROL FERNAND, *Breviary*, in *The Catholic Encyclopedia*, vol. 2, pp. 768–777.

CACCAMO DOMENICO, *Commendone Francesco*, in DBI, vol. 27 (1982), pp. 606–613.

CAI RAFFAELE, *Catherine de' Ricci*, in DSp, vol. 2 (1953), cols. 326–367.

Calapa Anna, *Le indicazioni del Concilio di Trento circa la predicazione e la loro incidenza nella prassi*, in *L'omelia. Atti della XXXVIII settimana di studio dell'APL. CLV*, Edizioni liturgiche, Rome, 2012, pp. 46–69.

Caravale Giorgio, *Il* Beneficio di Cristo *e l'Inquisizione romana: un caso di censure tardive* in *Cinquant'anni di storiografia italiana sulla Riforma e i movimenti ereticali in Italia (1950–2000)*, edited by Susanna Peyronel, Claudiana, Turin, 2002, pp. 151–173.

Cartotti Oddasso Adriana, *Caterina da Siena*, in BSS, vol. 3 (1962), pp. 996–1044.

Castellani G., *L'assistenza religiosa nell'armata di Lepanto (1570–1572). Con documenti inediti*, in "Civiltà Cattolica," 4 (1936), pp. 470–481; 1 (1937), pp. 39–49 and 433–443; 2 (1937), pp. 259–269 and 538–547.

Certeau (de) Michel, *Borromeo Carlo*, in DBI, vol. 20 (1970), pp. 260–269.

Cervini Fulvio, *Pio V, Vasari e l'arte "medievale,"* in *Il tempo di Pio V. Pio V nel tempo*, edited by F. Cervini and C. E. Spantigati, pp. 193–218.

Chapman John H., *The Persecution under Elizabeth*, in "Transactions of the Royal Historical Society," 9 (1881) pp. 21–43.

Charriere Ernest, *Négociations de la France dans le Levant*, Imprimerie Nationale de France, Paris, 1850, vol. 2, pp. 252–254.

Chiodi Luigi, *L'eresia protestante a Bergamo nella prima metà del Cinquecento e il vescovo Vittore Soranzo*, in "Rivista di Storia della Chiesa in Italia," 35 (1981), pp. 456–485.

Cicala Marco, *L'Affaire don Carlos. Leggenda nera arrivata fino a Verdi*, in "La Repubblica," 1 February 2017.

Civale Gianclaudio, *Francesco Borgia e gli esordi della pastorale gesuitica nei confronti dei soldati*, in *Francisco de Borja y su tiempo: Política, religión y cultura en la Edad Moderna*, edited by Hernán and María del Pilar Ryan, Albatros Ediciones, Valencia-Rome, 2011, pp. 207–222.

Civale Gianclaudio, *Religione e mestiere delle armi nella Franca dei primi torbidi religiosi. Il "Pedagogue d'armes" del gesuita Emond Auger (1568)*, in "Bibliothèque d'Humanisme et Renaissance," 74 (2012), pp. 505–533.

Claeys-Bouuaert Fernand, *Bulle In Coena Domini*, in DDC, II (1937), cols. 1132–1136.

Colosio Innocenzo, *Jean-Baptiste Carioni*, in DSp, vol. 1 (1937), cols. 153–156.

Colosio Innocenzo, *I Mistici italiani dalla fine del Trecento ai primi del Seicento*, in *Grande Antologia Filosofica*, edited by Umberto Antonio Padovani, Marzorati, Milan, 1954.

COLOSIO INNOCENZO, *Appunti sulla spiritualità domenicana*, in *Saggi sulla spiritualità domenicana*, Libreria Editrice Fiorentina, Florence, 1961, pp. 25–33.

COLOSIO INNOCENZO, *Alcuni dei principali punti teorici, pratici, metodologici, storici difesi su questa Rivista nei suoi primi quattordici anni*, in "Rivista di ascetica e mistica," nn. 5–6 (December 1969), pp. 416–456.

COMPARATO VICTOR IVO, *Calini Muzio*, in DBI, 16 (1973), pp. 725–727.

CONSTANT JOSEPH, *William Allen*, in DHGE, vol. 2, cols. 599–607.

CONSTANT JOSEPH, *Angleterre*, in DHGE, vol. 3 (1924), col. 204.

COZZI GAETANO, *sub voce*, in DBI vol. 40 (1991), pp. 757–777.

CRISTIANI, *Socinianisme*, in DTC, vol. 14 (1941), pp. 2326–2334.

CRIVELLI CAMILLO, *Anglicane, Ordinazioni*, in EC, vol. 1 (1948), cols. 1271–1273.

CRUZ-JESUS (DE LA) TOMAS, *Santa Teresa de Jesús. Actualidad. Panorama editorial. Estudios biográficos. Estudios doctrinales*, in "Ephemerides Carmeliticae," 19 (1968), pp. 9–44.

DE BLAAUW SIBLE, *Pio V e la liturgia*, in *Il tempo di Pio V. Pio V nel tempo*, edited by F. Cervini and C. E. Spantigati, pp. 80–81.

DE BOER WIETSE, *Carlo Borromeo*, in DSI, vol. 1, pp. 278–282.

DE CARO GASPARE, *Baglioni Astorre*, in DBI, vol. 5 (1963), pp. 197–199.

DE CARO GASPARE, *Burali, Scipione*, in DBI, vol. 15 (1972), pp. 370–376.

DE CARO GASPARE, *Caetani Onorato*, in DBI, vol. 16 (1973), pp. 205–209.

DE MARIA ENRICO, *Il canto gregoriano nelle scelte e nei corali di Pio V*, in *Il tempo di Pio V. Pio V nel tempo*, edited by F. Cervini and C. E. Spantigati, pp. 255–266.

DEGERT ANTOINE, *Procès de huit évêques français suspects de calvinisme*, in "Revue des Questions Historiques," 38 (1904), pp. 61–108.

DEGERT ANTOINE, *Une ambassade périlleuse de François de Noailles en Turquie*, in "Revue Historique," 159, 2 (1929), pp. 225–260.

DEL RE NICCOLÒ, *Storey*, in BSS, vol. 12 (1990), cols. 36–38.

DEL RE NICCOLÒ, *Vessillo e Vessillifero di Santa Romana Chiesa*, in *Mondo Vaticano*, Libreria Editrice Vaticana, Vatican City, 1995.

DITCHFELD SIMON, *Il Papa come pastore? Pio V e la liturgia*, in *Pio V nella società e nella politica*, pp. 159–178.

DONADELLI CLAUDIA, *Nunziature apostoliche*, in DSI, vol. 2, pp. 1119–1124.

DUKE ALASTAIR, *From King and Country to King or Country? Loyalty and Treason in the Revolt of the Netherlands*, in "Transactions of the Royal Historical Society," 32 (1982), pp. 113–135.

Dupré Theseider Eugenio, *Caterina da Siena*, in DBI, vol. 22 (1979), pp. 361–379.

Errera Andrea, *Difesa*, in DSI, vol. 1, pp. 479–481.

Eszer Ambrogio, *Il concetto della virtù eroica nella storia*, in *Sacramenti, liturgia, cause dei santi. Studi in onore del cardinale Giuseppe Casoria*, Editoriale Comunicazioni Sociali, Naples, 1992, pp. 605–636.

Feci Simona, *Pio V*, in DSI, vol. 2, pp. 1213–1215.

Feci Simona, *Foscarari Egidio*, in DBI, vol. 49 (1997), pp. 280–283.

Feci Simona, *Pio V*, in DBI, vol. 83 (2015), pp. 814–825.

Filesi Teobaldo, *Enrico, figlio del re del Congo, primo vescovo dell'Africa Nera*, in "*Euntes Docete*: Commentaria Urbaniana," 19 (1966), pp. 365–385.

Filipazzi Antonio, *L'influsso di Gian Matteo Giberti attraverso l'azione di Nicolò Ormaneto*, in *Atti del Convegno di studi Gian Matteo Giberti*, pp. 73–87.

Fiorani Luigi, *Il carisma dell'ospitalità*, in *La storia dei Giubilei*, Giunti, Rome, 1998.

Firpo Massimo, *Morone Giovanni*, in DBI, vol. 77 (2012), pp. 66–74.

Firpo Massimo, *San Pio V e il miracolo del crocefisso*, in Firpo Massimo, *Storie di immagini. Immagini di storia*, pp. 219–230.

Firpo Massimo - Simoncelli Paolo, *I processi inquisitoriali contro Savonarola (1550) e Carnesecchi (1566-1567). Una proposta di interpretazione*, in "Rivista di Storia e Letteratura religiosa," 18 (1982), n. 2, pp. 220–221.

Fontaine Michelle M., *For the Good of the City: The Bishop and the Ruling Elite in Tridentine Modena*, in "Sixteenth Century Journal," 28, 1 (1997), pp. 29–43.

Fossier François, *Clemente VII*, in DSP, vol. 1, pp. 330–333.

Fragnito Gigliola, *Paolo III*, in DBI, vol. 81 (2014), pp. 98–107.

Fragnito Gigliola, *Pio V e la censura*, in M. Guasco - A. Torre (edited by), *Pio V nella società e nella politica del suo tempo*, pp. 129–158.

Frajese Vittorio, *Filippo Neri*, in DBI, vol. 47 (1997), pp. 741–750.

Francesca dell'Immacolata Madre M., *Le origini apostolico-patristiche della Messa cosiddetta "tridentina,"* in V. Nuara, O.P. (edited by), *Il Motu Proprio "Summorum Pontificum" di S.S. Benedetto XVI*, vol. 3, pp. 93–131.

Francesco Borgia, Saint, *Lettera ai prepositi provinciali della Compagnia*, in *Monumenta Historica Societatis Jesu*, vol. 38, *Sanctus Franciscus Borgia*, IV, Typ. Gabrielis Lopez del Horno, Matriti, 1910.

Francesco Borgia, Saint, *Lettera ai prepositi provinciali della Compagnia*, in *Monumenta Historica Societatis Jesu*.

FRIEDENSBURG WALTER, *Giovanni Morone und der Brief Sadolets an Melanchthon vom 17. Juni 1537*, in "Archiv für Reformationsgeschichte," 1 (1903), pp. 372–380.

FRUTAZ AMATO PIETRO, *Messale*, in EC, vol. 8 (1952), col. 836 (cols. 831–840).

GAETA FRANCO, *Barbarigo Agostino*, in DBI, vol. 6 (1964), pp. 50–52.

GAGNEBET MARIE-ROSAIRE, *L'Enseignement du Magistère et le problème du surnaturel*, in "Revue thomiste," 53 (1953), pp. 5–27.

GARCÍA-VILLOSLADA RICARDO, *Erasme*, in DSp, vol. 4 (1960), col. 933.

GASTI FULVIO, *L'immagine di Pio V negli scritti biografici del 1712*, in C. BERNASCONI (edited by), *San Pio V nella Storia*, pp. 59–79.

GIAMPIETRO NICOLA, *A cinquant'anni dalla riforma liturgica della Settimana Santa*, in "Ephemerides liturgicae," 3 (2006), pp. 293–332.

GIOMETTI CRISTIANO, *Nuvolone Francesco*, in DBI, vol. 79 (2013), pp. 23–25.

GIORDANO SILVANO, *Sisto V*, in EP (2000), pp. 202–222.

GIUDICI GIOVANNI, *La tensione riformatrice di Pio V nella Chiesa del suo tempo*, in C. BERNASCONI (edited by), *San Pio V nella Storia*, pp. 33–37.

GOMBRICH ERNST H., *Celebrations in Venice of the Holy League and of the Victory of Lepanto*, in *Studies in Renaissance and Baroque Art presented to Anthony Blunt*, Phaidon, London-New York, 1967, pp. 62–68.

GORCE MAXIME, *Catherine de Sienne*, in DSp, vol. 2 (1953), cols. 327–348.

GORIA FEDERICO ALESSANDRO, *La bolla* De non infeudando *del 1567: politica antinepotistica e tutela del demanio ecclesiastico*, in AA. VV., *Le Carte del Diritto e della Fede*, Atti del convegno di studi, Alessandria, 16–17 June 2006, edited by E. Mongiano, G.M. Panizza, Società di Storia e di Archeologia, Alessandria, 2008, pp. 93–105.

GRECO GAETANO, *Gaetano di Thiene*, in DBI, vol. 51 (1998), pp. 203–207.

GUASCO MAURILIO, *La formazione del clero: i seminari*, in G. CHITTOLINI - G. MICCOLI (edited by), *Storia d'Italia, Annali*, vol. 9, pp. 629–715.

GULLINO GIUSEPPE, *Duodo Francesco*, in DBI, vol. 42 (1993), pp. 30–32.

HAGENEDER OTHMAR, *Il potere di deposizione del principe: i fondamenti canonistici*, in *Il sole e la luna. Papato, Impero e regni nella teoria e nella prassi dei secoli XII e XIII*, Italian translation, Vita e Pensiero, Milan, 2000, pp. 165–211.

HAMSHERE CYRIL, *The Ridolfi Plot 1571*, in "History Today," 26 (2014), pp. 32–39.

HEINZ ANDREAS, *Gregorio Magno e la liturgia romana*, in *Gregorio Magno nel XIV centenario della morte* (Rome, 22–25 October 2003), Accademia Nazionale dei Lincei, Rome, 2004.

HEINZ ANDREAS, *Liturgie e culture tra l'età di Gregorio Magno e il pontificato di Leone III*, in *Aspetti rituali, ecclesiologici e istituzionali*, edited by Renata Salvarani, Libreria Vaticana, Vatican City, 2012, pp. 282–290.

IENI GIULIO, *"Una superbissima sepoltura": il mausoleo di Pio V*, in *Pio V e Santa Croce di Bosco. Aspetti di una committenza papale*, edited by G. Ieni, Carlenrica Spantigati, Edizioni dell'Orso, Alessandria, 1985, pp. 31–48.

IMBART DE LA TOUR PIERRE, in *Les origines de la Réforme*, vol. 3: *L'Evangelisme (1521–1538)*, Slatkine, Geneva, 1978 (1914).

INGEBORG WALTER, *Burckard Johannes*, in DBI, vol. 15 (1972), pp. 405–408.

IOLY ZORATTINI PIETRO, *Ebrei*, in DSI, vol. 2, pp. 523–524.

IPPOLITI ALESSANDRO, *Fontana, Domenico*, in DBI, vol. 48 (1997), pp. 638–643.

JEDIN HUBERT, *L'importanza del decreto tridentino sui seminari nella vita della Chiesa*, in "*Seminarium*," 3 (1963), pp. 396–412.

JEDIN HUBERT, *Il Concilio di Trento e la riforma dei libri liturgici*, in *Chiesa della fede*, pp. 390–425.

JOHN PAUL II, Apostolic Exhortation *Catechesi Tradendae*, 16 October 1979, n. 13, in *Insegnamenti*, vol. 2/2 (1979).

JOHN PAUL II, Angelus del 20 febbraio 1994, in "L'Osservatore Romano," 22 February 1994.

JOHN PAUL II, Apostolic Letter *Latamur Magnopere* of 15 August 1997, promulgating the *Catechism of the Catholic Church*, in *Insegnamenti*, 20, 2 (1997), pp. 120–126.

JONG (DE) JAN L., *The painted decoration of the Sala Regia in the Vatican. Intention and reception*, in *Functions and Decorations: Art and Ritual at the Vatican Palace in the Middle Ages and the Renaissance*, edited by T. Weddigen, S. De Blaauw, B. Kempers, Brepols-Biblioteca Apostolica Vaticana, Tournhout-Vatican City, 2003.

JORGE ENRIQUE, *Santa Teresa de Jesús y el B. Ignacio de Azevedo. Martirio y profecía*, in "Manresa," 43 (1971), pp. 79–90.

JUNGHANS HELMAR, *Der Einfluss des Humanismus auf Luthers Entwicklung bis 1518*, in "Luther-Jahrbuch," 37 (1970), pp. 37–101.

JUSTIN, SAINT, *Apologia*, 1, 65–67. Latin text in *Prex Eucharistica. Textus e variis liturgiis antiquioribus selecti*, edited by A. Hänggi, I. Pahl, Fribourg, 1968 (Spicilegium Friburgense, 12), pp. 71–72.

KLINGSHIRN WILLIAM E., *Isidore of Seville's Taxonomy of Magicians and Diviners*, in "Traditio," 58 (2003), pp. 59–90.
KOLLER ALEXANDER, *Porcia, Bartolomeo*, in DBI, vol. 85 (2016), pp. 27–30.

LANZ ARNOLDO M., *Canisio Pietro*, in EC, vol. 9, cols. 1451–1453.
LANZETTI RAÚL, *Francisco Foreiro, o la continuidad entre el Concilio de Trento y el catecismo romano*, in "Scripta Theologica," 16, 1–2 (1984), pp. 451–458.
LAVENIA VINCENZO, *Tra Cristo e Marte. Disciplina e catechesi del soldato cristiano in epoca moderna*, in: *Dai cantieri alla storia. Liber amicorum per Paolo Prodi*, edited by G. Paolo Brizzi and Giuseppe Olmi, Il Mulino, Bologna, 2007, pp. 37–54.
LAVENIA VINCENZO, *Sisto di Siena*, in DBI, vol. 93 (2018), pp. 12–15.
LECLERCQ HENRI, *Bréviaire romaine*, in DACL, vol. 2 (1910), cols. 1262–1316.
LEONARDI CLAUDIO, *Alcuino e la scuola palatina: le ambizioni di una cultura unitaria*, in *Medioevo latino. La cultura dell'Europa cristiana*, edited by Francesco Santi, Sismel-Edizioni del Galluzzo, Florence, 2004, pp. 191–217.
LESURE MICHEL, *Notes et documents sur les relations vénéto-ottomanes 1570–1573*, in "Turcica," 15 (1972), pp. 134–164; 8 (1976), pp. 117–156.
LEVI ANNA - ROTH CECIL, *Joseph Nassì, duca di Nasso, e i Savoia*, "La Rassegna Mensile di Israel," 34, 8 (August 1968), pp. 464–474.
LOMPART GABRIEL, *Gaetano da Thiene. Estudios sobra un reformador religioso*, in "Regnum Dei," 24 (1968), pp. 1–325.
LOPETEGUI LEON, *San Francisco de Borja y el plan misionel de san Pio V. Primeros pasos de una Congregación de Propaganda Fide*, in "Archivum Historicum Societatis Iesu," 11 (1942), pp. 1–26.
LÓPEZ VELA ROBERTO, *Inquisizione spagnola*, in DSI, vol. 2, pp. 827–845.
LÖW GIUSEPPE, Canonizzazione, in EC, vol. 3 (1949), cols. 571–607.
LÖW GIUSEPPE, *Liturgia*, in EC, vol. 7 (1951), cols. 1443–1444.
LUTHER MARTIN, *De Captivitate Babylonia*, in WA, vol. 6, pp. 512, 514–518, 523.
LUTHER MARTIN, *Contra Henricum Regem Angliae* (1522), in WA, vol. 10b.

MANDONNET PIERRE, *Cano Melchior*, in DTC, 2, 2, cols. 1537–1540.

MANGENOT EUGÈNE, *Catéchisme*, in DTC, vol. 2 (1932), cols. 1895–1968.

MARCHETTI VALERIO, *Campeggi Camillo*, in DBI, vol. 17 (1974), pp. 439–440.

MARCOCCHI MASSIMO, *La personalità di Pio V e le direttive religiose, disciplinari e culturali delle Costituzioni del collegio Ghislieri*, in *Il Collegio universitario Ghislieri*, pp. 93–129.

MARCORA CARLO, *Nicolò Ormaneto Vicario di san Carlo*, in *Memorie storiche della Diocesi di Milano*, 8 (1961), pp. 209–590.

MAZZILLI SAVINI MARIA TERESA, *Da Papa Pio V all'iconografia di San Pio V: come è espressa la sua canonizzazione*, in C. BERNASCONI (edited by), *San Pio V nella Storia*, pp. 81–110.

MAZZONE UMBERTO - TURCHINI ANGELO (edited by), *Le visite pastorali. Analisi di una fonte*, in "Annali dell'Istituto Storico Italo-Germanico," 18, Il Mulino, Bologna, 1985.

MCNALLY ROBERT E., *Pope Adrian VI (1522–23) and Church Reform*, in "Archivum Historiae Pontificiae," vol. 7 (1969), pp. 253–285.

MENCHI SEIDEL, *Origine e origini del Sant'Uffizio*, in *L'inquisizione: atti del simposio internazionale*, pp. 291–322.

MESSINA PIETRO, *Del Monte Innocenzo*, in DBI, vol. 38 (1990), pp. 138–141.

MESSINA PIETRO, *Del Monte Pietro*, in DBI, vol. 38 (1990), pp.146–148.

MESSINA PIETRO, *De Torres, Ludovico*, in DBI, vol. 39 (1991), pp. 478–483.

MICHEL ALBERT, *Miracle*, in DTC, vol. 10 (1929), cols. 1789–1859.

MIELE MICHELE, *Pio V e la presenza dei domenicani nel corso della sua vita*, in *Pio V nella società*, pp. 27–48.

MILANO ATTILIO, *Battesimi di ebrei a Roma dal Cinquecento all'Ottocento*, in *Scritti in memoria di Enzo Sereni. Saggi sull'ebraismo romano*, edited by D. Carpi, A. Milano e U. Nahon. Fondazione Sally Mayer, Jerusalem, 1970.

MOLS ROGER, *Clement VII*, in DHGE, 12 (1953), cols. 530–534.

MORI ELISABETTA, *I Ghislieri a Roma da Pio V all'Ottocento: vicende familiari e patrimoniali ricostruite attraverso il riordinamento del loro archivio*, in "Bollettino dei Musei Comunali di Roma," 2, 1988, pp. 35–46.

MORI ELISABETTA, *L'Archivio del ramo romano della famiglia Ghislieri*, in "Archivio della Società Romana di Storia Patria," 18 (1995), pp. 118–171.

MORONI GAETANO, *Bandiera*, in *Dizionario di erudizione*, vol. 3, pp. 86–90.

MORONI GAETANO, *Nunzio apostolico*, in *Dizionario di erudizione*, vol. 58, pp. 151–172.

MUÑOZ TOMÁS LOPEZ, *Sesso, Carlo di*, in DSI, vol. 3, pp. 1416–1417.

MUSSELLI LUCIANO, *Il Collegio Ghislieri*, in *Almum Studium Papiense. Storia del l'Università di Pavia*, edited by D. Mantovani, vol. I, *Dalle origini all'età Spagnola*, tome II, Monduzzi Editore, Bologna, 2013, pp. 947–959.

NEGRUZZO SIMONA, *Pio V e la formazione dei giovani*, in C. BERNASCONI (edited by), *San Pio V nella Storia*, pp. 23–32.

NEGRUZZO SIMONA, *I collegi della controriforma: il caso pavese*, in *Dai collegi medievali alle residenze universitarie*, Clueb, Bologna, 2010, pp. 43–54.

NERI VALERIO, *Magia e divinazione in Isidoro di Siviglia (Etym. VIII, 9)*, in *Ravenna Capitale Uno sguardo ad Occidente Romani e Goti - Isidoro di Siviglia*, Maggioli, Santarcangelo di Romagna, 2012, pp. 147–160.

NICHOLLS GUY, *Historique des prières du canon romain*, in *Aspects historiques et théologiques du missel romain. Actes du cinquième colloque d'études historiques, théologiques et canoniques sur le rite romain* (Versailles, November 1999), Centre International d'Etudes Liturgiques, Paris, 2000, pp. 129–158.

O' DONOHOE JAMES, *The seminary legislation of the Council of Trent*, in *Il Concilio di Trento e la Riforma tridentina*, I, Herder, Rome-Freiburg, 1963, pp. 157–172.

ORO JOSÉ GARCÍA, *Observantes, recoletos, descalzos: la monarquía católica y el reformismo religioso del siglo xvi*, in *Actas del Congreso Internacional Sanjuanista*, Avila, 23–28 September 1991, *Junta de Castilla y León*, Valladolid, 1993, pp. 53–97.

PACCHIANI GEREMIA, *Manifestazioni protestantiche a Bergamo*, in "La Scuola cattolica," 58 (June 1935), pp. 323–347.

PALAZZINI PIETRO, *Tortura*, in EC, vol. 12 (1954), cols. 342–343.

PANOFSKY ERWIN, *Il movimento neoplatonico a Firenze e nell'Italia settentrionale*, in *Studi di iconologia* (1939), Einaudi, Turin, 1999, pp. 184–235.

PANZERI GIANLUIGI, *Carlo Borromeo e la figura del Vescovo della Chiesa tridentina*, in "La Scuola Cattolica," 124 (1996), pp. 685–731.

PARISELLO INNOCENZO, *Simonia*, in EC, vol. 2 (1953), col. 643 (642–646).

PARKER GEOFFREY, *The place of Tudor England in the messianic vision of Philip II of Spain*, in "Transactions of the Royal Historical Society," 13 (2002), pp. 187–221.

PASTORE ALESSANDRO, *Giulio II*, in DBI, vol. 57 (2001), pp. 17–26.

PASTORE STEFANIA, *Alumbradismo*, in DSI, vol. 1, pp. 47–51.

PASTORE STEFANIA, *In Coena Domini*, DSI, vol. 2, pp. 774–775.

PAUL VI, Speech of 17 November 1979, in *Insegnamenti*, vol. 3/2 (1979), pp. 1177–1189.

PELLEGRINI MARCO, *Leone X*, in DBI, vol. 64 (2005), pp. 513–523.

PENZI MARCO, *La politica francese di Pio V: tra riforma cattolica e guerra contro l'eresia*, in M. GUASCO - A. TORRE (edited by), *Pio V nella società e nella politica del suo tempo*, pp. 251–276.

PETER DAMIAN, SAINT, *Liber Gomorrhianus*, in PL, vol. 145, cols. 159–190, Italian translation, *Liber Gomorrhianus*, Edizioni Fiducia, Rome, 2015.

PETRUCCI FRANCA, *Colonna, Marcantonio*, in DBI, vol. 27 (1982), pp. 371–383.

PICOTTI GIOVANNI BATTISTA - SANFILIPPO MATTEO, *Alessandro VI*, in EP, vol. 3, pp. 13–22.

PIETRI CHARLES, *Damase évêque de Rome*, in *Saecularia Damasiana*, Libreria Editrice Vaticana, Vatican City 1986, pp. 29–58.

PIUS VI, Allocuzione *Quare Lacrimae* of 17 June 1793, in *Bullarii Romani Continuatio*, pp. 2627–2637.

POCIŪTĖ DAINORA, *L'arginamento dell'eterodossia riformata nel Granducato di Lituania e in Polonia: il trattato Orthodoxa fidei confessio di Mikołaj Pac*, "pl.it/ rassegna italiana di argomenti polacchi," 8 (2017), pp. 5–21.

PRESTON PATRICK, *St Pius V (1504–72) and St. Caterina De' Ricci (1523–90): Two Ways of Being a Saint in Counter-Reformation Italy*, in *Studies in Church History*, vol. 47 (*Saints and Sanctity*), Cambridge University Press online, 2011, pp. 208–227.

PROSPERI ADRIANO, *Bonelli Michele*, in DBI, vol. 10 (1969), pp. 766–774.

PROSPERI ADRIANO, *Clemente VII*, in DBI, vol. 26 (1982), pp. 222–259.

PROSPERI ADRIANO, *Campeggi*, in DSI, vol. 1, pp. 252–253.

QUARANTA CHIARA, *Paleario Aonio*, in DBI, vol. 80 (2014), pp. 412–417.

RANKIN MARK, *Richard Topcliffe and the Book Culture of the Elizabethan Catholic Underground*, in "Renaissance Quarterly," Summer 2019, pp. 492–536.

REBECCHINI GUIDO, *After the Medici. The New Rome of Pope Paul III Farnese*, in *I Tatti Studies*, 11 (2007), pp. 147–200.

REGAZZONI MAURO, *L'epoca della Riforma e della Controriforma*, in *Storia della spiritualità italiana*, edited by Pietro Zovatto, Città Nuova, Rome, 2002.

Ricossa Francesco don, *L'eresia ai vertici della Chiesa*, in "Sodalitium," 93 (1994), pp. 33–46.

Ries Julien, *Gnosticisme*, in DHGE, vol. 21 (1986), cols. 264–281.

Righi Davide, *Dall'Ordo Missae di Pio V all' Ordo Missae di Paolo VI. Contesti storici e prospettive teologico-liturgiche*, in "Rivista di teologia dell'evangelizzazione," 13 (2009), pp. 9–37.

Ristori Renzo, *Caterina de' Ricci*, in DBI, vol. 22 (1979), pp. 359–361.

Rodríguez García Pedro, *La cuestión histórico-doctrinal del Catecismo Romano*, in "Scripta Theologica," 17 (2), (1985), pp. 467–486.

Romano Davide, *Pole Reginald*, in DBI, vol. 84 (2015), pp. 526–533.

Romeo Giovanni, *Pio V nelle fonti gesuite*, in M. Guasco - A. Torre (edited by), *Pio V nella società e nella politica del suo tempo*, pp. 111–127.

Romito Fiorenzo, *Musica sacra*, in EC (1952), col. 1552.

Rosa Mario, *Adriano VI*, in EP, vol. 3 (2000), pp. 64–70.

Rotondò Antonio, *Biandrale Giorgio*, in DBI vol. 10 (1968), pp. 257–264.

Rotondò Antonio, *Carnesecchi Pietro*, in DBI, vol. 20 (1977), pp. 466–476.

Saitta Armando (edited by), Atti del *Convegno internazionale sull'Inquisizione nei secoli XVI e XVII: metodologia delle fonti e prospettive storiografiche*, October 1981, in "Annuario dell'Istituto storico italiano per l'età moderna e contemporanea," vols. 35–36 (1983–1984) and vols. 37–38 (1985–1986).

Santarelli Daniele, *La riforma della Chiesa di Paolo IV nello specchio delle lettere dell'ambasciatore veneziano Bernardo Navagero*, in "Annali dell'Istituto Italiano per gli Studi Storici," 20 (2003/2004), pp. 81–104.

Santus Cesare, *Tiziano*, in DSI, vol. 3, pp. 1575–1576.

Scaduto Mario, *Laìnez e l'indice del 1559. Lullo, Sabunde, Savonarola, Erasmo*, in "Archivum Historicum Societatis Iesu," 24 (1955), pp. 3–32.

Scaramella Pierroberto, *Sodomia*, in DSI, vol. 3, pp. 1445–1450.

Scaramella Pierroberto, *Pio V e la repressione dell'eresia nell'Italia meridionale*, in M. Guasco - A. Torre (edited by), *Pio V nella società e nella politica del suo tempo*, pp. 69–94.

Scattola Merio, *Domingo de Soto e la fondazione della scuola di Salamanca*, in "Veritas. Revista de filosofía," 54, 3 (2009), pp. 52–70.

Schneider Athanasius, *Il significato degli ordini minori nella Sacra Liturgia*, in V. Nuara, O.P. (edited by), *Il Motu Proprio "Summorum Pontificum" di S.S. Benedetto XVI*, vol. 3, pp. 54–70.

SCHOECK RICHARD, *The Fifth Lateran Council: Its Partial Success and Its Larger Failures*, in *Reform and Authority in the Medieval and Reformation Church*, edited by G. F. Lytle, Catholic University of America Press, Washington, D.C., 1981, pp. 99–126.

SCOLARI ALBERTO CARLO, *Le cappelle delle Reliquie e del Rosario nella chiesa del convento di S. Croce in Bosco Marengo*, in *Pio V e Santa Croce di Bosco*, pp. 63–83.

SCORZA RICK, *Vasari's Lepanto frescoes: apparati, medals, prints and the celebration of victory*, in "Journal of the Warburg and Courtauld Institutes," 75 (2012), pp. 141–200.

SEGRE RENATA, *Il mondo ebraico nei cardinali della Controriforma*, in *Italia Judaica: gli ebrei in Italia tra Rinascimento ed età barocca*, Atti del convegno (1984), Ministero per i Beni Culturali e Ambientali, Rome, 1986, pp. 119–138.

SERLUPI CRESCENZI MARIA, *L'appartamento di San Pio V*, in *Il Palazzo Apostolico Vaticano*, edited by Carlo Pietrangeli, Nardini, Florence, 1992, pp. 147–150.

SOLERA DENNJ, *I crocesignati e le origini della famiglia del Sant'Uffizio romano*, in "Studi Storici," January–March 2019, pp. 71–102.

STELLA ALDO, *Guido da Fano eretico del secolo XVI al servizio del re d'Inghilterra*, in "Rivista di storia della Chiesa in Italia," 13 (1959), pp. 196–238.

STELLA ALDO, *L'età postridentina* in *Diocesi di Padova*, edited by Pierantonio Gios, Editrice Gregoriana, Padua, 1996.

STICKLER ALFONSO MARIA, *Sacerdozio e regno nelle nuove ricerche attorno ai secoli XII e XIII nei decreti e decretalisti fino alle decretali di Gregorio IX*, in *Sacerdozio e regno da Gregorio VII a Bonifacio VIII*, Pontifical Gregorian University, Rome, 1954, pp. 1–26.

STOW KENNETH R., *More than meets the eye. Pius V and Jews*, in *Dominikaner und Juden/Dominicans and Jews*, edited by Elias H. Fullenbach and Gianfranco Miletto, De Gruyter, Berlin, 2014.

SURIAN MICHELE, *Relazione di Roma del clariss. Sig. Michel Soriano, tornato ambasciatore da Papa Pio V l'anno 1571*, in STEPHANI BALUZII - JOHANNIS DOMINICI MANSI (edited by), *Miscellanea*, IV, Apud Vincentium Junctinium, Lucae, 1764.

SZCZUCKI LECH (edited by), *Faustus Socinus and His Heritage*, Polish Academy of Sciences, Krakow, 2005, pp. 29–51.

TARRAGO RAFAEL E., *Bloody Bess: The Persecution of Catholics in Elizabethan England*, in "Logos: A Journal of Catholic Thought and Culture," 7, 1 (Winter 2004), pp. 117–133.

TELLECHEA IDÍGORAS JOSÉ IGNACIO, *Don Carlos de Seso y el arzobispo Carranza. Un veronés introductor del protestantismo en España*, in Miscellanea Card. *Giuseppe Siri*, edited by Raffaele Belvederi, Tilgher, Genoa, 1973, pp. 63–124.

TENENTI ALBERTO, *La Francia, Venezia e la Sacra Lega*, in G. BENZONI (edited by), *Il Mediterraneo nella seconda metà del 500*, pp. 393–408.

TEODORI RAISSA, *Lancellotti Scipione*, in DBI, vol. 63 (2004), pp. 305–306.

TESTORE CELESTINO, *Catechismo*, in EC, vol. 3 (1949), cols. 1118–1125.

TESTORE CELESTINO, *Azevedo (de) Ignazio*, in BSS, vol. 3 (1963), cols. 388–389.

TESTORE CELESTINO, *Felton Giovanni*, in BSS, vol. X (1991), cols. 614–615.

TRAPÈ AGOSTINO, *De gratuitate ordinis supernaturalis apud theologos augustinenses litteris encyclicis "Humani generis" praelucentibus*, in "Analecta Augustiniana," 21 (1951), pp. 217–265.

UCCELLI PIER ANTONIO, *Dell'eresia in Bergamo nel* XVI *secolo e di frate Michele Ghislieri inquisitore in detta città indi col nome di Pio V pontefice massimo e santo*, in "La Scuola cattolica," 3 (1875), pp. 222–236, 249–262, 559–569.

VALENTINO DI S. MARIA, *Teresa, santa*, in BSS, vol. 12 (1990), pp. 395–419.

VAN MEERBEECK LUCIENNE, *Commendone Francesco Giovanni*, in DHGE, vol. 13 (1956), pp. 367–378.

VANNI ANDREA, *Da chierico teatino a cardinale inquisitore. Breve profilo di Bernardino Scotti*, in "Rivista di Storia della Chiesa in Italia," 65 (2011) 1, pp. 101–119.

VENTURA ANGELO, *Bragadin Marcantonio*, in DBI, vol. 13 (1971), pp. 686–689.

VIGLIONE MASSIMO, *Il problema della crociata dal II Concilio di Lione alla morte di Pio II (1274–1464)*, in "Ricerche di Storia sociale e religiosa," 54 (1998), pp. 201–263.

VILLANI PASQUALE, *La visita apostolica di Tommaso Orfini* [sic] *nel Regno di Napoli (1566–1568). Documenti per la storia dell'applicazione del Concilio di Trento*, in "Annuario dell'Istituto storico italiano per l'età moderna e contemporanea," 8 (1956), pp. 5–79.

VIVANTI CORRADO, *La congiura d'Amboise*, in *Complots et conjurations dans l'Europe moderne. Actes du colloque international organisé à Rome, 30 septembre–2 octobre*

1993, a cura di Yves M. Bercé e Elena Fasano Guarini, École Française de Rome, 1996.

WALDSTEIN WOLFGANG, *Le mouvement liturgique de Dom Guéranger à la veille du Concile Vatican II*, in Centre International d'Études Liturgiques, *La Liturgie: Trésor de l'Eglise*, Paris, 1995, pp. 163–182.

WALZ ANGELO, *San Tommaso d'Aquino dichiarato dottore della Chiesa nel 1567*, in "Angelicum," 55 (1967), pp. 145–173.

WICKI JOSEF, *Nuovi documenti attorno ai piani missionari di Pio V nel 1568*, in "Archivum Historicum Societatis Iesu," 37 (1968), pp. 408–417.

Index of Names

Index of Names

Index of Names

Index of Subjects

Index of Subjects

About the Author

Roberto de Mattei is a Catholic historian who has taught in several Italian universities. Between 2003 and 2011, he served as vice president of the National Research Council, the highest Italian scientific institution. He is president of the Lepanto Foundation and is the editor of the magazine *Radici Cristiane* and the news agency Corrispondenza Romana. He is the author of thirty-five books, including *The Second Vatican Council: An Unwritten Story* (2011), translated into eight languages, and *Love for the Papacy & Filial Resistance to the Pope in the History of the Church* (2019). He has received many awards, including membership in the Order of St. Gregory the Great from the Holy See for his service to the Roman Catholic Church. He is married with five children.

Sophia Institute

Sophia Institute is a nonprofit institution that seeks to nurture the spiritual, moral, and cultural life of souls and to spread the Gospel of Christ in conformity with the authentic teachings of the Roman Catholic Church.

Sophia Institute Press fulfills this mission by offering translations, reprints, and new publications that afford readers a rich source of the enduring wisdom of mankind.

Sophia Institute also operates the popular online resource CatholicExchange.com. *Catholic Exchange* provides world news from a Catholic perspective as well as daily devotionals and articles that will help readers to grow in holiness and live a life consistent with the teachings of the Church.

In 2013, Sophia Institute launched Sophia Institute for Teachers to renew and rebuild Catholic culture through service to Catholic education. With the goal of nurturing the spiritual, moral, and cultural life of souls, and an abiding respect for the role and work of teachers, we strive to provide materials and programs that are at once enlightening to the mind and ennobling to the heart; faithful and complete, as well as useful and practical.

Sophia Institute gratefully recognizes the Solidarity Association for preserving and encouraging the growth of our apostolate over the course of many years. Without their generous and timely support, this book would not be in your hands.

www.SophiaInstitute.com
www.CatholicExchange.com
www.SophiaInstituteforTeachers.org